OXFORD MEDIEVAL TEXTS

HISTORIA ECCLESIE ABBENDONENSIS

THE HISTORY OF THE CHURCH OF ABINGDON

HISTORIA ECCLESIE ABBENDONENSIS

THE HISTORY OF THE CHURCH OF ABINGDON

Volume I

EDITED AND TRANSLATED BY
JOHN HUDSON

CLARENDON PRESS · OXFORD

OXFORD
UNIVERSITY PRESS

Great Clarendon Street, Oxford OX2 6DP

Oxford University Press is a department of the University of Oxford.
It furthers the University's objective of excellence in research, scholarship,
and education by publishing worldwide in

Oxford New York

Auckland Cape Town Dar es Salaam Hong Kong Karachi
Kuala Lumpur Madrid Melbourne Mexico City Nairobi
New Delhi Shanghai Taipei Toronto

With offices in

Argentina Austria Brazil Chile Czech Republic France Greece
Guatemala Hungary Italy Japan Poland Portugal Singapore
South Korea Switzerland Thailand Turkey Ukraine Vietnam

Oxford is a registered trade mark of Oxford University Press
in the UK and in certain other countries

Published in the United States
by Oxford University Press Inc., New York

First published 2007

British Library Cataloguing in Publication Data

Data available

Library of Congress Cataloging in Publication Data

Data available

Typeset by Anne Joshua, Oxford
Printed in Great Britain
on acid-free paper by
Biddles Ltd, King's Lynn, Norfolk

ISBN 978-0-19-929937-9

1 3 5 7 9 10 8 6 4 2

PREFACE

Sir Frank Stenton, on the first page of his *Early History of the Abbey of Abingdon*, commented of the Rolls Series edition of the *Chronicon Monasterii de Abingdon* that 'in 1858 little work had been done upon Old English diplomatic, and it would not be expected that the editor's criticism of the land-books in the series should have value at the present time. It is more serious that he cannot be trusted implicitly to give the exact reading of his texts . . . The whole plan of the edition, by which the latest MS. was adopted for the text, is faulty.' The present volume, along with its companion published in 2002, seeks to remedy these faults. My edition and translation of the *History* appear soon after Susan Kelly's edition of the Abingdon Anglo-Saxon Charters, published by the British Academy in 2000–1. Her work has been invaluable to me; she is in many ways the co-editor of the present volume.

The other debts accumulated in twenty years of working on the *History* would shame the most extravagant of medieval abbots. I have seen off many OMT series editors. Particular thanks are due to John Blair, whose knowledge of the local history is incomparable and whose advice and encouragement have been invaluable. Rosalind Love worked through text and translation of this volume at the stage when it was most helpful to me. James Binns and Michael Lapidge have also given guidance, particularly with Latin. And Barbara Harvey provided the initial inspiration for me, and continued to give advice, particularly on monastic food, long after she ceased to be a general editor of OMT.

Christine Rauer and Rob Bartlett at St Andrews worked through the whole text and improved it greatly. Simon Keynes answered queries, shared unpublished work, and provided me with a printout from microfilms of the manuscripts. Julian Harrison shared his knowledge of the manuscripts with me very generously.

Thanks are also due to, amongst others, Julia Crick for help on Geoffrey of Monmouth and many other matters, Susan Reynolds for comments on the use of 'vassallus', Julia Smith, Michael Winterbottom, Martin Brett, Magnus Ryan, Barbara Rosenwein, Tessa Webber for improvements to my manuscript descriptions, Richard Sharpe,

Katie Lowe, Simone Macdougall, Bob and Betty Kerr, Clare Brown for advice on matters medical and the miraculous, Alex Woolf for leads concerning Abbán/Aben, David Dumville, Stephen Baxter, the late Patrick Wormald, and James Campbell. The library staff at the British Library, Corpus Christi College Cambridge, Corpus Christi College Oxford, Lambeth Palace, the Bodleian, and St Andrews—in particular the Inter-Library Loan staff—have been extremely helpful. John Ball of the St Andrews IT staff saved me during crises small and enormous. Berta Wales, the secretary of the Mediaeval History Department at St Andrews, has helped in a myriad of ways. Anne Gelling at OUP has always been encouraging and patient, Bonnie Blackburn a marvellous copy-editor. Visits to Libraries in Oxford and London were made easy and enjoyable by Paul and Vanessa Brand. My younger daughter, Anna, is yet to share her older sister's delight in the swings now on the abbey grounds at Abingdon, but to her and to my wife Lise this volume is dedicated.

J.G.H.H.

St Andrews
August 2006

CONTENTS

MAP

ABBREVIATED REFERENCES

Accounts of the Obedientiars	*Accounts of the Obedientiars of Abingdon Abbey*, ed. R. E. G. Kirk (Camden Soc., NS li; 1892)
Anglo-Saxon Charters, ed. Robertson	*Anglo-Saxon Charters*, ed. A. J. Robertson (2nd edn., Cambridge, 1956)
Anglo-Saxon Wills, ed. Whitelock	*Anglo-Saxon Wills*, ed. D. Whitelock (Cambridge, 1930)
Anglo-Saxon Writs, ed. Harmer	*Anglo-Saxon Writs*, ed. F. E. Harmer (Manchester, 1952)
ANS	*Anglo-Norman Studies*
ASC	*Anglo-Saxon Chronicle*
ASE	*Anglo-Saxon England*
Barlow, *Edward the Confessor*	F. Barlow, *Edward the Confessor* (London, 1970)
Barlow, *The Godwins*	F. Barlow, *The Godwins* (Harlow, 2004)
Bede, *Ecclesiastical History*	Bede, *Ecclesiastical History of the English People*, ed. B. Colgrave and R. A. B. Mynors (OMT, 1969)
Berkhofer, *Day of Reckoning*	R. F. Berkhofer, *Day of Reckoning: Power and Accountability in Medieval France* (Philadelphia, 2004)
Biddle *et al.*, 'Early history'	M. Biddle, G. Lambrick, and J. N. L. Myres, 'The early history of Abingdon, Berkshire, and its abbey', *Medieval Archaeology*, xii (1968), 26–69
Bishop Æthelwold, ed. Yorke	*Bishop Æthelwold: His Career and Influence*, ed. B. Yorke (Woodbridge, 1988)
Blair, *Anglo-Saxon Oxfordshire*	J. Blair, *Anglo-Saxon Oxfordshire* (Stroud, 1994)
Blair, 'Minsters of the Thames'	J. Blair, 'The Minsters of the Thames', in J. Blair and B. Golding, eds., *The Cloister and the World: Essays in Medieval History in Honour of Barbara Harvey* (Oxford, 1996), pp. 5–28
BM Facs.	*Facsimiles of Ancient Charters in the British Museum*, ed. E. A. Bond (4 vols., London, 1873–8)
Chaplais, 'Royal Anglo-Saxon "chancery"'	P. Chaplais, 'The royal Anglo-Saxon "chancery" of the tenth century revisited', in H. Mayr-Harting and R. I. Moore, eds., *Studies in Medieval*

	History presented to R. H. C. Davis (London, 1985), pp. 41–51
Charters of Abingdon Abbey	*Charters of Abingdon Abbey*, ed. S. E. Kelly (2 vols., Oxford University Press for the British Academy, 2000–1)
Charters of the Early West Saxon Kingdom, ed. Edwards	*The Charters of the Early West Saxon Kingdom*, ed. H. Edwards (British Archaeological Reports, British Series cxcviii, 1988)
Chatsworth	Chatsworth cartulary, in *Two Cartularies of Abingdon Abbey*, ed. C. F. Slade and G. Lambrick (2 vols., Oxford Historical Society, NS xxxii, xxxiii, 1990–2)
Chronicon abbatiæ Rameseiensis	*Chronicon abbatiæ Rameseiensis*, ed. W. D. Macray (London, 1886)
Clarke, *English Nobility*	P. A. Clarke, *The English Nobility under Edward the Confessor* (Oxford, 1994)
Clayton, *Cult*	M. Clayton, *The Cult of the Virgin Mary in Anglo-Saxon England* (Cambridge, 1990)
CMA	*Chronicon monasterii de Abingdon*, ed. J. Stevenson (2 vols., London, 1858)
Councils and Synods	*Councils and Synods with other Documents relating to the English Church: I. A.D. 871–1204*, ed. D. Whitelock, M. Brett, and C. N. L. Brooke (2 vols., Oxford, 1981)
DB	*Domesday Book seu Liber censualis Wilhelmi Primi Regis Angliae*, ed. A. Farley and H. Ellis (4 vols., London, i–ii, 1783; iii–iv, 1816)
DMLBS	Dictionary of Medieval Latin from British Sources, ed. R. E. Latham *et al.* (London and Oxford, 1975–)
Dodwell, *Anglo-Saxon Art*	C. R. Dodwell, *Anglo-Saxon Art: A New Perspective* (Manchester, 1982)
Domesday Geography of South-East England, ed. Darby and Campbell	*The Domesday Geography of South-East England*, ed. H. C. Darby and E. M. J. Campbell (Cambridge, 1962)
Dumville, 'Annalistic writing at Canterbury'	D. N. Dumville, 'Some aspects of annalistic writing at Canterbury in the eleventh and early twelfth centuries', *Peritia*, ii (1983), 23–57
Dumville, *English Caroline Script*	D. N. Dumville, *English Caroline Script and Monastic History: Studies in Benedictinism, A.D. 950–1030* (Woodbridge, 1993)
Edward the Elder, ed. Higham and Hill	*Edward the Elder, 899–924*, ed. N. J. Higham and D. H. Hill (London, 2001)

EHD	*English Historical Documents*, i: *c.*500–1042, ed. D. Whitelock (2nd edn., London, 1979); ii: 1042–1189, ed. D. C. Douglas and G. W. Greenaway (2nd edn., London, 1981)
EHR	*English Historical Review*
EPNS	English Place Names Society
Fleming, 'Christ Church Canterbury's Anglo-Norman cartulary'	R. Fleming, 'Christ Church Canterbury's Anglo-Norman cartulary', in C. W. Hollister, ed., *Anglo-Norman Political Culture and the Twelfth-Century Renaissance* (Woodbridge, 1997), pp. 83–155
Gelling, *Early Charters of Thames Valley*	M. Gelling, *The Early Charters of the Thames Valley* (Leicester, 1979)
Gerchow, *Die Gedenküberlieferung*	J. Gerchow, *Die Gedenküberlieferung der Angelsachsen* (Berlin, 1988)
Gesetze, ed. Liebermann	*Die Gesetze der Angelsachsen*, ed. F. Liebermann (3 vols., Halle, 1903–16)
Gransden, 'Traditionalism and continuity'	A. Gransden, 'Traditionalism and continuity during the last century of Anglo-Saxon monasticism', *Journal of Ecclesiastical History*, xl (1989), 159–207
Gretsch, *Intellectual Foundations*	M. Gretsch, *The Intellectual Foundations of English Benedictine Reform* (Cambridge, 1999)
Handbook of British Chronology	*Handbook of British Chronology*, ed. E. B. Fryde, D. E. Greenway, S. Porter, and I. Roy (3rd edn., London, 1986)
Heads of Religious Houses	*The Heads of Religious Houses: England and Wales*, i: *940–1216*, ed. D. Knowles, C. N. L. Brooke, V. C. M. London (2nd edn., Cambridge, 2001)
Henry of Huntingdon, *Historia Anglorum*	Henry, archdeacon of Huntingdon, *Historia Anglorum*, ed. D. E. Greenway (OMT, 1996)
Hudson, 'Abbey of Abingdon'	J. G. H. Hudson, 'The abbey of Abingdon, its *Chronicle* and the Norman Conquest', *ANS*, xix (1997), 181–202
John, *Orbis Britanniae*	E. John, *Orbis Britanniae* (Oxford, 1966)
John of Worcester, *Chronicle*	John of Worcester, *Chronicle*, ed. R. R. Darlington and P. McGurk (3 vols., OMT, 1995–)
Keynes, *Atlas of Attestations*	S. D. Keynes, *Atlas of Anglo-Saxon Attestations* (Dept. of Anglo-Saxon, Norse and Celtic, Cambridge, 1995)
Keynes, *Diplomas*	S. D. Keynes, *The Diplomas of King Æthelred 'the Unready' 978–1016* (Cambridge, 1980)

Keynes, '"Dunstan B" charters'	S. Keynes, 'The "Dunstan B" charters', *ASE*, xxiii (1994), 165–93
Keynes, 'Studies'	S. D. Keynes, 'Studies on Anglo-Saxon Royal Diplomas', unpublished fellowship dissertation (2 vols., Trinity College, Cambridge, 1976)
Lapidge, 'Æthelwold as scholar and teacher'	M. Lapidge, 'Æthelwold as scholar and teacher', in *Bishop Æthelwold*, ed. Yorke, pp. 89–117
Lapidge, *Cult of St Swithun*	M. Lapidge, *The Cult of St Swithun* (Winchester Studies 4.ii, Oxford, 2003)
Lawson, *Cnut*	M. K. Lawson, *Cnut: The Danes in England in the Early Eleventh Century* (Harlow, 1993)
Liber Eliensis	*Liber Eliensis*, ed. E. O. Blake (Camden Society, 3rd Ser. xcii; 1962)
Liber Vitae, ed. Keynes	*The Liber Vitae of New Minster and Hyde Abbey Winchester*, ed. S. D. Keynes (Early English MSS in Facsimile, xxvi; Copenhagen, 1996)
Lyell	Lyell cartulary, in *Two Cartularies of Abingdon Abbey*, ed. C. F. Slade and G. Lambrick (2 vols., Oxford Historical Society, NS xxxii, xxxiii, 1990–2)
Maitland, *Domesday Book and Beyond*	F. W. Maitland, *Domesday Book and Beyond* (Cambridge, 1897)
Miller, *Ely*	E. Miller, *The Abbey and Bishopric of Ely* (Cambridge, 1951)
NMT	Nelson's Medieval Texts
OMT	Oxford Medieval Texts
Oxford Dictionary of Popes	*The Oxford Dictionary of Popes*, ed. J. N. D. Kelly (Oxford, 1986)
Oxford Dictionary of Saints	*The Oxford Dictionary of Saints*, ed. D. H. Farmer (Oxford, 1978)
PL	*Patrologia Latina*
Porter, 'Æthelwold's bowl'	D. W. Porter, 'Æthelwold's bowl and *The Chronicle of Abingdon*', *Neuphilologische Mitteilungen*, xcvii (1996), 163–7
Regularis Concordia	*Regularis Concordia*, ed. T. Symons (NMT, 1953)
Robinson, *Times of St Dunstan*	J. A. Robinson, *The Times of Saint Dunstan* (Oxford, 1923)
Salter, 'Chronicle roll'	H. E. Salter, 'A chronicle roll of the abbey of Abingdon', *EHR*, xxvi (1911), 727–38
Sawyer	P. H. Sawyer, *Anglo-Saxon Charters: An Annotated List and Bibliography* (London, 1968; rev. S. E. Kelly, http://www.trin.cam.ac.uk/chartwww/esawyer.99/esawyer2.html)

Scott, *Early History of Glastonbury*	J. Scott, *The Early History of Glastonbury* (Woodbridge, 1981)
Stenton, *Early History*	F. M. Stenton, *The Early History of the Abbey of Abingdon* (Reading, 1913)
Thacker, 'Æthelwold'	A. Thacker, 'Æthelwold and Abingdon', *Bishop Æthelwold: His Career and Influence*, ed. B. Yorke (Woodbridge, 1988), 43–64
TRE	*Tempore regis Edwardi* (in the time of King Edward)
VCH	*Victoria County History*
William of Malmesbury, *Gesta pontificum*	William of Malmesbury, *De Gestis pontificum Anglorum Libri Quinque*, ed. N. E. S. A. Hamilton (London, 1870)
William of Malmesbury, *Gesta regum*	William of Malmesbury, *Gesta regum Anglorum*, ed. R. A. B. Mynors, R. M. Thomson, and M. Winterbottom (2 vols., OMT, 1998–9)
Williams, '*Princeps Merciorum gentis*'	A. Williams, '*Princeps Merciorum gentis*: The family, career and connections of Ælfhere, ealdorman of Mercia, 956–83', *ASE*, x (1982), 143–72
Wormald, 'Æthelwold and his Continental counterparts'	P. Wormald, 'Æthelwold and his Continental counterparts: Contact, comparison, contrast', in *Bishop Æthelwold*, ed. Yorke, pp. 13–42
Wormald, 'Lawsuits'	P. Wormald, 'A handlist of Anglo-Saxon lawsuits', *ASE*, xvii (1988), 247–81
Wulfstan, *Life of Æthelwold*	Wulfstan of Winchester, *Life of St Æthelwold*, ed. M. Lapidge and M. Winterbottom (OMT, 1991)

INTRODUCTION

I. COMPOSER, TITLE, AND PURPOSE

THE *History of the Church of Abingdon* in its first surviving version traces the development of the abbey and its estates from its reputed foundation just before the time of King Ceadwalla of Wessex (685–8) until the abbacy of Walkelin (1158–64). Given that the death of Walkelin is not mentioned, composition probably ceased before his demise. It seems plausible that the first manuscript now surviving, London, British Library, Cotton Claudius C. IX, was also the first fair copy, written probably in the 1160s.[1]

1. Composer

The composer of the *History* is anonymous.[2] Sir Frank Stenton argued that 'an examination of Claudius C ix shows conclusively that it is a copy of a work written by one who was an inmate of Abingdon monastery before the year 1117'.[3] He based this argument on two key passages. The first concerns events following the death of Abbot Faritius:

> Moreover, we were without an abbot for four years, but had every abundance of provisions and clothing. Indeed, a venerable man from amongst us, named Warenger, had charge of this house. He had enjoyed the office of prior from the time of Abbot Reginald, ruled us vigorously, and always tended us as single-mindedly as the kindest mother.[4]

Here the first person plural could be used in an impersonal sense, just as it is stated that 'when King Æthelstan was holding the monarchy of

[1] See below, vol. ii. p. xvii n., for completion before the coronation of Henry II's son, the Young King, in June 1170, and for a passage in the main hand, following the text of the *History*, written after 1166. On writs included in the *History* which have sometimes been dated later than 1164 on the basis of witnessing by John of Oxford, see vol. ii, p. xvii n. 1. Cross-references to whole chapters in the present volume are by chapter number, to more specific passages by page number. References to vol. ii are by page number.

[2] I choose to call him composer rather than, say, author or compiler, in order to emphasize that his work involved both original composition and the gathering of existing material.

[3] Stenton, *Early History*, p. 4.

[4] Vol. ii. 224. Stenton, *Early History*, p. 5, states that 'interpreted strictly, this passage would mean that the writer was a member of the house of Abingdon already before the death of abbot Rainald in 1097'.

the principality of the whole of England, that is in the year 930 from the Incarnation of Christ, we received Cynath as abbot of Abingdon'.[5] Stenton's second passage, however, is more persuasive. Again it concerns Faritius: 'We saw him buy more than sixty silk cloths.' Unless the first person plural here is simply copied from a pre-existing note, it almost certainly indicates that the composer actually witnessed events in Faritius's time.[6] This would mean that the monk who composed the *History* had been in the abbey, or at least witnessed some affairs of the abbey, for forty-five to fifty years by the time of the completion of the *History*. Whilst quite an impressive twelfth-century lifespan, this duration is far from impossible. It would make the composer an approximate contemporary of Robert earl of Leicester (1104–68).[7] The *History*, therefore, is the work of a man who had lived through the events at least from the time of Abbot Faritius, and who may well have known monks present in the abbey in 1066. We cannot date his death, only note that the *History* ceases before that of Walkelin on 10 April 1164. Given that Book II of the *History* has no *explicit*, whereas Book I does, it is plausible that the composition of the *History* ended when the composer died.[8]

The composer's role in the monastery is not certain, but he may well have had a connection to the sacristy. This is plausible because of the connections between that office, documentation, and relics, the last being another of the *History*'s concerns.[9] Whilst the *History*

[5] See below, p. 34.

[6] Vol. ii. 72. Such uses of the first person plural are quite characteristic of the composer's style; see below, p. xxxvi.

[7] Robert provides an interesting warning about relying on memory even for events within a lifetime. According to Orderic, whom we may presume to be accurate, he was born in 1104, when Henry I was king of England; *The Ecclesiastical History of Orderic Vitalis*, bk. xi, c. 6, ed. M. Chibnall (6 vols., OMT, 1969–80), vi. 46. The Abingdon *History*, however, reports that in the time of Henry II, Robert 'testified that he had seen a full market [at Abingdon] in the time of King Henry [I], and, what's more, when he was still a boy and was being raised at Abingdon in the time of King William [presumably Rufus]'; vol. ii. 312. This extension of Robert's life need not necessarily be confusion or distortion by the compiler of the *History*; on the remembering of age and the tendency of the old to have presented themselves as still older at least in numerical terms, see K. Thomas, 'Age and authority in early modern England', *Proceedings of the British Academy*, lxii (1976), 205–48, esp. pp. 234–5.

[8] See below, p. clxxx, for the arrangement of folios by the scribe as the work came to its close.

[9] See vol. ii, p. xviii; also *CMA* ii. 375. See Keynes, *Diplomas*, p. 152, for a glossarist at Abingdon linking the office of *scriniarius* (custodian of relics) with that of *cancellarius*; the gloss is from the first half of the 11th century; for words of caution on the significance of this, see Chaplais, 'Anglo-Saxon "chancery" of the tenth century revisited', p. 42. Note also the combination in one manuscript of document and liturgical work at Sherborne in

displays no especial interest in lands and rights associated with the sacristy, particularly significant is the leading role which Richard the sacrist plays towards the end of the work.[10] This may only indicate Richard's importance in the affairs of the whole abbey, but taken with the other indications, reinforces the likelihood of a connection between the composer and the sacristy. This would be a connection he may have shared with his Peterborough counterpart as historian of church and estates, Hugh Candidus.[11]

2. Title and purpose

I have adopted as the title of the work that given at the start of Book II in this first manuscript, the 'History of this church of Abingdon'. Book I had described itself in both *incipit* and *explicit* simply as 'Book I of the lands of this church of Abingdon'. Similar works survive from various other monasteries during the twelfth century, with titles that vary between manuscripts of the same text, and between texts. From Ramsey there is a 'Liber benefactorum', from Ely the 'Historia Eliensis insule', from Battle the 'Liber de situ ecclesie Belli et de possessionibus sibi a rege Willelmo et ab aliis quibuslibet datis'.[12] Such texts are linked to cartularies and to the *Gesta abbatum* tradition that in England goes back to Bede.[13] Volumes combining narrative and document had previously existed in Francia,[14] and emerge from

the mid-12th century, as discussed by F. Wormald, 'The Sherborne "Chartulary"', in D. J. Gordon, ed., *Fritz Saxl 1890–1948: A Volume of Memorial Essays from his Friends in England* (London, 1957), pp. 101–19; at p. 106 he suggests that the binding of the Sherborne manuscript indicates a book for the sacristy.

[10] Vol. ii. 280–90. The original of one of the bulls of Eugenius III survives with the annotation 'Memoriale magistri Galfridi trenchebise'. The hand is quite similar to that of the *History*, but certain letter formations are different. The person responsible for the annotation presumably had a role in the keeping of documents. However, the differences in the script prevent any confident association of the annotator with the scribe of the *History* and any identification with the composer of the *History* would have to be simply speculative.

[11] J. A. Paxton, 'Charter and Chronicle in Twelfth-Century England: The House-Histories of the Fenland Abbeys', Ph.D. diss. (Harvard University, 1999), p. 96. For parallels in France, see Berkhofer, *Day of Reckoning*, pp. 36, 47.

[12] *Chronicon abbatiæ Rameseiensis*, p. 3 (note, however, that this title is present only in a 14th-century manuscript, not a 13th-century one); *Liber Eliensis*, Prologue, ed. Blake, p. 1; *The Chronicle of Battle Abbey*, ed. E. Searle (OMT, 1980), p. 66.

[13] See e.g. J.-P. Genet, 'Cartulaires, registres et histoire: L'exemple anglais', in B. Guenée, ed., *Le Métier d'historien au moyen âge: Études sur l'historiographie médiévale* (Paris, 1977), pp. 95–129; M. Sot, *Gesta episcoporum, gesta abbatum* (Typologie des sources du moyen âge occidental, xxxvii; Turnhout, 1981); E. M. C. van Houts, *Local and Regional Chronicles* (Typologie des sources du moyen âge occidental, lxxiv; Turnhout, 1995).

[14] F. L. Ganshof, 'L'Historiographie dans la monarchie franque sous les mérovingiens et les carolingiens', in *La storiografia altomedievale* (Settimane di studio del Centro Italiano

the late eleventh-century in England.[15] The multiplication of charter histories and their particular prevalence in England in the twelfth century can be explained by a variety of possible reasons, such as the desire for written evidence, the impact on church landholding of the events of King Stephen's reign (1135–54), and the formulaic nature of English charters, which required background to be provided by additional narrative. The various texts differ in some instances significantly in both form and content, for example the extent to which they reproduce charters or the interest they show in the miraculous.[16] However, they are linked by shared themes and purposes. Such themes are sometimes made explicit when the work has a Preface, as for example at Ely, Ramsey, and Battle. Then the emphasis is on elements such as preservation of information in writing, protection of rights, and the desire to gather documents into one book.[17]

sull'alto medioevo, xvii; Spoleto, 1970), pp. 631–85, at 657–9; R.-H. Bautier, 'L'Historiographie en France aux xe et xie siècles', ibid., pp. 793–850, at 809–22 and esp. pp. 817–20; P. J. Geary, *Phantoms of Remembrance: Memory and Oblivion at the End of the First Millennium* (Princeton, 1994), pp. 81–133; Berkhofer, *Day of Reckoning*, pp. 10–89. See also e.g. *Chronique de l'abbaye de Saint-Riquier (Ve siècle–1104)*, ed. F. Lot (Paris, 1894).

[15] *Hemingi Chartularium Ecclesiae Wigorniensis*, ed. T. Hearne (2 vols., Oxford, 1723); N. R. Ker, 'Hemming's cartulary: A description of the two Worcester Cartularies in Cotton Tiberius A. xiii', in R. W. Hunt, W. A. Pantin, and R. W. Southern, eds., *Studies in Medieval History Presented to Frederick Maurice Powicke* (Oxford, 1948), pp. 49–75; Fleming, 'Christ Church Canterbury's Anglo-Norman cartulary'. We know of at least one pre-Conquest estate history in England, although not one including full documents, that is, the Old English version of the *Libellus Æthelwoldi* concerned with Æthelwold's acquisitions for Ely; see *Liber Eliensis*, ed. Blake, pp. xxxiii–xxxiv, 72–117, 395–9. A new edition and translation is promised by Simon Keynes and Alan Kennedy. The statement in *Chronicon abbatiæ Rameseiensis*, Pref., ed. Macray, p. 4, that part of the composer's purpose was to bring diverse documents together in one place strongly suggests that he at least was not reliant on an earlier cartulary. See also *Hemingi Chartularium*, ed. Hearne, i. 285, on Wulfstan ordering the gathering of records into volumes.

[16] Unfortunately, we know little about the ways in which these histories were used, for example whether they were consulted, read from beginning to end, studied by individuals, or read aloud to a wider audience. A hint that the works may at times have been read from start to finish is given in B286: 'Moreover, we have carefully placed in the proper places each charter of each king reigning in succession and also of all others conferring their endowments on this house. But if indeed any mortal man wonders about the above lands and possessions, now given, now taken away, but now recovered and possessed, let him read the books in order, and he will find nothing contrary there which ought justly to lead his mind to doubt.' A suggestion, although possibly formulaic, that the works might be heard as well as read comes in the Preface to the Ramsey *Liber benefactorum*; *Chronicon abbatiæ Rameseiensis*, Pref., ed. Macray, pp. 4–5.

[17] *Liber Eliensis*, Prologue, ed. Blake, p. 1; *Chronicon abbatiæ Rameseiensis*, Pref., ed. Macray, pp. 3–5; *Chronicle of Battle Abbey*, ed. Searle, p. 32. See also Geary, *Phantoms of Remembrance*, p. 86, who argues that the motivation of the compilers of *Traditionsbücher* was threefold: legal, historical, and sacral.

The Abingdon *History* has no Preface and so the composer's purpose must be abstracted from the text. The desire to record events, rights, and claims for those in the future is clear both in the subject matter and in occasional statements within the narrative:

I have spoken for this reason, so that some day, through a man given by God, the just resumption of the other part [of a disputed church] should occur that much more swiftly, because the unjust seizure is found recorded in writing.[18]

Past experience is said to have taught the value of written record, as when the monastery fell into neglect in the tenth century:

despite the impact of such unforeseen evils, the books of deeds [i.e. documents] containing the possessions of the church were preserved—assuredly by God's foresight—so that the restorers of the possessions and afterwards their successors could have evidence of times of old.[19]

Outside events might be recorded, but mainly if they affected the abbey's own position, for the prime subject of record was the lands and rights of the abbey.[20] Of particular interest may have been early material which could be included or constructed on issues or places which were matters of dispute in the twelfth century. Thus an early narrative, developed from a forged charter, mentions the oppressions of the king's huntsmen and the links between Abingdon and the estate of Sutton. In the twelfth century disputes occurred with the men of the royal manor of Sutton and the abbey obtained from Henry I a writ forbidding Nigel d'Oilly and all his huntsmen and marshals of the court from lodging at Abingdon's land of Wheatley.[21] Late in Book I it is emphasized that Sparsholt 'has remained to this day in the fee of the church', whilst Book II shows it later being disputed.[22]

It was also wished that the abbot should be elected by the convent, free of outside interference and in accordance with the *Rule* of St Benedict. Such a right of election according to the *Rule* is included in pre-Conquest diplomas which appear in the *History*,[23] and also

[18] Vol. ii. 258. See also e.g. vol. ii. 292.

[19] See below, p. 46.

[20] For outside events being recorded largely for their own sake, see e.g. cc. 109, 118; vol. ii. 16.

[21] See below, p. 14; vol. ii. 120, 166–72.

[22] See below, pp. 212–14; vol. ii. 52, 182–6. *De abbatibus* describes the land as a reacquisition by Abbot Faritius in the early 12th century; *CMA* ii. 288. Note also disputes concerning Leckhampstead, cc. 120, 136; vol. ii. 56–8, 196–8; and renders of herrings, c. 141; vol. ii. 174–6.

[23] See below, pp. 62, 96, 146.

features in some narratives. According to the *History*, Edward the Confessor had to persuade the abbey to accept the aged Bishop Rodulf as their abbot:

> So that the monks would, out of respect both for God and himself, receive and treat honourably Rodulf, inasmuch as he was already of ripe old age, the king gave them permission rather to elect as his successor whomsoever they wished from amongst themselves when Rodulf died. The king was obeyed. Submission of due reverence was fittingly paid by the brethren to Rodulf. But the royal promise by no means deceived them thereafter.[24]

Although the *History* records that Æthelwold was appointed by King Eadred, acting 'by the counsel of his leading men and especially the advice of his mother Eadgifu', it clearly states that he had been appointed canonically.[25] Such an issue may have been of immediate concern in the time of Walkelin, whom the *History* presents as Henry II's nominee, whilst another Abingdon text, *De abbatibus*, states that Henry gave him the abbey on the intervention of his queen. The *History* is careful to present the two abbots as enthusiastic restorers of the abbey's possessions and thus fitting abbots.[26]

The *History* is also concerned with the protection of the abbey and monks against bad or weak abbots. This was particularly important under Walkelin given Abbot Ingulf's recent alienations of property, alienations condemned by the *History*. It is even possible that the *History* was written in response to a more pro-abbatial account of the abbey's affairs presented by another Abingdon text, *De abbatibus*, if, as is plausible, a version of that text was completed in Ingulf's time.[27] Concern with conventual rights would also fit with the likely origin of the *History* within the sacristy, one of the obediences or specially endowed offices of the monastery.[28] Obvious to the audience of the *History* may have been parallels between recent figures and earlier ones, for example between Ingulf and the late tenth-century abbot Eadwine, whose abbacy was said to have involved considerable losses, or between Walkelin and Abbots Wulfgar and Æthelwine as restorers of property.[29]

[24] See below, p. 198.

[25] See below, p. 48.

[26] The writing of the *History* in MS C coincided with the Becket dispute, itself partly caused by the nature of Becket's appointment and by conflicts over the resumption of church lands.

[27] See below, p. lvi.

[28] See vol. ii, pp. lxxxv–lxxxvii.

[29] Eadwine c. 96; Wulfgar c. 97; Æthelwine c. 111; Ingulf vol. ii. 290–6; Walkelin vol. ii. 296–8. Note the explicit comparison of Faritius with Æthelwold and Wulfgar in vol. ii. 66. Not just recent events but old documents could be recorded to make the convent's case. An Anglo-Saxon charter's anathema against future alienation of the land given could

The *History*, therefore, has as a further concern the recording of the deeds of abbots, providing *exempla* of good or bad pastorship. Protection and acquisition of lands remains the central issue, but other matters, such as the church buildings, ornaments, and relics, also merits mention.[30] In the most important cases character sketches, brief or in rare instances extended, are added to descriptions of deeds.[31]

The moral and exemplary purpose of the *History* extended beyond its treatment of abbots. A small number of miracle stories illustrating monastic virtues appear in Book I.[32] The fate of evil laymen is described, at times with relish. Take the case of Froger, sheriff of Berkshire in the wake of the Norman Conquest and oppressor of Abingdon:

> afterwards the vengeance of God, the Governor of all things, punished the ungoverned advances of that powerful man over those whom he had oppressed, so that royal justice took away from him the tyrannical right by which he was raised up, and as long as he lived it was changed into universal contempt by his neediness and stupidity. In these his afflictions, he presents a clear model for those to come that a place dedicated to the guardianship of the Queen of Heaven and consecrated in memory of the holy men who founded it and inhabited it should be revered rather than ravaged.[33]

Most important of all in the *History*'s depiction of relations with the outside world is the position of the king.[34] Right from the start of the *History* instances are given of the benefit of good relations between king and monastery.[35] The problems of the breakdown of such relations are illustrated by other cases, such as those of Alfred and William Rufus.[36] Examples are also given of kings who turned from antagonism to patronage: Ine, Coenwulf, and in particular Æthelred.[37] Above all,

easily be read to apply to the abbot, bound as he was by his abbatial oath to protect and regather the abbey's property. See vol. ii, p. xl on the abbot's oath.

[30] See below, pp. clxvi–clxxvii; vol. ii, pp. ci–civ. Building work receives less attention in Book I of the *History* than in Book II.

[31] The extended character sketches are devoted to the dominant figures of each book, Æthelwold and Faritius; see cc. 24, 27; vol. ii. 64–6.

[32] cc. 29, 30; see also below, p. 218. See vol. ii. 32 for the prior, 'inspired by divine prompting', saving the monks from the collapse of the church tower.

[33] See below, p. 228. See also e.g. vol. ii. 104–6.

[34] Note also the link to the papacy established by the references to Pope Leo III, a link which was to be particularly important in Stephen's reign; see below, pp. 14, 18, 64, 96, 146; vol. ii. 264–80.

[35] See below, pp. 2–6; also e.g. 56 (feasting with the king at Abingdon).

[36] See below, p. 32; vol. ii. 60–2.

[37] cc. 3–7, 9, 97.

there are the exemplary relations enjoyed with kings by the two heroes of the *History*, Abbots Æthelwold and Faritius.

The *History* helped to form in monks' minds their image of their house's past and of the community of monks and associated benefactors. It may have been intended to record the names of donors for their liturgical commemoration. Such a link is made more explicit in the preface of the equivalent text from Ramsey, which certainly by the fourteenth century was entitled *Liber benefactorum*.[38] At least in the late eleventh century there seems to have been a different text at Abingdon fulfilling this purpose, as shown by Earl Hugh of Chester's demand that in return for his gift 'I may be your brother, and my wife and father and mother be in your prayers, and . . . we all be written in the Book of Commemorations'. Whether the existence of such a text should be seen as reducing the liturgical significance of the *History* is uncertain; at Canterbury in the late eleventh century cartulary and obituary list co-existed and were closely related in material and probably purpose.[39]

II. COMPOSITION OF THE *HISTORY*: (A) MS C

1. Possible precursors of the *History*

London, British Library, Cotton Claudius C. IX preserves the first surviving text of the *History*, but did the composer of this text rely heavily on an earlier version? It has been suggested that he must have 'used some now lost abbatial history, possibly a pre-Conquest one'. Evidence for this view comes from comparison of various post-Conquest chronicles, and the detail in some, such as the Abingdon *History*, on pre-Conquest matters compared with the vagueness of others. Charters and oral tradition might explain this precision, but the detailed quality of the account of mid-eleventh-century events, together with 'the precise detail and vivid touches in some of his narrative', have been taken to suggest an extended narrative source.[40] An alternative view is that 'the collection in Claudius C IX seems

[38] See *Chronicon abbatiæ Rameseiensis*, Pref., ed. Macray, pp. 3–4.

[39] Vol. ii. 24–6. For obituary lists containing notes of donors and donations, see R. Fleming, 'Christchurch's sisters and brothers: An edition and discussion of Canterbury obituary lists', in M. A. Meyer, ed., *The Culture of Christendom: Essays in Medieval History in Commemoration of Denis L. T. Bethell* (London, 1993), pp. 115–53; id., 'Christ Church Canterbury's Anglo-Norman cartulary', pp. 103–6.

[40] Gransden, 'Traditionalism and continuity', p. 193.

originally to have been compiled in the 1130s, though the manuscript itself was probably written in the 1160s'.[41]

Given that no earlier texts survive, conclusions on this point must be cautious. The absence of a Preface is a further problem. It might either have referred to an earlier work, or have specified the need to assemble diverse documents into a single book, thus implying the lack of a prior version. The *History* does include references to earlier texts, but these appear to be specific documents referring to lands, not more extended narratives. Given such references, the silence on narratives may, but need not, be significant. There are mentions of the *gesta* of individual abbots, but these need only be references to sections of the

[41] Keynes, *Diplomas*, p. 10 n. 12; id., 'Studies', i. 70–5. Keynes's argument rests primarily on the relationship between the *History* as in MS C and the additions made at the abbey to the *Chronicle* of John of Worcester and preserved in Lambeth Palace Library 42. At p. 72, Keynes places considerable emphasis on the statement in the Lambeth manuscript that the writer knew nothing certain concerning the period between the death of Hræthhun and the reign of Æthelstan (see John of Worcester, *Chronicle*, ii. 610); 'This remark has no parallel in C ix, and indeed we find in that work a considerable amount of information about the history of Abingdon in the later ninth and early tenth centuries.' In fact there is very little in MS C concerning Abingdon in this period, although this is rather concealed by Stevenson's edition, which relies on MS B. The treatment of the Danes in c. 14 has no information concerning Abingdon. It is followed by two charters, neither of which concerns gifts directly to Abingdon. There is then a very short narrative concerning Alfred, which does not fit well with John of Worcester's picture of that king. Next, in c. 18, comes another charter recording a gift not directly to Abingdon, followed by very brief mention in c. 19 of the death of Edward the Elder and the accession of Æthelstan. There follows a mention of Abbot Cynath and then charters of Æthelstan. The Abingdon addition to John of Worcester shows knowledge both of Cynath and of three of the four estates that Æthelstan gave; the fourth estate could quite easily have been omitted by accident. At p. 75, Keynes suggests that *History*'s 'account of events occurring during the reigns of Stephen and Henry II is somewhat confused'. This is not the case; rather the writer has, for example, sometimes kept together his accounts of particular disputes, an arrangement confused by the reviser of the *History*, who favoured a more strictly chronological arrangement. As suggested below, p. xxv, this very integration of material of different periods creates problems for Keynes's argument. At p. 75, Keynes also suggests that the work had been compiled in the 1130s 'with a few additions relating to the reigns of Stephen and Henry II'. Even setting aside the post-1135 material integrated into the sections of the *History* devoted to the period before 1135, these 'few additions' from the accession of Stephen amount, in the present edition, to at least sixty-two pages (ii. 260–321—the date of events in ii. 254–61 is not certain but in part these pages cover events certainly after 1135). The section from the death of Faritius in 1117 to that of Henry I in 1135 amounts to thirty-eight pages (ii. 224–61), but some of these concern events after the accession of Stephen and indeed after that of Henry II. There is thus no reduction in the proportionate amount of space devoted to the later period. The exceptional period is that of the abbacy of Faritius, 1100–17. The arguments on the development of the *History* put forward in F. Langer, *Zur Sprache des Abingdon Chartulars* (Berlin, 1904), esp. pp. 12–16, notably for earlier versions being compiled in 1054 × 1100 and in Henry II's reign, are not convincing.

History on the deeds of specific abbots, not to separate and pre-existing texts.[42]

Moreover, the extent of pre-Conquest memory is not all that great. Setting aside the exceptional case of Æthelwold, the increase in narrative only really starts about fifty years before the Conquest, and even then the treatment of abbacies is considerably less detailed than for those after 1071 and particularly after 1100. There is no equivalent to the very detailed treatment of Ætheric, bishop of Dorchester (1016–34), in the Ramsey history, let alone the activities of Æthelwold in the *Liber Eliensis*, which certainly was based on an earlier text surviving in Latin as the *Libellus Æthelwoldi*.[43] There are other possible explanations for the relatively good chronology of the Anglo-Saxon period and its growing detail and colour in the eleventh century: these include use of the *Anglo-Saxon Chronicle*, the probable existence of notes of individual events and transactions, the certain existence of a *Book of Commemorations* at least in the late eleventh century, and above all the interpretation of a large body of charters, some of which themselves display an interest in history.[44]

Can it be shown that the composer in the 1160s was responsible for putting together the whole *History*, rather than just being responsible for the period after, say, 1130 or the death of Faritius in 1117? Although no abbacy is again treated at such great length as that of Faritius, there is no major shift in the form of the *History*, with its combination of narrative and document. Rather there is general consistency from the first half of the eleventh century onward.[45] All references to 'the present day' or equivalent phrases could refer to

[42] See below, p. 222; vol. ii. 78, 308. Likewise, there is no shift in form or style after 1130; see below, pp. xxxiii–xxxvii.

[43] Chronicon abbatiæ Rameseiensis, cc. 70–82, ed. Macray, pp. 120–48. See Gransden, 'Traditionalism and continuity', p. 194: 'the great detail of these passages and their lively tone suggest that the chronicler copied them from some now lost Life of Ætheric'. For the *Libellus Æthelwoldi*, see above, n. 15.

[44] If a *Book of Commemorations*, with only brief notes of donors and perhaps gifts, was an important source, the process in relevant instances would be one of fresh composition rather than rewriting. Note Fleming, 'Christ Church Canterbury's Anglo-Norman cartulary', p. 92. The same would apply concerning any type of list of donors, whether or not connected to commemoration; see the suggestions in *Stoke by Clare Cartulary, BL Cotton Appx. xxi*, ed. C. Harper-Bill and R. Mortimer (3 vols., Suffolk Charters, iv–vi; 1982–4), iii. 51–3.

[45] See below, p. lxxii, for a possible increase in pre-existing short texts concerning disputes and transactions, together with a decline in the number of diplomas, causing the change at that point. On the structure of Book II in MS C, see vol. ii, pp. xxx–xxxvii.

Walkelin's time, although they need not do so.[46] The rare occasions on which the *History* seems to display factual error may also be significant. There may be confusion between Rufus and Henry I in a dispute involving a knight named Rainbald at the end of the eleventh and the start of the twelfth century. Such confusion seems more explicable in a text composed in the 1160s than in one written some decades earlier.[47]

It can moreover be demonstrated that certain sections of the *History* were at the very least rewritten and possibly composed some time after the events they describe. A few Anglo-Saxon matters, particularly concerning landholding, are explained for a later audience.[48] A chapter dealing with matters of Æthelred's reign looks forward to William of Normandy's conquest of England.[49] Rufus's treatment of vacancies is presented as a past evil:

> At that time there was an unspeakable custom practised in England, that if any person among the prelates of churches departed life, the church honour was assigned to the royal treasury. And this was done with the church of Abingdon, as with others.[50]

Furthermore, the extensive account of a long-running dispute over Marcham involving the king's dispensers and stretching from the reign of Rufus to that of Henry II, although dispersed in Book II, has a coherence as a whole.[51] Cross-references within the text reinforce this impression.[52] Such features demonstrate that any earlier narrative materials had at least been significantly rewritten.

Interventions in the first person plural may also be significant,

[46] See below, pp. 28, 114 (referring to monks in general rather than those individuals introduced by Æthelwold), 182, 198, 212, 218; vol. ii. 52, 54, 244, 258.

[47] See vol. ii. 58 and n. 138.

[48] See esp. below, p. 208: 'for he who had in his possession such writing could thereby dispute more confidently for any land'. See also pp. 212, 218, and note vol. ii. 6 for a reference to 'those known as thegns'. See below, p. clvii, for anachronistic language concerning Anglo-Saxon land-holding and lordship.

[49] c. 109. Note also e.g. vol. ii. 16 referring to Henry son of William I as 'then a youth'; vol. ii. 62 referring to Robert count of Meulan as 'the elder'.

[50] Vol. ii. 60.

[51] Vol. ii. 52–4, 234–44, 306–8. Note also an account of a dispute of Stephen's reign which mentions 'King Henry the younger, who reigned after Stephen', vol. ii. 282; similarly the reference to 'Ingulf—then abbot of the church', vol. ii. 280. Reference such as that at vol. ii. 174 to 'the time of Abbot Faritius' may indicate that the passages were written after the abbacy of the abbot named. See also below, pp. xxxvi, lxxi.

[52] See below, n. 126, for such cross-references in the first person plural; also e.g. pp. 48, 190, 208, 222; vol. ii. 2, 58, 306.

although they do not prove that the same composer was intervening each time. A passage dealing with events in Abbot Walkelin's time looks back to matters which 'we recorded above, among the deeds of the venerable Abbot Vincent'. This refers the reader back to a passage which itself begins with a reference back to the vacancy after the death of Faritius 'as we have recorded above'.[53] Whilst necessarily somewhat impressionistic, other aspects of stylistic consistency also suggest a single composer. There is some consistency of vocabulary, in terms of certain words and phrases being used frequently, and of less frequently used words appearing far apart.[54] Given that the composer was drawing on earlier written texts, rewriting did not necessarily produce absolute stylistic consistency.[55] Occasional sentences interrupt the narrative flow, suggesting possible interpolation in earlier short texts.[56] However, any such stylistic variations or awkward interpolations work at the level of individual chapters and are not indications of an extended *History* pre-existing that preserved in our earliest manuscript.

The most plausible view of the composition of the *History* is, therefore, that MS C does indeed preserve the first extended Abingdon text combining charter and narrative, that it was being composed in the time of Abbot Walkelin, and that it drew on a variety of sources, including relatively short and specific texts recording events and transactions.

2. Sources for the composition of Book I

What, then, were the sources that the composer used for his Book I? Let us deal first with narratives. Matters concerning, for example, royal succession were probably drawn from a version of the *Anglo-Saxon Chronicle*. It could be that the *Chronicle* of John of Worcester was the source, but it should be noted that the dating of the council of Kirtlington to Easter is present in the *Anglo-Saxon Chronicle* and the

[53] Vol. ii. 234, 308.

[54] See below, e.g. 'callidus' p. 196, vol. ii. 280; 'in articulo temporis' p. 140, vol. ii. 82; note also vol. ii. 6 'tali in articulo huius fortune'. See further, below, pp. xxxiii–xxxvii.

[55] It is, for example, interesting to see that a word such as *manerium* is not introduced into the text dealing with events before the mid-11th century: below, pp. 198, 212; cf. p. 244 in the revised version of the *History*.

[56] For example, in dealing with Stigand's machinations concerning lands in Gloucestershire when he was bishop of Winchester, it is mentioned that William I later imprisoned him for life, a statement of no immediate relevance to the passage; below, p. 196. The final sentence of the chapter also seems somewhat detached and obscure.

History, but not in John of Worcester.[57] An Abingdon manuscript of John of Worcester, in the same hand as the *History*, does survive, and includes various additions specifically concerning Abingdon, most of which also appear in the text of the *History*. The best explanation of the shared Abingdon passages and of the lack of influence of the core text of the Worcester *Chronicle* on the *History* is that the scribe came to John of Worcester after he had completed the *History*.[58]

The composer of the *History* appears to have known Wulfstan of Winchester's *Life of St Æthelwold*. However, he did not choose to copy passages from it in the way that some authors did, for example William of Malmesbury in his *Gesta pontificum*.[59] Most notably there is not the copying which appears in the Abingdon manuscripts of John of Worcester's *Chronicle* or in the later version of the *History*.[60] Rather, the earlier manuscript of the *History* includes two miracle stories which also appear in the *Life*. In both cases, the *History*'s version is distinct from the *Life*'s, probably best taken as new composition based on material in the *Life*.[61] The closest to direct verbal copying comes in the *History*'s chapter 'Concerning Queen Eadgifu', where it is mentioned that 'at the start of the construction of the monastery [King Eadred] measured the foundations of the work with his own hand [*ipse fundamenta faciendi operis propria metiretur manu*]'. In the *Life*, one of the shared miracle stories had taken place on a day when the king visited the monastery to oversee the building works and 'with his own hand he measured all the foundations of the monastery [*mensusque est omnia fundamenta monasterii propria manu*]'.[62] The verbal parallels are close enough both to establish the composer of the *History*'s knowledge of the *Life* and to confirm that elsewhere he deliberately chose not to copy from it.

[57] *ASC*, 'B' and 'C', *s.a.* 977; below, p. 136; John of Worcester, *Chronicle*, ii. 428. Likewise the account of Harthacnut's death, below, p. 186, does not use information available from John of Worcester, *Chronicle*, ii. 532–4.

[58] John of Worcester, *Chronicle*, ii. 609–15, iii. 307–8; see below, pp. 4, 14, 46, 52, 54, 116, 138, 176, 178, 186, 194, 198, 220; vol. ii. 64, 70, 224, 228. The treatment of Æthelwold in c. 24 is related to, though lengthier than, the Abingdon addition in John of Worcester, *Chronicle*, ii. 610. See below, pp. lviii–lix, on the relationship of the manuscripts; below, p. xli, on MS B's use of John of Worcester.

[59] See Wulfstan, *Life of Æthelwold*, ed. Lapidge and Winterbottom, pp. cxliii–clxvii, esp. clviii–clix.

[60] See below, pp. xli, lviii.

[61] See cc. 29 and 32, Wulfstan, *Life of Æthelwold*, cc. 12 and 14, ed. Lapidge and Winterbottom, pp. 22–8; cf. below, p. lviii, on MS B's direct quotation from the *Life of Æthelwold*.

[62] See below, p. 56; Wulfstan, *Life of Æthelwold*, c. 12, ed. Lapidge and Winterbottom, p. 22.

Rather than extended narratives, it is documents and above all charters or diplomas which are the major written source for the *History*. The version in MS C contains seventy-four pre-1066 documents, five of which appear only in that manuscript.[63] All relate to lands which were either part of the endowment in 1066 or were claimed as having been once part of the endowment. Twenty-one, largely from the mid-tenth century, are in favour of individuals, and most appear to be genuine documents that came to the abbey when the lands concerned passed to it.[64] The remaining documents all explicitly concern grants which the *History* presents as having been made to the monastery. The majority are royal diplomas from the period 930–1054. There are also charters supposedly from the earliest years of the house, but probably related to a minster at Bradfield, and some other spurious charters from the eighth and ninth centuries.[65]

Whereas at Glastonbury an early cartulary was available for the composition of a history in the twelfth and early thirteenth centuries, it would appear that the composer of the *History* was working from originals.[66] Of one document the *History* states that 'we have found what follows written in English in almost worn-away letters'.[67] The originals almost all survived to be consulted again by the reviser of the *History*, and minor difference of order of documents between the two versions of the *History* may suggest slight shuffling of documents within bundles.[68] The documents were probably kept in chests, as is

[63] For what follows, see below, Concordance 1. Those appearing only in MS C are cc. 5, 6, 10, 25, 113; see below, p. xlvi, on their omission from MS B. My figure of seventy-four does not include c. 2, and counts cc. 3 and 4 as a single document.

[64] See also Keynes, *Diplomas*, pp. 10–11, 33–4. There are no instances like those at St Augustine's, Canterbury, where the lay beneficiary's name was simply changed to that of the church in order to record the transfer; see *Charters of St Augustine's Abbey, Canterbury, and Minster-in-Thanet*, ed. S. E. Kelly (Anglo-Saxon Charters, iv; Oxford, 1997), pp. ciii–civ.

[65] For Bradfield: cc. 3, 4, 5, 6, 7; other 8th- and 9th-century charters: cc. 8, 10, 11, 12, 13, 15, 16, 18. Blair, 'Minsters of the Thames', p. 22, suggests—on the basis of Susan Kelly's inferences—that Bradfield was perhaps originally founded as early as the 660s and was the centre of a *familia* of daughter houses; 'this may therefore have been a minster of very considerable importance, but there is no indication in the later history of the church that it remained of any account in the late Anglo-Saxon period and after'.

[66] See Scott, *Early History of Glastonbury*, pp. 6, 19; L. Abrams, *Anglo-Saxon Glastonbury: Church and Endowment* (Woodbridge, 1996), pp. 14–18, 31–4, on the early Glastonbury cartulary, the precise dating of which is difficult. She points out, p. 17 n. 44, that we cannot be sure that the relevant passages in the Glastonbury *De antiquitate* were the work of William of Malmesbury rather than interpolations. On the development of the *De antiquitate*, see Scott, *Early History of Glastonbury*, pp. 34–9.

[67] See below, p. 136. See below, p. clxxxiv, on the collection of boundary clauses.

[68] See below, pp. xliv–xlvii.

revealed by the story of the will of Archbishop Ælfric being found in one of the abbey's chests in the late eleventh century.[69] Such chests may have been kept in the sacristy, and perhaps have been associated with the church's relics.

The range of charters that appears in MS C is the product of a process of selection, linked to the establishment of Abingdon's landed endowment.[70] To take one example, the composer knew that King Æthelred had given his thegn Beorhtric eight hides at Leverton, which Edward the Confessor later gave to Abingdon. He may have learnt of this from a note associated with Edward's charter, but it is more likely that he knew of Æthelred's charter, which would later be included in the revised *History*.[71] However, the composer of the earlier version chose to include only the Confessor's charter for Abingdon, presumably considering this sufficient evidence of title. Indeed, in no case does MS C include both a charter recording the gift of land to Abingdon and an earlier charter recording that single piece of land being given to an individual.[72] Only when there was no charter recording the transfer to Abingdon did he include the most recent of the charters transferring land to an individual; presumably the assumed subsequent transfer of that charter to the monastery was deemed sufficient title.

When copies in MS C can be compared with surviving originals, they are generally revealed as of good quality.[73] The proem was on

[69] Vol. ii. 50.

[70] See also Keynes, *Diplomas*, pp. 10–11. See below, p. cxxxi, for the possibility that the existence at Abingdon of more than one storage chest might help to explain differences between the selection of documents included in MS C and in MS B. Cf. Robinson, *Times of Saint Dunstan*, p. 78, on relics being stored in chests at Glastonbury, and the production of two relic lists, one arranged by chest, the other by subject. Chroniclers elsewhere likewise did not necessarily use all the documentation available to them; see Berkhofer, *Day of Reckoning*, pp. 54–5, on Hariulf at Saint-Riquier.

[71] cc. 134–5, B228. Note also the omission of the charter recording the Confessor's grant of Sandford to Earl Godwine, B271; cf. the inclusion of the charter in his name granting land there to Abingdon, c. 132, on which see also below, p. cxix; the omission of the charter recording Æthelred granting five hides in Chilton to Byrhtwold bishop of Ramsbury, B239; cf. the inclusion of the charter in the Confessor's name granting land there to Abingdon, c. 133. See also Keynes, *Diplomas*, p. 12.

[72] Note, however, the will of Archbishop Ælfric recording his grant of Dumbleton to Abingdon, and the charter concerning Dumbleton in the preceding chapter; cc. 104, 105. Note also the mention of various estates in two charters in King Coenwulf's name, below, cc. 10, 11.

[73] *Charters of Abingdon Abbey*, pp. lvi, lx, states that MS C has less of a tendency to modify personal names and Old English words than would be displayed in the later revision. Note also that Latin readings in charters in MS C which differ from those in MS

several occasions omitted, particularly perhaps when it repeated the formulae of a nearby charter.[74] On the other hand, some lengthy proems were retained,[75] whilst shorter ones often reiterate the utility of writing for the preservation of memory.[76] In addition, boundary clauses were routinely omitted, but the same manuscript includes a quire of boundary clauses, copied in the same hand as the *History*.[77] Usually witness lists were considerably abbreviated; the longer of the witness lists in this version may indicate charters of particular importance, especially the privilege of Æthelred and to a slightly lesser extent that of Edgar.[78]

Charters were also sources for narrative passages in the *History*. The comment that Alfred, in taking away from the abbey the place in which it was situated, was 'rendering inappropriate compensation to the victorious Lord for the victory that he had enjoyed', derives from a charter in Eadred's name.[79] Elsewhere charters were a source of information rather than phraseology. The very first chapter of the *History* states that

> we have learnt from a record of bygone events which man of old was the original founder of this monastery: that Cissa king of the West Saxons gave the site for the monastery to be built for the worship of almighty God to a certain Hæha, a man of the religious life and abbot, and also to his sister, named Cilla, and that very many endowments and possessions were conferred on it by royal gift, for the necessities of life of those living therein.[80]

The 'record of bygone events' is probably the charters which immediately follow. The chapter concerning Abbot Hræthhun and

B are sometimes supported by the 16th-century copies; see e.g. below, p. 38, for 'adaugeat' rather than 'adaugebat', p. 66 'sit' rather than 'ait' (*Charters of Abingdon Abbey*, no. 22, 52). Cf. the treatment of Anglo-Saxon charters noted by Fleming, 'Christ Church Canterbury's Anglo-Norman cartulary', pp. 93–6. See below, p. 36, for MS C taking what was in fact a capital P to be an Anglo-Saxon wynn. Note also the number of scribal errors in cc. 129–30, and see below, p. xxxi, on the translation of Ælfric's will.

[74] cc. 16, 22, 60, 61, 69, 77, 81, 83, 85, 98 (where the omission makes the start of the charter somewhat awkward), 135.

[75] e.g. c. 104.

[76] e.g. cc. 8, 20.

[77] See below, p. clxxxiv.

[78] cc. 60 and 98, the latter of which omits the thegns who witnessed; cf. the much abbreviated witness list to c. 37, Eadwig's privilege. Note also c. 20.

[79] See below, pp. 32, 50.

[80] Stenton, *Early History*, pp. 16–17, notes that 'the form Hean, which alone appears in Abingdon documents, merely represents an oblique case of this name [Hæha], treated as a nominative by scribes to whom the declensions of Old English had become unfamiliar'.

his protection of the abbey from the oppressions of King Coenwulf's servants almost certainly arises from the relevant charter in Coenwulf's name; a story of a specific episode has been used to explain what is in fact a not unusual immunity clause.[81] Æthelred's charters suggested oppressions suffered by the house whilst those from Æthelwold's time gave an early version of the house's history.[82]

Other types of documents too acted as sources for the *History*. Only one will specifically making a grant to Abingdon appears in the *History*, that of Archbishop Ælfric of Canterbury.[83] It appears in MS C only in a Latin version, whereas the revised *History* also includes the Old English. The Latin text omits some details, makes some errors of translation, and omits the exact terms of an agreement involving St Albans and a layman, presumably of little interest to Abingdon.[84] Further grants may have been known from wills that do not appear in the *History*. They may have been lost, or excluded from the *History* because they were in the vernacular or because they were less impressive documents than diplomas. Alternatively, if Abingdon was not the main beneficiary, it may not have received or recorded the entire will but only a short statement of the relevant gift.[85]

Vernacular documents may have recorded other gifts, such as that of Chalgrave and *Bulthesworthe*, which is accompanied in the *History* by a list of witnesses. There is a Latin summary of a vernacular text recording Abbot Æthelwold and Bishop Brihthelm's exchange of Kennington and Curbridge, a text which appears in full in the later manuscript.[86] Such vernacular charters and records of individual

[81] cc. 9, 11, on which see also *Charters of Abingdon Abbey*, pp. cxcv–cxvi, and below, p. 14 n. 47. Gransden, 'Traditionalism and continuity', p. 198, suggests that a charter of the Confessor could underlie the *History*'s account of how Lewknor was acquired from Queen Edith (c. 121)

[82] See cc. 37, 60, 98, 99, 102.

[83] c. 105. Ælfric's will may have come to Abingdon because he was initially buried there; John of Worcester, *Chronicle*, ii. 613. The 'testament' of Abbot Hæha, c. 7, concerns Bradfield.

[84] See K. A. Lowe, 'Latin versions of Old English wills', *Journal of Legal History*, xx (1999), 1–24, at pp. 5–6, who concludes that it 'is salutary to note the carelessness with which the translator handled details of less importance to the foundation [i.e. Abingdon] while on the face of it giving a full and accurate account of the will's contents'.

[85] See e.g. cc. 107, 108; also *Charters of Abingdon Abbey*, pp. 579–83. Lowe, 'Latin versions of Old English wills', p. 4, notes that such incorporation of material from wills into Latin narrative also occurs at Ely and Ramsey.

[86] See below, p. 76. There may also have been boundary clauses with an existence separate from diplomas; *Charters of Abingdon Abbey*, p. xlvi. In addition, the Latin account of a gift by Ceadwalla at the start of the *History* translates a vernacular text that came to be appended to a diploma; c. 2 and n. 5; see also Gelling, *Early Charters of the Thames Valley*, no. 142.

bequests can be grouped with the type of short memoranda and notes that may underlie other passages of the *History*.[87] Very occasionally such reliance on earlier memoranda can be proved. Thus the *History*'s section concerning the acquisition of Kingston from Ealdorman Ælfhere translates a vernacular text preserved in the quire of MS C devoted to boundary clauses.[88] Elsewhere reliance on earlier short texts, Latin or vernacular, can only be suggested on less definitive grounds. Forms of dating by solar cycle or concurrents, unique within the *History*, may be one indication.[89] Vocabulary choice or phraseology may be suggestive,[90] but in general the process of rewriting from any earlier notes seems to have been quite thorough. Whatever their precise nature, and whatever their relationship to the text of the *History*, it seems very likely that an increase in the number of pre-existing notes contributed to the change in form of the *History* from the first half of the eleventh century, with increased narrative and the appearance of accounts of disputes.[91]

In addition, the composer of the *History* could have heard accounts of some events that had taken place late in the period covered in Book I from old monks who had either experienced the events themselves or in turn heard them from their elders.[92] When Abbot Adelelm (1071–83) was seeking to establish the abbey's rights, one of his greatest helpers was Ælfwig, priest at the royal vill of Sutton Courtenay and a *Domesday* tenant of the abbey. Amongst Ælfwig's qualities was excellent memory of past events. In 1091 × 1094, the church of Sutton Courtenay was given to the abbey, and it was arranged that Ælfwig was to be succeeded by his son, should the son

[87] In general, see the various non-royal vernacular documents collected in *Anglo-Saxon Charters*, ed. Robertson. For a different way of using such notes, see Fleming, 'Christ Church Canterbury's Anglo-Norman cartulary', pp. 91–2.

[88] c. 93; see also below, p. lxi, for attempts to associate this text with a 'house narrative'.

[89] Vol. ii. 18, 108.

[90] For unusual vocabulary, see e.g. the use of 'datio' in the account of a gift by Henry d'Aubigny; vol. ii. 146. This is the only use of the word in the *History*, although it could, of course, be a slip for 'donatio'. The list of relics compiled on the order of Faritius uses the word 'contestor' with reference to St Malo; vol. ii. 222. The word does not appear in *DMLBS*, although R. E. Latham, *Revised Medieval Latin Word-List from British and Irish Sources* (rev. edn., London, 1980), s.v. 'contest/atio litis', does include 'contestator' with a reference to the ninth century. The relic list may have been wrongly copied into the *History*, or may include an otherwise extremely rare form.

[91] See below, p. lxxii, for this change of form. See also below, p. xxxvi, on verses being copied into the *History*

[92] See above, p. xv, on the possible date of the composer's entry to the monastery; see also vol. ii, pp. xx–xxi.

survive him. If we assume that the son did outlive Ælfwig, he may well have lived into the time when the composer of the *History* was at Abingdon, giving the composer a potential link to the late Anglo-Saxon past, its events, and its traditions.[93]

3. Style of narrative sections of the *History*

Finally, in this consideration of the work of the composer of the first version of the *History*, let us briefly examine the style of the narratives for which he was responsible. In general, the prose is clear and quite simple. Slips or infelicities of grammar do occur but are few.[94] The historic present is sometimes employed for quite extended passages, sometimes for just part of a sentence.[95] There are only occasional minor flourishes, such as the juxtaposition 'just' and 'unjust' in the phrase 'sed non patitur Deus sicut iusta sic iniusta diu subsistere'.[96] No clear literary model is used for the initial laudatory depiction of Faritius, for example, and we have already seen that the composer avoided direct derivation from the *Life of Æthelwold*.[97] If there is a major influence on his style, it is the mass of charter material that he has digested.

Some preference for classicizing or, perhaps more accurately, Romanizing vocabulary is displayed. *Imperium* and related words are common. Sometimes employed to mean order or command,[98] *imperium* is most commonly used to mean kingship, dominion, or reign,[99] as it also is in Anglo-Saxon charters.[100] It is also used in adjectival form as an impressive alternative to *regius* or *regalis*.[101] Cnut is said to have ruled Denmark, Norway, and England 'imperialiter' in a passage which also mentions his visit to Rome and his giving of laws.[102] The phrase 'res publica' is used to refer to public or royal property,[103] to the common good in need of protection,[104] and also to the public or worldly affairs and property of the monastery.[105] The

[93] Vol. ii. 4, 36–40.

[94] See below, p. 178 ('Hec uero nominata . . . ex ea genuit'); p. 188 ('Abbendoniam requisitum abbatem ueniunt').

[95] See below, e.g. pp. 136–8, 174; vol. ii. 22.

[96] Vol. ii. 240.

[97] See above, p. xxvii; vol. ii. 64–6.

[98] e.g. below, pp. 138, 224; vol. ii. 6, 16, 182.

[99] e.g. below, pp. 10, 32; vol. ii. 26, 58, 174, 180 ('ante suscepti imperii monarchiam').

[100] See e.g. below, p. 18, for 'anno imperii nostri'.

[101] See below, p. 196, vol. ii. 4, 50, with reference to the crown or to orders.

[102] See below, p. 184. The title *basileus*, which I translate as 'emperor', appears only in charters in the *History*, not in narrative sections.

[103] See below, p. 4.

[104] Vol. ii. 6.

[105] Vol. ii. 4, 104.

adjective *publicus* is used not only in the sense of 'open' or 'public' in a formal context[106] but also of 'official' or even 'state': letters were sent 'ad comprouinciales publicarum administrationum exactores [to the local officials of public administration]',[107] and there are references to 'publica moneta [public money]'.[108]

There are also occasional uses of vocabulary from Romano-canonical private law. Thus a grant is made 'de proprio fratrum fructuario', rather than the more common phrases such as 'a dominio monachorum'.[109] However, whilst such words are on occasion used, they do not seem to carry any strict technical sense. Likewise, the terms *possessio* and *proprietas* feature in the text, but are not contrasted in the way that was becoming significant in legal thinking in England at this very time, to distinguish between possession and ownership.[110] *Proprietas* barely figures in the text, although it is once used in the sense of right or ownership disputed between two parties.[111] *Possessio* appears considerably more often but is largely used in the narratives to refer to physical possessions,[112] rarely to the enjoying of possession.[113] Even in this latter case, possession is probably not being consciously contrasted with ownership.[114]

The composer was willing to use words unknown or not common in classical Latin. In the latter category come, for example, the words

[106] See e.g. vol. ii. 56 'publico eis interminato maledicto', 172 'publico in conspectus iterare', 220 'nisi publica satisfactione et restitutione penituerint'. See also vol. ii. 22, 30, for 'ratiotinatione publica' and 'ratiocinatu publico'. Cf. e.g. below, p. 16, vol. ii. 4, for use of *publice*.

[107] Vol. ii. 144; note also vol. ii. 62, particularly on Hugh of Buckland being sheriff and 'publicarum iusticiarius compellationum', which may mean something like 'pleas of the crown'.

[108] Vol. ii. 36, 50.

[109] Vol. ii. 56; it is probable 'proprio' is here an adjective, 'fructuario' a noun, although this cannot be certain. Occasionally a phrase is used that is neither common in contemporary English law nor a term from learned law, but perhaps had a certain learned ring; see vol. ii. 62 for 'delegatio commendaticia'. I would like to thank Magnus Ryan for his help on this point.

[110] M. G. Cheney, '*Possessio/proprietas* in ecclesiastical courts in mid-twelfth-century England', in G. S. Garnett and J. G. H. Hudson , eds., *Law and Government in Medieval England and Normandy* (Cambridge, 1994), pp. 245–54.

[111] See below, p. 210.

[112] See below, e.g. pp. 2, 14, 46, 92, vol. ii. 4, 6, 26.

[113] See below, p. 190. Charters also sometimes use 'possessio' in a more abstract sense, but not in contrast to ownership; e.g. below, p. 36. Note also charters using phrases such as 'in eternam possessionem': e.g. below, pp. 68, 86.

[114] Cf. the background in learned law of Thomas of Marlborough, author of the equivalent *History* of Evesham; Thomas of Marlborough, *History of the Abbey of Evesham*, ed. J. E. Sayers and L. Watkiss (OMT, 2003), pp. xv–xxvii.

'infortunium' and 'commanipulares', both used in the account of oppressions of the church by William Rufus.[115] Likewise, the chapter introducing Abbot Faritius twice uses the extremely uncommon comparative of the quite rare word 'procurate'.[116] Post-classical vocabulary also features in legal terminology, for example 'inuestitura', with reference both to possession of the abbey and possession of land. In the latter sense it is once glossed with another medieval term 'id est saisitionem [that is, seisin]'.[117]

The writer sometimes states that he is introducing vernacular usages with reference to place and personal names. He mentions the watercourse at Botley 'quem uulgo "Lacche" appellant' and a man '"Scalegrai" uulgariter nominatus'.[118] He also occasionally refers to common usage in other contexts. Once he explains the words 'quadraginta manipuli [forty bundles]', with the gloss 'quos uulgo garbas uocant [commonly called sheaves]'.[119] Likewise he interestingly glosses the phrase 'in capite', referring to land held directly from the lord, with the words 'ut uulgo loquatur'.[120]

As already noted, the writer does not favour rhetorical flourishes, and nor does he make much use of recurrent phrases. Those that are used often come as warnings or notification to men of the future to pay attention to what has been described, for example 'let men in future see what should be guarded against concerning this' and 'so let all guard against the frauds of a perjurer, and guard against sending a letter to the friend of fraud by such a representative'.[121] Likewise, allusions to other texts are rare within the narratives. There are very

[115] Vol. ii. 60; for *infortunium*, see also below, pp. 46, 138, 222. I translate the words as 'misfortune' and 'barrack-mates' respectively.

[116] Vol. ii. 66; vol. ii. 70 uses 'procurate'.

[117] See below, pp. 32 (possession of abbey), 198, 224, vol. ii. 10, 88 (with gloss).

[118] Vol. ii. 20, 286. See also below, pp. 32 'que uulgari onomate Abbandun dicitur', 2092 'que Sandford uulgo uocitatur', 212 'qui uulgo mons Albi Equi nuncupatur', this last of course being a Latin rendering; see also vol. ii. 246 'qui uulgariter Mora dicitur'. Cf. the common practice in Anglo-Saxon charters of including a phrase such as 'qui uulgariter uocitatur' with reference to a place or another name; e.g. below, pp. 36, 50 ('uillam que uulgari onomate Aebbandun dicitur').

[119] Vol. ii. 34.

[120] Vol. ii. 100. Historians now normally confine the phrase 'in chief' to reference to those holding directly of the king. Regarding the vernacular, note also the significant use of vernacular words in the list of entitlements of monastic servants that appears in the continuation of the *History* in MS B. Several are Old French, but the term 'scepinga', meaning allotment, may be a Latinized form relating to the OE 'scyp', meaning a patch of cloth and by analogy a patch of land; vol. ii, Appendix II.

[121] See below, p. 210 'uideant posteri quid inde cauendum sit', vol. ii. 106 'caueant ergo omnes periuri fraudes, caueantque tali legato mittere breue fraudis amico'.

occasional biblical allusions, and a phrase such as 'there is no medicine against death' sounds proverbial.[122] As for use of verse, it is possible, although uncertain, that the composer of the *History* was responsible for the brief metrical obituary of Abbot Wulfgar. He was quoting rather than composing the inscription on the reliquary given by Cnut to Abingdon, and probably also a verse obituary of Aubrey and William de Ver.[123] In general, however, the text is unornamented by allusion or quotation, even compared with other fairly similar and undecorated texts such as the *Book of the Foundation of the Monastery of Walden*.[124]

More characteristic of the text are first-person interventions, in singular and plural.[125] Some of these are within cross-references[126] or brief explanations such as 'lest I delay with many details',[127] or slight flourishes such as 'let us turn our pen to . . .'.[128] Further instances of narratorial interventions are statements that matters are recounted as a warning to men in future and comments on the purpose of writing.[129] Others still are comments on the source or extent of the writer's knowledge: 'we have learnt from a record of bygone events'; 'as to what caused the evil of this misfortune, nothing true has come to my notice'; 'likewise, concerning the same land, we have found what follows written in English in almost worn-away letters'; 'I saw the perpetrators of the damage which was inflicted suffer equal

[122] Vol. ii. 82. For biblical quotations and allusions, see below, p. 387, and vol. ii. 400.

[123] See below, pp. 176–8; vol. ii. 90; the introductory phrase 'Horum itaque sepultorum epitaphium hic annexuimus' strongly suggests that this is a quotation rather than a composition by the compiler of the *History*. It is possible that the obituary might have been carved on a tomb; cf. below, p. xli, for the obituary of Ceadwalla, and see R. J. Bartlett, *England under the Norman and Angevin Kings* (Oxford, 2000), p. 598. Professor Richard Sharpe (personal communication) comments that the style 'is competent but the amount of rhyme between caesura and end of line fits in with twelfth-century decadent taste in hexameters'.

[124] *The Book of the Foundation of Walden Monastery*, ed. D. Greenway and L. Watkiss (OMT, 1999), pp. lxvi–lxvii, 207.

[125] Note also other forms of narratorial comment, for example a linking of peace with evil behaviour, below, p. 220: 'now peace was bestowed following the excessive and long-lasting oppressions of the Danes, those distresses were forgotten and everyone rushed to commit improper and presumptuous deeds'.

[126] See above, p. xxv; also e.g. below, pp. 48, 162, 208, 222, vol. ii. 58, 306. Note also the use of the first person plural to refer to the monks or monastery as a whole: below, p. 34 ('we received Cynath as abbot'), vol. ii. 146, 224, 238.

[127] See below, p. 192. See also e.g. below, pp. 76, 94, 194.

[128] Vol. ii. 8, 72.

[129] e.g. vol. ii. 46, 106; also above, p. xxxv. Cf. vol. ii. 6–8 for what seems to be a deliberate attempt, through a certain allusiveness of style, not to accuse particular individuals of wrongdoing.

misfortune at a later time'; 'this Giralmus was afterwards led astray by I know not what cause'.[130] Finally some instances combine these various purposes, whilst aiming to reinforce trust in the writer: 'I have related these matters concerning a man now dead, and no one will suspect me of wishing to flatter ashes. Let us pass hence to other matters.'[131]

Very occasionally the writer uses the second person, as when he says that a few years after the restoration of the abbey in the mid-tenth century 'you might see the whole monastery honourably built and richly endowed'.[132] He rarely employs direct speech, exceptions being miracle stories deriving from the *Life of St Æthelwold*, the story concerning Queen Edith and the grant of Lewknor, and some words of Faritius.[133] The impression of a general avoidance of stylistic device in the first version of the *History* will be confirmed as we now turn to the work of the reviser, preserved in London, British Library, Cotton Claudius B. VI.

(B) MS B

London, British Library, Cotton Claudius B. VI comes from the second quarter or perhaps the middle of the thirteenth century. The version of the *History* which it preserves comes from after the death of Abbot Hugh in 1221, since he is referred to as 'uir bone memorie', 'a man of blessed memory'. Although a passage in Book I of the *History* appears to allude to his building works at the abbey, the only one of his deeds explicitly mentioned is his journey overseas and acquisition of a confirmation charter from Richard I in 1190.[134] The possibility thus arises of at least one intermediate manuscript, written soon after that date and only very slightly revised when transcribed in MS B. The textual relationship of MSS C and B gives no definitive answer to this question. Some errors in MS B do suggest that it derives from MS C, but the derivation could be via an intervening manuscript in which the errors had appeared.[135] Likewise internal

[130] See below, pp. 2, 46, 136, vol. ii. 60, 284. See also vol. ii. 70–2 on matters the compiler had heard from others or seen himself.

[131] Vol. ii. 290.

[132] See below, p. 56. See also vol. ii. 64.

[133] See below, pp. 52, 54, 192, vol. ii. 218.

[134] See below, p. 360, vol. ii. 370–2. For the date of Hugh's death, see *Heads of Religious Houses*, pp. 25, 241.

[135] See below, pp. 114, 156, 182, 222, vol. ii. 24, 92. Corrections within the revised version's new sections need not indicate an intervening manuscript but only copying from notes, wax, or a draft: see e.g. below, p. 268.

references within the passages that MS B added to the original version of the *History* do not make it clear whether it is the first revised manuscript. For example, references to 'the present day' give no help with specific dating.[136] Events and documents which one might have expected to be included, for example Abbot Hugh's inclusion in a group of King John's messengers to Rome in 1200, and the obtaining of a confirmation bull from Innocent III, are not mentioned.[137] On the other hand, there are also very significant omissions in the continuation up to 1190, including various bulls of Alexander III.[138] These omissions show that silences after 1190 need not indicate that the *History* was originally revised soon after that date. Marginalia in MS C in the hand that was used to give guidance to the rubricator of MS B show that at the very least the reviser made direct use of MS C.[139] This does not rule out the existence of an intervening manuscript but reinforces the sense that it is unnecessary to posit such a lost text.

Again there is no surviving Preface to help us with regard to the identity or background of the reviser, or his purpose, although the now lost first folios of the manuscript may have included such a Preface.[140] The reviser was presumably a monk of Abingdon. Apart from the continuation from the time of Walkelin to the confirmation by Richard I, the main changes that he made were for the period before the late tenth and early eleventh centuries. The first complete chapter of narrative shared by the two manuscripts concerns Osgar, abbot from 963 to 984,[141] although the reviser had earlier drawn on MS C's narratives without reproducing them at length.[142] The next shared narrative also concerns Osgar, and thereafter there is a fair amount of common material and common order, with additional charters and some changes to the narrative appearing in MS B.[143] However, it is only from the description of a dispute over Leckhampstead in the time of Edward the Confessor that MS B really becomes a

[136] See below, pp. 268, 282, 328, 356.

[137] *Rotuli Chartarum in Turri Londinensi Asservati, 1199–1216*, ed. T. D. Hardy (London, 1837), p. 99. Lyell, no. 25, issued on 7 Mar. 1200.

[138] Lyell, nos. 19–22; Chatsworth, no. 87; *CMA* ii. 313–14; vol. ii. 398–9.

[139] See below, p. clxxxiii.

[140] The missing start of the text likewise prevents us knowing whether it was given a title by the reviser; the *incipit* and *explicit* of the individual books provide no help.

[141] c. 71, B209.

[142] e.g. c. 36, B113.

[143] c. 93, B213. The charter in the preceding chapter in MS C appears as B211, with another charter as B212. B214 and B215 draw on cc. 95 and 96. B 216 and B 217 are copies of cc. 97 and 98.

simple copy of MS C with minor textual variations and very occasional additions.[144]

Consistency of style indicates that the revision was the work of one person.[145] Descriptions of the coming of the Anglo-Saxons, of the Danes in the ninth century, and to an extent of their successors under Swein at the end of the tenth and the start of the eleventh, show similarities.[146] The same allusions from Vergil and from the Bible appear in additions early in the *History* and in the continuation after the death of Walkelin.[147] Use of words such as 'magnate' and 'baron' with reference to the Anglo-Saxon period suggest at least a thorough rewriting of any early sources and probably new composition, as also does routine employment of the phrase 'in pure and perpetual alms' with reference to any lands given to the abbey.[148]

1. Sources for the revision

The reviser of the *History* treated the narratives in the earlier version in various ways. Some were omitted. Although it may have appeared in the lost folios at the start of MS B, MS C's opening passage on the site and foundation of the monastery was probably omitted as part of the provision of a new foundation story. Omission of other passages is harder to explain, notably the miracle stories associated with Æthelwold.[149] With one exception in Edward the Confessor's time, all the short passages prefacing charters were cut or replaced with new passages.[150]

In other cases, too, MS B replaces the passages in MS C with an alternative passage on the same matter, as with the death of Harthacnut.[151] However, with the exception of confusion over two narratives

[144] c. 120, B259.

[145] See below, pp. liii–lv; note especially the consistent use of the phrase 'quid multa?'

[146] See below, pp. 236, 266, 354.

[147] See below, p. 276 and vol. ii. 354, for 'dum adhuc uitales carperet auras'; below, p. 250 and vol. ii. 344, for 'uiscera misericordie'.

[148] Magnates: below, pp. 262, 276, 292, and also vol. ii. 328 ('magnatuum hominum'); barons: below, pp. 252, 282; 'in puram et perpetuam elemosinam': below, pp. 246, 248, 252, etc.

[149] cc. 29–33. Note also c. 94.

[150] The exception is c. 134, B274.

[151] c. 118, B256. Note also the different narratives concerning Bishop Hræthhun; c. 9, B17. For Hræthhun there is a third version in the Abingdon additions to the Worcester *Chronicle*; John of Worcester, *Chronicle*, ii. 610, as well as a brief account in *De abbatibus*, *CMA* ii. 274. Note also that the account of Thomas of Hurstbourne and the vacancy after the death of Abbot Roger in the *History* in MS B is very different from that in MS C, fo. 179, added after the *History* in a different hand, probably of the end of the 12th century; see vol. ii. 358–70, *CMA* ii. 297–9 respectively.

concerning Robert d'Oilly, such complete replacement of narratives ceases in the mid-eleventh century.[152] There are also passages where the reviser draws on the phraseology of MS C, but rewrites to varying degrees. There is one instance of this before the tenth century, where a few words are shared.[153] Then both limited and more extensive sharing occurs for passages from the late tenth century,[154] and there is some very extensive common wording in chapters relating to the time of the Norman Conquest.[155]

Besides such replacement or rewriting, MS B also adds narratives for which there was no equivalent in MS C.[156] What were the sources for such narratives? [157] If, as I would argue, a version of the Abingdon text now known as *De abbatibus* existed prior to the revision of the *History*, it may well have suggested matters requiring discussion.[158] Most notable is the lengthy treatment of developments concerning King Coenwulf, his sisters, and Culham, more extensive and elaborate than the short passage in *De abbatibus*. There are some verbal parallels but these are very limited.[159] The Frankish embassy to Æthelstan's court that contributed to Abingdon's relic collection does not appear in MS C, but does appear in *De abbatibus* and MS B.[160] Both mistakenly refer to Hugh, duke of the Franks and count of Paris, as Hugh Capet, king of France, but other verbal similarities are small. For the reviser of the *History*, *De abbatibus* may have been a source of material and subjects, but not of words.[161]

[152] Vol. ii. 32–4, 326–30.

[153] See below, pp. 28, 266.

[154] B214, B215 cf. cc. 95, 96, show sentences in common. See B243, cf. c. 109, for a section with some verbal parallels as well as some differences of subject matter; it also has some verbal parallels to B37. See also B245, B248, B249, B250.

[155] B285, B290.

[156] Apart from brief introductions to gifts, the new narratives in MS B are B1–B8, B11–B13, B15–B16, B19, B21, B25, B27, B29, B31, B38–B39, B46, B62, B63, B112–B113, B174, B207–B208, B233, B252, B289, B291, vol. ii, Appendices I and II.

[157] For the period after 1071, see vol. ii, pp. xxxviii–xl.

[158] See also below, p. lxxxvii, on Aben or Abben, the founder of Abingdon in *De abbatibus* and in the revised *History*. However, it is uncertain whether the Abben story would have appeared in any early version of *De abbatibus*; see below, p. lxxxv, for the suggestion that knowledge of Abben may have arrived at Abingdon in 1180. Compare also c. 14, B37, and *CMA* ii. 276 on the degree of destruction attributed to the Danes by MS C, MS B, and *De abbatibus* respectively.

[159] B16, *CMA* ii. 274. *De abbatibus* uses the phrase 'liberam et quietam ab omni seculari seruicio'; the *History* uses 'liberam ab omni humano seruitio et seculari exaccione'.

[160] B62, *CMA* ii. 276–7.

[161] In the account of Helenstow, verbal parallels again are very scarce, but note *CMA* ii. 269, 'quarum ipsa mater et abbatissa extitit', below, p. 244, 'quarum in posterum mater extitit et abbatissa'. For comparison of the *History* and *De abbatibus*, see also vol. ii. 344–6; cf. *CMA* ii. 291–2.

The reviser preferred rather more literary sources, and for the early period of Abingdon's *History* he drew upon two. One was Geoffrey of Monmouth's *Historia regum*, short passages of which appear at the start of his account.[162] The other is Bede's *Ecclesiastical History*, which is a possible source of information for the first two surviving chapters of the revised *History* and certainly provides information and some words for the next three chapters, including the text of Ceadwalla's epitaph.

For further information on national matters, the reviser drew on the *Chronicle* of John of Worcester. The two texts share the error of calling Offa of Mercia's son Ecgberht rather than Ecgfrith, and both state that the Danes came from the Danube.[163] The reviser drew on John of Worcester not just for material but actual words in his praise for Edgar, and in his accounts of Æthelred's consecration, Edward the Confessor's anointing, and William the Conqueror's coronation.[164] He may well have been using the copy of John of Worcester by the scribe of MS C, although he did not include any of the additional Abingdon passages that appear in the John of Worcester manuscript but not in MS C of the *History*.[165]

Unlike the compiler of MS C, the reviser drew verbatim on Wulfstan of Winchester's *Life of Æthelwold* for his account of Æthelwold's restoration of Abingdon, and more briefly for a passage concerning Æthelwold's building of his church, although not for his account of the saint's early life.[166] He explicitly referred to the *Passion*

[162] See below, p. 232, for quotation from Geoffrey, pp. 234, 242, for knowledge derived from Geoffrey; also below, p. liii.

[163] See below, pp. 250, 266 (cf. c. 14), John of Worcester, *Chronicle*, ii. 226, 280. Neither feature of MS B could derive from any existing version of the *Anglo-Saxon Chronicle*.

[164] See below, pp. 328, 346, 362, 370.

[165] It is possible that the reviser used the work of William of Malmesbury and/or Henry of Huntingdon, which could have provided him with the names of the Viking leaders Hinguar and Ubba, below, p. 266. A text of Henry of Huntingdon for the period 1132–54 may have been copied at Abingdon, although this depends on the questionable argument that there was a second Abingdon manuscript of John of Worcester, Cambridge, Corpus Christi College 92; see below, p. lviii, and Henry of Huntingdon, *Historia Anglorum*, ed. Greenway, pp. cxxvi–cxxvii. It is conceivable that the reviser's notion that Siward was made bishop of Rochester was derived from William of Malmesbury's *Gesta pontificum*, but it is equally likely that William and the reviser independently came to the same erroneous explanation of an episode that must have seemed very confusing to later eyes; see below, p. ciii. There are also parallels to *De antiquitate Glastonie ecclesie*, notably in the story of King Lucius and Pope Eleutherius and in the mentions of Pope Leo and King Coenwulf, but there is no clear evidence for direct borrowing; see below, pp. cxii, 232, and also Scott, *Early History of Glastonbury*, pp. 27–8. Overall, there is no compelling reason to believe that the reviser used William of Malmesbury or Henry of Huntingdon.

[166] B84, B207; cf. c. 24, B83.

and *Life* of Edward the martyr with reference to the translation of Edward's relics to Abingdon, although the surviving texts of the *Passio* do not mention the translation.[167]

Further narratives may derive from notes and memoranda.[168] There is no obvious source for the account of Wulfric Spot's foundation of Burton. It is possible that Abingdon had a copy of his will, although the provision for the payment to the king mentioned in the *History* differs from that in his surviving will; perhaps a related document or a summary note was in Abingdon's possession.[169] The account of Æthelwold's works as abbot states that the reviser learnt 'from the witness of ancient books [*librorum*]' about a gift of a gold chalice and perhaps about his giving other ornaments. These 'books' could resemble the surviving Old English account of Æthelwold's gifts to Peterborough.[170] Another set of notes may have concerned miracles, notably concerning disputes over the meadow at Berry and over the mill at Cuddesdon, and the dreams of Abbot Siward and—somewhat later—Robert d'Oilly.[171] However, even if these stories do have earlier textual bases, they are consistent in style with the rest of the revision and with one another.[172] It is best to take them as new compositions, with a textual or oral basis.

Oral traditions and sources are occasionally revealed in the revised

[167] See below, p. 358. There is an outside possibility that the same text may have influenced the reviser's treatment of Edward's death. B214 states that 'Edwardo rege Anglorum dolo Ælfthriþe nouerce sue ad celestia per martirium translato'. The relevant passage in the existing version of the *Passio* also uses the words 'nouerce sue' and 'dolo', but they are some sentences apart, and any suggestion of influence must be extremely tentative; C. E. Fell, *Edward King and Martyr* (Leeds, 1971), p. 4 line 17, p. 5 line 2. The focus on Ælfthryth might also come from John of Worcester, *Chronicle*, ii. 428.

[168] Note, however, that the routine passages prefacing royal charters to individuals and stating that the recipients passed on the gift to Abingdon display no knowledge of documents beyond that shown in MS C; see also *Charters of Abingdon Abbey*, pp. cxxxv–cxxxvi.

[169] B233; see also *Charters of Abingdon Abbey*, p. 98. The form of the word 'Chantuarie' might suggest copying from a written text. Note also B168, which records a gift without including a charter. Various explanations are possible. The charter may have been lost, the gift recorded in some form of note rather than a charter, or even—if the gift really was made on the same day as that recorded in B167—a note made on the same piece of parchment as the record of the other gift. Note also the knowledge of a dispute in Abbot Ingulf's time for which no documentation is included; vol. ii. 344.

[170] See below, p. 338; *Anglo-Saxon Charters*, ed. Robertson, no. 39.

[171] B63, B252, B291, vol. ii. 326–30. Note also the dream of the boy Nicholas in *De abbatibus*; *CMA* ii. 285.

[172] Note the presence of Romano-canonical language below, p. 256, resembling that at p. 284. Note also the use of the phrase 'a sompno expergefactus' in the story of Siward's dream, 'expergefactus a sompno' in that of Robert d'Oilly's dream; below, p. 360, vol. ii. 330.

History. Differing oral traditions, rather than texts, may emerge in the account of the finding of the Black Cross at Helenstow: 'it was not, as some say, deposited there by Constantine the Great, who was made emperor in that area. It is more plausible that it was sent there by his well-wishers, the Britons, whom he had taken with him when setting out for Rome.'[173] Dunstan was 'reputed' to have made two bells with his own hands.[174] The reviser had learnt of the size of cheese provisions going back to Æthelwold's time 'from the testimony of aged men'.[175] Oral tradition probably also preserved knowledge of Æthelwold's drink provision, which had merited the composition of a riddle early in the eleventh century.[176]

Discussions about the abbey's past, including its foundation, may have stimulated the reviser's thoughts in other ways. He was aware that the quite low-lying position of the abbey is hard to reconcile with a place-name ending in the English *dun*, and that this problem would disappear if the place-name element were the Irish *dún*: 'For we have learnt from our contemporaries that, according to the language of the Irish, Abingdon is interpreted "house of Aben"; but according to the language of the English, Abingdon commonly means "the hill of Aben".' Although this is of course invention, linked to a foundation story involving the Irish monk Abben, James Campbell has pointed out that the speculation 'is chiefly interesting for what it suggests about its author's possibly having Irish contacts, perhaps such as might have put him onto the possibilities that St Abbán might offer to Abingdon'.[177] It may even be that the contact can be identified. In 1180 Lawrence O'Toole, archbishop of Dublin, spent three weeks at Abingdon before following Henry II to Normandy. Amongst his disciples, and perhaps a companion at Abingdon, was Albinus O'Mulloy. Albinus may later have been author of the *Life* of Abbán, a *Life* that would mention that saint's coming to Abingdon. It is possible that Lawrence's visit was the occasion when the story of Abben, Aben, or Abbán began to enter the Abingdon foundation tradition, and perhaps when Abingdon entered the Irish stories of St Abbán.[178]

[173] See below, p. 242.

[174] See below, p. 338.

[175] See below, p. 340.

[176] Porter, 'Æthelwold's bowl'.

[177] See below, p. 234. J. Campbell, 'The debt of the early English Church to Ireland', in P. Ní Chatháin and M. Richter, eds., *Ireland and Christendom* (Stuttgart, 1987), pp. 332–46, at 340.

[178] *Vitae Sanctorum Hiberniae*, ed. C. Plummer (2 vols., Oxford, 1910), i. 12–13; R. Sharpe, *Medieval Irish Saints' Lives: An Introduction to the Vitae sanctorum Hiberniae* (Oxford, 1991), pp. 352–3.

Even when drawing on the above sources, therefore, the revised version of the *History* contains a significant amount of new composition. Indeed, some of the new narratives did not copy existing texts even when they were available. Thus the treatment of Æthelwold's early life could have been, but was not, copied from the *Life of St Æthelwold*.[179] In other cases, the new compositions deal with matters not discussed elsewhere, and were most likely constructed to explain current concerns. The account of Abbot Siward's contemplation of rebuilding the church and the dream that persuaded him against this course of action was probably inspired by matters of importance in Abbot Hugh's time.[180]

Before assessing further the motivation for, and character of, such new or rewritten narratives, we must deal with the reviser's other main set of sources, charters. MS B contains approximately twice as many pre-Conquest documents as MS C.[181] The texts in the great majority of cases include the type of material excluded or much reduced in MS C: proems and expositions, boundary clauses, witness lists.[182] The reviser appears to have sought out the full charters wherever possible.[183] When the reviser simply copied from the earlier version of the *History*, it may well be because no original had survived.[184]

There are signs that the copying of charters into MS B was undertaken with some care. This is apparent in the accuracy of transcription and the common orthography displayed, for instance, in King Eadwig's charter concerning Milton,[185] and also in more complicated matters. For example, Oswald appeared as a witness to a charter immediately after the archbishop of Canterbury and thus in the position appropriate to the archbishop of York. However, the charter is dated 968 and Oswald only became archbishop in 970. The

[179] B83.

[180] B252, and see below, pp. l–li. See also B207 and vol. ii. 332–8 concerning food provision.

[181] See Concordance 2, *Charters of Abingdon Abbey*, p. xlviii.

[182] See *Charters of Abingdon Abbey*, p. lx, for the reviser's habit of tidying up witness lists.

[183] See *Charters of Abingdon Abbey*, pp. xlviii, lx. The reviser may also have had access to alternative abbreviated versions from those that appear in MS C. B18 has better place-name forms than c. 11, although no witness list. It remains possible that the place-name forms may have come from some further source.

[184] B28, B49, B50. These charters were presumably lost between the composition of the earlier version of the *History* and its revision. Given that such losses are exceptional, the composition of the *History* was clearly not regarded as making the originals redundant.

[185] c. 50 (B139); see also c. 55 (B127).

title that followed his name in MS B has been erased, presumably to remove the anomaly.[186] On the other hand, copies in MS C can on occasion give readings preferable to those in MS B.[187] In addition, some of the rearrangement of the order of charters in MS B in fact worsens the chronological pattern of the *History*. Thus a charter of Æthelbald of Mercia is wrongly reassigned to Æthelbald of Wessex, King Æthelred of Wessex and King Eadred are confused, and the Myton charter of Cnut that specifically mentions Abbot Siward appears in the context of his predecessor, Æthelwine.[188]

Some readings in Æthelred's great charter of 993 may give an indication of the reviser's varied working method, or at least that of his scribe. MS C gives the readings 'iusta' and 'renouande', the original charter 'iuste' and 'renouate'. MS B gives 'iusta' corrected to 'iuste', 'renouande' corrected to 'renouate'.[189] Given that these are two corrections of the same type, this seems to be more than a matter of simple scribal slips. Rather in this charter, for these readings at least, the revision seems to have worked from MS C and corrected from the original charter rather than starting with the original.[190] Such a procedure seems different from that employed when he was copying Eadwig's Milton charter, for example.

As already noted, sixty-nine pre-Conquest documents appear both in MS C and MS B.[191] Of these, a small number appear twice in MS B. In some cases, these are charters that MS B includes in full in their correct chronological place and then copies from MS C in a shortened

[186] B196 (*Charters of Abingdon Abbey*, no. 107). There are no witnesses in the version in MS C, c. 90.

[187] See above, p. xxix.

[188] B30, B32, B89, B93, B246; cf. cc. 8, 16, 113. Also leading to confusion was the decision by the reviser to change the order of two charters in Æthelstan's name, concerning Sandford-on-Thames and Swinford. An error arose, in that MS C's version of the Swinford charter stated that the bounds were to be found in a charter for Cumnor; MS B left this statement in its version of the Sandford charter, but it makes no sense in the context of that estate; see cc. 20–2, B48–B50, *Charters of Abingdon Abbey*, nos. 25–7.

[189] See below, pp. 146, 148, *Charters of Abingdon Abbey*, no. 124. Other readings cited in the *apparatus criticus* also show the proximity of MS B to MS C rather than to the original in the case of this charter.

[190] See also a charter of King Æthelred of Wessex that appears in two versions in MS B; c. 16, B32, B89 (*Charters of Abingdon Abbey*, no. 15). At one point the fuller version in MS B gives the reading 'principi' altered to 'principe', the latter being the reading in the abbreviated version of the charter in MS C; the abbreviated version in MS B gives 'principi', which is also the better reading grammatically. It may be that the full version was checked against the short version in MS C. Alternatively, this may be a simple scribal slip, not caused by copying.

[191] See above, p. xxviii.

version in the context of a later discussion of the land.[192] Confusion over kings' names helps to explain other repetitions.[193] Elsewhere, the reviser may simply have failed to realize that the full text that he had before him in the original was soon after to appear in MS C.[194]

MS B leaves out a very few charters that appear in MS C. Two of the four charters involving Abbot Hæha are omitted. This may be a matter of choice.[195] However, folios are missing early in MS B and these could have included the charters concerned. This explanation would involve some chronological awkwardness, as both charters that appear only in MS C are in the name of Ine, and the missing folios would more logically contain documents in the name of King Ceadwalla. This likelihood is reinforced by the text in MS B following the missing folios referring to Ceadwalla granting 'the goods enumerated above', although no such enumeration of goods survives.[196] However, it remains possible that the missing folios could have referred to grants by Ceadwalla as well as including the missing charters. It is even possible that those charters would have appeared in Ceadwalla's name, given that the two manuscripts differ in their attribution of a further charter to Ceadwalla or Ine.[197] That MS B once contained versions of the two Hæha charters on folios now lost remains the most plausible explanation of their apparent omission.

One of the charters in King Coenwulf's name is omitted in MS B. In MS C it is rather awkwardly positioned between the narrative concerning the king's oppressions of Abingdon and his charter of confirmation prohibiting such oppressions. The reviser may simply

[192] See the charters concerning Sparsholt and Whitchurch, cc. 139–140, B184, B238, B279–B280. That the duplicate short versions in MS B are copied from MS C is shown, for example, by variant readings and shared witness lists in c. 139 and B279, cf. B184 (*Charters of Abingdon Abbey*, no. 97).

[193] See c. 137 and B277, a short version in King Eadwig's name of a charter that appears in a full version in King Edmund's name in B72. The full version appears in the chronologically correct place, the short version in the context of the dispute over Leckhampstead. MS B repeats in fuller form a charter of King Æthelred of Wessex because the reviser mistook the king's name for Eadred; c. 16, B32, B89.

[194] See c. 135, B257 (full version), B275, where the confusion may be explained by the omission of the proem and exposition in the shortened version. See also c. 133, B258 (full version), B288, although in this case confusion is less explicable because both versions start at same place.

[195] See *Charters of Abingdon Abbey*, pp. lxi–lxii, 4, at the last of which Kelly argues that 'it can probably be assumed that he deliberately edited out these two documents, perhaps because they were so much concerned with Bradfield rather than Abingdon, perhaps because the information they contained tended to contradict in detail the material in [*Charters of Abingdon*, no. 4], the longest and most impressive of the four documents'.

[196] See below, p. 244.

[197] c. 3, B9.

have chosen to omit the intrusive charter to improve the narrative flow, or have set it aside and then unintentionally failed to include it.[198] He may well have omitted a charter in King Edmund's name concerning Culham because it seemed to question the continuing attachment of that land to Abingdon.[199] It should, however, also be noted that this charter just precedes MS C's record of the death of Edmund. It is with Edmund's death that MS B splits MS C's Book I into two books. The division between Book II and Book III in MS B certainly caused confusion in its text, and it is possible that confusion also occurred here, leading to unintentional omission of the charter.[200] MS C and MS B each contain a charter of Cnut concerning Myton, but they are different charters.[201] It may be that the reviser had an original for his version of the charter, but not for that which had appeared in MS C, and therefore chose to include just the former. However, apart from such speculation, there is no obvious explanation for the manuscript differences in this case.[202]

MS B contains seventy-one documents that had not appeared in MS C, two of which are included twice.[203] Besides the Myton charter, just two further diplomas recording grants to Abingdon appear only in MS B, whilst an Old English record of an exchange appears in full in the vernacular in MS B, only in Latin summary in MS C.[204] Both the diplomas are of King Æthelred, and both could well have appeared on a folio now missing from MS C.[205] It may well be that the reviser added no further diplomas directly in favour of Abingdon.

The great bulk of the additional charters are to lay grantees. Of the eight charters of Edmund in MS B recording grants not to Abingdon, only two appear in MS C. Of these two, one appears in the context of the later dispute concerning Leckhampstead and there only in King

[198] c. 10.

[199] c. 25; see *Charters of Abingdon Abbey*, pp. lxii, 47. Note that the charter in c. 10 also included Culham amongst the lands it granted

[200] See also below, p. cxiv, on confusion in MS B's revision of the treatment of Edmund.

[201] c. 113, B246.

[202] The omission of two writs of King Stephen in MS B is most likely a simple error; vol. ii. 262–4.

[203] See Concordance 2. The swift repetition of the narrative and charter concerning Padworth appears to be a simple error; B151, B152, B156, B157. The two versions of Eadwig's grant of Hanney to Ælfric display some significant differences; B133, B161, *Charters of Abingdon Abbey*, no. 55.

[204] c. 44, B142 (*Charters of Abingdon Abbey*, no. 76).

[205] B219, B231. The boundaries of the former but not the latter appear in the quire of MS C devoted to boundary clauses. B231 is oddly placed amongst charters concerning lands that passed indirectly to Abingdon.

Eadwig's name. The other also has textual problems and in MS C is wrongly positioned, after King Eadwig's charters.[206] It is hard to establish the criteria that the reviser used to decide which additional charters to include. It does appear he chose to omit some, in that two diplomas in favour of laymen but associated with other Abingdon documents survive as sixteenth-century copies of originals, not in the *History*.[207] In general, though, the impression is that the reviser wished to include as many additional documents as possible. Approximately half of these additional diplomas for laymen, nearly all dating from the 940s and 950s, have a link to Abingdon through the estate history.[208] There are often later documents for these estates appearing in both MSS of the *History*, the composer of the earlier version having apparently considered that a single later document, often in favour of the abbey itself, was a sufficient title-deed.[209] The earlier documents would have been deposited at Abingdon when the estate passed to the abbey. Very occasionally MS B includes a charter for an estate to which no reference is made in Book I of MS C, but which was an Abingdon possession in *Domesday Book*.[210] Given that other, non-*Domesday* evidence for an Abingdon connection can sometimes be very slight but persuasive, in the case of some further estates for which MS B includes charters there may have been a connection to Abingdon for which no evidence survives.[211] However, it is probable that the reviser of the *History* also included many diplomas concerning lands that had no connection with the monastery.[212] The inclusion of such documents, whilst unusual, was not unique.[213] The reason for their

[206] cc. 58, 137. One other charter, c. 25, only appears in MS C.

[207] *Charters of Abingdon Abbey*, nos. 43, 62. One is a grant to Æthelmær *praeses* of land in Chetwode and Hillesden, Buckinghamshire, and the other a grant to Brihthelm, bishop-elect, of lands in Church Stowe, Northamptonshire; *Charters of Abingdon Abbey*, nos. 43, 62 respectively. It is just possible that these charters had come to be wrongly associated with Abingdon documents after the time of the *History*. Abingdon did have an interest in lands in Hillesden, but there is no known link to Chetwode or Church Stowe.

[208] See Concordance 2, and below, pp. cxxvi–cxlix, on the charter evidence for the development of the endowment.

[209] See above, p. xxix.

[210] e.g. Garford, B66, and Benham, B137; it should be noted that the latter may well have been a post-Conquest acquisition; see below, p. cli n. 818.

[211] e.g. *Bultheswrthe*, on which see c. 106, B55.

[212] See below, pp. cxxvi–cxxxi; Concordance 2; Keynes, *Diplomas*, pp. 12–13.

[213] See Keynes, *Diplomas*, p. 13 n. 21: 'Besides the compiler of B vi, the only cartularists prepared to admit a number of apparently "unrelated" diplomas into their collections were the compilers of National Library of Wales, Peniarth 390, and B. L. Add. 15350, from Burton and the Old Minster Winchester respectively; there are, however, isolated examples of such diplomas preserved from other archives.'

preservation at Abingdon will be considered further in the context of the abbey's endowment.[214]

2. Purposes of revision

Two main problems arise in seeking to explain the purpose of the revision of the *History*. First, there is no surviving Preface in which the reviser explains his position. Second, there is the problem of telling when the main process of revision occurred. Was it soon after 1190, when the history recounted ceases, or was it later, perhaps following the death of Abbot Hugh? Given this uncertainty it is necessary to proceed with caution, in particular when looking outside the form, style, and content of the text.

First, one may set the rewriting of the *History* in the context of disputes from the 1160s to the time of the writing of MS B. Some of these concerned the external rights of the church. A dispute in 1223 over the liberty of the church and its hundredal jurisdiction may well have caused renewed attention to be paid to the *History*.[215] Continuing conflict between the men of Culham and the men of Sutton, which reached the king's court in 1212, may explain the still greater attention paid to those two estates in the later version of the *History*.[216] In addition, during Hugh's abbacy there were major internal problems within the monastery, concerning, amongst other matters, the rights of obedientiaries, the allowances of servants, and matters relating to food and drink. According to the bishop of Salisbury, the settlement, concerning servants and their stipends, had involved investigation in ancient books.[217] Such disputes and such investigations fit well with the concern displayed in the revised *History* with food and drink allowances,[218] with the inclusion of a list of stipends as established by an investigation in the late 1180s,[219] and

[214] See below, p. cxxvi.

[215] *Curia Regis Rolls* (in progress, HMSO 1922 to the present), xi. 189 (no. 941); it begins 'Abbas de Abendon' queritur quod Henricus de Scaccario vicecomes contra libertatem ecclesie sue, qua ecclesia sua a conquestu Anglie usque nunc usa est, injuste vexat eum . . .'. Note also Henry III's confirmation issued in 1230 concerning Hormer hundred; Lyell, no. 102; Chatsworth, no. 350; MS C, fo. 178^{r-v}.

[216] *Curia Regis Rolls*, vi. 390–1. For increased attention to Culham and Sutton in MS B, see B11 (establishing that Sutton had once been an Abingdon holding), B16 (privileges of Culham), B64 (establishing continuing ownership of Culham).

[217] Lyell, no. 167 (p. 106); see generally Lyell, nos. 166–8.

[218] B207, vol. ii. 332–8.

[219] Vol. ii. 358–70.

with the copying in the same hand as the revised *History* of a tract on the offices of the monastery.[220]

Another concern may have been the paying for privileges, including that obtained from Richard I, and the suggestion that Abbot Hugh had acquired the abbacy in improper fashion. Gerald of Wales wrote of an abbot of Abingdon who dating shows must have been Hugh that he 'had been promoted to his abbacy from the post of kitchener, through a bribe of 1500 marks which he had given to a prince'.[221] Sensitivity concerning payment to the king may come out in the *History*'s treatment of the purchase of a privilege from King Coenwulf. The earlier version states: 'Therefore Bishop and Abbot Hræthhun, thinking that the king was a man to be approached through money rather than swayed by prayers, offered him £120 besides one hundred hides at the royal vill of Sutton, situated near Abingdon.'[222] In the later version this expands to the following:

> To do this more confidently, he took with him gold and silver to the value of £120, judging that this would provide for him the most powerful persuasion and the greatest salve in obtaining the king's love. When this was done, he offered the king for the good of peace that tiny amount of silver and gold [*illud tantillulum argenti et auri*], and in addition one hundred hides situated at the royal vill of Sutton, close to Abingdon.[223]

The substantial payment of £120 thus becomes a 'tiny amount of silver and gold'.

Thirdly there is the rebuilding of the church, which was a feature of Hugh's abbacy.[224] This probably underlies the long story of Siward's plan to replace Æthelwold's church, and in particular Æthelwold's advice to Siward in a dream:

> 'it is not for your time to demolish my work or build another. So that you may display greater faith in my sayings, wait very diligently, that a certain future father and shepherd of this monastery will come from overseas, who will demolish this work and begin a new one; but he will not complete this.

[220] *CMA* ii. 336–417.

[221] Gerald of Wales, *Speculum ecclesiæ*, dist. ii. c. 29, in *Opera*, ed. J. S. Brewer *et al.* (8 vols., London, 1861–91), iv. 92. Identification of the anonymous abbot as Hugh is certain because he appears in Gerald as a contemporary of Roger abbot of Evesham, 1190–1213.

[222] See below, p. 14.

[223] See below, p. 256.

[224] See e.g. *De abbatibus*, *CMA* ii. 293; Salter, 'Chronicle roll', p. 729; *Chronicle of the Monastery of Abingdon, 1218–1304*, ed. J. O. Halliwell (Berkshire Ashmolean Society, Reading, 1844), p. 1; Biddle *et al.*, 'Early history', p. 48.

[Abbot Reginald] After this man, indeed, there will also come two other men likewise shepherds of the monastery, who—greatly needed—will busy themselves doing many good deeds both about building and about other matters relating to this monastery. [Faritius and Vincent] When they yield to death, for a very long period of time there will be no future pastor and abbot in this monastery who will in similar fashion strive to increase this monastery with good deeds. In most recent times, indeed, there will likewise be a future abbot of this monastery who will embrace this monastery in "the bowels of Christ" with such emotion that piling good things on good, destroying buildings and rebuilding them for the better, adorning the church, preserving the ordered life, diminishing nothing of the customs but rather augmenting them, God-fearing, strong in behaviour, outstanding in holiness of life, a pious father and worthy of being called shepherd, in peace of heart will await the peace of eternity. [Hugh]'[225]

The replacement of earlier church buildings, even the discussion of which had—according to *De abbatibus*—brought Abbot Adelelm to a painful end, was an issue that required careful legitimation both in dream and in writing.[226]

Let us move from the necessarily speculative relationship with outside events to the reasons for rewriting that can be found within the text of the *History*. Some have already been discussed. There was the desire to include a mass of charters that the reviser knew had been excluded, and to supply linking passages explaining their relevance by the fact that the lands concerned had become part of the church's endowment.[227] Likewise, the reviser dealt with material found in other narrative sources, such as *De abbatibus*.[228]

Partly on the basis of these additional sources, the reviser chose to add further detail to the *History*'s account.[229] Such details might refer to chronology,[230] to the names of participants,[231] to the course of events,[232] or to the accumulation of lands or wealth.[233] Earl

[225] B252.

[226] For Adelelm's fate, see *CMA* ii. 284.

[227] See above, p. xliv. For a lengthier than usual explanation of the relevance of a charter to a grantee other than Abingdon, see B13.

[228] See above, p. xl. Note also the insertion of miracle stories; B38, B63, B291, vol. ii. 326–30.

[229] Note also e.g. below, p. 294, on Æthelwold's illustrious stock, p. 354 on Dunstan's prophecy. The additions are not always accurate; see below, p. 362, for the reviser mistakenly naming Rochester as the see to which Siward was appointed.

[230] See below, pp. 254, 266, 294, 368; cf. 14, 28, 44, 220 respectively.

[231] See below, p. 266; cf. p. 28.

[232] See below, p. 292; cf. p. 48.

[233] See below, p. 356; cf. p. 178; Æthelwine's gift of a cross added.

Godwine's role in the move of Siward from Abingdon to Canterbury is specified, Godwine's death and the succession of Harold noted, and the nature of Harold's claim to the throne outlined.[234] Sometimes the reviser made explicit the link between general and Abingdon history, as when he specified that the Danes destroyed the abbey in the ninth century, or associated the fate of Abbot Eadwine with the later return of the Danes.[235]

Sometimes, however, detail was cut. The specific accusation that King Coenwulf dined at the expense of the inhabitants of Abingdon possessions was removed,[236] as was the statement that Eadred 'canonically' appointed Æthelwold abbot of Abingdon, although the later version did carefully mention Dunstan's consent to the royal action.[237] In the account of the late tenth and early eleventh centuries, there is an occasional tendency to cut material unrelated to Abingdon, notably an outline of the Norman claim to the English throne and a description of Cnut's wide rule.[238]

More notable than differences in narrative detail, however, are changes in structure, terminology, and style. The division between the early history of the church and the tenth-century reform is emphasized by MS C's Book I being split into two books in MS B. The basis for the arrangement of Edgar's charters is made explicit, presumably to help the reader.[239] New narratives bring out links between pre- and post-Conquest history, notably with reference to building and food arrangements.[240] Phraseology is improved in the terms of the reviser's times, with a new reference to the 'freedom of the English Church',[241] and with repeated and anachronistic use of the phrase 'in pure and perpetual alms' with reference to grants made before the Conquest.[242]

[234] See below, pp. 362, 364, 368.

[235] See below, pp. 268, 346; cf. pp. 28, 138.

[236] See below, p. 254; cf. p. 14; the reviser's reformulation seems also to play down the criticism that the king could be swayed by money.

[237] See below, p. 48; cf. p. 296. The later version does not repeat the statement at p. 44 that King Æthelstan commended Æthelwold to Bishop Ælfheah of Winchester. This is the more surprising given the importance of Ælfheah in Wulfstan, *Life of Æthelwold*, cc. 7–9, ed. Lapidge and Winterbottom, pp. 10–14.

[238] See below, pp. 172, 184. Note also below, p. 138; cf. p. 346.

[239] B174.

[240] B207, B252, vol. ii. 66, 72, 332–40, 344.

[241] See below, p. 254. Vol. ii. 346 seems to use the phrase 'libertas ecclesiastica' in the general sense of 'ecclesiastical liberty' rather than just with reference to the freedom of Abingdon.

[242] For use in MS B, see above, n. 148; in MS C Book I does not use phrases based on 'in elemosina'.

More generally, the reviser seems to have regarded the earlier version of the *History* as too plain in style. Take as a first example the treatment of Abbot Hræthhun's dealings with King Coenwulf. The chapter in MS B, but not in MS C, contains an allusion to Juvenal's *Satires*. The reviser also widens the vocabulary used by employing phrases that occur in learned law, such as 'dilatory exceptions'.[243] And it is in this section that the reference to the 'freedom of the English Church' appears.

This chapter reflects stylistic elaborations made more widely by the reviser. As already noted, he drew on a variety of written sources. Above all, he may have desired to use Geoffrey of Monmouth to link the story of Abingdon to the longer history of Britain.[244] In addition there were changes in vocabulary choice. It is not simply that the reviser preferred some words that do not appear in the earlier version, or are unusual within it, such as 'memoratus' and 'quamplurimus'.[245] Rather, the reviser's vocabulary is deliberately wider, introducing words such as 'magnatus' and 'gaza'.[246] Some inspiration was drawn from charters for less usual vocabulary, such as 'pincernarius'.[247] The reviser also had a range of recurring phrases.[248] Some refer to the process of writing or address the reader concerning the narrative:

[243] See below, p. 254, 'nunc blandiciis cauillatoriis, nunc fulminantibus minis, quasi excepcionibus dilatoriis'; cf. p. 14; see also below, p. 284, 'de aliquibus exceptionibus dilatoriis aut cauillatoriis uel obscuris placitis subterfugiis'. Cf. Peter of Blois, Sermon no. 65, *PL* ccvii. 774: 'non cavillationibus argues, non dilatoriis exceptionibus ages'.

[244] Note also the Galfridian matter at the start of *De abbatibus*, prior to the section printed by Stevenson; London, British Library, Cotton Vitellius A. XIII, fos. 83^r–84^r. The Geoffrey-related material there is more extensive than that which appears in MS B of the *History*, but the opening of the revised *History* is lost. It is hard to tell at what date the Galfridian material entered *De abbatibus*, and therefore the question of the influence between that text and MS B cannot be answered. Stories such as that in Geoffrey of the derivation of the name Britain from its founder Brutus may have encouraged Abingdon to seek a founder with an appropriate name.

[245] For the very occasional appearance of 'memoratus' in MS C, see below, p. 222 and vol. ii. 238. Below, p. 318, provides the only use of the word 'mansatus' to appear in the *DMLBS*, in the form 'mansatorum'. One may suspect that the scribe confused 'mansarum' and 'cassatorum'.

[246] See below, pp. 262, 274, 276, 292, vol. ii. 328.

[247] See below, p. 324, 'pincernarius', deriving from 'propincernarius' in B170 (*Charters of Abingdon Abbey*, no. 79). See also p. 310, '[architec]tandum', deriving from the relevant charter at p. 74; the mistaken form in the narrative may indicate that the scribe was unfamiliar with the word.

[248] See e.g. below, pp. 296, 344, for 'uita angelica'; pp. 236, 272, 360, for a recurrent use of 'accumulare'; pp. 254, 338, 368, 370, for 'quoad' with a comparative adverb and 'posse'; pp. 260, 268, 272, 326, 354, 358, vol. ii. 344, for 'quid multa?' (cf. in MS C 'quid plura' in a charter of King Ecgberht of Wessex, p. 24). Note also repeated use of the phrase 'as was then the custom'.

'Now it remains for us to turn our pen, which moves back and forth, to King Ceadwalla's successors, and to describe succinctly both their bad and their good deeds, according to the extent of our knowledge.'[249] Pairs of words are linked to rhetorical effect, for example 'tam effectiuum quam affectiuum'.[250] Particularly notable are circumlocutions for death: 'de carnis exuto ergastulo [left the prison of the flesh]',[251] 'uiam uniuerse carnis ingresso [gone the way of all flesh]',[252] 'cessit in fatum [yielded to death]'.[253]

Such phrases are part of the reviser's process of adding biblical, liturgical, and literary allusions to the text.[254] Certain important passages, such as the description of Æthelwold's early career, are particularly rich in allusion.[255] Not surprisingly, the Bible was the reviser's favoured source, although some passages described, for example, as 'the word of the Lord' are not direct biblical quotations.[256] Amongst classical writers, he quoted only from Juvenal's *Satires* and Vergil's *Aeneid*; in neither case need he have direct knowledge of the full work.[257] Likewise, phrases derived from or

[249] See below, pp. 244, 272, 370.

[250] See below, p. 308.

[251] See below, pp. 232, 238, 262.

[252] See below, pp. 234, 250, 272, 276, 284, 294, 338, 344, 356, vol. ii. 354.

[253] See below, pp. 250, 252, 260, 264, 326, 354, 360, vol. ii. 370.

[254] See pp. 254 (cf. p. 14), 268 (cf. p. 28), 326 (cf. p. 94), 354 (cf. p. 172), vol ii. 326–30 (cf. ii 32–4).

[255] B83. One problem that arises is the close parallels with a *Life* of Mary Magdalene and Martha, attributed to Hrabanus Maurus but now regarded as a 12th-century Clairvaux production. The parallels seem too great to be accidental; B83 'Iste uero Æþelwoldus *non solum genere illustrem uerum etiam titulo spectabilem* et omni sanctitate plenam *lineam traxit nobilitatis. Vigebant* autem in ipso *ingenii* pariter *et industrie bona* acceptabilia, *adeptaque in puerilibus annis plena litterarum scientia, nature* institucionum bona uenustissime *accumulauit honestas. Inueniebantur* etiam in eo *corporis miranda uenustas*, *morum acceptissima gratia*, *eloquiorum gratissima luculentia, adeo ut et species et mores et gratia* in adolesce⟨n⟩te Æþelwuoldo uiderentur ad inuicem *emula sibi probitate certare*'; *Life* of Mary and Martha, c. 1, *PL* cxii. 1433, 'Pater eius Theophilus, natione Syrus, *non solum genere illustrem, verum etiam titulo spectabilem* et administratione clarissimam *nobilitatis lineam traxit*. . . . *Vigebant* in iis tribus *ingenium*, simul *et industria bona*, et *adepta in puerilibus annis litterarum* Hebraicarum *plena scientia*. Bona *nature*, industriamque atrium, *cumulauit honestas*; in singulis enim *inueniebatur corporum miranda uenustas*, et *morum acceptissima gratia*, et *eloquiorum gratissima luculentia*; *adeo ut* uiderentur ad inuicem *et specie, et moribus, et gratia, aemula sibi probitate certare*.' However, there is no other evidence for a copy of the *Life* of Mary and Martha being known at Abingdon, and I have been unable to trace a common source for the two passages. On the *Life*, see V. Saxer, 'La "Vie de sainte Marie Madeleine" attribuée au pseudo-Raban Maur, oeuvre claravalienne du XIIe siècle', in *Mélanges Saint Bernard* (Dijon, 1954), pp. 408–21; *The Life of Saint Mary Magdalene and of her Sister Saint Martha*, trans. D. Mycoff (Kalamazoo, 1989).

[256] See below, pp. 294, 340.

[257] See below, pp. 254, 276, vol. ii. 328, 332, 354.

influenced by learned law, such as 'ius merum',[258] or the tag 'attestante lege qua dicitur mortuo mandatore, respirat mandatum',[259] were used to enrich the text's style, although they need not reflect any great legal learning.

Some further narratorial interventions appear, for example at the close of MS B's Book I,[260] and in exposition of miracle stories such as that of a speaking crucifix:

> For it is not to be doubted that an image may speak, nor does it merit wonder if God, who takes back and bestows, who created everything from nothing (that is, not from pre-existing matter), should bring forth from an inanimate creation a ringing voice, as if brought forth from the windpipe, who once wondrously assigned Balaam to an ass so that at first it kicked back against the prophet and then with a living voice admonished him not to go further on the way. These are your works, good Jesus, to whom praise and glory.[261]

A further characteristic is the much greater use of various types of direct speech. The reader hears King Ceadwalla's internal addressing of God, the discussions between King Coenwulf and his sisters leading to the foundation of Helenstow, Æthelwold's persuasion of the dreaming Siward, the conversations within and following Robert d'Oilly's nightmare, and debate over Faritius's provisions for the monks.[262]

Not all is a matter of elaboration.[263] There is no newly composed verse.[264] The miraculous element is removed from the story of the coming of St Edward the martyr's relics to Abingdon.[265] Some statements are clarified in terms of grammar or phraseology.[266] Yet overall, the reviser's intention is clear: not so much to change the core themes and purpose of the work as to render more impressive a relatively plain text.

[258] See below, p. 284, 'undiluted right'.

[259] See below, p. 256, 'in accordance with the law whereby it is said that with the death of the one ordering, the order breathes its last'.

[260] See below, p. 292 (cf. p. 46).

[261] See below, p. 272.

[262] See below, pp. 238, 250–2, 358–60, vol. ii. 328–30, 332–6. Note also the brief statements at pp. 248, 284.

[263] The praise of King Alfred's learning, below, p. 48, does not appear in MS B, increasing the consistency of the negative portrayal of Alfred.

[264] See below, p. 240, for the copying of Ceadwalla's epitaph. In B245 and B249 brief verses are cut from the equivalent passages in c. 111.

[265] B250.

[266] See e.g. B37; cf. c. 14 for simplification of grammar; B243; cf. c. 109 for some clarification of phraseology.

III. OTHER SOURCES RELATING TO THE ABBEY OF ABINGDON UP TO 1071

1. Abingdon sources

The evidence of the *History* can be supplemented from other sources, some from Abingdon, others from elsewhere. Of the texts closely associated with Abingdon the most helpful is the text known as *De abbatibus Abbendonie*, although its heading in the thirteenth-century manuscript is 'Excepciones Simonis de primis fundatoribus Abbendoniæ et de abbatibus Abbendoniæ que etiam bona queve mala fecerunt [Simon's extracts concerning the first founders of Abingdon, the abbots of Abingdon, and their good and bad actions]'.[267] It starts 'In principio erat Verbum', and goes on to treat Brutus and his coming to Britain. Only after dealing with other matters, such as the invasion by Julius Caesar, does it come on to the foundation of Abingdon by Abben. It then deals with the abbots up to and including Hugh (1189/90–*c.*1221). In its existing form, the text may well come from the Abingdon daughter house at Colne, Essex, the affairs of which are treated at length in its final chapter. In general, *De abbatibus* has been regarded as a later, less significant, work than the *History*.[268] However, such a position may need modification. It is arguable that the surviving text contains an earlier core, going back at least to the mid-twelfth century. The text's final chapter differs in certain ways from the rest of the text in its material, notably in its focus on Colne, and in its manuscript form, particularly its use of frequent, usually alternating, red and green initials. Furthermore, Abbots Faritius, Vincent, and Ingulf all have sections with headings in the form 'Concerning Abbot N. and the goods he conferred on us'. Whilst there is a similar heading for Abbot Hugh, the abbots of the period 1158–89/90 are briefly treated in a section headed 'Concerning abbots after Ingulf'. It seems plausible that a text that once ended with Ingulf has been extended during the time of Abbot Hugh.[269] It may well be that other material, for example concerning Brutus and Abben, was also incorporated in the late twelfth or early thirteenth

[267] Given the contents of the tract, the use of the word 'excepciones' in the title should not be taken to indicate that the work is simply a set of extracts from other Abingdon histories.

[268] See e.g. Stenton, *Early History*, p. 1.

[269] In vol. ii, p. xxiii, I suggest that the first version of the *History* and a version of *De abbatibus* completed in Ingulf's abbacy may be seen as providing competing views of Ingulf, one from the convent's side, one from the abbot's.

century, but this process cannot be securely dated.[270] One therefore cannot tell when subject matter shared by *De abbatibus* and the later but not the earlier version of the *History* became current at Abingdon.

De abbatibus deals with many matters which appear in the *History*, on occasion only in the revised version. In general it is briefer than the *History*, but sometimes it differs in detail or perspective and occasionally it adds notable material.[271] For example, it states that King Ine, having repented of his earlier seizure of Abingdon's possessions, gave 3,750 pounds of silver for building churches at Abingdon and Glastonbury.[272] Whereas the *History* simply mentions that King Offa gave Goosey to Abingdon, *De abbatibus* states that he gave it in exchange for the island of Andersey, and that his son died on that island.[273] Most notably of all, it provides descriptions of the churches built by Hæha and Æthelwold.[274]

There are also several later versions of Abingdon history in diverse manuscripts.[275] Oxford, Corpus Christi College 255 contains extracts made by Brian Twyne in 1606 from a roll written after 1361, itself extracted from various Abingdon works including 'le landbok', which appears to have been the revised version of the *History*.[276] The list of abbots in London, British Library, Cotton Julius C. VII,

[270] It has been suggested above, p. xliii, that the presence of Abben in the stories concerning the earliest history of the abbey may derive from a visit of Archbishop Lawrence O'Toole in 1180. Note also the confusion displayed in *De abbatibus* over the meaning of legal terms, below, p. clviii, perhaps suggesting a later date for the passage concerned.

[271] See below, p. lxxxv, on the foundation of the abbey.

[272] *CMA* ii. 272. Cf. *De antiquitate Glastonie ecclesie*, c. 41, Scott, *Early History of Glastonbury*, p. 96, for Ine giving 2,640 pounds of silver for the building of a chapel at Glastonbury.

[273] *CMA* ii. 273. *Charters of Abingdon Abbey*, p. cciii, states that 'it is tempting to believe the Andersey dimension, for the island had a long history of royal association'. Such royal association might also explain the development of a story to this effect.

[274] *CMA* ii. 272–3, 277–8.

[275] The Chatsworth manuscript containing an Abingdon cartulary also includes a list of abbots in a 16th- or 17th-century hand, stating that Hæha began to build in 685 and died in 730; Chatsworth, p. 324. Note also London, British Library, Cotton Caligula A. VI, fo. 229^{v}, for extracts 'ex historia monasterii de Abendonia' made by John Joscelyn in the 16th century.

[276] Note esp. the reference to Siward wishing to destroy Æthelwold's church, but being deterred; Salter, 'Chronicle roll', p. 729. The reference to only one version of the *History* suggests that the fuller and more highly decorated MS B was the more important of the two manuscripts in the later medieval period. For the roll's other sources, see Salter, 'Chronicle roll', pp. 730–1. Salter, p. 727, dates the roll to 1361, presumably on the grounds that this is the last date mentioned in it; a more cautious dating would be to the abbacy of Peter de Hanney, who was elected in 1361 and was abbot until 1399.

fo. 305^{r-v}, is headed 'ex rotulo antiquo de Abendon [from an ancient roll of Abingdon]', perhaps the same record as mentioned in the Oxford Corpus MS. There are also other fourteenth-century historical works with Abingdon entries.[277] However, none of these late works add significantly to the *History*, and details in which they differ from it may derive from misunderstanding, not additional knowledge.[278]

More significant is the copying of the *Chronicle* of John of Worcester at Abingdon. Two manuscripts of John's *Chronicle* contain Abingdon additions, London, Lambeth Palace 42 and Cambridge, Corpus Christi College 92. The former is in the same hand as the *History* and is clearly an Abingdon manuscript.[279] Its additions concerning Abingdon sometimes share text with the *History*, sometimes are copied from the *Life of St Æthelwold*, sometimes are verbally independent.[280] Cambridge, Corpus Christi College 92 was copied from various manuscripts, including Lambeth Palace 42. It contains most of the Abingdon additions, sometimes in the text, sometimes in the margin.[281] It is not certain that this should be considered an Abingdon manuscript except in the sense that the Lambeth manuscript was one of its exemplars. It seems plausible that it was either copied at Abingdon for another house, or that Lambeth Palace 42 was temporarily taken from Abingdon for copying. If the text was not intended for Abingdon, this would help to explain the variable fashion in which the Abingdon additions are treated.[282]

The copy of the *Chronicle* in Lambeth Palace 42 runs to 1131, but the manuscript itself is from the later twelfth century. It contains a list of archbishops of Canterbury the last of whom is Thomas Becket,

[277] See also Cambridge, Trinity College 993; on which see M. R. James, *The Western Manuscripts in the Library of Trinity College, Cambridge* (4 vols., Cambridge, 1900–4), ii. 414–15.

[278] See e.g. Salter, 'Chronicle roll', p. 728, on 'Guiatus' (i.e. Abbot Cynath) being responsible for recovering all that Hinguar and Ubba had taken away, and being associated with the miracles mentioned in B38 and B39.

[279] See John of Worcester, *Chronicle*, ii, pp. xli–xlv. See also below on the decoration of the two manuscripts and of Oxford, All Souls College 18.

[280] John of Worcester, *Chronicle*, ii. 609–15, iii. 307–8. The extended new composition *s.a.* 948 provides a short history of the house, including yet another version of the oppressions by King Coenwulf in the time of Abbot Hræthhun. There is also another version of the miracle story concerning the boy Ædmer (cf. below, c. 30) and a different account of Æthelwold.

[281] See John of Worcester, *Chronicle*, ii, pp. liii–lix.

[282] See ibid. ii. 609–15, iii. 307–8. The other contents of this manuscript show only that it was later at Peterborough.

indicating that the list was composed before 1170, or at least before the election of Thomas's successor in 1173. Likewise, the list of kings does not contain Henry the young king, son of Henry II, again pointing to a date of 1170 or before. Although the lists could have been copied later without being updated, Lambeth Palace 42 was already available for copying at the time of production of Corpus Christi College 92, which probably predates 1181.[283] It seems likely, therefore, that the Lambeth manuscript is almost exactly contemporary with the earlier manuscript of the *History*, in the period 1164–70.[284]

It therefore cannot be determined on manuscript dating grounds whether the John of Worcester manuscript derived material from the *History* or vice versa.[285] If it is significant that the *History* does not use the main text of John and hence was written without access to his work, the Abingdon additions in Lambeth Palace 42 would be largely drawn from MS C.[286] Other additions in Lambeth Palace 42 could derive from the *History* without being verbatim extracts, for example *s.a.* 963, 984, 1048, 1049. Very occasionally additional detail is provided, perhaps because explanation was needed; for example the addition *s.a.* 1006 specifies that Archbishop Ælfric, having been buried at Abingdon, was moved to his own see under Cnut.

Next amongst narrative texts which may have a strong Abingdon

[283] John of Worcester, *Chronicle*, ii, p. lviii, seems willing to take the presence of Alexander III as the final entry in a list of popes and Richard of Dover in a list of archbishops of Canterbury as evidence that the scribe was working before the death of Alexander III in 1181.

[284] Cf. John of Worcester, *Chronicle*, ii, p. xlv, where it is argued that the Lambeth manuscript of John of Worcester and MS C of the *History* 'must be dated on palaeographical grounds to the late twelfth century, and this late date stands in the way of any attempt at identifying the scribe of the two manuscripts with the compiler of the Abingdon chronicle and L's Abingdon entries'. Given acceptance of a date of *c.*1180 for the relevant section of Cambridge, Corpus Christi College 92, and the willingness to use final entries in lists of office holders for the dating of that manuscript, the balance of evidence points to my suggested date of *c.*1164–70 for MS C of the *History*, unless it can be established that a hand of *c.*1164–70 can be securely distinguished from one of 'the late twelfth century', including one of before 1181.

[285] It is possible that for at least some of the shared entries there was an earlier source. See below, p. lxi, on the recording of Sidemann's death, and note the use within it of the word 'humatur', a word that is not the usual one for burial in either the Abingdon *History* or John of Worcester. Other speculations are possible, for example that Abingdon had an earlier, now lost, copy of John of Worcester to which the Abingdon additions were made; the additions then were used in the composition of the *History* and the whole John of Worcester text was copied into the manuscript now in Lambeth Palace Library.

[286] Note, though, that the compiler of the first version of the *History* often did not copy directly from sources that it seems certain he did know, such as the *Life of Æthelwold*; see above, p. xxvii.

connection is the *Anglo-Saxon Chronicle*. Since the sixteenth century, version C of the *Chronicle* has been associated with Abingdon.[287] The exact nature, and indeed the very existence, of such a connection have, however, been a matter for debate. For example, Simon Keynes has commented that the entries for 985, 990, 1016 relating to Abingdon show only that a common ancestor of versions CDE passed through Abingdon, whilst noting that the manuscript of the C version 'may have come from the abbey'.[288] David Dumville has commented that C was 'probably written early in 1045 at Abingdon', and was a derivative of an earlier version annotated at Abingdon. Abingdon's contribution to earlier composition, however, may only have amounted to marginal or interlinear annotation.[289] Katherine O'Brien O'Keeffe has commented on the limited nature of the Abingdon entries, for example contrasting them with the treatment of Peterborough in version E.[290] She concludes that

> the negative evidence against an Abingdon origin for C (its silence on the circumstances of its refoundation, the perfunctory mention of Æthelwold, Osgar, and omission of some eleventh-century abbots) though not convincing on its own, tells in concert with the palaeographical and positive textual evidence.[291]

She therefore rejects the Abingdon origin of version C. The attribution of version B of the *Chronicle* to Abingdon rests wholly on its relationship to version C,[292] and hence O'Brien O'Keeffe's conclu-

[287] See *The Anglo-Saxon Chronicle: A Collaborative Edition*, v: *MS. C*, ed. K. O'Brien O'Keeffe (Cambridge, 2001), p. lxxiv.

[288] S. D. Keynes, 'The declining reputation of King Æthelred the Unready', in D. Hill, ed., *Ethelred the Unready: Papers from the Millenary Conference* (British Archaeological Reports, British Series lix, 1978), pp. 227–53, at 232. For other arguments, see e.g. Gransden, 'Traditionalism and continuity', p. 192; *The Anglo-Saxon Chronicle: A Collaborative Edition*, x: *The Abingdon Chronicle A.D. 956–1066*, ed. P. W. Conner (Cambridge, 1996), pp. xxxiv–xxxvi.

[289] Dumville, 'Annalistic writing at Canterbury', pp. 27–9.

[290] *Anglo-Saxon Chronicle: MS. C*, ed. O'Brien O'Keeffe, p. lxxviii; see also pp. lxiii, lxxi, and esp. p. lxvii on the modesty of version C's notice concerning Æthelwold and on the absence of a mention of Osgar. At p. lxxix she argues that there is no reason to take the mention under 977 of the burial of Bishop Sidemann of Crediton at Abingdon as a sign that version C is an Abingdon text. See further her comments at p. lxxiv: 'the second [argument for association of version C with Abingdon] accepts John Joscelyn's identification of C as an Abingdon manuscript in the list of Chronicle manuscripts he prepared between 1565 and 26 January 1567'. She points out, p. lxxvi, that it is unclear why Joscelyn made this association, when Talbot, Leland, and Bale had not done so.

[291] *Anglo-Saxon Chronicle: MS. C*, ed. O'Brien O'Keeffe, p. lxxxix.

[292] *The Anglo-Saxon Chronicle: A Collaborative Edition*, iv: *MS. B*, ed. S. Taylor (Cambridge, 1983), p. xi. See also Dumville, 'Annalistic writing at Canterbury', p. 40.

sions call into question version B's Abingdon link as well. At present, therefore, it is best to conclude that a version or versions of the *Anglo-Saxon Chronicle* were known at Abingdon and annotated there, but to leave open the question of whether the abbey was at any point responsible for the composition of the main entries on national history.

O'Brien O'Keeffe's questioning of the attribution of version C to Abingdon is one problem with an attempt by Patrick Conner to isolate the Abingdon contribution to the *Anglo-Saxon Chronicle* in its C version, and to link this contribution to an Abingdon 'house narrative'.[293] The evidence for this house narrative rests heavily on the passage of the Abingdon *History* concerning the burial of Bishop Sidemann, and its relationship to the equivalent passage in the *Anglo-Saxon Chronicle* versions B and C.[294] Conner notes similarities to the memorandum in the *History* concerning the exchange of land at Kingston with Ælfhere. This leads him to reject the obvious explanation that the *History*'s passage derived from the *Chronicle*, and to conclude that

> If the Latin version of the Sidemann obit was based on the Old English text in MS. B or C of the *Anglo-Saxon Chronicle*, then numerous hypotheses are necessary to explain why the Old English version of the Ælfhere memorandum is similar to the *Chronicle* text. The circumstances are best explained if a 'house-narrative' or collection of memoranda which existed from *ca* 975 (or alternatively from Abingdon's refoundation in 956) was drawn on by the different persons who updated [the root manuscript of B and C], who compiled MS. Cotton Claudius C. ix, and who copied MS Cotton Claudius B. vi.[295]

Differences in the treatment of the death of Edward the martyr and the accession of Æthelred in the earlier and revised versions of the

[293] *Anglo-Saxon Chronicle: Abingdon Chronicle*, ed. Conner, pp. xi–xii: 'My goal in this *editio princeps* of the *Abingdon Chronicle* has been to reconstruct Abingdon's probable contribution to the *Anglo-Saxon Chronicle*. That is to say, I have tried, with the help of MSS. B, D, and E, and various kinds of textual analysis, to isolate those parts of MS. C which most probably either originated at Abingdon and were copied into the later recensions, or were altered significantly at Abingdon for inclusion in MS. C.' At p. xvi he argues that versions B, C, D, and E 'all contain texts from a single source, which we believe to have been comprised of a series of chronicling activities which took place in Abingdon in 956 × 978, in 1044, and at more or less regular intervals thereafter until *post* 1066'.

[294] See below, c. 94; *ASC*, 'B' and 'C', *s.a.* 977; *Anglo-Saxon Chronicle: Abingdon Chronicle*, ed. Conner, p. xl.

[295] *Anglo-Saxon Chronicle: Abingdon Chronicle*, ed. Conner, pp. xli–xlv, quotation at p. xliv; below, c. 93. See also p. xlv for comparison of *ASC*, 'C', *s.a.* 978, 979, with c. 95 below.

History also lead him to suggest that they were drawing on different segments of the house narrative.[296]

These arguments for an Abingdon 'house narrative' are not, however, persuasive.[297] One might, for example, have expected relevant passages to appear in Abingdon additions to John of Worcester, but apart from that concerning Sidemann they do not. It is best to see the Sidemann passage in John of Worcester as linked directly to the *History*; neither gives the exact date of death, which does appear in the *Anglo-Saxon Chronicle*.[298] Linguistic similarities to the Ælfhere memorandum appear less significant than Conner makes out. The differences in the accounts of Edward the martyr's death and Æthelred's accession are explicable in terms of the reviser's usual practices, not needing a lost source as explanation.[299] Likewise, omissions in *Anglo-Saxon Chronicle* version C, for example concerning the coming of Æthelwold to Abingdon or the abbacy of Æthelsige, do not seem to fit reliance on a house narrative.[300] It is, indeed, sometimes hard to see precisely what Conner means by a 'house narrative'. If it was an extensive text, one might imagine something like the *Libellus Æthelwoldi* at Ely, and no such text existed at Abingdon, at least by the time of the composition of the *History*. If, however, the house narrative may, as Conner suggests, 'have been no more than a series of memoranda', this certainly fits my arguments above on the composition of the *History*.[301] However, the memoranda were probably written on various single sheets, not in continuous narrative form. This certainly is the implication of the statement that the compiler of the *History* 'found' the Ælfhere memorandum 'written in English in almost worn-away letters'.[302]

Let us now move from possible Abingdon narratives to charters. Nine Abingdon charters survive as medieval single sheets, of which

[296] *Anglo-Saxon Chronicle: Abingdon Chronicle*, ed. Conner, pp. xlvi–xlviii.

[297] See also *Anglo-Saxon Chronicle: MS. C*, ed. O'Brien O'Keeffe, pp. lxxx–lxxxix.

[298] John of Worcester, *Chronicle*, ii. 613.

[299] See above, p. xl. The phrase 'Nec multo post . . .', upon which Conner comments at pp. xlvi–xlvii, occurs elsewhere in MS C of the *History*, below, pp. 44, 210, vol. ii. 74, and does not seem to require the special explanations sought by Conner.

[300] The discussion of Siward in *Anglo-Saxon Chronicle: Abingdon Chronicle*, ed. Conner, pp. lix–lx, does not really explain why, for example, the putative house narrative would influence only the reviser of the *History*. Likewise the discussion of the annals for 1065–6 does not consider the likelihood that the composer of MS C in the 1160s derived information from a version of the *Anglo-Saxon Chronicle* without basing his text directly upon it or upon a 'house narrative'.

[301] See *Anglo-Saxon Chronicle: Abingdon Chronicle*, ed. Conner, p. lxii.

[302] c. 93; see also *Charters of Abingdon Abbey*, p. 449.

seven are presumed originals.[303] The two directly in favour of Abingdon and three of those in favour of laymen appear in both manuscripts of the *History*, four others in favour of laymen just in MS B.[304] The selection surviving may simply be a matter of chance, with many others being burnt in the later Middle Ages in a dispute between the citizens and abbey of Abingdon.[305] Further originals, though, did survive until the Dissolution, and Robert Talbot copied twelve at some point before 1558.[306] Of these, three are found in no other source.[307] I have found no obvious explanation why particular originals survived when others were lost.[308]

The two Abingdon cartularies contain little pre-Conquest material. Both have a 1336 *Inspeximus* of Edward III that includes a charter in King Coenwulf's name absent from the *History*.[309] The Lyell cartulary alone contains an extract from the same Coenwulf charter in a thirteenth-century legal document, and the writ of Edward the Confessor granting sake and soke.[310] It also includes an extract from the *Quo warranto* enquiries showing that in the late thirteenth century the abbey had a charter in the name of the Confessor that it produced as evidence of its ownership of Lewknor.[311]

Finally, there are Abingdon texts that tell us about the liturgical and intellectual life of the abbey. Most notable of these is Cambridge, Corpus Christi College 57, which includes, amongst other important texts, a copy of the *Rule* of St Benedict and a martyrology, into the margin of which have been copied Abingdon obits.[312] There are also

303 See *Charters of Abingdon Abbey*, p. xlvi.

304 Gifts directly to Abingdon: cc. 67 (= B206), 98 (= B217); to laymen: cc. 46 (= B131; the single sheet should possibly be dated to the 11th century), 50 (= B139), 55 (= B127), B97, B150, B186, B225 (a 13th-century copy).

305 See Stenton, *Early History*, p. 43.

306 *Charters of Abingdon Abbey*, pp. xlvii, lxiii–lxv. The copying of the charters was not always accurate, and nor are the single sheets always closer in readings to the versions in MS B rather than MS C.

307 See below, pp. lxvii–lxix.

308 A possible exception may be c. 98, Æthelred's confirmation charter, a document of special importance.

309 Lyell, nos. 141, 523; Chatsworth, no. 361 (= *Charters of Abingdon Abbey*, no. 10); see below, p. lxviii.

310 Lyell, nos. 70, 539.

311 Lyell, no. 538, *Placita de Quo Warranto*, ed. W. Illingworth (London, 1818), pp. 664–5; see also c. 121

312 On this manuscript, see below, pp. clxxv–clxxvi. Note also the post-Conquest kalendar, Cambridge, University Library, Kk. i 22, fos. 1^v–7^r. For procedure at Abingdon, see *Liber Vitae*, ed. Keynes, pp. 59–60: 'the obits were copied in the mid-eleventh century into the margins of the abbey's martyrology, presumably in connection with the approved procedure for commemoration of departed brethren in the chapter Office'.

shorter texts, such as a letter to a priest Ælf., almost certainly the Ælfwine who became bishop of Winchester, and a riddle concerning the drink measure for the monks.[313]

2. Other sources

What of non-Abingdon texts? Starting with those from before 1066, there is the important vernacular account, probably by Æthelwold, of monasticism in England up to the tenth-century reform.[314] In a portion now lost but the contents of which are suggested by William of Malmesbury's *Life of Dunstan*, this very likely mentioned a visit to Abingdon by Edgar when he was young. Seeing the ruins, and learning of their background, he swore that if he ever became king he would restore the monastery, and others like it, to their original state.[315] The surviving portion of the vernacular account records the refoundation of the abbey, focusing on Edgar's fulfilment of his vow and his ordering that 'a glorious minster' be built there within three years.[316] Also of obvious importance is the *Life of Æthelwold*, written in 996 or soon after by Wulfstan, a monk and priest who became precentor of the Old Minster, Winchester.[317] The *Anglo-Saxon Chronicle*, besides versions B and C, provides very limited information, almost entirely about the succession to the abbacy. *Lives* of St Swithun by Lantfred and Wulfstan mention a Byrhtferth, *prepositus* (that is, prior) of Abingdon, who was blind for fifteen

[313] M. Förster, 'Die altenglische Glossenhandschrift Plantinus 32 (Antwerpen) und Additional 32246 (London)', *Anglia*, xli (1917), 94–161, at pp. 153–4; for the association with Abingdon, N. R. Ker, *Catalogue of Manuscripts containing Anglo-Saxon* (Oxford, 1957), pp. 2–3. Porter, 'Æthelwold's bowl'.

[314] *Councils and Synods*, i. 143–54. Gretsch, *Intellectual Foundations*, p. 232 n. 18, suggests a date in the mid-960s for the text as preserved. Cf. Gransden, 'Traditionalism and continuity', p. 203 n. 233, for criticism of the attribution to Æthelwold and the suggestion that 'the narrative was at least revised after the Conquest'. For the contents of the text, see also Wormald, 'Æthelwold and his Continental counterparts', p. 40.

[315] William of Malmesbury, *Life of Dunstan*, bk. ii, c. 2, *Saints' Lives*, ed. M. Winterbottom and R. M. Thomson (OMT, 2002), p. 238. *Charters of Abingdon Abbey*, p. xxxviii n. 15, points out that the vernacular account 'may represent a very early mythologising of Abingdon's recent past'. Alternatively, the story of the visit could simply be true.

[316] *Councils and Synods*, i. 147–8. The focus on Edgar is increased by the statement that at his succession there had been only one monastery living in regular fashion, and that was Glastonbury, where Edmund had established monks; *Councils and Synods*, i. 148–9.

[317] Wulfstan, *Life of Æthelwold*, pp. xiii–xvi. See above, pp. xxvii, xli–xlii, on its use in the *History*. The *Life*'s account of Eadred's restoration was taken on by *Liber Monasterii de Hyda*, ed. E. Edwards (London, 1866), pp. 151–2, and note also p. 180; see Wulfstan, *Life of Æthelwold*, pp. clxv–clxvi.

years. Various cures failed, and he then went barefoot as a pilgrim to the body of St Swithun at Winchester and was cured. According to Wulfstan he held his position in the time of Abbot Osgar and looked after the abbey's estates [*prouiderat . . . rura monasterii*].[318]

Particularly significant among non-narrative sources is the *Liber Vitae* of New Minster, Winchester. The greater part of the *Liber Vitae* was produced by a monk called Ælfsige, at New Minster, in 1031.[319] A consolidated list in this work, rather than any Abingdon-produced source, provides most of our knowledge of the names of pre-Conquest Abingdon monks, for whom the Winchester monks were to offer prayer.[320] Our knowledge of one aspect of abbots' activity is increased by their appearances as witnesses to royal charters.[321] Finally, wills record various gifts to Abingdon, the documents presumably not being preserved at the house because Abingdon was not the main beneficiary or, as in the case of Archbishop Ælfric, the place of burial.[322]

As for post-Conquest sources for the Anglo-Saxon history of Abingdon, the most notable narratives are those of William of Malmesbury. His *Gesta regum* contains an account of the Frankish mission to Æthelstan's court at Abingdon,[323] and also mentions Abbots Æthelwold and Siward.[324] The *Gesta pontificum* records the foundation of the abbey, the disasters it suffered under the Danes and Alfred, and the refoundation under Eadred. After mentioning Æthelwold and Osgar its section on Abingdon passes directly to the coming of Faritius. Elsewhere in the *Gesta pontificum*, William copied the *Life of Æthelwold*'s version of the miracle story involving the monk Ælfstan, placing it amongst the deeds of the bishops of Ramsbury, the see to which Ælfstan would be appointed. Further

318 Lantfred, *Life of Swithun*, c. 28, Lapidge, *Cult of St Swithun*, p. 316; Wulfstan, *Life of Swithun*, c. 11, Lapidge, *Cult of St Swithun*, p. 526. Neither Abingdon sources nor the New Minster *Liber Vitae* mention Byrhtferth.

319 *Liber Vitae*, ed. Keynes, p. 15.

320 Ibid., fos. 26^{v}–27^{r}.

321 See below, pp. xciii–cvi. Note also Sawyer, no. 1425, a lease from St Albans to a widow named Tova and her son of land at Great Tew, Oxfordshire, witnessed by, amongst others, the abbot and whole congregation of Abingdon. The document can be dated to 1049 × 1052.

322 See above, p. lix, for Archbishop Ælfric's burial at Abingdon.

323 William of Malmesbury, *Gesta regum Anglorum*, bk. ii, c. 135, ed. Mynors *et al.*, i. 218; see also his *Gesta pontificum*, bk. v, c. 246, ed. Hamilton, p. 397. See above, p. 000, for William's *Life of Dunstan* preserving matter from the vernacular account of monastic reform.

324 *Gesta regum*, bk. ii, cc. 149, 197, ed. Mynors *et al.*, i. 242, 352.

treatment of Æthelwold appears in William's section on the bishopric of Winchester, and he also recorded in his section on Shaftesbury that part of the body of Edward the martyr was taken to Abingdon.[325]

Other post-Conquest historians had less to say about Abingdon.[326] The *Chronicle* of John of Worcester, except for the Abingdon additions, adds little, although interestingly it does refer to Abbot Eadwine, maligned in the *History*, as 'the venerable monk Eadwine'.[327] Henry of Huntingdon just mentioned that Edgar, on Æthelwold's advice, built the abbey of Abingdon on the Thames.[328] Orderic Vitalis placed Oswald at the centre of reform, and states that 'with the help of Dunstan and Æthelwold, both holy men, he first established regular discipline at Glastonbury and Abingdon'.[329]

Much more useful than the snippets in such historians is the evidence of *Domesday Book*, which, as we shall see, is essential to analysis of the abbey's endowment. Archaeology can be helpful, for example with regard to land use and economic development at Abingdon and in some of its estates.[330] Unfortunately, the 1922 excavation of the abbey site was, in Martin Biddle's words, 'inadequate even by comparison with other amateur excavations of its day', and can provide us with only limited help on the pre-Conquest buildings.[331]

3. Omissions from the *History*'s account

This survey of other sources for the history of the abbey has already indicated that there are some omissions in the *History*'s account. Particularly notable is the absence of mention of Edgar's visit to Abingdon when he was young.[332] Our knowledge of Æthelsige,

[325] *Gesta pontificum*, bk. ii, cc. 75, 83, 86, 88, ed. Hamilton, pp. 166, 181, 188, 191–2. See also *Gesta pontificum*, bk. i, c. 20, ed. Hamilton, p. 32 and n. 5, for Ælfric archbishop of Canterbury, wrongly being said to have been abbot of Abingdon.

[326] Very brief mentions include e.g. the Waverley annals reference to Abingdon's foundation by Ceadwalla in 688; *Annales monastici*, ed. H. R. Luard (5 vols., London, 1864–9), ii. 153.

[327] John of Worcester, *Chronicle*, ii. 434. At ii. 552–4 he attributes to Edward the Confessor the ejection of Bishop Spearhafoc, previously abbot of Abingdon, from the see of London.

[328] Henry of Huntingdon, *Historia Anglorum*, bk. v, c. 25, ed. Greenway, p. 320.

[329] Orderic, *Ecclesiastical History*, bk. iv, ed. Chibnall, ii. 242.

[330] See e.g. G. Astill, 'The towns of Berkshire', in J. Haslam, ed., *Anglo-Saxon Towns in Southern England* (Chichester, 1984), pp. 53–86, at 73 (and plan on p. 74); *Archaeology at Barton Court Farm, Abingdon, Oxon.*, ed. D. Miles (Council for British Archaeology Research Report, 1; 1984); T. G. Allen, 'A medieval grange of Abingdon Abbey at Dean Court Farm, Cumnor, Oxon', *Oxoniensia*, lix (1994), 219–447.

[331] Biddle *et al.*, 'Early history', p. 61; see also below, p. clxvi.

[332] See above, p. lxiv.

probably abbot of Abingdon between 1016 and 1018, comes from the *Anglo-Saxon Chronicle*, not the *History*.[333] It is strange that the burial of Archbishop Ælfric is not mentioned in the *History*, although it does appear in the Abingdon additions to John of Worcester's *Chronicle*.[334] It is only from *De abbatibus* that we know of Æthelwold constructing a new watercourse and building organs for use in church.[335] Several gifts mentioned in surviving wills are not recorded in the *History*.[336]

We also know of documents that did not appear in the *History*, although it is very hard to tell if their omission was intentional, accidental, or a matter of survival. The abbey archive would once, and in the 1160s may well still, have included a very significant number of Anglo-Saxon wills, leases, and writs.[337] If these did survive until the 1160s, they may have been omitted because they appeared no longer relevant or because they were in the vernacular. However, the comment on the poor state of the Ælfhere memorandum may indicate that others had not survived.[338] Some charters too may not have survived until the composition of the *History*. Most notable is a statement in the *Life of Æthelwold* that by Osgar's time the abbey had over 600 hides, 'and it was further underpinned by the granting of privileges of perpetual liberty, written on God's and the king's authority. They are kept there to this day, sealed with gold leaves.'[339] Such a document may well have resembled the resplendent New Minster charter.[340] Had such a charter existed at the time of the composition of the *History*, the compiler would surely have mentioned it.

However, we also know of charters which did survive until the time of the composition of the *History* but do not appear within it: these are preserved in later copies.[341] The revised version of the *History*

[333] See below, p. c.

[334] John of Worcester, *Chronicle*, ii. 613: 'et sepultus est Abbendonie unde monachus extiterat sed regnante Kanuto rege ad sedem suam translatus'.

[335] *CMA* ii. 278; see also below, p. clxviii, for the description in *De abbatibus* of Æthelwold's church.

[336] See below, p. cxlvii.

[337] See *Charters of Abingdon Abbey*, p. xlix.

[338] c. 93.

[339] Wulfstan, *Life of Æthelwold*, c. 21, ed. Lapidge and Winterbottom, p. 36. See also below, c. 39, which mentions a charter of Eadwig concerning *Earmundesleah*, but is not followed by that charter; this could be because the charter did not survive at the time of composition. For lost documents, see further *Charters of Abingdon Abbey*, Appendix I.

[340] Sawyer, no. 745; *The Golden Age of Anglo-Saxon Art*, ed. J. Backhouse, D. H. Turner, and L. Webster (London, 1984), plate iv.

[341] See also *Charters of Abingdon Abbey*, p. l. Sixteenth-century copies of two grants not directly to Abingdon survive in a group with Abingdon charters; see above, p. lxiii.

records that 'King Eadwig gave to Brihthelm, his kinsman, Stowe amounting to five hides, and he by the king's consent gave it to God and the blessed Mary and the house of Abingdon and the monks serving God there, on the same terms as above'.[342] The closing statement suggests that the reviser had no charter available, yet a copy of a lost original was made in the sixteenth century, and one is left wondering how the reviser knew of the grant if he did not have the charter.[343] Likewise two charters directly to Abingdon exist in later copies, one in a sixteenth-century single sheet, the other an *inspeximus* of Edward III.[344] The former is a charter in King Eadwig's name granting twenty hides at Tadmarton to Abingdon. If it was in existence by the time of the *History*'s compilation, it is not clear why it was omitted.[345] The second charter, in King Coenwulf's name and granting land at Culham to Abingdon, was, it has been suggested, a product of the later twelfth century, and may have underlain the reviser's story of Coenwulf, his sisters, and the passing of Culham to Abingdon. If so, one might have expected it to appear in the revised *History*, just as Coenwulf's charter concerning demands by his officials coexisted with its related narrative. An alternative and preferable possibility would be that the charter draws on the revised *History*, perhaps in a process of fabrication linked to the obtaining of a bull from Gregory IX (1227–41) confirming to the abbey Culham and its chapel.[346] As we shall continue to see, the composition of history at Abingdon had long taken place in the context of documents rather than narrative accounts.[347] The forged Culham charter may be one

[342] B155.

[343] *Charters of Abingdon Abbey*, no. 62.

[344] Ibid., nos. 68 and 10 respectively.

[345] *Charters of Abingdon Abbey*, p. 289, may explain the circumstances of forgery, but these do not explain the omission of the charter from the *History*. It may be that accidental omission was more likely when several documents of similar supposed date existed for one estate, as in the case of Tadmarton.

[346] *Charters of Abingdon Abbey*, no. 10. See ibid., pp. 46–8, which has some inconsistency as to dating. Cf. Gelling, *Early Charters of the Thames Valley*, p. 125, who suggests that the *History*'s passage 'was presumably the main basis of the forgery'. See also *Charters of the Early West Saxon Kingdom*, ed. Edwards, pp. 187–9. The charter records Coenwulf's grant of Culham to Abingdon, made at the request of his two sisters, whom it names as 'Keneswyth' and 'Burgenilde', probably Coenswith or Cwenthryth and Burghild. Coenwulf in fact had daughters named Cwenthryth and Burghild. The former he appointed abbess of Reculver and Minster-in-Thanet, and Susan Kelly has suggested that 'it is possible that he set up another of his offspring in a minster on the Upper Thames, perhaps at Culham or perhaps at Abingdon (or perhaps between the two, on Andersey)'; *Charters of Abingdon Abbey*, pp. ccv–ccvi, 48–9. For Coenwulf and his officials, see cc. 9, 11, B17, B18.

[347] See below, p. lxxxii.

piece of evidence that such composition did not cease with the completion of the revised version of our *History*.

IV. STRUCTURE OF THE *HISTORY* UP TO 1071

The earlier version of the *History* is divided into two books. Book I ends with the imprisonment of Ealdred, the last abbot elected before the Norman Conquest, and with the oppressions by various invaders. Book II begins with William I's appointment as abbot of Adelelm, a monk from Jumièges. The division thereby focuses attention on abbatial change. The revised version is divided differently. Book I is brought to an end with the 'third destruction of the monastery' in King Eadred's time. The earlier version has a brief summary at this point, and the revival under Eadred and Æthelwold is marked by large decorated initials, but there is no stronger structural division.[348] The change re-emphasizes the place of the successive destructions and reforms of the house in the structuring of the view of the past. Book II in the revised version stretches from the reign of Eadred to the Battle of Hastings. This shifts the focus from change in the abbey, as in the earlier version, to change in the kingdom. However, the shift to Book III is somewhat muddled. After the division he had made at Hastings, the reviser returned to events of the Confessor's reign, before dealing again with the king's death, the Conquest, and its aftermath up to the account of Ealdred's capture and the Norman oppressions, copied from MS C. He then inappropriately reproduced MS C's statement that 'Here begins Book II of the History of the church of Abingdon', and moved on to events under Abbot Adelelm.

In the earlier version of the *History* Book I is thirty-one folios long, Book II forty-one and a half folios. The preponderance is thus on the post-Conquest period. The introduction in particular of many more Anglo-Saxon charters changes this in the revised version of the *History*. Book I ends on fo. 32^{v} by the most recent foliation, Book II runs from fo. 32^{v} to fo. 117^{v}, Book III from fo. 117^{v} to 177^{v}. Therefore in the earlier version approximately three-sevenths of the text concerns the period before the appointment of Abbot Adelelm in 1071, four-sevenths the period after. In the revised version, approximately two-thirds of the text concerns the period before the appointment of Adelelm, one-third the period after.

[348] See below, p. 292, cf. p. 46; for the large initials in MS C, see fo. 111^{r}.

The text is further divided into sections, each normally with a rubricated heading. Use of headings is not entirely consistent. For example, in the earlier version of the *History* narratives prefacing charters sometimes have a heading of their own, sometimes do not. It would appear that the scribe only gradually established his practice, as use of headings in these circumstances becomes consistent in the second half of Book I.[349] Headings occasionally appear in the margin,[350] perhaps as an afterthought, whilst MS B sometimes uses headings consisting only of rubricated minims.[351] In addition, there are sections with no heading, sometimes through the fault of the scribe or rubricator.[352]

1. MS C

Abbacies, reigns, and structure

The earlier version of the *History* begins with a brief account of the geographical situation of the abbey, but thereafter has a largely chronological arrangement. Particularly until the time of Æthelwold, abbacies feature less prominently in the structure of the *History* than they do in Book II. For example, kings' reigns rather than abbacies predominate in the treatment of the late ninth and early tenth centuries. The discussion of Æthelwold's youth owes its location in the text to his link to Æthelstan, and his coming to the abbacy appears in a section headed 'Concerning the restoration of this church in the time of King Eadred'.[353] The organizational importance of kings no doubt stems from the preponderance of the royal charter material and the scantiness of knowledge concerning abbots. From the time of Æthelwold, however, Book I comes to share Book II's abbacy-by-abbacy structure.

The space devoted to each period and abbacy varies, as can be seen from the following table:

349 Without heading: see e.g. cc. 18–19, 42–3, 60–1; with heading: cc. 34, 40, 45, etc.; consistent use of heading from c. 68 (although note an exception at cc. 103–5).

350 e.g. MS C, fo. 128r (cc. 106, 107), MS B, fo. 5r (B5).

351 B276, B278, B281–B283.

352 See below, pp. 260, 264, 280, 316, 330, 346, 362, 368, 370.

353 cc. 24, 27.

Period	*Chapters*	*Duration*	*Approx. proportion of total words of Book I*
Haeha	1–7	670s-728	4%
Mercian kings	8–11	716–821	5%
Wessex kings to Edward the Elder	12–18	802–924	5%
Æthelstan to Eadred's accession	18–26	924–46	6%[354]
Æthelwold	27–70	c.954–63	29%
Osgar	71–95	963–84	10%
Eadwine	96	985–90	less than 0.5%
Wulfgar	97–111	990–1016	16%[355]
Æthelwine	111	1016/18–30	1%
Siward	112–19	1030–44	4.5%[356]
Æthelstan	119–23	c.1044–7	4%[357]
Spearhafoc	124	c.1047–51	less than 1%
Rodulf	125	1051–2	less than 0.5%
Ordric	126–43	1052–66	10%[358]
Ealdred	143–4	1066–71	3%

One sees immediately the centrality of Æthelwold's abbacy to Book I of the *History*, although its predominance does not match that of Faritius's rule in Book II.

It is hard to see any clear principles of arrangement within accounts of abbacies. With the partial exceptions of those concerning Æthelwold, Ordric, and Ealdred, the accounts are too brief to have allowed any clear chronological arrangement, except with regard to the ordering of charters.[359] As we have already seen, flashbacks and anticipations help to integrate the various sections, as does the use of cross-references.[360]

354 Note that c. 24 concerns Æthelwold.

355 I have taken into account the portion of the missing folio that can be reconstructed, but some text is still missing so the figure should be very slightly higher.

356 Note that further material concerning Siward, after his abbacy, appears in cc. 120, 122.

357 Very little of this concerns Abbot Æthelstan himself.

358 This figure includes cc. 137, 139, 140, charters not from the time of Abbot Ordric.

359 In the case of Ordric, we have the first grant of privilege to the abbey associated by the compiler with the succession of a new abbot, and it appears in the appropriate place at the start of the abbacy; c. 127.

360 See above, pp. xxv, xxxvi.

Documents and narrative

Whilst a few of the charters in the *History* contain elements of historical narrative,[361] in general the distinction between document and narrative is clear. Just under a quarter of Book I is made up of narrative, the remainder of documents.

Period	*Chapters*	*Approx. proportion narrative rather than document*
Haeha	1–7	17%[362]
Mercian kings	8–11	19%
Wessex kings to Edward the Elder	12–18	18%
Æthelstan to Eadred's accession	18–26	18%[363]
Æthelwold	27–70	16%
Osgar	71–95	25%
Eadwine	96	100%
Wulfgar	97–111	17%
Æthelwine	111	100%
Siward	112–19	30%
Æthelstan	119–23	91%
Spearhafoc	124	100%
Rodulf	125	100%
Ordric	126–43	34%
Ealdred	143–4	100%

Thus the proportion of narrative to document varies between abbacies, but there is a significant shift in the early eleventh century. Up to the coming of Abbot Æthelwine just under one-fifth of the text consists of narrative, from the time of Abbot Æthelwine a little less than three-fifths. Once again, we see Book I becoming markedly more similar in characteristics to Book II.[364]

In general a link is provided between related documents and narratives. This may take the form of a simple narrative prefacing the charter or a sentence following the charter. These make a

[361] See e.g. pp. 4–6, 142; cf. M. Chibnall, 'Charter and Chronicle: The use of archive sources by Norman historians', in C. N. L. Brooke *et al.*, eds., *Church and Government in the Middle Ages* (Cambridge, 1976), pp. 1–17.

[362] I here take all of c. 4 as constituting document rather than narrative.

[363] Note that c. 24 concerns Æthelwold.

[364] See vol. ii, pp. xxxv–xxxvi. Note that post-Conquest charters were often shorter than pre-Conquest ones, and this affects the proportion of the text taken up by documents.

statement such as 'and then the beneficiary gave it to Abingdon'.[365] Occasionally there is a more developed link, notably in the case of King Coenwulf's privilege for Abingdon, which seems to have formed the basis of an extensive narrative in the *History*.[366] Another more sophisticated link is provided with regard to the charters of Edgar and Æthelred granting Sparsholt and Whitchurch respectively. These appear in the portion of the text devoted to Abbot Ordric (1042–66) and follow an explanation about monks holding and having freedom to dispose of patrimonies.[367] There are also, however, charters that are included without any introduction or explanation.[368]

Within reigns there is a logic to the order of charters. In Æthelstan's reign, four royal charters appear, the first dated 930, the others 931, and then a document recording a grant by Æthelstan the 'senator'.[369] The one charter of Eadred directly to Abingdon in MS C appears some sections before his one charter for a layman.[370] Likewise for Eadwig, Edgar, and Æthelred, their main confirmation charters come first, followed by those recording grants directly to Abingdon, and then those recording grants to individuals that are said to have passed to the abbey.[371] In the case of Eadwig and Æthelred the distinction between the second and third type of charter is made explicit. Take Eadwig: 'From this point let us note briefly the following lands which were given not by that king to the abbey, but rather by those to whom he had granted the option of giving them freely to whomsoever they might wish.'[372] Within the groups, the ordering is basically chronological, although with some

[365] On the reliability of these statements, see below, pp. cxxvi–cxxix.

[366] cc. 9 and 11. See above, pp. xxx, liii, for words and phrases from charters being used in narratives.

[367] cc. 138–40.

[368] cc. 13, 86, 117.

[369] cc. 19–23.

[370] cc. 28, 35.

[371] Amongst Eadwig's charters, c. 44 has a transitional place, as the land concerned was not given directly to Abingdon but soon passed to the church through an exchange. See below, p. lxxviii, on MS B making explicit the arrangement of Edgar's charters.

[372] See below, p. 76. See also below, p. 162, concerning Æthelred's charters. Cf. vol. ii. 72 on Faritius: 'let us turn our pen to his deeds outside, making this distinction: each is to be arranged in order, first those things which previously were deemed to belong to others, and by his endeavour became the church's own; then those which had once been the church's own, but which had been dispersed by other less sound rulers of the monastery, and were completely alienated from the abbey's property, but were now restored by him'.

lapses.[373] A group of three charters of Edgar concerning grants unusually distant from the monastery appear together. The first is from 961, the year before the preceding charter, which had concerned Hendred in Berkshire. However, chronological order is restored after this brief slip, and indeed the remaining two charters concerning more distant estates may simply be appearing in their appropriate chronological place, not being grouped for reasons of geography.[374] After the reign of Æthelred, the chronological arrangement of charters ceases, at exactly the time when their numbers diminish and also as the proportion of narrative in the *History* increases. Those documents that do appear are often located in the context of a dispute to which they are relevant, even at the expense of chronology.[375]

Thus the *History* before the time of Æthelwold lacks a significant continuous narrative. Only three pre-Æthelwoldian abbots are mentioned, Hæha, Hræthhun, and Cynath. Even into Æthelred's reign the *History* is really a collection of charters, linked by sentences referring to the gifts in the charters and punctuated with very occasional further narratives, on the foundation of the house, the coming of the Danes, changes of king and abbot, and on Æthelwold himself. Then from the time of Æthelred, and particularly from the last sections devoted to gifts and events of his reign, the text becomes much closer in form to Book II, combining numerous and varied narratives with a still very significant number of documents.[376]

2. MS B

Abbacies, reigns, and structure

In MS B, as in MS C, the early history of the church is structured around reigns as much as around abbacies. Moreover, whilst abbacies again become more significant from the time of Æthelwold, viewers of the text continue to have their eyes drawn to the illustrations of kings in the text.

The space devoted to each abbacy is as follows:

[373] e.g. c. 52, a charter dated 957, precedes cc. 53–6, all charters dated 956.

[374] cc. 67, 69, 70; note that cc. 64, 65, were charters recording grants in Hampshire, dated 961 and 962.

[375] The first instance is c. 137.

[376] The change becomes clear particularly from c. 106.

Period	*Chapters*	*Duration*	*Approx. proportion of total words of Book I*
Abben	B1–3	uncertain	1%[377]
Hæha	B4–11	670s–728	2%
Mercian kings	B11–24	716–821	3%
Wessex kings to Edward the Elder	B25–46	802–924	6%
Æthelstan to Eadred's accession	B46–81	924–46	13%
Æthelwold	B82–209	c.954–63	45%
Osgar	B209–14	963–84	2%
Eadwine	B215	985–90	—
Wulfgar	B216–45	990–1016	16%
Æthelwine	B245–51	1016/18–30	1.5%
Siward	B251–6	1030–44	2%
Æthelstan	B256–63	*c.*1044–7	2.5%
Spearhafoc	B264	c.1047–51	—
Rodulf	B265	1051–2	—
Ordric	B266–85	1052–66	4%
Ealdred	B285–92	1066–71	2%

These proportions can be compared with those in MS C:

Period	*B total %*	*C total %*
Abben	1	—
Hæha	2	4
Mercian kings	3	5
Wessex kings to Edward the Elder	6	5
Æthelstan to Eadred's accession	13	6
Æthelwold	45	29
Osgar	2	10
Eadwine	—	0.4
Wulfgar	16	16
Æthelwine	1.5	1
Siward	2	4
Æthelstan	2.5	4

[377] Abben: fo. 4; note that some further relevant material would have been contained in missing folios. Hæha: fos. 5^{r}–7^{r}; note that further relevant material would have been contained in missing folios. Mercian kings: fos. 7^{r}–11^{v}. Wessex kings: fos. 11^{v}–18^{r}. Æthelstan to Eadred succession: fos. 18^{r}–32^{v}. Æthelwold: fos. 32^{v}–85^{r}. Osgar: fos. 85^{r}–87^{r}. Eadwine: fo. 87^{r-v}. Wulfgar: fos. 87^{v}–106^{r}. Æthelwine: fos. 106^{r}–107^{v}. Siward: fos. 107^{v}–109^{v}. Æthelstan: fos. 109^{v}–112^{v}. Spearhafoc: fo. 112^{v}. Rodulf: fo. 112^{v}. Ordric: fos. 112^{v}–117^{r}. Ealdred: fos. 117^{r}–119^{v}.

Period	*B total %*	*C total %*
Spearhafoc	—	0.7
Rodulf	—	0.3
Ordric	4	10
Ealdred	2	3

Three major changes regarding the distribution between abbacies have been made to the earlier version of the *History*. First is the still greater emphasis on the period of Æthelwold's abbacy. Indeed, material that had appeared within Osgar's abbacy in MS C appears within Æthelwold's in MS B, markedly diminishing the proportion of the text devoted to Osgar. Second is the notable increase in space given to the reigns of Æthelstan, Edmund, and Eadred. Third is the diminution in the proportion of the text devoted to Ordric's abbacy. All these changes of emphasis are related to the increase in the numbers of charters recording gifts to beneficiaries other than Abingdon. These particularly swell the portions of text from the time of Æthelstan to that of Æthelwold. They have no such effect on the account of Ordric's abbacy, leaving it relatively diminished in comparison with earlier periods.

Any chronological element remains limited in the narratives even of the abbots to whom relatively larger amounts of space are allocated. The treatment of Æthelwold remains divided between his early life, his abbacy, and his elevation to Winchester and later death. The new sections on his building work, his gifts to the church, and his food and drink provisions are simply placed at the end of the portion of the text covering his abbacy, and dated to the time of Edgar.[378] Cross-references, anticipations, and flashbacks continue to provide coherence to the text.[379]

[378] Note vol. ii, p. xxxi on the sections concerning Faritius, Vincent, and Ingulf each ending with their endowment of the offices of the abbey.

[379] See e.g. B7 (to a missing portion of the text), B40, B83, B113, B207 (references to the Norman Conquest, Stephen's reign, and an implicit link to the later description of Faritius's provisions concerning food), B290.

Documents and narrative

Period	*Chapters*	*Approx. proportion narrative rather than document*
Abben	B1–3	100%
Hæha	B4–11	60%
Mercian kings	B11–24	55%
Wessex kings to Edward the Elder	B25–46	35%
Æthelstan to Eadred's accession	B46–81	15%
Æthelwold	B82–209	just below 10%
Osgar	B209–14	20–25%
Eadwine	B215	100%
Wulfgar	B216–45	slightly over 5%
Æthelwine	B245–51	15–20%
Siward	B251–6	40–45%
Æthelstan	B256–63	40%
Spearhafoc	B264	100%
Rodulf	B265	100%
Ordric	B266–85	30%
Ealdred	B285–92	85%

These proportions can be compared with those in MS C:

Period	*B total %*	*C total %*
Abben	100	—
Hæha	60	17
Mercian kings	55	19
Wessex kings to Edward the Elder	35	18
Æthelstan to Eadred's accession	15	18
Æthelwold	just below 10	16
Osgar	20–25	25
Eadwine	100	100
Wulfgar	slightly over 5	17
Æthelwine	15–20	100
Siward	40–45	30
Æthelstan	40	91
Spearhafoc	100	100
Rodulf	100	100
Ordric	30	34
Ealdred	85	100

There is new narrative early in MS B. However, the overall proportion of document to narrative is even higher in MS B than MS C, with narrative making up just under one-fifth of the text.

Charters with no related narrative are much more common than in MS C, particularly in the reigns of Edgar and Æthelred.[380] Again, however, narratives are often linked in a simple way to the charters, with narrative passages either introducing or following documents.[381] Narrative could also be used to improve or supplement documentary evidence in various ways. This might be in the routine inclusion of the phrase 'in pure and perpetual alms' in the introduction to the gift. In the case of King Edmund's grant of Culham to the royal woman Ælfhild, the mixture of narrative and document is more complicated. The heading states that the section will be the 'Charter of King Edmund concerning Culham', and such a charter appeared in MS C. However, in MS B, the main text of the charter is not given; instead the bounds of Culham are preceded by a narrative stating that the grant of Culham to Ælfhild was only for her life.[382] The change reinforces MS B's emphasis on the special connection between the abbey and Culham.[383]

The principles of arrangement of charters are largely similar to those employed in MS C. Indeed, it is now made explicit for King Edgar's charters:

> Now, indeed, we have thought it necessary to mention this munificent king's generous gifts towards this most sacred house of Abingdon, and also its liberties and those of the possessions pertaining to that abbey, strengthened by his authority. To be placed first is his privilege, next the charters whereby he confirmed subsequent possessions to this house, third the charters of his men who by his consent conferred charters[384] on this house confirmed by Edgar's charters, which from that time until the present remain unshaken and by the grace of God will maintain their strength forever. Fourth, indeed, we place the charters both of him and of his men confirming our former possessions.[385]

[380] See esp. B179–B206, B217–B232.

[381] On the reliability of these statements, see below, pp. cxxvii–cxxix.

[382] B64.

[383] For the vocabulary of some narratives being influenced by the charter concerned, see above, p. liii.

[384] It seems likely that the scribe here meant to write 'terras' (lands) or some such word, rather than 'cartas' (charters).

[385] B174. The four groups are respectively B175; B176–B183; B184–B196; B197–B206, the last group in fact being charters of the king, not of his men.

In Æthelred's case, the charters recording gifts made directly to the abbey are divided from other charters by the rubricated heading 'These are the lands which King Æthelred gave to his followers, and they by the king's consent gave to the church of Abingdon.'[386]

Let us look, then, at the arrangement of charters of kings from Æthelstan onwards, the period for which there are sufficient charters to allow significant analysis. The standard order until the death of Æthelred is again (i) general privileges, where issued; (ii) charters recording grants direct to the abbey; (iii) charters recording grants to followers. For Cnut there are no charters to his followers included, whilst by the Confessor's time the charters are much more closely integrated into the narrative.

What of the ordering of charters within this basic framework? Charters from Æthelstan's reign recording grants directly to the abbey appear in chronological order, largely following the arrangement in MS C. The earlier version of the *History* included no grants by Æthelstan to his followers, but several are added in MS B. They do not appear in chronological order, with one charter in particular interrupting any chronological sequence.[387] There are no charters from Edmund recording direct grants to Abingdon. For the grants to followers, the reviser soon starts to provide a chronological ordering made explicit in the narratives preceding charters. His aim is largely, although not perfectly, achieved.[388] No such explicit attempt at chronology is made for Eadred's charters. Only one directly for Abingdon is included, and whilst the grants to followers in the 940s precede those of the 950s, there is no great effort at a chronological arrangement.[389] For Eadwig there is again an explicit effort at chronological arrangement by year of issue, lasting throughout the grants directly to the abbey and extending into those to his followers. It is very largely successful, helped by the vast preponderance of charters issued in 956. Apparent mistakes could be through scribal omission of a final minim in some dates.[390] Perhaps the sheer

[386] B222.

[387] B59; note also B57, which lacks a dating clause.

[388] For slips, note B69 wrongly saying that B70 (a charter of 942) was issued in the same year as B68 (a charter of 940), and confusion at B76–B80.

[389] Note further the mistaken inclusion of two charters of King Æthelred of Wessex; B89, B93.

[390] For example, the *anno Domini* date in B123 (*Charters of Abingdon Abbey*, no. 53) may be missing a minim, the presence of which would reconcile this date with the indiction and the witness list.

repetitiveness led the reviser part way through the collection of Eadwig charters to abandon the statement that the grant was made in the same year as the preceding one, although it does reappear in a narrative that unexpectedly is followed by no charter.[391]

Efforts to arrange Edgar's charters are not entirely successful. MS C's largely chronological ordering of charters direct to Abingdon is not retained. Likewise, the grants to followers are not chronologically ordered. The promise of a fourth grouping, 'the charters both of him and of his men confirming our former possessions', is not entirely fulfilled. The charters gathered thus are all grants by the king directly to the abbey; none are charters of his men. All the charters, or all but one, do concern lands no longer held by the abbey in the twelfth or thirteenth centuries.[392] However, several other charters concerning such lands had been included in the third group, grants by the king to his followers that were said to have passed to Abingdon.[393] The fourth group again lacks chronological order, an order that could have been derived with relative ease not just from their dating clauses but also from their arrangement in MS C.

Only two charters of Edward the martyr appear, and the one directly in favour of the abbey precedes the one to a bishop.[394] Æthelred's charters are then arranged with a competence not displayed in relation to Edgar's. The charters directly in favour of the church retain MS C's sound chronology, and the chronological arrangement of the charters to the king's followers is largely successful.[395] As with MS C, efforts at chronological arrangements thereafter cease, as charters play a reduced part in the *History* and the form of its organization changes.

The revised *History* thus provides more narrative in its early stages than had MS C. Information from Geoffrey of Monmouth, for example, together with a different foundation story, shape the work's opening, and are followed by fuller accounts of kings, including the long narrative concerning Coenwulf and his sisters. Thereafter, the revised *History* comes to be dominated by charters, generally linked by short narratives concerning the gifts. A group of narratives deals with events relating to the Viking attacks of the

[391] B155.

[392] Of the places mentioned in those charters, only in Hendred did Abingdon have lands in the 12th or 13th century; see B202, B203, vol. ii. 388. However, the later lands may not be those that Edgar granted to Abingdon; see *Charters of Abingdon Abbey*, pp. 224–5.

[393] e.g. B185, B188.

[394] B211, B212.

[395] B227 appears to be wrongly positioned.

later ninth century,[396] but this does not mark a lasting shift in form. Rather, charters continue to dominate, their increased numbers also raising the proportion of the text devoted to the period from Æthelstan to Æthelred. There are only occasional narratives not related to the charters, most notably the sections concerning Æthelwold. The shift to a form much closer to that in MS B's Book III occurs in the first half of the eleventh century. This is the same point at which the change occurs in MS C, as is logical since this is the very time when MS B becomes an only slightly modified copy of MS C.

3. Foundation history

To bring these considerations of sources and structure together, it is helpful to undertake a case study of the use of sources on a particularly difficult and not necessarily typical issue, the foundation of the abbey. I will deal first with the medieval development of the foundation legends and then consider modern analyses of the same subject.[397]

Development of the foundation legends

Medieval writers, like modern historians, faced a particular problem for Abingdon: Bede made no mention of Abingdon, whereas he did refer to Ely and to *Medehamstead*, as he called what would later be Peterborough.[398] Nor do other early sources fill the gap, as at Glastonbury, which is mentioned in St Boniface's letter collection.[399] Also lacking were famous relics or impressive remains of buildings.[400]

It is, indeed, only from Æthelwold's time that we can begin to identify the various strands of the Abingdon foundation legends.

[396] B37–B40.

[397] For comparative purposes, see e.g. A. G. Remensnyder, *Remembering Kings Past: Monastic Foundation Legends in Medieval Southern France* (Ithaca, NY, 1995); Paxton, 'Charter and Chronicle'.

[398] Note, however, Miller, *Ely*, pp. 8–9, on the limits of Bede as a source for later tradition at Ely; he comments that the composer of the *Liber Eliensis* 'desired to establish a venerable antiquity for the privileges enjoyed by his church in his own day; and to vindicate for those privileges some sort of continuity from St Etheldreda's day'.

[399] See *Monumenta Germaniæ Historica: Epistolarum tomus iii* (Berlin, 1892), p. 388 (no. 101).

[400] The legends of the Black Cross seem to begin in the time of Æthelwold; see below, p. lxxxvi. See above, p. lxiv, on Edgar seeing the ruins of Abingdon. Note that the *Life of Æthelwold* does not mention the remains of any great church buildings.

Æthelwold displayed a considerable interest in the history of monasticism in general and of certain monasteries in particular.[401] The former is most obvious in the vernacular account of the monasticism in England of which he appears to have been author, the latter most clearly displayed in charters. His interests included the decline of monasticism since the golden age of Bede, and the associated fate of monastic property and privileges.

Æthelwold sought historical backing for his efforts to restore and accumulate monastic lands and liberties. At Abingdon, this project manifested itself in three groups of charters. One was the forgery, quite probably in Æthelwold's time, of supposedly pre-tenth-century charters for Abingdon. These may have been based on early records, but were assembled in a way that seems to reveal Æthelwold's concerns.[402] Thus one of the charters in King Coenwulf's name talks of Abbot Hræthhun redeeming lands 'from servitude established by the hands of strangers [*a manu extraneorum*]', a notion of central importance to Æthelwold.[403] It may also be in Æthelwold's time that a second group of records, in this case concerning a foundation at Bradfield, were assimilated into Abingdon traditions, providing a seventh-century origin and the name of a first abbot, Hæha, and a founding king, Cissa. However, it should be noted that these named individuals appear in other accounts of the foundation only in the twelfth century.[404]

Perhaps significantly, their names are not present in the third relevant group of charters, the major privileges in the names of Eadwig, Edgar, and Æthelred. Whilst the authenticity particularly of the first two of these is controversial, it is reasonable to take their account of Abingdon's past as that developed in the time of

[401] See Wormald, 'Æthelwold and his Continental counterparts', pp. 39–40; also *Charters of the Abbey of Abingdon*, p. clxix.

[402] See below, p. cxxv, on links between Coenwulf, Pope Leo III, and privileges relating to churches. See also *Charters of the Abbey of Abingdon*, p. 26, on c. 8, a charter recording grants by King Æthelbald of Mercia and King Æthelheard of Wessex: 'The transformation of such a document into a full-scale statement about Abingdon's early holdings could perhaps be considered against the background of Æthelwold's campaign to reconstruct the ancient endowment.'

[403] See below, p. 16. Note the use of 'extraneorum' in the *Orthodoxorum* charters, below, pp. 62, 96, 146.

[404] On these charters and their place in the *History*, see Stenton, *Early History*, pp. 15–16, who suggests that 'provisionally, at least, we may fairly look to Malmesbury as the immediate source of the early formulas employed in the first charters of the Abingdon series'; *Charters of the Early West Saxon Kingdom*, ed. Edwards, pp. 168–77, 195–6; *Charters of Abingdon Abbey*, p. cxcvi. On the dating of their composition, see below, pp. cciv–ccv.

Æthelwold.[405] Four key points emerge. Ceadwalla is the earliest king mentioned, and to him is attributed the gift of land at Abingdon 'to our Lord and His mother Mary'. Secondly, the abbey had been freed 'of every yoke of earthly service . . . by our Catholic predecessors, that is by St Leo the Pope and by Coenwulf the Catholic king, as is contained in the old privilege obtained by Abbot Hræthhun'.[406] Thirdly, the kings' predecessors '(deceived by diabolical avarice) had unjustly built themselves a royal building' on the site of the abbey. And, finally, it was King Eadred who 'restored to the church of God the land called Abingdon' and 'forbade that any king seek hospitality therein or ever construct a building' there.

The *Life of Æthelwold*, written *c.*1000, does not concern itself with the abbey's foundation. It states only that at Abingdon 'there had of old been a small monastery', which by King Eadred's time had become 'neglected and forlorn'.[407] No further evidence on foundation legends emerges until the twelfth century. It is in William of Malmesbury's *Gesta pontificum*, written in the 1120s, that Cissa appears, wrongly identified as the father of Ine: 'Cissa father of Ine, and soon Ine himself, king of the West Saxons, and many kings from the start established [*fundauerunt*] the monastery of Abingdon.'[408] This statement appears in simplified form in John of Worcester: 'Cissa father of Ine established Abingdon.'[409] The tradition became well established, with, for instance, Ralph Diceto naming Cissa as the founder of Abingdon in his list of pre-Conquest founders of churches.[410]

[405] For the authenticity of the charters, see below, pp. cxcix–cciv. For historical material in charters from Thorney and Ely, see Sawyer, nos. 779, 792, and Thacker, 'Æthelwold', p. 54.

[406] *Charters of Abingdon Abbey*, e.g. p. cxciii, accepts the possibility that Æthelwold was here making 'reference to ancient documentation, in the form of a privilege of immunity in the names of Pope Leo III and King Coenwulf of Mercia'.

[407] Wulfstan, *Life of Æthelwold*, c. 11, ed. Lapidge and Winterbottom, p. 18. It is difficult to tell what significance should be attached to the use of the diminutive 'monasteriolum' in this context, given the chronological vagueness of the reference to the past and the desire to magnify Æthelwold's achievement.

[408] William of Malmesbury, *Gesta pontificum*, c. 88, ed. Hamilton, p. 191.

[409] John of Worcester, *Chronicle*, ii. 538, and see ii. 538 n. 1 on the relationship to William of Malmesbury. Probably drawing on the *History*, the Abingdon manuscripts of John of Worcester provide a brief addition under the year 688: King Ine 'completed [*perfecit*] the monastery called Abingdon, which the noble man Cissa and King Ceadwalla had begun'; John of Worcester, *Chronicle*, ii. 609.

[410] Ralph de Diceto, *Opera historica*, ed. W. Stubbs (2 vols., London, 1876), ii. 211; Ralph describes Edgar as the endower of the monastery.

This brings us to the version of the *History* in MS C. Cissa again appears as the founder, but with much more detail:

Cissa king of the West Saxons gave the site for the monastery to be built for the worship of almighty God to a certain Hæha, a man of the religious life and abbot, and also to his sister, named Cilla, and . . . very many endowments and possessions were conferred on it by royal gift, for the necessities of life of those living therein. Both Hæha and Cilla were ennobled by royal lineage.

Following Cissa's death, he was succeeded by Ceadwalla, who gave twenty hides to Abingdon. The subsequent chronology is somewhat uncertain, in part because of a lack of clarity in the *History* as to the role of particular individuals.[411] The foundation came under threat from Ine, successor of Ceadwalla, who took away the endowment before a monastery had been built, but then changed his mind and gave back the land to Hæha and Cilla. Hæha too reportedly vacillated in his devotion to the monastery:

But now, less than five years after taking these vows, and desiring to change and be released from his decisions, he has taken King Ine as his helper regarding the inheritance that he has claimed back. I have willingly yielded regarding these matters, and restore in full that land and the monasteries which, as I have said, we built. . . . Moreover, I have undone and mercifully remitted the monk's vow that he had sworn me, in the presence of the venerable Bishop Hædde, and Abbot Aldhelm, and Wintra, and all our *familia* in the church.[412]

This portion of the text ends with the 'Testament' of Abbot Hæha, granting land to Cilla, and with the departure of King Ine for Rome. The compiler has thus sought to combine the association with Kings Cissa and Ine, which we have seen in William of Malmesbury, with the importance given to King Ceadwalla in the Abingdon charters.[413] He has then struggled to integrate these kings with documentary material to form a coherent narrative. That documentary material is primarily concerned with a foundation at Bradfield but crucially has been taken to provide the name of a founding abbot and evidence for an early landed endowment.

[411] Note the discrepancy between c. 3 and B9 as to whether the charter is of Ceadwalla or Ine.

[412] It is unclear who is the narrator of this passage; one possibility is Cilla.

[413] See also *Charters of Abingdon Abbey*, pp. cxcvi–cxcvii. Stenton, *Early History*, pp. 8–9, is no doubt right to argue that the *History*'s account is too incoherent for the documents to have been forged by the compiler himself.

The Abingdon *De abbatibus* provides a substantial and interesting account of the foundation.[414] However, dating its composition, and hence assessing its significance in the development of the legends, is problematic. Even if a version of *De abbatibus* was composed in the 1150s or 1160s, as suggested above, it was clearly rewritten and extended in the thirteenth century, and this rewriting may have involved not just continuation but the introduction of new material earlier in the text. It is therefore just possible that the version in *De abbatibus* is very slightly earlier than that in MS C of the *History*. It is much more likely to be later than MS C, and could even be later than the version in MS B. It begins with Abben, the son of a noble, who escaped a slaughter of great men carried out by Hengist at Stonehenge, a slaughter in which Abben's father died. Terrified, he lived for a while with the wild animals in a wood in southern Oxfordshire, eating small plants (*herbis*) and roots. Having nothing to drink, he prayed and God gave him a spring that could still be seen at the time of writing. Men heard of his holiness and flocked to him. Then they built him a small dwelling and chapel in honour of St Mary. To escape the company of men, Abben left and set out for Ireland, where he died a good death. The hill where he lived received the name Abingdon, and is the hill situated next to Bayworth and Pinsgrove, both of which are in Sunningwell parish.

Then, under Centwine, king of the West Saxons (676–?685), there was a noble man and sub-king (*regulus*) named Cissa, who was lord of Wiltshire and most of Berkshire. His 'metropolis', or royal centre, was at Bedwyn, Wiltshire, and he built a fortification to the south of there called, from his own name, *Cyssebui* (probably in the place now called Chisbury Camp).[415] Hæha and Cilla were Cissa's nephew and niece. When he heard it preached that it was easier for a camel to pass through the eye of a needle than for a rich man to enter heaven, Hæha turned from earthly to heavenly things. He went to his uncle and asked to be granted a place to build a monastery and gather brothers. Cissa agreed to his request, and the place Hæha found for his

[414] *CMA* ii. 268–73.

[415] Stenton, *Early History*, p. 18, argues that 'the fact that the inventor of this identification found it necessary to travel fifty miles before he could find a place with which the name of Cissa could be brought into relation shows conclusively that his personality was not inferred from local nomenclature nearer home'. He was therefore willing to believe that 'the Abingdon tradition has preserved a trace of authentic fact, and that in the traditional Cissa the true name is recorded of one of the obscure sub-reguli whose rule in Wessex is attested by the evidence of Bede'.

monastery was that which Abben had left. There he built a monastery in 675. Cissa gave many gifts and possessions to that place, and Hæha granted to it a part of his inheritance. His sister, with the king's consent, used part of her inheritance and built a nunnery next to the Thames at Helenstow, where she was abbess.[416] She had a cross made which incorporated part of a nail of the Lord, to be placed on her chest after her death. This was the Black Cross which would be found in Æthelwold's time.[417] Out of reverence for that cross, the nunnery was dedicated in honour of the Holy Cross and St Helen. After Cilla's death, the nuns were moved to Wittenham or perhaps Wytham,[418] and then because of the war between Offa of Mercia and Cynewulf of Wessex were again dispersed, the writer knew not whither.

Hæha's initial efforts to build a monastery and domestic buildings for the monks at the aforesaid site of the hill of Abingdon proved unsuccessful, as repeatedly what was built one day fell down the next. Then a hermit who lived in the wood of Cumnor recounted to Hæha a vision he had experienced which advised that the monastery should be built elsewhere, at *Seuekesham*.[419] Hæha obeyed the advice, and moved to the new site next to the Thames, five years after having begun work. During that time Cissa had died and been buried at the first site, but was moved to the new one. He was succeeded by Ceadwalla, from whom Hæha successfully requested that he grant the place that Cissa had bestowed for the building of the monastery. The king also ordered that the place be called Abingdon for ever more. Ine took away all of Cissa and Ceadwalla's grants, but repented and restored them and more, as well as giving 3,750 pounds of silver to build churches at Abingdon and Glastonbury. Hæha died in the time of Ine's successor, Æthelheard (726–?740), and was succeeded by Abbot Conan.[420]

[416] See also below, p. clxx.

[417] *CMA* ii. 269–70.

[418] The place-name evidence here is not certain. *De abbatibus* uses the form 'Witthe-ham', the version of the story in MS B uses 'Witham'; *CMA* ii. 269, below, p. 244. The latter is the form used for Wittenham below, p. 264. See *VCH*, *Berkshire*, iv. 427, for the name of the Harcourt family house, 'Wytham Abbey', being taken as linked to the story that the nuns of Helenstow went to Wytham. Note, however, that p. 244 states that 'a fort was then built on the hill at *Witham*, on account of which the nuns withdrew from that place'; see e.g. *VCH*, *Berkshire*, iv. 381, for a hill-top fort at the Wittenham Clumps.

[419] See *Charters of Abingdon Abbey*, p. cxcviii: 'The place-name *Seouecesham* has not been preserved . . . but its first element, a personal name *Seofoca*, is also found in Seacourt in Wytham (*Seofecanwyrth*, "Seofoca's homestead")'.

[420] There follows the description of Hæha's church, on which see below, p. clxvi.

The account in MS B of the *History* is unfortunately mutilated. After missing folios, the surviving text begins with the conversion of Lucius king of Britain, before moving on to the foundation of Abingdon. Again this is put down to Aben, or Abben, but here he is not a British noble but an Irish monk.[421] MS B states that

after some time passed, moreover, this man came to the court of the most distinguished king of the Britons, where he was received in praiseworthy fashion and magnificently honoured by everyone, and he became so privileged in the king's love that the latter rejoiced that he had discovered in Abben another Joseph. Furthermore, in response to his prayers, that Abben obtained from the king of the Britons most of the region of Berkshire, within which, by the consent of the king and the counsel of the kingdom, he happily founded a monastery on which he conferred the name Abingdon, alluding either to his own name or that of the place. For we have learnt from our contemporaries that, according to the language of the Irish, Abingdon is interpreted 'house of Aben'; but according to the language of the English, Abingdon commonly means 'the hill of Aben'. . . . The venerable man Abben gathered there a plentiful multitude of monks, that is three hundred monks or more who served God there in constant devotion; he was not merely in charge of them as prior and abbot but rather benefited them all in every respect, striving according to the *Rule* of St Benedict rather to be loved than feared. Indeed in his final days, when he was white-haired, the holy man Abben followed in the footsteps of Christ, and, spurning the glory of the world for the love of Him and taken by the sweetness of his native soil, sought Ireland. There, by the disposition of divine clemency, he ended his life in holy religious living.[422]

The monastery was situated between two streams, just beyond Sunningwell, and survived until the coming of the Saxons.

Two folios are then missing, and next we are flung into the reign of Ceadwalla. Following an account of his visit to and death in Rome, we are given a description of '*Seuekesham*, afterwards called Abingdon':

Here was a royal seat, to this place people gathered when the important and difficult business of the realm was discussed. From the earliest times of the Britons it was also a place of religion, in the time both of pagan religion and

[421] Cf. the Irish monk Maildubh who, according to the *Gesta pontificum*, founded Malmesbury; William of Malmesbury, *Gesta pontificum*, bk. v, c. 189, ed. Hamilton, pp. 333–5; see also Bede, *Ecclesiastical History*, bk. v, c. 18, ed. Colgrave and Mynors, p. 514. It is notable that Faritius in his *Life* of Aldhelm had mentioned 'Meldun' as founder of Malmesbury, but no link can be constructed between this reference and the development of the story of Abben; *PL* lxxxix. 69.

[422] See below, p. 234, on which note above, p. xliii.

of Christian. Also in this city was considerable evidence of Christianity from the religious life of the ancient Britons, as mentioned above, for crosses and images, which were found buried in various places in this village, provide proof of this.[423]

There follows an account of the Black Cross different from that in *De abbatibus*.[424] We first hear of Hæha and Cilla in the context of Ceadwalla's favour to the nunnery Helenstow. The later fate of the nunnery is similar to that related in *De abbatibus*, with the additional information that 'a fort was then built on the hill at *Witham*, on account of which the nuns withdrew from that place'. Cissa is mentioned for the first time in the context of King Ine's actions: 'At first he [Ine] decreed to make void the gifts and endowments of his predecessors Cissa and Ceadwalla and also the greatest part of the inheritance of Hæha the abbot particularly to the monastery of Abingdon, but afterwards he returned to his senses and repented his deed.'[425] Ine's grant is said to have taken place in Hæha's presence. Ine's charter of restoration follows, and itself is followed by the 'Testament' of Abbot Hæha granting land to Cilla.

The lost folios make very difficult the interpretation of this account, let alone full analysis of its relationship to those in MS C and *De abbatibus*. Cissa, Hæha, and Cilla had presumably appeared in those folios, as may those charters only surviving in MS C. Likewise there is no explicit reference to the shift of site, although Abben's foundation is said to have been near Sunningwell, the later foundation at *Seuekesham*. Nevertheless, the sense that the story of Abben was tacked on at the start through the desire for an appropriately named founder is reinforced by the way in which the conclusion to MS B's Book I summarizes the duration of the monastery up to its lying in ruins in the 940s. It does not look back to Abben, but states that 'from the time, indeed, of Cissa and Ceadwalla and also Ine, kings of the West Saxons, through whose patronage that monastery was first raised and constructed, right up to this third destruction of that monastery, 240 years are calculated to have passed'.[426] Here the key figures in the foundation legend remain those prominent in William of Malmesbury and in the earlier version of the *History*.

We thus see a core to the Abingdon traditions, but also separate stories, some of which become joined more or less firmly to the core.

[423] See below, p. 240–2. [424] B7. [425] B8.

[426] See below, p. 292; the figure 240 years is taken from MS C, where it refers to the time from Ine to the demise of the monastery following the death of Edmund.

Present at least from the time of Æthelwold is the vital position of Ceadwalla. At some point Cissa becomes associated with Abingdon. This may well arise from knowledge of the Bradfield charters, although it is also possible that an existing association of Cissa and Abingdon was the reason why the Bradfield charters came to be associated with the house. With these charters come the first founder Hæha and his sister Cilla. Finally, Aben or Abben, British noble or Irish monk, was made to be the founder whose personal name explains the place name of the monastery. However, his story remains prefatory to the history of the house beginning in the time of the West Saxon kings.[427]

The early history of the abbey

From these various stories, and from any other evidence, can we construct a plausible picture of the foundation of Abingdon?[428] The account of the Black Cross does seem to describe an early Anglo-Saxon artefact, probably 'one of those open-work disc-headed pins which have been found on several sites of the late 7th and 8th centuries, including that of Hilda's monastery at Whitby'.[429] There had also been a pagan Anglo-Saxon cemetery nearby. Probably by chance, therefore, the reviser may have been correct in his statement that Abingdon was not merely a royal seat but 'also a place of religion, in the time both of pagan religion and of Christian'.[430]

Abbot Hæha too may have some historical basis. A Hæha appears in a Malmesbury witness list of the early eighth century, and as this name is otherwise unique, it seems appropriate to assume that the

[427] For relevant later medieval material, see Biddle *et al.*, 'Early history', p. 32; note esp. Oxford, Corpus Christi College 255, fos. 54^r–55^r. The short, later medieval accounts draw on those in both versions of the *History* and in *De abbatibus*, although some make occasional additions, for example pointing out that Sevekesham was named after a pagan, Sevecus, whereas Abingdon was named after a Christian, Abben. The abbot's defence in his impeachment in 1368 mentioned Ceadwalla's original grant of Abingdon itself to the monastery.

[428] Note also *Charters of Abingdon Abbey*, pp. cxcviii, 5, linking the Æbbe or Æbba whose personal name must underlie the place-name Abingdon with the St Ebbe to whom a church in Oxford is dedicated.

[429] Biddle *et al.*, 'Early history', p. 27.

[430] B6. See Blair, 'Minsters of the Thames', p. 21: 'recent excavation shows that the town, including both St Helen's and the abbey, lie within the ramparts of a late Iron Age valley-fort'; Biddle *et al.*, 'Early history', pp. 26–7, on Roman and early Anglo-Saxon settlement and the pagan cemetery; P. Rahtz, 'Gazetteer of Anglo-Saxon domestic settlement sites', in D. M. Wilson, ed., *The Archaeology of Anglo-Saxon England* (London, 1976), pp. 405–52, at 408, on sunken-featured buildings of early Saxon date being recorded close to St Helen's church.

Abingdon and Malmesbury references are to the same man.[431] Quite possibly he was abbot of Bradfield, near Reading. His presence in the Abingdon story results from the incorporation of information from Bradfield documents which had passed into Abingdon hands.[432] It is possible but unprovable that an early minster at Abingdon came into existence as a cell of Bradfield, and that this might explain the survival of the Hæha charters at Abingdon.[433] However, it should also be noted that the Hæha/Cissa element does not become apparent in the foundation legends until the twelfth century, and is not present in the tenth-century documents.[434] It may therefore be only during the twelfth century that the Bradfield documents came to be regarded as part of the Abingdon foundation story.[435]

A sceptical line may also be appropriate for the story of the shift of site.[436] It does not appear in the tenth-century evidence, but may not have been appropriate there. More significantly, it does not appear in MS C, which surely would have included it had it been a central part of Abingdon tradition. Because of the lost folios in MS B, we are left entirely reliant on the version in *De abbatibus*, with its features such as the mention of Stonehenge and the appearance of the hermit. Such features might be described as legendary, suggesting lengthy if not necessarily reliable tradition. However, they might equally be called romantic, in the sense of being shared with twelfth-century and later works written under the influence of Geoffrey of Monmouth. These influences came into play when it was felt necessary to explain the lack of an obvious hill at the monastery's site, and also to reconcile the present monastic site with the mention in an Anglo-Saxon charter

[431] Sawyer, no. 245; Stenton, *Early History*, pp. 16–17.

[432] See above, p. lxxxii. Note also Hæha's connection to land in Bradfield in his 'will', below, p. 10. *Charters of Abingdon Abbey*, p. 7, speculates that the charter in c. 6 suggests three stages in the foundation of Bradfield; (i) its setting up quite soon after conquest by King Wulfhere of Mercia; (ii) confiscation of the land by Ine in the context of a West Saxon reconquest of the area; (iii) restoration by Ine when he was told, perhaps by Theodore, that the land belonged to the church.

[433] *Charters of Abingdon Abbey*, pp. cci–ccii.

[434] See also *Charters of Abingdon Abbey*, p. cci: 'It seems that there is good reason to believe that one or more minster communities were established at Abingdon in the period before the first Viking Age. Whether they should genuinely be associated with Hæha and his sister Cilla remains an unresolvable question.' Cf. Stenton, *Early History*, pp. 18–19, who puts more trust in the account in MS C of the *History*.

[435] On the possible date of the construction of these documents, see below, pp. cciv–ccv.

[436] See Stenton, *Early History*, p. 3; O. G. S. Crawford, 'Abingdon', *Antiquity*, iv (1930), 487–9; M. Gelling, 'The hill of Abingdon,' *Oxoniensia*, xxii (1957), 54–62; R. Forsberg, 'Review Article: An edition of the Anglo-Saxon charter boundaries of Berkshire', *Studia Neophilologica*, li (1979), 139–51; *Charters of Abingdon Abbey*, p. cxcvii.

boundary clause of an *Abbendun* that must have been somewhere in the north of Sunningwell parish, close to Boars Hill.[437] Any puzzlement at least on the first of these two issues was dealt with more economically—if not necessarily more convincingly—in the first version of the *History* with its statement that 'the hill of Abingdon is situated on the north side of the river Thames, where it passes by the bridge of the town of Oxford, and from the hill the same name is bestowed on the monastery positioned not far off'.[438]

In the end, we may be best to rely on our earliest evidence giving an account of the Abbey's past, not the *History* in either version or *De abbatibus*, but the tenth-century Abingdon charters. These looked back to Ceadwalla in the second half of the seventh century as the endower of the house. He can be linked to the founding of other new minsters and is certainly a plausible candidate to have been founder of Abingdon. However, with Bede's silence on Abingdon, there is no secure proof as to who founded the abbey or when.[439]

4. Perceptions of the past in the Abingdon *Histories*

Various key points have emerged in the foregoing analyses. The first is the vital role of charters in the construction and expression of Abingdon views of the past. In the tenth century, charters had

[437] c. 28 (which does not include the boundary clause), B85, *Charters of Abingdon Abbey*, no. 51A. The charter is almost certainly not genuine. The boundary clause appears in the quire of MS C devoted to such clauses; fo. 196^r, *Charters of Abingdon Abbey*, p. 585 (no. 1). One may wonder whether the contact with the Irish visitors in 1180 stimulated interest in the sense of the place-name, and created dissatisfaction with the earlier explanation, and indeed the earlier version's use of the rather tautologous 'Mons abbendone'.

[438] See below, p. 2; also p. 4. The present site of Abingdon could be described as on the north side of the Thames, but the reference to the bridge is problematic for that site, unless it could be taken to mean the bridge of the Oxford road, which seems excessively speculative. Again the description of the position of the hill might better fit a site in the north of Sunningwell parish. My rejection of the story in *De abbatibus* does not mean that there was in fact no shift of site, but rather is an argument that the evidence for such a shift is insufficient. One may further wonder whether separate sites with local traditions of religious observance were being combined in a single narrative through the story of the shift; note that the revised version of the *History*, below, p. 240, states that *Seuekesham* 'was also a place of religion, in the time both of pagan religion and of Christian'. Such a combining into a single narrative would be encouraged by the fact that the reviser probably knew that such shifts of site had taken place in much more recent history, and may have known that they formed part of more recent foundation stories; note, for example, the parallels of the Abingdon foundation story in *De abbatibus* to the involvement of hermits and the shifts of site in the foundation story of Kirkstall; see E. Freeman, *Narratives of a New Order: Cistercian Historical Writing in England, 1150–1220* (Turnhout, 2002), pp. 137–46.

[439] On Ceadwalla as a plausible founder, see *Charters of Abingdon Abbey*, p. cxcvi.

recalled vital moments in the abbey's development. In the twelfth century the compiler of the *History* found no coherent narrative for the pre-Æthelwoldian history, but sought to construct some narratives from charters.[440] Even names of Abingdon abbots were lacking; when Abbot Cynath was found in a charter granting him Dumbleton, the *History* makes him an abbot of Abingdon, although he was probably abbot of Evesham.[441] The second feature to emerge is the existence of certain structural points in the two versions of the *History*. There was the original foundation, or foundations; the destruction in the time of the Danes and King Alfred; the demise of the church in the mid-tenth century; its refoundation under Æthelwold; the Norman Conquest and the coming of Adelelm, the first abbot appointed by a Norman king; and the abbacy of Faritius. The third feature is the use of the past to justify present situations or claims. At the same time, in internal affairs at least, the past was not entirely binding. This attitude is clearest in the revised *History*. Faritius was justified in his changes to Æthelwold's food and drink allowances on the grounds that he was improving them.[442] Most notable of all, whereas *De abbatibus* has Abbot Adelelm die an unpleasant death because he disrespectfully wished to replace Æthelwold's church, the revised *History* established Æthelwold's miraculous advance approval for rebuilding in the twelfth and thirteenth centuries.[443] In this case, prophecy and history combine to legitimize the present.

V. PARTICIPANTS IN THE *HISTORY* UP TO 1071

My aim in this section is not to provide complete biographies of all who appear in the *History*, although particularly in the case of abbots I provide supplementary information from other sources. Rather, my main purpose is to examine the *History*'s presentation of participants, and their role within its account of the development of the abbey and its endowment. In the process the differences between the two versions of the *History* will be further illuminated.

[440] See above, p. lxxxiv; also *Charters of Abingdon Abbey*, p. xxxvi.

[441] *Charters of Abingdon Abbey*, p. 98.

[442] B207, vol. ii. 332–8. Note also the neutral tone with which the revised *History* presents Abbot Vincent's use of the wealth stripped from St Æthelwold's retable to secure confirmation of the liberty of the church; vol. ii. 338–40. Such action could be justified by precedents, notably in the actions of Æthelwold himself; Wulfstan, *Life of Æthelwold*, c. 29, ed. Lapidge and Winterbottom, pp. 44–6.

[443] B252, *CMA* ii. 284.

1. Abbots of Abingdon

Abbots, with kings, are the most prominent individuals in the pre-Conquest part of the *History*. The reputed founder abbots of Abingdon, Abben and Hæha, have already been considered. *De abbatibus* states that Hæha was succeeded by Conan, but gives no further information about the latter save mentioning his death.[444] It is possible that he should be associated with an Abbot Cumma who appears in a charter of King Æthelbald contained in both manuscripts of the *History*.[445] However, the *History* tells us no more about him, and again he does not appear in the tenth-century material on the abbey's early history. A Cumma, given no title, witnesses two eighth-century charters, neither of which is genuine; they may, nevertheless, give some indication of men active as witnesses in the 730s–740s.[446] It is possible that the charter of Æthelbald originally mentioned only Cumma as its beneficiary, not Abingdon. Cumma's church need not have been Abingdon, and the transformation of the grant into a summary of Abingdon's early estates may have occurred in Æthelwold's time.[447]

MS C gives much more prominence to the third and final abbot who is mentioned before the time of Æthelstan, Hræthhun. He, moreover, is the first abbot to be mentioned in the tenth-century charters that touch on the abbey's history. MS C describes him as a 'most prudent man . . . [who] governed that monastery in the most secure peace as long as he lived'. In particular, he obtained papal protection from Leo III (795–816) against infringements by royal officials, and two very substantial charters from King Coenwulf (796–821).[448] Only one of these charters calls him abbot. The other simply refers to him as Bishop Hræthhun, although associating him with the community of Abingdon. An Abbot Hræthhun witnesses two charters of 814, although his house is not specified.[449] It does seem plausible that he was abbot of Abingdon. Certainly he was bishop of Leicester

[444] *CMA* ii. 272–3. [445] c. 8.

[446] Sawyer, nos. 242, 256; *Charters of Abingdon Abbey*, p. ccxii.

[447] *Charters of Abingdon Abbey*, p. 26. The charter on which this forgery in Æthelbald's name was based could have passed into Abingdon's possession with the acquisition of Watchfield; *Charters of Abingdon Abbey*, p. 103.

[448] See below, pp. 14–22, *CMA* ii. 274; according to the revised *History* and *De abbatibus*, considerable expense was involved. See also Stenton, *Early History*, pp. 27–8 (although note that he does not differentiate the versions of the *History*); Edwards, *Charters of the Early West Saxon Kingdom*, pp. 185–6.

[449] Sawyer, nos. 173, 177.

from some point between 814 and 816. MS C tells us that he retained the abbacy of Abingdon after becoming bishop, which fits with the chronology of charter witnessing. In contrast, *De abbatibus* states that Hræthhun bishop of the Mercians ruled the abbey of Abingdon and afterwards was made its abbot, whilst MS B states that 'in King Offa's time a certain bishop named Hræthhun, driven from the kingdom of the Mercians by indignities and force of enmity, renounced his bishopric and became a monk in the monastery of Abingdon, afterwards being made abbot and father'.[450] *De abbatibus* seems to place his death in the time of King Coenwulf, that is before 821.

The same text, but neither version of the *History*, names Hræthhun's successor as Ealhhard, and places the latter's death in Alfred's reign (871–99), in which case he would have been extremely old.[451] It is possible, however, that *De abbatibus* had simply drawn Ealhhard's name from a witness list of a charter of 868 preserved at Abingdon.[452] No source mentions any further abbot of Abingdon before the reign of King Æthelstan (924–39).

According to MS C, in the time of Æthelstan 'we received Cynath as abbot of Abingdon', whilst MS B recalled King Æthelstan's generosity to Abingdon, 'then governed by Abbot Cynath'.[453] Both then include that king's charter recording the grant of Dumbleton to Cynath 'the archimandrite'. The charter does not mention Abingdon, and is not authentic in its present form.[454] In contrast to MS C, *De abbatibus* records that it was Edward the Elder who gave the abbey to a monk called Cynath, the latter dying in Æthelstan's time.[455] According to Stenton the name Cynath 'represents a late contraction of an unrecorded O. E. Cynenoth'.[456] It should also be noted that the form looks like Old English or Anglo-Latin spellings of the Gaelic name Cinaed (Kenneth).[457] The existence of an early tenth-century

[450] *CMA* ii. 273, below, B12.

[451] *CMA* ii. 275–6.

[452] c. 15, and see *Charters of Abingdon Abbey*, p. ccxii.

[453] See below, pp. 34, 278. Cynath is also mentioned in an Abingdon addition to John of Worcester; John of Worcester, *Chronicle*, ii. 610.

[454] c. 19, B47, *Charters of Abingdon Abbey*, no. 22 (which gives an addition in Edgar's name surviving only in a 16th-century copy).

[455] *CMA* ii. 276. Stenton, *Early History*, pp. 33–4, identifies Cynath with the Guiatus mentioned in a 14th-century Abingdon text as recovering everything that Inguar and Ubbar the Danes had seized; Salter, 'Chronicle roll', p. 728.

[456] Stenton, *Early History*, p. 34.

[457] See e.g. Symeon of Durham, *Historia regum*, cc. 48, 113, *Opera omnia*, ed. T. Arnold (2 vols., London, 1882–5), ii. 45–6, 130 (Cynoht, Cynoth, Kynath). I owe this point to Alex Woolf.

Abbot Cynath at some monastery is supported by the appearance of a 'Kenod abba' in the confraternity book of St Gallen, in a context linked to the visit of Bishop Cenwold of Worcester in 929.[458] However, the man concerned was probably not abbot of Abingdon, the *Historia* simply having derived his abbacy from the charter concerning Dumbleton. Most likely he was abbot of Evesham.[459]

De abbatibus names a certain Godescale [i.e. Gottschalk] as Cynath's successor as abbot of Abingdon during Æthelstan's reign. It places his death in the time of King Eadred and has him immediately succeeded by Æthelwold.[460] King Æthelstan, from the relics given by Hugh Capet, gave the abbot a nail from the Crucifixion, and many other things to be kept in the monastery of Abingdon. MS B mentions Godescealc abbot of Abingdon in the context of land at Culham in 940, and he also appears in the witness list of a charter of Æthelstan. Another charter in the name of Æthelstan, recording a gift to Abingdon for use of monks there 'under the charge of Godescealc the priest', appears in both versions of the *History*.[461] Both charters are spurious, but it is possible that one of the Continental priests associated with Æthelstan did have control of a secular minster at Abingdon. *De abbatibus* and MS B wrongly transform him into an abbot. Thus it would seem that before the coming of Æthelwold, we may only know of one true abbot of Abingdon, that is Hræthhun.

St Æthelwold has been much studied elsewhere, and information from the *History* only supplements other sources, most notably the *Lives*.[462] Æthelwold was from an aristocratic background and grew up

458 S. Keynes, 'King Athelstan's books', in M. Lapidge and H. Gneuss, eds., *Learning and Literature in Anglo-Saxon England: Studies Presented to Peter Clemoes on the Occasion of his Sixty-Fifth Birthday* (Cambridge, 1985), pp. 143–201, at 200.

459 *Charters of Abingdon Abbey*, p. 98; Robinson, *Times of St Dunstan*, pp. 35–40; see also the witness lists of Sawyer, nos. 394, 395.

460 *CMA* ii. 276–7. F. M. Stenton, *Anglo-Saxon England* (3rd edn., Oxford, 1971), p. 444, points out that this is a German name, never current in pre-1066 England. 'Godescealc' was presumably one of the number of foreign churchmen living in English religious houses at this time; see M. Wood, 'The making of King Æthelstan's empire: An English Charlemagne?', in P. Wormald *et al.*, eds., *Ideal and Reality in Frankish and Anglo-Saxon Society: Studies Presented to J. M. Wallace-Hadrill* (Oxford, 1983), pp. 250–72, at 261–4. See also *Charters of Abingdon Abbey*, pp. ccxii–ccxiii, 109; Thacker, 'Æthelwold', p. 46.

461 cc. 20, B49 (*Charters of Abingdon Abbey*, no. 26), B64.

462 See esp. *Bishop Æthelwold*, ed. Yorke; Wulfstan, *Life of Æthelwold*, ed. Lapidge and Winterbottom, pp. xxxix–li; *Charters of Abingdon Abbey*, p. ccxiv. Æthelwold was prominent as the first abbot in the witness lists of numerous royal charters, and later attested as bishop; see Keynes, *Atlas of Attestations*, tables XLIV, XLVII, XLVIII, LV. Note that he witnessed Eadwig's charters even following the division of the kingdom with Edgar.

in Winchester. He spent some time in the household of King Æthelstan, and was ordained by Ælfheah bishop of Winchester. He went to the newly founded monastery of Glastonbury to study under Dunstan, first as a monk and then as prior. During Eadred's reign, according to the *Life*, he decided to go overseas, to get a better grounding in monastic life, but the king, persuaded by his mother, gave Æthelwold the monastery of Abingdon.[463] Possibly during Eadred's reign he gave instruction to the future King Edgar.[464] In 963 he was appointed bishop of Winchester. He was a great founder and reformer of monasteries, the most famous being at Abingdon, Peterborough, Ely, Thorney, Crowland, and Winchester.[465] Æthelwold was a 'very sound' Latinist,[466] and was the composer of the *Regularis Concordia*, the monastic customary for reformed houses. He was also associated with writing in the vernacular, notably the account of his acquisitions at Ely, his translation of the *Rule* of St Benedict, and his history of monasticism and reform in England that may have acted as a preface to his translation of the *Rule*.[467] He died on 1 August 984.[468]

What of the Abingdon narratives' treatment of Æthelwold? Within the *History*, his abbacy is central for the Anglo-Saxon period, as that of Abbot Faritius is for the post-Conquest. MS C places its account of his youth and his appreciation by King Æthelstan after its charters of that king.[469] It notes that Æthelstan commended Æthelwold to Bishop Ælfheah of Winchester, before mentioning the succession of Edmund and the destitution of Abingdon. Soon after, following the accession of Eadred, the narrative returns to Æthelwold, recording that he took the habit at Glastonbury under Dunstan. Eadred, acting particularly on the advice of his mother, appointed Æthelwold abbot of Abingdon. Following a charter of Eadred, it then devotes four

[463] Wulfstan, *Life of Æthelwold*, cc. 10–11, ed. Lapidge and Winterbottom, p. 18; note also William of Malmesbury, *Gesta pontificum*, bk. ii, c. 75, ed. Hamilton, p. 166. His appointment cannot be dated exactly; see Wulfstan, *Life of Æthelwold*, ed. Lapidge and Winterbottom, pp. xliii–xliv.

[464] See *Regularis Concordia*, Prooem. 1, ed. Symons, p. 1; John, *Orbis Britanniae*, pp. 159–60; Lapidge, 'Æthelwold as scholar and teacher', p. 98.

[465] See also Thacker, 'Æthelwold', p. 58.

[466] For Æthelwold's learning, see esp. Lapidge, 'Æthelwold as scholar and teacher', with comments on his Latin at pp. 90, 102 n. 85. For his role in the composition of charters, see below, p. cxcvii.

[467] Wormald, 'Æthelwold and his Continental counterparts', p. 40; Gretsch, *Intellectual Foundations*.

[468] Wulfstan, *Life of Æthelwold*, c. 41, ed. Lapidge and Winterbottom, p. 62.

[469] c. 24; this section does not appear in MS B.

chapters to events within the monastery during his abbacy.[470] In particular, it notes how he sent his monk, Osgar, to Fleury to be instructed in its monastic customs; how his holy reputation attracted men to the stricter way of life at Abingdon; and how he summoned skilled men from Corbie, whom his own monks were to imitate in reading and chanting. Thereafter for his abbacy it provides only short narratives as an accompaniment to charters, referring to his acquisition of privileges and lands. A chapter is devoted to his election to the bishopric of Winchester, his replacement of clerics there with monks, and his establishment of new monasteries, which he propagated as shoots from the fertile vine of Abingdon.[471] Finally, it mentions his death in King Æthelred's reign, when his protection for churches was particularly needed.[472]

The later version gives an independent account of Æthelwold's youth, praising in hagiographical fashion his birth, disposition, appearance, and abilities.[473] Drawing on the *Life of Æthelwold*, it then mentions his move to Glastonbury under Dunstan. Next it turns to King Eadred's favour for Æthelwold, and again draws upon the *Life* for its account of his foundation of Abingdon.[474] Following accounts and charters recording various gifts, a further independent narrative mentions the continuing favour Æthelwold enjoyed under Eadred's successor Eadwig, and the privilege he obtained.[475] After further records of gifts, another independent narrative comments that King Edgar, 'instructed by the blessed St Dunstan and by St Æthelwold', provided great support and patronage for the monastic reform of the Church.[476] Following further charters, MS B then devotes a lengthy chapter to Abingdon under Æthelwold.[477] It mentions his building of the church there, his dispatch of Osgar to Fleury, his enrichment of the abbey with texts and ornaments (some made by himself), and his arrangement concerning food and drink allowances. It then gives his prayer for the protection of the house, before reproducing MS C's chapter on his elevation to the bishopric of Winchester.[478] Its record of his death is also drawn from MS C.[479]

The account in *De abbatibus* of Æthelwold's abbacy gives markedly

[470] cc. 29–32. See above, p. xxvii, on their relationship to the *Life of Æthelwold*.
[471] c. 71.
[472] See below, p. 138.
[473] B83.
[474] B84.
[475] B113.
[476] See below, p. 326–8.
[477] B207.
[478] B208–B209. The latter is the first chapter that the reviser copied in full from the earlier version of the *History*.
[479] See below, pp. 138, 346.

more prominence to his building work, notably including a description of the church that he had constructed.[480] It records the discovery of the Black Cross, found when work was going on in the Thames next to the monastery.[481] Like MS B, it describes the ornaments that he made for and gave to the church, and his provisions concerning food and drink. It also mentions his foundation of monasteries elsewhere and his imposition upon them of Abingdon customs. It states that 'he made the *Rule* of St Benedict come from the monastery of Fleury', and in further chapters mentions his election to Winchester and his death.[482]

Finally, it should be noted that the Abingdon manuscripts of the *Chronicle* of John of Worcester contain, under the year 948, a lengthy entry concerning Æthelwold not present in the other texts of John's *Chronicle*. This draws significantly upon passages from Wulfstan's *Life of Æthelwold*, and shares passages with the *History*. However, it also includes independent narrative, notably providing another account of Abbot Hræthhun and his dealings with the officials of King Coenwulf.[483] Much more briefly, under 963, the same manuscripts mention that Æthelwold brought Abingdon monks to the Old Minster at Winchester, and include the same passage as the *History* concerning Abbot Osgar's succession and the consecration of the church at Abingdon.[484]

Osgar (963/4–84) has already been mentioned as a monk whom Æthelwold brought from Glastonbury to Abingdon and sent to Fleury. Neither version of the *History* gives a strong impression of his abbacy, the earlier version's account of his death only calling him 'of pious memory'.[485] *De abbatibus*—with no apparent shame—states that in his time monks of Abingdon stole the relics of St Vincent, the head of St Apollinaris, and many other relics from the monks of Glastonbury.[486] Osgar was a frequent attestor of royal charters in Edgar's reign and in the first two years of Æthelred's, when he appears as first witness.[487] However, he does not appear as a witness to any of the five charters of King Edward the martyr. William of

[480] *CMA* ii. 277–80. See below, p. clxviii, for Æthelwold's building work.

[481] See above, p. lxxxvi.

[482] On the copy of the *Rule* brought from Fleury, see also below, p. clxxvi.

[483] John of Worcester, *Chronicle*, ii. 609–13.

[484] Ibid., ii. 613.

[485] See below, pp. 114, 138, 346.

[486] *CMA* ii. 280; for general background, see P. Geary, *Furta Sacra: The Theft of Relics in the Central Middle Ages* (rev. edn., Princeton, 1990).

[487] Keynes, *Atlas of Attestations*, tables LV, LXI.

Malmesbury briefly mentioned him in the *Gesta pontificum* as completing the work of his master, Æthelwold.[488] The Abingdon version of John of Worcester's *Chronicle* places his death in 984.[489]

The *Anglo-Saxon Chronicle* version E places in 984 the installation of the next abbot, Eadwine, whereas version C and John of Worcester place it in 985, suggesting a vacancy after the death of Osgar.[490] *De abbatibus* completely ignores Eadwine, perhaps because of the means whereby he came to the abbacy. It was bought for him by his brother, Ealdorman Ælfric, probably Ælfric Cild.[491] Without explicit personal criticism of Eadwine, both versions of the *History* present his abbacy as a time of considerable losses. It should, however, be noted that a later chapter attributes to his time a grant to Abingdon of land at Chalgrave and *Bulthesworthe*.[492] He also witnessed several royal charters.[493] After almost six years as abbot he died on 17 April 990.[494]

According to the *History*, Eadwine's successor Wulfgar (990–1016) brought the king to favour Abingdon, notably leading to a reversal of losses of land and a confirmation of privileges. It describes him as 'a perspicuous man of the greatest probity, and needed for the restoration of the church's liberty in that threatening crisis', and comments that the 'alertness of Abbot Wulfgar's industry' helped Abingdon to avoid losses during the Danish invasions of Æthelred's reign.[495] This contrasts with the comment in *De abbatibus* that in Æthelred's time the Danes destroyed all of England and especially obliterated Abingdon.[496] Wulfgar regularly witnessed royal diplomas between 993 and 1016, and may have acted as a draftsman for royal documents in favour of Abingdon.[497] He died on 18 September

[488] William of Malmesbury, *Gesta pontificum*, bk. ii, c. 88, ed. Hamilton, pp. 191–2.

[489] John of Worcester, *Chronicle*, ii. 613. He died on 24 or 28 May; *Charters of Abingdon Abbey*, p. ccxiv.

[490] John of Worcester, *Chronicle*, ii. 434, where Eadwine is referred to as a 'uenerabilis monachus'.

[491] See below, p. 138 (also John of Worcester, *Chronicle*, ii. 613), for reference to 'maior domus regie Ælfricus quidam prepotens'. MS B includes this passage but changes the name to Eadric; below, p. 346. On the problem of identity, see below, p. cxxiii. The purchase by Ealdorman Ælfric is also mentioned in a charter of Æthelred, below, p. 144.

[492] c. 106.

[493] Keynes, *Atlas of Attestations*, table LXI.

[494] For the day of death, see Gerchow, *Die Gedenküberlieferung*, p. 337.

[495] cc. 97, 110. The *Anglo-Saxon Chronicle* notes his succession in 990. See also vol. ii. 66.

[496] *CMA* ii. 280. On the reliability of this statement, see below, p. cxliv.

[497] *Charters of Abingdon Abbey*, p. ccxv, Keynes, *Atlas of Attestations*, table LXI; see below, p. cxcvii.

1016.[498] Whilst the later version of the *History* states only that he went the way of all flesh, the earlier records that 'the devoted flock that piously treated and loved him performed his funeral rites in mourning'.[499] Wulfgar is also mentioned by Wulfstan in his *Life of St Swithun*. Wulfstan speaks of him as the current ruler of Abingdon,

> known to everyone through his outstanding and kindly virtues by the nickname *Niger*, but who as Wulfgar is radiant of mind and handsome in appearance; he watches over the flock entrusted to him with his admonitions and prayers, and he rejoices in the Lord through the increase of his goodly sheepfold.[500]

The succession to the abbacy then becomes confusing. According to both versions of the *History* and *De abbatibus*, Wulfgar was succeeded by Æthelwine.[501] However, the *Anglo-Saxon Chronicle* versions C and E give Æthelsige as Wulfgar's successor.[502] Version E alone mentions Æthelsige's death in 1018, and the succession of Æthelwine. Given the date at which they were written, these entries probably should be preferred to the *History* as sources on abbatial succession. Yet problems remain, in that an Abbot Æthelsige witnessed four royal diplomas between 1018 and 1026.[503] This of course could be a different man from the one recorded in *Anglo-Saxon Chronicle* version E as dying in 1018. Other possibilities must be entirely speculative, for example that Æthelsige was not made abbot in 1016 but given custody of Abingdon until an abbot was appointed. Æthelsige then continued elsewhere as an abbot. *Anglo-Saxon Chronicle* version E would then have misinterpreted his departure from Abingdon as his death; version C knew that he did not die in 1018, and here has the support of the witnessing pattern.

498 *Heads of Religious Houses*, p. 24; his death is also noted in an Abingdon addition to John of Worcester; John of Worcester, *Chronicle*, ii. 614.

499 See below, p. 176.

500 Wulfstan, *Life of St Swithun*, c. 11, Lapidge, *Cult of St Swithun*, p. 526. No other source mentions Wulfgar's nickname, and the New Minster *Liber Vitae*, ed. Keynes, fo. 26^{v}, simply calls him 'Wulfgar abbas'.

501 See below, pp. 176, 356, *CMA* ii. 280. See below, p. 182, and *Charters of Abingdon Abbey*, pp. 542–3, for a grant to the abbey by a man named Æthelwine, who could be, but probably is not, the abbot of that name.

502 See also Dumville, 'Annalistic writing at Canterbury', pp. 27–8, who explains the differences in terms of the copying of marginal or interlinear annotations made at Abingdon; *Anglo-Saxon Chronicle: MS. C*, ed. O'Brien O'Keeffe, pp. lxvii–lxviii, agrees that differences result from the copying of annotations but sees them as evidence that MS C of the *Anglo-Saxon Chronicle* was not written at Abingdon.

503 Keynes, *Atlas of Attestations*, table LXVII.

The two versions of the *History* agree on the assertiveness of Æthelwine with regard to justice, and on his closeness to King Cnut, a view expanded upon in one of the Abingdon manuscripts of John of Worcester's *Chronicle*. Notably he made a reliquary for saints' relics, along the lines of and almost as large as one that Cnut had made for the relics of St Vincent.[504] Royal charters between 1019 and 1032 record Abbot Æthelwine as a witness, but it cannot be told when this is the Abingdon Æthelwine or a namesake from Athelney.[505] The Abingdon Æthelwine died on 24 or 25 February 1030.[506]

Æthelwine's successor, Siward, had been a monk of Glastonbury. One of the Abingdon manuscripts of John of Worcester records that Siward succeeded to the abbacy in 1030. He witnessed royal diplomas with the title abbot between 1032 and 1045 or slightly later,[507] and in the case of one Abingdon charter in MS C his attestation includes the statement that he had composed the document ['presentem scedulam gaudens composui'].[508] The *History* praises him for his 'vigour in both worldly and ecclesiastical matters', but the later version adds that he contemplated replacing the church built by St Æthelwold before coming to his senses on the subject.[509]

In 1044, however, according to versions C and E of the *Anglo-Saxon Chronicle*,

> Archbishop Eadsige [of Canterbury] resigned the bishopric because of his infirmity, and consecrated to it as bishop Siward, abbot of Abingdon. He did this with the permission and by the advice of the king and of Earl Godwine. Otherwise it was known to few people before it was done, because the archbishop suspected that somebody else would ask for it, or purchase it, whom he less trusted and favoured, if more people knew about it.[510]

504 c. 111, B245, B249. See also John of Worcester, *Chronicle*, ii. 614, with words shared with the *History* italicized: 'Quem rex Kanutus pro laudabilis uite merito secretorum suorum conscium efficiens a noxiis sese retrahere ac recta appetere eius suasionibus studebat. Hinc et cenobium Abbendonense a rege diligitur et muneribus eius cumulatur, nam inter alia sua donaria capsam *de argento et auro* parari *fecit* in qua sancti *Vincentii leuite et martiris reliquie* col*locarentur*'.

505 Keynes, *Atlas of Attestations*, table LXVII.

506 For the year, see John of Worcester, *Chronicle*, ii. 614; for 24 Feb., see Gerchow, *Die Gedenküberlieferung*, p. 336; for 25 Feb., see Cambridge, University Library, Kk. i 22, fo. 2r.

507 Keynes, *Atlas of Attestations*, tables LXVII, LXXIII; the latest charters are Sawyer, nos. 1011 and 1471.

508 c. 117, on which see *Charters of Abingdon Abbey*, pp. 552–3.

509 See below, pp. 178, 358–60.

510 On the obscure allusiveness of this passage, see N. P. Brooks, *The Early History of the Church of Canterbury* (Leicester, 1984), pp. 299–300.

In royal charters of 1045–8, with Eadsige absent Siward witnesses as archbishop, taking precedence over the archbishop of York.[511] When Eadsige does appear, Siward witnesses as bishop, and does not take precedence over the archbishop of York.[512] Likewise, two vernacular documents were witnessed by 'Archbishop Eadsige and Bishop Siward', and bishop is his title in a writ concerning the Leckhampstead dispute.[513]

Later writers seem on occasion to have been perplexed by this situation, improper as it would have appeared to them. William of Malmesbury in his *Gesta regum* gave a quite similar account to that of the *Anglo-Saxon Chronicle*.[514] In his *Gesta pontificum* he added that Siward was ungrateful to Eadsige, even depriving him of necessary food, and so lost his position as successor designate. To lessen his shame and loss, he was given the bishopric of Rochester.[515] John of Worcester did not mention Siward's appointment in 1044, although the main text of his *Chronicle* does record his death, entitling him 'corepiscopus' of Archbishop Eadsige.[516] This passage is omitted in the Abingdon copies of John's *Chronicle*, which replace it with the statement that Siward, who had been performing the duties of the archbishop ('archiepiscopi uices moderans'), fell ill, was taken from Canterbury to Abingdon, and, after two bed-bound months, died and was buried there.[517] As for Siward's appointment at Canterbury, a passage common to the Lambeth Palace manuscript of John of Worcester and to the earlier version of the *History* is not entirely clear to us in its treatment of the matter. It states that Eadsige, with the consent of the king and the leading men of the realm, 'pontificatus decorauit apice, ac patriarchatus sui uice ipsum fungi instituit'.[518] 'Pontificatus' might mean bishopric or archbishopric; if the former, it might still mean Canterbury, or just 'a bishopric'. The phrase

[511] Keynes, *Atlas of Attestations*, table LXXII.

[512] Sawyer, no. 1010, Siward witnesses as bishop, following Eadsige as archbishop of Canterbury and Ælfric as archbishop of York; Sawyer, no. 1014, Siward witnesses as bishop, after Archbishop 'Æti' (presumably Eadsige), Archbishop Ælfric, and Eadnoth bishop of Dorchester.

[513] *Anglo-Saxon Charters*, ed. Robertson, nos. 102, 103 (= Sawyer, nos. 1472, 1473); c. 120.

[514] William of Malmesbury, *Gesta regum*, bk. ii, c. 197, ed. Myers *et al.*, i. 352.

[515] William of Malmesbury, *Gesta pontificum*, bk. i, c. 21, ed. Hamilton, p. 34.

[516] John of Worcester, *Chronicle*, ii. 552; note R. A. L. Smith, 'The place of Gundulf in the Anglo-Norman Church', *EHR*, lviii (1943), 257–72, at p. 261.

[517] John of Worcester, *Chronicle*, ii. 614.

[518] See below, p. 186; John of Worcester, *Chronicle*, ii. 614.

'patriarchatus sui uice fungi' might mean that Siward was to be Eadsige's successor, or to just to undertake his duties. When recounting the dispute over Leckhampstead, the *History* refers to Siward as 'bishop', as in the writ concerning the same dispute.[519] The later version of the Abingdon *History* refers to Siward being 'consecrated as bishop of Rochester'.[520] The Abingdon *De abbatibus* keeps much to the *Anglo-Saxon Chronicle*, stating that, with Edward the Confessor's consent, Siward was made archbishop of Canterbury.[521]

What are we to make of this? To treat Siward simply as coadjutor to Eadsige is to downplay his position, given that both the *Anglo-Saxon Chronicle* and royal charters make it clear that in Eadsige's absence he was treated as archbishop.[522] However, the witness lists also make it clear that when Eadsige was present, Siward was his subordinate and bishop. Later writers could concentrate on this subordinate position, rather than explicitly treat the irregularity of Siward's substitution into the archbishopric. The association of Siward with Rochester in the *Gesta pontificum* and the revised Abingdon *History* may stem from confusion with an Abbot Siward of Chertsey who became bishop of Rochester.[523] In the end, Eadsige outlived Siward, who in 1048 fell ill, resigned his position at Canterbury, and returned to Abingdon, where he died within two months, on 23 October. He left to the abbey Wittenham and the furnishings of his chapel.[524]

When Siward moved to Canterbury, he was replaced by the sacrist, Æthelstan.[525] The *History* praises him, notably for his charity during a famine.[526] He witnessed royal charters in 1044–5, but died on 29 March 1047 or 1048.[527] Following Æthelstan's death the king appointed as abbot a monk of Bury St Edmunds called Spearhafoc,

[519] See below, p. 188. [520] See below, p. 362.

[521] *CMA* ii. 281, which may, of course, draw on the *Anglo-Saxon Chronicle*.

[522] See also Brooks, *Canterbury*, p. 300.

[523] See *ASC*, *s.a.* 1058; it does not mention the house of which Siward had been abbot.

[524] c. 122. See also John of Worcester, *Chronicle*, ii. 614; *ASC*, 'C', *s.a.* 1048. Siward's burial at Abingdon is also mentioned by Gervase of Canterbury in his *Actus pontificum: The Historical Works of Gervase of Canterbury*, ed. W. Stubbs (2 vols., London, 1879–80), ii. 362.

[525] c. 119. *De abbatibus* mentions only that he was Siward's successor; *CMA* ii. 281.

[526] See below, p. 194–6.

[527] c. 123. Keynes, *Atlas of Attestations*, table LXXIII. For the day of his death, Gerchow, *Die Gedenküberlieferung*, p. 336; for the day and year, see *ASC*, 'C', *s.a.* 1047 but with the indication that the death took place in 1048, John of Worcester, *Chronicle*, ii. 614, which places the death in 1048.

a name meaning Sparrowhawk. The *History*, the Abingdon manuscripts of John of Worcester, and *De abbatibus* comment on his skills as a gold- and silver-smith.[528] This view is supported by Goscelin's *Historia translationis S. Augustini*, which recounts a miracle in which he lost a precious ring belonging to Queen Edith, wife of Edward the Confessor. At St Augustine's, Canterbury, he prayed to St Liudhard, whose relics were there, and the ring was found. The writer notes that Spearhafoc 'fashioned statues of immense size and beauty . . . of Liudhard and his venerable queen, Bertha, which he solemnly erected over the saint's tomb'.[529] As abbot, Spearhafoc leased South Cerney, Gloucestershire, to Stigand, then bishop of Winchester, but was unable to resume the land.[530] During his abbacy, he witnessed only one royal charter, in 1050.[531]

Spearhafoc's abbacy came to an end in 1051 when, according to the *History*, he

> was promoted by the king to be bishop for the city of London. Then, at a time when he had, by the king's allocation, plenty of gold and chosen gems acquired for fashioning the imperial crown, he stuffed money-bags full with riches from the bishopric, left England in secret, and did not appear again. God's vengeance brought such ends for those by whose trickery the Church was diminished for their own profit.[532]

De abbatibus states that the king entrusted [*commisit*] the bishopric of London to Spearhafoc, but he left England secretly and never reappeared.[533] John of Worcester attributed to King Edward the ejection of Spearhafoc from London; interestingly, there are no additions concerning Spearhafoc peculiar to the Abingdon manuscripts of John's *Chronicle*.[534] The 'C' version of the *Anglo-Saxon Chronicle* also mentions Spearhafoc's appointment to London, whilst the 'D' version goes on to say that 'it was taken from him before he was consecrated'. The 'E' version gives a considerably fuller account. Following the promotion of Robert de Jumièges, Edward the Confessor gave London to Spearhafoc. On Robert's return from Rome, where he had been to collect his pallium,

[528] For his abbacy, see c. 124; John of Worcester, *Chronicle*, ii. 614; *CMA* ii. 281. For succession in 1048, see also *ASC*, 'E'; the Waverley annals follow the *ASC*, but add that his abbacy lasted two years, *Annales monastici*, ii. 183.

[529] Goscelin, *Historia, miracula et translatio S. Augustini*, c. 32, *PL* clv. 46.

[530] c. 124; see also below, p. clxiii.

[531] Keynes, *Atlas of Attestations*, table LXXIII, Sawyer, no. 1022.

[532] See below, p. 196.

[533] *CMA* ii. 281.

[534] John of Worcester, *Chronicle*, ii. 552–4.

Abbot Spearhafoc met him . . . with the king's writ and seal to the effect that he was to be consecrated bishop of London by the archbishop. But the archbishop refused and said that the pope had forbidden it him. Then the abbot went to the archbishop again about it and asked for ordination as bishop, and the archbishop refused him resolutely and said that the pope had forbidden it him. Then the abbot went back to London and occupied the bishopric that the king had given him; he did this with the king's full permission all that summer and autumn.

The *Chronicle* then tells of the coming of Eustace of Boulogne to England, the fall of the Godwine family, and the king's putting away of the queen, Earl Godwine's daughter, before stating that 'Abbot Spearhafoc was expelled from the bishopric of London, and William the king's priest was consecrated to it'.

Spearhafoc was replaced as abbot by Bishop Rodulf, a royal kinsman. The *History* describes him as aged and long a bishop in Norway.[535] He was probably a Norman, the bishop who participated in Olaf Haraldson's missionary work in Norway.[536] Again the king seems to have imposed his nominee on the abbey, but according to the *History* Edward had to make a concession, that after his death they might 'elect as his successor whomsoever they wished from amongst themselves'. Rodulf died within two years of his appointment, and was succeeded by Ordric, an Abingdon monk.[537] This may suggest that, at least in the short term, the royal promise about election held. Certainly he was welcome to the monastery:

a man of middle age and charming affability, a monk of the church of Abingdon, was received by them as abbot, with the king's approval, and to the immense joy of everyone. Since he was greatly loved by the king, he obtained affirmation by his edict of very many things necessary for the liberty of the church.

The *History* also praises him at the time of his death:

after he had honourably governed the house entrusted to him, and had returned home from the shrine of the princes of the apostles (to which he had

[535] See below, p. 198; see also *De abbatibus* (*CMA* ii. 281), the Abingdon addition at John of Worcester, *Chronicle*, ii. 615, *ASC*, 'E', *s.a.* 1048 (*rectius* 1051).

[536] See L. Abrams, 'England, Normandy and Scandinavia', in C. Harper-Bill and E. M. C. van Houts, eds., *A Companion to the Anglo-Norman World* (Woodbridge, 2003), pp. 43–62, at 56–7; T. Graham, 'A runic entry in an Anglo-Saxon manuscript from Abingdon and the Scandinavian career of Abbot Rodulf (1051–2)', *Nottingham Medieval Studies*, xl (1996), 16–24, who pays particular attention to a runic addition in Cambridge, Corpus Christi College 57.

[537] See below, p. 198; also John of Worcester, *Chronicle*, ii. 615.

gone for the sake of devotion), he was worn out by a long-lasting illness and was allotted his final day.[538]

Like the *History*, *De abbatibus* reinforces the impression of a successful abbacy by recording various acquisitions in Ordric's time.[539] Ordric witnessed royal charters between 1050 and 1065.[540] He died early in 1066, probably on 23 January.[541]

The final abbot appointed before the Norman Conquest, during the reign of Harold II, was Ealdred.[542] He had been provost or perhaps prior of the abbey. He accepted the Conquest and swore oaths of loyalty to King William. He protected the abbey's mill at Cuddesdon against the threat from the men of the bishop of Lincoln.[543] With considerable effort he regained certain lands which had been forfeited to the king by the abbey's man, the priest Blæcmann, and—says the *History*—'he might also perhaps have extricated others which had passed from the lordship of the church to the right of another, had he not incurred the king's anger, to his own and the church's misfortune'.[544] The men of Abingdon unsuccessfully supported a rising against William:

The king's anger was so directed against their lord, that is Abbot Ealdred . . . that by the king's order he was immediately placed in captivity at Wallingford castle. A little while later he was taken from that place and for safekeeping committed into the hands of Bishop Walkelin of Winchester, with whom he remained as long as he lived.[545]

De abbatibus states that it was mentioned to King William that Ealdred was plotting against him with the Danes.[546] Ealdred died in 1071.

[538] See below, p. 220.

[539] *CMA* ii. 281–2.

[540] Keynes, *Atlas of Attestations*, table LXXIII.

[541] 23 Jan. is the *obit* in Cambridge, University Library, Kk. i 22, fo. 1^v; *Heads of Religious Houses*, pp. 24, 241. Cambridge, Corpus Christi College 57, fo. 44^r, records the burial [*depositio*] of an abbot 'O' on 23 Jan.; Gerchow, *Die Gedenküberlieferung*, p. 335. B287, and a dry-point addition in the margin of MS C, fo. 135^r, dates his death to 'around the feast of St Vincent', that feast falling on 22 Jan. His death is also recorded in the Lambeth Palace manuscript of John of Worcester; John of Worcester, *Chronicle*, ii. 615.

[542] cc. 143–4. He was also called Brihtwine; see below, p. 227 n. 517. According to *De abbatibus*, it was in Ealdred's time that Queen Edith gave Lewknor for the boy monks, but this differs from the *History*'s account; *CMA* ii. 283, cf. c. 121.

[543] B291.

[544] See below, p. 222. See also p. 372, where it is said he was kindly received by King William.

[545] See below, p. 226.

[546] *CMA* ii. 283.

2. Monks of Abingdon

Very few monks of Abingdon are mentioned by name in the *History*.[547] Besides those who became abbot, we learn of two, Ædmer and Ælfstan, through miracle stories from the time of Æthelwold.[548] We also learn that Ælfric, archbishop of Canterbury from 995 to 1005, had been a monk of Abingdon.[549] The later version of the *History* draws on the *Life of St Æthelwold* to name 'certain clerics in minor orders' who followed Æthelwold to Abingdon, namely Osgar (the future abbot), Foldbriht, and Frithegar from Glastonbury, Ordbriht from Winchester, and Eadric from London.[550] Foldbriht's identity is uncertain, although he may well have become abbot of Pershore.[551] Frithegar too may have become an abbot, possibly of Evesham, whilst Ordbriht certainly became abbot of Chertsey and later was bishop of Selsey.[552] Of Eadric it is only known, from the Winchester *Liber Vitae*, that he was a priest.[553] Finally, we hear of two monks in the Confessor's reign, Godric and Leofric, who had inherited lands at Sparsholt and Whitchurch respectively.[554]

3. Kings

Throughout the Anglo-Saxon and the post-Conquest periods, Abingdon was closely associated with kings. Its location may have made it a suitable place to shift from road travel in Wessex to river travel along the Thames. Abingdon's role as a royal meeting place and

[547] See also below, p. clxxi. See above, p. lxiv, for Wulfstan's *Life of St Swithun* mentioning a prior named Byrhtferth; p. lxv, for the Winchester *Liber Vitae*. Æthelgar, who became abbot of New Minster, Winchester, in 964, and was later bishop of Selsey, had probably been a monk of Abingdon; see *Liber Vitae*, ed. Keynes, pp. 26–32.

[548] cc. 29, 30. For the story involving Ælfstan, see Wulfstan, *Life of Æthelwold*, c. 14, ed. Lapidge and Winterbottom, pp. 26–8; William of Malmesbury, *Gesta pontificum*, bk. ii, c. 83, ed. Hamilton, p. 181. Ælfstan went on to become abbot of Old Minster, Winchester, and then bishop of Ramsbury.

[549] See below, p. 166; also William of Malmesbury, *Gesta pontificum*, bk. i, c. 20, ed. Hamilton, p. 32, who wrongly says that Ælfric had been abbot of Abingdon; John of Worcester, *Chronicle*, ii. 613.

[550] See below, p. 298.

[551] *Heads of Religious Houses*, pp. 58, 252; see also below, p. cciii.

[552] *Heads of Religious Houses*, pp. 38, 244. On Frithegar, see Williams, '*Princeps Merciorum gentis*', pp. 169–70.

[553] *Liber Vitae*, ed. Keynes, p. 95. He appears as the sixth name in the Abingdon list, straight after the abbots, suggesting that he held a position of some prestige within the abbey; *Liber Vitae*, fo. 26^{v}.

[554] c. 138.

residence is particularly prominent in the later version of the *History*. This states of *Seuekesham*, afterwards called Abingdon, that 'here was a royal seat, to this place people gathered when the important and difficult business of the realm was discussed'.[555] It was at Abingdon that Æthelstan received messengers from Hugh, duke of the Franks.[556] The later version of the *History* also tells us that in King Eadred's time the neglected church had only forty hides at Abingdon, the royal estate being one hundred hides.[557] The king then gave his hundred hides 'with excellent buildings' to the abbot and monks. Likewise a charter in Eadwig's name states that Eadred had restored to the church the land called Abingdon, 'on which our predecessors (deceived by diabolical avarice) had unjustly built themselves a royal building'.[558] It sounds as if, just before Eadred gave Abingdon to Æthelwold, a royal meeting place and building were coupled with a minster closely associated with the king. Such a close association remained when the minster became a reformed monastery.[559]

It is uncertain whether the meeting place or royal building were the same as, related to, or separate from a royal residence at Andersey, an island between two branches of the Thames close to the abbey. According to *De abbatibus*, King Offa came to Andersey, liked the look of it, and ordered that royal houses [*domus*] be built there. In exchange he gave the monks Goosey.[560] The same source notes the problems caused by the royal huntsmen and others staying in the king's houses on Andersey during the time of King Coenwulf. Abbot Hræthhun gave the king Sutton and 120 pounds of silver to be free of such oppression. The king accepted the arrangement, and ordered that the monks have the place in perpetuity.[561] The two versions of the *History* tell similar stories of oppressions by Coenwulf's men, and the subsequent settlement, but neither the narratives nor the related

555 See below, p. 240.

556 B62, William of Malmesbury, *Gesta regum*, bk. ii, c. 135, ed. Mynors *et al.*, i. 218. See Sawyer, no. 552a, for a charter of Eadred issued at 'the royal vill of Abingdon' in 950. The grant was in favour of Barking, and was witnessed by three abbots including Dunstan; it does not mention Æthelwold. Note also charters issued close to Abingdon, for example at Sutton Courtenay; Sawyer, nos. 338a, 993 (= c. 117, B254).

557 See below, p. 296.

558 See below, p. 64, on the authenticity of which see below, pp. cxcix–cciv; see also cc. 60, 98. The same charters prohibited that any future king construct a building there.

559 See below, p. 56, for a claim that Eadred was accustomed to come to the church at Abingdon, and for him feasting there. See also Thacker, 'Æthelwold', pp. 56–7. Cf. the close association of monastery and palace at Winchester.

560 *CMA* ii. 273.

561 *CMA* ii. 274.

charter make any specific mention of Andersey.[562] The reason for, and significance of, *De abbatibus*'s focus on Andersey must remain unclear. Certainly, despite the grant mentioned in *De abbatibus*, the association of Andersey with kings continued. *De abbatibus* reports King Æthelstan staying there at the time of the mission from Hugh, duke of the Franks.[563] At the end of the Anglo-Saxon period it had been obtained by a priest called Blæcmann, who built a church there.[564] However, when Abbot Ealdred regained control of various of that priest's lands from William I, part of Andersey was excepted and 'that place lasted until Abbot Faritius's time as a royal haven'.[565] In the post-Conquest period it was described as 'crammed on all sides with sundry small buildings', although by the start of the twelfth century at least Blæcmann's foundation was in decay.[566]

Sir Frank Stenton analysed the importance of Abingdon and Abingdon evidence to the eighth- and ninth-century struggles between Mercia and Wessex.[567] Here my interests are more limited, looking simply at what the narrative sections of the *History* tell us about kings and about Abingdon views of the past. The place in the Abingdon foundation stories of Cissa, described in the *History* as king of the West Saxons, has been discussed above.[568] The earlier version of the *History* refers to Ceadwalla, king of Wessex between 685 and 688, succeeding Cissa. It also mentions his grants to the abbey, and his departure for Rome.[569] The later version of the *History* treats his conversion and his baptism at Rome at considerably greater length, including the epitaph inscribed on his tomb.[570] The two versions of the *History* give separate descriptions of the decision by Ceadwalla's successor, Ine, first to annul earlier grants and then to restore and indeed increase the endowment.[571] The later version specifies that he

[562] cc. 9, 11, B17, B18.

[563] *CMA* ii. 277.

[564] c. 136. It is unclear whether Blæcmann's acquisition of Andersey had any connection with his links to the royal house and the Godwine family; see below, p. cxxii.

[565] See below, p. 372.

[566] Vol. ii. 72–4.

[567] Stenton, *Early History*; see esp. p. 21: 'in the eighth century Berkshire was a border county'. See also Thacker, 'Æthelwold', pp. 44–5; Blair, *Anglo-Saxon Oxfordshire*, pp. 43, 54–6; *Charters of Abingdon Abbey*, pp. cciv–ccvi, where it is pointed out that the Thames was not a defensible border and Berkshire not a necessary geographical entity.

[568] See above, pp. lxxxv–xcii.

[569] cc. 2–3. See also above, p. xci.

[570] B4–B5. See also *De abbatibus*, *CMA* ii. 271.

[571] cc. 2–7, B8–B10. An addition in the Abingdon manuscripts of John of Worcester states 'et ⟨Ine⟩ monasterium quod dicitur Abbendona, quod prius uir nobilis Cissa et rex Ceadwala inceperunt, perfecit'; John of Worcester, *Chronicle*, ii. 609.

was the first donor of Sutton to the abbey.[572] According to both versions of the *History*, again in distinct passages, Ine left for Rome, entrusting the kingdom to Æthelheard.[573]

Æthelheard is not mentioned in any other narrative section, although a charter in his name and that of King Æthelbald of the Mercians is included.[574] MS B gives just the succession in Wessex from Æthelheard to Cuthred to Sigebert and to Cynewulf, who was defeated in battle by Offa of Mercia.[575] The same war was also responsible for the withdrawal of nuns, formerly of Helenstow, from *Witham*, where a fort was built.[576] A critical view of Offa is also suggested when it states that he 'seized [*usurpauit*] for himself everything which had been subjected to Cynewulf's jurisdiction, from the Icknield Way between the town of Wallingford and Ashbury in the south to the river Thames in the north'.[577] However, the *History* also mentions his gift of Goosey, without suggesting (as does *De abbatibus*) that it was in return for Andersey.[578]

MS C does not mention the succession of Offa's son, Ecgfrith. His brief reign is noted in MS B and *De abbatibus*, but both refer to him as Ecgberht; the error may be derived from John of Worcester.[579] MS B also records that 'after Cynewulf king of the West Saxons was killed by Cyneheard, brother of his predecessor Sigeberht, his own brother Beorhtric succeeded him'. It continues that Beorhtric gave Easton, Hampshire, to one of his nobles, who in turn gave the land and associated charter to Abingdon. It also includes a similar transaction concerning Hurstbourne, Hampshire. Finally it records Beorhtric's death, which from other sources can be placed in 802.[580]

Ecgfrith of Mercia's successor Coenwulf features significantly in both versions of the *History*. In a narrative derived in part from a spurious charter of Coenwulf, MS C tells of the oppressions that he and his men inflicted on Abingdon, and the successful resistance by

572 See below, p. 246.

573 See below, pp. 10, 246.

574 c. 8, B30.

575 B12.

576 See below, p. 244; see above, p. lxxxvi, on the problem of identifying the place concerned as Wittenham or Wytham.

577 See below, p. 246. Given that the passage only appears in MS B, Stenton, *Early History*, p. 23, is rather misleading in attributing this passage to 'the twelfth-century historian of Abingdon'. On the description of the border, see also Stenton, *Early History*, p. 25.

578 See above, p. lvii.

579 See above, p. xli.

580 B13, B14, B19, B20, B25. *Handbook of British Chronology*, p. 23. On the significance of these charters of Beorhtric to the question of Mercian control of Wessex at this time, see Stenton, *Early History*, p. 29; *Charters of Abingdon Abbey*, p. 29.

the head of the monastery, Hræthhun.[581] Coenwulf is presented as resistant to papal orders, and in this context, MS C comments that Hræthhun deemed the king a man to be persuaded by money rather than prayers. MS B gives its own but similar account of this dispute and the consequent royal privilege.[582] However, its account is preceded by another chapter in which the king 'full of piety and "the bowels of mercy"', granted his sisters lands at Culham for life, so they might live there in God's service. The lands thereafter were to pass to Abingdon.[583] MS B then lists some of Coenwulf's successors, recording gifts and charters associated with Berhtwulf king of Mercia (840–?852).[584]

Thereafter, the focus is on kings of Wessex, with the rise to dominance of Ecgberht. In contrast to MS C, where Ecgberht, Æthelwulf, and Æthelred are mentioned only through their charters,[585] MS B devotes a chapter to Ecgberht and his connection to Abingdon. He 'received in submission all the kings of the whole of Albion', was devoted to Abingdon, and granted it Marcham.[586] His son Æthelwulf is noted for a gift which passed to Abingdon, and his 'general privilege for all the churches of his realm, to whom he distributed by shares the tenth part of the lands of his realm in pure and perpetual alms. The first and foremost of them was the house of Abingdon.'[587] MS B also praises Æthelwulf's son and successor, Æthelbald, for his love of Abingdon and his confirmation and grant to it.[588] However, the charter it then attributes to him belongs in fact

[581] c. 9; also the charters in cc. 10 and 11. See further below, p. ccv.

[582] B16–B18; the link between B16 and B17 is somewhat awkward. The version of the story in *De abbatibus* does not link the dispute to its mention of the abbot's trip to Rome, rather stating that he set off with the king and bishop's permission; *CMA* ii. 274.

[583] Another version of the story of Coenwulf's sisters appears in *De abbatibus*, *CMA* ii. 274. See also above, p. lxviii, for a charter in Coenwulf's name referring to his gift of Culham to Abingdon made at the request of his sisters. A mutilated passage in *De abbatibus* records the burial at Abingdon of either Coenwulf or Abbot Hræthhun; *CMA* ii. 274–5.

[584] B21–B24, the treatment of the succession not being entirely accurate; cf. *De abbatibus*, *CMA* ii. 275.

[585] cc. 12, 13, 16. See also c. 15 for a charter of Æthelwulf's daughter Æthelswith, queen of the Mercians, recording the gift of Lockinge; her husband was King Burgred of Mercia. The same charter, with a brief introductory narrative, appears in B33–B34. Cf. *De abbatibus* which attributes the gift to a man called Cuthwulf, with the king's consent; *CMA* ii. 275.

[586] B25; note the mistake concerning Ecgberht's relationship to his predecessor. *De abbatibus* says that a very rich man gave Marcham to Abingdon, with Ecgberht's consent; *CMA* ii. 275.

[587] B27–B28. For Æthelwulf, see also *De abbatibus*, *CMA* ii. 275.

[588] B29.

to the eighth century, and is correctly positioned in MS C.[589] Æthelbald's brother and successor Æthelberht is treated ambivalently: 'Although he reigned for little time, that is five years, and in the generous giving of endowments did not provide sufficiently profitably for his soul's salvation, nevertheless, he did strive incessantly to take care of the protection of the Church.'[590]

To the reign of the next king, Æthelred (865/6–71), is attributed a gift of land at Wittenham, and the coming of the Danes. The latter drove out the monks from Abingdon and so destroyed the house 'that nothing is reported to have remained there besides the walls'.[591] Matters were made worse by King Alfred, who, according to MS B, 'piled evils on evils, like Judas amongst the twelve', and took Abingdon violently away from the monastery.[592] MS C does not mention the destruction of the monastery by the Danes, but does note Alfred's taking of Abingdon.[593] Several chapters later, however, it refers to Alfred as 'the most learned king in liberal letters'.[594] Alfred's son, Edward the Elder, is merely named in MS C. MS B, which refers to him as 'king of the whole of England', presents him making two gifts that passed, together with the associated charters, to Abingdon. In fact the first of these was a gift of Edward the Confessor.[595] Edward the Elder's third wife, Eadgifu, would later feature as a prominent influence in favour of the monastery: she 'cherished the abbot and monks with the greatest love. Sometimes she showered quantities of her wealth on them, at other times she sought her son's favour for them by assiduous persuasion.'[596]

MS C does not give any lengthy account of Edward's son and successor Æthelstan, but is favourable in its tone. It describes him as 'holding the monarchy of the principality of the whole of England'.[597] It is under Æthelstan that an abbot, Cynath, is again named, and

[589] c. 8, B30.

[590] See below, p. 264.

[591] See below, p. 268.

[592] See below, p. 272.

[593] c. 17. William of Malmesbury, *Gesta pontificum*, bk. ii, c. 88, ed. Hamilton, p. 191, supports the *History*'s negative picture of Alfred in relation to Abingdon: 'Elfredi tempore regis, cum barbarica ubique Dani discursarent petulantia, edifitia loci ad solum complanata. Tum rex, malorum preventus consiliis, terras, quecunque appendices essent, in suos suorumque usus redegit.' See also *De abbatibus*, *CMA* ii 275–6.

[594] See below, p. 48; MS B does not include this description.

[595] See below, pp. 32–4, B42–B45. Note that the gift of Farnborough by Alfred's daughter, Æthelflæd, lady of the Mercians, is wrongly placed before the Danish invasions in B35–B36.

[596] See below, p. 56; see also cc. 27, 28, B82, B84.

[597] See below, p. 34.

charters record royal gifts directly to the abbey.[598] It also notes the king's favour to the young Æthelwold, and his commending of him to Bishop Ælfheah of Winchester.[599] As usual, MS B is more expansive, indeed is moved to some rhetorical heights. Æthelstan was 'of such piety and holiness of life' that

> he strove unceasingly to expend the utmost care and the greatest diligence in rebuilding again numerous destroyed churches. Amongst these he embraced with such great sincerity and so great a privilege of love the monastery of Abingdon, then governed by Abbot Cynath, that not only did he enrich it with various ornaments but also endowed it with extensive possessions.[600]

The text goes on to record various of his gifts and charters which passed directly or indirectly to Abingdon.[601] It also mentions him 'holding his full court at Abingdon', and receiving a Frankish embassy. The messengers brought various gifts and relics, the latter of which—this version of the *History* states—King Æthelstan gave to Abingdon, 'concealed with all honour in a silver reliquary'.[602]

After mentioning Æthelstan's favour for Æthelwold, the earlier version of the *History* goes on to state that

> not long after, that king was allotted the end of his life and bequeathed the highest position to his brother Edmund. After his death (*post cuius obitum*), the monastery of Abingdon was reduced to such forlornness that all possessions belonging to it were subjected to royal lordship and it was utterly destitute of monks.

Although grammatically ambiguous, the reference would appear to be to the death of Æthelstan, and this is made clear in the related Abingdon passage in John of Worcester.[603] Whilst MS C does not explicitly criticize Edmund, and records his death without significant comment, it does include a charter recording him making a gift of Culham to the royal matron Ælfhild.[604] The *History* states that she made the church heir of the possession, readers having already been

598 cc. 18–22. 599 c. 24. 600 See below, p. 278.

601 B47–B61. See also *De abbatibus* for his gifts to the abbey; *CMA* ii. 276.

602 B62. *De abbatibus* also mentions the gifts from Hugh, and Æthelstan's death; *CMA* ii. 276–7. However, it says that Hugh sent gifts 'because his wife was Æthelstan's sister'.

603 See below, p. 46; John of Worcester, *Chronicle*, ii. 610; cf. below, p. 292, for the version in the revised *History*. Wulfstan, *Life of Æthelwold*, c. 10, ed. Lapidge and Winterbottom, p. 16, passes quite swiftly over Edmund's reign. For Edmund being turned against Dunstan, see *Vita Sancti Dunstani auctore B*, c. 13, *Memorials of Saint Dunstan, Archbishop of Canterbury*, ed. W. Stubbs (London, 1874), p. 23.

604 cc. 25, 26.

informed that Culham had earlier been a long-standing possession of Abingdon. This grant, together with the lack of praise for Edmund compared with his predecessor and successor, reinforces the impression that it was his reign that was regarded as a period of 'desolation' for the abbey.

The later version of the *History* does not include MS C's passage on the decline of the abbey following Æthelstan's death. Indeed, it mentions Edmund's confirmation of Watchfield to the abbey, on condition that the abbey grant Culham to Ælfhild for life. It also records numerous gifts and charters of Edmund that passed indirectly to Abingdon. Finally, it records his death at the hands of his butler.[605] It goes on to state that:

> After his death, as we have learnt from the testimony of ancient books, the monastery of Abingdon was reduced to such a forsaken state that, with all its possessions subjected to royal lordship by the sceptre-bearing power, it was entirely destitute of monks. However, nothing true or worthy of recounting has come to our notice as to the causes of this evil misfortune and the occurrence of so unexpected a downfall. Concerning this matter we judge it more useful and also more honourable to remain for the moment wisely silent on such desolation, rather than to make something public which cannot easily be proved to be true or plausible.

It is unclear why the reviser attributed this decline to the period after Edmund's death, whereas MS C specifies that it was after Æthelstan's; it may, for example, arise from his need to include the charters of Edmund which he had found, or indeed may stem from the grammatical ambiguity of the earlier version noted above. However, the version in MS B makes poor sense given the revival that the abbey was about to enjoy following Edmund's death. It is also notable that MS B does not provide an impressive illustration of Edmund, as it does for his predecessor and successors.[606]

The two versions reunite in their praise for Edmund's successor, Eadred; indeed it is with Eadred—'the repairer of the house of Abingdon and most faithful restorer of its stolen possessions'—rather than with St Æthelwold that MS B starts its second book.[607] Both

605 B64–B81.

606 See below, pp. clxxxix–cxc.

607 See below, p. 294; the focus soon switches to Æthelwold. Keynes, '"Dunstan B" charters', p. 188, speculates on what he admits is very limited evidence that Eadred may have intended to be buried at Glastonbury or Abingdon, and that therefore Glastonbury or Abingdon was the intended burial place mentioned in his will as the recipient of gifts of precious objects and treasure; *Charters of Abingdon Abbey*, p. xxxvii n. 10, is duly sceptical of this suggestion.

versions emphasize his love for Æthelwold. On his mother's advice, Eadred gave Abingdon to Æthelwold and endowed the abbey with estates.[608] According to MS C, 'at the start of the construction of the monastery [the king] measured the foundations of the work with his own hand, and then in excellent fashion made gifts to them with royal generosity'.[609] MS C includes one gift and charter of Eadred that passed indirectly to Abingdon, MS B many more.[610] The latter also notes the recognition of his holiness at his death, especially announced to Abbot Dunstan by a heavenly voice.[611]

Privileges, gifts, and charters of Eadred's successor, Eadwig, feature extensively in MS C, but it makes no comment on him.[612] MS B also includes numerous privileges, gifts, and charters, but is more forthcoming in its personal comment on the king.[613] In Eadwig's sight, Æthelwold 'found such grace that the king provided his assent, both effective and affectionate, to all his requests for the promotion of the house of Abingdon'.[614]

Eadwig was succeeded by his brother Edgar. Rather surprisingly, neither version of the *History* mentions his contacts with Abingdon before his succession.[615] Both versions of the *History* record his gifts and charters concerning lands that passed directly or indirectly to Abingdon.[616] MS C speaks of 'the bountiful generosities of this king in relation to this monastery', and of the reverence and love in which he held Æthelwold, although such praise is not significantly more extensive than that bestowed upon Eadred.[617] In praising Edgar the

[608] cc. 27–8, B84–B85. See also below, p. 56, for Eadred continuing to visit the church.

[609] See below, p. 56; see also Wulfstan, *Life of Æthelwold*, cc. 10–12, ed. Lapidge and Winterbottom, pp. 16–24; William of Malmesbury, *Gesta pontificum*, c. 88, ed. Hamilton, p. 191, for Eadred as the initiator of the revival of Abingdon.

[610] B86–B111.

[611] B112, and see below, p. cxx. Like that of Edgar, Eadred's death appears in the Abingdon kalendar, Cambridge, University Library, Kk. i 22, fo. 5^{r}.

[612] cc. 36–56. Whether this silence results from hostility on Eadwig's part towards reforming monasticism must be uncertain; see e.g. Thacker, 'Æthelwold', p. 52. Likewise it cannot be told whether the grants that Eadred, according to a charter in his name, intended to come into effect after his death were fulfilled or not; see below, p. cxxxviii. Problems for Abingdon may have arisen with the division of the kingdom between Eadwig and his brother Edgar in 957, the dividing line being the Thames; see *Charters of Abingdon Abbey*, p. xxxviii. Note that *De abbatibus* states that Edgar succeeded Eadred, omitting any mention of Eadwig; *CMA* ii. 280.

[613] For gifts and charters, see B114–B172.

[614] See below, p. 308. The description of his death is neutral; below, p. 326.

[615] See above, p. lxiv, on his seeing the church's ruins and his vow to restore the house, p. xcvi, on the possibility that Æthelwold was his tutor.

[616] cc. 60–70, 72–90; B174–B206.

[617] See below, p. 94. See also p. 114 concerning the expulsion of clerics from

later version of the *History* returns to the higher rhetorical style of its description of Æthelstan.[618] Whilst comments such as that on his accession he 'strove in constant meditation "to shed the old man with his deeds"' suggest reservations about his life before he came to the throne, it is fulsome praise which characterizes its description of his kingship. The praise continues in its brief mention of his death: 'Edgar, most illustrious king of the English, happily went the way of all flesh'.[619]

MS C gives a brief description of the murder of Edgar's successor, Edward the martyr, noting his simple life and attributing the killing vaguely to 'the treachery of wicked men'.[620] MS B describes him as

> a man whose memory should be commemorated. Through the passage of time . . . that man exerted power by both the seriousness of his behaviour and the holiness of his life, so that before he had suffered the fate of mankind, placed on earth he was seen by all to live the angelic life.[621]

It goes on to attribute his martyrdom to 'the trickery of his stepmother Ælfthryth'.[622]

Both versions of the *History* note in shared narrative, as well as in their copies of his own great charter of 993, the bad counsel and the hostility to the church of the next king, Æthelred II. In particular they record his reversal of his father's gifts and his giving of the abbacy to Eadwine in return for payment.[623] The earlier version also calls him an 'unwarlike' king, who met the Danish invaders with money, not arms. In the face of such weakly resisted invasions Abingdon's possessions were endangered.[624] However, another chapter appearing in both versions of the *History* recounts that Abbot Wulfgar managed to persuade Æthelred to favour Abingdon, so that

Winchester, and their replacement by Abingdon monks. *De abbatibus* does not comment on Edgar, *CMA* ii. 280.

[618] B173. Below, p. 328, calls him a 'munificent king', p. 336 'most illustrious'.

[619] See below, p. 344. His death on 8 July also appears in the Abingdon kalendar, Cambridge, University Library, Kk. i 22, fo. 4v; note also Gerchow, *Die Gedenküberlieferung*, p. 337, for Cambridge, Corpus Christi College 57, fo. 67v, recording the 'depositio Eadgari' on 8 July.

[620] c. 95. See c. 116, B250, for his relics being brought to Abingdon.

[621] See below, p. 344.

[622] See below, p. 346. The mention of Edward in *De abbatibus* is very brief; *CMA* ii. 280.

[623] c. 95, 96, 98, B214, B215, B217. *De abbatibus* passes no comment on Æthelred; *CMA* ii. 280.

[624] See below, p. 140. See below, p. cxliv, for the statement in *De abbatibus* that Abingdon was destroyed by the Danes under Swein.

he admitted his errors, compensated the abbey for its losses, and issued a confirmation charter.[625] Both versions of the *History* go on to record further of his gifts that supposedly passed directly or indirectly to the abbey.[626] The earlier version also mentions his marriage to Emma of Normandy in 1002, his departure to Normandy in December 1013 or January 1014, his return after King Swein's death in February 1014, and the end of 'the troubled king' amidst Cnut's invasion and English disloyalty after thirty-six years of his reign 'embroiled in diverse dangerous events'. The later version mentions Dunstan's prophecy of the troubles of the reign, Æthelred's flight to Normandy, and copies the earlier version's section on his death.[627] Both versions share a description of the struggles of Æthelred's son, Edmund Ironside, against the Danes, but make no mention of any relations between him and Abingdon.[628]

The *History* notes only the brevity of the rule in England of Æthelred's rival, King Swein.[629] The Danish invaders as a group are condemned for their barbarity and the *History* appears to include Swein in this condemnation,[630] but no such accusation is made against his son Cnut. Rather, the earlier version of the *History* mentions that he 'ruled Denmark, Norway, and England with a just and strong hand as becomes an emperor', that he visited Rome, and issued laws.[631] Cnut became a patron of Abingdon under the influence of Abbot Æthelwine and of his successor Siward.[632] Particularly notable was a gold and silver reliquary he had made in honour of St Vincent, but he also gave two very resonant bells.[633] His grants of estates were less notable. Both versions of the *History* include a charter recording the grant of the church of St Martin, Oxford, and two hides at Lyford, while they each include a different charter concerning Myton.[634] Of Cnut's successor, Harold Harefoot, MS C says only that he was 'instituted as king', had been born of a concubine, and died after five years. MS B does not even call him

[625] c. 97, B216.

[626] cc. 100–4, B219–B232, B234, B237–B239.

[627] cc. 109–10, B243–B244.

[628] See below, pp. 174, 356.

[629] See below, pp. 174, 356.

[630] See below, pp. 174, 354.

[631] See below, p. 184. For Cnut's visit or visits to Rome in 1027 and possibly again around 1030/1, see Lawson, *Cnut*, pp. 100, 102–4. On his laws, see Lawson, *Cnut*, pp. 61–3, 204–10.

[632] On Cnut's respect for Siward, see below, p. 358; there is no equivalent passage in MS C.

[633] See the related passages below, pp. 176–8, 356. See also *De abbatibus*, *CMA* ii. 281.

[634] cc. 113, 114, B246, B247. *De abbatibus* does not mention Cnut's grants of lands; *CMA* ii. 281.

king, mentioning only his parentage and his death.[635] Next came Harthacnut, son of Cnut and Queen Emma. Both versions of the *History* include his charter concerning Farnborough.[636] The earlier version alone criticizes him for his taxation, and his treatment of the corpse of Harold Harefoot, which he ordered 'to be dug up and sunk in a place of deepest filth'. Punishment for such wrongdoing was swift, and the text reports with satisfaction that soon afterwards he collapsed and died during a feast at a royal palace.[637]

The same version of the *History* reports the subsequent delight at the succession of Edward the Confessor, son of Æthelred.[638] MS B at the equivalent point calls him Harthacnut's brother, son of Æthelred and Emma. It also provides a fuller account of his accession. It refers to him as 'the most blessed Edward', and in the heading of the following section as 'St Edward'.[639] In different passages, both versions of the *History* mention his part in the appointment of Abbot Siward to take on the duties of the archbishop of Canterbury.[640] A passage common to the two manuscripts describes a visit to Abingdon by Edward, his mother, and his wife, and the consequent gift of Lewknor.[641] Other gifts, charters, writs, and confirmations by Edward are also recorded.[642] Less popular with the composer of the *History* was Edward's practice of choosing abbots for Abingdon, the monk and goldsmith Spearhafoc and the aged bishop Rodulf, both of whom had pre-existing connections with the king. Disapproval of such practice is indicated by the *History* recording that Edward promised that the abbey should thereafter elect as abbot whomsoever they wished from themselves.[643] MS C's account of Edward's reign closes with the dedication of Westminster Abbey and his death. This passage also appears in MS B, which later, in a second chapter headed 'Concerning the death of King Edward', refers to him 'having been translated to the heavens'.[644]

[635] See below, pp. 184, 360. Cf. the very brief account of the succession in *De abbatibus*; *CMA* ii. 281.

[636] cc. 116–17, B253.

[637] See below, p. 186.

[638] See below, p. 186.

[639] See below, p. 362. *De abbatibus* calls him 'gloriosus rex'; *CMA* ii. 283.

[640] See below, pp. 186, 362; see also *De abbatibus*, *CMA* ii. 281.

[641] c. 121, B261; see also *De abbatibus*, *CMA* ii. 283.

[642] cc. 121, 127–35, B257, B258, B267–B271 (the last of which does not appear in MS C), B273–B280, B287–B288; note also *De abbatibus*, *CMA* ii. 281–2.

[643] cc. 124–5, B264–B265; note also the different tone of the *History* concerning the succession of Abbot Ordric; c. 126, B266. Cf. the lack of comment in *De abbatibus*, *CMA* ii. 281.

[644] See below, pp. 220, 370; the phrase is also used of Edward the martyr below, p. 346.

Edward's successor Harold had already appeared in the *History* as a benefactor of Abingdon. Edward had given him four hides at Sandford-on-Thames but at Harold's request had then given them to Abingdon.[645] Passages common to both versions of the *History* state in a neutral fashion that 'to [Edward the Confessor] succeeded as king Earl Harold, son of Earl Godwine', and describes Tostig as 'brother of our King Harold', thereby distinguishing the latter from the king of Norway. Harold's victory at Stamford Bridge is reported, whilst his defeat at Hastings is put down to over-confidence.[646] There seems no effort, therefore, to deny the legitimacy of Harold's kingship, although a passage which appears only in the later version of the *History* refers to Harold as Edward's successor without entitling him king.[647]

Neither version of the *History*, in their accounts of the events of 1066, present William as a usurper.[648] However, when mentioning King Æthelred's marriage to Emma of Normandy, the earlier version of the *History* had traced the descent therefrom of William 'who later attacked England and seized [*usurpauit*] for himself the kingship there'. The later version of the *History* states that Harold 'argued' that he had a better claim to the throne because Edward had left him the kingdom on account of their kinship.[649] It also adds a passage concerning William's coronation that is drawn from the *Chronicle* of John of Worcester. John's passage concludes with the promises that William made at that coronation, to which the *History* adds a comment of its own: 'All these things he swore but he held none of them.' Rather, he deposed almost all the bishops and abbots, and almost all the English nobles fled the country and their lands were forfeited.[650] Apart from these passages, criticism of William is muted.

[645] cc. 131–2, B271–B273. This description of the stages of the gift differs somewhat from the more common instances where the king is referred to as giving land to a layman and the layman as giving it to the church with the king's consent. Possibly the transaction in this case was of different form, possibly it was best after 1066 not to attribute gifts to Earl Harold even with the Confessor's consent. These circumstances would also have provided an incentive for the forgery of a charter recording Edward's grant direct to Abingdon, rather than relying simply on possession of the genuine charter recording Edward's gift of Sandford to Earl Godwine; B273. Note also below, pp. 222–4, concerning Kingston.

[646] See below, pp. 220–2, 366–8.

[647] See below, p. 370. See also *De abbatibus*, *CMA* ii. 283.

[648] See below, pp. 222, 368, 370. On the *History* and the Norman Conquest, see also J. G. H. Hudson, 'The abbey of Abingdon, its *Chronicle* and the Norman Conquest', *Anglo-Norman Studies*, xix (1997), 181–202.

[649] See below, pp. 174, 368.

[650] See below, p. 372. Note also the positive presentation of Robert d'Oilly's wife in the miracle story concerning Robert in MS B, vol. ii. 328–30. She was Ealdgyth, daughter of Wigod of Wallingford; Blair, *Anglo-Saxon Oxfordshire*, p. 174.

Resistance to the lordship of men from overseas is recorded in a passage shared by both versions, but the same section says that the men of Abingdon 'ought to have favoured King William's side' rather than join the rebels as they did. However, the *History* goes on to note the king's anger against their lord, Abbot Ealdred, which may imply criticism.[651] In general, the strongest criticism is for those associated with William, rather than for the king himself. It had already noted that William's queen had exacted precious ornaments from the church, whilst the later version also recorded that certain monks and sacrists of Jumièges deceitfully took to Normandy very many ornaments associated with Æthelwold.[652]

The differing treatment of kings in the two versions of the *History* illustrates many of the characteristics of the revision.[653] Indeed, but for the lack of explicit statement or external evidence, it would be tempting to associate the rewriting of the *History* as manifested in MS B with either efforts to obtain a royal confirmation or a royal visit to Abingdon.[654] Take the key structural points of the work. The *History* now ends with a royal charter, that of Richard I. Book II is made to start with Eadred, and end with William I's victory at Hastings. Comments on kings are also changed. It is Eadred not Æthelwold who is called the third restorer of the church, whereas the earlier version—although clear on Eadred's importance—only said that the restoration took place in his time.[655] The closeness of abbots to the king is still further emphasized, from the instance of Abben onwards.[656] Indeed portions of the *History* start to read like a treatise offering advice to, and *exempla* of, kings.

Seized by a deadly illness, King Eadred fell into his sickbed, which he did not leave until, by disposition of the just Judge of the world, he breathed out

[651] See below, pp. 226, 374.

[652] See below, pp. 224, 340. See also vol. ii p. lxvi.

[653] Note also e.g. the focus on kings in B8; the extended account of Edmund's death in B81.

[654] If we reject the notion that there was an intervening manuscript between the two surviving ones, or if we simply concentrate on the production of MS B regardless of an intervening manuscript, we would have to look to visits by Henry III. He visited Abingdon frequently, at least once a year between 1220 and 1224, and then in 1227, 1228, 1231, 1232, 1234, 1235, 1238, 1240, 1241, 1245, 1246, 1251, 1255, 1257, 1258, 1260, and 1263; see T Craib, *The Itinerary of King Henry III, 1216–1272*, ed. S. Brindle and S. Priestley (English Heritage, n.d.), pp. 30–4, 37–8, 41–2, 44–5, 48–51, 53–4, 58, 60, 62–4, 66.

[655] See below, pp. 48, 294. Note also the considerable increase in space devoted to Æthelstan and Eadred in MS B because of the increased number of their charters included; B46–B63, B82–B112.

[656] B2 concerning Abben, B25 Ecgberht, B46 Æthelstan, B113 Eadwig, B251 Cnut.

his final breath [955]. Indeed, there slipped from Heaven a voice which notified the blessed Dunstan abbot of Glastonbury—who was travelling and hurrying as quickly as possible the sooner to see that flock—of the blessedness of Eadred's death and how he had suffered the fate of mankind, saying 'King Eadred sleeps in the Lord'. Oh how happy the life of a king which is commended by such a happy attestation![657]

Edgar's great virtues are described by the reviser, as are those of Edward the martyr, whilst William the Conqueror receives criticism.[658] Focus on the king was further intensified by the provision of illustrations of rulers, greatly enriching the physical appearance of the manuscript and a fitting accompaniment to the increased richness of the text.[659]

4. Others

Many further participants in the *History* appear only incidentally, for example as figures in national history.[660] Others appear only once or only very briefly, for example because of involvement in a dispute.[661] A few people are specified as having been buried at Abingdon: Sidemann bishop of Crediton, who died in 977; Ælfstan bishop of Wilton and former monk of Abingdon, whose death the *History* dates to 980; Eadwine, probably the ealdorman of Sussex who died in 982; and a royal woman named Ælfhild.[662]

Tenants

The tenants of the abbey, so prominent in the *History* for the post-Conquest period, are rarely visible in the Anglo-Saxon portion even though *Domesday Book* reveals that many of the lands held by tenants in 1086 had already been granted out before the Conquest.[663] There are a few exceptions, such as Brihtmund and his family, tenants of Leckhampstead, and Thorkell, who held lands at Kingston Bagpuize.[664] Also according to the *History*, the wealthy priest Blæcmann

[657] See below, p. 308.

[658] See below, pp. 326 (cf. p. 95), 344 (cf. p. 132), 372 (cf. p. 222).

[659] See below, pp. clxxix–cxc.

[660] See below e.g. p. 232 on the conversion; p. 236 on Vortigern; p. 242 on Constantine and Helen; p. 266 on Hinguar and Ubba; p. 282 on Hugh, duke of the Franks; pp. 172, 354, on archbishops of Canterbury; pp. 220, 368, on Harold Hardrada.

[661] See e.g. below, p. 190, on an evil reeve.

[662] See below, pp. 52–4, 138, 172, 286; *ASC*, 'C', *s.a.* 977, 982. See also below, p. 194, for Abbot Siward.

[663] See below, p. cliv, for alienation; above, p. lxvii, for the *History*'s lack of documents recording leases.

[664] See below, pp. 188–90, 208–10, 220.

'had become the man of the church and held from it Sandford, Chilton, and Leverton', a statement partially supported by *Domesday Book*.[665] His flight with Gytha, mother of King Harold, suggests that he may have had a connection with the Godwine family.[666]

Donors

Many people in addition to kings are mentioned in the *History* as donors to the abbey. There are, for example, several notable gifts by women, some probably known from records of their bequest.[667] In most cases the donors appear simply as recipients of royal lands who are said to have passed these gifts on to Abingdon, statements that need to be treated with considerable caution.[668] Many such donors only appear once or twice, and in the absence of surnames or other identification it is often difficult to decide if two or more appearances of the same name refer to one or more individuals.[669] Here I wish only to deal with a few men who may have been important patrons.[670]

First there is Ealdorman Ælfhere of Mercia and his family. Ælfhere was probably the pre-eminent ealdorman in Edgar's reign, and was later remembered by some as a despoiler of monasteries in his ealdordom after Edgar's death.[671] The *History* records Æthelwold

[665] c. 143. See also cc. 136, B290; *DB* i, fos. 59^{r} (where he is said to have held Chilton from Harold *in alodio*), 156^{v}. Note also e.g. *DB* i, fo. 160^{r}, for a Blæcmann having held Boycott in Oxfordshire; E. A. Freeman, *The History of the Norman Conquest of England* (6 vols., Oxford, 1867–79), iv. 144 n., states that this land 'doubtless belongs to our Blæcman'. It may be significant that the 1086 holder was called 'Reinbaldus', who might be identified with the Abingdon knight Rainbald, prominent in the *History*; see vol. ii, esp. pp. lxiii–lxiv, 54–8.

[666] See also *Charters of Abingdon Abbey*, p. clxi.

[667] cc. 25, 57–8, 106–7, B64. It has been suggested that these grants are evidence either for a revival of a minster for women dedicated to St Helen, or for female religious living there with some unofficial arrangement with the monks of Abingdon; M. A. Meyer, 'Patronage of West Saxon royal nunneries in late Anglo-Saxon England', *Revue bénédictine*, xci (1981), 332–58, at pp. 345–6; id., 'The queen's demesne in later Anglo-Saxon England', in Meyer, ed., *Culture of Christendom*, pp. 75–113, at 94 and n. 79, P. Halpin, 'Women religious in late Anglo-Saxon England', *Haskins Society Journal*, vi (1994), 97–110, at p. 104. These claims are not necessary to explain the existing evidence; see S. Foot, *Veiled Women* (2 vols., Aldershot, 2000), ii. 20: 'All that can be said with confidence is that during the tenth century religious women occupied estates to which Abingdon Abbey laid claim at the Conquest.'

[668] On such passages, see below, pp. cxxvi–cxxix.

[669] See e.g. c. 55, B122–B123, B126–B127, for Beorhtric, a thegn.

[670] For a more extensive treatment of these men, see *Charters of Abingdon Abbey*, pp. clxxiii–cxcii. For other donors, see footnotes to the relevant donations.

[671] *Charters of Abingdon Abbey*, p. clxxxv. He died in 983. See Williams, '*Princeps Merciorum gentis*'.

obtaining Cuddesdon from him, Osgar acquiring Kingston.[672] His widow, Eadflæd, may also have been a patron of Abingdon.[673] Ælfhere's brother Ælfheah was probably made ealdorman of central Wessex in 959 and was buried at Glastonbury following his death in 971. The extent of his donations is uncertain. The earlier version of the *History* attributes to a thegn named Ælfheah the gift of Buckland, the later version the gifts of Farnborough, Compton, and Lyford.[674] These may be references to one thegn or two, and the thegn may or may not be the future ealdorman of central Wessex. Moreover, even if all these lands were held by the future ealdorman Ælfheah, it is again impossible to demonstrate that he himself was responsible for giving them to Abingdon.[675] Further brothers called Eadric and Ælfwine may have been the thegns of those names who received various grants that appear in the *History* and are there said to have passed to Abingdon.[676] Their brother-in-law was Ælfric *Cild* who succeeded Ælfhere as ealdorman of Mercia in 983. The name Ælfric is a common one so it is impossible to tell whether, for example, the Ælfric who received Bayworth from King Eadwig and is said to have made Abingdon his heir was indeed Ælfric *Cild*, let alone whether he did leave Bayworth to Abingdon.[677] He was, quite probably, the very powerful man who bought the abbey for his brother, Abbot Eadwine, although Ælfric ealdorman of Hampshire is also a candidate.[678]

Another possible significant donor to Abingdon may have been Wulfric Cufing, who indeed may have been connected to Ealdorman Ælfhere's family.[679] The evidence for his role as donor is that a large number of estates which later belonged to Abingdon had once been his, and that a significant number of charters in the revised version of

[672] cc. 45–6, 93. See also B147–B148. *Charters of Abingdon Abbey*, p. clxxxvi, appears sceptical of the suggestion that Ælfhere gave Cuddesdon to Abingdon.

[673] c. 107; see also *Charters of Abingdon Abbey*, pp. clxxxvi, 580–1. See also below, pp. 152, 158, for conflict probably between this Eadflæd and her brother-in-law Ælfric *Cild*.

[674] cc. 51–2, B56–B57, B73–B74, B104–B105.

[675] See below, p. cxli.

[676] Eadric: cc. 47–8, 137, B145–B146, B151–B152, B156–B157, B164–B165, B189. Ælfwine: cc. 49–50, 89–90, B108–B109. See also *Charters of Abingdon Abbey*, pp. clxxxvii–cxc.

[677] c. 53. See also e.g. B132–B133 concerning Hanney. *Charters of Abingdon Abbey*, p. cxci, concludes that 'there is therefore no evidence that Ælfric was a direct patron of Abingdon (although it seems possible that some of his family estates passed to the abbey through his brother, if Abbot Eadwine was indeed his brother)'.

[678] c. 96, B215. See also *Charters of Abingdon Abbey*, pp. cxc–cxci; Keynes, *Diplomas*, p. 177 n. 91.

[679] On Wulfric, see *Charters of Abingdon Abbey*, pp. clxxiv–clxxxv.

the *History* record grants to him.[680] He had probably started to attend the witan in the 930s, but most of the charters recording grants to him come from Eadred's reign. However, he forfeited in the late 950s, perhaps for reasons connected with the division of the kingdom between Eadwig and Edgar. He was restored to his lands in 960 and the charter recording his restoration appears in MS B.[681] Six of the eight Berkshire estates that this charter mentions were in Abingdon's possession in *Domesday Book*. However, this does not prove that Wulfric gave them to Abingdon, and in one case, that of Boxford, it can be demonstrated that it first passed to another thegn, Ælfwine, who may have been the brother of Ealdorman Ælfhere, as mentioned above.[682]

There is also some evidence for a connection between the Godwine family and Abingdon, although their contribution to the endowment that the church enjoyed in 1066 was limited.[683] Queen Edith gave the abbey land at Lewknor.[684] Earl Harold was said to favour Abingdon in the case over Leckhampstead.[685] He persuaded Edward the Confessor to give Abingdon four hides at Sandford, and encouraged Thorkell to become the abbey's man 'concerning himself together with his land which is called Kingston'.[686] The *History* tells us that after 1066

> the men of the abbey of Abingdon, while they ought to have favoured King William's side, changed their minds and opinions and hastened armed to where they had learnt that the king's enemies were situated. En route they were surrounded, captured, imprisoned, and very wretchedly afflicted.[687]

Such opposition to William might indicate support for Harold, perhaps not surprising in the case of men such as Thorkell.[688] Here one must be careful to distinguish the relationships and attitudes of the monastery from those of at least some of their tenants.

[680] cc. 34–5, B65–B66, B86–B87, B90–B91, B96–B97, B100–B101, B106–B107, B158–B159, B171–B172.

[681] B186 (*Charters of Abingdon Abbey*, no. 86).

[682] cc. 89–90. This and other evidence leads *Charters of Abingdon Abbey*, p. clxxxi, to suggest that 'it is important to consider whether this kin-group [i.e. Ælfhere's] may not have inherited or acquired a major portion of Wulfric's Berkshire holdings, and themselves transmitted it to Abingdon'.

[683] Note that Abingdon lands at Drayton may have fallen into the hands of the Godwine family by 1066; see below, p. 349 n. 311. Godwine's support for Siward's move to Canterbury may arise from a personal link to the abbot, not from favour to Abingdon; see above, p. ci.

[684] c. 121.

[685] c. 136; see also c. 120.

[686] cc. 131–2, 143, B271–B273, on which see above, p. cxix n. 645.

[687] c. 144.

[688] See above, p. cxxii, on Blæcmann, vol. ii. 24 n. 56 on Eadnoth the staller.

Royal officials

There is little hint in the Anglo-Saxon portion of the *History* that royal officials would be a source of trouble for Abingdon as they clearly were in the post-Conquest period. The story of King Coenwulf, his huntsmen, and reeves may reflect twelfth-century concerns, although the burden of royal huntsmen was also a problem for minsters in the ninth century.[689] Immediately after the Conquest, sheriff Froger emerged as a leading oppressor of the abbey, and there was also conflict involving the king's chaplain, Peter, who was keeper of the vacant bishopric of Lincoln.[690] It is unclear whether the relative pre-Conquest silence is a sign of better relations with royal officials or, perhaps more likely, a product of the scarcity of dispute records.

Major churchmen

Several major churchmen appear in the pre-1071 part of the *History*. Only one pope is mentioned in relation to Abingdon. This was Leo III, from whom Abbot Hræthhun obtained protection against the oppressions of King Coenwulf.[691] The importance already attached to this papal intervention before the writing of the *History* is clear from the later tenth-century royal privileges.[692] The Winchcombe archive has a fragment of a privilege of the same pope confirming Coenwulf's rights over minsters that he had acquired or inherited. It could be that he really did intervene with regard to Abingdon as well as Winchcombe, or it could be that a copy of the Winchcombe privilege was later known at Abingdon and misinterpreted to form the basis of the privilege mentioned in the charters and the *History*.[693]

More prominent in the *History* than popes are archbishops of Canterbury. There is Archbishop Eadsige who in his infirmity called Abbot Siward to his aid.[694] Archbishop Stigand appears as opponent of Abingdon when bishop of Winchester, and his imprisonment by William I is recorded, perhaps with some pleasure.[695] Most prominent

[689] See below, c. 9.
[690] See c. 144, B291.
[691] cc. 9, 11, B17, B18.
[692] cc, 37, 60, 98.
[693] See *Charters of Abingdon Abbey*, p. cciv, which also mentions a Glastonbury document in this context; *De antiquitate Glastonie ecclesie*, cc. 49, 50; Scott, *Early History of Glastonbury*, pp. 106–8.
[694] c. 119, B256.
[695] See below, p. 196. The *History* never refers to Stigand as archbishop, although it is not clear whether this is significant in general, or indeed specifically with regard the problem of the witnesses of c. 132, where he is titled bishop when he appears as first witness to a charter dated 1054.

of all is Dunstan, who, according to the earlier version of the *History*, received Æthelwold at Glastonbury, gave counsel concerning his expulsion of clerics from Winchester, joined in the consecration of the church at Abingdon, and ordered that Bishop Sidemann be buried at the abbey.[696] The reviser added that he consented to Æthelwold's election to Winchester, received a heavenly announcement of the death of King Eadred, gave instruction to King Edgar, consecrated Edward the martyr, and, whilst he was crowning King Æthelred, prophesied the great change that the kingdom was to undergo. Amidst all this activity, he also, we are told, made with his own hands two large bells for Abingdon.[697]

VI. ENDOWMENT, ADMINISTRATION, AND LAW UP TO 1071

1. Abingdon's estates

Evidence

Although the abbey may well have enjoyed a wide variety of sources of income, our evidence for its endowment is very largely confined to its lands. The most useful evidence of income from these is provided by *Domesday Book*. However, rather than work back from *Domesday*, I now follow the pattern of the *History* and deal in turn with the reputed early endowment, losses suffered during the Viking Age, the endowment during the time of Æthelwold, changes in the period from the death of Edgar in 975 until 1066, and finally the impact of the Norman Conquest. This arrangement will help us to analyse the pattern and the plausibility of the *History*'s account of the development of the endowment.

The nature of the evidence leads to many difficulties of interpretation. Non-diploma documents, for example wills and leases, have almost entirely been lost. Moreover, there are no genuine diplomas recording grants directly to Abingdon before the time of the Viking attacks, and problems of authenticity with a significant number of tenth- and eleventh-century diplomas for Abingdon.

As for the diplomas with beneficiaries other than Abingdon, these are accompanied almost always in MS C and often in MS B by a statement that the beneficiary gave the land to the abbey. Some are

[696] cc. 37, 71, 83, 94.
[697] See below, pp. 296, 308, 326, 338, 346, 354.

specific and very plausible, but most are routine.[698] Although in the case of diplomas in MS C it can generally be shown that the land was to have some Abingdon connection, and although the fact that the compiler included the statements as a matter of perhaps uncritical routine need not necessarily mean that they are always inaccurate, the routine statements in MS C may on occasion obscure the time when and the processes whereby the lands passed to the abbey. The *Libellus Æthelwoldi*, for example, suggests that purchase played a much greater part in the assembling of the lands of an Æthelwoldian house than the *History*'s record of voluntary patronage would allow.[699]

The statements in MS B that beneficiaries passed their lands to Abingdon must be treated with still greater scepticism.[700] They are formulaic and indeed in some portions of his text the reviser simply includes diplomas without the formulaic gloss. The lack of critical thought by the reviser as to whether or how lands passed to Abingdon can be demonstrated. King Æthelred of Wessex's charter granting ten hides in Wittenham to his noble named Æthelwulf appears in both versions of the *History*. MS C follows it with the statement that 'this church afterwards possessed that land by gift of Bishop Siward, together with his document'. MS B reproduces this statement, but also contradicts it in adding one of the standard passages, apparently through simple routine:

> Not forgetful of the above favour, Æthelwulf gave and firmly granted that village to the house of Abingdon, with everything entirely pertaining to it, by the consent and will of the king, together with the king's charter expressing that gift and the manner of giving, and in most reverent devotion he offered the king's charter on the altar of Abingdon, for greater protection, in honour of God and the blessed Mary.[701]

[698] For more specific statements, note e.g. cc. 44, 104; see also *Charters of Abingdon Abbey*, pp. cxxxiii–cxxxiv. Keynes, 'Studies', p. 87, suggests that some of the estates recorded in charters to individuals may have been 'given by eleventh-century kings (who are otherwise poorly represented by authentic charters), if we imagine that the grants were effected by the transfer of earlier title-deeds, perhaps accompanied by writ'. One might, however, have expected the narratives in the *History* to record such royal grants in the 11th century, when narratives are growing in number and detail, and may have been based on earlier notes.

[699] For purchases, see cc. 33, 93; see also *Charters of Abingdon Abbey*, pp. cliii, clxx–clxxii, for possible parallels to other houses.

[700] See also *Charters of Abingdon Abbey*, pp. cxxxiv–cxxxvi, where the emphasis is primarily upon scepticism as to the timing of donation to Abingdon. A curious instance is B65, which does not specify that the land passed to the church, even though Garford certainly was part of Abingdon's later endowment.

[701] c. 16, B31–B32. MS C's statement could be based on a written source such as a will. Note also *Charters of Abingdon Abbey*, p. cxxxv, on Wormleighton.

If one concludes from such lack of consistency and accuracy that all such routine statements in MS B should be ignored unless there is other supporting evidence, this considerably reduces our knowledge of the process of endowment at Abingdon, particularly in the tenth century.

Rejection of the routine statements, however, need not mean that there was in no case a link between such lands and Abingdon. Some of the charters do concern estates once associated with the abbey, but then lost, alienated, or exchanged. Lands might be lost to straightforward depredations or to permanent alienation of effective control through perpetuation of leases; in neither case would the charter necessarily be lost. Similarly bequests to the church that allowed the grantor or his heir continued but finite tenure might never pass to the church, despite the transfer of the charter. Other estates may have been broken up or combined. If the lands were then given away, the older diplomas may not have been transferred with the new units of land. Such a policy of alienation might have been undertaken, for example, with regard more distant estates.[702] For all these reasons, lands might not form part of the abbey's later endowment, but a twelfth- or thirteenth-century compiler of a *History* would wish to include relevant charters to show the existence of a claim, and might indeed include any available charters on the assumption that they related to lands in which the abbey had once had an interest.

Such explanations, though, have their problems. The evidence for a policy of alienation of distant estates is limited.[703] If there was any policy of permanent alienation, it was likely that the charter would normally pass with the land.[704] Even if an estate was broken up or merged in the process of alienation, the obsolete charter may sometimes have been destroyed. Other charters make clear the concern that disputes would arise from the existence of older documents: 'and so we wish that this charter, by our power, may condemn in every way older landbooks, if they are found, so that they may nowhere prevail at all against our authority'.[705] And if lands were lost through dispute, but Abingdon kept the charter and preserved its claim, it is hard to see why so many of the relevant charters appear only in MS

[702] See *Charters of Abingdon Abbey*, pp. cxlvi–cxlvii, cxlix–cli, clxiii–clxv. The argument put forward there for a deliberate retrenchment does not always differentiate sufficiently clearly between complete alienation and a policy of leasing; see esp. p. clxiv on South Cerney, the lease of which seems to have been quite a short one.

[703] See below, pp. cxlv–cxlvii.

[704] Note also c. 137, *Charters of Abingdon Abbey*, p. cxxxvi.

[705] c. 140.

B. This would be particularly true of lands lost through a process of extension of leases leading to eventual alienation, as in the case of South Cerney.[706] It is best to treat with scepticism MS B's statements that the lands concerned passed to Abingdon not just with regard to timing of the transfer but with regard to its actually ever having occurred.[707]

Why, then, do the charters concerning lands that may never have passed to Abingdon appear in the revised *History*, and why are they only in that version? We probably need to seek multiple explanations, rather than a single one. One possibility is that lay people placed their charters in monasteries for safe keeping, a practice which we certainly know existed later in the Middle Ages.[708] King Eadred was said to have entrusted numerous documents to Dunstan for safe keeping at Glastonbury.[709] This is presented as a sign of special favour to Dunstan, but it may be a gloss put on a more common practice by an author intent on praising Dunstan. Alternatively, similar special favour may have been shown to Æthelwold and some other Abingdon abbots.

Such an explanation still does not explain why so many charters were retained at Abingdon, rather than being retrieved by the landholders. Permanent handing over of a charter might risk loss of the estate, given the close association of transfer of land and transfer of document.[710] However, there are further possible explanations. The charters could come to the abbey with monks, either possessing the charters to prove their own right to property or holding them on behalf of their families.[711] A particular source of charters may have been Englishmen entering the monastery after 1066, although in the absence of the names of monks this is speculative. However, there are

[706] See below, p. cxlv, clxiii. The same problem arises with regard charters given as earnest for a bequest, that bequest never being fulfilled but leaving Abingdon with at least a claim to the land; cf. *Charters of Abingdon Abbey*, p. cli.

[707] Cf. *Charters of Abingdon Abbey*, p. cliii: 'it would be wrong to treat these diplomas as unconnected with the endowment; their connection might be peripheral, but they should not be relegated from the discussion because they do not bear on the state of the endowment in 1066'.

[708] Stenton, *Early History*, p. 43, Keynes, *Diplomas*, p. 12 and n. 20. See also below, p. cxcvi n. 1086.

[709] *Memorials of Saint Dunstan*, ed. Stubbs, p. 29.

[710] *Charters of Abingdon Abbey*, p. cxxxix, points out that 'Dunstan was required to convey the treasures (and presumably the landbooks) to the king's death-bed when he fell ill'. See *Charters of Abingdon Abbey*, pp. cxxxvii–cxl, for further criticisms of the 'safe-deposit' theory, p. clxxvi, for acceptance that it may be a possibility at least in a particular case.

[711] See esp. c. 138; also *Charters of Abingdon Abbey*, p. clii.

just hints in the case of abbots that lands or at least charters that appear in the *History* may have been linked to them personally rather to the abbey. A charter of Edmund granting thirty hides at Waltham, Berkshire, to his thegn Ælfsige, and another of Æthelred granting eight hides at Waltham to Ælfgar *prepositus*, appear in MS B. The revised *History* says in the first instance that Ælfsige passed land and charter to Abingdon, but there is no other evidence of a connection between Abingdon and Waltham. However, the estate was associated with royal goldsmiths, and it could be that the presence of the charters in the Abingdon archive came about through Abbot Spearhafoc, himself a royal goldsmith.[712]

More charters and lands still may have been associated with Æthelwold rather than with Abingdon. Suggestive evidence exists concerning Washington in Sussex, for which MS B includes a charter granting it to a layman. MS B also includes Edgar's charter recording his grant of twenty-four hides at Washington to Æthelwold, and the charter makes no mention of Abingdon as grantee.[713] Æthelwold went on to exchange land at Washington for estates that he used to found Thorney and Peterborough.[714] A similar association with Æthelwold may explain the presence in the revised *History* of Eadwig's grant to a layman of the nearby estate of Annington.[715] We also know that Æthelwold had other lands in what is now West Sussex, although at some distance from Washington and Annington, because part of the gift he made to King Edgar in return for the site of the monastery at Ely was sixty hides at Harting. The lands, according to the *Libellus Æthelwoldi*, had been given to Æthelwold by his lord, who the *Liber Eliensis* says was King Æthelstan.[716] Other lands mentioned in the Abingdon *History* may also have had an association with Æthelwold personally rather than, or as well as, with Abingdon. MS C includes Eadwig's grant of Cuddesdon to Ealdorman Ælfhere, and follows it

[712] B67–B68, B237; *Charters of Abingdon Abbey*, p. 136.

[713] B95, B205. For people depositing valuables at Abingdon after the Norman Conquest see also below, p. 226; however, the *History* comments that many of these were taken away by the Normans.

[714] *Anglo-Saxon Charters*, ed. Robertson, no. 37. *Charters of Abingdon Abbey*, pp. cxliv–cxlv, comments that 'it may be that a new landbook was drawn up for Wulfstan, while the earlier charters for Washington (now technically obsolete) remained in Æthelwold's personal archive and later passed into the archive of Abingdon, where they were preserved because of the connection with Æthelwold'.

[715] B150. *Charters of Abingdon Abbey*, p. 278, comments that 'it is possible that the landbook for the estate had passed through Æthelwold's hands at some time after 956'.

[716] *Liber Eliensis*, bk. ii, c. 4, ed. Blake, p. 76.

with an unusually circumlocutory statement of how the land passed to Abingdon: 'And so the holy father Æthelwold, with the king's permission, acquired this land from that ealdorman, with the charter given to him by the king, and thus that land came to this church.'[717] The evidence of the *Libellus Æthelwoldi* suggests that confusion was possible between gifts to Æthelwold and gifts to Ely, and the situation at Abingdon may have been the same.[718]

These are possible explanations of the presence at Abingdon of charters concerning lands not associated with the abbey.[719] The compiler of MS C chose to include only charters concerning lands that could be linked to the church, but he may not have been the originator of such selectivity. It is possible, for example, that different groups of documents were stored in separate bundles or perhaps separate chests. The reviser would then have added a further bundle or bundles. Although in some cases evidence of an Abingdon link may have been lost, I shall therefore work on the premiss that charters appearing only in MS B, with or without a formulaic statement that the property concerned passed to the abbey, do not constitute secure testimony of an Abingdon interest in the lands unless there is further supporting evidence.

Claims concerning the early endowment

There is no firm evidence for the early endowment of Abingdon. The earliest charters probably concern a minster at Bradfield, not Abingdon. The early charters for Abingdon are not authentic, and the claims made in the late tenth century not necessarily to be trusted. Indeed, if the early charters were put together in the time of Æthelwold, they too constitute evidence for tenth-century claims regarding the early endowment, not evidence for that endowment itself.[720]

[717] c. 46; note that this sentence does not appear in B131. Note also B185 (*Charters of Abingdon Abbey*, no. 101) recording Edgar's gift of Aston Upthorpe, to his queen, Ælfthryth. There is no other evidence, apart from the presence of this charter and B76 (*Charters of Abingdon Abbey*, no. 36) in the later version of the *History*, that Abingdon had lands in the area. However, the queen did have a close association with Æthelwold and one may wonder whether the land or the charter passed to him on some basis. In 1086 it was again held by a churchman with close royal connections, Regenbald the chancellor; *DB* i, fo. 63^r.

[718] Differing views over what belonged to Æthelwold and what belonged to Ely may be one of the problems underlying the dispute in *Liber Eliensis*, bk. ii, c. 19, ed. Blake, p. 95.

[719] See also below, p. cxcvi n. 1086, for the possibility that copies of charters drafted at Abingdon were kept.

[720] See also *Charters of Abingdon Abbey*, p. clxvi.

The supposedly early evidence provides the following information.[721] Ceadwalla gave twenty hides and specified woods to Abingdon. Later, Ceadwalla or Ine restored to Abbot Hæha 173 hides next to Abingdon. A further document, to be associated with Bradfield, confirms the restoration and makes further grants, producing a total—it claims—of 273 hides. Another charter of Ine grants Hæha fifteen hides in Bradfield, fifteen in Basildon, twenty-five in Streatley, and eighty in *Earmundesleah*, and yet another Ine charter gives back to Hæha and Cilla forty-five hides at Basildon, Bradfield, and Streatley.[722]

Moving on from these diplomas linked to Hæha and Bradfield, Æthelbald of Mercia confirmed to Abingdon earlier king's gifts amounting to 250 hides on the west bank of the Thames and twenty on the east, and added twenty-seven hides in Watchfield and ten by Ginge Brook.[723] With these grants we are moving on to lands in which Abingdon had a provable later interest. The dealings with King Coenwulf suggest that Abingdon may have had a hundred hides at Sutton Courtenay,[724] whilst two diplomas of Coenwulf mention lands including core elements of the later Abingdon estate as recorded in the later tenth century and in *Domesday*. The first mentions 310 hides at Abingdon, ten at Longworth, eighteen at *Aclea*, *Northtuna*, and *Punningstoce*, fifteen at Sunningwell, ten at Eaton, ten at Sandford, thirty at Denchworth and Goosey, Culham 'with all the places pertaining to Abingdon', ten hides at Ginge, and ten at Leckhampstead.[725] The second does not in general give hidages but lists

Culham, Kennington, Hinksey, Cumnor, *Earmundesleah*, Eaton, Sunningwell, Sandford amounting to ten hides, Wootton, Ginge, Denchworth, Charney, Goosey, Fernham, Watchfield, Shrivenham, Bourton, Leckhampstead, Boxford, Welford with its appendages, Wickham with its fields as King Ceadwalla remitted, with the whole wood which is called Speen, Poughley, *Trinlech*, and Easton, with all minor plots pertaining to the aforementioned places.[726]

[721] cc. 2–6. See also c. 7, the 'testament' of Hæha, which grants Cilla forty-eight hides at Bradfield, fifty-five hides at Ashdown, eighty-three at *Earmundesleah*, a total—it says—of 183 hides.

[722] A narrative in MS B claims that Ine gave Sutton Courtenay to Abingdon; B11.

[723] c. 8.

[724] cc. 9, 11, B17–B18.

[725] c. 10. For comments, see *Charters of Abingdon Abbey*, pp. 38–41.

[726] c. 11. Only Bourton, Fernham, and Shrivenham appear in no other document in the Abingdon archive.

A charter in the name of Ecgberht of Wessex, which appears in both manuscripts of the *History*, records the king granting fifty hides at Marcham to Abingdon,[727] whilst a passage of narrative in MS B attributes to Offa the gift of Goosey.[728] In addition, some charters appearing in MS C record grants said to have passed to the abbey involving lands that were later part of the endowment.[729]

What then of the charters of the reform period? A charter in Eadred's name notes Alfred's removal of Abingdon and its appurtenances from the abbey, and restores Abingdon immediately and ten hides in Ginge, ten in Goosey, thirty in Longworth, and thirty in Cumnor after his death.[730] A charter in Eadwig's name mentions the restoration of land at Abingdon once given by Ceadwalla, whilst the equivalent in Edgar's name reproduces this passage and also confirms ten hides in Ginge, fifteen in Goosey, thirty in Longworth, and five in *Earmundesleah*.[731] All these places had appeared in the charters in Coenwulf's name. In contrast, documents recording individual grants to Abingdon, for example Eadwig's quite possibly authentic charter concerning Ginge, do not present the grants as restorations.[732]

It is impossible to come to any secure conclusion on the extent of the early endowment of Abingdon. A list such as appears in the charter in Coenwulf's name may be based on some early written source, may rest on oral tradition, or may have been at least largely a later invention.[733] The *History*'s claim that records survived the period of the Danes and Alfred is surely not a product of real knowledge but a deduction based on the existence of documents dated to before that period. That Æthelwold may have supported his efforts to obtain lands from the king with charters, including ones to laymen backed with a statement that the lands had passed to Abingdon, need not indicate that all those lands had been part of

[727] c. 12, B25–B26. For Culham, see also *Charters of Abingdon Abbey*, no. 10, probably forged after the revision of the *History*.

[728] See below, p. 248.

[729] cc. 15 (Lockinge), 16 (Wittenham). For charters only in MS B concerning lands said to have passed from donees to Abingdon, see B14 (Easton, Hampshire), B20 (Hurstbourne, Hampshire), B22 (lands in Gloucestershire), B24 (possibly Pangbourne, Berkshire), B36 (Farnborough, Warwickshire or Berkshire), B93 (Balking, Berkshire).

[730] c. 28. Abingdon is assessed at twenty hides, Ginge ten, Goosey ten, Longworth thirty, Cumnor thirty.

[731] cc. 37, 60; see also c. 98. See also c. 39 for Eadwig giving *Earmundesleah*. See *Charters of Abingdon Abbey*, pp. cii–cciv, clix, clxv–clxix, for the relevant estate histories.

[732] c. 42. See also c. 81 concerning Cumnor.

[733] See also *Charters of Abingdon Abbey*, pp. clxviii–clxix, 44.

the early endowment.[734] Only very unusually do we have relevant evidence from a source away from Abingdon, and even then it is not necessarily of a wholly reliable type. A charter in Edward the Elder's name confirms to the Old Minster, Winchester, fifty hides in Hurstbourne, Hampshire, which, it says, had been acquired by King Ecgberht from Bishop Hræthhun and the community of Abingdon in return for fifty hides in Marcham, Berkshire. However, it is possible that the Winchester diploma may be from Æthelwold's time, so its status as independent or as early evidence is questionable.[735]

Losses in the later ninth century

If the extent of the early endowment of Abingdon is uncertain so too must be any estimate of losses in the first Viking period. The earlier of the versions of the *History* does not blame losses on the Danes but rather on Alfred. Drawing on a charter in Eadred's name, it states that 'he took away from the aforesaid monastery the village in which the monastery is situated, called by the vernacular name Abingdon, with all its appendages, rendering inappropriate compensation to the victorious Lord for the victory which he had enjoyed'.[736] The reviser blamed both the Danes and Alfred for damaging the house and its lands. The Danes

> entirely drove out the monks and destroyed with hostile hand, leonine ferocity, and detestable greed the sacrosanct and venerable house of Abingdon, which so many holy kings and such authoritative men, of whom we have spoken above, had founded and endowed with various endowments, so that nothing is reported to have remained there besides the walls.[737]

Alfred

> indeed piled evils on evils, like Judas amongst the twelve, and violently took away from that monastery the village in which it is situated, commonly called Abingdon, with all its appendages, rendering inappropriate compensation to the victorious Lord for the victory which he had enjoyed against the defeated Danes at Ashdown.[738]

[734] For an example where there are surviving hints of an earlier connection, see *Charters of Abingdon Abbey*, pp. clxvi–clxvii, concerning Hurstbourne. More generally, see *Charters of Abingdon Abbey*, p. clxix.

[735] Sawyer, no. 358, *Charters of Abingdon Abbey*, p. 53.

[736] c. 17. [737] B37. [738] B40.

De abbatibus states that, in the time of Edward the Elder, the few monks who remained after the Danish attacks had only Culham, and the church of Wickham and the church of Cumnor.

Whilst it is very plausible that Abingdon's endowment suffered in the course of the wars between the kings of Wessex and the Danes, to tie these narratives to specific estates lost must be speculative because of the lack of secure early evidence concerning Abingdon's lands.[739] Moreover, the compilers of the *History* were regarding the ninth-century church very much in a twelfth- or thirteenth-century light. If one thinks of the church of Abingdon at the time of the Danish invasions as a royal minster, royal removal of lands looks rather different.[740] In royal eyes it may well have been justifiable, particularly if Danish attacks had disrupted the religious life or even destroyed the church itself.

The early tenth century

The earlier version of the *History* presents four charters of Æthelstan in favour of Abingdon, together with one of the noble Æthelstan 'senator', giving lands at Dumbleton, Aston Somerville, Shellingford, Sandford-on-Thames, Swinford, and Uffington.[741] All these places except for Aston Somerville were part of the later Abingdon endowment, but none of the charters can be accepted as genuine.[742]

The case of Dumbleton, furthermore, illustrates other problems that arise in dealing with even the charters presented in the *History* as making gifts directly to Abingdon. First, the charter specifies that the gift is to Abbot Cynath, making no mention of Abingdon as the recipient. Cynath was probably in fact abbot of Evesham.[743] Secondly, a sixteenth-century single-sheet copy of the charter, but not the versions in the *History*, includes as a postscript a confirmation of the land concerned to Bishop Osulf of Ramsbury, who had been

[739] Cf. D. N. Dumville, 'Ecclesiastical lands and the defence of Wessex in the first Viking-Age', in his *Wessex and England from Alfred to Edgar* (Woodbridge, 1992), pp. 29–54, esp. p. 40 n. 55, and R. Fleming, 'Monastic lands and England's defence in the Viking Age', *EHR*, c (1985), 247–65. Both the source criticism of the former and the general argument of the latter may be acceptable.

[740] See above, p. xcv, below, p. clxx, *Charters of Abingdon Abbey*, pp. ccviii–ccix.

[741] cc. 19–23.

[742] See below, p. ccvi. Swinford was probably included within the abbey's large manor of Cumnor in *Domesday*; *DB* i, fo. 58^{v}. The common land at Aston Somerville may have been perceived as part of the estate at Dumbleton, also explaining why the heading of the section only mentions Dumbleton.

[743] See above, p. xcv.

granted it by Abbot Cynath.[744] Thirdly, a narrative in the earlier version of the *History* says that 'this village was given by King Æthelstan to that monastery but, as we have said above, was afterwards taken away by others'. Unfortunately its account of the loss of the land may have been recorded on the lost folio between cc. 101 and 102; the revised *History* says that it was given to Ælfric by Wulfric Spot, whose predecessors had unjustly taken it from the abbey. According to a royal charter in 1002, Dumbleton had returned to King Æthelred when a woman forfeited it for fornication. It then passed to Abingdon through the will of Archbishop Ælfric, to whom King Æthelred had granted it.[745] It may be that this pattern of gift, loss, and restoration is correct, but doubts may be raised by the lack of authenticity of Æthelstan's charter, and it is possible that the land only came to Abingdon rather later than Æthelstan's reign.

MS B adds a large number of early tenth-century charters recording grants to laymen, who, it was stated, donated them to Abingdon. Whilst some may have passed to Abingdon, they may have done so later than these passages suggest.[746] For example, MS B includes a charter of Edward the Elder recording his grant of Hardwell to Tata son of Æthelhun, a gift which an accompanying passage says Tata passed to Abingdon. Neither this charter nor this narrative appears in the earlier version of the *History*, which attributes the gift of Hardwell to the will of Eadwine, probably the ealdorman of Sussex, whilst *De abbatibus* attributes the gift to a man called 'Edwi' in the time of Abbot Ordric, 1052–66.[747] This later gift by Eadwine or Edwi, not an immediate transfer by Tata, would have brought the charter to Abingdon.

Kings may have continued to exploit lands possibly once associated with the church. For example, King Edmund granted Culham to the royal lady Ælfhild.[748] The reviser of the *History* omitted this charter and claimed that Edmund's grant had only been for life, with reversion to the monks' own use, but this is likely to reflect the

[744] *Charters of Abingdon Abbey*, no. 22.

[745] cc. 103–5.

[746] B53–B54 may be one instance where the routine note that the gift passed to Abingdon is in fact correct. For lands that may never have passed to Abingdon, see e.g. B60–B61, B79–B80. See also below, p. 93 n. 215, on cc. 57–8 in MS C; and note *Charters of Abingdon Abbey*, no. 43.

[747] B44–B45, c. 108, *CMA* ii. 282. For gifts that later passed to Abingdon, see also B56–B59.

[748] c. 25; see also B69 concerning *Earmundesleah*, which may earlier have been an Abingdon possession.

reviser's concerns rather than tenth-century arrangements.[749] Overall, the evidence for tenth-century royal or other endowment of Abingdon before the mid-940s is thin. We may sympathize with the person who composed the passage in the Abingdon copy of the *Chronicle* of John of Worcester stating that he knew nothing certain of what happened to the monastery between the death of Coenwulf and the reign of Æthelstan.[750]

Endowment in the period of Æthelwoldian reform

According to the *Life of St Æthelwold*, when Eadred came to the throne in 946, monastic religion at Abingdon was 'neglected and ruined, its buildings poor, and its estate consisted of only forty hides of land. The remainder of the estate, which lies adjacent to it and consists of a further hundred hides, was the king's possession and under his royal control.'[751] Forty hides, although small by later standards, was still an endowment of some significance. Eadred then gave 'his royal possession in Abingdon, that is the hundred hides, with excellent buildings, to the abbot and brethren to increase their everyday provisions, and he gave them much monetary help from his royal treasury. His mother sent them presents on an even more lavish scale.'[752] Then when Osgar was made abbot, the *Life* tells us, 'the place was enriched by the gift of six hundred and more hides'.[753]

What of the *History* and its charter material? Whilst proceeding chronologically, I shall classify gifts in various ways. I distinguish between gifts in the *Domesday* core area of Abingdon's endowment, Berkshire and Oxfordshire, and gifts elsewhere. I also distinguish between gifts recorded in charters directly to Abingdon and those said to have been given to Abingdon by a charter's beneficiary. Amongst the latter group, I separate those appearing in MS C

[749] B64. See also Thacker, 'Æthelwold', pp. 46–7.

[750] John of Worcester, *Chronicle*, ii. 610: 'Post cuius discessum quid huic loci contigerit usque ad gloriosi principis Æthelstani imperium quia nusquam certi quicquam addiscere potui, suo meus stilus caruit officio.'

[751] Wulfstan, *Life of Æthelwold*, c. 11, ed. Lapidge and Winterbottom, pp. 18–20; the passage is copied in B84.

[752] Wulfstan, *Life of Æthelwold*, c. 11, ed. Lapidge and Winterbottom, p. 20; the passage is copied below, p. 296, making an explicit association with Eadred's charter, c. 28, B85.

[753] Wulfstan, *Life of Æthelwold*, c. 21, ed. Lapidge and Winterbottom, p. 36. By the standards of medieval chroniclers' figures the number seems a reasonably accurate one when compared with the gifts made to Abingdon in the time of Æthelwold and Osgar, as listed below, pp. cxxxix–cxlii.

from those appearing only in MS B. In both cases I note whether there is an additional reason to believe the statement that the land passed to Abingdon.

Royal grants directly to Æthelwold's house probably began under Eadred. Whilst there is no explicit bequest to Abingdon in his will, and his great charter recording his restorations to Abingdon is quite possible a forgery, the latter may support the *Life*'s statement concerning his generosity to Abingdon.[754] Eadred was

> to have full enjoyment of the appended lands which pertain to that village in diverse places, that is Ginge (ten hides), Goosey (ten hides), Longworth (thirty hides), Cumnor (thirty hides), with the permission of the aforenamed abbot and the brothers subjected to him, for necessary purposes through the days of my life. When, though, the period of my life has passed, these with all their accessories are to be brought back perpetually to that village and subjected to the aforesaid monastery.

That such lands are also recorded as being granted by Eadwig or Edgar in charters of those kings may, but need not, show that Eadred's gift did not take effect.[755] Æthelwold, in his vernacular account of monasticism, criticized Eadred's brother and successor Eadwig for, amongst other faults, 'distributing the lands of the holy Church to rapacious strangers', but there is no such criticism in the Abingdon *History*.[756] Rather Eadwig is presented as having made grants to the monastery, involving Abingdon, five hides at *Earmundesleah*, twenty at Hinksey, Seacourt, and Wytham, and ten at Ginge, as well as sixty yokes of woodland at Hawkridge to provide wood for building the abbey church.[757] Our lack of certainty concerning the early endowment of the church makes it hard to tell how far such grants were restorations, how far they were new gifts, how far they came from royal lands, how far the interests of other parties were affected.[758]

[754] The heading to c. 28, Eadred's charter, includes twenty hides at Abingdon, whereas the charter specifies no hidage for that place. The rest of the lands granted totalled eighty hides, so the heading has made the total one hundred, matching the amount that Eadred is said to have given in the *Life of Æthelwold*.

[755] See Thacker, 'Æthelwold', p. 52.

[756] See above, p. cxv.

[757] See cc. 37–43; see notes to the appropriate sections for problems of authenticity with these charters. Another charter, a quite skilful fabrication not present in the *History* but preserved in a 16th-century copy of a lost single sheet, records King Eadwig giving twenty hides in Tadmarton to Abingdon in 956; *Charters of Abingdon Abbey*, no. 68, and see also above, p. lxviii. Note also c. 44 for Eadwig giving permission for Æthelwold's exchange of Curbridge for Kennington.

[758] See above, p. cxxxiii; Thacker, 'Æthelwold', p. 53.

Giving accelerated under Edgar, although the authenticity of some of his diplomas remains a problem. His gifts include more distant lands from the monastery, but let us start with grants of lands in Berkshire and Oxfordshire. One of his early actions, in 958, may have been to grant ten hides in Ginge, fifteen in Goosey, thirty in Longworth, and five in *Earmundesleah*. This may have been a reiteration of grants possibly made by Eadred and Eadwig, as already mentioned.[759] He also made the following gifts:

Chapter	*Place*	*Hidage*	*Date*	*Charter authenticity*
62	Drayton	20	960	probably authentic
66	Hendred	3	962	probably authentic
73	Hendred	10	964	suspicious
75	Marcham	50	965	suspicious
77	Denchworth	2	965	suspicious
79	Fyfield	25	968	possibly authentic
81	Cumnor	30	968	possibly authentic
83	Hanney	10	968	possibly authentic
85	Oare	10	968	possibly authentic
86	Beedon	5	965	suspicious

Let us now move on to gifts of more distant lands. Charters in Edgar's name record him making the following grants:[760]

Chapter	*Place*	*Hidage*	*Date*	*Charter authenticity*
61	Bedwyn, Wiltshire	73	958	very suspicious
64	Hurstbourne, Hampshire	50	961	probably genuine
65	Southampton, Hampshire	various rights	962	probably genuine
67	Ringwood, Hampshire	22	961	uncertain
69	Burbage, Wiltshire	20	961	uncertain
70	Easthall, Sussex	5	963	probably authentic

In addition, Ælfgifu, a woman of royal descent, bequeathed Chesham, Buckinghamshire, to Abingdon between 966 and 975.[761]

Turning now to gifts for which the *History* provides charters supplemented by the statement that the beneficiary gave the land to Abingdon, all those appearing in MS C concern lands in Berkshire or

[759] c. 60; see above, p. cxxxviii.

[760] See above, p. cxxx, on his grant of Washington to Æthelwold.

[761] *Anglo-Saxon Wills*, ed. Whitelock, no. 8, pp. 118–19. The will survives in the cartulary of St Swithun's, Winchester.

Oxfordshire, and in all cases a definite link can be established between the abbey and the lands concerned. The gifts may be summarized as follows:

Chapter	*Donor*	*Donee*	*Place*	*Hides*	*Date*	*Charter authenticity*
57–8[762]	Edmund	Sæthryth noble matron	Winkfield	11	942	authentic
34–5	Eadred	Wulfric thegn[763]	Chieveley	25	951	authentic
44	Eadwig	Brihthelm priest	Kennington	—	956	authentic
45–6	Eadwig	Ælfhere ealdorman	Cuddesdon	20	956	suspicious
47–8	Eadwig	Eadric thegn	Welford	22	956	authentic
49–50	Eadwig	Ælfwine thegn	Milton	15	956	probably authentic
51–2	Eadwig	Ælheah thegn	Buckland	10	956	possibly authentic
53	Eadwig	Ælfric thegn	Bayworth	25	956	authentic
54	Eadwig	Byrhtnoth thegn	Tadmarton	10	956	probably authentic
55	Eadwig	Beorhtric thegn	Tadmarton	5	956	probably authentic
56	Eadwig	Byrhtnoth noble	Tadmarton	5	956	authentic
137	Eadwig[764]	Eadric thegn	Leckhampstead	10	—	modified
139	Edgar	Æthelsige chamberlain	Sparsholt, etc.	10	963	modified
88	Edgar	Wulfstan thegn	Whistley	10	968	probably authentic
90	Edgar	Ælfwine thegn	Boxford	10	968	suspicious

[762] As a charter of Edmund, this is out of chronological order in MS C. It may be so situated because the compiler believed that Sæthryth gave the land to Abingdon in Æthelwold's time. In MS B, it appears among the charters of Edmund, B78.

[763] The earlier version of *History* did not specify that Wulfric gave this land to Abingdon; the reviser spelt this out, B100.

[764] MS B includes both this shortened version of the charter and a full version that has King Edmund as the grantor; B72, B277. *Charters of Abingdon Abbey*, p. 156, states of the full version that the charter 'seems to be authentic'. I here include it under Eadwig because

It is hard to tell whether the donees really were the people responsible for passing the lands to Abingdon,[765] although notably in the cases of Welford and Leckhampstead it is specified that they made their grants to Abingdon when they were dying, whilst Ælfric is said to have made Abingdon heir to Bayworth after his death. In these cases additional notes or records may have underlain the *History*'s more precise statements. On the other hand, the case of Sparsholt may warn against acceptance of the *History*'s routine statements. The *History* contains a charter of Edgar recording his gift of Sparsholt to Æthelsige his chamberlain, but makes clear that the estate passed to Abingdon only in the mid-eleventh century.[766]

Similar problems of chronology may apply to grants recorded only in MS B even when there is an association between Abingdon and the lands concerned. Nevertheless, the grants may usefully be summarized as follows:

Chapter	*Donor*	*Donee*	*Place*	*Hides*	*Date*	*Charter authenticity*
B87	Eadred	Wulfric thegn	Stanmore[767]	10	947/8	probably authentic
B91	Eadred	Wulfric *miles*	Denchworth	5	947	authentic
B97	Eadred	Wulfric thegn	Welford	18	949	authentic
B99	Eadred	Ælfsige thegn and wife Eadgifu	*Æscesburh*[768]	33	953	authentic
B107	Eadred/ Eadwig	Wulfric thegn	Boxford	10	958?	questionable
B123	Eadwig	Beorhtric thegn	Hendred	10	955/6	probably authentic
B133	Eadwig	Ælfric royal kinsman	Hanney	20	956	authentic
B137	Eadwig	Ælfsige thegn	Benham	25	956	authentic

my concern is the earlier version of the *History*'s presentation of the building up of the endowment.

[765] An exception is Brihthelm's exchange of Kennington with Æthelwold; c. 44.

[766] cc. 138–9.

[767] Stanmore was almost certainly included in Abingdon's holding in Beedon in *Domesday*; *DB* i, fo. 58^{v}; *Charters of Abingdon Abbey*, p. 174.

[768] i.e. Uffington, see below, p. 44 n. 112.

Chapter	*Donor*	*Donee*	*Place*	*Hides*	*Date*	*Charter authenticity*
B154	Eadwig	Æthelnoth thegn	Fyfield	13	956	authentic
B159	Eadwig	Wulfric thegn	Charlton	5	956	authentic
B165	Eadwig	Eadric thegn	Longworth	30	958	probably authentic
B167	Eadwig	Eadwold thegn	Drayton	10	958	probably authentic
B170	Eadwig	Cynric cup-bearer	*Cern*[769]	2	958	probably authentic
B172	Eadwig	Wulfric thegn	Denchworth	5	958	probably authentic
B190	Edgar	Brihtheah deacon	Kingston	7	970	probably authentic

In addition MS B includes charters for places in Berkshire and Oxfordshire for which there is no other evidence of Abingdon interest: in order of appearance, Curridge, Compton, Barkham, and *Weonfelda* granted by Eadred; Padworth granted by Eadwig; and Aston Upthorpe, Ardington, Ducklington granted by Edgar, as well as various of the estates restored to Wulfric Cufing in 960.[770]

As for places outside Berkshire and Oxfordshire, notably fewer have any other connection to Abingdon:

Chapter	*Donor*	*Donee*	*Place*	*Hides*	*Date*	*Charter authenticity*
B148	Eadwig	Ælfhere *senator*	Wormleighton, Warwickshire[771]	10	956	probably authentic
B194	Edgar	Eadwine thegn	Moredon, Wiltshire[772]	20	962	probably authentic

[769] These could be the two hides which *Domesday* records Abingdon holding in Pusey; see below, p. 325 n. 239.

[770] B103, B105, B109, B111, B152, B157, B185, B186, B193, B195. It cannot be told whether it is significant that Barkham and Compton both had a *TRE* tenant named Ælmer; *DB* i, fos. 57^r, 61^r. The two references may be to the same man, and he could also be identified with the Ælmer who held land in Charlton and Buckland, the latter probably as a tenant of Abingdon; *DB* i, fos. 57^r, 59^v. It is conceivable that he or his predecessors had had a tenurial relationship with Abingdon for the other lands but one hidden by *Domesday*. Alternatively he could be an Abingdon tenant who deposited diplomas in the abbey, perhaps at the time of the Conquest; see above, p. cxxix.

[771] In fact the land probably passed to Abingdon by grant of King Æthelred, below, p. cxlvii.

[772] See below, p. cxliii, for the connection between Moredon and Abingdon.

In addition MS B includes records gifts of places outside Berkshire and Oxfordshire for which there is no other evidence of Abingdon interest: in order of appearance, Washington in Sussex given by Eadred;[773] Pyrford in Surrey, Annington in Sussex, Church Stowe in Northamptonshire, *Æscmere* in Hampshire given by Eadwig; Linslade in Buckinghamshire and *Hamstede*, perhaps also in Buckinghamshire, given by Edgar.[774]

Reduction of estates after 975

The question of whether Abingdon ever received and held those estates for which there is no evidence of an Abingdon connection apart from the testimony, often formulaic and sometimes demonstrably flawed, of the revised version of the *History* is closely tied to the question of losses following the death of Edgar. There are some explicitly recorded losses. A charter of Æthelred states that

> My father King Edgar, whilst he was reigning, granted some of the lands to almighty Christ and his mother St Mary for the monastery which is called Abingdon, for the redemption of his soul, that is Bedwyn with everything pertaining to it, Hurstbourne with all its appendages, Burbage and all the revenues belonging to it. These lands were forthwith violently taken away from the aforementioned holy monastery according to the decision and order of all the leading men, and at their command were subjected to my power. Whether they did this justly or unjustly, they themselves may know. Then, when my brother left this wretched world and received the reward of never-ending life predestined for him by God, I, with Christ's assent, received lordship both of the royal lands and at the same time those pertaining to kings' sons.[775]

This removal of lands by Edward the martyr is the only Abingdon loss for which there is specific and definitely authentic early evidence. Another case may involve land at Moredon, which a probably authentic charter of Edgar records that king granting to his thegn, Eadwine. It then apparently passed to Abingdon.[776] Next, a dubious charter of Æthelred, which may be a considerably later fabrication or a contemporary production, states that

[773] See above, p. cxxx, for the link of this estate to Æthelwold.

[774] B95 (on the connection of which to Æthelwold see above, p. cxxx), B146, B150, B155 (and *Charters of Abingdon Abbey*, no. 62, surviving in a 16th-century copy), B168, B188, B189. See also B191, B192, B222.

[775] c. 99 (p. 150).

[776] B194.

a certain knight named Ælfgar, my reeve and favourite, unjustly acquired a village of the most holy mother Mary of the monastery of Abingdon, named by the inhabitants Moredon, twenty hides, in the time that is of Abbot Eadwine, with my consent although unjustly, and he gave it to his wife Ælfgifu as a hereditary gift of dower.[777]

Such an instance may be taken to support the statement in the earlier version of the *History* that in the time of Abbot Eadwine (985–90) 'the monastery of Abingdon, which had been extremely rich a little before, now met with loss of a great many of its possessions', although other evidence is lacking.[778] *De abbatibus* tells us that the Vikings completely destroyed Abingdon in Æthelred's time, but it is significant that such an attack is mentioned by neither version of the *History*, nor are there any stated losses of lands resulting from these attacks.[779]

So much for direct evidence for losses. There is also the question of the fate of lands for which there is strong evidence that Abingdon was given them before the death of Edgar, but which did not form part of the *Domesday* endowment. Most notable are Edgar's large grants of lands distant from Abingdon.[780] We have already seen that Bedwyn and Burbage in Wiltshire and Hurstbourne in Hampshire, amounting to 143 hides, were taken away by Edward the martyr on the grounds that Edgar should not have granted them as he did.[781] Also lost by 1066 were lands and rights in Southampton, twenty-two hides at Ringwood in Hampshire, and five hides in Easthall, Sussex. In addition, lands in at least one of the charters to an individual rather than directly to Abingdon do seem to have passed to the abbey and then been lost, those at Moredon, as mentioned above. Even though restored to Abingdon by Æthelred, they were not held by the abbey in 1066.

If other lands mentioned in charters to individuals really did pass to Abingdon, the scale of the losses between 975 and 1066 was very

777 See below, p. 160.

778 See below, p. 140.

779 *CMA* ii. 280. *Charters of Abingdon Abbey*, p. xlii, concludes that an attack on Abingdon in the first decade of the 11th century cannot be ruled out, but any disruption must have been short-lived.

780 Although some of the charters concerned are questionable, others are genuine, and questions over charter authenticity need not lead to denial that the grants were actually made. See also *Charters of Abingdon Abbey*, p. cliii: 'King Edgar was absurdly generous to the abbey, bestowing upon the community farflung estates in Sussex and Hampshire; other donors in Abingdon's golden age may have poured out similarly inconvenient largesse. Over the course of little more than a century this complex accumulation of property was transformed into a compact and manageable endowment in Berkshire and Oxfordshire.'

781 For this and the remainder of this paragraph, see also above, p. cxxxix.

considerable. However, we have already seen that the routine statements that the grantee passed the lands to Abingdon need to be treated with scepticism, and have concluded that at least in the case of MS B the routine statements by themselves should not be deemed sufficient evidence of an Abingdon connection.

What explanations, then, can be given for loss of the estates which we know were in Abingdon's possession? One is depredation, quite possibly what the lay claimants of such lands would have considered justified seizure following Edgar's unjustified favour to monasteries, just as Edward the martyr did with Bedwyn, Burbage, and Hurstbourne. Another is loss through disputes in court under a less favourable regime. It is very plausible that, following the death of Edgar, Abingdon, like other monasteries, lost lands to local landowners in disputes in or out of court, or failed to receive lands that had been promised to them.[782]

Another possibility is of deliberate retrenchment of the estate, alienating more distant properties whilst retaining the Berkshire and Oxfordshire core for reasons of convenience.[783] Alienation of Church lands was condemned by the reformers. Æthelwold, in his vernacular account of monasticism, implored his successors to increase the observance of the holy rule, and went on

> Nor is any one of them to presume through the devil's prompting or through any avarice to diminish God's patrimony or with any ill-will to seek how it may be diminished, either in estates or in any other possessions, lest through poverty and penury the fire of holy religion should become lukewarm and grow completely cold.[784]

In practice, nevertheless, lands were granted away, perhaps with a preference for exchange rather than sale or simple gift.[785] Leases for a set period were acceptable, but might be repeatedly extended or lead to the loss of lands:

> Stigand, bishop of the city of Winchester, who then indeed had care of the archbishopric of Canterbury (for with its ruler dead that place lacked governance), as a crafty pleader extracted from Spearhafoc the land called

[782] See also *Charters of Abingdon Abbey*, pp. clxviii, clxxii.

[783] See ibid., esp. p. clxv; note also Clarke, *English Nobility*, pp. 53–60, who argues that such consolidation was a hallmark of long-established estates.

[784] *Councils and Synods*, i. 152; also i. 153–4, addressed to abbesses. See further *Charters of Abingdon Abbey*, p. cxlvii. Note also e.g. *Wulfstan's Canon Law Collection*, ed. J. E. Cross and A. Hamer (Cambridge, 1999), p. 84.

[785] See *Charters of Abingdon Abbey*, p. cxlviii.

Cerney, situated in Gloucestershire, to be entrusted to him for a set time. As repayment, at the time of the restitution he would add in perpetual gift to the church of Abingdon his own property of Aston, a village neighbouring Lewknor. But when he had acquired what he sought, he neither restored what had been entrusted to him, nor discharged the payment for what had been entrusted.[786]

However, the evidence for a policy of retrenchment of distant estates is limited.[787] If one concentrates on lands either given directly to Abingdon or for which further evidence for an Abingdon link exists, the number of estates is not large, even if the hidage is.[788] It is, moreover, notable that the majority of these distant estates were the subject of known disputes: Bedwyn, Burbage, Cerney, Hurstbourne, Moredon.[789] Given our limited knowledge of pre-Conquest disputes, this is a significant number, suggesting perhaps that other unknown disputes led to further losses of lands: the disputes involving all but Cerney are known only from charters of Æthelred with their characteristic narrative sections and such charters cease as a source of evidence for Abingdon after Æthelred. Comparison with other abbeys too suggests the possibility of extensive loss through disputes.[790] Burton had lost much of its original 1002 endowment by 1066, and the cause may well have been lay depredation; it may be significant that the *Life and Miracles of Saint Modwenna* records the saint's vengeance against a violator of the monastery whom *Domesday Book* shows to have held lands that had formed part of the abbey's

[786] See below, p. 196. *Charters of Abingdon Abbey*, pp. clxiv–clxv, takes this as part of the policy of relinquishing more distant properties. However, leasing was not the same as relinquishing, and the case in fact might better be taken as evidence for the unplanned loss of distant properties, at least in terms of complete as opposed to temporary alienation from the church. See below, pp. cliv–clv, for the lack of later evidence that there was a preference for leasing more distant estates.

[787] Analysis of the *Domesday* tenants of the distant estates that the *History* links to Abingdon does not reveal to me any significant pattern, except perhaps that several were associated with the Godwine family, an association that is not necessarily surprising given the extent of their estates. See esp. *DB* i, fo. 28^r, for Earl Gyrth holding Washington; fo. 32^r, for Harold holding Pyrford from King Edward; fo. 39^r, for Tostig holding Ringwood. There is no evidence to explain this pattern in terms of the Godwine family using Abingdon as a deposit for their charters (see *Charters of Abingdon Abbey*, p. cxlii) or of them having seized the lands from Abingdon.

[788] See above, p. cxxxix.

[789] cc. 99, 102, 124.

[790] Miller, *Ely*, pp. 24–5, states that the widest extent of that abbey's lands was in the first decades of the eleventh century. *Domesday Book* reveals that by 1066 there had been losses in Essex, Cambridgeshire, and Norfolk, although Miller does not provide an explanation for those losses.

early endowment.[791] At Abingdon the loss of distant estates may have been the result of external pressure rather than internal planning.

Acquisitions between 975 and 1066

Although Edgar's problematic grants of the lands associated with the royal family, together with his twenty hides at Ringwood, are of an exceptionally large scale, grants outside Berkshire and Oxfordshire did not cease with his death. When Æthelred reversed his policy of taking lands from the Church, his charter for Abingdon announced that he had retained Bedwyn, Burbage, and Hurstbourne but gave in compensation Wormleighton in Warwickshire and Cerney in Gloucestershire, as well as Farnborough, Berkshire, and an unidentified place called Perry.[792] He also restored twenty hides at Moredon, Wiltshire, and a small estate at Cricklade in the same county.[793] Archbishop Ælfric bequeathed lands in Dumbleton, Gloucestershire, where Abingdon had lands in *Domesday Book*.[794] Notes in the *History* record that women named Ælfgifu and Eadflæd had bequeathed lands at *Bulthesworthe*, Chalgrave in Bedfordshire, and Hillesden in Buckinghamshire, to Abingdon, although these were not retained by 1066.[795] Likewise absent from the Abingdon *Domesday* holding are three hides at Myton, Warwickshire.[796] Eadwine of Caddington bequeathed to Abingdon land at *Pirian*, which he had bought from the abbey; the context in the will suggests that it may have been in Bedfordshire or Hertfordshire.[797] The overall impression is that Abingdon continued to be happy to receive grants outside Berkshire and Oxfordshire, although their scale was in general smaller than before 975. Such grants are not dissimilar from those received after

[791] Geoffrey of Burton, *Life and Miracles of St Modwenna*, c. 44, ed. R. J. Bartlett (OMT, 2002), p. 184.

[792] c. 99, on which see Keynes, *Diplomas*, pp. 177–8; see also c. 101 concerning Cerney. Wormleighton was no longer an Abingdon estate in 1066.

[793] c. 102.

[794] cc. 104–5, *DB* i, fo. 166^r.

[795] cc. 106–7.

[796] c. 113, B246.

[797] S. Keynes, 'A lost cartulary of St Albans Abbey', *ASE*, xxii (1993), 253–79, at p. 276; Sawyer, no. 1517. Eadwine's will can be dated to *c.*1050. *Charters of Abingdon Abbey*, p. 507, takes *Pirian* to be the same place which Æthelred had granted to Abingdon in 999; see below, p. 152. If so, the land had been given to Abingdon at the end of the 10th century, alienated or lost, and then restored by Eadwine, although we cannot tell whether Eadwine's bequest came into effect. However, it should be noted that *Pirian*, or Perry, is a not uncommon place-name and it is possible that we are dealing with two places of the same name.

the Conquest.[798] Again this weighs against ideas of a policy of retrenchment.

Kings also continued to give lands in Berkshire and Oxfordshire, and these were much better retained:

Chapter	*Donor*	*Place*	*Hidage*	*Date*	*Charter authenticity*
92	Edward	Kingston	7	975 × 978	uncertain
B219[799]	Æthelred	Arncott	2	983	probably authentic
B231[800]	Æthelred	Drayton	3	1000	probably
		Sutton	2		spurious
114	Cnut	Lyford; minster of St Martin, Oxford, and land[801]	2	1032	probably authentic
117	Harthacnut	Farnborough	10	1042	uncertain[802]
121	Queen Edith	Lewknor	—[803]	reign of Confessor	—
132	Edward	Sandford	4	1054	spurious
133	Edward	Chilton	5	1052	probably spurious
135	Edward	Leverton	8	1050	probably spurious

In at least these last three cases it is difficult to tell whether the lands really were granted to Abingdon before the Conquest, or whether after the Conquest the abbot succeeded in persuading the king to allow them to the abbey; only in the case of Sandford did *Domesday Book* attribute clear title to the abbey in 1066.[804] The *History* also

[798] In the better-documented period after 1066 we know that there were considerable difficulties in retaining grants such as that of Hill in Warwickshire; see vol. ii. 26, 136, and *Rotuli Curiæ Regis*, ed. F. Palgrave (2 vols., London, 1835), i. 70, 240–1, ii. 143, 347; *Curia Regis Rolls*, i. 139, 257, 300, 399, 456, 463.

[799] This charter may have appeared on a missing folio of MS C.

[800] This charter may have appeared on a missing folio of MS C.

[801] See also J. Blair, 'Saint Frideswide's monastery: Problems and possibilities', *Oxoniensia*, liii (1988), 221–58, at p. 226, for Abingdon's possible temporary acquisition of St Frideswide's in Cnut's time.

[802] On the problem of whether this constituted a new gift, see below, p. 185 n. 415.

[803] *DB* i, fo. 156^{v}, gives the hidage as seventeen in 1086.

[804] *DB* i, fo. 59^{r}, states that Blæcmann held Chilton from Harold 'in alodio' and held Leverton 'in feudo'; in the case of Leverton Blæcmann's lord is not made explicit, although it may be implied that it was the abbot, from whom the 1086 tenant held. See *DB* i, fo. 156^{v} for Sandford.

records grants by people other than kings. Abbot Osgar purchased twenty hides at Kingston from Ealdorman Ælfhere.[805] Eadwine, probably the ealdorman of Sussex, bequeathed lands at Beedon and Hardwell.[806] A woman named Eadflæd gave land at Wickham and Winkfield, and the monk Godric Cild gave land at Sparsholt.[807] *De abbatibus*, but not the *History*, records a gift of Garsington, Oxfordshire, and an unidentified *Hamestede*.[808]

The revised *History* also continues to include charters to individuals, sometimes supplemented by the statement that the beneficiary gave the land to Abingdon. Some concern places with a further association to Abingdon:

Chapter	*Donor*	*Donee*	*Place*	*Hides*	*Date*	*Charter authenticity*
B212	Edward	Ælfstan bishop	Kingston	13	975 × 978	possibly authentic
B224	Æthelred	Wulfgar	Drayton and Sutton	3 1.5	983	authentic
B228	Æthelred	Beorhtric thegn	Leverton	8	984	authentic
B229	Æthelred	Leofwine thegn	Wootton	10	985	authentic
B225	Æthelred	Wulfric thegn	Dumbleton	2.5	995	authentic
104	Æthelred	Ælfric archbishop	Dumbleton	24	1002	probably authentic
140	Æthelred	Leofric thegn	Whitchurch	10	1012	uncertain
B239	Æthelred	Byrhtwold bishop	Chilton	5	1015	probably authentic
B271	Edward	Godwine earl	Sandford	4	1050	authentic

For others there is no further evidence of a link to Abingdon.[809]

805 c. 93, hidage possible altered. The *History* places the transaction in the reign of Edward the martyr.

806 c. 108.

807 cc. 107, 138–9.

808 *CMA* ii. 282; *Charters of Abingdon Abbey*, p. 583 (xi).

809 B43 (Sevington, Wiltshire), B223 (Charlton, Berkshire), B226 (*Osanleia*), B227 (Ardley, Oxfordshire), B230 (Benson, Oxfordshire), B232 (Little Haseley, Oxfordshire), B237 (Waltham St Lawrence, Berkshire).

The Domesday TRE endowment

Domesday Book allows the following estimates of the annual values of Abingdon lands in 1066:

County	*Approx. annual income*	*Hidage*[810]
Berkshire	*c.*£380–420	just over 510
Oxfordshire	slightly over £60	—
Gloucestershire	£12	—[811]

Domesday thus suggests a total income *TRE* of about £450–90. Abingdon was probably the eighth wealthiest monastery in England.[812]

The great bulk of Abingdon estates was in Berkshire, in which county it was the largest landholder. There was particular concentration in west Berkshire. This region included the valuable northern areas, notably the Vale of the White Horse, which had the best land in the county, as well as the less rich area of the central downlands.[813] The core of the estate was Hormer hundred, in a loop of the Thames, where the abbey was the only significant, or perhaps the only, landholder in 1066.[814] *Domesday* records its division into two huge manors, Barton and Cumnor, whilst mentioning other settlements within those holdings.

The abbey also had significant lands in Oxfordshire. It had more property in Oxford than in Wallingford, Berkshire.[815] Of its seven Oxfordshire manors, three were close to Oxford, Lower Arncott north-east of Oxford, Lewknor in the east of the county, and

[810] I give rounded figures and ranges because of the problems of making precise *Domesday* calculations from incomplete or problematic information: note e.g. the absence of a *ualet* for Chilton, *DB* i, fo. 59^r; the absence of an entry for Culham; disputed possession of Fawler; lack of clarity as to whether the value of mills, etc. is included in the totals, on which see H. C. Darby, *Domesday England* (Cambridge, 1977), p. 210.

[811] On the possibility of an Abingdon interest in the Wiltshire borough of Cricklade, see *Charters of Abingdon Abbey*, pp. 530–1.

[812] See vol. ii, p. lxxv for this position in 1086; that in 1066 was probably similar.

[813] See *Domesday Geography of South-East England*, ed. Darby and Campbell, pp. 261, 282–3. See also *Archaeology at Barton Court Farm*, ed. Miles. Note also below, p. 240, on Abingdon being 'surrounded with the richest farmlands, flourishing meadows, abundant fields, and milk-giving herds'. Whether or not this is a topos, it may also represent observation.

[814] The exception may be Shippon, on which see *DB* i, fo 58^v; vol. ii. 24.

[815] Note that the position of Abingdon properties in later medieval Oxford shows that they were almost all in what seems to have been the Anglo-Saxon *burh*, suggesting early acquisition; Blair, *Anglo-Saxon Oxfordshire*, pp. 160–1.

Tadmarton and Barford St Michael in its north.[816] The Gloucestershire estates were limited to Dumbleton and the disputed land of South Cerney.

The immediate impact of the Conquest, before the coming of the first Norman appointed abbot, Adelelm, involved the loss of some estates with Henry de Ferrers seizing Fyfield and Kingston.[817] Neither was to be regained by the abbey. However, by 1086 the *Domesday* annual income had risen to between £510 and £540.[818]

Rights and income other than land

Information on sources of revenue other than land are scarce. Occasional wills not included in the *History* mention money gifts, with, for example, a man called Æthelwold leaving twenty mancuses of gold to Abingdon for his brothers.[819] *Domesday Book* supplements the *History* and other narrative sources concerning other secular resources.[820] Thus it shows the importance of fisheries and woods in the area.[821] Mills were a particularly significant area for investment, the scale of which is not revealed by the *History* but by *Domesday*: it records Abingdon having twenty-seven mills in Berkshire, four in Oxfordshire, and one in Gloucestershire. The dispute over Cuddesdon mill included in the revised version of the *History* shows the efforts that could be expended on protecting these valuable sources of revenue. *De abbatibus* reveals new mills being built below the *curia*, and a new channel for a millstream being dug in Æthelwold's time, uncovering the Black Cross in the process.[822] The *History* also reveals some commercial rights, in a charter of Edgar concerning Southampton and in the narrative concerning the duty of one hundred herrings to be paid from each ship of the citizens of Oxford to the monks' cellarer for passing through a newly cut channel of the

[816] Note that *Domesday* does not mention Culham; see below, p. clxi.

[817] See below, pp. 222–4; see Hudson, 'Abbey of Abingdon', pp. 190, 196.

[818] See vol. ii, p. lxxiv. For general changes of value in Berkshire and Oxfordshire, see also *Domesday Geography of South-East England*, ed. Darby and Campbell, pp. 209, 260; for hidage reduction in Berkshire, ibid., pp. 249–50. It is possible that Abingdon acquired Hoe Benham, Berkshire, after the Conquest, although it is not clear at what date; vol. ii. 156 n. 378.

[819] *Anglo-Saxon Wills*, ed. Whitelock, no. 12; see also no. 10, for Ealdorman Æthelmær giving two pounds to Abingdon. See below, p. clxix, for gifts of ornaments.

[820] On woodland, meadows, pastures, fisheries, and mills in the area, see *Domesday Geography of South-East England*, ed. Darby and Campbell, pp. 262–71.

[821] For woods being mentioned in the *History*, see e.g. c. 2.

[822] *CMA* ii. 270, 278–9, on which see Biddle *et al.*, 'Early history', p. 47.

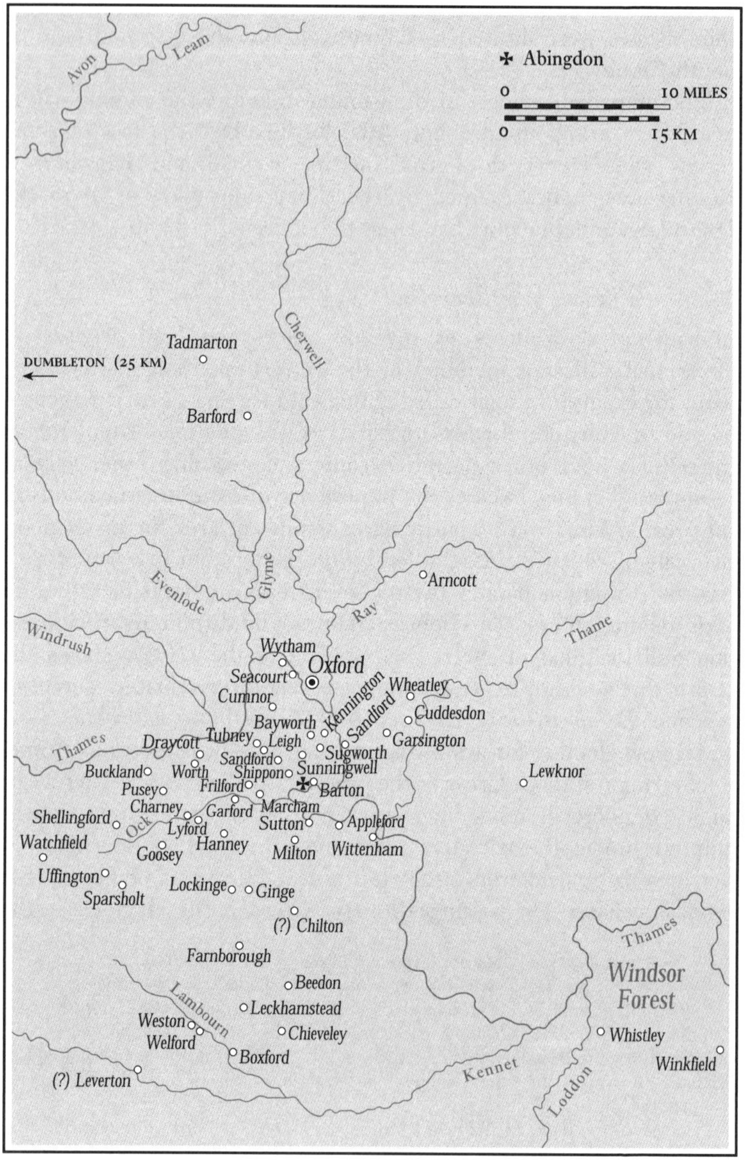

MAP 1. *TRE* Abingdon estates named in *Domesday*

Thames.[823] The abbey may in addition have enjoyed some revenue from jurisdictional privileges, to be considered later.[824]

There may also have been various ecclesiastical rights, for example pensions from churches with links to Abingdon, perhaps extending back to the pre-Æthelwoldian minster.[825] Particularly close ties were enjoyed with the church of Culham, ties for which both versions of the *History* provide ancient bases.[826] The abbey may also have received revenues from tithes, although there is no evidence for this in the Anglo-Saxon period.[827]

2. Estate administration

This section is intended to provide only background to the information in the *History* on the control of Abingdon's estates, not a full economic analysis of estate exploitation.[828] However, it must be noted that the information provided by both the *History* and *Domesday* is demonstrably limited, for example with regard to arrangements within complex estates and to changing settlement and estate patterns.[829]

Demesne and tenants

As stated earlier, the *History* is notably restricted in its interest in the abbey's pre-Conquest tenants. Nevertheless, both the limited Abingdon evidence and analogies with other monasteries suggest that

[823] cc. 65, 141.

[824] See below, pp. clviii–clix; for suggestions on the significance of such income, see S. P. J. Harvey, 'The extent and profitability of demesne agriculture in England in the later eleventh century', in T. H. Aston *et al.*, eds., *Social Relations and Ideas: Essays in Honour of R. H. Hilton* (Cambridge, 1983), pp. 45–72.

[825] See Thacker, 'Æthelwold', p. 48: 'Such a community must have had a large dependent territory or *parochia* over which it exercised certain well-defined rights, including a monopoly over burials, claims to church scot, etc. The area of this *parochia* would have corresponded with the administrative unit focused on the estate with which the church was associated, in this instance, presumably, the great royal estate of *Earmundesleah*.'

[826] B16, B64; see also below, p. clx.

[827] Cf. vol. ii, p. lxxx.

[828] Such an analysis would rely very largely on *Domesday Book*, not the *History*; see above, p. cli, on the number of mills owned by Abingdon being revealed only by *Domesday*.

[829] See e.g. the case of lands given to the knight Hermer during the reign of William I; vol. ii. 8. *Charters of Abingdon Abbey*, p. clix, concludes that this instance 'forms a reminder that the internal economy of the Abingdon manors may have been far more intricate than is now apparent. If the Denchworth holding was a detached portion of the Uffington manor, then we should take into account the possibility of other such associations which might result in some Abingdon holdings being concealed within *Domesday* entries for distant manors.' See also *Charters of Abingdon Abbey*, p. clxii.

leasing of lands was very important. *Domesday* records various Abingdon tenants whom it describes as being prohibited either from going where they wished [*non potuit ire quo uoluit*] or from withdrawing [*non potuit ab eo recedere*].[830] These were probably leaseholders, holding the equivalent of what at Ely were called thegnlands.[831] The Abingdon entries also mention people who could go where they wished but none were Abingdon tenants, and in two cases they are specified as holding *in alodio*, which may indicate the holding of bookland.[832]

Domesday provides information on the proportion of land that had been granted out by the abbey. For Berkshire the information is quite extensive, and indicates that roughly a quarter of lands by value was held by tenants. This figure is approximately similar to that for 1086.[833] In Oxfordshire the proportion held by tenants *TRE* is only about one-seventh, but the information on *TRE* arrangements is very limited, so the figure is likely to be a significant underestimate.[834] Where it provides sufficient information, *Domesday* also indicates very similar patterns of estates having been alienated in 1066 and 1086. Of the Berkshire estates given individual *Domesday* entries, all that were alienated in 1086 had also been alienated in 1066. Only Buckland had a tenant named for 1066 and not 1086. In contrast, some of the lands presented as subsidiary units within large manors did specify tenants for 1086 but not for 1066. This may simply be an omission, but in other cases it is specified that the land had been of the demesne supply of the monks, strongly suggesting a change in landholding terms between 1066 and 1086.[835] There is no clear

[830] All Berkshire, unless otherwise stated: (i) 'non potuit ire quo uoluit': Norman in Seacourt; thegn in Wytham; Norman in Beedon; Ælfgeard's sons in Lyford; (ii) 'non potuit ab eo recedere': Ælfward the priest and Leofwine the goldsmith in Shippon; Leofwine and Norman in Barton and Dry Sandford; Wulfric in Bayworth; six Englishmen in Sugworth, Sunningwell, and Kennington; Brihtwine, Ælfric, and a reeve in Leckhampstead, Weston, and Boxford; five thegns in Frilford; Eadwine the priest in East Hanney; Siward in Sandford-on-Thames (Oxfordshire). See *DB* i, fos. 58^{v}–59^{r}, 156^{v}. Silence on the terms of tenure need not indicate that other tenants were free to go or withdraw.

[831] On thegnlands, see Miller, *Ely*, pp. 51–3; some may have been administrative tenures, others leases or the product of commendation. A reference in the *History* to 'vavassours' land' may indicate that the term thegnland was in use at Abingdon before the Conquest; vol. ii pp. lix, 50.

[832] *DB* i, fos. 58^{v} (Edith at Benham), 59^{r} (Blæcmann at Chilton, as Harold's tenant, and Eadric at Fawler as the king's tenant).

[833] See vol. ii, p. lxxv.

[834] Named *TRE* tenants held lands worth a total of £8. 15*s* in Sandford-on-Thames; *DB* i, fo. 156^{v}.

[835] Goosey and Hanney, *DB* i, fo. 59^{r}.

pattern of nearby estates being kept in demesne and distant ones being alienated, although there is some concentration of alienated lands on the south side of the Berkshire downs.

Estate administration

Whilst fixed division of revenues between convent and abbot, and endowment of obedientiaries, were post-Conquest developments, it is possible that some revenues were allocated for specific purposes, as the *History* indicates was the case with the assignment of Lewknor to the boy monks' morning repast.[836] How, then, were the demesne estates providing for monastic needs administered? A memorandum probably from the mid-thirteenth century lists seven manors that from ancient times were appropriated to the convent for the provision of food supplies: Cumnor, Barton, Marcham, Charney, Uffington, Lockinge with Farnborough, and Milton.[837] On each lived monks known as 'reeves of the manors [*prepositi maneriorum*]'. At fixed times each sent from his estate a contribution towards the provisioning of the monastery. The arrangement lasted for a long time, but was eventually changed because the monks stationed on the manors were living in a less regular fashion than was fitting.

The memorandum has been analysed by Gabrielle Lambrick.[838] All seven estates were pre-Conquest, and all were in north Berkshire, five being within ten miles of the abbey. All were held at least partially in demesne in *Domesday* and continued to be so held. She notes the similarity to the system at Cluny, but points out that it was unusual in England and might well be out of line with tenth-century reform ideals. She therefore suggests that it was unlikely to have been introduced by Æthelwold, and puts forward as a possible candidate Osgar, who had knowledge of Fleury and possibly of other French houses deriving practices from Cluny. Alternatively it might have been introduced from *c.*1000 when, according to *De abbatibus*, the Danes wiped out the abbey. The situation in the years before the Conquest, she suggests, seems to have been that this group of manors together with others were held in demesne and supplied food farms for the monastery, including the abbot. Some would have been held by the monk reeves, others farmed

[836] On division of revenues and endowment of obedientiaries, see vol. ii, pp. lxxxiii–lxxxvii. For Lewknor, see c. 121. *Accounts of the Obedientiars*, pp. 36–7, has income from Lewknor in the kitchener's account.

[837] Chatsworth, no. 405, G. Lambrick, 'Abingdon Abbey administration', *Journal of Ecclesiastical History*, xvii (1966), 159–83, at pp. 182–3.

[838] Lambrick, 'Administration', pp. 161–5.

by laymen or other monks.[839] The seven manors were probably transferred to the abbot's management later, when a division of revenues between abbot and convent was negotiated.[840]

However, it must be said that there is no strong early evidence for this system. As Lambrick notes, it was very much against reform ideals: the proem to the *Regularis Concordia* states that monks are not to visit properties of the monastery except if great necessity or reasonable discretion required.[841] If such ideals rule out Æthelwold as the inventor of the system, they surely equally rule out Osgar. More acceptable would be lay reeves rather than monks. In this case, the system would fit the type of farming of lands that we know existed elsewhere.[842] For this we have some Abingdon evidence earlier than the memorandum, although still well after the Anglo-Saxon period. MS C includes a list of revenues of the chamber, written in the same hand as the *History*, and therefore probably from before *c.*1170. It includes the entry: 'from abbey's manors, which make nine and a half months, 52s. 3d.'.[843] Another list in MS C, probably in a late twelfth-century hand, deals with the kitchener's revenues and mentions Cumnor, Marcham, Charney, Uffington, Milton, Shellingford, Lockinge, Wittenham, and Appleford, 'which make one month of farm, and Cuddesdon which makes a half month of farm'.[844] What we have

[839] Lambrick, 'Administration', p. 165 n. 1, interprets the *History*'s account of Blæcmann's holdings at Sandford, Chilton, and Leverton in this way. She also suggests that Godric Cild was farming Sparsholt from his father Eadric *TRE* and inherited it on his father's death; 'the abbey thereupon claimed that it had passed to the monastic community to which the monk belonged, and he may have been allowed to continue farming the estate in the abbey's interest'. The *History* gives only very limited support for this interpretation of arrangements at Sparsholt; c. 138. *DB* i, fo. 59^r, mentions neither Eadric nor Godric farming the land from the abbey.

[840] Lambrick, 'Administration', p. 161, where she suggests that the change took place 'during the last quarter of the eleventh century or thereabouts'.

[841] Ibid., p. 162; see *Regularis Concordia*, proem. 12, ed. Symons, p. 8: 'Villarum autem circuitus, nisi necessitas magna compulerit et necessariae rationis discretio hoc dictauerit, uagando nequaquam frequentent.'

[842] R. V. Lennard, *Rural England, 1086–1135* (Oxford, 1959), p. 131. It should also be noted that the evidence from Cluny is less clear for 10th-century practice than Lambrick makes out. Evidence for small numbers of monks living on collections of properties known as *decanie*, where goods were collected before being sent to the mother house, exists from the mid-12th century, but earlier arrangements for *obedientie* are much less clear; see M. Hillebrandt, 'Le Doyen à Cluny: Quelques remarques sur sa terminologie et son histoire', *Annales de Bourgogne*, lxxii (2000), 397–428. I would like to thank Barbara Rosenwein for her help on this point.

[843] *CMA* ii. 326; on the list, see vol. ii, p. xxvi.

[844] *CMA* ii. 307, on which see vol. ii, p. xxvi. The list includes all the manors that appear in the memorandum in the Chatsworth cartulary.

then is nine named manors—including all seven named in the later memorandum—owing a month's farm, and one owing half a month.[845] Again there is no early evidence to support this, the only significant *Domesday* statements being that Goosey and Hanney were 'of the monks' food' in 1066.[846] However, the type of system suggested by these late twelfth-century customs is similar to that which existed at other houses and may have existed at Abingdon before 1066.[847]

3. Law and disputes

The dispute records and the narratives that make the *History* such a valuable source on post-Conquest law are far less numerous for the Anglo-Saxon period.[848] Moreover, composition or rewriting of such narratives by the compiler of the *History* was likely to introduce more significant anachronism regarding the earlier period. Indeed, one of the uses to which the Anglo-Saxon portions of the *History* can be put is to suggest how Anglo-Saxon law was perceived in the time of Henry II and beyond.[849] The earlier version recounts that

> a certain rich man named Thorkell, by the witness and advice of Earl Harold, did homage to the church of Abingdon and Abbot Ordric concerning himself together with his land which is called Kingston. Indeed, it was then permitted to any free man to do so, so that the lordship of the aforesaid village would be dependent on the perpetual right of this church.[850]

In this instance, an anachronistic term, homage, is being used in an attempt to describe an Anglo-Saxon practice, commendation. In one of the passages introducing charters to laymen in MS B twelfth- or thirteenth-century language is casually used to describe the grant: 'King Alfred gave to a loyal man of his, named Deormod, the village

[845] Conceivably the central estate at Barton provided the remaining two and a half months, although the present list mentions Barton paying the particular render three times a year. On Barton having the sense of central farm, see R. J. Faith, *The English Peasantry and the Growth of Lordship* (Leicester, 1997), pp. 36–7, 42.

[846] *DB* i, fo. 59^{r}. Cf. the relatively early evidence on farming at Ely contained in the *Liber Eliensis*, bk. ii, c. 84, ed. Blake, pp. 152–3, and discussed by Miller, *Ely*, pp. 37–43.

[847] Lennard, *Rural England*, p. 131 and n. 1. See Wulfstan, *Life of St Swithun*, c. 11, Lapidge, *Cult of St Swithun*, p. 526, saying that a *prepositus* called Byrhtferth had looked after estates of the abbey (*prouiderat . . . rura monasterii*) in the time of Abbot Osgar.

[848] See above, pp. xxxiv, lv, on the limited influence of learned law on the vocabulary of the *History*.

[849] See also below, p. 192, for use of the phrase 'in misericordia . . . incidit', 'fell into mercy', in the context of a case in the reign of the Confessor.

[850] See below, p. 222.

called Appleford, for his service and homage.'[851] The Latin translations of Old English documents also provide interesting information, although it cannot be told whether the translations were the work of the compiler.[852] For example, the terms 'sace and socne [sake and soke]' are translated as 'litigium [lawsuit]' and 'exquisitionem [search, investigation]', the latter an unusual term in England and not a very good match for soke.[853]

Jurisdictional rights of the reformed house

The phrase 'sake and soke' appears in the first of a pair of writs in Edward the Confessor's name. The writ grants Abbot Ordric for Abingdon 'sake and soke, toll and team, and *infangentheof*, inside borough and outside borough, *hamsocn* and *grithbrice* and *foresteal* over his own land'.[854] Sake and soke may have involved jurisdiction similar to that of the hundred court, except perhaps in excluding any rights of capital punishment. Toll and team were the rights to take tolls and to supervise the processes of proof concerning possession of chattels. *Infangentheof* was the right to execute thieves caught red-handed within the privileged land, after summary trial. *Hamsocn* concerns assault on a person in a house, or perhaps on the house, *grithbrice* breach of the peace, and *forsteal* obstruction, particularly of royal officials.[855] Doubts have been expressed about the authenticity of this writ, but there are not sufficient difficulties to make certain that it should be rejected.[856] Some doubts could arise from minor slips or changes made in copying. It may be significant that the last three privileges are not mentioned in *De abbatibus*'s summary of Edward's grant, but *De abbatibus* struggled with the meaning even of the more common privileges and may have omitted the others either because of ignorance of their meaning or because it was providing

[851] See below, p. 274.

[852] See also use of the phrase 'secundum patrie Anglie morem', 'according to the custom of the land of England', in the Latin version of the will of Archbishop Ælfric, with no equivalent in the Old English version; c. 105, B235 (*Charters of Abingdon Abbey*, no. 133).

[853] cc. 127–8. For 'exquisitio', cf. *Gesetze*, ed. Liebermann, i. 213. *De abbatibus* gives the more imaginative translation of sake and soke as, respectively, 'conflictus' and 'assaltus'; *CMA* ii. 282. Note also c. 127 for MS B's confusion over the spelling of *infangentheof*; the incorporation into the word of the 'v' which MS C had used as a key within its translation suggests that the scribe of MS B did not frequently employ the term.

[854] c. 127.

[855] N. D. Hurnard, 'The Anglo-Norman franchises', *EHR*, lxiv (1949), 289–327, 433–60, at pp. 302–10.

[856] *Anglo-Saxon Writs*, ed. Harmer, pp. 123–31.

only a summary.[857] Likewise, it may cast suspicion on the Confessor's writ that his successors' grants are less specific; William I's writ simply grants all customs as the abbot could show by writ or charter that the abbey had had by gift of King Edward, whilst that of William II grants only 'sake and soke and all its customs, as well and fully as it best and most fully had in the time of King Edward and of my father'.[858] However, the detail of Edward's writ may have rendered later repetition unnecessary. Parallels to other writs make it plausible that Edward's grant should be accepted as authentic.[859]

A second writ granted that Abbot Ordric and the monastery 'are to have and possess freely Hormer hundred, in their own power for ever more. And thus that no sheriff or court reeve may have any soke or court there without the abbot's own order and grant.'[860] It has been strongly argued that all Anglo-Saxon writs with such exclusion clauses are bogus.[861] No such clause appears in William II's writ that mentions the hundred or in those from the earlier part of Henry I's reign. Rather it first appears in a writ of Henry I datable to 1126 × 1127, issued in the context of a dispute between the king and Abbot Vincent, and that dispute would provide a context for the forgery of the writ in Edward's name.[862] Whether this forgery involved creating the whole writ or just improving a grant of the hundred by the addition of an exclusion clause cannot be told.

Overall, Abingdon's secular jurisdictional privileges were not extensive compared with some of the other great monasteries established in the tenth century, for example Ely.[863] Nor is there any other evidence of the abbot having a court that decided land cases, as he would after the Norman Conquest. It is possible that some such court might have dealt with disputes over leases. However, in the only case for which we have extensive information, that concerning Leckhampstead, the issue of hereditary right was raised

[857] *CMA* ii. 282; see above, p. clviii n. 853.

[858] Vol. ii. 2, 20.

[859] See esp. *Charters of Abingdon Abbey*, p. 573.

[860] c. 129.

[861] P. Wormald, 'Lordship and justice in the early English kingdom: Oswaldslow revisited', in W. Davies and P. Fouracre (eds.), *Property and Politics in the Early Middle Ages* (Cambridge, 1995), pp. 114–36, esp. pp. 128–9.

[862] Vol. ii. 230–2.

[863] Cf. e.g. Miller, *Ely*, pp. 25–35; also Hurnard, 'Anglo-Norman franchises', esp. pp. 316–27, 446–7. See also below, cc. 9, 11, 12, B17, *Charters of Abingdon Abbey*, no. 10, for privileges claimed in charters in King Coenwulf's name; below, p. ccv, on the dating of these forgeries.

and the case was settled 'in an assembly of high-ranking men', most likely a royal or shire court.[864]

Abingdon established some ecclesiastical privileges, although these too were limited compared with those of certain other houses that were prominent in the tenth-century reform movement.[865] The *Orthodoxorum* charters of privileges emphasize the abbey's right to elect its own abbot. Even if the earlier charters of the series, in the names of Eadwig and Edgar, are not genuine, such freedom of election may have been one of Æthelwold's main concerns as abbot. Æthelred affirmed the right after his appointment of Eadwine.[866] Again when Edward the Confessor appointed the aged Bishop Rodulf as abbot of Abingdon, the monks extracted a promise that they 'elect as his successor whomsoever they wished from amongst themselves when Rodulf died'.[867]

The other privileges particularly prominent in the later version of the *History* were those enjoyed by Culham. They supposedly derived from the time of King Coenwulf. For example,

> the abbot alone according to the favour of the privilege may choose and constitute a man experienced in law to hear diligently and bring to a canonical decision complaints and pleas concerning both criminal and other matters pertaining to ecclesiastical law.
>
> From that time, too, the priest or cleric of the church of Culham was to receive the chrism on the vigil of Easter by the hand of the sacrist in the church of Abingdon, to use for baptism and the sick. Moreover, when the parson or vicar of that church yields to death, the abbot of Abingdon, by his own authority and not by the consent or counsel of the archbishop or bishop or archdeacon or dean or any ecclesiastical official, will give the parsonage or vicarage to whom he wishes, without presentment being made to the diocesan or another.[868]

[864] See below, pp. 188, 210. For an interpretation of this case, see A. G. Kennedy, 'Disputes about *bocland*: The forum for their adjudication', *ASE*, xiv (1985), 175–95, at pp. 188–9.

[865] Abingdon was not exempt from episcopal supervision, as would become particularly clear during the disputes of the early 13th century; see above, p. xlix. For the diocesan bishop being behind Æthelred's oppression of the church, see below, p. 142. For a brief introduction to the background of monastic exemption, see B. H. Rosenwein, *Negotiating Space: Power, Restraint, and Privileges of Immunity in Early Medieval Europe* (Ithaca, 1999), pp. 32–6.

[866] See below, pp. 62, 96, 146; also John, *Orbis Britanniae*, p. 172; Thacker, 'Æthelwold', p. 53.

[867] c. 125. Note also *De abbatibus* on Siward's responses concerning episcopal benediction; *CMA* ii. 281. See above, p. l, for one of the possible motives of the reviser of the *History* being to re-emphasize freedom of abbatial election.

[868] See below, p. 252; see also *Charters of Abingdon Abbey*, no. 10.

It seems likely that Culham did enjoy privileges from an early period, but the exact nature of those privileges must remain uncertain.[869] By the later Middle Ages, Culham was an ecclesiastical peculiar under the abbot's direct control and had special rights of sanctuary.[870] In addition, Culham would be exempt from royal taxation, and geld exemption could even be an explanation for the lack of reference to Culham in *Domesday Book*.[871]

Substantive law

Although its evidence is limited, the *History* does provide some interesting snippets of information, particularly about the law of landholding. Some are preserved in charters, most notably King Æthelred's charter concerning the resumption from Abingdon of certain lands that pertained to the king's sons, vital evidence on royal landholding arrangements.[872] Others appear in narratives, thus raising anxiety about anachronism. Nevertheless, most concern the mid-eleventh century rather than earlier periods, and it is interesting that it was believed to have been 'the custom among the English that those monks who wished might receive goods and patrimonies, enjoy them, and do with them as they pleased'.[873]

We are told something of the way in which land transfers were believed to have been made.[874] Charters passed with lands, and the revised version of the *History* repeatedly states that the charter was placed on the altar of the church, thus symbolizing the transfer.[875]

[869] See e.g. Thacker, 'Æthelwold', p. 45, for the argument that 'there seems no good reason to reject these traditions out of hand, and they find some confirmation in the fact that Culham long remained very closely linked with the abbey'. Arguments based on working back from later arrangements are criticized e.g. by E. Cambridge and D. Rollason, 'Debate: The pastoral organization of the Anglo-Saxon Church. A review of the "Minster Hypothesis"', *Early Medieval Europe*, iv (1995), 87–104.

[870] Thacker, 'Æthelwold', p. 49; *VCH*, *Oxfordshire*, vii. 35.

[871] See *VCH*, *Oxfordshire*, vii. 30–2; *Charters of Abingdon Abbey*, pp. ccv, 47–8. On ecclesiastical peculiars in the later Middle Ages, see R. N. Swanson, 'Peculiar practices: The jurisdictional jigsaw of the pre-Reformation Church', *Midland History*, xxvi (2001), 69–95. *Charters of Abingdon Abbey*, p. clxiv, suggests that 'it may have been Culham's complete identification with the abbey (and perhaps with Hormer Hundred) that led to its omission from the Domesday survey'.

[872] c. 99. See P. Wormald, '*On þa wæpnedhealfe*: Kingship and royal property from Æthelwulf to Edward the Elder', in *Edward the Elder*, ed. Higham and Hill, pp. 264–79, esp. pp. 271, 274.

[873] See below, p. 212.

[874] See above, pp. cxxvii, cxlv, for purchases and exchanges.

[875] See e.g. B42, B44, which state that the donor 'as was then the custom, as a symbol of this gift placed the king's charter (through which he had all his right in that land) on the altar of the blessed Mary at Abingdon'.

Whilst such statements are given in routine fashion, and are in part intended to show why the charters ended up at Abingdon, some such ceremony seems plausible. In one case the routine statement is expanded to include direct speech by the donor:

> Lulla, desiring before his death to make Christ his heir, with the consent of King Beorhtric and the counsel of authoritative men, gave and granted to God and St Mary and the house of Abingdon and the monks serving God there the aforesaid village, that is Easton, and placed on the altar of the blessed Mary at Abingdon that charter whereby King Beorhtric had confirmed that land to him. At that time this had greater efficacy and confirmatory power than anything else that he could do concerning that land. And as a sign of complete agreement he pronounced in English 'All my right which I had in Easton I give to St Mary in Abingdon'.[876]

The routine mention of royal consent again may not be based on any detailed knowledge of Anglo-Saxon law, and may be included because of later practice, but neither of these reasons precludes the possibility that the consent of Anglo-Saxon kings was on occasion sought for grants of bookland.

There is some information about leases, including possible ambiguity over their duration:

> a custom in those days got out of control, to considerable future damage: anyone offering plenty of gold or silver would receive by purchase a portion of land amounting to three or five hides, or a whole village, in various places of the abbey, under the cover that permission to possess this land was to extend for the lives of three, or two, men.[877]

The rather awkward ending may be significant in the context of the dispute over Leckhampstead, where the church was insistent that the original lessee's wife should count as one of the three lives for which the lease should last. It is possible that in some cases lay lessees may not have counted the widow in this way.[878]

Disputes

Leases were a prominent issue in the small number of dispute narratives in the pre-Conquest part of the *History*.[879] Apart from

[876] B13.

[877] See below, p. 218.

[878] See below, p. 190. Other leases were for a shorter period than even a single life, for example that of South Cerney to Bishop Stigand; below, p. 196. See also above, p. cxxix, below, p. clxiii.

[879] I omit disputes not directly involving Abingdon, as recorded in some charters copied into the *History*; see esp. B227 (= *Charters of Abingdon Abbey*, no. 125, trans. *EHD*, i. no. 118). Note also the dispute concerning Lewknor, but not directly involving Abingdon; c. 121.

the account of the early conflict with King Coenwulf, the case concerning Leckhampstead is the first dispute narrative to appear in the earlier version of the *History*.[880] A lease of South Cerney also produced a dispute, on the outcome of which the *History* is rather obscure; *Domesday Book* only records that it was claimed by Abingdon but 'all the shire testified that Archbishop Stigand had held it for ten years in King Edward's time'.[881] Fyfield was leased for three lives to the sheriff Godric but lost to Henry de Ferrers after the Conquest.[882]

Apart from disputes over leased lands, the later version of the *History* also includes quarrels involving a meadow and—after the Norman Conquest—a mill.[883] The latter in particular is a type of dispute that would feature strongly in later parts of the *History*. Also like several later disputes, it involves conflict with a royal official.[884]

We learn something of disputing procedures in and out of court. Most notable is the use of documents in court, for example the production of a landbook by Abingdon's opponent Brihtwine in the dispute concerning Leckhampstead:

> Brihtwine . . . had hitherto possessed the land at Leckhampstead without the monks' permission, and he was behaving in particularly loud-mouthed fashion since he had the land-book, that is the document of the estate described. For he who had in his possession such writing could thereby dispute more confidently for any land.[885]

It is unclear why Brihtwine, if he was only the successor of a lessee as the abbey claimed, had come into possession of the document. Nevertheless, his strong position may explain why, despite the *History* presenting the abbey as victorious in dispute, *Domesday Book* records Brihtwine as the abbot's tenant of Leckhampstead in the time of King Edward.[886] The same case is also interesting for Bishop, formerly Abbot, Siward's use of a letter to send his evidence

[880] cc. 9, 120, 136.

[881] See below, p. 196; *DB* i, fo. 169^{r}.

[882] See below, p. 224; see also the general statement, below, p. 218–20, concerning problems arising from leases.

[883] B63, B291.

[884] It may be significant that it appears at the stage where the text was quite possibly starting to draw on earlier notes or memoranda. For another clash with a royal official, see below, p. 228, involving Froger the sheriff.

[885] See below, p. 208. Brihtwine was, according to the *History*, the brother of the third tenant by a lease for three lives. At his brother's death, the land should have returned to the church, but Brihtwine was refusing to give up the land and claiming it instead by hereditary right; c. 120.

[886] *DB* i, fo. 58^{v}.

concerning a case, an instance of a practice for which there are few surviving parallels.[887] One may also wonder whether the dispute would have arisen, or have been so serious, had not Siward moved from Abingdon to Canterbury.

However, the most striking example for procedure in court, appearing only in the later version of the *History*, is the use of a shield, sheaf of wheat, and candle to determine possession of a meadow at Berry, disputed with men of Oxfordshire.[888] The shield floated down the Thames, miraculously indicating Abingdon's possessions. The use of such a procedure in a dispute during the reign of Edmund is unprovable; if based on any early record, its absence from the first version of the *History* is hard to explain. The supernatural, however, is involved in other judicial contexts as well. The later version of the *History* attributes to the Black Cross particular power, which would have been relevant in judicial contexts: 'it is so holy that no one who has taken an oath on it can affirm a lie without punishment and mortal danger, for it is believed to have been smelted and made in large part from nails of the Lord'. If such a view was widely shared, it is an interesting instance of the type of popular beliefs that would have been of considerable importance in the administration of justice but are rarely recorded.[889] The same version of the *History* records Abbot Ealdred taking the relics of St Vincent to confront the men of the bishopric of Lincoln in their dispute over Cuddesdon mill:

When, indeed, by judgment of the judges present it came about that the abbot was to make an oath on the relics which he had brought that his side was the more just, he knelt and stretched upwards his right hand. When, lo, on the opponents' side the firm ground began to shake, the hard ground to soften, so much so that the feet of the horses became stuck in the softness. Also a very strong wind plucked the spears from the hands of those holding

[887] See esp. S. D. Keynes, 'The Fonthill Letter', in M. Korhammer, ed., *Words, Texts and Manuscripts: Studies in Anglo-Saxon Culture presented to Helmut Gneuss on the Occasion of his Sixty-fifth Birthday* (Cambridge, 1992), pp. 53–97.

[888] B63. On this case, see also above, p. xlii; EPNS, *Berkshire*, ii. 454. For parallels with an episode in *Beowulf*, see A. Orchard, *A Critical Companion to 'Beowulf'* (Woodbridge, 2003), pp. 102–3; C. Tolley, '*Beowulf*'s Scyld Scefing episode: Some Norse and Finnish analogues', *Arv*, lii (1996), 7–48, at p. 11; R. North, *Heathen Gods in Old English Literature* (Cambridge, 1997), pp. 182–94. H. M. Chadwick, *The Origin of the English Nation* (Cambridge, 1907), p. 279, stated that the story 'must have been founded upon some ritual practice current among the peasantry of the district'.

[889] B7. See e.g. J. G. H. Hudson, *The Formation of the English Common Law* (Harlow, 1996), p. 159, on popular belief concerning ordeal.

them, and threw them into the air, dashed them against one another and broke them by the force of the wind, in a marvellous sight.[890]

Finally, the Leckhampstead dispute shows resort to the supernatural not to decide a case but to ensure that a decision be observed:

Not long afterwards, when Hereman the diocesan bishop of this place was dedicating the church then constructed at the cemetery entrance, amongst the rest of the things which were there held to be admitted or excluded by episcopal office, he excluded from the community of Christianity and struck with perpetual anathema all who from that time strove in any way for the extraction of the aforesaid land from the sustenance of the monks living at Abingdon.[891]

VII. MONASTIC BUILDINGS AND LIFE UP TO 1071

1. Dedication

As soon as we have any secure information, we know that the abbey of Abingdon was dedicated to St Mary. However, our sole evidence for this for the period before the mid-tenth century comes from forged charters and later narratives. This may lead to some caution as to the early dedication, because at least some abbeys, including Worcester, had a change of dedication to Mary in the tenth century.[892] Interestingly, the privilege for Abingdon in King Eadwig's name refers to the abbey, 'situated in the well-known place called by the noble name of Abingdon by local inhabitants of this race, and held to be dedicated to the mother of our Lord Mary, ever Virgin, and also to the blessed Peter prince of the apostles and to his fellow apostle Paul'.[893] Whether or not the charter as it stands is authentic, it seems unlikely that this unusual reference to Peter and Paul would be a result of later composition. However, there is no other strong evidence for an early dedication to these apostles.[894]

[890] See below, p. 374.

[891] See below, p. 210.

[892] Clayton, *Cult*, pp. 132–4. She modifies her views somewhat in 'Centralism and uniformity versus localism and diversity: The Virgin and native saints in the monastic reform', *Peritia*, viii (1994), 95–106. An alternative possibility is that Abingdon, like other early minsters, may at one stage have had a pair of churches, one dedicated to Peter and Paul, the other to Mary. Mary then emerged as the main dedication, attached to the abbey church. See J. Blair, 'Anglo-Saxon minsters: A topographical review', in J. Blair and R. Sharpe, eds., *Pastoral Care before the Parish* (Leicester, 1992), pp. 226–66, at 250–6.

[893] See below, p. 62.

[894] See also c. 94 for Bishop Sidemann being buried at Abingdon in the chapel dedicated to St Paul.

2. Buildings

Evidence for the abbey buildings is poor. The written sources are late and limited, the archaeological investigation inconclusive. An excavation in 1922 was poorly executed. It uncovered on the site of the Norman abbey an Anglo-Saxon church, the dimensions of which may have been at least 200 feet long by 57 feet wide, possibly with an east-end apse. This building has been variously interpreted as Æthelwold's minster, an earlier church possibly of the ninth century, or a post-Conquest building.[895]

Pre-Æthelwoldian church

The existence of a round church seems to have been associated with the Virgin Mary, with a possible example at Hexham in the early eighth century, and there is some evidence for such a church at Abingdon.[896] Unfortunately, neither version of the *History* gives us a description of the pre-Conquest church buildings, although a description of the earliest church may have appeared in the lost early folios of the revised version. Instead, we have to rely on *De abbatibus*, which describes churches that it attributes to the founder, Hæha, and the refounder, Æthelwold. Hæha's *monasterium* was 120 feet long and round in east and west. It was built where the monks' cellar currently was, in such a way that the altar stood where the *lavatorium* was now situated. About it were twelve cells for the twelve monks, and the same number of chapels. There was a high surrounding wall rather than a cloister. According to a later passage in *De abbatibus*, the Danes destroyed the *monasterium*, but the cells and chapels survived to be found by Æthelwold, who ordered that they be preserved.[897]

[895] Biddle *et al.*, 'Early history', pp. 63–4; *Charters of Abingdon Abbey*, p. xxxix.

[896] See Clayton, *Cult*, p. 137, who notes further evidence from Bury and St Augustine's, Canterbury; R. Krautheimer, 'Sancta Maria Rotunda', in *Studies in Early Christian, Medieval, and Renaissance Art* (London, 1969), pp. 107–14; R. Gem, 'Towards an iconography of Anglo-Saxon architecture', *Journal of the Warburg and Courtauld Institutes*, xlvi (1983), 1–18, esp. at pp. 8, 11. Neither the *History* nor *De abbatibus* gives any description of the monastery associated with Abben.

[897] *CMA* ii. 272–3, 277. E. Fernie, *The Architecture of the Anglo-Saxons* (London, 1983), p. 110, argues that the description of the *monasterium* concerns the whole site, not just the church; he draws a contrast with the *ecclesia* mentioned at *CMA* ii. 273. The ellipsis within his translation may slightly alter the sense of the passage, and he does not deal with the later passage concerning Danish destruction. See also *CMA* ii. 270, where the 'officinas monachorum' are referred to as distinct from the 'monasterium'. The earlier version of the *History* does not mention destruction of the church by the Danes, but the later version tells

It is hard to know how much trust to place in this description. As we have seen, archaeology provides no help. The passage in *De abbatibus* is followed by a description of clothing, food, and other practices within the monastery, which seem highly unlikely to have any early source.[898] If *monasterium* does, as seems likely, refer to the church, it might indicate a longitudinal church, with apses at both east and west ends; however, this would make Abingdon the first church on this plan north of the Alps, which may also instil doubt.[899] That the rounded ends of Hæha's *monasterium* bears some resemblance to *De abbatibus*'s description of Æthelwold's own church, to be discussed below, may also instil scepticism. If, on the other hand, *monasterium* is taken to refer to the whole site, such a sub-circular precinct does seem plausible for an early religious community, but at 120 feet would be extremely small.[900] If preserved by Æthelwold, memory of it may have passed down into the written record. However, it need not have been the work of the founder, and it has been suggested that *De abbatibus* may be describing 'arrangements which would have characterized many, perhaps all, of the grander ecclesiastical communities in the period before reform', that is perhaps in the earlier tenth rather than the seventh century.[901]

The fate of the early abbey church, whatever its form, is not recorded with any certainty. The later version of the *History*, like *De abbatibus*, attributes to the Danes the destruction of Hæha's church but this is not specified in the earlier version of the *History*. It has been suggested that the early buildings may have survived to form part of a group with Æthelwold's church, but if these included the early church it may be the more surprising that we hear so little of its form and nothing of its later demise in the *History*.[902]

us that 'nothing is reported to have remained there besides the walls'; below, p. 268. For a description of a possibly rather similar group of buildings at Christchurch minster, Hampshire, see J. Blair, *The Church in Anglo-Saxon Society* (Oxford, 2005), p. 516.

898 *CMA* ii. 273.

899 Fernie, *Architecture of the Anglo-Saxons*, p. 110.

900 See e.g. Biddle *et al.*, 'Early history', p. 43; R. J. Cramp, 'Monastic sites', in Wilson, ed., *Archaeology of Anglo-Saxon England*, pp. 201–52, at 216; Blair, 'Anglo-Saxon minsters: A topographical review', p. 235, with other relevant comments at pp. 227, 230 on geography, pp. 235–46 on the reuse of Roman sites.

901 Thacker, 'Æthelwold', p. 48.

902 See Gem, 'Iconography', p. 8 n. 42; he does not there discuss the account in *De abbatibus* of the Danish destruction of all but the cells and chapels, *CMA* ii. 277.

Æthelwold's church

Æthelwold's own vernacular account of reform states that Edgar ordered that a glorious minster be built at Abingdon within three years, but does not describe the resultant building.[903] The *Life of St Æthelwold* specifies that the new church was built on the existing site and was measured out for Æthelwold by King Eadred himself.[904] Such action suggests that the church may have been started from scratch, rather than modifying an existing building. Æthelwold worked on the site himself, and 'one day, when the man of God was toiling at building work, a huge post fell on him, knocking him into a pit. He broke almost all his ribs on one side, and would have been completely shattered but for the pit breaking his fall.'[905] Unfortunately, the *Life* gives no description of the church, saying that it is better seen than described.[906] The earlier version of the *History* repeats the story of Eadred measuring out the foundations and records the dedication of the church in 963.[907] However neither it nor the revised version describes the church.[908] We are again left to rely on *De abbatibus*, which states 'Cancellus rotundus erat; ecclesia et rotunda, duplicem habens longitudinem quam cancellus; turris quoque rotunda erat'.[909] If *rotundus* means 'round ended', we have a description notably similar to that given for Hæha's church.[910] If *rotundus* means 'round', the meaning is different: 'the chancel was round, the nave also round and twice the length of the chancel, and a tower too was round'. Thus we appear to have a centrally planned building, perhaps related in design to the palace chapel at Aachen.[911]

[903] *Councils and Synods*, i. 148.

[904] Wulfstan, *Life of Æthelwold*, c. 13, ed. Lapidge and Winterbottom, p. 24. According to Leland, Faritius moved 'the olde churche that stode then more northerlye where now the orchard is', the old church presumably being that of Æthelwold; *The Itinerary of John Leland in or about the Years 1535–1543*, ed. L. T. Smith (5 vols., London, 1906–10), v. 76.

[905] Wulfstan, *Life of Æthelwold*, c. 15, ed. Lapidge and Winterbottom, p. 28. The church concerned is not specified but the position of the chapter in the *Life* would suggest Abingdon.

[906] Wulfstan, *Life of Æthelwold*, c. 13, ed. Lapidge and Winterbottom, p. 24.

[907] See below, pp. 56, 116; also John of Worcester, *Chronicle*, ii. 611.

[908] B207 would be the obvious place for such a description. B252 mentions the church, but gives no physical sense of it. See below, B118–B119, for a grant relating to the building of the church.

[909] *CMA* ii. 277–8.

[910] Biddle *et al.*, 'Early history', p. 45.

[911] See Gem, 'Iconography', pp. 7–12; Fernie, *Architecture of the Anglo-Saxons*, p. 109, noting his comments on the tower; Thacker, 'Æthelwold', p. 57, who also states that 'one possibility is that like Æthelwold's reconstructed Old Minster at Winchester it had a large circular or perhaps double-apsed west work with a complex of chapels and facilities for the display of relics and for royal ceremonial'.

At least by 977 there was a *porticus* chapel on the north, where Bishop Sidemann was buried.[912]

Other buildings

From narratives, we also learn in passing of other monastic buildings. The revised version of the *History* contains accounts of two miracles said to have occurred in the refectory in the time of the Danes, which may be an imposition of later arrangements or may give some indication of the existence of other monastic buildings in the second half of the ninth century.[913] Æthelwold's inspection of the monastery, according to the earlier version of the *History*, took him to the kitchen [*coquina*]. However, the monk cooking there was doing so for craftsmen or workmen rather than monks, and it is notable that the version of the story in the *Life* does not use the word kitchen.[914] In the time of Edward the Confessor we hear of the king and queen visiting all the domestic buildings of the monks, and seeing the boy monks eating in the refectory.[915] In the same reign a church was dedicated at the cemetery entrance.[916]

Ornaments

Abingdon texts tell us a considerable amount about the ornaments that decorated the interior of the church. Particularly prominent are reliquaries.[917] Also mentioned are liturgical vestments and vessels, as well as splendid gospel books.[918] The revised *History* gives a lengthy account of Æthelwold's contribution. Of especial note was a silver retable, worth £300, but his gifts also included a chalice, crosses, and cloths of silver and gold.[919] MS B also says that Æthelwold made a

[912] *ASC*, 'C', *s.a.* 977. For another, eastern, porticus chapel having existed but been demolished by the end of the 11th century, see vol. ii. 30. For the possibility of a chapel dedicated to St Vincent, see below, p. 286. According to the revised version of the *History*, Abbot Siward (1030–44) contemplated demolishing this church, but this is not mentioned in the earlier version or in *De abbatibus*, and (as suggested above, p. l) the reviser's passage may reflect 13th-century concerns rather than 11th-century reality; B252.

[913] B38–B39.

[914] c. 29; cf. Wulfstan, *Life of Æthelwold*, c. 14, ed. Lapidge and Winterbottom, p. 26.

[915] c. 121.

[916] See below, p. 210.

[917] See below, pp. 172, 176–8, 194, 356. On reliquaries, see Dodwell, *Anglo-Saxon Art*, pp. 195–201.

[918] See below, pp. 172, 194, 356; note the mention of bells below, pp. 178, 356. See Dodwell, *Anglo-Saxon Art*, pp. 180–7 on vestments, 203–9 on vessels, 201–3 on books and bindings.

[919] See below, pp. 338–40. According to *De abbatibus*, engraved (*sculpta*) on the retable were the twelve apostles and perhaps the Virgin; *CMA* ii. 278. Dodwell, *Anglo-Saxon Art*, p. 209, refers to it as a 'frontal'. For crosses four feet high, see *CMA* ii. 278; Dodwell,

form of timbrel 'to arouse greater devotion on festival days', and constructed two bells 'with his own hands'.[920] Many such ornaments fell victim to the Norman Conquest, a notable oppressor being William I's queen.[921]

3. Monastic life

Abingdon before Æthelwold

The sources give very little specific information on life in the church of Abingdon before the tenth century. If it is to be trusted at all, the foundation story, with Hæha's equivocation over his monastic vows, may suggest a situation where boundaries between secular and monastic were confused, as suggested by Bede's *Letter to Egbert*.[922] It is also possible that the *History* is right to associate the early foundation with a nunnery at St Helens. The local settlement pattern and the discovery of the cruciform disc-headed pin later known as the Black Cross might provide evidence for such a nunnery.[923]

In the eighth and ninth centuries Abingdon was in the contested border area between Mercia and Wessex, and it seems likely that Abingdon was a royal minster, first under the control of Mercia and then of Wessex.[924] The scale of the minster, and even the effect of

Anglo-Saxon Art, p. 212, notes that the text does not make any comment suggesting they were unusually large, although it should be added that such comment might not be expected of *De abbatibus*.

920 Dodwell, *Anglo-Saxon Art*, pp. 49–50, is sceptical of statements that Æthelwold himself made sophisticated ornaments.

921 See below, p. 224; see also p. 340. See further Dodwell, *Anglo-Saxon Art*, ch. 8, esp. pp. 221–2, on the impact of the Norman Conquest.

922 c. 4.

923 For a cautious suggestion of this possibility, see Blair, *Anglo-Saxon Oxfordshire*, pp. 64–5; also *Charters of Abingdon Abbey*, p. cci, 'what relationship [the pre-Æthelwoldian minster] would have had with St Helen's is impossible to discover. Perhaps we should see the two centres as respective components of a double monastery, with the men living separately from the women.' The stronger suggestion by Meyer, 'Patronage', pp. 345–6, is criticized by Foot, *Veiled Women*, i. 51 n. 80. For St Helen's as an early minster, see Biddle *et al.*, 'Early history', p. 29, and Thacker, 'Æthelwold', p. 50, who both raise the possibility that the later parochial rights of St Helen's may show its early importance. For criticism of the method of working back from later parochial rights, see Cambridge and Rollason, 'Pastoral organization of the Anglo-Saxon Church', e.g. p. 102: 'Payments for chrism, which could only be supplied by the bishop, were not an archaic due in the late eleventh century but a significant element of episcopal income. Their organization may therefore have been of recent date.'

924 See above, p. cix, on the border region. Thacker, 'Æthelwold', p. 47, suggests that the minster would have been occupied by 'a group of secular priests or canons, who lived in separate houses drawing separate incomes from the communal property, and who, in the tolerant circumstances of the ninth-century Anglo-Saxon church, may even perhaps have married'.

Viking attacks on the area, are uncertain. Nevertheless, certainly by Æthelstan's reign, as we have seen, Abingdon was an important royal centre. Associated with a royal residence or palace would have been a royal minster, and it is possible that the minster was headed by one of Æthelstan's favoured Continental clerics, Godescealc.[925]

The earlier version of the *History* states that 'after [Æthelstan's] death [939], the monastery of Abingdon was reduced to such forlornness that all possessions belonging to it were subjected to royal lordship, and it was utterly destitute of monks', whilst the later puts the decline after the death of Edmund (946).[926] However, as we have seen, the *Life of St Æthelwold* mentions a continuing endowment of forty hides even in the period of destitution. The *History* may well exaggerate the scale of decline in order to highlight Æthelwold's achievement.[927]

Æthelwold and after: material life

The existing close association of Abingdon with the king made it a particularly suitable place for Eadred to give Æthelwold to build up his monastery.[928] The fourteenth-century chronicler John of Glastonbury dated the refoundation of Abingdon to 954, but his source, if any, is unknown, and earlier evidence cannot provide such an exact date.[929] Nevertheless, the association with Eadred's reign (946–55) is supported by the *Life of St Æthelwold* and its account of that king measuring out the foundations of the new abbey.[930]

De abbatibus states that there were fifty monks at Abingdon in Æthelwold's time, although the Winchester *Liber Vitae* gives the names of only forty-one Abingdon monks in the period up to 1030.[931]

925 See below, pp. 38, 286; see above, pp. xcv, cvii.

926 See above, p. cxiv.

927 Wulfstan, *Life of Æthelwold*, c. 11, ed. Lapidge and Winterbottom, pp. 18–20; the passage is copied below, p. 296. See also *Charters of Abingdon Abbey*, p. ccix; Thacker, 'Æthelwold', p. 51, argues that 'almost certainly . . . the church which Æthelwold came to rule and reform in 955 had only ten years before been a substantial minster associated with an important royal residence'.

928 Cf. Stenton, *Early History*, pp. 50–1, who stated that 'so far as we can see it was only chance that directed that Abingdon should be the scene of Æthelwold's labours'. He notes that there were other monasteries in Berkshire, and that 'we have no warrant for the assumption that Abingdon, when Æthelwold received it, differed in any significant way from any of these little houses'.

929 Wulfstan, *Life of Æthelwold*, ed. Lapidge and Winterbottom, p. xliv.

930 Wulfstan, *Life of Æthelwold*, c. 12, ed. Lapidge and Winterbottom, p. 22; see also *Charters of Abingdon Abbey*, pp. xxxvi–xxxvii.

931 *CMA* ii. 279; *Liber Vitae*, ed. Keynes, pp. 95–6, fos. 26^{v}–27^{r}. See above, p. cxxii n. 667, for rejection of the idea that some form of female community existed at Abingdon in the 10th century.

The monks for the new monastery came from various places, the *Life of St Æthelwold* naming Glastonbury, Winchester, and London.[932] According to the earlier version of the *History*, 'to follow the stricter way of life, very many men of God, from diverse parts of England and instructed in different manners of reading and singing, heard of the holiness of Æthelwold, came to him and were received'.[933] This stricter way of life was in part liturgical, as will be discussed shortly, but also presumably covered matters such as food provision. However, whilst Æthelwold is generally regarded as the most austere of the English reformers, it should be noted that our twelfth- and thirteenth-century narratives give instances of him alleviating the strictness of the *Rule* in certain ways. According to *De abbatibus*, he did so in order to attract the rich to become monks.[934] Most notable is the account in the revised version of the *History* of his provisions concerning food and drink. Some historians have treated this with scepticism, seeing it as a justification for laxities in life at the time of writing. However, it may be that greater trust should be placed at least in the general thrust of the account, not least because an early eleventh-century riddle appears to celebrate the generosity of Æthelwold's drink provision.[935]

As for the standards of life at Abingdon after the abbacies of Æthelwold and Osgar, the *History* provides little comment. Notably neutral in tone is the statement with reference to a mid-eleventh-century practice that was certainly not acceptable at the time of writing: 'it was then the custom among the English that those monks who wished might receive goods and patrimonies, enjoy them, and do with them as they pleased'.[936] The additional food provision for boy monks is also recorded.[937] However, we cannot gain an overall picture of either declining or maintained standards, and the *History* did not endeavour to provide one.

[932] See above, p. cvii.

[933] See below, p. 54.

[934] *CMA* ii. 279. See further Thacker, 'Æthelwold', p. 56.

[935] B207. For doubts, see Knowles, *Monastic Order*, pp. 716–17; *Charters of Abingdon Abbey*, p. xl. For greater acceptance, see Porter, 'Æthelwold's bowl', and Lapidge, 'Æthelwold as scholar and teacher', p. 106 and n. 105, where he comments 'that the information as transmitted includes a number of Old English words and expressions (e.g. *bolla Æthelwoldi*) which are unlikely to have been fabricated by a thirteenth-century chronicler'.

[936] See below, p. 212; Gransden, 'Traditionalism and continuity', p. 191, gives this as an example of diversity of custom, and describes it as 'perilously near to property owning by individual monks'. See also Knowles, *Monastic Order*, pp. 80–1 and n. 4.

[937] c. 121.

Æthelwold and after: liturgical life and learning

The Virgin Mary, to whom the abbey was dedicated, was naturally of considerable importance in the devotions of Æthelwold and of Abingdon. Whilst her Assumption limited the number of possible relics, at least by the early twelfth century Abingdon was claiming possession of Marian clothing relics.[938] The tenth-century reformers promoted considerable liturgical devotion to the Virgin, as is apparent, for instance, from the *Regularis Concordia* as well as from monastic dedications.[939] At Abingdon we have evidence for such devotion continuing beyond the initial period of reform, for a Marian poem was dedicated to Siward, abbot from 1030 to 1044.[940]

The church of Abingdon acquired relics of saints other than Mary even before the coming of Æthelwold. The revised version of the *History* recounts the Frankish embassy to Æthelstan's court in 926, bringing him as gifts

> precious relics to be treated with all reverence and also to be venerated, specifically part of a thorn of the crown and part of a nail of the Lord, and the standard of St Maurice the most glorious martyr and commander of the Theban legion, with a precious finger of St Denis the martyr. . . . The aforesaid King Æthelstan gave those relics, concealed with all honour in a silver reliquary, to this most sacred house of Abingdon.[941]

The same event was recorded by William of Malmesbury, who stated that the piece of the crown of thorns and a piece of Christ's cross passed to Malmesbury. What we have is competition between at least two houses for precious relics.[942] In the early twelfth century the list

[938] Vol. ii. 220; for the limits to Marian relics, see Clayton, *Cult*, p. 131.

[939] See Clayton, *Cult*, esp. pp. 62–8, 89, 110, 121.

[940] See ibid., pp. 106–8; the poem was added (probably between 1030 and 1044) to a copy of Boethius' *De Consolatione Philosophiae*, written at Abingdon *c.*1000. Clayton states, pp. 106–7, that 'the poem consists of a set of Latin verses, written in the form of a circular maze, which can be read in either of two ways: by following the path of the maze, which gives one arrangement of lines, or according to the circles, which gives a different arrangement. The seven concentric circles reflect the sevenfold heaven into which, the author prays, Siweard, the dedicatee of the verses will be introduced.' It is not strictly necessary that the poem was composed at Abingdon. It could have been written elsewhere with a dedication to Siward, and then copied into the Abingdon manuscript.

[941] B62. If this version of the story is true, the passing of the standard of Maurice provides some evidence of interest in Roman martyrs at Abingdon in the 10th century; see also vol. ii, p. civ and n. 588. On relics at Abingdon before 1066, see also I. G. Thomas, 'The Cult of Saints' Relics in Medieval England', Ph.D. thesis (London, 1975), pp. 150–5.

[942] William of Malmesbury, *Gesta regum*, bk. ii, c. 135, ed. Mynors *et al.*, i. 218–20. For possible additional competition from Exeter, see L. H. Loomis, 'The holy relics of

of relics drawn up for Abbot Faritius included the holy nail and the finger of St Denis, but not the others mentioned in this passage.[943]

Æthelwold himself displayed considerable interest in relics.[944] In later Abingdon writings this manifested itself most importantly in his association with the finding of the Black Cross. However, it should be noted that this episode is mentioned neither in the *Life of St Æthelwold* nor the earlier version of the *History*. Nor, still more strikingly, does the relic appear in Abbot Faritius's list.[945] The earlier version of the *History* does mention the presence at Abingdon of relics of St Vincent, for which King Cnut provided a reliquary.[946] The later version adds the story of their spectacular use by Abbot Ealdred in the dispute concerning the mill at Cuddesdon.[947] The presence of relics of Vincent at Abingdon is confirmed by the early and independent evidence of an Anglo-Saxon list of saints' resting places.[948] According to Abbot Faritius's list, the relics consisted of an arm, a thigh bone, part of a shoulder blade, and a rib. They had, the *History* tells us, been acquired in the time of King Edgar. *De abbatibus*, more dramatically, tells us that they were stolen from Glastonbury in Abbot Osgar's time.[949] Again we have competition concerning

Charlemagne and King Athelstan: The lances of Longinus and St Mauricius', *Speculum*, xxv (1950), 437–56, at pp. 446–50.

[943] Vol. ii. 220–2. This need not indicate the truth of the *History*'s story, but might indicate that the story reflects 12th-century relic holdings.

[944] On Æthelwold and relics, see also Thacker, 'Æthelwold', p. 61, and S. J. Ridyard, *The Royal Saints of Anglo-Saxon England* (Cambridge, 1988), pp. 106–14. On Æthelwold obtaining Edgar's permission to transfer relics from neglected sites, see the 'Lives of Saint Thancred and Saint Torhtred', in *Liber Vitae: Register and Martyrology of New Minster and Hyde Abbey, Winchester*, ed. W. de Gray Birch (London, 1892), p. 286.

[945] I take the 'small part of a nail' to be the relic acquired from Æthelstan, not that used in the making of the Black Cross; vol. ii. 220. Cf. Thacker, 'Æthelwold', p. 60: 'it seems reasonable to suppose that the story [of the Black Cross] was current in Æthelwold's time, and that the veneration of the cross in the new community represents an attempt to link it with early monasticism at Abingdon'. The feast of St Helen (18 Aug.) was observed at Abingdon, but was not unique to that monastery and need not be specifically associated with the relic of the Black Cross; *English Benedictine Kalendars after A. D. 1100*, ed. F. Wormald (2 vols., Henry Bradshaw Soc., lxxvii, lxxxi; 1939, 1946), i. 26.

[946] See below, p. 176; also p. 356. See below, p. 286, for a chapel dedicated to St Vincent. Vincent, the proto-martyr of Spain, died in 304; *Oxford Dictionary of Saints*, p. 391. On his cult, see further Thacker, 'Æthelwold', p. 60 n. 132

[947] B291, above, p. clxiv.

[948] D. W. Rollason, 'Lists of saints' resting-places in Anglo-Saxon England', *ASE*, vii (1978), 61–93, at p. 91.

[949] Vol. ii. 70, 200, *CMA* ii. 280; also stolen were the head of St Apollinaris and many other relics. Cf. William of Malmesbury on Glastonbury's acquisition of the relics, *De antiquitate Glastonie ecclesie*, c. 62, Scott, *Early History of Glastonbury*, p. 130; see also *Gesta regum*, bk. ii, c. 160, ed. Mynors *et al.*, i. 260. Thacker, 'Æthelwold', p. 61, suggests that 'it

possession of relics. Similarly Shaftesbury and Abingdon both claimed possession of the relics of Edward the martyr, and the earlier version of the *History* provided a miracle to support Abingdon's position. In the time of Cnut,

> the relics of St Edward, king and martyr, were moved to Abingdon. And when their carrier afterwards resolved to take them away from there, not far from the church on his journey, by God's will he was stopped in his tracks and could go no further. Thus the sacred relics were brought back to the church and are preserved therein to this day.[950]

Abbot Faritius's list of relics also includes a shoulder blade, arm, finger, and some hairs of Æthelwold himself. His cult presumably developed at Abingdon as well as elsewhere soon after his death, and he appears prominently in a calendar perhaps written at Abingdon in *c.*1000 and certainly in the abbey's possession by the mid-eleventh century.[951] The revised *History* includes a prayer plausibly attributed to Æthelwold and most likely preserved at Abingdon since his time.[952]

Besides relics, a further manifestation of the cult of the saints was the observance of feast days. According to the later version of the *History*, Æthelwold replaced mead with wine at dinner for the principal feasts observed at Abingdon: Christmas, Easter, Whitsun, the Assumption of St Mary and her Nativity, the birth of the apostles Peter and Paul, the feast of All Saints.[953] The same calendar that names Æthelwold also includes various early saints, and their commemoration may reflect Æthelwold's own interests.[954]

The manuscript containing the calendar is of the greatest importance as evidence of learning and liturgical life in late Anglo-Saxon Abingdon.[955] It includes a heavily annotated copy of the *Rule* of St

looks therefore as if Eadgar may have come into possession of relics of St Vincent and divided them between Glastonbury and Abingdon'. On Faritius's treatment of the festivals of St Apollonaris and Vincent, see vol. ii, p. cvi. The head of Apollinaris does not appear in Faritius's relic list.

950 c. 115; cf. B250. Faritius's relic list includes 'the greatest part of St Edward'; see vol. ii. 222. William of Malmesbury stated that parts of Edward's body were taken from Shaftesbury to Leominster and Abingdon; *Gesta pontificum*, bk. ii, c. 86, ed. Hamilton, p. 188.

951 Thacker, 'Æthelwold', pp. 62–3; on the manuscript, Cambridge, Corpus Christi College 57, see below; on the cult, see Wulfstan, *Life of Æthelwold*, ed. Lapidge and Winterbottom, pp. cxii–cxliii. *De abbatibus* records Abbot Ingulf (1130–58) building a chapel dedicated to St Æthelwold; *CMA* ii. 291.

952 B208.

953 See below, p. 342.

954 See Thacker, 'Æthelwold', pp. 62–3.

955 Cambridge, Corpus Christi College 57; for what follows, see esp. M. R. James, *A Descriptive Catalogue of Manuscripts in the Library of Corpus Christi College, Cambridge*

Benedict, two texts associated with the Carolingian reformer Benedict of Aniane, and the *Diadema monachorum* by the early ninth-century author Smaragdus of Saint-Mihiel, again associated with Carolingian reform circles. Such works were used within the monastery, for example for daily communal reading in the chapter. There were also insertions relating to monastic customs and liturgy, and two formulae used to announce the death of members of the community.

The manuscript contents illustrate the influence of Frankish monasticism on liturgical life at Abingdon. *De abbatibus* states that Æthelwold had the *Rule* brought from Fleury. The earlier version of the *History* is not so specific, but states that Æthelwold sent Osgar to Fleury for instruction, from which the monk 'returned with other fellow soldiers and kindly imparted by teaching what he had learnt'.[956] It also records that Æthelwold, 'wishing them to sing praise to God in church with a harmonious voice, summoned from the monastery of Corbie (situated in France and with a very high reputation for ecclesiastical discipline at that time) highly skilled men whom his own monks might imitate in reading and chanting'.[957] Such Frankish, and in particular Fleury, influence was also of wider influence within monastic reform, notably manifest in the *Regularis Concordia*, a text very closely linked to Æthelwold.

Liturgy was central to monastic life, and there is evidence that monks of Æthelwold's *familia*, at least in his time as bishop of Winchester, had to carry out not only the normal monastic offices

(2 vols., Cambridge, 1912), i. 114–18; Gerchow, *Die Gedenküberlieferung*, pp. 244–52, 335–8; Thacker, 'Æthelwold', pp. 54–5; Wormald, 'Æthelwold and his Continental counterparts', p. 31; Gretsch, *Intellectual Foundations*, pp. 252–4. This Abingdon copy is one of five 10th- or 11th-century English manuscripts of the *Regula S. Benedicti abbatis Anianensis siue Collectio capitularis*; Wulfstan, *Life of Æthelwold*, ed. Lapidge and Winterbottom, p. lvii.

[956] *CMA* ii. 278; below, p. 54. See also Wulfstan, *Life of Æthelwold*, c. 14, ed. Lapidge and Winterbottom, p. 26; below, p. 336. For continuing links to Fleury, see Gretsch, *Intellectual Foundations*, pp. 369–70; Lapidge, *Cult of St Swithun*, pp. 220–1, on the possibility of a book belonging to Lantfred, a Frankish monk who had come from Fleury to Winchester, being with Osgar at Abingdon probably in period 974 × 984. Lantfred's own works included the *Translatio et miracula S. Swithuni*; see Lapidge, *Cult of St Swithun*, pp. 218–24. Æthelwold based his translation of the *Rule of St Benedict* on a Fleury version of rule. The date of the translation is uncertain; Gretsch, *Intellectual Foundations*, p. 260, implies that Æthelwold probably brought it with him to Abingdon from Glastonbury. The Fleury version is not that copied in Cambridge, Corpus Christi College 57, which seems to have two exemplars, one Carolingian and the other English, the latter based on an 8th-century Worcester manuscript.

[957] See below, p. 54. For Æthelwold's concern with music, see also *De abbatibus*, which states that he built organs for Abingdon with his own hands; *CMA* ii. 278. See Lapidge, *Cult of Swithun*, pp. 382–3, for organs and Church reform.

but also considerable private devotions.[958] As for other aspects of learning, the position at Abingdon is not entirely clear. We have already seen that the extent of historical writing in Anglo-Saxon Abingdon is a matter of dispute.[959] There was no Abingdon hagiography, no celebrated scholar particularly associated with the house, and only a small number of manuscripts.[960] However, this impression could be deceptive, being partly a matter of survival, partly linked to the departure of the best Abingdon scholars to Winchester and other houses associated with Æthelwold. Moreover, it has been suggested that Æthelwold may well have compiled his gloss on the Royal Psalter while at Abingdon.[961] There are also reasons for believing that there were links between Abingdon and the vernacular gloss on Aldhelm's *De Virginitate*.[962] Although not of interest to the later compiler and reviser of the *History*, such an emphasis on use of the vernacular was a key feature of Æthelwoldian reform.[963]

VIII. MANUSCRIPTS

1. MS C: London, British Library, Cotton Claudius C. IX

Contents (* indicates work of the scribe of the *History*)[964]

fo. 1^{r} Notarial copy of letters patent of Elizabeth I[965]

fo. 1^{v} Pressmarks

fo. 2^{r} Cottonian title page

fo. 3^{r} Cottonian list of contents

[958] Lapidge, 'Æthelwold as scholar and teacher', p. 105.

[959] See above, pp. lx–lxii.

[960] See also *Charters of Abingdon Abbey*, pp. xl–xli; Wulfstan, *Life of Æthelwold*, ed. Lapidge and Winterbottom, p. lxi. Cf., for example, the attribution of the *Life* of Oswald to Byrhtferth, monk of Ramsey. Note also Dumville, *English Caroline Script*, pp. 18, 26, 153–5, on the lack of use of Caroline minuscule at Abingdon until the mid-11th century, whereas it was used at Winchester from the time of Æthelwold.

[961] Gretsch, *Intellectual Foundations*, pp. 263, 266, 274, suggests that Æthelwold compiled his gloss on the Royal Psalter in his time at Glastonbury or Abingdon, with some evidence pointing to Abingdon. See also Dumville, *English Caroline Script*, p. 14 n. 33.

[962] Gretsch, *Intellectual Foundations*, p. 377. Note also ibid., p. 426: 'The origin of the glosses in Æthelwold's circle at Glastonbury (and perhaps Abingdon) also leave it beyond reasonable doubt that it was Æthelwold and Dunstan who were responsible for placing the study of Aldhelm in a central position in the late Anglo-Saxon curriculum, and that it was the intellectual milieu of King Æthelstan's court which inspired them to do so.'

[963] See also Ker, *Catalogue of Manuscripts containing Anglo-Saxon*, no. 2, for a manuscript of the *Excerptiones de Prisciano* with Latin and Old English glosses, which he says (p. 3) is 'almost certainly from Abingdon'.

[964] See also Julian Harrison's description of the manuscript at ⟨http://molcat.bl.uk⟩.

[965] This is a former pastedown.

fos. 4^{r}–12^{r} Hugh of Saint Victor, *Chronicle* (Worcester, s. xii^{2})
fos. 12^{v}–17^{v} Annalistic chronicle (Worcester, s. xii^{2})
fos. 18^{r}–102^{v} William of Malmesbury, *Gesta regum Anglorum* (Battle Abbey, s. xiii^{i})
fos. 102^{v}–103^{r} Award of Norham, 1291
fo. 104^{r} Cottonian title page: 'Historia Abbatiæ Abbendonensis de rebus & terris eiusdem ecclesiæ duobus distincta libris'
fos. 105^{r}–177^{r} *Historia ecclesie Abbendonensis* (s. xii^{2})*
fos. 177^{v}–178^{r} Confirmation charter of Richard I (s. xii^{ex})
fo. 178^{r} Notification of agreement between the abbot of Abingdon and Peter son of Herbert de Forc, 5 Nov. 1232 (s. xiii^{med})
fo. 178^{r-v} Charter of Henry III (s. xiii^{med})[966]
fo. 179^{r-v} Proceedings following the death of Abbot Roger (s. xii^{ex})[967]
fos. 179^{v}–182^{r} Customs relating to obedientiaries (s. xii^{ex})[968]
fo. 182^{r} Lists of (i) hides in Berkshire pertaining to abbey; (ii) knights holding of abbey (s. xiii)
fo. 182^{v} Memorandum of dues owed by John de Courtney (s. xiii^{ex})
fo. 183^{r} Customs relating to obedientiaries, continued (s. xii^{ex})[969]
fo. 183^{r-v} Bull of Alexander III, 1177 (s. xii^{ex})[970]
fo. 184^{r-v} Charter of William, dean and chaplain of Salisbury, 1220–36/7 for Abingdon (s. xiii^{med})
fo. 185^{r} blank
fo. 185^{v} Arrangements concerning the provision of wine (s. xiii^{2})[971]
fo. 186^{r-v} Arrangements for the admission of novices (s. xiii^{2})[972]
fo. 187^{r} Names of tenants holding lands in Wallingford, which pertain to the abbot's chamber (s. xii^{2})
fo. 187^{r} Decree concerning matters done in accordance with the greater part of the chapter (s. xiii)[973]
fo. 187^{r} Principal feast days, on which the abbot was accustomed to eat in the refectory (s. xiii^{ex})

[966] This is a different hand from that earlier in fo. 178^{r}.

[967] Printed *CMA* ii. 297–9, *English Lawsuits from William I to Richard I*, ed. R. C. van Caenegem (2 vols., Selden Society, cvi, cvii; 1990–1), no. 570. This continuation does not pick up the narrative at the point where the *History* ceases. Its later date of composition, after the coronation of the Young King in 1170, is indicated by its use of 'Henricus secundus' for Henry II, rather than the *History*'s 'Henricus iunior'.

[968] Printed *CMA* ii. 299–309.

[969] Printed ibid., pp. 312–13.

[970] Printed ibid., pp. 313–14.

[971] Printed ibid., pp. 314–17.

[972] Printed ibid., pp. 317–20.

[973] Decrees of Third Lateran Council (1179), c. 16. The passage also appears in the Decretals of Gregory IX, X 3.11.1.

fos. 187^{v}–190^{r} Lists concerning lands and tenants of the church of Abingdon in Berkshire (s. xii^{2})*[974]

fo. 190^{r} *Domesday* entries concerning Winkfield and Whistley (s. xii^{ex}/s. xiii^{1}); four lines in early modern hand

fo. 190^{r-v} Abingdon response to 1166 inquest into knight service (s. xii^{2})*[975]

fo. 191^{r} List of lands and tenants (s. xii^{2})*[976]

fo. 191^{v} Custom of wood to be gathered for fuel (s. xii^{2})*[977]

fos. 191^{v}–192^{r} Dues owed to the monks' kitchen (s. xii^{2}, with near contemporary addition)*[978]

fo. 192^{r} Refectorer's dues and obligations (s. xii^{ex})[979]

fo. 192^{v} Rents of the altar (s. xii^{2})*[980]

fo. 192^{v} Rents of the chamber (s. xii^{2})*[981]

fo. 193^{r} Rents of the almoner (s. xii^{ex})[982]

fo. 193^{r} Bull of Pope Alexander III (s. xii^{ex})

fo. 193^{r} Rent of the precentor (s. xii^{ex})[983]

fo. 193^{r-v} Rent of the infirmary (s. xii^{ex})[984]

fo. 193^{v} Rent pertaining to the fabric of buildings (s. xii^{ex})[985]

fos. 193^{v}–194^{r} Rent of the hostillar (s. xii^{ex}/s. xiii)[986]

fo. 194^{r-v} Memorandum concerning tenants and lands (s. xiii)[987]

fo. 194^{v} Rents due to the almoner (s. xiii)[988]

fo. 195 late medieval or early modern parchment leaf

fos. 196^{r}–202^{v} Boundary clauses for Abingdon charters (s. xii^{2})*

fo. 203^{r} Charter of Edward I for Abingdon (s. xiv)

fo. 203^{r} Charter of Henry III for Abingdon (s. xiv)

fos. 204^{r}–209^{v} Early modern Abingdon indexes, notes, letters, on paper

fo. 210 medieval/early modern parchment pastedown (lifted)

[974] Printed vol. ii. 379–89; see also D. C. Douglas, 'Some early surveys from the abbey of Abingdon', *EHR*, xliv (1929), 618–25, at pp. 623–5.

[975] Printed vol. ii. 389–91.

[976] Ibid., pp. 391–4.

[977] Ibid. pp. 394–5; *CMA* ii. 321–2.

[978] Printed vol. ii. 395–6; *CMA* ii. 322–4.

[979] Printed *CMA* ii. 324.

[980] Printed vol. ii. 397; *CMA* ii. 324–5.

[981] Printed vol. ii. 398; *CMA* ii. 326–7.

[982] Printed *CMA* ii. 327–8.

[983] Printed ibid., p. 328.

[984] Printed ibid., p. 328.

[985] Printed ibid., p. 329.

[986] Printed ibid., pp. 329–30.

[987] Printed ibid., pp. 330–2.

[988] Printed ibid., pp. 332–4. This passage is in the same hand as the preceding memorandum concerning tenants.

Date and history of the manuscript

As argued earlier, the section of MS C devoted to the Abingdon *History* probably dates from the 1160s.[989] Given that the *History* goes up to the early part of that decade, the existing manuscript is most likely the first fair copy of the work.[990] The post-Reformation history of the Abingdon portion of the manuscript is uncertain until it was acquired by Sir Robert Cotton, probably by 1610. It was he who brought the Abingdon material together with the other historical works that now form Cotton Claudius C. IX.[991]

Physical description of the History *portion of MS C*

The text of the *History* is written in two columns, with normally thirty-eight lines per column.[992] The writing rises from the top ruled line. The written area is approximately 225–35 × 155–65 mm. The first four quires, each of four bifolia, form Book I of the *History* (fos. 105–35).[993] Quires 5 to 11 form Book II of the *History* (fos. 136–77).[994] It is notable that the last two 'quires' are in fact each a single bifolium, suggesting that the scribe was making preparation for the end of the work.

An Arabic numeral foliation from 1 to 74 at the centre of the upper margin of the recto predates the bringing together of the various elements of MS C, and extends from the opening of the *History* to

[989] See above, p. xv.

[990] The physical stages of writing out historical texts in the 12th century require further study. For the use of wax tablets for a draft, see Eadmer, *The Life of St Anselm*, ed. R. W. Southern (NMT, 1962; corrected reprint OMT, 1979), p. 150. For a surviving author's draft, with corrections, interlineations, marginal text, and spaces left blank for names or improvements, see *Cronicon Richardi Divisensis de tempore regis Richardi primi*, ed. J. T. Appleby (NMT, 1963), pp. xviii–xxiv.

[991] For the general context of Cotton's interests, see E. M. C. van Houts, 'Camden, Cotton, and the Chronicles of the Norman Conquest of England', in C. J. Wright, ed., *Sir Robert Cotton as Collector* (London, 1997), pp. 238–52; at p. 248 she points out that Cotton obtained the *Ramsey Chronicle*, the *Liber Eliensis*, Hemming's cartulary, and both manuscripts of the Abingdon *History*. C. G. C. Tite, '"Lost or stolen or strayed": A survey of manuscripts formerly in the Cotton Library', in Wright, ed., *Sir Robert Cotton as Collector*, pp. 262–306, at 266, points out that in the early 1620s Cotton owned Oxford, Bodleian Library, Digby 96, the Abingdon manuscript of the *Meditations of Godwin*.

[992] There are thirty-nine lines on fos. 119^{v} and 120^{r}; thirty-seven lines on fos. 132^{v} and 133^{r}; thirty-six lines on fo. 169^{v}. In the portions by the main scribe after the *History*, there are normally thirty-eight lines per column, although only thirty-seven at fos. 201^{v} and 202^{r}.

[993] One folio of quire 3 is missing, between fos. 126 and 127.

[994] Quire 5 consists of four bifolia and one single folio; quire 6 of three bifolia; quire 7 of five bifolia; quires 8 and 9 each of three bifolia and a single folio.

include the charter of Richard I. It is then replaced by separate foliations for the different sections that follow. An emended version of the foliation of the *History* then appears at the top right-hand corner of the recto. A further ink foliation of the whole manuscript at the top right-hand corner of the recto has been superseded by a modern pencil foliation at top and bottom right-hand corners.[995] A folio is missing from the manuscript between the present fos. 126 and 127.[996]

The *History* in MS C contains only one illustration, a depiction of Abbot Faritius as part of an initial A at the start of the account of his abbacy at fo. 144^{r}. The illustration is in gold and red, outlined in green and on a blue background. In addition, there is a large zoomorphic initial M in gold and other colours at the start of Book I, large decorated initials at the start of the sections on the restoration of the church under Eadred and Æthelwold and of the charter in Eadred's name which follows, a large initial A in gold and other colours at the start of Book II, and two drawings of the papal rota of Eugenius III.[997] There are also secondary initials in red, green, and light blue, with varying degrees of elaboration.[998]

Rubrication is in the same hand as the main text. All section headings are rubricated.[999] Within the main text, whole words are sometimes in red ink. Some are place-names, most are personal names, in particular those of Anglo-Saxon kings within charters.[1000] Kings' names also very occasionally appear in red outside charters.[1001] Abbots too appear in red ink, most notably Æthelwold and Faritius.[1002] Initials

[995] This refoliation is dated 21 Jan. 1970 at the end of the manuscript.

[996] This was fo. 23 in the early foliation. I can find no obvious reason why it was removed.

[997] fos. 105^{r}, 111^{r}, 170^{v}, 171^{v}. The same decorator may have been responsible for the major decorated initials in Oxford, All Souls College 18, but that manuscript—although it could be an Abingdon product—was not written by the same scribe.

[998] For such initials following headings, see e.g. fos. 113^{v}, 115^{v}, 118^{v}. To fo. 108^{v} the initials are alternately in red and green. At fo. 108^{v} there is a blue initial, and thereafter there is no predominant ordering of colours. The larger of these initials following headings sometimes appear in the margin; e.g. fos. 105^{r} (central margin), 107^{r}, 119^{r}.

[999] Note the four lines of rubricated text, probably over an erasure, at fo. 105^{r} (heading to c. 2); the four and a half lines at fo. 111^{r} (heading to c. 28); almost four lines at fo. 135^{v} (*explicit* to Book I); three lines at fo. 143^{v} (heading for the chapter introducing Faritius, vol. ii. 64).

[1000] For place-names, note fos. 114^{r} (Ginge), 118^{v} (Drayton). Henry I's name is rubricated in two places on fo. 159^{r}, the first being in a charter.

[1001] Note fo. 118^{r} Edgar; fo. 159^{r} Henry I.

[1002] Æthelwold, fos. 111^{r}, 113^{v}, 114^{r}, 114^{v}, 117^{v}, 118^{r}, 118^{v}, 119^{r}, 124^{r}; Faritius, fos. 148^{v}–164^{v}; also Abbot Vincent, fos. 164^{v}–167^{r}; Ingulf fo. 168^{r}. Note also: fo. 118^{r} Dunstan; fo. 124^{v} Pope Leo, King Coenwulf, Abbot Hræthhun; fos. 124^{v}, 126^{v} Abbot Wulfgar; fo. 124^{r} Virgin Mary.

of witnesses are added in red, green, or blue,[1003] although on occasion the rubricator, having added those in red, forgot to return with another colour.[1004]

Other words are emphasized by the use of capitals, often within charters.[1005] The names of kings, abbots, the Virgin Mary, and other saints are on occasion made prominent in this way.[1006] So too are place names.[1007] Likewise whole words at the start of a charter, of a heading, or of a section quite frequently are capitalized.[1008] On other occasions, just part of a word is capitalized, again often names or the start of sections.[1009]

The scribe has a few orthographic habits worth noting. The tailed 'e' is used almost invariably at the start of the word 'ecclesia',[1010] and frequently but far from invariably where one would expect the form 'ae' in classical Latin.[1011] It also appears inappropriately for the ablative 'e' ending.[1012] The form 'v' as opposed to 'u' is used occasionally in lower case, for example as the second letter of a word the initial of which is to be added by the rubricator.[1013] The Latin word for shire, 'vicecomitatus' is often spelt with an opening 'v', the words 'uxor' and 'ui' sometimes are, and there are other

[1003] Note also the crosses following witnesses at fo. 159^r^.

[1004] At fo. 127^r^ (c. 102) the rubricator provided the initials of the witnesses in red but forgot to return with another colour to fill in the capital of the 'Ego', which preceded each name. Also there are examples of the rubricator forgetting to add initials, especially at the start of a line; see e.g. fos. 115^v^, 120^v^, 127^r^ (cc. 48, 70, 104).

[1005] Capitalization and rubrication of names does not seem to have been determined in any simple fashion by the copying of originals. Take Æthelred's *Orthodoxorum* charter, c. 98, the original of which is London, British Library, Cotton Augustus ii. 38. This has some names, of kings and of the Virgin Mary, in capitals in a different black ink, and other personal and place-names in capitals in the usual ink. MS B makes no such distinctions. MS C has some names in red and in capitals, but these include Abbots Wulfgar and Æthelwold. The Virgin Mary only once appears in red. Abbot Eadwine appears in capitals in the original, but not in MS C, and similarly place-names and even St Benedict are not distinguished by case or colour in MS C. At most the original suggested the distinguishing of some words by case and colour; it certainly did not determine the forms adopted in the *History*.

[1006] e.g. fos. 105^r^, 106^r^, 109^r^, 113^r^, 117^v^, 129^r^, 141^v^, 155^r^, 155^v^, 156^r^ and many other examples. There are exceptions; see e.g. fos. 105^v^, 122^r^, 122^v^.

[1007] e.g. fos. 106^r^, 110^r^, and many other examples.

[1008] e.g. fos. 106^r^, 113^v^, 115^v^, 126^v^, and many other examples. Note 'Amen' capitalized at fos. 110^v^, 126^v^.

[1009] Capital N may be particularly common; e.g. fo. 115^r^.

[1010] For irregularity of usage see the charters of Nigel d'Oilly and Henry I concerning *Abbefeld* at fo. 150^r^.

[1011] See e.g. fo. 160^r^, lines 4 and 5.

[1012] See fo. 162^r^.

[1013] e.g. fo. 106^v^ (opening of c. 9), 108^v^ (opening of c. 18), fo. 109^r^ (opening of c. 19).

occasional instances.[1014] Very occasionally words beginning 'on . . .' appear in the aspirated form 'hon . . .': 'honeris', 'honerosus', 'honere'.[1015] Likewise the pronoun 'is' sometimes appears as 'his'.[1016] The exceptional form 'monakis' in a 'Cirograph concerning the land of Chesterton' may reflect the original from which the scribe was copying.[1017]

The manuscript has various marginalia in later medieval and early modern hands. Two groups of marginalia are of particular significance for us. One is in a small hand writing in brown ink, the other in a larger hand in dry-point. Both appear to be hands that gave guidance to the rubricator of MS B, and the marginalia in MS C appear in the main text of MS B.[1018] Such annotations indicate that the compiler of MS B was making direct use of MS C, although it cannot absolutely rule out the additional existence of another, intervening manuscript.

Material following the History

The *History* is followed by a copy of the confirmation charter of Richard I in a slightly later hand, followed by diverse other material, with fos. 179–85 perhaps forming a separate booklet. This in turn is followed by what may be another booklet, including a group of administrative texts by the main scribe.[1019] Why these appear here rather than within the *History* is uncertain. They may have been deemed inappropriate in form for that text, but the

1014 'Vicecomitatus': fos. 138^r, 151^v, 152^r, 160^v; other uses: e.g. 'vicecomitibus' fos. 138^r, 152^r, 'vidente' fo. 152^v.

1015 See below, pp. 20, 24, 180, 190, 216, ii. 14.

1016 See below, p. 132; vol. ii. 34, 106, 196; note also 'hisdem' for 'isdem', vol. ii. 188, 280.

1017 vol. ii. 200.

1018 Given that the marginalia in MS C are sometimes erased, identification can be difficult. However, for the small, brown ink hand, see esp. fo. 154^r, and note also fos. 154^v, 166^v. For the dry-point hand, see esp. fos. 129^v (cf. heading to B252), 135^r (see B285), 162^v (see vol. ii. 214), and note also fos. 131^v, 135^v. The identity of the dry-point hand in the two manuscripts is clear by comparing MS C, fos. 129^v and 131^v with MS B, fo. 155^r.

1019 See vol. ii, App. III. Keynes, 'Studies', p. 77, associates the *Domesday* related administrative lists with the early 12th-century case heard in the treasury at Winchester, vol. ii. 168–70, but this association is unprovable. The quire with the administrative lists consists of five bifolia, of which the outside one could be an addition; fos. 186–95. The administrative lists start on the verso of the second of the five bifolia; fo. 187^v. If the lists formed a separate booklet, and the current outmost bifolium is an addition, this would have left the recto of its first folio initially blank, although it was subsequently written upon; fo. 187^r. This and the preceding set of diverse texts probably had an early existence separate from the *History*, having once been foliated 1–16 in Arabic numerals.

History does contain ornament and relic lists and allocations to obedientiaries whilst the reviser entered administrative texts into his account.[1020]

The final medieval quire contains vernacular boundary clauses, most of which can be shown to have been extracted from royal diplomas.[1021] In one case the survey is followed by a vernacular agreement concerning the sale of land at Kingston Bagpuize to the abbey; a Latin version of the agreement had already appeared in the *History*.[1022] The majority of the clauses come from charters that appear in both versions of the *History*, some from charters that are only in MS B. Sets of bounds concerning Charney Basset and Wormleighton, however, do not apparently derive from either version of the *History*.[1023] The boundary clauses provide good coverage for estates that the abbey held in 1066, and it is possible that no boundary clauses were available for the *TRE Domesday* estates not covered.[1024] It is unclear whether the collection of boundary clauses was put together by the compiler of the *History*, or what relationship its compilation had to the writing of the *History*.[1025] For example, there are only limited similarities of arrangement of the boundary clauses to the order of charters in the *History*. It could be that the order derives at least in part from the organization of the original charters into bundles within the abbey's archive chests.[1026]

The medieval section of MS C concerning Abingdon therefore is made up of the *History* and what may have been three separate booklets, two of which contain work by the scribe of the *History*. The

[1020] Vol. ii. 214–24, 322–6, 336–8, 358–70.

[1021] The boundary quire consists of three bifolia and a single folio; fos. 196–202. It was once foliated 1–7 in Arabic numerals, again suggesting an existence separate from the *History*. On this collection of boundary clauses, see *Charters of Abingdon Abbey*, pp. xlvi, lvi–lvii, 590–1; Keynes, 'Studies', pp. 77–87.

[1022] c. 93, *Charters of Abingdon Abbey*, p. 589 (no. 50).

[1023] *Charters of Abingdon Abbey*, nos. 71A, 150, pp. 588 (no. 35), 590 (no. 54).

[1024] See Keynes, 'Studies', p. 86, for Whistley, Sandford-on-Thames, and Beedon. Note that some charters appear in MS C without their boundary clauses appearing in this collection; see esp. the group of charters concerning lands outside Berkshire and Oxfordshire given by Edgar; cc. 67, 69, 70. None of this group recorded a *Domesday* possession of Abingdon. In other cases the *History* contained more than one charter concerning a place, whereas the boundary quire contains only one boundary clause; e.g. Ginge, cc. 42, 60, *Charters of Abingdon Abbey*, p. 585 (no. 3).

[1025] Clearly the *History* concentrated primarily on Latin material, the boundary clause collection on vernacular, but this need not mean that the latter was produced by a process of excision as the composer looked through his sources and put together the *History*.

[1026] On the organization of the collection of boundary clauses, see *Charters of Abingdon Abbey*, p. 591.

date at which these additional sections became physically attached to the *History* cannot be determined with certainty.

2. MS B: London, British Library, Cotton Claudius B. VI

Contents

fo. 1^{r} Cottonian binding instruction
fo. 1^{v} Pressmarks
fo. 2^{r} Cottonian contents page
fo. 3^{r} Battle scene (s. xv^{med}). Initial; rest of text erased[1027]
fo. 3^{v} French text, with three line erasure in col. 1
fos. 4^{r}–177^{v} *History of the Church of Abingdon* (s. $xiii^{2/4}$)
fos. 178^{r}–202^{v} Treatise on obedientiaries (s. $xiii^{2/4}$)

Date and history of the manuscript

MS B was written by a scribe probably working in the second quarter or perhaps the middle of the thirteenth century.[1028] It has been suggested that the illustrations are unlikely to be later than the 1220s or 1230s, which would be within the range suggested by the script.[1029] The same scribe was responsible for the treatise on the obedientiaries of the abbey that follows the *History* in the manuscript.

We know rather more of the later history of MS B than of MS C. It belonged to Sir Thomas Parry (d. 1616), who held various former Abingdon estates amongst his lands in Berkshire. The manuscript was later in the possession of Robert Erskine, Viscount Fenton and first earl of Kelly, who had acquired various Berkshire estates through his marriage to a member of the Norreys family, lords of Hormer hundred and Cumnor. It then passed to a Mr Powell of Sandford and

[1027] N. Morgan, *Early Gothic Manuscripts [I]: 1190–1250* (Oxford, 1982), p. 89. See also M. P. Brown, 'Sir Robert Cotton, collector and connoisseur?', in M. P. Brown and S. McKendrick , ed., *Illuminating the Book: Makers and Interpreters. Essays in Honour of Janet Backhouse* (London, 1998), pp. 281–95, at 294: 'A strikingly carefully executed example of text erasure is to be found in Claudius B.vi, fol. 3, where a fifteenth-century French miniature and initial have been left floating in disembodied fashion on the page, presumably intended to accommodate a Cottonian inscription (in similar fashion to Nero A. II, fol. 2) and to act as a decorative frontispiece to a chronicle and the Cartulary of Abingdon Abbey. A curious three-line text erasure also occurs on the verso of the leaf. Something of a pattern of usage for leaves from this French volume can be observed. They are frequently used, in their painstaking partially erased state, to preface volumes containing combined chronicles and cartularies, as in Cleopatra D.ii (the Cartulary of Guisborough Priory), which also has a three-line erasure on its verso.'

[1028] See above, p. xxxvii, for it presumably being written after the death of Abbot Hugh, since it refers to him as a 'man of blessed memory'.

[1029] Morgan, *Early Gothic Manuscripts*, pp. 89–90.

thence to Thomas Allen (1542–1632), an Oxford scholar who possessed at least five former Abingdon manuscripts. From him MS B passed to Sir Robert Cotton, and is included in the catalogue of his library begun in 1621.[1030]

Physical description of the History *portion of MS B*

The text is written in two columns. The writing rises from the top ruled line. The standard written area is approximately 220–5 × 135–40 mm. In general there are thirty-eight lines per column, although fo. 31^{r} has only thirty-two lines, fo. 31^{v} only thirty-one.[1031] Fo. 81^{r}, which like fo. 31 is on thinner parchment, has the text in an unusual arrangement, with three additional lines at the bottom, the last two stretching across both columns. The manuscript is too tightly sewn to be certain of quiring without disbinding. Chapter numbers in roman numerals from 5 to 52 appear in the margins on fos. 4^{r}–19^{r}. However, these are not original, because they are by the same hand as roman numeral page/folio numbers that were added after the loss of early folios.[1032]

Some folios are missing. Probably two folios are lacking at the start, so that the *History* begins in what may have been its fourth chapter.[1033] After the first surviving folio of the *History*, two further folios are missing between the current fos. 4 and 5. Further folios are missing between the current fos. 130 and 131, and between fos. 160 and 161. These folios were presumably taken because they contained illustrations of Henry I and Stephen. Those between fos. 4 and 5 may have contained an illustration of Ceadwalla. The folios at the start, too, may have contained desirable illustrations.

It is very hard to tell what would have appeared in the missing folios at the start of the work. A Preface is one possibility, or general material such as appears at the start of *De abbatibus* in London,

[1030] *Charters of Abingdon Abbey*, pp. lii–iii, lviii. Allen may also have been the source of Cotton's Abingdon single-sheet diplomas.

[1031] Note that fo. 31 is on thinner parchment than normal, although not uniquely so; fo. 36 is also on thinner parchment, but has the normal number of lines. There are other exceptions; thus fos. 10^{r}, 11^{r}–13^{v}, 14rb, 14^{v}–19^{r} have thirty-seven lines per column, 19^{v} thirty-six, 20^{r-v} thirty-seven, 23ra forty, 28^{v} thirty-seven, 81^{v} thirty-seven, 92^{r}–95^{v} thirty-nine, 110ra thirty-nine, 140^{r-v} thirty-seven. Thirty-eight lines per column remains normal in *De obedientiariis*. The text at the end of the *History*, fo. 177^{v}, is written in one column down the centre of the page.

[1032] See fos. 4^{r}–19^{r}. At fo. 10^{r} there is a shift from numbering by page to numbering by folio.

[1033] Certainly the first of the roman numeral chapters is 'V'; fo. 4^{r}.

British Library Cotton Vitellius A. XIII, fos. 83^{r}–84^{r}. The next pair of missing folios must have completed the account of the Saxon invasion, and then probably dealt with the foundation story involving King Cissa, Abbot Hæha, and his sister Cilla. The text must also have recorded gifts by Ceadwalla, since a surviving passage that follows refers to Ceadwalla's gifts 'enumerated above'.[1034] It may also have included two early charters that only survive in MS C.[1035] The contents of the remaining two missing folios can be reconstructed from MS C, since they concern the period for which MS B is very much a direct copy of MS C.

The earliest page/folio numbering is, as noted above, in roman numerals. Subsequent Arabic numeral foliations at the centre and the right-hand corner of the top of the recto are superseded from fo. 101^{r} by modern pencil foliation and there is also modern pencil foliation throughout at the bottom right-hand corner of the recto.[1036]

Initials at the start of sections and sometimes at the start of charter boundary clauses are large, and usually red flourished with blue or blue flourished with red, generally in an alternating series.[1037] Initials within sections, if coloured, are plain red or blue, and these same colours are sometimes used for initials of witnesses' names or of the word 'Ego' or for a cross preceding a witness.[1038]

Rubrication is in the same hand as the main text. All section headings are rubricated. However, apart from subheadings such as 'Mete (boundaries)' or 'testes (witnesses)',[1039] MS B does not follow MS C's repeated rubrication of whole words outside headings. Guidance for the rubricator is provided on occasion in dry-point or in small, informal script in brown ink. In both cases this writing is generally in the margin, although sometimes it is apparently the main scribe using his normal ink who provides a small letter where a coloured initial is to appear.[1040]

[1034] See below, p. 244.

[1035] cc. 5, 6.

[1036] The Arabic numeral foliation at the centre of the top of the recto may be late medieval or early modern, that at the right-hand corner 18th century.

[1037] For exceptions, see fos. 119^{v}–120^{r} for two large blue initials in a row. See also fo. 118^{r} for a large initial half in blue and half in red (cf. fo. 178^{r}, the start of *De obedientiariis*); fos. 127^{v}, 176^{v}, for large initials in red without blue decoration; fo. 176^{v} for a small blue initial at the start of a section.

[1038] See also fo. 155^{v} for coloured initials of church vestments, vessels, and ornaments, fos. 156^{v}–157^{r} for initials of saints.

[1039] e.g. fos. 11^{r}, 18^{v}, 30^{v}, 107^{r}, 114^{v}, 115^{r}.

[1040] See e.g. fos. 22^{v}, 25^{v}, 118^{r}, 129^{v}.

Other words are emphasized by capitals, although not with the same frequency as in MS C. Notable amongst these again are kings' names in charters,[1041] and also singled out is the word 'testes' at the start of witness lists.[1042] On other occasions it is just parts of words or individual letters that appear in capitals.[1043]

Again a few orthographical habits should be noted. Anglo-Saxon runic forms are more common than in MS C,[1044] although they are not always used when they might be.[1045] An Anglo-Saxon form of the letter 'g' is often used in Old English personal and place names, although not consistently so.[1046] It is also used for the words 'geldum', 'gildum', and 'geldare',[1047] and in passages of Old English even outside boundary clauses.[1048] The form 'v' as opposed to 'u' is used occasionally in lower case.[1049] The scribe of MS B also on occasion uses a compound form of the letters 'Th' at the start of place and personal names.[1050] With slightly more frequency than in MS C, although still far from commonly, words normally beginning with vowels appear in aspirated form, for example 'his' for 'is'.[1051] In contrast, at one point MS B gives 'onorifice' where MS C gives the standard 'honorifice'.[1052]

The manuscript has various marginalia in later medieval and early modern hands. There are various words and letters to provide guidance for the rubricator, most commonly in a small informal hand in brown ink,[1053] also in black ink,[1054] with increasing frequency

1041 e.g. fos. 6^v^, 31^r^.

1042 e.g. fos. 114^v^, 115^r^, for red capitals for 'testes'. Note also e.g. Archbishop Oda's name capitalized in a witness list at fo. 44^r^.

1043 See e.g. fos. 13^v^, 39^r^.

1044 see e.g. cc. 22, 23.

1045 See e.g. c. 101, where a runic form is used for Wulfgar's name in the 16th-century copy where it is not used in MS B; also c. 50, where the original uses a wynn in King Eadwig's name, but MS B does not.

1046 e.g. fos. 14^r^, 22^v^, 24^r^, 142^v^, 151^r^, 153^v^, 156^r^, and many other examples. For inconsistent usage, see e.g. fo. 45^v^. The scribe was presumably very familiar with the form from the Anglo-Saxon charters he was copying.

1047 e.g. fos. 137^r^, 148^v^, 149^v^, 163^r^.

1048 e.g. 'gife' at fo. 7^v^.

1049 e.g. fos. 141^r^, 171^r^. The scribe also with some frequency uses 'uu' for 'w'; I have standardized the text to the latter form.

1050 See fos. 6^r^, 138^v^, 148r, 150^v^, 151^v^, 173^v^.

1051 Aspirated forms in both MSS; below, p. 132, ii. 34, 106, 188, 196, 280; aspirated form just in MS B: below, pp. 138, 224 ('his' for 'iis'); vol. ii. 8, 36, 168. See also p. 262 for 'Hæthelwlfo', p. 292 for 'Hine', p. 334 for 'Hedgari'. However, see 'honeris' in MS C and pp. 20 and 24 being corrected to 'oneris' in MS B.

1052 c. 64 (MS B fo. 78^r^).

1053 e.g. fos. 9^r^–10^v^, 38^v^, 39^v^, 112^v^, 113^r^.

1054 e.g. fos. 174^r^, 175^r^.

in dry-point or pencil,[1055] and in the main hand.[1056] Sometimes these guiding notes are fully or partially erased.[1057] On other occasions these hands provide indications of corrections that are made in the main text.[1058]

Illustrations

MS B is punctuated with portraits of kings and queens that normally appear at the start of the first charter issued by them.[1059] Their later desirability is suggested by the removal of some folios that would have contained such portraits. On average they are approximately two-thirds of a written column wide. The smallest, of Æthelflæd, lady of the Mercians, and of Cnut, stretch down for nine lines of writing, the largest, of Edgar, sixteen lines. The rulers are depicted against burnished gold backgrounds, crowned, seated, and in a variety of postures. Some are holding a sceptre, normally but not always in the right hand. Others hold a sword in their right hand. Some have an index finger extended, normally towards the start of the accompanying charter in their name. Others have their open hand outstretched in a similar direction. Henry II has the first and second fingers of his right hand extended, in a gesture resembling that of benediction. The style of illustrations, it has been suggested, resembles that of the Huntingfield Psalter, and, given that the Psalter was produced in Oxford, may derive from the same workshop.[1060]

There is no illustration of King Edmund, but at the point of his

[1055] e.g. fos. 117^{r}, 118^{r}, 119^{r}. Later in the manuscript the rubricator sometimes failed to follow the dry-point guidance and did not provide a heading, e.g. fos. 155^{r}, 161^{r}.

[1056] e.g. fos. 34^{r}, 102^{r}.

[1057] e.g. fos. 48^{r}, 49^{r}, 63^{r}.

[1058] e.g. fos. 33^{r}, 36^{r}, 64^{r}, 112^{r}, 112^{v}, 113^{r}, 123^{r}, 139^{r}, 155^{v}, 156^{v}.

[1059] Fos. 6^{r} Ine (sceptre in right hand), 9^{v} Coenwulf (index finger of right hand extended), 12^{r} Ecgberht (sword), 13^{r} Æthelbald (sceptre in right hand), 14^{r} Æthelswith (index finger of left hand extended), 14^{r} Æthelflæd (sceptre in right hand, open left hand outstretched), 18^{r} Æthelstan (open left hand outstretched), 33^{v} Eadred (sceptre in right hand, legs crossed), 43^{r} Eadwig (sceptre in right hand, index finger of left hand extended), 63^{r} Edgar (index finger of right hand extended), 85^{v} Edward the martyr (sword, index finger of left hand extended), 87^{v} Æthelred (sword), 106^{r} Cnut (sceptre in right hand, index finger of left hand extended), 108^{v} Harthacnut (sword, index finger of left hand extended, pointing downwards and away from start of charter), 109^{v} Edward the Confessor (sceptre in right hand, index finger of left hand extended), 119^{v} William I (sceptre in right hand, index finger of left hand extended), 124^{r} William II (sword, index finger of left hand extended), 169^{v} Henry II (first and second fingers of right hand extended, sceptre in left hand), 176^{v} Richard I (sword).

[1060] Morgan, *Early Gothic Manuscripts*, pp. 77–9, 89–90, illustrations 107, 109, 111, 113. For a comparative context, see S. Lewis, *The Art of Matthew Paris in the Chronica Majora* (Aldershot, 1987), ch. 3; she mentions Cotton Claudius B. VI at pp. 140, 143, 491 n. 16.

death, mentioned at the start of Book II, there is a large initial 'I' at the top of which there is a king's head, by the same artist as was responsible for the other royal portraits.[1061] There is also a depiction—in blue ink—of the Black Cross at the start of the account of its finding,[1062] and drawings of the papal rota of Eugenius III within two of his bulls.[1063]

IX. EDITIONS AND TRANSLATION

The Rolls Series edition of the *History* was based on the later of the two manuscripts, and also manages to conflate the two versions in confusing fashion.[1064] The edition has been long criticized, most notably by Stenton.[1065] The main text in the present edition is based on the earlier of the manuscripts, with variant readings from the later manuscript and from 'original' charters noted.[1066] Only the most significant variants from later copies of charters are recorded.[1067] In the present volume, where the two versions of the *History* differ considerably, the later version is set out in an appendix, with its independent narratives edited in full, its charters and those narratives derived from the earlier version of the *History* calendared.[1068] The

[1061] fo. 32^{v}. [1062] B7, fo. 5^{v}. [1063] fos. 164^{v}, 165^{v}.

[1064] See further Hudson, 'Abbey of Abingdon', pp. 182–4, 187–8, 200–2.

[1065] Stenton, *Early History*, p. 1 n. 1: 'The editing of these texts does not bear detailed criticism. In 1858 little work had been done upon Old English diplomatic, and it would not be expected that the editor's criticism of the land-books in the series should have value at the present time. It is more serious that he cannot be trusted implicitly to give the exact reading of his texts. . . . His identifications of sites mentioned in the course of the work are often wildly inaccurate and have misled many subsequent scholars. The whole plan of the edition, by which the latest MS. was adopted for the text, is faulty.' Edwards, in *Charters of the Early West Saxon Kingdom*, p. 166, comments that Birch's edition of the Anglo-Saxon charters was an improvement on Stevenson's.

[1066] I have not footnoted where the original alone uses 'ae' or 'æ' when MSS C and B use 'e'; these variants are readily available in *Charters of Abingdon Abbey* and in *BM Facs.* When a section of the *History* survives in only one manuscript and I emend that manuscript's reading in my edition, I use the abbreviation MS when giving the manuscript reading in the *apparatus criticus*, to distinguish these instances from variants deriving from a second manuscript. Marginal references to MS C appear at the appropriate folio break. Those to MS B appear at the break when the text is being edited in full, or at the appropriate first section heading when the text is being calendared. The same practices are followed for marginal references to Stevenson's edition.

[1067] The variants in later copies are readily available in *Charters of Abingdon Abbey*. That volume, as it is interested in presenting the best possible texts of the charters, bases its texts on originals where available; in contrast, my interest is to present the texts as they exist in the *History*.

[1068] In the case of chapters in MS B very largely derived from MS C, a combination of calendaring and editing is employed to allow clear understanding of the text: see below, B214, B215, B248, B285, B287, B290.

charters, generally edited from MS B, are easily available in Susan Kelly's edition of the *Charters of Abingdon Abbey*.[1069] In Volume 2, where the two versions of the *History* are much closer together, additions and continuation in the later manuscript are placed in appendices. A further appendix in Volume 2 includes administrative documents written in the earlier manuscript by the scribe of the *History*. The present edition therefore includes all the work of the main scribe in MS C except the quire of boundary clauses; these clauses are readily available via the *Charters of Abingdon Abbey*.

In the great majority of cases I have inserted section breaks and headings in the text only when these are clear in the manuscripts through rubricated headings, represented by italics in the present edition.[1070] Very occasionally, I have introduced a break when a heading seems to have been omitted in the manuscripts because of the position on the page, for example the top of a new column.[1071] Occasionally the scribe's normal process of division into sections seems to have broken down, leading to more diffuse sections than usual.[1072] On occasion I have divided such sections where there is a marked change of subject matter,[1073] particularly when there is a scribal indication of a shift, for example a large initial.[1074] The decision in such cases as to when to divide is necessarily somewhat arbitrary.[1075]

Minor matters of orthography, such as the use of 'c' or 't', have been standardized according to the preferred usage of MS C, even though this manuscript was not always consistent. I have not noted MS B's variants in such matters. In the appendices based solely on

[1069] To avoid unnecessary overlap with Susan Kelly's work, and also awkwardness of formatting, the invocations and proems, and the boundary and dating clauses and witness lists that MS B includes for charters that also appear in MS C are simply footnoted with a reference to *Charters of Abingdon Abbey*, rather than being given in the *apparatus criticus*. The text as in MS B should therefore be reconstructed by working from the Appendix, using its cross-references to *Charters of Abingdon Abbey* and the text as in MS C, and using the *apparatus criticus* of each to obtain MS B's readings. In the case of B285 the variants from c. 143 are sufficient that I have printed MS B's text in full, even though it is only a revision of MS C's version.

[1070] I have not italicized single rubricated words introducing a witness list or boundary clause. The chapter numbers are my own, and their series continues uninterrupted where folios are missing in the manuscript.

[1071] See e.g. cc. 103, 109, 136, 138, B23, B31, B55, B56, B85, B142, B143, B258, vol. ii. 252.

[1072] See e.g. cc. 115, 141, 143.

[1073] See e.g. cc. 115–16.

[1074] e.g. c. 122.

[1075] e.g. cc. 18, 136, might have been split at points where there was a large initial, but I have treated them as single sections.

MS B, I have followed that manuscript's customary practices, rather than standardizing according to the preferred practice of MS C. I have reproduced place-names as they appear in the manuscripts, noting MS B's variants. There are considerable problems in expanding place-names, and I have sought a solution that neither obscures the sense of the narrative sections of the text by retaining numerous unextended place-names, nor renders the edition unhelpful to those interested in early place-name forms. If MS C gives an abbreviated form that leaves the core of the place-name clear but removes only the ending, I have adopted MS B's reading when the latter provides a complete word. Otherwise, I have followed MS C's most common usage. This can produce a spurious certainty when the decision is made on the basis of very few or no instances of the full name.[1076] The ablative of adjectival forms of place-names regularly, although not universally, appears as '-e', not '-i'. In the appendices, I have followed the practice of MS B in its prevalent place-name forms. Both manuscripts are inconsistent in the use of figures or words for numbers. In the *History*, I have standardized usage as words for small numbers, except when referring to amounts of money. In the various administrative lists in the appendices to Volume 2, I follow the practices of those lists.

Paragraphing is consistent between text and translation. Where possible, sentences in the translation correspond with those in the Latin text, but not infrequently such strict correspondence would lead to a quite inappropriate translation, with an excessively Latinate succession of clauses.[1077] My aim has been to give a straightforward translation, retaining the flavour of the Latin even if this seems at times to produce a rather legalistic prose; thus not every 'supradictum' has been translated but enough to reflect the tone of the Latin. Likewise I have kept sufficient of the Graecisms in Æthelstan's charters to retain their flavour, with words such as archimandrite. I have also tended to favour consistency of translation of particular words.

This preference for consistency of translation relates to the main

[1076] Note also e.g. MS C's consistent use of the abbreviated form 'Dorob'nensis'; in extending this abbreviated version I have adopted the standard form 'Dorobernensis'.

[1077] The text at various points uses the historic present, but I do not reproduce this in the translation, since it would produce an inconsistent use of tenses, sometimes even within a single sentence; see e.g. vol. ii. 22. D. D. James, 'A Translation and Study of the "Chronicon Monasterii de Abingdon"', Ph.D. thesis (Rice University, 1986), is unsatisfactory, not least in its reliance upon Stevenson's edition.

problem of translation arising from the *History*. In the earlier version, we have a twelfth-century text recording matters going back to the seventh. To make matters more problematic, it also contains documents from before the twelfth century. How, then, should one translate a word such as *comes*? Various possibilities arise. One could use 'ealdorman' in all instances up to the early eleventh century, and then earl; or ealdorman in the documents composed up to the early eleventh century, and earl in all other instances. However, I have chosen to translate consistently as 'earl', since I find it highly unlikely that the composer of the *History* made any distinction between earl and ealdorman, and therefore I use the word normally applied in twelfth-century situations.[1078] For the same reason, and perhaps still more controversially, I have usually rendered *miles* as knight, even when used of the Anglo-Saxon period. Sometimes, however, standard usage renders consistency of translation too awkward even if one considered it appropriate; I therefore render *dux* as 'ealdorman' or as 'duke' when appropriate, and *comes* as 'count' when it is a continental title. The word *minister* I translate varyingly according to context, 'thegn', for example, in Anglo-Saxon charters but elsewhere as 'official' or 'servant'.[1079] Equally problematic are words such as *monasterium*, which might on occasion best be rendered 'minster' but again I normally render it 'monastery' because I do not think the composer of the *History* would consistently have distinguished between what are now called 'monasteries' and 'minsters'.[1080] Similarly the word *uilla* could cover a multiplicity of types of settlement. There might be an argument for translating it only as 'village' with reference to nucleated settlements. However, to retain consistency of translation, and to avoid the rather archaic or

[1078] The appropriateness of such a translation particularly in narrative sections is unusually clear-cut when one has phrases such as 'comites et barones' used with reference to the Anglo-Saxon past: see e.g. below, pp. 252, 282. In its portion devoted to the Anglo-Saxon period, MS C uses *barones* only in the translations of the Confessor's writs; below, p. 200.

[1079] Note also *princeps*: translated as 'noble' below, pp. 12, 20, 24, 30, 44, 76, 90, 100, 172, 258, 260, 262, 264, 266, 286, 300, 312; vol. ii. 264; as 'prince' below, pp. 14, 28, 48, 174; vol. ii. 50, where the word refers to the king, and vol. ii. 266, 272, in papal privileges; at p. 136 I have translated it as 'ealdorman' because that is the word in the Old English original; at p. 224 as 'ruler' because it there may refer to king, queen, and nobles; at p. 282 as 'commander' with reference to St Maurice.

[1080] See e.g. below, p. 244, concerning Helenstow. There are exceptions, as when the word forms part of a phrase such as New Minster. At p. 180 'monasteriolum' is rendered 'little minster'; at vol. ii. 254 and 296 'monasterium' is rendered as 'minster' with reference to St Aldate's, Oxford.

awkward-sounding 'vill' or 'township', I have usually opted for 'village', indicating a rural settlement, area, or group of people.[1081]

Translating Old English names also presents problems, as we have later twelfth-century Latin versions of names from the preceding centuries. In order to ensure consistency between the two volumes, I have normally used the standard Old English form (e.g. 'Alfwius' becomes Ælfwig).[1082] Sometimes, however, the Latin would allow more than one Old English form, in which case the possibilities are given in footnotes. Where the Latin text gives a twelfth-century name beginning 'Egel-' or 'Egil-', suggesting the contemporary vernacular, I retain that form in the translation, whilst footnoting the Old English form beginning Æthel-. When the name appears in the *History* for an earlier period, I use the form Æthel-.

In general, notes are provided only on the first appearance in the *History* in each volume of a person, place, or subject; this first reference can be located through the index. I have attempted to provide notes on everyone named in the text, although in some cases this has proved impossible since I have found nothing more about them. I have not, however, provided such notes for people who appear *only* as witnesses of royal or papal documents, since their appearance bears little or no relationship to the history of the abbey of Abingdon. The footnotes provide guidance on the authenticity of Anglo-Saxon charters, generally through a summary of Kelly's views as presented in *Charters of Abingdon Abbey* and through the noting of any different opinions. There is some further discussion of particular charters in the appendix to this Introduction. This approach to questions of authenticity reflects both the difficulty of obtaining definitive answers and the primary interest of this edition in twelfth- and thirteenth-century Abingdon views of the past.

[1081] Note also p. 218: 'a custom in those days got out of control, to considerable future damage: anyone offering plenty of gold or silver would receive by purchase a portion of land amounting to three or five hides, or a whole village [*trium aut quinque terre portionem hidarum, siue uillam integram*]'.

[1082] For ease of cross-reference, I have also sought to make rare forms consistent with those in the index of *Charters of Abingdon Abbey*.

APPENDIX: ANGLO-SAXON CHARTERS

Abingdon is one of the major archives of documents from Anglo-Saxon England. There are slightly fewer than 150 documents, including two royal writs in the vernacular, one episcopal writ in Latin, one will and three records of other land transactions in the vernacular, and three other documents. The great majority of documents, however, are royal diplomas. There are forty-eight royal diplomas purporting to come from before the mid-tenth century refoundation, mostly to laymen or churchmen with no known connection to Abingdon, and thirty-eight diplomas recording grants of land or privileges to the refounded monastery or its abbot.[1083]

The Abingdon charters have been very extensively and authoritatively analysed in Susan Kelly's two-volume edition for the British Academy Anglo-Saxon Charters Series, *Charters of Abingdon Abbey* (2 vols., 2000–1). The existence of Kelly's edition, and the concerns of the present volumes, have determined the nature and extent of my own treatment of the charters. In the preceding Introduction my main concern was the position of the charters within the *History* and their role in its composition. In the footnotes to the charters I have often been able simply to refer to or to summarize Kelly, whilst noting, where appropriate, differing opinions.[1084] Nevertheless, it will here be helpful to discuss relatively briefly the related issues of charter production, authenticity of certain charters, and dating of forgery.

1. Charter production

The question of whether Anglo-Saxon royal diplomas were produced in a central royal chancery or locally, notably by ecclesiastical beneficiaries, has been a controversial one. Given the lack of definitive evidence, conclusions have to be drawn from the form of charters themselves. Thus common characteristics shared between charters of

[1083] *Charters of Abingdon Abbey*, pp. xlvi, lxix, lxxi; also below, Concordances.

[1084] See *Charters of Abingdon Abbey*, pp. lxvii–lxviii, for assessment of the authenticity of the single-sheet charters relating to Abingdon and the *History*. *Charters of Abingdon Abbey*, p. lxviii, notes that almost all the charters in the Abingdon archive that are dubious or suspicious are grants directly to the abbey, not to individuals.

different monastic houses may suggest central drafting, common characteristics shared between charters of only one house may suggest beneficiary drafting, as well as possible forgery. There are also intermediate positions, for example that scribes at one or more monastic houses may at times have taken responsibility for a significant proportion of royal diplomas, not just those for their own house.

Central control of the production of most charters, although not necessarily always production in a royal chancery independent of any monastic houses, does seem to have been a feature of the mid- to late tenth century, to which a great number of the *History*'s charters making grants directly to Abingdon are dated.[1085] It is possible that Abingdon was one monastic centre that had responsibility for production of charters not only for royal grants to itself but also to other beneficiaries. This is of importance not only for the processes of royal charter production but also for the authenticity of the charters in the *History*.[1086] Susan Kelly has pointed out that 'the close formulaic links between [the tenth-century reform period] Abingdon charters have a clear implication: the majority, if not all of them, would appear to have been drawn up in the abbey'.[1087] Such formulaic

[1085] See the summary in *Charters of Abingdon Abbey*, pp. lxxiii–lxxxii. R. Drögereit, 'Gab es eine angelsächsische Königskanzlei?', *Archiv für Urkundenforschung*, xiii (1935), 335–436, and Keynes, *Diplomas*, pp. 14–28, argue for the importance of a royal chancery; P. Chaplais, 'The Anglo-Saxon chancery: From the diploma to the writ', in F. Ranger, ed., *Prisca Munimenta: Studies in Archival and Administrative History presented to Dr A. E. J. Hollander* (London, 1973), pp. 43–62, and 'Royal Anglo-Saxon "chancery" of the tenth century revisited', argues for monastic production with royal control. Neither party believes in absolute consistency of practice; see e.g. Keynes, *Diplomas*, p. 81. A further problem in considering the role of a chancery is that scribes working directly in the royal household may have had as their main product writs rather than diplomas, the survival rate of writs being very small for the period before 1066; Chaplais, 'Anglo-Saxon chancery', pp. 60–1; 'Royal Anglo-Saxon "chancery" of the tenth century revisited', pp. 43–4, is cautious on this possibility.

[1086] It is just conceivable that such drafting practices could also relate to the presence of 'alien' diplomas in the Abingdon archive, if the grant never came into final effect, if the beneficiary left the document at the monastery for safe keeping, or if copies were kept at Abingdon. *Charters of Abingdon Abbey*, no. 43, records a grant by King Eadred of land in Buckinghamshire to Æthelmær *praeses*. It does not appear in the *History*, but was preserved among the 16th-century copies of Abingdon documents. Its phraseology is similar to a charter for Barking, issued at the royal 'uillula' of Abingdon; Sawyer, no. 552a. One may wonder whether the Æthelmær charter too was produced at Abingdon and for some reason remained or returned there in some form; however, it does have a notarial subscription by Bishop Æthelwold of Dorchester. For the possibility that Glastonbury retained copies of charters drafted there, see Keynes, '"Dunstan B" charters', p. 188. *Charters of Abingdon Abbey*, p. 179, provides an alternative reason for the presence in the Abingdon records of the charter to Æthelmær, based on the history of the estates concerned.

[1087] *Charters of Abingdon Abbey*, p. lxxii.

interrelation and drafting in the abbey led Simon Keynes to conclude that 'there are strong grounds for suspecting that many were produced there not in the years given by the diplomas themselves but rather were concocted subsequently on the basis of a few authentic diplomas in the archives, presumably to serve as direct evidence of the abbey's interest in the estates'.[1088] Kelly is more willing to accept the possibility of Abingdon drafting of authentic charters, for example noting shared formulation of charters concerning lands in the Abingdon region but not for the abbey.[1089] It may also be significant that of the five charters recording grants directly to Abingdon in Abbot Wulfgar's time, four have witness lists, three of which attribute to him a role in the drafting of the charter.[1090]

Of especial concern has been the role in the production of charters early in Edgar's reign of a scribe who has been christened 'Edgar A' and who has been associated with Abingdon and even with Æthelwold himself.[1091] Of the eight diplomas dated between 960 and 963 surviving as apparent originals, five were the work of this scribe. The arguments for an association with Abingdon rest on a variety of bases: script; shared formulae;[1092] the fact that two of the five are preserved in the Abingdon archive; a subscription stating that Æthelwold 'depinxi' one document;[1093] the two-stage process of drawing up

[1088] Keynes, *Diplomas*, pp. 11–12.

[1089] *Charters of Abingdon Abbey*, p. lxxix: 'these links *may* be coincidental, but *could* suggest local production'; see also pp. lxxxii–lxxxiii.

[1090] cc. 98, 101, 102, *Charters of Abingdon Abbey*, nos. 124 ('hoc sintagma triumphans dictaui'); 128 ('gaudens dictaui', this phrase only appearing in MS B, not in the 16th-century copy); 135 ('hanc kartulam gaudenti corde composui'). The exceptions are cc. 99, B231, *Charters of Abingdon Abbey*, nos. 129 (which has no witness list), 130 (which just uses the verb 'conlaudo'). In the witness list of B232, King Æthelred's charter recording the grant of Little Haseley to his thegn Godwine, it is stated that 'Ego Wlfgar abbas dictaui'; see *Charters of Abingdon Abbey*, no. 131, p. 510. See further *Charters of Abingdon Abbey*, pp. cxxix–cxxx, where it is stated (p. cxxix) that 'the hypothesis of contemporary (or near contemporary) in-house production receives support from some later diplomas in the archive which seem to show the domestic formulation maturing and evolving in later decades'.

[1091] *Charters of Abingdon Abbey*, pp. cxv–cxxxi; Keynes, *Diplomas*, pp. 70–9; Drögereit, 'Königskanzlei', p. 416; P. Chaplais, 'The origin and authenticity of the royal Anglo-Saxon diploma', in Ranger, ed., *Prisca Munimenta*, pp. 28–42, at 42. Other leading churchmen may have had a role in writing charters; see esp. Keynes, '"Dunstan B" charters', for Dunstan and Glastonbury; also below, p. 110 n. 247, for the possibility of Bishop Oswald being composer and scribe of attestations to the original of Edgar's charter concerning Ringwood, c. 67.

[1092] See below, p. cxcix, on the *Orthodoxorum* charters, and also *Charters of Abingdon Abbey*, p. cxviii.

[1093] B186 (= *Charters of Abingdon Abbey*, no. 86).

the charter recording King Edgar's grant of land at Ringwood to Abingdon in 961.[1094] The palaeographical evidence in fact is not strong, and there could be other explanations for shared formulae, for example the scribe being in the personal service of the king.[1095] However, it does seem significant that Æthelwold attests all five surviving 'Edgar A' originals, but is not a witness of the other three originals from the key period, 959–63. As Kelly pithily puts it, 'when "Edgar A" was unavailable, then so was Æthelwold'.[1096] This need not mean that the charters are Abingdon productions. Rather they may be linked to Æthelwold as a member of the royal circle. Nor need he have been responsible for the physical writing of the charter, but rather have been its composer; this may be the meaning of the word 'depinxi' which follows his attestation in the earliest of the five 'Edgar A' originals, the charter of restoration to Wulfric Cufing which is also preserved in the revised version of the *History*.[1097] Whatever the form of Æthelwold's input, the pattern of witnessing does suggest a link between him, at the time he was abbot of Abingdon, and the 'Edgar A' charters. And unless one believes that monks were as stationary as the *Rule* hoped, the scribe who wrote the charters could quite easily have been an Abingdon monk accompanying Æthelwold.[1098] Given the nature of Edgar's regime, and the role of the reformers within it, the distinctions between royal and devolved production or central and monastic scribes may be potentially misleading.[1099]

[1094] *Charters of Abingdon Abbey*, pp. 358–9.

[1095] Keynes, *Diplomas*, p. 75.

[1096] *Charters of Abingdon Abbey*, p. cxix. One difficulty with this view is that the charters of 'Edgar A' show some similarities to a charter of Edgar when he was only king of the Mercians, at a time when Æthelwold appears to have been in the circle of Eadwig, not Edgar; Sawyer, no. 681, Keynes, *Diplomas*, pp. 75–6. However, it is also possible that 'Edgar A' could have adopted earlier formulations when he came to be associated with Edgar; note also Keynes's qualification to his own arguments at *Diplomas*, p. 76 n. 153.

[1097] B186 (*Charters of Abingdon Abbey*, no. 86). Given the varying addition of verbs to attestations, the silence as to Æthelwold's drafting role in the other 'Edgar A' charters does not seem to me significant. Keynes, *Diplomas*, p. 71, argues that 'there is some justification for regarding "Edgar A" not only as the scribe but also as the draftsman' of the relevant charters. However, a close association between Æthelwold and a scribe might have a similar effect.

[1098] Cf. Keynes, *Diplomas*, pp. 74–5: 'it emerges therefore that a single person was made responsible for the drafting and writing of the majority of [Edgar's] diplomas issued in the opening years of the reign, and certainly of more than one would expect were his services only exploited when the king was in the vicinity of Abingdon or if the beneficiaries were required to make their own arrangements for the production of the diplomas in their favour'.

[1099] This seems the best way of solving the apparent problem stated at *Charters of Abingdon Abbey*, p. cxxv: 'The idea of independent local production of royal diplomas seems incompatible with Keynes's vision of strong royal government which kept a firm

2. Authenticity

If a person or persons associated with Abingdon had particular input into the production of some of Edgar's charters, this may have implications for the authenticity of charters to the abbey showing a close formulaic interrelationship that might otherwise be a cause for suspicion. It is also possible that after a period of close association with the king through 'Edgar A', Abingdon could have had a continuing accepted but more independent role in charter production in certain circumstances in later years. Such complex interrelationship of the central and the local, the royal and the monastic, may encourage greater acceptance of questionable Abingdon charters.[1100]

Of particular concern have been the so-called *Orthodoxorum* charters, which derive their title from the opening word of several of the group. They are also of importance in the discussion of 'Edgar A' because it is arguable that one of the influences upon his style of charter were the earliest Abingdon *Orthodoxorum* charters.[1101] This would support 'Edgar A''s association with Æthelwold and Abingdon.

There are six *Orthodoxorum* charters. Three are for Abingdon, in the names of Eadwig, Edgar, and Æthelred. The other three are for Pershore, Worcester, and Romsey.[1102] The Worcester charter is a clear forgery. The charter of Æthelred for Abingdon is generally regarded as an authentic original.[1103] Our main concern here will be the two earlier Abingdon examples, although the Pershore text is also relevant. In general the charters of Eadwig and Edgar have been rejected, as being based on Æthelred's charter. However, Eric John has argued for their authenticity, with the reservation that a clause concerning estates may be interpolated in Edgar's charter.[1104] More

control on charter-production for legal and constitutional reasons.' Æthelwold and his like were part of 'strong royal government'. In addition, this debate raises the question of how far the strength of late Anglo-Saxon government was made possible in part by the co-opting of local governmental and administrative procedures, a process that I consider in another context in 'Faide, Vengeance et Violence en Angleterre (ca. 900–1200)' (Collection de l'École Française de Rome, 357, 2006).

1100 See also *Charters of Abingdon Abbey*, pp. cxxv, cxxx.

1101 See *Charters of Abingdon Abbey*, pp. cxxiv, 358–9.

1102 For Abingdon, see cc. 37, 60, 98; for other houses, Sawyer, nos. 786, 788, 812.

1103 Note, however, that Dumville, *English Caroline Script*, p. 135 n. 100, suggests that there are 'some advanced features' in the script of the charter in Æthelred's name, and that 'one may wonder whether these add to the textual reasons for uncertainty about the authenticity of this diploma'.

1104 John, *Orbis Britanniae*, pp. 181–209, with discussion of the interpolation at p. 195.

recently Kelly has argued in great detail for their acceptance.[1105] My intention here is to summarize the arguments and to add some comments.

The argument for rejection of the early charters, and their reliance on that of Æthelred, is succinctly put by Keynes.[1106] First, the proem typical to the charters is textually related to and developed from two charters of 961 and 962, and therefore later than the supposedly earliest *Orthodoxorum* charters. Secondly, a clause in four of the *Orthodoxorum* charters deals with earlier seizure of lands: 'At that time when the lands, which I have devoutly restored to the Lord through this new privilege, had been unjustly taken from the holy church of God, some perfidious men seized the hereditary charters and issued new ones for themselves.'[1107] Keynes takes this as suitable for reference to the seizures of the 980s. If the clause had been devised in the time of Eadwig or Edgar, 'it would assuredly be a strange coincidence if . . . [it] was found still to be appropriate for use in 993'. Thirdly, there are miscellaneous lesser suspicious features about all the charters except that of Æthelred, features that cumulatively produce doubt concerning authenticity. Finally there are apparently minor but in fact significant points of contact between [Æthelred's diploma for Abingdon] and other diplomas produced in the 990s, suggesting that its formulation was contemporary and generally current rather than derivative and perhaps restricted to Abingdon.

Kelly responds to these points as follows. First, the proem of Æthelred's charter, damaged in the original and not present in the *History*'s copies, appears to be a variant on the usual *Orthodoxorum* formula, and therefore is less likely to be the immediate model for the other diplomas.[1108] Whilst the lengthy proem of Eadwig's charter is

[1105] *Charters of Abingdon Abbey*, pp. lxxxiv–cxv; at p. xcviii she states that 'there are thus better grounds for accepting [Eadwig's diploma] as an authentic privilege of 959, probably drawn up by Æthelwold himself or by a close associate, than for rejecting it as a product of the 990s or later'; at p. civ that 'once more, there seems more reason than not to accept [Edgar's diploma] as a genuine document of late 959, a reiteration and expansion of [Eadwig's]; it has a very convincing witness-list, and its contents are not out of place in the historical context'. At pp. cii–civ she argues that the clause in Edgar's charter which Eric John saw as an interpolation might also be explained by Eadwig having failed to fulfil the terms of Eadred's will.

[1106] Keynes, *Diplomas*, pp. 98–100.

[1107] See below, p. 146.

[1108] *Charters of Abingdon Abbey*, p. lxxxvii. Kelly also there points out that Æthelred's charter is considerably longer than the other Abingdon ones, containing the king's regrets about specific earlier events. She therefore argues that 'if we are searching for a basic model for this group, then there seems to be good grounds for focusing on [Eadwig's charter for more typical of documents later in the century, it is not impossible for an earlier charter, especially one issued on an important occasion. The first *Orthodoxorum* charters could be early work of 'Edgar A', or linked to his work, rather than being based on that work.[1109] Secondly, the clause concerned with lost lands could refer to the dispersal of estates prior to the coming of Æthelwold.[1110] Thirdly, the minor suspicious features in the Eadwig and Edgar Abingdon charters may be explicable in ways that do not require the documents to be considered forgeries.[1111] As for the 'points of contact' with other charters of the 990s, this could just show the influence of the *Orthodoxorum* charters in that decade, and there are also points of contact with earlier charters.[1112]

It should also be pointed out that the charters' concerns, notably the free election of abbots and the confirmation of ancient freedoms, are rather different from those of most royal diplomas.[1113] They are quite probably the types of grant that Æthelwold was particularly keen to get, although this of course need not establish the authenticity of the documents.[1114] However, for such grants the form of the diplomas may have been particularly influenced by the beneficiary, whether or not we see 'Edgar A' as linked to Abingdon and responsible for the two early Abingdon *Orthodoxorum* charters.[1115] This is

Abingdon], supposedly the earliest of the six documents. This represents the charter-type in its purest form, and it would be possible to see the other examples as documents as evolving from it.' It remains possible that the Eadwig charter was forged on the basis of Æthelred's and then the others derived from it.

[1109] Ibid., pp. lxxxviii, lxxxix.

[1110] Ibid., p. cii; see also Æthelwold's account of monasticism, *Councils and Synods*, i. 146, 152–3.

[1111] See *Charters of Abingdon Abbey*, p. xcvi, on Oda witnessing Eadwig's charter, which leads to problems with the date; however, his name does not appear in the earlier copy, in MS C. See p. xcviii on the problem of the incarnation date of Edgar's charter, pp. xcix–ci on its witness list.

[1112] Ibid., pp. xc–xcii.

[1113] Ibid., p. lxxxvi. Such concerns were of course central to the reform movement. The different concerns may have affected the form of the documents, taking them away from typical royal diplomas; cf. the charters 'in gold letters' referred to above, p. lxvii.

[1114] It could be significant that the Eadwig and Edgar diplomas specify free election after the death of Æthelwold. In fact the next vacancy at Abingdon came not with Æthelwold's death but his move to the bishopric of Winchester. A retrospective forgery would have been made in the knowledge of this.

[1115] *Charters of Abingdon Abbey*, p. xciii. John, *Orbis Britannie*, p. 207: 'The shape of these charters can be confidently attributed to Æthelwold in his Abingdon days. They throw some light on how and why the monastic charter went out of "chancery", as we know it started to do in Edgar's day. These charters represented a new and exotic type of privilege owing much more to continental than English precedent; consequently it is not particularly true of the historical element within the charter, a feature that would fit with Æthelwold's known interests. Given that Æthelwold in his vernacular account of monasticism is critical of Eadwig, the existence of a genuine Eadwig *Orthodoxorum* charter would explain why Eadwig had to have a prominent and accepted position in the history of Abingdon as expressed in charters. The tradition critical of Eadwig would, furthermore, make him a somewhat surprising grantor of a forged charter. Also notable is the emphasis on Mary in the proems of the *Orthodoxorum* charters, an emphasis that would fit an association with Abingdon and with Æthelwold.[1116] Again this is far from proving that the charters in Eadwig and Edgar's names are genuine, but it does help to explain why the spread of *Orthodoxorum* style proems is limited. The two other possibly genuine *Orthodoxorum* charters are both to monasteries with Marian dedications, Pershore and Romsey.

To these arguments concerning the diplomatic of the charters I wish to add only three points, again none of which is decisive as to the authenticity of the charters. First, the charters of Eadwig and Edgar both use the following phrase:

> after the death of the outstanding Abbot Æthelwold [*abbatis egregii*], in whose times, with Christ's aid, this restoration of liberty was granted, the entire congregation of the aforementioned monastery may by suitable counsel choose someone for themselves, according to the regular institutions of the blessed Benedict, and, choosing him from that body of brothers, justly appoint him abbot.[1117]

Æthelred's charter refers just to 'the aforesaid Abbot Wulfgar' where these charters refer to 'the outstanding Abbot Æthelwold'. It is conceivable that the latter phrase would be more appropriate for a dead abbot, just as a charter of Eadwig concerning woodland at Hawkridge refers to 'the *Rule* of the outstanding Abbot

surprising that men like Æthelwold, who enjoyed the king's highest confidence, should be left to draft their own documents and ensure that what they wanted for their houses should be properly expressed in explicit formulas.' Note also that to the name of Abbot Wulfgar in the witness list of the Æthelred charter is attached the phrase 'hoc sintagma + triumphans dictaui'. *Charters of Abingdon Abbey*, p. cxiv, concludes that Æthelred's charter for Abingdon 'is most easily understood as a diploma written at Abingdon, probably by Abbot Wulfgar . . . in the aftermath of a campaign to have Abingdon's ancient liberties and immunities recognized and confirmed'.

[1116] *Charters of Abingdon Abbey*, pp. xciii–xcv.

[1117] See below, pp. 62, 96. The Pershore charter, Sawyer, no. 786, uses the same phrase of Abbot Foldbriht.

Benedict'.[1118] If so, the phrase would indicate a forger capable of use of an inappropriate phrase. However, Eadwig's Hawkridge charter, which Kelly accepts as most likely genuine, does refer to 'the most devout Abbot Æthelwold', so at least some epithets could be attributed to a living abbot. A second point is that whilst Æthelred's *Orthodoxorum* charter does mention Æthelwold's role in the refoundation of Abingdon, its historical section concentrates on King Coenwulf, Pope Leo, Abbot Hræthun, and King Ceadwalla, whilst also mentioning more recent kings as donors. It is arguable that a historical section composed after Æthelwold's death might have found a way of mentioning him in this passage. Thirdly, it may be significant that another of the *Orthodoxorum* charters is for Pershore.[1119] The charter is in Edgar's name and is dated to 972. It may be notable that the charter is written in a neat square miniscule, the typical script of Edgar's charters. The Æthelred *Orthodoxorum* charter of 993 for Abingdon is in Caroline script. The writer of the Pershore charter may have been a sophisticated forger with a good grasp of the appropriate script for an appropriate date, or—perhaps more likely—he may have been writing before the shift to the routine use of Caroline script in royal diplomas.[1120] Also perhaps significant is that the abbot of Pershore was named Foldbriht. This is a very unusual name, and he was most likely the monk of that name whom Æthelwold brought from Glastonbury to Abingdon.[1121] If so, one is faced with the choice of believing either that the first *Orthodoxorum* charter was drawn up for Abingdon in the 990s, and that forgery of 'earlier' charters based on Æthelred's then took place not only at Abingdon but also at other monasteries, or that *Orthodoxorum* charters existed earlier, and spread from Abingdon, for example to Pershore through an Abingdon monk, Foldbriht. Further supporting, although not decisive evidence, may come from

[1118] See below, p. 74. The epithet for Æthelwold and Foldbriht could of course be an interpolation. In the whole corpus of Anglo-Saxon diplomas, the phrase in the form 'abbatis egregii' only appears in these three Abingdon charters and their Pershore equivalent.

[1119] See *Charters of Abingdon Abbey*, pp. cvi–cxi; at p. cxi Kelly concludes that 'there seems good reason to accept that [the Pershore diploma] is more likely to be an original than a late forgery based on [Æthelred's charter for Abingdon.]'

[1120] *Charters of Abingdon Abbey*, p. cvii, which also notes that Neil Ker and Pierre Chaplais accepted the script as appropriate for 972. See also above, p. cxcix n. 1103, for David Dumville's concern about the dating of the Abingdon charter because of its script.

[1121] See above, p. cvii, also *Charters of Abingdon Abbey*, p. cx. Foldbriht was abbot of Pershore *c.*970–*c.*984; *Heads of Religious Houses*, pp. 58, 252.

the witness list of the Pershore charter; the name of Abbot Osgar of Abingdon—who had been a companion of Foldbriht in their move from Glastonbury to Abingdon—is accompanied by the word 'dictaui'.[1122] The possibility of the authenticity of the pre-Æthelred *Orthodoxorum* charters must at the very least remain open.

3. Dating of forgery

The forging of charters was part of the process whereby the monks of Abingdon created a written record of their past. However, the dating of forgeries is very difficult, particularly if they survive only in cartulary copies. Furthermore, forgeries often drew on earlier documents, and the more skilful the forger the harder it will be for us to date his work. One possibility is to look for external circumstances that might have encouraged forgery, most notably disputes. At least in the case of Abingdon, however, this is problematic. Dispute accounts often make no mention of documents, even when there are charters in the *History* that one might have expected to be used. Moreover, the great increase in recording of disputes after the Norman Conquest may encourage the association of forged charters with that period when they could have been created in the context of earlier, unrecorded disputes.

I shall concentrate on the following charters: those linked to Bradfield; a charter in the name of King Coenwulf, dated 821, and mentioning Pope Leo and Abbot Hræthun; three charters in Æthelstan's name making grants directly to Abingdon; some charters of the Confessor.

Bradfield charters

Various suggestions have been made as to the date of the construction of the Bradfield documents.[1123] Stenton suggested that 'the compiler of [the document which appears as cc. 3 and 4 in the *History*] was acquainted with the Anglo-Norman general charter of confirmation, the continental *pancarte*'.[1124] However, this document is of such irregular form that a debt to the Continental *pancarte* seems an unnecessary explanation. It is possible that the texts as they now exist were put together only when the monks of Abingdon wished to add

[1122] See also Chaplais, 'Royal Anglo-Saxon "chancery" of the tenth century revisited', p. 50.

[1123] cc. 3–7 (= *Charters of Abingdon Abbey*, nos. 1–4).

[1124] Stenton, *Early History*, p. 11 n. 1.

Hæha, Cilla, and Cissa to their foundation story, which may have been as late as the twelfth century. In that case, however, it is surprising that only one of the charters actually mentions Abingdon.[1125] It is more likely that the documents were confected from early records at Bradfield, and later co-opted by Abingdon and employed to give the early foundation a documentary history. The mention of Abingdon may have been inserted as part of the process of co-opting.[1126] Whether this process was complete before or after the first recorded mention of Cissa in connection with the abbey's foundation must remain uncertain.[1127]

Charter in the name of King Coenwulf of Mercia, dated 821

Two charters in the name of King Coenwulf appear in MS C, one being omitted from the revised *History*.[1128] It is the charter that appears in both versions of the *History* that is our particular concern here. It formed the basis of the narratives concerning the oppressions by Coenwulf's servants that appear in the *History*, *De abbatibus*, and the Abingdon John of Worcester, and records the activities of Abbot Hræthun and Pope Leo. It is closely related to the version of Abingdon history that appears in the *Orthodoxorum* charters, a version of history that must therefore have been existence by 993, quite possibly by 959, and should probably be associated with Æthelwold. Again this charter, and the other charter in Coenwulf's name, may be based on an earlier document, again possibly not in Abingdon's favour.[1129] Changes and additions would have been made, most notably a list of estates that Æthelwold may have been intent on claiming for the house. Thereby was created the 'old privilege obtained by Abbot Hræthun' mentioned in the *Orthodoxorum* charters

[1125] c. 4.

[1126] See *Charters of Abingdon Abbey*, pp. lxix–lxx, and notes to nos. 1–4.

[1127] Although the first mention of Cissa is in William of Malmesbury rather than an Abingdon source, it is very plausible that William knew of foundation stories from Abingdon. Note also Stenton's suggestion, *Early History*, pp. 15–16, that Malmesbury lay behind some early forgeries contained in the Abingdon archive, and his raising of the possibility that Faritius provided the link between the houses.

[1128] cc. 10–11, B18, *Charters of Abingdon Abbey*, nos. 8 and 9. On the forgery, probably in the 13th century, of another Coenwulf charter relating to Culham, see above, p. lxviii.

[1129] See also *Charters of Abingdon Abbey*, pp. lxx, cciv, notes to nos. 8 and 9. *Charters of Abingdon Abbey*, p. cciv, takes the mention in c. 10 of a grant to redeem lands 'a manu extraneorum' as possibly significant of the date of forgery, since 'the theme of restoration would have been dear to Æthelwold's heart'.

as recording the liberties granted by Pope Leo and King Coenwulf.[1130]

Æthelstan charters for Abingdon

Three charters dated 931 and in the name of King Æthelstan record grants of Shellingford, Swinford, and Sandford-on-Thames to Abingdon.[1131] All have diplomatic features of post-960 charters. Sandford was one of the lands that the abbey had to reclaim after the Norman Conquest, and Susan Kelly suggests that this provides the circumstance for forgery. This case might be supported by the additional existence of a forged charter of the Confessor granting Sandford to Abingdon. However, there are other possible explanations for the forging of the Sandford charter,[1132] and the post-Conquest history of the estates would provide no such explanation for the Swinford or Shellingford forgeries. Shellingford was a *Domesday* holding of Abingdon, and there is no sign of it having been disputed. Swinford does not appear in *Domesday* but probably formed part of Abingdon's manor of Cumnor.[1133] It is possible that the Æthelstan charters were forged before the Conquest in unknown circumstances.[1134]

Charters in the name of Edward the Confessor

Finally we come to the three charters in the Confessor's name recording grants directly to Abingdon.[1135] The estates concerned are Leverton, Chilton, and Sandford-on-Thames. All these estates came into the hands of the priest Blæcmann, who fled England after the Conquest. The *History* then tells us that 'whatever had been his was taken back into the king's hand, as a fugitive's. Therefore with great effort the abbot [Ealdred] obtained restitution of these aforesaid lands from the king.'[1136] However, *Domesday* shows that Abingdon's claim to the estates before 1066 was far from clear. Blæcmann held

[1130] The word *uassallus* is used below, p. 20, in a way that seems appropriate for the pre- rather than the post-Conquest period; see below, p. 21 n. 63.

[1131] cc. 20–2, *Charters of Abingdon Abbey*, pp. lxx–lxxi, nos. 25–7 and notes.

[1132] See above, p. cxix n. 645.

[1133] VCH, *Berkshire*, iv. 400.

[1134] See also c. 19, and notes to *Charters of Abingdon Abbey*, no. 22, on the complex history of a charter in Æthelstan's name recording a grant of various lands to Abbot Cynath.

[1135] cc. 132, 133, 135, *Charters of Abingdon Abbey*, p. lxxi, nos. 145–7 and notes. See above, p. clix, on the writs of the Confessor.

[1136] See below, pp. 208, 222.

Leverton 'in feudo', but no lord is specified.[1137] He held Chilton from Earl Harold 'in alodio'. Only of Sandford is it specified that he held it from Abingdon.[1138] It is just possible that the lands were already contentious before 1066, creating the circumstances for the production of the charters. Early production may be suggested by the care with which the witness list of the Leverton charter is constructed: Kineweard, apparently the contemporary reeve of Berkshire, was substituted for Godwine, probably reeve of Oxford, who appears in the witness list upon which that of the Leverton charter may be based.[1139] Nevertheless, the most likely circumstance for the forgery of the charters is during the post-Conquest efforts to regain the lands.[1140]

The above survey has not brought definitive conclusions about the dating of forgeries, and indeed suggests that unknown circumstances may have prompted the construction of documents. However, it does seem likely that the time of Æthelwold was one period of documentary concoction, particularly of documents that would feature in the historical accounts of the early house and would also provide a basis for claims relating to the supposed early endowment. The aftermath of the Norman Conquest may be another period of retrospective improvement of the archive, although in this case through documents referring to individual disputed estates.[1141] It is likely that some improvement of earlier documents continued in the twelfth century, for example in the case of Edward the Confessor's grant of the hundred of Hormer.[1142] Any case for further fabrication by the compiler of the earlier version of the *History*, particularly of charters

[1137] It is possible that the abbey or abbot is implied by the preceding portion of the entry, concerning the 1086 tenant.

[1138] *DB* i, fos. 59^{r}, 156^{v}.

[1139] See *Charters of Abingdon Abbey*, p. 566.

[1140] See above, p. cxix n. 645, for the suggestion that after 1066 a genuine charter recording Edward the Confessor's grant of Sandford to Earl Harold may not have been considered sufficiently secure proof of title.

[1141] The problems of assessing the authenticity of charters, and of attributing a date to any process of forging, are also demonstrated by three problematic charters for which Kelly suggests post-Conquest circumstance that might have prompted forgery, but the boundary clauses of which seem linguistically appropriate for their 10th-century date: cc. 79 (concerning Fyfield), 83 (concerning Hanney), 101 (concerning South Cerney), *Charters of Abingdon Abbey*, pp. 435–6, 439, 442, 501–2. Even if the charters are post-10th century products, it is possible that they were produced for unrecorded disputes, or, in the case of South Cerney, for a recorded dispute taking place before 1066.

[1142] See above, p. clix.

relating to the early history of the house, is less persuasive, notably because of the awkwardness of the foundation story in MS C; had the compiler of the *History* had the choice of the form and content of his earliest documents, a less problematic tale might have been expected.[1143]

[1143] See Keynes, 'Studies', pp. 74, 92–6, for the suggestion that the compiler of the first version of the *History* may have been responsible for the concoction and altering of some documents. The argument relates in part to the interrelated nature of the Edgar charters, which Keynes, 'Studies', p. 96, thinks may indicate 'that texts might be concocted and altered during the process of compiling an historically-orientated survey'. For the early charters, notably those of Ecgberht and Æthelwulf of Wessex, Keynes, 'Studies', p. 74, finds it significant that the reviser derived his texts directly from MS C, which may 'suggest that the documents did not exist in a separate form'. There are of course other possible explanations why the charters did not survive until or were not used in the revision of the *History*.

MANUSCRIPT SIGLA

A	Anglo-Saxon single-sheet diploma (individual details in historical notes)
B	London, British Library, Cotton Claudius B. VI
C	London, British Library, Cotton Claudius C. IX
CCCC	Cambridge, Corpus Christi College 111

TEXT AND TRANSLATION

[i. 1 n.] C fo. 105r ⟨*I*⟩*ncipit liber primus terrarum huius ecclesie Abbendonensis, continens annos .ccccxiiii..*

1. Mons Abbendone ad septemtrionalem plagam Tamese fluuii ubi pretermeat pontem Oxenefordis urbis situs est, a quo monasterio non longe posito idem nomen inditum.[1] Quis autem antiquorum illius primum institutor fuerit monimento ueterum accepimus:[2] quod Cissa rex occidentalium Saxonum Heano cuidam religiose uite uiro ac abbati, simulque sorori eiusdem, Cille nomine, locum ad omnipotentis Dei cultum construendi cenobii dedit, collatis ad hoc regio munere plurimis beneficiis et possessionibus, ob uite necessarium inibi fore degentium.[3] Vterque siquidem regio nobilitabatur genere. Verum non multo post, antequam designato insisteretur operi, rex ipse uita functus est.[4]

[i. 8 n.] 2. *Ceadwalla uero ei succedens, uiginti cassatos Deo omnipotenti et monachis ibidem seruientibus dedit, sicque in fine scripti sui de eadem uilla, scilicet Abbendun, ait:*[5]

Silua que uocatur Ædeleahing[6] et alia Colmonora[7] et Geatescum[8] pertinent his uiginti hidis, quos ego ipse modo partim equitando, modo partim nauigando large mensus sum, tum mihi tum omnibus meis successoribus, pro Deo et pro seculo. Ceterum quisquis demonis instinctu de his diminuerit que ego Deo et sancte Marie deuota mente in perpetuum largitus sum, Christus illius potentiam diminuat hic et in euum, nisi cum perfecta emendatione adimpleat et restituat ea que a Deo abstulit.

[1] For the location of the monastery, see above, p. xci.

[2] This phrase probably refers to the charters that follow, rather than to a narrative record; see above, p. xxiii.

[3] King Cissa may be an otherwise unknown sub-king in Wessex; *Charters of Abingdon Abbey*, p. 17. Hæha was probably the Abbot Hæha who witnessed Ine's privilege to the churches of Wessex in 704; Sawyer, no. 245. Cilla is a short form of Ceolswith, the name by which she is called below, p. 8. On these individuals, and for the statements here and in the following chapters about the foundation and early endowment of Abingdon, see above, p. lxxxiv.

[4] The date of Cissa's death is not known.

[5] Sawyer, no. 1603; *Charters of Abingdon Abbey*, no. 51B. Ceadwalla was king of Wessex 685–8, when he abdicated and went to Rome. He died in 689; *Handbook of British Chronology*, p. 22. For his place in Abingdon's later perception of its endowment, see above, p. cix. Rather than this heading and Latin text, MS B contains a vernacular version, preceded by a description of the bounds of the vill of Abingdon. It appears not in this early position in the *History* but at the end of a charter in Eadred's name included only in MS B;

Here begins Book I of the lands of this church of Abingdon, covering four hundred and fourteen years.

1. The hill of Abingdon is situated on the north side of the river Thames, where it passes by the bridge of the town of Oxford, and from the hill the same name is bestowed on the monastery positioned not far off.[1] Moreover, we have learnt from a record of bygone events[2] which man of old was the original founder of this monastery: that Cissa king of the West Saxons gave the site for the monastery to be built for the worship of almighty God to a certain Hæha, a man of the religious life and abbot, and also to his sister, named Cilla, and that very many endowments and possessions were conferred by royal gift for this purpose, for the necessities of life of those living therein.[3] Both Hæha and Cilla were ennobled by royal lineage. However, not long after, the king himself died, before he could press on with the intended work.[4]

2. *Ceadwalla indeed succeeded him, and gave twenty hides to almighty God and the monks serving there, as he says at the end of his document concerning that village, i.e. Abingdon.*[5]

The wood called *Ædeleahing*[6] and the other at *Colmonara*[7] and *Geatescum*[8] pertain to these twenty hides, which I myself have measured extensively partly on horseback, partly by boat, both for myself and for all my successors, with regard to God and the world. However, if anyone, at a demon's prompting, diminishes what I have devoutly bestowed in perpetuity on God and St Mary, may Christ diminish his power now and for eternity, unless he makes good with perfect restitution and restores what he took from God.

below, B85 (*Charters of Abingdon Abbey*, no. 51, 51A). The vernacular bounds and version of this passage also appear in MS C, fo. 196^{r}, in the quire devoted to such clauses; *Charters of Abingdon Abbey*, p. 585 (no. 1). The charter is almost certainly a forgery, and the vernacular passage may have been added from another source, probably in the 12th or 13th c.; see *Charters of Abingdon Abbey*, p. 212. Kelly, at p. 212, notes the suggestion of P. R. Kitson, that the language of the bounds suggests that they were composed in the second half of the 11th c.

[6] i.e. Æthelheah's wood; EPNS, *Berkshire*, ii. 462. This and the following places were presumably detached appurtenances of Abingdon.

[7] This probably means charcoal-burner's slope or ridge, and 'was the name of the N. and N.W. slope of the W. end of Boar's Hill'; EPNS, *Berkshire*, ii. 462–3.

[8] i.e. 'Geat's valley', 'valley of the gate', or Yatscombe; *Charters of Abingdon Abbey*, p. 216, EPNS, *Berkshire*, ii. 460.

[i. 9 n.] Abeunte Ceadwalla Romam, Ine successit in regnum.[9] Qui primo predecessorum suorum donationes irritas facere decreuit, deinde facti penitens, de suis etiam easdem longe uberius auxit.[10]

B fo. 6r 3. (B9) | *Carta Ceadwalle[a] regis.*[11]

[i. 9] In nomine Domini Dei nostri Ihesu Christi saluatoris. Ea que [i. 10] secundum decreta canonum salubriter decernuntur quamuis sermo tantum ad testimonium sufficeret, tamen pro incerta futuri temporis ambiguitate, firmissima litterarum astipulatione roborentur. Quapropter ego Ceadwalla,[b] [12] rex Westsaxonum,[c] terram iuxta Abbendone[d] .clxxiii. cassatorum Hean abbati libenter reddidi quam Cissa B fo. 6v rex sibi ac Cillan sorori | sue atque abbatisse aliquando dederat.

Sed Ini[e] rex eandem terram postea, dum regno potiretur, diripiens ac rei publice restituit, nondum constructo monasterio in ea nec ullo admodum oratorio erecto.[13] Rursus[f] ad edificandum [g]in ea[g] monasterium eidem Hean,[h] patricio tunc temporis suo, eandem terram redonauit, dicens:

4. (B9) [a]*Carta Ini regis.*[a]

Ego Ini,[b] monarchus[c] Saxonie, regnante Domino, regalia gubernans sceptra, terram quam predecessores[d] mei, Cissa et ceteri, Hean[e] patricio sueque germane Cillan dedisse noscuntur, iterum cum consilio plurimorum reddo et relinquo.[f] [14]

Deinde predictus patricius Hean se cum omni facultate sua et prefata terra omnipotentis Dei seruitio subdidit, meque[15] ad construendum monasterium illud in loco supra nominato, id est iuxta Ebbendune,[g]

3 [a] Ine *B* [b] Ini *B* [c] Saxonum *B* [d] Abbendune *B* [e] Ina *B* [f] autem *add. B* [g–g] *om. B* [h] Heano *B*

4 [a–a] *om. B* [b] Ina *B* [c] monarc *B* [d] predecessoris *B* [e] Heano *B* [f] relinco *B* [g] Abbendune *B*

[9] Ine was king of Wessex 688–*c.*726. Like Ceadwalla, he abdicated and went to Rome; *Handbook of British Chronology*, p. 22.

[10] A similar sentence appears in the Abingdon copies of the Worcester *Chronicle*; John of Worcester, *Chronicle*, ii. 610.

[11] This and the next section constitute Sawyer, no. 241; *Charters of Abingdon Abbey*, no. 4. In its present form it is clearly a fabrication, but parts were almost certainly based on genuine early records; *Charters of Abingdon Abbey*, p. 16. Edwards, in *Charters of the Early West Saxon Kingdom*, p. 174, suggests that the charter 'may represent an early attempt to write an account of the early history of Abingdon'. For the links of this and the other Hæha charters to the minster at Bradfield, see above, p. xxviii.

[12] Both Edwards, in *Charters of the Early West Saxon Kingdom*, p. 175, and *Charters of Abingdon Abbey*, p. 16, prefer Ine as the correct reading, given in MS B; MS C would have

Ceadwalla left for Rome and Ine succeeded to the kingdom.[9] First he decided to render void his predecessors' gifts, then he repented of so doing and from his own possessions increased them far more richly.[10]

3. (B9) *Charter of King Ceadwalla.*[11]
In the name of the Lord God, our saviour Jesus Christ. Although the spoken word by itself suffices as testimony for those matters soundly decided according to the decrees of the canons, still, because of the uncertain doubt of times to come, they are to be strengthened by the firmest corroboration of written letters. Therefore I, Ceadwalla[12] king of the West Saxons, have willingly given back to Abbot Hæha the land of 173 hides next to Abingdon which King Cissa had once given to him and Cilla his sister and abbess.

But afterwards, when King Ine acquired the kingdom, he took away that land and restored it to the public property, without a monastery yet having been built on it nor any church at all erected.[13] He gave that land back again to the same Hæha, then his nobleman, to build a monastery on it, saying:

4. (B9) *Charter of King Ine.*
I, Ine, monarch of the Saxon land, who, with the Lord reigning, control the royal sceptres, by many men's counsel again give back and relinquish the land which my predecessors, Cissa and others, are known to have given to Hæha the nobleman and his sister Cilla.[14]

Then that nobleman Hæha subjected himself with all his wealth and the aforementioned land to the service of almighty God, and chose me[15] to build that monastery in the place named above, that is next to

changed the name to simplify the apparent chronology of grants. However, it should be noted that in general MS C shows less tendency to alter or confuse names than does MS B; see below, pp. 210, 288, 300, 302, 322, 348, 366. The present narrative in either form is, in Kelly's words, 'repetitive and self-contradictory', and it seems impossible to make a compelling case for preferring one or other name.

[13] *Charters of Abingdon Abbey*, p. 18, argues plausibly that Ine took back the land *because* the beneficiaries had not fulfilled an undertaking to build a monastic church, but the document does not make the causal link quite so explicit. On the *History*'s use of the phrase *res publica*, see above, p. xxxiii. The *History* regularly uses the word *oratorium* to refer to a whole church, rather than a specific part.

[14] The language in this sentence clearly does not belong to Ine's time. For example, Anglo-Saxon kings only started to use the word 'monarchus' to refer to themselves in the 10th c.; *Charters of Abingdon Abbey*, p. 18.

[15] The identity of the first-person narrator in this section is not clear; for tentative speculation that it could be Cilla, see *Charters of Abingdon Abbey*, pp. 19–20.

regulariterque regendum illud abbatem elegit. Sponteque sua seipsum meo regimonio[h] commisit uotoque monachico astringens.[i] At nunc, nondum euoluto ad integrum quinquennio ex quo hec uota uouit, soluenda immutare decreta cupiens, Inique regem in suffra-
C fo. 105v gium sibi repetite hereditatis | assumpsit. Quibus ego libenter cessi, prefatamque terram et monasteria que construximus, ut dixi, in toto retribuam.[16] Insuper et de orientali parte fluminis Tamise uiginti cassatos, quos mihi Cuthredus regulus et Merciorum rex Æilredus[j]
[i. 11] necnon et Ini rex Saxonum tradiderunt,[17] adiciam; decem quoque cassatos secus uadum Bestlesford[18] et centum in Bradanfeltha[k] [19] (ubi monasterium erexi), quos Ini et Coenred[l] simul dederunt pariter, tribui; qui fiunt simul .cclxxiii. cassatos.[20] Votum autem monachi quod mihi spopondit relaxans clementer indulsi, presente uenerando antistite Hedde necnon Aldelmo abbate et Wintra et omni familia nostra in ecclesia.[21] Si quis uero contra hoc decretum abbatatus uenire temptauerit, uel has donationes regum religiosorum, tirannica fretus potestate, uiolenter demere uel auferre satagerit, sciat se coram Christo rationem in ultimo uiuorum et mortuorum examine redditurum. Scripta est uero hec cautionis singrapha anno ab incarnatione Christi .dcxcix., indictione duodecima.[m]

5. *Carta Ini regis.*[22]

Ego Ini, rex Westsaxonum, ob indulgentiam criminum meorum, aliquam terram ad ecclesie munificentiam libenter impendo. Dispensante enim Domino, Hean abbati in potestate concessa fuerat in

[h] regimini, *corr. from* regimonio *B* [i] constringens *B* [j] Ethelredus *B* [k] Bradenfeld *B* [l] Conred *B* [m] *see Charters of Abingdon Abbey, p. 16, for the witness list in B*

[16] Such a release from monastic vows and an apparent return of property to secular purposes would be highly irregular. *Charters of Abingdon Abbey*, pp. 18–20, suggests that, if Cilla is the narrator here, what may have happened is that Hæha was freeing himself of vows of subordination to her, thereby allowing himself independence as an abbot and control of properties. Man and land were thus not returning to the secular world. However, as *Charters of Abingdon Abbey*, p. 20, points out concerning this hypothesis, 'in the absence of external evidence there seems to be little chance of establishing its validity'. See also *Charters of the Early West Saxon Kingdom*, ed. Edwards, pp. 175–6.

[17] See *Charters of Abingdon Abbey*, p. 20, for the possibility that the sub-king Cuthred should be identified with the kinsman of King Cenwealh of Wessex whom the *ASC*, *s.a.* 648, records as receiving 3,000 hides near *Æscesdune* from that king; note also *ASC*, *s.a.* 661. Æthelred was king of the Mercians 675–704; *Handbook of British Chronology*, p. 16. The land concerned may be in what became southern Oxfordshire; *Charters of Abingdon Abbey*, p. 20.

[18] Berkshire. See EPNS, *Berkshire*, ii. 513; note also *Charters of Abingdon Abbey*, p. 8. It had no later association with Abingdon.

Abingdon, and to govern it as abbot according to the Rule. Of his own accord he entrusted himself to my control and bound himself with a monastic vow. But now, less than five years after taking these vows, and desiring to change and be released from his decisions, he has taken King Ine as his helper regarding the inheritance that he has claimed back. I have willingly yielded to them, and restore in full that land and the monasteries which, as I have said, we built.[16] On top of this I add twenty hides to the east of the river Thames which Cuthred the sub-king and Æthelred king of the Mercians and also Ine king of the Saxons bestowed on me;[17] also I have bestowed ten hides by the ford at Basildon[18] and one hundred hides in Bradfield[19] (where I erected the monastery) which Ine and Coenred together jointly gave; these together make 273 hides.[20] Moreover, I have undone and mercifully remitted the monk's vow that he had sworn me, in the presence of the venerable Bishop Hædde, and Abbot Aldhelm, and Wintra, and all our *familia* in the church.[21] If anyone attempts to go against this decision of the abbacy or, relying on tyrannical power, strives violently to take away or steal these gifts made by devout kings, let him know that he will render account before Christ at the Last Judgement of the living and the dead. This charter of undertaking was written in the year 699 from the Incarnation of Christ, the twelfth indiction.

5. *Charter of King Ine.*[22]

I, Ine king of the West Saxons, for the indulgence of my wrongs, willingly bestow some land for the endowment of the church. For, by the Lord's disposition, land in four areas had been granted to Abbot

[19] Berkshire. The place was probably the site of an early minster, but certainly from the 10th c. the land there was in lay hands and had no later association with Abingdon; *Charters of Abingdon Abbey*, p. 7.

[20] Coenred was Ine's father and perhaps a sub-king of Wessex; *Charters of Abingdon Abbey*, p. 21; *Handbook of British Chronology*, p. 22. The arithmetic whereby the figure 273 hides was reached is obscure.

[21] Hædde was bishop of the West Saxons 676–*c.*705; the famous writer Aldhelm was abbot of Malmesbury; Wintra was abbot of Tisbury, Wiltshire; *Charters of Abingdon Abbey*, pp. 18–19.

[22] Sawyer, no. 239; *Charters of Abingdon Abbey*, no. 2. Again it is a fabrication, but again probably with a genuine documentary base; see *Charters of Abingdon Abbey*, p. 9; *Charters of the Early West Saxon Kingdom*, ed. Edwards, p. 172. The date of fabrication is uncertain, and Edwards, p. 174, suggests that 'nothing in this charter is of identifiably tenth-century or later date, and it may be that it is a forgery produced fairly early, possibly at the monastery of Bradfield itself.' Neither this charter nor the following one appears in MS B, whereas normally the compiler of the later version included more documentary material; for possible explanations, see above, p. xlvi.

[i. 12] quatuor partibus terre,[a] id est in Bradanafel quindecim cassatuum, et quindecim cassatuum apud Bestlesforda, et manentium quinque et uiginti cuius uocabulum est Stretlee, et octoginta cassatos apud Æaromundeslee.[23] Que scilicet donationes ut firmius ac tenatius reliquum durarent in euum, etiam coram summis pontificibus, id est Brihtwallo archiepiscopo et Daniele episcopo,[24] peracte sunt, necnon et cespites horum locorum pro ampliore firmitate libro superposui quem ipsi duo prefati episcopi in manibus suis tenuerunt.[25] Porro ut firmior prefate donationis largitio inextricabili tenacitate iugiter seruaretur, etiam testes adiunximus quorum nomina subter tenentur inserta. Si quis uero contra hec nostre diffinitionis decreta, proprie temeritatis pertinatia fretus, uiolenter uenire nisus fuerit, nouerit se in tremendo ultime discussionis examine coram iudice Christo, equa discretionis lance singulorum facta librante, rationem redditurum. Signum manus[b] Ini regis Westsaxonum +. Signum manus Ethelredi regis Merciorum +. Signum manus Ethelfrith. Ego Daniel seruus seruorum Dei hanc donationem confirmaui +. Hec carta scripta est tercio nonas mensis Iulii, indictione duodecima, anno ab incarnatione Christi .dclxxxvii..[26] Ego Winberctus hanc cartam scripsi et subscripsi +.[27] Hec terra prefata iugiter ecclesie sancte Marie in Ebbandune subiecta sit.[28]

6. *Item alia carta Ini regis.*[29]

Ego Ini, rex Westsaxonum, pro anime mee remedio, reddidi terram quinque et quadraginta cassatorum[30] Hean patricio et Ceolswiðe,[31] ad monasterium construendum; que terra appellatur in Bradanfelda et

5 [a] *rectius* terra? [b] *last three letters over erasure MS*

[23] *Charters of Abingdon Abbey*, p. 9, suggests this sentence may be an interpolation. Note the difference in the hidages attributed to Basildon and Bradfield compared with above, p. 6. *DB* i, fo. 62^r, records Streatley, Berkshire, as held by Asgar the staller from King Edward for twenty-five hides *TRE*. The exact location of the eighty hides at *Earmundesleah* is uncertain, but most likely included land at Appleton, Eaton, and Bessels Leigh, and quite possibly elsewhere in Hormer hundred, Berkshire; EPNS, *Berkshire*, ii. 443–4, *Charters of Abingdon Abbey*, p. 11.

[24] Berhtwald was elected archbishop of Canterbury in 692, consecrated in 693, and died in 731; Daniel was bishop of Winchester *c.*705–44; *Handbook of British Chronology*, pp. 213, 223.

[25] For similar ceremonies, see Sawyer, nos. 1164, 1804–6.

[26] 687 was in fact the fifteenth indiction. The confusion could result from a scribal error, with 'xv' being misread as 'xii'. However, Ine did not succeed Ceadwalla until 688, whilst the churchmen involved in the conveyancing ceremony only came to office after 687. For other problems with the dating and witness list, see *Charters of Abingdon Abbey*, pp. 10–11.

[27] Wynberht was to be abbot of Nursling. Here and in two other charters (Sawyer, nos. 243, 1164) his subscription connects him to the writing of the charter. In the present context the phrasing presumably derives from a genuine early West Saxon charter; *Charters*

Hæha's control, that is fifteen hides in Bradfield, and fifteen hides at Basildon, and twenty-five hides named Streatley, and eighty hides at *Earmundesleah*.[23] So that these gifts might last more securely and steadfastly for ever more, this was carried out in the presence of the highest prelates, that is Archbishop Berhtwald and Bishop Daniel,[24] and also for greater security I placed turfs from these places on a book which those two bishops held in their hands.[25] Further, we have also added the witnesses whose names are listed below, so that the bestowal of this gift may be perpetually preserved with insoluble steadfastness. If anyone indeed, relying on the stubbornness of his own temerity, strives to come violently against these decisions of our decree, let him know that he will render account at the awe-inspiring trial of the Last Judgement before Christ the Judge, when the unbiased distinguishing scales weigh everyone's deeds. Sign of the hand of Ine king of the West Saxons +. Sign of the hand of Æthelred king of the Mercians +. Sign of the hand of Æthelfrith. I Daniel servant of the servants of God have confirmed this gift +. This charter was written on 5 July, the twelfth indiction, the year 687 from the Incarnation of Christ.[26] I Wynberht wrote and subscribed this charter +.[27] This aforementioned land is to be perpetually subject to the church of St Mary in Abingdon.[28]

6. *Likewise, another charter of King Ine.*[29]

I, Ine king of the West Saxons, for the cure of my soul, have given back land amounting to forty-five hides[30] to Hæha the nobleman and Ceolswith,[31] for building a monastery; that is, the land described as in

of the Early West Saxon Kingdom, ed. Edwards, pp. 12–13, 173–4; *Charters of Abingdon Abbey*, pp. 10–11.

[28] This sentence was probably added later, if the fabrication was put together at Bradfield; *Charters of the Early West Saxon Kingdom*, ed. Edwards, p. 174.

[29] Sawyer, no. 252; *Charters of Abingdon Abbey*, no. 1, which, at pp. 4–5, argues that the present text needs to be treated sceptically, as 'a patchwork of ancient records'. Edwards, in *Charters of the Early West Saxon Kingdom*, p. 168, argues that it 'appears to be basically authentic, although a few anachronistic details suggest some later interpolation'. Given the interpolations she notes, Edwards is not in fact far from Kelly's 'patchwork' conclusion. Stenton, *Early History*, pp. 12–13, believed it could be a fragment of a genuine charter of Ine. However, his demonstration that it 'does not resemble the ordinary work of a twelfth-century forger' does not preclude the arguments of Edwards and Kelly. This charter, like the previous one, is omitted from MS B. For the possible circumstances of Ine's restoration of lands, see above, p. xc n. 432.

[30] Note the difference of hidage from the preceding charter, where Bradfield and Basildon are said to have had fifteen hides each, Streatley twenty-five.

[31] To be identified with Hæha's sister, called by the short form Cilla in the other documents. The difference of name form suggests dependence on different original records.

Bestlesforda, et alia que nominatur Stretlea, cum omnibus ad se pertinentibus. Cui donationi testes affuerant Ebba,[32] Æthilbald, et
[i. 13] Eadfrith filius Iddi,[33] et cum iussione episcoporum Cedde, Germani, Winfridi.[34] Quam terram primus dederat Eadfrith filius Iddi super altare in ecclesia que ibi constructa est, pro anima eius. Ego Theodorus, seruus Dei, archiepiscopus consensi et subscripsi.[35]

7. **(B10)** [a]*Testamentum Heani abbatis.*[a] [36]

Ego Hean, dispensante Domino abbas, aliquam terre possessiunculam
B fo. 7r (que mihi ex munificentia parentum meorum, qui regni guber|nacula
C fo. 106r potiri noscuntur, in potestate concessa fuerat)[37] | in loco cuius uocabulum est Bradanfeld, cum adiacentibus, nec minus aliis sicut infra signatum est locis, ac conditione Cillan sorori mee ad possidendum contuli,[b] ut post obitum meum, si ipsa superstes uixerit, disponat et regat cum Dei timore; et post se ad istum monasterium omnino reddat. Si uero omnipotentis Dei iudicio, me uiuente, uite sue sortem disposuerit, ius eiusdem loci et dispensatio mihi cedat. Supradicte uero quantitas terre in Bradanfeld octo et quadraginta cassatuum[c] est, in Escesdune quinque et quinquaginta,[38] in loco qui uocatur Æarmundeslea[d] tres et octoginta. Summa simul redacta in[e] .clxxxiii. cassatos colligitur.[39] Si quis ergo definitionem[f] hanc a me factam unacorditer,[g] canonice, et ecclesiastice, a rege Ini necnon et ab episcopo Daniele roboratam, irritam facere temptauerit, sciat se coram Christo rationem redditurum.

[h]Anno ab incarnatione Domini .dccxxviii. rex Ine, relicto imperio ac Æthelhardo commendato, Romam profectus est.[h] [40]

7 [a–a] Testamentum Heani antequam abbas efficeretur *B* [b] *corr. from* contulit *B* [c] cassatorum *B* [d] Earmundeslea *B* [e] *om. B* [f] diffinitionem *B* [g] *corr. from* una concorditer *B* [h–h] *om. B*

[32] See above, p. lxxxix n. 428.

[33] For comment on these names, see *Charters of Abingdon Abbey*, p. 5; the witnesses cannot be identified with otherwise known individuals. Edwards, in *Charters of the Early West Saxon Kingdom*, p. 169, takes this as evidence that 'the first lot of witnesses are genuine'. However, they could have been copied from a document now lost.

[34] Probably three successive bishops of the Mercians: Jaruman (?662–?667), Chad (669–72), Wynfrith (672–672 × 676); *Handbook of British Chronology*, pp. 218, 220. Edwards, in *Charters of the Early West Saxon Kingdom*, p. 169, in supporting her general acceptance of the authenticity of the document, states that 'the list of bishops appears to be an interpolation'.

[35] Edwards, in *Charters of the Early West Saxon Kingdom*, p. 169, comments that 'Theodore's subscription is also likely to be a later addition'.

[36] Sawyer, no. 1179; *Charters of Abingdon Abbey*, no. 3. Despite the rubric given in the

Bradfield and Basildon, and the other land named Streatley, with everything pertaining to them. Present as witnesses to this gift had been Æbba,[32] Æthelbald, and Eadfrith son of Iddi,[33] and by the command of the bishops Chad, Jaruman, Wynfrith.[34] Eadfrith son of Iddi had first given this land on the altar in the church which was built there, for his soul. I Archbishop Theodore, servant of God, have consented and subscribed.[35]

7. (B10) *Testament of Abbot Hæha.*[36]

I, Hæha, abbot by the Lord's disposition, have conferred on my sister Cilla that she may possess a small piece of land in the place named Bradfield (which land had been granted into my control by the munificence of my kin, who are known to have the governance of the realm),[37] with what belongs to it, and no less the other places as indicated below, on the condition that if she survives me and lives on after my death, she may dispose and rule with the fear of God; and after her it is to return completely to that monastery. But if by the judgement of almighty God she should chance to die in my lifetime, the ownership and administration of the place will fall to me. The extent of that land is forty-eight hides in Bradfield, fifty-five in Ashdown,[38] eighty-three in the place called *Earmundesleah*. The overall total is 183 hides.[39] If anyone therefore attempts to make null this decision taken by me wholeheartedly, canonically, and in accord with church law, and strengthened by King Ine and also by Bishop Daniel, let him know that he will render account in Christ's presence.

In the year of our Lord 728 King Ine left and entrusted dominion to Æthelheard and set out for Rome.[40]

History, this is not a typical Anglo-Saxon will and it does not record a post-obit gift. Its degree of authenticity is problematic. Edwards, in *Charters of the Early West Saxon Kingdom*, pp. 170–2, argues for substantial authenticity; *Charters of Abingdon Abbey*, pp. 12–13, is rather more sceptical.

[37] The reference is probably to Ine, but possibly also to Eadfrith; *Charters of the Early West Saxon Kingdom*, ed. Edwards, p. 171. *De abbatibus* also shows Hæha's royal connections, as nephew of Cissa; *CMA* ii. 269.

[38] This probably refers to the entirety of the Berkshire Downs; see EPNS, *Berkshire*, i. 2–4. See also above, p. 6 n. 17, on *ASC*, *s.a.* 648,

[39] Again the arithmetic is incorrect. One possible way of rectifying it would be to take the reference to Bradfield to include all the lands mentioned in Ine's charter in the previous chapter, totalling forty-five not forty-eight hides. However, hidages for particular estates in these charters are notable for their inconsistency.

[40] Æthelheard was king of Wessex 726–?740; *Handbook of British Chronology*, p. 22. Cf. MS B's longer account, below, B12.

B fo. 13r **8. (B30)** [a]*Carta regum Æðelbaldi et Æthelhardi.*[a] [41]

[i. 38] Domino regnorum regna regenti, iura imperiorum disponenti,[b] [i. 39] semper gloria. Precedentium etenim temporum antiquitate ac diuersitate succedentium imperiorum, a predecessoribus prouide plura disposita ignorantie caligine iccirco cassabuntur, dum litterarum[c] notis origo institutionum minime deprehenditur tradita.[42] Ne qua uero ex accidenti obiectione posteris dissensio oriatur, prout pridem censuit peritorum constitutio, ueluti uice testamenti stilo edenda ac iure sunt hereditaria successoribus relinquenda, ut seculis et generationibus ueritas in preteritis actibus declaretur. Quamobrem utile uisum ac necessarium fore iudicauimus dilucide huic sceduli[d] describere quantitatem terre monasterii fundati[e] in honore sancte Dei genitricis Marie semper uirginis, situm e latere montis Ebbandune,[f] cui uenerabilis presidet usque hodie abbas Cumma.[43] Nam ex utraque parte fluuii Tamise cis citra suis antecessoribus ad ius monasterii prefati quedam territoria collata fuerant. Plaga predicti fluminis occidentali data in Dei oblatione terra his Saxonum regibus, Cissa, Ceadwalla, Ini; quantitate huius numeri .ccl. cassatuum continetur. Plaga uero orientali Mercie [. . .][g] potentissimi reges, ad sustentationem Dei seruorum suprafato monasterio, terram hac supputatione manentium uiginti, qui additis uocabulis inspiciantur Æthelred, Cuthred, Coenred. Insuper et rex Æthelbaldus suam specialiter oblationem monasterio eidem obtulit locoque in Wacenesfel,[h] septem[i] et uiginti cassatos dedit, alibi quoque iuxta riuum Geenge decem erogauit.[44] Prescriptas quoque preteritorum regum donationes, una cum suis presulibus et principibus sed et optimatibus, perhenniter Dei cultui eodemque monasterio prefato firmauit, quorum nomina [i. 40] subscriptionibus annexa declarantur. [j]Æthelbaldus Brittannie Anglorum monarchus[45] preformatas propinquorum sed et regum

8 [a–a] Carta Aðelbaldi regis West Saxonum de Wachenesfeld *B* [b] disonenti *B* [c] literarum *B* [d] *corr. from* scedule *C*; ceduli *B* [e] fundato *B C* [f] Abbedune *B* [g] .cclxxiiii. *B; the erasure in C is too small to allow this figure* [h] Wacenesfeld, *altered to* Wachenesfeld *B* [i] sex et uiginti *B, the figures in both MSS being in Roman numerals* [j–j] *see Charters of Abingdon Abbey, p. 23, for the witness list in B*

[41] Sawyer, no. 93; *Charters of Abingdon Abbey*, no. 5. This again is a fabrication, based in part on early records; see *Charters of Abingdon Abbey*, pp. 24–5. Æthelbald was king of Mercia 716–57; *Handbook of British Chronology*, p. 16. Note that MS C correctly places the supposed transaction in the earlier 8th c., whereas the reviser wrongly identified the donor as Æthelbald of Wessex, and places the charter in the mid-9th c. The presence of the king of Wessex and of West Saxon bishops suggests a period of co-operation between Mercia and Wessex, whereas Berkshire was often disputed territory between the two realms.

8. **(B30)** *Charter of Kings Æthelbald and Æthelheard.*[41]

To the Lord ruling the kingdoms of kingdoms, disposing of the rights of empires, always glory. And indeed, with the antiquity of past times and the diversity of succeeding empires, very many matters arranged prudently by our predecessors will be broken by the darkness of ignorance, in that the beginnings of arrangements were not caught and set down in written letters at all.[42] Lest, indeed, a dispute may arise among later men from some objection which occurs, as an undertaking of experienced men formerly decreed, hereditary possessions should be made known in writing like a testament and be left by right to successors, so that the truth concerning past deeds may be declared to the future ages and generations. Therefore it has seemed useful and we have judged it necessary to describe clearly in this document the extent of the land of the monastery founded in honour of the holy mother of God Mary, ever Virgin, situated to the side of the hill of Abingdon, over which the venerable Abbot Cumma presides to this day.[43] Territories on both sides of the river Thames, on the near side and on the far, had been conferred on that monastery's ownership by his ancestors. On the western bank of that river land totalling 250 hides had been given as an offering to God by these kings of the Saxons: Cissa, Ceadwalla, and Ine. And on the eastern bank [. . .] the most powerful kings of Mercia (who may be identified by the further names Æthelred, Cuthred, and Coenred) had given to the sustenance of God's servants in that monastery, land reckoned at twenty hides. In addition, King Æthelbald specially presented his own offering to that monastery and gave twenty-seven hides in Watchfield, and elsewhere he also bestowed ten hides next to Ginge Brook.[44] Also he confirmed the above gifts of past kings perpetually to the worship of God and to the above monastery, together with his prelates and nobles and leading men, whose names are declared attached in the subscriptions. Æthelbald monarch of the English of Britain[45] by this sign + has confirmed the gifts of his

[42] The formulation of this proem is characteristic of 10th- or 11th-c. charters; *Charters of Abingdon Abbey*, p. 25.

[43] On Abbot Cumma, see above, p. xciii.

[44] Watchfield and Ginge, Berkshire. For details of Ginge Brook, see EPNS, *Berkshire*, i. 10. *Charters of Abingdon Abbey*, pp. 26–7, suggests that the document upon which the fabrication was based may have concerned a simple gift by King Æthelbald of Watchfield and Ginge, or of just the latter. Certainly Ginge and maybe Watchfield could have been early possessions of Abingdon. *DB* i, fo. 59^r, records Abingdon holding Watchfield for twenty hides *TRE*, fo. 59^v Abingdon holding Ginge for ten hides *TRE*.

[45] This is probably a later 10th-, certainly not an 8th-c. royal title; *Charters of Abingdon Abbey*, p. 25.

donationes hoc signo + firmauit. Ego Daniel plebi Dei famulus canonica subscriptione manu propria + firmaui. Ego Wor episcopus hanc donationem + subscripsi. Ego Forthere episcopus in Banesinga uilla,[46] iubente rege, crucis signum + infixi. Ego Walcstod episcopus signum crucis + ad confirmationem imposui. Ego Æthelhardus rex hanc suprafatam donationem sancto hoc signo + una cum comitibus
C fo. 106v supter nominatim | descriptis roboraui, in expeditione ultra fluuium Sabrina aduersus Britonum gentem.[j]

[i. 21 n.] 9. *De temporibus Rethuni abbatis.*[47]

Succedentibus nonnullis postea annis, Kenulfo rege regnante,[48] illius cenobii possessiones uenatores et aucupes regis frequentare earumque incolas passim predari ac si licitum foret in consuetudinem sibi usurparunt,[a] rex ipse prefectique illius eorundem incolarum expensis penes ipsos epulari atque equos suos depascendos, cum custodibus eorum, illis sepius committere. Cenobii illius primas illo tempore Rethunus dicebatur, episcopi et abbatis officio functus. His se suaque infestis huiusmodi negotiis impeti egre ferens, uirum Dei, Leonem summum Romane sedis pontificem, adiit ac de suarum rerum detrimento eum consuluit.[49] Ille conquerentem, affabili lenitate consultum, remittit ad propria sue auctoritatis cum apicibus quibus Anglie principem hortabatur ecclesie libertati intendere, portitorem litterarum suarum, uti probum deceret uirum, uereri. Ea si fecerit, laudi sibi salutique fore. Audito itaque rex pape Romani mandato, cum inficiari potius quam exequi id estimaretur, tardante aliquandiu illius progressu mandati, Rethunus episcopus et abba appetendum hominem pecunia ratus precum uotis minus flexibilem, optulit ei .cxx. libras preterea et centum manentes ad uillam regalem Suttun,[50]

9 [a] *corr. from* usurparant *MS*

[46] *Charters of Abingdon Abbey*, p. 25, suggests that this is probably the royal vill of Benson, Oxfordshire.

[47] Cf. below, B17, dealing with the same matters. The content of these chapters probably derives from Coenwulf's privilege in the next chapter but one. The extended narrative, distinctive at this stage of the text, may also reflect concerns closer to the time of the composition of the *History*; see above, p. cxxv. On the issues mentioned in the chapter, see Blair, *Church in Anglo-Saxon Society*, p. 132.

[48] Coenwulf was king of Mercia 796–821; *Handbook of British Chronology*, p. 17. An identical passage ('Succedentibus . . . rege') appears in the Abingdon copies of the Worcester *Chronicle*; John of Worcester, *Chronicle*, ii. 610.

[49] Leo III was pope 795–816; see *Oxford Dictionary of Popes*, pp. 97–9.

[50] Sutton Courtenay, Berkshire. A similar phrase appears in the Abingdon copies of the Worcester *Chronicle*; John of Worcester, *Chronicle*, ii. 610. *Charters of Abingdon Abbey*, p. 44, argues that 'medieval and modern historians have taken this . . . to refer to 100 hides at Sutton Courtenay: but the wording suggests that the treasure and land was actually

relatives and also of the kings, as listed above. I Daniel servant to the people of God have confirmed + with canonical subscription by my own hand. I Bishop Wor have subscribed + this gift. I Bishop Forthhere have affixed this sign of the cross + at the village of *Banesinga*,[46] at the king's order. I Bishop Walhstod have imposed the sign of the cross + for confirmation. I King Æthelheard have strengthened this above-mentioned gift with this holy sign +, together with my companions described by name above, during the expedition beyond the river Severn against the Britons.

9. *Concerning the times of Abbot Hræthhun.*[47]

Some years later, during the reign of King Coenwulf,[48] the king's huntsmen and fowlers wrongfully made into a custom that they should frequent the possessions of that monastery and everywhere plunder their inhabitants, as though this were permitted. The king himself and his reeves made it a custom to dine at the expense of those same inhabitants who were under their power, and very often to commit to them their horses for pasturing, with their keepers. The head of the monastery at that time was called Hræthhun, and he fulfilled the office of bishop and abbot. He took it ill that he and his possessions were subject to harmful impositions of this kind, and so he went to the man of God, Leo, the highest bishop of the Roman see, and consulted him concerning the harm to his possessions.[49] After advising him with courteous gentleness, Leo sent the complainant home with letters of his own authority in which he urged the prince of England to pay heed to the liberty of the church and to show respect to the bearer of his letters, as befits a righteous man. If he acted thus, it would be good for his reputation and salvation. When the king heard the Roman pope's instruction, he considered that it should be rejected, not followed, and so for some time progress regarding the instruction was delayed. Therefore Bishop and Abbot Hræthhun, thinking that the king was a man to be approached through money rather than swayed by prayers, offered him £120 besides one hundred hides at the royal vill of Sutton,[50] situated near

transferred *to* the royal vill at Sutton Courtenay'. However, the word 'ad' was quite frequently used to mean 'at' with reference to a place-name, as in the charter which follows and also below, p. 82. It remains very plausible that the view of the later version of the *History*, below B11, and of *De abbatibus*, *CMA* ii. 274, that land at Sutton was given to the king, is correct. *TRE* it was in the king's hands and answered for twenty-three hides and one virgate, apart from one hide which was held by the father of Ælfwig the priest, probably from Abingdon; *DB* i, fos. 57^{v}, 59^{r}. Counter-payments for grants were not uncommon; see J. Campbell, 'The sale of land and the economics of power in early England: Problems and possibilities', *Haskins Society Journal*, i (1989), 23–37.

prope Abbendonam sitam; ad hec et Deo uota pro illo magnopere libari. Quorum omnium gratia, adeo animum regis ad beniuolentiam uir ille sibi captauerat ut decretum publice sanciretur ne quisquam domus regie officialium uel prefectorum aut episcoporum in posses-
[i. 22 n.] sionibus ecclesie Ebbendunensi pertinentibus ultra iam aliquid lucri siue seruitutis[b] requireret, immo libertas ex integro omnibus eis perpetuaretur.

[i. 24] **10.** *Carta Kenulfi regis.*[51]

Anno Dominice incarnationis .dcccxi., Cenulfi uero regis Merciorum anno undeuicensimo[52] a tempore quo accepit a Deo sibi regnum concessum. Cum fratribus in monasterio quod dicitur Ebbendune unanimiter a paruo usque ad magnum [a]statuentibus et concedentibus,[a] ⟨dedimus⟩ Rethuno religioso abbati uel eius heredibus in dominium proprium ad habendum siue fruendum terram in monasterio quod dicitur Ebbanduna liberam .cccx. manentes;[53] Wyrðe decem manentes,[54] ad Aclea et ad Norðtuna et Punningstoce octodecim manentes, pro eius amabili pecunia ac deuotione quam erga nos gerebat.[55] Fuimus enim in sinodo in loco qui dicitur Celichyð, coram optimatibus nostris, et in pecunia dedit quod ualuit .cxx. libras, et cum centum mansionibus redemit iam agros a seruitute collocatas[b] a manu extraneorum:[56] in primis ad Sunnigwellan quindecim manentes, ad Eatune decem manentes, ad Sandforda decem manentes, ad Denceswyrðe et ad Goseie triginta manentes, etiam Culanham cum omnibus locis ad Ebbandune pertinentibus, ad Gainge decem et ad Lechamstede decem manentes.[57] Hoc scitote non solum pro anime mee sed pro totius gentis Merciorum salute

[b] seruitatis *MS*

10 [a–a] statuentes et concedentes *MS* [b] *rectius* collocata?

[51] Sawyer, no. 166; *Charters of Abingdon Abbey*, no. 8. This charter does not appear in MS B; see above, p. xlvi. It is a fabrication, possibly put together in the context of Æthelwold's efforts to reassemble what he regarded as the ancient endowment of Abingdon. Æthelwold probably had access to a privilege of Coenwulf for Abingdon or perhaps another house. Charters of Eadwig, Edgar, and Æthelred, below, pp. 62–4, 96, 146, mention Pope Leo and King Coenwulf freeing Abingdon from secular burdens, a grant recorded in a 'uetustum priuilegium'. That *priuilegium* may be the genuine document on which this and the next charter are based; see *Charters of Abingdon Abbey*, pp. cciii–cciv, 38–9. An early source is suggested, for example, by the spelling of the place-name Chelsea.

[52] 811 was in fact the fifteenth or sixteenth year of Coenwulf's reign. The text may refer to an otherwise unknown Chelsea synod in 811. This is not improbable as several known synods were held at Chelsea, annually in the later 780s, in 799, 801, and 816. Alternatively, the AD date may be wrong, the regnal date correct, in which case the meeting is that of 816; see *Charters of Abingdon Abbey*, pp. 38–9.

Abingdon. In addition he thought that God should be strongly petitioned concerning that matter. Thanks to all these methods, Hræthhun gained the king's good will to such an extent that the latter publicly ordained a decision that no official of the royal household or reeve or bishop should hereafter seek any profit or servitude in the possessions pertaining to the church of Abingdon, but rather that freedom wholly be perpetuated for all of them.

10. *Charter of King Coenwulf.*[51]

In the year of our Lord 811, and in the nineteenth year of Coenwulf king of the Mercians[52] from the time at which he received the kingdom granted to him by God. By the unanimous decision and grant of the brethren in the monastery which is called Abingdon, from small to great, we have given to Hræthhun the devout abbot and his heirs to have and enjoy free in their own lordship the land in the monastery which is called Abingdon 310 hides;[53] ten hides at Longworth,[54] eighteen hides at *Aclea*, *Northtuna*, and *Punningstoce*, in return for the pleasing money and devotion which he bore towards us.[55] For we were in a synod at a place called Chelsea, in the presence of our leading men, and he gave us money worth £120, and also with one hundred hides he now redeemed lands from servitude established by the hands of strangers:[56] first at Sunningwell fifteen hides, at Eaton ten hides, at Sandford ten hides, at Denchworth and at Goosey thirty hides, also Culham with all the places pertaining to Abingdon, at Ginge ten and at Leckhampstead ten hides.[57] Know that I will do this for the salvation not only of my soul but also of all the Mercian

[53] *Charters of Abingdon Abbey*, p. 39, suggests that 'this confusing and ambiguous detail is an insertion, an example of the land-totals which revisors of the Abingdon muniments sometimes added in improbable places'. The Latin of the opening and to a lesser degree of this whole charter is problematic, notably in terms of tenses and verb forms.

[54] Berkshire. In the later 10th c. Abingdon claimed thirty hides in Longworth as part of its early endowment; below, p. 50. *DB* i, fo. 59^{r}, records Abingdon holding Longworth for thirty hides *TRE*; by 1086 the assessment had been reduced to eight hides.

[55] *Aclea*, *Nothtun*, and *Punningstoke* conceivably may have been or become associated with Longworth, although the name endings may make this unlikely; *Charters of Abingdon Abbey*, p. 39.

[56] See above, p. lxxxii, on this phrase in the context of Æthelwold's reform.

[57] Sunningwell, Eaton, Sandford (probably Dry Sandford), Denchworth, Goosey, and Leckhampstead are all in Berkshire, Culham in Oxfordshire. *Charters of Abingdon Abbey*, p. 40, suggests that Culham was an addition to an existing list. All except Eaton and perhaps Denchworth were *Domesday* estates of Abingdon, and Abingdon's lands at Denchworth may have been entered under Goosey; *DB* i, fos. 58^{v}, 59^{r}, vol. ii. 8 n. 15. No genuine charter associates Abingdon and Eaton; see also below, B178. *DB* i, fo. 61^{v}, shows that Eaton was not in Abingdon's hands *TRE*, and was held by Miles Crispin in 1086. Abingdon later received the tithe of Eaton; vol. ii. 210.

facturum. Has terras in perpetuum liberaliter adquisiuit[c] a grauitudine comitum et a durissima seruitute regum, et sancte Dei genitricis ecclesie liberaliter illas seruire subiunxit. Proinde mandamus, per auctoritatem semper uirginis Marie et per signum sancte crucis in qua
[i. 25] omnis uictoria consistit, ut inantea nullus eum inquietare presumet
C fo. 107r uel eius successores conquassare audeat, | sed cum firma pace et securitate prenominatos agros possideant ac gubernent, et post cuicumque ipsis placuerit dimittant. Ego Coenwlf, rex Merciorum, has terras liberabo ab omni seruitute, magno uel modico, regum, principum, episcoporum, pro salute anime mee et pro tota gente Merciorum, sicuti ab omni seruitute fuit liberata, et est cum his testibus utrorumque sexuum, monachorum uel secularium, ut hec nostra statuta firma permaneat in perpetuum. Hic infra caraxantur nomina testium: Ego Coenwlf rex consensi et subscripsi in sinodo et in loco qui dicitur Celichyð. Ego Wulfred archiepiscopus.

B fo. 9v **11. (B18)** *Priuilegium Kenulfi regis.*[a] [58]
In nomine [b]Dei et Domini[b] nostri Ihesu Christi ueri redemptoris mundi. Anno uero Dominice incarnationis .dcccxxi., indictione quarta decima, ego Kenulfus,[c] ab eodem Domino[d] nostro populis et tribubus preordinatus in regem, anno imperii nostri quinto et uicensimo, fui rogatus ab apostolica sede, per priuilegium domni apostolici gloriosissimi pape Leonis[e] et[f] Rethunum uenerabilem episcopum, ut sibimet [g]seu familie[g] que habitat in monasterio [h]quod situm est in Abbendonia quodque dedicatum[h] est in honore
[i. 26] sancte Marie semper uirginis et Dei genitricis Domine nostre, ut[i] illud monasterium seu[j] omnia loca que ad ipsum pertinere dinoscuntur, cum rebus mobilibus et inmobilibus, in notis causis et ignotis, in modicis et in magnis, in[k] Domini Dei omnipotentis et beatissimi Petri
B fo. 10r principis apostolorum, donans donabo perpetuis temporibus | eternam libertatem in sancte Trinitatis patrocinio omnia loca ad prefatum monasterium pertinentia, quorum infra nominantur nomina: [l]Culeham, Chenitun, Hengestesie, Cumenoran, Earmundesle, Eatun,

[c] adquisibit *MS*

11 [a] regis *om. B* [b–b] Domini et Dei *C* [c] Cœnulfus rex Merciorum *B* [d] Deo et domino *B* [e] Leonis pape *B* [f] per *add. B* [g–g] uel suis propinquis seu ipsa familia *B* [h–h] que sita est in Abbandune ecclesie quod [*over erasure, probably of* que] ibidem dedicata *B* [i] *this second* ut *appears to be redundant* [j] uel *B* [k] *the sense requires a noun such as* honorem *here* [l–l] Culanhom, Chenigtun, Hengesteseig, Cumanora, Earmundelæh, Eatun, Suniggawelle, Sondford, Wudtun, Gæging, Deniceswurþ, Ceornei, Goseg, Færhom, Wæchenesfeld, Scrivenanhom, Burgtuun, Læhhamstede, Boxora, Wælingford *B*

people. He acquired these lands in perpetuity, free from the imposition of earls and the most burdensome servitude of kings, and has harnessed them to serve freely the Church of the holy mother of God. Accordingly we instruct, by the authority of Mary, ever Virgin, and by the sign of the holy cross in which every victory dwells, that henceforth no one presume to trouble him or dare to crush his successors, but they are to possess and govern the aforenamed lands with firm peace and security, and afterwards to pass them on to whomsoever they wish. I, Coenwulf king of the Mercians will free these lands from all servitude, great or small, of kings, nobles, and bishops, for the salvation of my soul and for the whole people of the Mercians, just as they had been freed of all servitude, and it is with these witnesses of both sexes, monks and seculars, that this our firm decree may remain in perpetuity. The names of the witnesses are spelt out here below: I King Coenwulf have consented and subscribed in the synod and at the place called Chelsea. I Archbishop Wulfred.

11. (B18) *Privilege of King Coenwulf.*[58]

In the name of God and our Lord Jesus Christ true redeemer of the world. In the year of our Lord 821, the fourteenth indiction, I Coenwulf, preordained by the same Lord as king for peoples and tribes, in the twenty-fifth year of our dominion, was asked by the apostolic see, through the privilege of the most glorious apostolic lord Pope Leo and through the venerable Bishop Hræthhun, for him and for the community which lives in the monastery situated at Abingdon and dedicated in honour of St Mary, ever Virgin and mother of God, our Lady, that to that monastery and all the places which are known to pertain to it, with movable and immovable possessions, in known and unknown affairs, in small things and in great, I give and will give for ever more in honour of the Lord God almighty and of the most blessed Peter prince of the apostles eternal liberty under the protection of the Holy Trinity for all places pertaining to the aforementioned monastery, the names of which are specified below: I grant and will remit, as we have already said, perpetual liberty for Culham, Kennington, Hinksey, Cumnor, *Earmundesleah*, Eaton,

[58] Sawyer, no. 183; *Charters of Abingdon Abbey*, no. 9. Like the previous charter, it is a fabrication, possibly put together in the context of Æthelwold's efforts to reassemble what he regarded as the ancient endowment of Abingdon. The phrase 'nec rex pastum requirat' resembles one in the 10th-c. confirmations; below, pp. 64, 96, 146.

Sunningauuille, Sandford decem manentium, Wdetun, Geinge, Denicheswrde, Ceornei, Goseig, Fernham, Wacenesfeld, Scriuenham, Burgtun, Lechamstede, Boxora, Weliford[l] cum appenditiis suis,[m] Wicham cum suis campis sicut Ceadwalla[n] rex perdonauit, cum illa silua integra que dicitur Spene, [o]Pohanlech, et Trinlech, Eatun,[o] cum omnibus agellulis ad prefata loca pertinentibus,[59] concedens perdonabo, sicut prediximus, perpetuam libertatem. Et mandatum mandamus, in nomine Patris et Filii[p] et Spiritus Sancti, ut nullus superueniat hominum, superbia inflatus, nec rex suum pastum requirat uel habentes homines quos nos dicimus festigmen,[q] nec eos qui accipitres[r] portant uel falcones uel caballos ducunt siue canes, nec penam, mittere super eos quoquomodo audeat,[60] nec princeps nec
[i. 27] graphio[s] hanc lenitatem prefatam in alicuius honeris[t] molestiam[u] mutare audeat, aut in diebus nostris uel successorum nostrorum. Si pro aliquo[v] delicto accusatur homo Dei, ecclesie ille custos solus cum suo iuramento, si audeat, illum castiget.[w] [61] Sin autem, ut recipiat aliam iusticiam huius uicissitudinis conditionem, prefatum delictum cum simplo pretio componat.[62] Expeditionem cum duodecim uassallis et cum tantis scutis exerceant.[63] Antiquos[x] pontes[y] et arces renouent.[64] Ceterum plena et[z] integra libertate glorientur. Maxime cum ipsi diebus Dominicis septem[a] missas pro nobis saluberrimas offerant, et armis spiritualibus—centum psalteriis—contra inuisibiles hostes dimicare non cessent.[b] Si quis autem prescriptis statutis

[m] mid heora gebura tunum, *with* id est cum appenditiis suis *interlin. B* [n] Ceadwælla *B* [o–o] Wohanlæh, Trindlæh, Eastun, *with an OE wynn in the first word B* [p] fili *B* [q] fæstingmen *B* [r] ancipitres *B* [s] graffio *B* [t] oneris, *with deletion before first letter B* [u] molestia *B* [v] alico *B* [w] *corr. from* castigat *B* [x] *corr. from* antiquas *B* [y] *followed by* exerceat *del. B* [z] *interlin. B* [a] singulis, *in later hand, over erasure C* [b] *corr. from* cessant *B*

[59] Except for Culham, all these lands were in Berkshire. Wickham, together with its woodland appendages, was probably part of the large *Domesday* manor of Welford. Hinksey and Wootton probably formed part of the large *Domesday* manor of Cumnor. Apart from Eaton, Fernham, Shrivenham, and Bourton, all were Abingdon estates in *Domesday*; *DB* i, fos. 58v–59v. See above, p. 17 n. 57, on Denchworth.

[60] On such privileges, see e.g. Maitland, *Domesday Book and Beyond*, p. 272. For further charter references to *fæstingmen*, see Sawyer, no. 134, a charter of Offa granting privileges to the churches of Kent, and including a privilege similar to that here recorded for Abingdon; no. 186, a charter of Ceolwulf king of Mercia and Kent for Archbishop Wulfred. *EHD*, i. 515 n. 1, states that the 'term [*fæstingmen*] occurs only in charters, and seems to refer to those who had the right to claim lodging as they went about the king's business'. Another possibility is that it refers to some kind of surety; see e.g. W. H. Stevenson, 'Yorkshire surveys and other eleventh-century documents in the York Gospels', *EHR*, xxvii (1912), 1–25, at pp. 11–12, for 'festermen' in a Yorkshire context being sureties. This might make more sense as a vernacular equivalent of 'habentes homines', i.e. men who were to 'hold' another to a certain purpose.

Sunningwell, Sandford amounting to ten hides, Wootton, Ginge, Denchworth, Charney, Goosey, Fernham, Watchfield, Shrivenham, Bourton, Leckhampstead, Boxford, Welford with its appendages, Wickham with its fields as King Ceadwalla remitted, with the whole wood which is called Speen, Poughley, and *Trinlech*, and Easton, with all minor plots pertaining to the aforementioned places.[59] And we order and instruct, in the name of the Father and the Son and the Holy Spirit, that no man, puffed up with pride, may encroach, no king seek hospitality or the retainers whom we call *festigmen*, nor may he dare to impose upon them in any way those who carry hawks or falcons, or lead horses or dogs, nor any penalty.[60] Nor is a noble or official to dare to alter this aforesaid leniency by the infliction of any burden, whether in our day or our successors'. If any man of God is accused regarding any wrong, that custodian of the church alone is to correct him with his own oath, if he dares.[61] If not, moreover, that he may receive other justice as a settlement of this situation, let him pay for the aforementioned wrong with the simple price.[62] They are to do military service with twelve retainers and with as many shields.[63] They are to repair old bridges and fortresses.[64] For the rest, let them exult in full and complete liberty. And, especially since on Sundays they offer seven most beneficial masses for us, let them not cease to fight with spiritual weapons—one hundred psalters—against invisible enemies. Moreover, if anyone is not willing to obey the aforewritten

[61] This seems to mean that the abbot has jurisdiction over all his monks in such cases, or perhaps over the men of the abbey; see Maitland, *Domesday Book and Beyond*, pp. 275, 280.

[62] *Singulare pretium* (or '*angild*') was compensation or restitution to the wronged person, typically in a case of theft; see Maitland, *Domesday Book and Beyond*, pp. 274, 282, 290–2; J. Goebel, *Felony and Misdemeanor: A Study in the History of English Criminal Procedure* (New York, 1937), pp. 348–54. Maitland, *Domesday Book and Beyond*, p. 292, comments that 'the most detailed and at the same time the most hopelessly obscure information that we get is such as can be obtained from two Abingdon charters', that is the present one and that which appears in the following chapter. Cf. my translation with those suggested by Maitland, *Domesday Book and Beyond*, pp. 275, 292, and Goebel, *Felony and Misdemeanor*, p. 350 n. 51.

[63] For use of the word 'uassallus', or near equivalents, to mean retainer, see S. M. G. Reynolds, *Fiefs and Vassals* (Oxford, 1994), p. 332; *Charters of Abingdon Abbey*, p. 84; also Reynolds, pp. 84–105, for evidence from the Carolingian period. Note the reference to 'aulici uassalli' in *De abbatibus*; *CMA* ii. 274. For 'faselli' in the sense of follower, most likely military follower, see also Asser, *Life of Alfred*, cc. 53, 55, ed. W. H. Stevenson (Oxford, 1904), pp. 41, 44, with comment at pp. 254–5.

[64] This is the first mention in a charter in the *History* of the *trinoda necessitas*, on which see N. P. Brooks, 'The development of military obligations in eighth- and ninth-century England', in P. Clemoes and K. Hughes, eds., *England before the Conquest: Studies in Primary Sources presented to Dorothy Whitelock* (Cambridge, 1971), pp. 69–84.

noluerit obedire, sciat se alienum esse a consortio sancte Dei ecclesie et a participatione corporis et sanguinis Domini nostri Ihesu Christi per auctoritatem beati Petri apostoli, nisi digne emendauerit quod
C fo. 107v contra Dei ecclesiam fecisset. Dederunt enim pro huius|modi rei gratia in auro et[c] argento .cxx. libras et centum manentes ad uillulam[d] regalem que dicitur Suðtun.[65]

Que postquam uir ille prudentissimus patrauit, in summa quietis[e] securitate quoad uixit[f] cenobium illud gubernauit.

[i. 33] **12. (B26)** [a]*Carta Ecgberhti regis de Mercham et de ecclesie Abbendonensis*
B fo. 11v *libertate.*[a66]

B fo. 12r In nomine Dei et Domini nostri Ihesu Christi redemptoris mundi. Anno Dominice incarnationis .dcccxxxv., indictione tercia decima, ego Ecgbert,[b] rex occidentalium Saxonum, dedi monasterium illud[c] Mercham quinquaginta manentium ad Abbendune,[67] cum licentia et consensu totius nostre gentis et unanimitate[d] omnium optimatum.
[i. 34] Hec donatio fuit facta in Pascha in Dorchecestre,[e 68] et postera uice eandem donationem liberaliter in Natali confirmauimus, anno imperii nostri quarto et tricensimo. Et sic mandamus, in nomine Patris et Filii et Spiritus Sancti, ut nullus superueniat hominum ibi, superbia inflatus, nec rex suum pastum requirat uel habentes homines quos

[c] *followed by* in *interlin. B* [d] uillam *B* [e] pacis *B* [f] coaduixit *B*

12 [a–a] Carta Egbrihti regis Westsaxonum de Mercham *B* [b] Ecberht *B* [c] monasterium illud *from B, C being illegible because of erasure beneath blot. Two or three erased characters follow in B.* monasterium illud sic al. liber *in later hand in margin C* [d] unamitate *B* [e] Dorkecestre *B*

[65] It cannot be certain whether the final sentence should be seen as part of the probably 10th-c. fabricated document that the scribe of the *History* was copying, an endorsement (possibly translated), or an additional note, nor likewise what part it formed of any document upon which the 10th-c. fabricator of the present charter based his text. For comment on the transaction, see above, p. 14 n. 50.

[66] Sawyer, no. 278; *Charters of Abingdon Abbey*, no. 11, which, at pp. 51–4, judges this to be a fabrication, but with an underlying genuine diploma of Ecgberht, king of Wessex 802–39 (*Handbook of British Chronology*, p. 23). The genuine document may have concentrated on privileges, the grant of Marcham, Berkshire, being a later addition, as may have been some modifications to the privileges. Parts of the charter are identical to that of Coenwulf, above, c. 11, where appropriate notes are provided. Of the witnesses, only Ealdorman Wigferth could not appear in a charter of this date, unless in this instance he is an otherwise unknown ealdorman of that name; *Charters of the Early West Saxon Kingdom*, ed. Edwards, p. 194. Stenton, *Early History*, p. 30, argued that the section on judicial privileges was written 'at a time when the outlines of Old English law were becoming confused', by a man who 'was acquainted with the Norman *murdrum*'. At least the last part of this argument is not compelling; see also *Charters of the Early West Saxon Kingdom*, ed. Edwards, p. 193.

provisions, let him know that he is estranged from the fellowship of the holy Church of God and from participation in the body and blood of our Lord Jesus Christ by the authority of the blessed Peter the apostle, unless he fittingly makes amends for what he did against God's church. For they gave for the sake of this £120 in gold and silver and one hundred hides at the small royal vill called Sutton.[65]

After that most prudent man completed these matters, he governed that monastery in the most secure peace as long as he lived.

12. (B26) *Charter of King Ecgberht concerning Marcham and the liberty of the church of Abingdon.*[66]

In the name of God and of our Lord Jesus Christ redeemer of the world. In the year of our Lord 835, the thirteenth indiction, I, Ecgberht king of the West Saxons, have given to Abingdon that monastery at Marcham amounting to fifty hides,[67] with the permission and consent of all our people and the unanimous accord of all the leading men. This gift was made at Easter in Dorchester,[68] and on a later occasion we freely confirmed this gift at Christmas, in the thirty-fourth year of our dominion. And so we instruct, in the name of the Father and the Son and the Holy Spirit, that no man, puffed up with pride, may encroach there, no king seek hospitality or the retainers

Sawyer, no. 358, a charter for the Old Minster, Winchester, in the name of Edward the Elder, mentions that Ecgberht had given Abingdon fifty hides in Marcham in return for fifty hides at Hurstbourne. H. P. R. Finberg, *Lucerna* (London, 1964), p. 134, argues that although the present charter does not mention Hurstbourne, 'there is . . . no reason to doubt that the exchange took place'. However, it must also be noted that the Winchester charter may come from Æthelwold's time; *Charters of Abingdon Abbey*, p. 53. See below, c. 75, for a questionable charter of King Edgar, granting fifty hides in Marcham to Abingdon, for discussion of the area covered by these fifty hides, and for consideration of why *DB* i, fo. 58^{v}, records Abingdon as having twenty hides in Marcham *TRE*, as opposed to the fifty mentioned in the charters.

[67] Blair, 'Minsters of the Thames', pp. 20–1, argues that the words 'illud monasterium' could refer to a minster at Marcham. Marcham was the mother church of one chapel in the later Middle Ages, the site is appropriate for a minster, and archaeology suggests that the churchyard was once much larger. He suggests the possibility that 'Marcham was a genuinely early church, but a subsidiary element in the Abingdon complex rather than a free-standing minster'. However, at p. 7, he admits that the claims of Marcham to be a minster are 'dubious' and it may be simpler in terms of sense, although not of grammar, to take the words 'illud monasterium' to refer to Abingdon. Note also that the text in MS C is unclear, and the correct reading may not originally have been 'illud monasterium'.

[68] The place-name form may suggest that this is Dorchester-on-Thames, Oxfordshire; EPNS, *Oxfordshire*, i. 152. If so, this is significant for the extent of the power of the king of Wessex in 836. On the other hand, meetings on festivals were regularly held at Dorchester in Dorset. See further *Charters of Abingdon Abbey*, p. 52, for problems of interpretation. For the Devon place-name evidence, see EPNS, *Dorset*, i. 347.

nos[f] dicimus festigmen, nec eos qui accipitres portant uel falcones, uel caballos ducunt siue canes, nec penam mittere super eos quoquomodo[g] audeat, nec princeps nec graphio hanc lenitatem prefatam in alicuius honeris[h] molestiam mutare audeat, aut in diebus nostris uel successorum nostrorum. Si pro aliquo delicto accusatur homo Dei, ecclesie ille custos solus cum suo iuramento, si audeat, illum castiget. Sin autem ut recipiat alienam iusticiam, huius uicissitudinis conditionem, prefatum delictum cum simplo pretio componat. Quid plura? Ne cui hominum per uim aliquid ibi tribuatur, neque in palefridis neque in refectiones, sed ab his omnibus liber permaneat.[69] De illa autem tribulatione que witereden[70] nominatur sit libera, nisi tamen singuli[i] pretium soluerit ut talia accipiant.[71] Fures quoque quos appellant weregeld ðeofas, si foris rapiantur, pretium eius dimidium illi ecclesie et dimidium regi[j] detur; et si intus rapitur, totum reddatur ad ecclesiam. Similiter de hereditate peregrinorum, id est [k]Gallorum et Brittonum et[k] horum similium,[72] ecclesie reddatur. Pretium quoque sanguinis peregrinorum, id est wergeld,[l] dimidiam partem rex teneat, dimidiam ecclesie antedicte reddant.[73] Silua quoque omnis que illi ecclesie et suburbanis eius suppetit in omnibus causis sit libera, et non secetur ibi ad regis uel principis edificia aliqua pars materie, grossi[m] uel gracilis, sed ab omnibus defensa et libera maneat. Si quis autem
[i. 35] prescriptis statutis noluerit obedire, sciat se alienum esse a consortio sancte Dei ecclesie et a participatione corporis et sanguinis Domini nostri Ihesu Christi per auctoritatem beati Petri apostoli, nisi digne emendauerit quod contra Dei ecclesiam fecisset. [n]Ego Ecgbert rex +. Ego Æthelwlf filius regis +. Ego Ælfstan episcopus +.[74] Ego Rethun episcopus +. Ego Kinred episcopus +. Ego Wlflaf abbas +. Ego Eadwald[o] abbas +. Ego Wlfhar dux +. Ego Osmod dux +. Ego Wigferd

[f] *om. B* [g] quomodo *B* [h] oneris, *with deletion before first letter B* [i] *rectius* singulare? [j] *corr. by erasure, almost certainly from* regni *B* [k–k] *over erasure C* [l] weregeld *B* [m] *rectius* grosse [n–n] *see Charters of Abingdon Abbey, p. 51, for the witness list in B* [o] *corr. from* Eadwad *by interlin. in different ink C*

[69] *Charters of Abingdon Abbey*, p. 52, notes that in a similar clause, Sawyer, no. 271 for Rochester uses the word 'parafrithis', deriving from the late Latin *paraveredus*, 'a horse for extraordinary occasions, an extra post-horse'. The Abingdon text shows the influence of the later *palefridus*, and it is upon the Abingdon form that I base the translation.

[70] i.e. penal fines; *Charters of Abingdon Abbey*, p. 52. Only three other charters mention such payments: Sawyer, nos. 294, 294a; two of King Æthelwulf's 'First Decimation' diplomas from 844; and Sawyer, no. 1277, a charter issued by the bishop of Winchester in 877. Whilst both the charters in Æthelwulf's name are problematic, they may rest on a contemporary and authentic basic text; see *Charters of Malmesbury Abbey*, ed. S. E. Kelly (Oxford for the British Academy, 2006), pp. 80–7.

whom we call *festigmen*, nor may he dare to impose upon them in any way those who carry hawks or falcons, or lead horses or dogs, nor any penalty. Nor is a noble or official to dare to alter this aforesaid leniency by the infliction of any burden, whether in our day or our successors'. If any man of God is accused regarding any wrong, that custodian of the church alone is to correct him with his own oath, if he dares. If on the other hand, that he may receive justice from somebody else as a settlement of this situation, let him pay for the aforementioned wrong with the simple price. What more? That nothing is to be imposed there on any man by force, neither for palfreys nor for entertainment, but it is to remain free of all these.[69] Moreover, let it be free of the exaction that is called '*witerædeni*',[70] except, however, it pays the single price that they may receive such things.[71] If the thieves whom they call 'wergild thieves' are seized outside, half their price is to be given to that church and half to the king; if he is seized inside, all is to be rendered to the church. Similar payment is to be made to the church concerning the inheritance of pilgrims, that is of Frenchmen and *Brittones* and the like.[72] Also, the king is to have half the blood price (i.e. wergild) of pilgrims, and they are to render half to the aforesaid church.[73] Also all the wood associated with that church and its dependencies is to be free in all matters, and no portion of the timber, stout or thin, is to be cut there for the king's or a noble's buildings, but it is to remain protected and free from everything. If anyone is not willing to obey the aforewritten provisions, let him know that he is estranged from the fellowship of the holy Church of God and from participation in the body and blood of our Lord Jesus Christ by the authority of the blessed Peter the apostle, unless he fittingly makes amends for what he did against God's church. I King Ecgberht +. I Æthelwulf son of the king +. I Bishop Ælfstan +.[74] I Bishop Hræthhun +. I Bishop Coenred +. I Abbot Wulflaf +. I Abbot Eadwald +. I Ealdorman Wulfheard +. I Ealdorman Osmod +. I Ealdorman Wigferth +, and many others,

[71] The text of the latter part of this sentence may be corrupt, and its sense is not clear. 'The single price' may again refer to *angild*, restitution in cases of theft. However, Stephen Baxter (pers. comm.) suggests to me that 'singuli pretium' may rather be a one-off payment for the judicial privilege. For further interpretations of the clause, see Maitland, *Domesday Book and Beyond*, pp. 282, 290–2; Goebel, *Felony and Misdemeanor*, pp. 349–54.

[72] *Brittones* could refer to Welshmen or Bretons.

[73] Cf. *Ine*, 23.2, *Gesetze*, ed. Liebermann, i. 98, for an abbot or abbess sharing with the king the wergild of a slain 'elðeodigne', an outsider, foreigner, or perhaps pilgrim.

[74] There is no other record of a Bishop Ælfstan at this time, and Kelly suggests that the name is a mistake for Ealhstan bishop of Sherborne; *Charters of Abingdon Abbey*, p. 51.

dux +,[n] et multi alii hanc libertatem prescriptam, cum his testibus infra nominatis, firmiter in Ihesu Christo cum signaculo sancte crucis confirmantes roborauimus.

B fo. 12v **13. (B28)** [a]*Priuilegium Æthelwlfi regis.*[a] [75]

[i. 36] Ego Æthelwlf, gratia Dei occidentalium Saxonum rex, in sancta ac celeberrima Paschali sollennitate, pro mee remedio anime et regni prosperitate et populi ab omnipotenti Deo mihi collati,[b] consilium salubre cum episcopis, comitibus, et cunctis optimatibus meis perfeci, C fo. 108r ut decimam partem terrarum per regnum nostrum non solum | sanctis ecclesiis darem, uerum etiam et ministris nostris in eadem constitutis, in perpetuam libertatem habere, concessimus, ita ut talis donatio fixa incommutabilisque permaneat, ab omni regali seruitio et omnium secularium seruitute absoluta. Placuit autem Ælhstano episcopo Sciremburnensis ecclesie, et[c] Swithuno Wentane ecclesie episcopo, et ducibus communiter.[76] Hoc autem fecimus in honorem Domini nostri Ihesu Christi, et beate semper uirginis Marie, et omnium sanctorum, et Paschalis festi reuerentia, ut Deus omnipotens nobis et nostris posteris propitiari dignetur. Scripta est autem hec cartula anno ab incarnatione Domini nostri Ihesu Christi .dcccliiii., indictione secunda, die Paschali in palatio nostro quod dicitur Wiltun.[77] Qui autem augere uoluerit nostram donationem, augeat omnipotens Deus dies eius prosperos. Si quis uero minuere uel mutare presumpserit, noscat se ante tribunal Christi redditurum rationem, nisi [i. 37] prius satisfactione emendauerit. [d]Ego Æthelwlf rex. Ego Ælhstan episcopus. Ego Swithun episcopus. Ego Wlflaf abba. Ego Werferð abba. Ego Æthered et ego Ælfred filii regis consensimus.[d]

13 [a–a] Quomodo Aðelwlfus rex dedit decimam partem regni sui ecclesiis *B* [b] coati *B* [c] *om. B* [d–d] *see Charters of Abingdon Abbey, p. 65, for the witness list in B*

[75] Sawyer, no. 302; *Charters of Abingdon Abbey*, no. 14. Æthelwulf, son of Ecgberht, was king of Wessex 839–56/8; *Handbook of British Chronology*, p. 23. This is one of six Wessex charters (Sawyer, nos. 302–5, 307–8) concerned with a royal grant recorded in the *ASC*, *s.a.* 855/6: 'King Æthelwulf booked the tenth part of his land throughout all his kingdom to the praise of God and his own eternal salvation.' *Charters of Malmesbury Abbey*, ed. Kelly, pp. 65–79, concludes that 'it does seem to be very probable indeed that the common text / witness-list of the six "decimation charters" of 854 derives from a genuine document of the mid-ninth-century'; see also S. Keynes, 'The West Saxon charters of King Æthelwulf and his sons', *EHR*, cix (1994), 1109–49, at p. 1121. Compared with the others, the Abingdon

firmly in Jesus Christ with the sign of the holy cross, have confirmed and strengthened this above liberty, together with the witnesses named below.

13. (B28) *Privilege of King Æthelwulf.*[75]

I, Æthelwulf, by the grace of God king of the West Saxons, at the holy and most renowned solemn feast of Easter, for the cure of my soul and the prosperity of the kingdom and of the people conferred on me by almighty God, have concluded profitable consultations with my bishops, earls, and all my leading men, that I may give one-tenth of the lands throughout our kingdom not only to the holy churches, but also we have granted to our thegns constituted in the same to have in perpetual liberty, thus that such a gift may remain fixed and unchangeable, exempt from all royal service and all worldly servitude. This, furthermore, pleased Ealhstan bishop of the church of Sherborne and Swithhun bishop of the church of Winchester, and all the great men together.[76] Moreover, we did this in honour of our Lord Jesus Christ, and of blessed Mary, ever Virgin, and of all the saints, and in reverence of the feast of Easter, that almighty God may deign to be rendered favourable to us and our posterity. This charter, moreover, was written in the year of our Lord Jesus Christ 854, the second indiction, on Easter day in our palace which is called Wilton.[77] Moreover, whoever wishes to increase our gift, may almighty God increase his prosperous days. But if anyone takes on himself to diminish or change it, let him know that he will render account before the throne of Christ, unless previously he makes amends with compensation. I King Æthelwulf. I Bishop Ealhstan. I Bishop Swithhun. I Abbot Wulflaf. I Abbot Werferth. I Æthelred and I Alfred the king's sons have consented.

version is very abbreviated. Record of a specific grant to a beneficiary other than the abbey may have been excised, transforming the text into a general grant of privileges. It is notable that the version in MS B seems to have been copied from MS C; possibly no fuller version was available in Abingdon by the 13th c. *Charters of Malmesbury Abbey*, ed. Kelly, pp. 65–91, argues that the 854 decimation involved a grant of land, whereas the 844 decimation involved a 10 per cent tax reduction; see also Keynes, 'West Saxon charters', p. 1120,

[76] Ealhstan was bishop of Sherborne 816 × 825–67, Swithhun bishop of Winchester 852/3–862 × 865; *Handbook of British Chronology*, pp. 222, 223.

[77] For 'palaces', see P. Rahtz, 'Royal sites', in *The Blackwell Encyclopaedia of Anglo-Saxon England*, ed. M. Lapidge *et al.* (Oxford, 1999), pp. 399–401.

14. *De aduentu Danorum in Angliam.*[78]

Circa hec tempora,[79] Danorum ex gente nonnulli nauigio Angliam aduentare predam capere, hominum occisioni[a] instare, habitaculaque eorum exurere. Qui, cum pene ad internicionem ab Anglis sepius funderentur, suorum tamen compatriotarum[b] prosecutione numerosiore mox multitudine reparabantur. Tantus inesse eis regnandi siue dominandi in Anglia uidebatur appetitus, ut quodcunque oportuni uel importuni foret perpetiendum equo id animo transigeretur, dum modo imperitandi speratum ius sibi obuiaret. Nec tamen ad hoc leui quiuere prouentu attingere, siquidem ab illis non minus ducentis in eo sudatum annis.[80] Vnde Anglia, quondam plurimis fulta principibus (ut apud orientalium et occidentalium Saxonum, Merciorum et Northanhinbrorum, Cantiorum quoque nationes singuli reges essent), recrudescentibus erumpnis Danorum manu tantam sanguinis humani effusionem perpessa est ut uix in regno unus relinqueretur princeps, cuius ceteri consultu tuerentur. Eo urbes subuersas passim, [i. 38] succensos uicos, destructa monasteria, monimenta eorum plurimis in locis dant indicia, ubi parietum ac murorum reliquie hucusque spectantur.[81] Ita profligatis locorum habitatoribus, cum quies bellorum utcunque patraretur, loca a suis cultoribus pridem deserta ab aliis incoli ceperunt, commutato eorum dominatu et famulatu.

[i. 42] 15. (B34) [a]*Carta Æðelsiðe regine de Lacinge quindecim manentium.*[a82]

B fo. 14[r] Regnante in perpetuum Domino nostro Ihesu Christo. Ego Æðelsuið, regina Deo largiente Merciorum, cum consensu [b]et testimonio[b] meorum seniorum, concedens donabo Cuþwulfo [c]fideli meo[c] ministro [i. 43] aliquam telluris partem mee proprie potestatis, id est terram quindecim manentium in loco qui dicitur Lacinge,[d] pro eius humili[e] obedientia atque pecunia placabili, hoc est mille quingentis solidis argenti et auri uel quindecies centum siclis, ut habeat et possideat quamdiu uiuat perfruaturque uoluntarie, et (post finem illius termi-

14 [a] *ending involves erasure MS* [b] compatriatarum *MS*

15 [a–a] Carta Adelsuið regine de Lakinge *B* [b–b] *om. B* [c–c] fidelissimo *B* [d] Lakinge *B* [e] humi *B*

[78] Cf. MS B's different account, below, B37.

[79] The *ASC*, *s.a.* 855/6, states that King Æthelwulf's 'decimation' occurred in the same year that 'heathen men for the first time stayed in Sheppey over the winter'. B37 places the coming of Danes in the time of King Æthelred of Wessex (865/6–71), fitting with the *Anglo-Saxon Chronicle*'s mention of the coming of 'a great heathen army', *s.a.* 866/7.

[80] This presumably means that the Danes strove to obtain authority over England from the 9th c. until the success of Swein and Cnut in the early 11th.

14. *Concerning the coming of the Danes to England.*[78]

Around this time,[79] some men from the Danish people came to England by boat to take booty, to devote themselves to slaying men, and to burn their dwellings. Very often they were almost exterminated by the English, but nevertheless were soon revived in still greater numbers by their compatriots who followed them. They seemed to have such an appetite for reigning and ruling in England that with equanimity they went through any necessary suffering, opportune or inopportune, so long as they could obtain the right of ruling, which they desired. Nor were they able to attain this by easy progress, for they sweated at it for no less than 200 years.[80] Therefore, England, which once had been provided with the authority of many princes (as there were individual kings for the nations of the East and West Saxons, Mercians and Northumbrians, and also the men of Kent), suffered such an outpouring of human blood when troubles erupted again at the hands of the Danes that scarcely one prince remained in the kingdom, by whose counsel others might be protected. Evidence in many places, where remains of walls and buildings are observed to this day, gives reminders of these events, towns everywhere overthrown, settlements burnt, monasteries destroyed.[81] Thus, after the inhabitants of places had been overwhelmed and when peace from battles was achieved to any degree, places previously deserted by their cultivators began to be occupied by others, with their lordship and servitude having been changed.

15. (B34) *Charter of Queen Æthelswith concerning Lockinge, amounting to fifteen hides.*[82]

With our Lord Jesus Christ reigning in perpetuity. I, Æthelswith, by God's largesse queen of the Mercians, with the consent and testimony of my most influential men, grant and will give to Cuthwulf, my faithful thegn, a part of an estate under my own control, that is land amounting to fifteen hides in the place called Lockinge, for his humble obedience and his acceptable money, that is 1,500 shillings of silver and gold and 1,500 *sicli*, so that he may have and possess it as long as he lives and enjoy it of his own accord and (after his end and

[81] A similar sentence, with some variations, appears below, p. 268.

[82] Berkshire. Sawyer, no. 1201; *Charters of Abingdon Abbey*, no. 17, which, at p. 75, argues that 'there seems to be a very good case for accepting the charter's authenticity'. Æthelswith was the wife of Burgred of Mercia and daughter of Æthelwulf of Wessex. Her brother, Æthelred king of Wessex, is the first witness.

numque dierum) liberam relinquat cuicumque uoluerit, in sempiternam potestatem hereditatemque perpetuam.[83] Et hec donatio peracta[f] est anno Dominice incarnationis .dccclxviii., indictione prima. Et
C fo. 108v nos[g] datum precipimus omnibus seculi potestatibus, in nomine Dei | Patris et Filii et Spiritus Sancti, inuiolatum[h] seruare. His testibus subscribentibus et consentientibus,[i] quorum nomina post recitata conscribuntur. [j]+ Ego Ethered rex occidentalium Saxonum consensi
[i. 44] et subscripsi. Ego Ælfred frater regis consensi et subscripsi. Ego Brugred rex Merciorum consensi. Ego Æthelswit regina consensi et subscripsi. Ego Alhferð episcopus, ego Alhhard abbas, et multi alii consenserunt.[j]

Idem uir postea eandem terram huic ecclesie concessit.

[i. 41] **16. (B32)** [a]*Carta regis Ætheredi de Wittanham.*[a] [84]
B fo. 13v Ego Æthered,[b] gratia Dei occidentalium Saxonum rex, dono atque concedo dilecto ac uenerabili meo principi[c] Æthelwlfo terram decem cassatorum in loco qui appellatur Wittanham,[d] ut habeat atque possideat in perpetuam hereditatem cum omnibus utilitatibus ad eam pertinentibus in campis, pratis, pascuis, piscariis, quamdiu in hoc seculo uitam duxerit, et post finem uite illius heredi cuicumque placuerit liberam habeat donandi uel concedendi potestatem.[85] Hec quoque terra secura et immunis permaneat ab omni regali seruitio et omnium secularium seruitute preter expeditionem et pontis factione⟨m⟩[e] et arcis munitione⟨m⟩. Si quis hanc meam donationem augere et amplificare uoluerit, augeat omnipotens Deus dies eius prosperos. Si uero quis frangere uel mutare presumpserit, noscat se ante tribunal eterni iudicis in die iudicii rationem redditurum, nisi prius satisfactione emendauerit. Scripta est autem huius donationis cartula[f]

[f] pacta *B* [g] *om. B* [h] hec supradicta inuiolata *B* [i] cunsentientibus *B*
[j–j] *see Charters of Abingdon Abbey, p. 73, for the witness list in B*

16 [a–a] Carta Adelredi regis de Witthenham *B* [b] Æthelred *B* [c] principe *C*
[d] Withennam *B* [e] fractione *B C* [f] cartule *B*

[83] Cuthwulf's identity cannot be certain, although he may be the same man as the West Saxon thegn who attended the ratification of King Æthelwulf's 'decimation' at Winchester in 854; *Charters of Abingdon Abbey*, p. 75. Both versions of the *History* say that Cuthwulf gave the land to the church, but this could be later interpretation of what was in fact a 10th-c. acquisition; see *Charters of Abingdon Abbey*, pp. 75–6. *De abbatibus* attributes the gift to Cuthwulf, with the consent of King Æthelwulf; *CMA* ii. 275. Abingdon held East Lockinge for ten hides *TRE*, *DB* i, fo. 59v. *Siclus* means a shekel or coin, in this case presumably a penny.

the finish of his days) leave it free to whomsoever he wishes, in eternal power and perpetual inheritance.[83] And this gift was completed in the year of our Lord 868, the first indiction. And we order that all powers of the world preserve inviolate what has been given, in the name of God the Father and Son and Holy Spirit. With these witnesses subscribing and consenting, whose names are written listed below: + I Æthelred king of the West Saxons have consented and subscribed. I Alfred the king's brother have consented and subscribed. I Burgred king of the Mercians have consented. I Queen Æthelswith have consented and subscribed. I Bishop Ealhferth, I Abbot Ealhhard, and many others have consented.

The same man afterwards granted that land to this church.

16. (B32) *Charter of King Æthelred concerning Wittenham.*[84]
I, Æthelred, by the grace of God king of the West Saxons, give and grant to my beloved and venerable noble Æthelwulf land amounting to ten hides in the place called Wittenham, that he may have and possess it in perpetual inheritance with all revenues pertaining to it in fields, meadows, pastures, and fisheries, as long as he lives in this world, and let him have the free power of giving and granting to whatever heir he pleases after the end of his life.[85] Also let this land remain secure and immune from all royal service and all worldly servitude besides military service, and bridge making, and fortress fortification. If anyone wishes to add to and increase this my gift, may almighty God add to his prosperous days. But if anyone takes on himself to break or change it, let him know that he will render account before the throne of the eternal Judge on the Day of Judgement, unless he previously makes amends with compensation. Moreover, the charter of this gift

[84] Sawyer, no. 335; *Charters of Abingdon Abbey*, no. 15. MS B repeats this charter with invocation, proem, and different readings; below, B89. The latter full text gave the king's name as Æðred, so the compiler mistakenly placed it in the context of King Eadred; *Charters of Abingdon Abbey*, p. 68. A similar confusion of Eadred and Æthelred was made in B93 (*Charters of Abingdon Abbey*, no. 16). The present charter gives the date 862, although it is generally held that Æthelred became king of Wessex only in 865. However, Keynes, 'West Saxon charters', pp. 1129–30, suggests that King Æthelberht may have allowed Æthelred his brother some royal authority in Wessex even before his death. The charter therefore seems trustworthy. Little Wittenham, Berkshire, would at this time have been in the Wessex–Mercia border region and its grant to Ealdorman Æthelwulf may reflect its strategic importance; *Charters of Abingdon Abbey*, p. 69. Abingdon held Little Wittenham for ten hides *TRE*; *DB* i, fo. 59^r.

[85] Æthelwulf was an ealdorman, first in the sphere of the Mercian kings whose charters he attested between 836 and 845, and later in that of the West Saxon kings until his death in a battle at Reading in 871; *Charters of Abingdon Abbey*, p. 56.

anno Dominice incarnationis .dccclxii., in uilla regali que appellatur Mycendefr,[86] coram idoneis testibus quorum nomina subtus annexa
[i. 42] notantur: [g]Ego Ethered rex. Ego Ælfred frater regis. Ego Swithun Wentane ciuitatis episcopus. Ego Alhhard abbas, et multi alii.[g]

Eandem[h] uero terram dono Siwardi episcopi cum descriptione eius postea ecclesia ista possedit.[87]

[i. 50 n.] **17.** *De Ælfredo rege.*[88]

Igitur post mortem Ætheredi regis, frater eius Ælfredus suscepit imperium. Qui uillam in qua cenobium situm est, que uulgari onomate Abbandun dicitur, cum omnibus suis adiectiuis a predicto cenobio abstraxit, uictori Domino impares pro uictoria qua functus est reddens[a] taliones. Quo decedente, Ædwardus filius eius successit in regnum.

[i. 51] B fo. 16r **18. (B41)** [a]*Carta regis Ælfredi de Æppelford.*[a] [89]

Quicquid concedendum est [b]regali dono fidelibus[b] libello litterarum muniri debetur, quia fragilis hominis[c] memoria recedit et traditio litterarum semper ad memoriam reducit. Vnde ego[d] Ælfredus, Anglosaxonum[e] rex, cuidam meo[f] fideli nomine Deormodo unam quinque mansorum uillulam nomine Æppelford dono et concedo, pro alia terrarum particula quam incoli[g] Harandun[h] appellant.[90] Tali igitur iure hereditario illi trado et concedo ut post uite sue terminum cuicumque suo heredi siue alicui monasterio sanctorum in perpetuam tradat hereditatem, prout ipse uoluerit. Sit autem predicta[i] terra libera ab omni seculari seruitio exceptis tribus, expeditione populari, restauratione uiatici pontis, constructione regalis arcis. Si quis autem cupiditatis flamma accensus hunc nostrum libellulum frangere

[g–g] *see Charters of Abingdon Abbey, p. 67, for the witness list in B* [h] Tandem *B*

17 [a] reddente *MS; cf. below, c. 28*

18 [a–a] Carta Alfredi Regis West Saxonum de Appelford *B* [b–b] fidelibus regali dono *B* [c] hominum *B* [d] *om. B* [e] *altered by interlin. to* Anglorum Saxonum *B* [f] eo *B* [g] incole *B* [h] Haraendun *B* [i] presens *B*

[86] Hampshire. [87] For Siward's gift of Wittenham, see below, p. 194.

[88] This section does not appear in MS B, but its main sentence appears in expanded form in B40. On the *History*'s treatment of Alfred, king of Wessex, 871–99, see above, p. cxii. For the phraseology of this chapter, cf. below, p. 50, a charter of King Eadred; the present chapter almost certainly derives in part from that charter.

[89] Berkshire. Sawyer, no. 355; *Charters of Abingdon Abbey*, no. 18, which, at p. 80, concludes on diplomatic and linguistic grounds that the charter 'may be based on a genuine record from Alfred's time which was rewritten and reworked at Abingdon at a later date, in

was written in the year of our Lord 862, in the royal vill called Micheldever,[86] in the presence of suitable witnesses, whose names are noted attached below: I King Æthelred. I Alfred the king's brother. I Swithhun bishop of the city of Winchester. I Abbot Ealhhard, and many others.

And this church afterwards possessed that land by gift of Bishop Siward, together with his document.[87]

17. *Concerning King Alfred.*[88]
Therefore, after the death of King Æthelred, his brother King Alfred took up dominion. He took away from the aforesaid monastery the village in which the monastery is situated, called by the vernacular name Abingdon, with all its appendages, rendering inappropriate compensation to the victorious Lord for the victory that he had achieved. When he died, his son Edward succeeded to the kingdom.

18. (B41) *Charter of King Alfred concerning Appleford.*[89]
Whatever should be granted by royal gift to loyal men should be protected by a written document, since the fragile memory of man passes away and the handing down of letters always recalls to memory. Wherefore I, Alfred king of the Anglo-Saxons, give and grant to a loyal man of mine named Deormod a small village named Appleford amounting to five hides, in return for another small portion of land which the locals call Horn Down.[90] Therefore I hand over and grant it to him by such hereditary right that he may hand it over after the end of his life, just as he wishes, in perpetual inheritance to any heir of his or to any monastery of the saints. Moreover, let the aforesaid land be free of all worldly service except three, common military service, road bridge repair, and royal fortress construction. Moreover, if anyone fired by the flame of greed attempts to break this our document, let him be damned and

the time of Æthelred or later in the eleventh century'. Although the *History* goes on to say that Deormod gave it to Abingdon, this must be taken with caution. Another possible time of acquisition would coincide with the production of the present charter in its current form. Abingdon held Appleford for five hides *TRE*; *DB* i, fo. 59^r.

[90] Deormod witnessed Sawyer, no. 348, a charter in Alfred's name, as 'cellerarius', cellarer or perhaps steward. He is mentioned in the Fonthill letter (Sawyer, no. 1445), and as a thegn is a regular witness of royal charters between *c.*880 and *c.*909—the latest date of surviving charters of Edward the Elder. He may have become an ealdorman; *Charters of Abingdon Abbey*, p. 80. For the identification of *Harandun* with Horn Down, near East Hendred, see EPNS, *Berkshire*, ii. 480–1. *Charters of Abingdon Abbey*, p. 77, appears cautious about this identification. Horn Down may subsequently have become attached to the king's manor of Sutton Courtenay; EPNS, *Berkshire*, ii. 481.

temptauerit,[j] sit dampnatus atque sepultus in inferno inferiori cum Iuda apostata atque Pilato et cum omnibus qui iniuste possident
C fo. 109r sanctuarium Dei. [k] Et[l] hoc scriptum inuio|labilem firmitatem semper[m] obtineat. Ego rex primus regali sigillo confirmo,[n] meosque fideles ad
[i. 52] confirmandum[o] testes esse precipio. [p]+ Signum Ælfredi regis. Signum Ædwardi filii regis. Signum Deormod ministri.[p]

[q]Eandem terram postea idem uir Deo et sancte Marie concessit.

[i. 59 n.] Defuncto ergo Eadwardo rege, successit in regnum filius eius Æthelstanus.[91] Æthelstano itaque rege monarchiam principatus totius Anglie tenente, anno scilicet ab incarnatione Christi .dccccxxx., Cynatum Abbendonie accepimus abbatem fuisse.[92] Cuius regis dono idem abbas in Dumeltuna decem mansiones ad occidentalem fluuii Esingeburne et duas itidem mansiones ad orientalem eiusdem fluuii plagam ad Eastane, cum siluis, pratis, pascuisque suis, sed et in alio loco, id est Scæringaford et Sandford, quindecim cassatorum, Swineford quoque quinque manentium, consecutus est ecclesie sue ob honorem et cumulum.[q] [93]

[i. 60] **19. (B47)** [a]*Carta regis Æthelstani de Dumeltuna.*[a] [94]
B fo. 18r Summa polorum cacumina, ima quoque solorum fundamina, tetra
B fo. 18v necnon baratrorum tragedia,[b] alme[c] Tri|nitatis monarchia regnando ac regendo premendoque, auctor omnium Deus gubernat ethraliter, cuius uidelicet largiflue[d] liberalitatis munificentia Ethelstanum,[e] regem Albionis prestantissimum, solio sublimauit paterno, ac triquadri[95] orbis rumigerula pre ceteris ampliauit prerogatiua. Tali namque sceptrorum suffultus diademate, patronus regie[f] dignitatis

[j] tempauerit *B* [k] *see Charters of Abingdon Abbey, p. 77, for a vernacular passage in B stating that Deormod acquired the five hides from King Alfred for 50 gold mancuses, and again noting that the land was to be free of everything except military service and fortress construction* [l] *followed by* ut *B* [m] *om. B* [n] *corr. from* firmo *by interlin. B* [o] firmandum *B* [p–p] *see Charters of Abingdon Abbey, p. 77, for the witness list in B* [q–q] *om. B*

19 [a–a] Carta Aþelstani regis de Dumelt' *B* [b] tragœdia *B* [c] almæ *B* [d] largifluæ *B* [e] Æthelstanum *B* [f] regiæ *B*

[91] Edward (the Elder) was king of Wessex 899–924; Æthelstan 924–39; *Handbook of British Chronology*, pp. 24–5. The present paragraph does not appear in MS B, but cf. below, B46.

[92] On Cynath, see above, p. xciv.

[93] Dumbleton and Aston Somerville, Gloucestershire; Shellingford and Swinford, Berkshire. Abingdon held Dumbleton for seven and a half hides at the time of *Domesday*, with a further two and a half hides in Dumbleton or in Littleton in Dumbleton being in lay hands; *DB* i, fos. 166r, 167r, 167v, 168v. Swinford was probably included within the abbey's

buried in the lowest Hell with Judas the apostate and Pilate and with all who unjustly occupy the sanctuary of God. And may this writing always retain inviolable strength. I the king first confirm this with the royal mark, and I order my loyal men to be witnesses to the confirming. + Sign of King Alfred. Sign of Edward the king's son. Sign of Deormod the thegn.

The same man afterwards granted that land to God and St Mary.

Therefore when King Edward died, his son Æthelstan succeeded to the kingdom.[91] And so, when King Æthelstan was holding the monarchy of the principality of the whole of England, that is in the year 930 from the Incarnation of Christ, we received Cynath as abbot of Abingdon.[92] This abbot gained by King Æthelstan's gift, for the honour and increase of his church, ten hides in Dumbleton to the west of the river Isbourne and similarly two hides on the eastern side of that river at Aston, with their woods, meadows, and pastures, and also in another place, that is Shellingford and Sandford amounting to fifteen hides, and also Swinford amounting to five hides.[93]

19. (B47) *Charter of King Æthelstan concerning Dumbleton.*[94]
Reigning and ruling and dominating with the monarchy of the Holy Trinity, God the author of all things governs in heavenly fashion the highest summits of the poles, also the lowest foundations of the earth, and the foul tragedies of Hell; that is, by the munificence of His generous liberality He elevated Æthelstan, outstanding king of Albion, to his father's throne, and his special repute increased beyond others of the three-cornered earth.[95] Supported by such a diadem of sceptres, with unrestrained generosity of heart the

large manor of Cumnor in *Domesday*; *DB* i, fo. 58^{v}. Abingdon held twelve hides in Shellingford *TRE*; *DB* i, fo. 59^{v}. Aston Somerville was in lay hands; *DB* i, fo. 169^{v}. The Sandford mentioned here and in the charter in c. 21 is almost certainly Sandford-on-Thames, Oxfordshire, rather than Dry Sandford, Berkshire. *DB* i, fo. 156^{v}, records Abingdon having fifteen hides at Sandford-on-Thames, ten of which were held from the church by Blæcmann *TRE*, one by Siward.

94 Sawyer, no. 404; *Charters of Abingdon Abbey*, no. 22. This charter also survives in a 16th-c. copy of a lost single sheet, Cambridge, Corpus Christi College 111, pp. 171–3. That copy alone includes as a postscript a confirmation of the land concerned to Bishop Osulf of Ramsbury, who had been granted it by Abbot Cynath. *Charters of Abingdon Abbey*, p. 95, comments on the difficulty of the document's history, and concludes that it and the postscript 'include some genuine information about the early history of Dumbleton, but the diploma itself does not seem to be authentic as it stands'. Dumbleton eventually passed to Archbishop Ælfric of Canterbury and from him to Abingdon; see below, cc. 104–5.

95 For Aldhelm as the source of the word 'triquadrus', and the tracing back of it to Orosius, see Robinson, *Times of St Dunstan*, p. 58.

pannagericus gratuita cordis generositate Cynatho monastice conuersationis archimandrite[96] proprie possessionis tellurem duobus in locis iure hereditario perpetualiter condonauit, ac prefato abbati suisque post se heredibus, euuangelico prouocatus paradigmate taliter promulgante, 'Omni habenti dabitur, et habundabit',[97] perhenniter possidendam firmauerat. Hoc denique imperator magnanimus non pretio [g]philargirie, sed longeue[g] prosperitatis patrocinio ac paradisiace amenitatis[h] mercimonio more solito prestauerat gratis.
[i. 61] Hec scilicet loca hoc utuntur nomine: ad Domeltun[i] decem mansiuncule uidelicet[j] que sunt ad[k] occidentali parte fluminis Esingburnan, et due[l] communiter ad[m] orientali plaga eiusdem limphe, populari sorte diriuantur ad Eastune. Quinque nam locis habentur siluaticis ad Fleferth, dextra leuaque illi[n] riuuli qui uulgariter[o] Pidwella[p] uocitatur.[98] Huiusque loci usurpatio en[q] adoptat domnus abbas siluis, pratis ac pascuis, aratura ac reliquis illac rite subsidiis, ut perpetim possideat[r] ad Dumoltun[s] in posterum pio potissimum prosatori[99] ad[t] gloriam ac deinceps magnopere collatori[u] ad premium. Hec nempe condonatio peracta est nongentesimo atque tricesimo[v] laterculo Ihesualis infantie[w] summique prolis essentie, ac ter assis indictio copulatim coniungitur.[100] Huius pro certo largiflue[x] dapsilitatis locupletatio firma senatorum astipulatione[y] atque rata assertione,[z] uti infra caraxatur, quinto anno ex quo nobilissime gloriosus rex Angolsaxones[a] regaliter gubernabat tercioque postquam autentice[b] Northanhimbrorum Cumbrorumque blanda mirifici conditoris beniuolentia patrocinando sceptrine gubernaculum perceperat uirge[c]
C fo. 109v constat | esse, Christo to Theon suffragante,[101] salubriter adimpleta;
[i. 62] ac prisco certissime[d] diriuationis confinio circumcincta.[e] Hoc sup-
B fo. 19r plementum quoque huic singraphe rex famosissimus augmentabat, ut ne aliquis fraudulenta seductione hunc codicellum uetustis euincere ualeat libellulis. Si quis (quod absit) possessor agelluli fas

[g–g] philargiee seo longeuæ *B* [h] amænitatis *B* [i] Dumolan *B* [j] *om. B* [k] *om. B* [l] duæ *B* [m] *om. B* [n] illius *B* [o] uulgaliter *C* [p] Widwella *C*, Pidwuella *B* [q] ne *B*, en *CCCC* [r] pertineat *B* [s] Dumolatan *B* [t] *om. B* [u] cumlator *B* [v] tricentesimo *B* [w] infantiæ *B* [x] largifluæ *B* [y] adstipulatione *B* [z] adsertione *B* [a] Anglosaxones *B* [b] authentice *B* [c] uirgæ *B* [d] certissimæ, *corr. from* certissime *B* [e] *followed by* hoc modo dinoscitur, *and boundaries in B, for which see Charters of Abingdon Abbey, p. 93. The boundaries also appear in the quire of C devoted to such clauses, fo. 201v, Charters of Abingdon Abbey, p. 589 (no. 46)*

[96] 'Archimandrita' is a Graecism for abbot.

[97] Cf. Matt. 25: 29 'omni enim habenti dabitur, et abundabit'.

praiseworthy protector of royal dignity gave from his own possession an estate in two places perpetually by hereditary right to Cynath the archimandrite[96] of the monastic religious life, and, roused by the evangelist pronouncing the following advice: 'To whomsoever hath, to him shall be given, and he shall have more abundance',[97] he confirmed this to the aforementioned abbot and his heirs after him to possess eternally. The magnanimous ruler then in accustomed fashion presented this not for a price, out of love for money, but free of charge, as a defence for long-lasting prosperity and an exchange for heavenly loveliness. These places have the following names: Dumbleton, that is, ten small hides which are to the west side of the river Isbourne, and two in common land on the eastern side of that water, delegated by popular allocation to Aston. They are held with five wooded places at *Fleferth*, to the right and left of the stream commonly called the Piddle Brook.[98] The lord abbot took possession of this place with woods, meadows, and pastures, ploughing and the remaining revenues duly there, so that he might perpetually possess Dumbleton in future especially for the glory of the pious Procreator[99] and henceforth particularly for the reward of the bestower. This grant, then, was completed in the 930th year of Jesus' infancy and of the being of the highest offspring, and the indiction of a unit thrice combined together.[100] The enrichment of this assuredly bountiful munificence is agreed to have been advantageously completed by the firm support and strong corroboration of the senators, as is spelt out below, in the fifth year from when the glorious king was most nobly ruling the Anglo-Saxons in royal fashion and the third after he had authoritatively acquired by the pleasing benevolence of the wonderful Creator the governance of the sceptre-staff for the protecting of the Northumbrians and Cumbrians, with Christ the Lord's aid;[101] and it is encircled with this ancient boundary of most certain derivation. The most famous king also added the following supplement to this charter, that no one by fraudulent deceit be able to overcome this document with old writings. If (let it not be so) any possessor of the

[98] Alternatively, this could mean 'five [*mansiuncule*] are held in wooded places at *Fleferth*'; cf. below, p. 166. *Fleferth* was a large wooded area in Worcestershire, the woods here probably around Kington, near Flyford Flavell; *Charters of Abingdon Abbey*, p. 99.

[99] I follow the translation of the very unusual word 'prosator' in Aldhelm's letter to Heahfrith; Aldhelm, *The Prose Works*, tr. M. Lapidge and M. Herren (Ipswich, 1979), p. 160.

[100] i.e. the third indiction.

[101] The phrase 'to Theon' is another Graecism, meaning literally 'the God'.

diuinum profanando seu ius humanum uiolando deliquerit, alius eiusdem genealogie rationabilius agens regi supradicto in longinquam
[i. 63] perfruatur retributionem.[102] Augentibus uero hoc regale donatiuum dupla Deus adaugeat[f] bona; minuentibus necnon Sathan[g] cum satellitibus inferat dampna. Det Deus ne proueniat. Pax in euum seruantibus. [h]Ego Ethelstan rex et rector totius Brittannie ceterarumque Deo concedente gubernator prouinciarum hec dona uexillando conscripsi. + Wulfhelmus quoque archipresul, cum Rodwardo ceterisque pontificibus, consensi et subscripsi.[h] [103]

[i. 64] **20. (B48)** [a]*Carta regis Æthelstani de Scaringaford.*[a] [104]

Regnante in perpetuum Domino nostro Ihesu Christo, qui imperio Patris cuncta disponit, simul Sancti Spiritus gratia uiuificante. Quamuis enim uerba sacerdotum et decreta iudicum in robore firmitatis iugiter perseuerent, attamen pro incerta futurorum mutabilitate annorum cirogrophorum[b] testamento sunt roboranda. Quapropter ego Æthelstan, totius Brittannie basileus,[105] quandam telluris particulam, duodecim uidelicet cassatos, loco qui celebri ad Scaringaford nuncupatur uocabulo, Domino nostro Ihesu Christo sancteque eius ecclesie beate Dei genitricis Marie dicate[c] honori,[d] loco qui celebri ad Abbendune nuncupatur onomate ad usus monachorum Dei inibi degentium, cum omnibus utensilibus, pratis uidelicet et pascuis, Godescalco obtinente presbitero,[106] eterna largitus sum hereditate. Sit autem predictum rus omni terrene seruitutis iugo liberum tribus exceptis, rata uidelicet expeditione, pontis arcisue restauratione. Si
[i. 65] quis igitur hanc nostram donationem in aliud quam constituimus transferre uoluerit, priuatus a consortio sancte Dei ecclesie, eternis
B fo. 19v baratri incendiis lugubris iugiter cum Iuda prodi|tore eiusque complicibus puniatur, si non satisfactione emendauerit congrua quod contra nostrum deliquit decretum. Scripta est hec carta anno

[f] adaugebat *B* [g] Satan *B* [h–h] *see Charters of Abingdon Abbey, p. 94, for the witness list in B and CCCC*

20 [a–a] Carta regis Aþelstani de Xalingeforð *B* [b] *changed from* cirographorum *B* [c] dicata *B C* [d] *interlin. C*

[102] For speculation on the date of composition and the significance of this clause, see *Charters of Abingdon Abbey*, pp. 97–8. Its meaning is very obscure. It sounds as if it is going to be a standard penalty clause, but its second half perhaps seems to imply that a successor of the offender could regain control of the land by making compensation to the king.

[103] For the complexities of the witness lists in the manuscripts and the relationship of these complexities to the authenticity of the charter, see *Charters of Abingdon Abbey*, pp. 95–6.

tiny plot of land does wrong by profaning divine law or violating human right, another of the same line, who acts more reasonably towards the above-mentioned king, is to be placed in long-lasting recompense.[102] Moreover, for those increasing this royal gift, may God increase their goods twofold, and to those reducing it, may Satan with his satellites bring damnation. May God grant that this does not arise. Peace for ever to those preserving the gift. I Æthelstan, king and ruler of all Britain and by God's grant governor of other provinces, have underwritten these gifts by making the sign of the cross +. Also I Archbishop Wulfhelm, with Hrothweard and the other bishops, have assented and subscribed.[103]

20. (B48) *Charter of King Æthelstan concerning Shellingford.*[104]
With our Lord Jesus Christ reigning in perpetuity, who by the order of the Father disposes of all things, with the grace of the Holy Spirit at the same time giving life. For, however much the words of priests and the decisions of judges constantly persist in the strength of security, nevertheless because of the uncertain changeableness of future years they should be strengthened by the testimony of written documents. Therefore I, Æthelstan, emperor of the whole of Britain,[105] have bestowed as eternal inheritance a small portion of an estate, that is twelve hides, in the place called by the well-known name of Shellingford, with all associated resources, that is meadows and pastures, to our Lord Jesus Christ and to His holy church dedicated to the honour of the blessed Mary mother of God, in the place called by the well-known name of Abingdon, for the use of the monks of God living therein, under the charge of Godescealc the priest.[106] Moreover, let the aforesaid land be free of every yoke of earthly servitude except three, that is, fixed military service, and bridge and fortress repair. If, therefore, anyone wishes to change this our gift into something other than we have established, let the mournful man be removed from the fellowship of the holy Church of God and be endlessly punished in the eternal fires of Hell with Judas the betrayer and his accomplices, if he does not make amends with fitting compensation for what he has done wrong against our decision. This charter was written in the year of our Lord 931, the

[104] Sawyer, no. 409; *Charters of Abingdon Abbey*, no. 25, which, at p. 109, argues on diplomatic grounds that this was a forgery, from after the end of the 10th c.

[105] On the use of *basileus* as a royal title in 10th-c. England, see H. R. Loyn, 'The imperial style of the tenth-century Anglo-Saxon kings', *History*, xl (1955), 111–15, at pp. 111–12.

[106] On Godescealc, see above, p. xcv.

Dominice incarnationis .dccccxxxi., indictione quarta. Cuius etiam inconcusse firmitatis auctoritas his testibus roborata constat, quorum subtus nomina caracteribus depicta annotantur: [e]+ Ego Æthelstan, singularis priuilegii monarchia preditus, rex huius singraphe fulcimentum cum signo sancte semperque amande crucis corroboraui et subscripsi. + Ego Wulfelmus Dorobernensis ecclesie archiepiscopus
[i. 66] consensi et subscripsi. Ego Wulfstanus Eboracensis ecclesie archiepiscopus consensi et subscripsi.

Ego Ælfwine episcopus consensi.	Ego Osferth dux consensi.
Ego Birnstan episcopus consensi.	Ego Alfwold dux consensi.
Ego Sigelm episcopus consensi.	Ego Aldred dux consensi.
Ego Kenwald episcopus consensi.	Ego Oscbyrht dux consensi.
Ego Ælfheah episcopus consensi.	Ego Elfstan dux consensi.
Ego Adulfus episcopus consensi.	Ego Odda minister consensi.
Ego Odo episcopus consensi.	Ego Ælfehah minister consensi.
Ego Elfric abbas consensi.	Ego Ethelstan minister consensi.
Ego Edwine abbas consensi.	Ego Elfric minister consensi.
Ego Burhsige abbas consensi.	Ego Eadric minister consensi.[e] [107]

[i. 68] **21. (B50)** [a]*Carta regis Æthelstani de Sandford.*[a] [108]

B fo. 20[r] [b]Confirmat nos sacre auctoritatis scriptura, dicens 'Nudus egressus
C fo. 110[r] sum | ex utero matris mee et nudus reuertar illuc', et iterum 'Nichil intulimus in hunc mundum, uerum nec ab eo auferre quid poterimus'.[109] Quapropter,[c] lubrici potentatus non inmemor,[b] ego Æthelstan,[d] Christo conferente rex et primicerius totius Albionis, regni
[i. 69] fastigium humili presidens animo, ob remunerationem maioris premii aliquantulam[e] particulam quindecim comparatam cassatis, cui uocabulum certa astipulatione [f]Sandford profertur,[f] ad ecclesiam beate Marie genitricis Dei ac Domini nostri Ihesu Christi in loco qui

[e–e] *see Charters of Abingdon Abbey, pp. 107–8, for the witness list in B*

21 [a–a] Carta regis Athelstani de Sanford *B* [b–b] *om. B* [c] Qua propterea *MS* [d] Æðelstan *B* [e] *followed by* ruris *B* [f] profertur Sandford *B*

[107] For the boundaries of Shellingford recorded in MS C, fo. 200[v], in the quire devoted to such clauses, see *Charters of Abingdon Abbey*, no. 25A and p. 588 (no. 37). Those boundaries may well derive from the present charter, although unusually the version of the charter in MS B does not include a boundary clause.

[108] Sawyer, no. 408; *Charters of Abingdon Abbey*, no. 27. Apart from the place concerned, this document is almost identical to the next charter, concerning Swinford. *Charters of Abingdon Abbey*, p. 114, suggests that the present document was forged after the Conquest when the abbot sought the return of Sandford from William I; see below, p. 222. Equally

fourth indiction. The authority of this resolute confirmation, it is agreed, is strengthened by these witnesses, whose names depicted in letters are listed below: + I King Æthelstan, endowed with the monarchy of singular privilege, have corroborated and subscribed the authority of this charter with the sign of the holy and always to be loved cross. + I Wulfhelm archbishop of the church of Canterbury have consented and subscribed. I Wulfstan archbishop of the church of York have consented and subscribed.

I Bishop Ælfwine have consented.	I Ealdorman Osferth have consented.
I Bishop Beornstan have consented.	I Ealdorman Ælfwold have consented.
I Bishop Sighelm have consented.	I Ealdorman Ealdred have consented.
I Bishop Cenwold have consented.	I Ealdorman Æscberht have consented.
I Bishop Ælfheah have consented.	I Ealdorman Ælfstan have consented.
I Bishop Athulf have consented.	I Odda the thegn have consented.
I Bishop Oda have consented.	I Ælfheah the thegn have consented.
I Abbot Ælfric have consented.	I Æthelstan the thegn have consented.
I Abbot Eadwine have consented.	I Ælfric the thegn have consented.
I Abbot Biorhsige have consented.	I Eadric the thegn have consented.[107]

21. (B50) *Charter of King Æthelstan concerning Sandford.*[108]

The writing of sacred authority strengthens us, saying 'Naked came I out of my mother's womb and naked shall I return thither', and again 'We brought nothing into this world, and it is certain we can carry nothing out from it.'[109] Therefore, not unmindful of the transitoriness of power, I, Æthelstan, by Christ's appointing king and ruler of the whole of Albion, exercising this eminence of kingship humbly, willingly grant, with a view to payment of a greater reward, a small portion totalling fifteen hides, called by reliable statement Sandford, to the church of the blessed Mary mother of God and of our Lord

possible, however, is that the charter was forged before the Conquest as a result of unrecorded circumstances.

[109] Job 1: 21 'nudus egressus sum de utero matris meae et nudus reuertar illuc'; 1 Tim. 6: 7 'Nihil enim intulimus in hunc mundum: haud dubium quod nec auferre quid possumus.'

dicitur Abbandun ad usus ibidem fratrum Deo seruientium libenter concedo, obsecrans et precipiens in nomine Christi ut nemo successorum nostrorum superioris uel inferioris gradus hoc nostre deuotionis donum aliquo temeritatis aliquatenus instinctu dirumpat. Sit autem predicta tellus, quam ego cum consensu optimatum meorum prefato largitus sum cenobio, ab omni terrene seruitutis iugo libera, tribus his exceptis, rata uidelicet expeditione, pontis arcisue restauratione. Si quis autem, laruarico instinctus[g] spiritu, hoc donum uiolare immutareue[h] presumptuosus temptauerit, nisi digna satisfactione ante obitum suum reus penituerit, eternis baratri prostratus incendiis cum Iuda Christi traditore[i] eternaliter lugubris puniatur.[j]
B fo. 20v Scripta est[k] hec carta[l] anno | Dominice incarnationis .dccccxxxi., indictione quarta, huius[m] etiam inconcusse firmitatis auctoritas prescriptis in prima carta testibus consentientibus huius regis largitati.

[i. 66] **22. (B49)** [a]*Carta de Swinford.*[a] [110]

B fo. 19v [i. 67] Ego[b] Æthelstan,[c] Christo conferente[d] rex et primicerius totius Albionis, regni fastigium humili presidens animo, ob remunerationem maioris premii, aliquantulam ruris particulam quinque comparatam cassatis, cui uocabulum certa astipulatione [e]profertur Swinford,[e] ad ecclesiam beate Marie genitricis Dei ac Domini nostri Ihesu Christi in loco qui dicitur Abbandun ad usus[f] ibidem fratrum Deo seruientium libenter concedo, obsecrans et precipiens in nomine Christi ut nemo successorum nostrorum superioris uel inferioris gradus hoc nostre deuotionis donum aliquo temeritatis aliquatenus instinctu dirumpat.[g] Sit autem predicta tellus, quam ego cum consensu optimatum meorum prefato largitus sum cenobio, ab omni terrene[h] seruitutis iugo libera, tribus his exceptis, rata uidelicet expeditione, pontis arcisue restauratione. Si quis autem, laruarico instinctus spiritu, hoc donum uiolare uel immutare[i] presumptuosus[j] temptauerit, nisi
B fo. 20r dig|na satisfactione ante[k] obitum suum reus penituerit, eternis baratri prostratus incendiis cum Iuda Christi[l] proditore eternaliter lugubris puniatur. Termini uero huius prefate telluris in libro qui[m] ad Cumenoran[n] pertinet scripta habentur.[111] Scripta est siquidem hec

[g] *corr. from* instinctu *by interlin. C* [h] uel immutare *B* [i] proditore *B* [j] Termini uero huius prefate telluris in libro qui ad Cumanoran pertinet scripta habentur *add. B* [k] *followed by* siquidem *B* [l] cartula *B* [m] cuius *B*

22 [a–a] Carta regis Aþelstani de Swinford *B* [b] *see Charters of Abingdon Abbey, pp. 110–11, for the preceding proem in B* [c] Æðelstan *B* [d] conferrente *B* [e–e] Swynford profertur *B* [f] *corr., probably from* usum *C* [g] disrumpat *B* [h] terrenæ *B* [i] inmutare *B* [j] presumpturus *B* [k] *corr. from* tante *B* [l] *interlin. B* [m] *corr. from* que *B* [n] Cumanoran *B*

Jesus Christ in the place called Abingdon, for the use of the brethren serving God there, entreating and ordering in Christ's name that none of our successors, of higher or lower rank, prompted by any rashness break to any degree this gift of our devotion. Moreover, let the aforesaid estate, which I have bestowed on that monastery with the consent of my leading men, be free of every yoke of earthly servitude except these three, that is, fixed military service, and bridge and fortress repair. Moreover, if any presumptuous man, prompted by diabolical spirit, attempts to violate or change this gift, unless the offender does penance with worthy compensation before his death, let the mournful man eternally be laid down and punished in the eternal fires of Hell with Judas the betrayer of Christ. This charter was written in the year of our Lord 931, the fourth indiction, the authority of this resolute confirmation being with the witnesses recorded above in the first charter consenting to the largesse of this king.

22. (B49) *Charter concerning Swinford.*[110]

I, Æthelstan, by Christ's appointing king and ruler of the whole of Albion, exercising this eminence of kingship humbly, with a view to payment of a greater reward, willingly grant a small portion of land totalling five hides, called by reliable statement Swinford, to the church of the blessed Mary mother of God and of our Lord Jesus Christ in the place called Abingdon, for the use of the brethren serving God there, entreating and ordering in the name of Christ that none of our successors, of higher or lower rank, prompted by any rashness break to any degree this gift of our devotion. Moreover, let the aforesaid estate, which I have bestowed on that monastery with the consent of my leading men, be free of every yoke of earthly servitude except these three, that is, fixed military service, and bridge and fortress repair. Moreover, if any presumptuous man, prompted by diabolical spirit, attempts to violate or change this gift, unless the offender does penance with worthy compensation before his death, let the mournful man eternally be laid down and punished in the eternal fires of Hell with Judas the betrayer of Christ. The boundaries, indeed, of this aforementioned estate are to be found recorded in the landbook that pertains to Cumnor.[111] This charter, indeed, was

[110] Sawyer, no. 410; *Charters of Abingdon Abbey*, no. 26. Like the preceding charter, this is a forgery.

[111] The charter concerned is probably c. 81, B177; *Charters of Abingdon Abbey*, no. 111; the boundaries also appear in the quire of MS C devoted to such clauses, fo. 197^{v}; *Charters of Abingdon Abbey*, p. 586 (no. 12).

cartula anno Dominice incarnationis .dccccxxxi., indictione quarta, cuius etiam inconcusse firmitatis auctoritas [o]prescriptis in prima carta testibus consentientibus huius regis largitati.[o]

[i. 70] B fo. 20[v] **23. (B52)** *Carta Æthelstani[a] senatoris de Offentuna.*[112]

Ego Æthelstan senator scripto inserui istam terram de Vffentune ad ecclesiam sancte Marie de Abbenduna in diebus Ethelstani[b] regis. Et hoc[c] fuit testimonio Kynsii episcopi de Berrucscire, et Wlfhelmi[d] archiepiscopi et Rodwardi[e] episcopi, et multorum aliorum C fo. 110[v] episcoporum, | abbatum,[f] atque principum qui ibi congregati erant ubi ista uilla ad ecclesiam sancte Marie in Abbendona concessa fuit.[113] Archiepiscopus etiam Wlfhelmus[g] et omnes episcopi et abbates qui ibi simul aderant excommunicauerunt a Christo et ab omni communione Christi et omni Christianitate qui unquam hoc donum immutauerit uel istam terram diminuerit, in pascuis siue metis, ut sit ipse missus et dimersus in inferno inferiori sine fine. Et dixit omnis populus qui ibi aderat 'Fiat, fiat, Amen'.

[i. 90] **24.** Qua tempestate[114] adolescentulus quidam, etate quidem iuuenculus, moribus uero grandeuus, Æthelwoldus nomine, plurima Æthelstani regis familiaritate fulciebatur. Quem quia rex uirtutum emulum, litterarum cupidum, et ad hec ingenio uigere optimo cernebat, presuli Wintoniensi Ælfego, in Dei rebus tunc spectabili uiro et interdum prophetali spiritu decorato, eum spiritualibus exercitiis imbuendum commendauit; ratus (quod uerum erat) magnum quiddam de eo in ecclesia futurum fore.[115] Nec multo post, rex ipse finem uite sortitur

[o–o] *see Charters of Abingdon Abbey, pp. 111–12, for the witness list in B*

23 [a] Aþelstani *B* [b] Æthelstani *B* [c] *om. B* [d] Wulfhelmi *B* [e] Rodwuardi *B* [f] abbatumque *B* [g] Wulfhelmus *B*

[112] Berkshire. Sawyer, no. 1208; *Charters of Abingdon Abbey*, no. 28. MS B gives the Latin text followed by boundaries in the vernacular and then an Old English version of the Latin text. The *History* in MS C just gives the Latin text, the boundaries and the Old English text appearing in the quire devoted to such clauses, fo. 196[r–v]; *Charters of Abingdon Abbey*, p. 585 (no. 2). MS B precedes the charter with a brief narrative; see below, B51. *Charters of Abingdon Abbey*, pp. 117–18, takes the Latin charter to be a translation of the Old English, concluding that the document 'is a forgery, with personal names derived from more than one source and an entirely fictitious description of the conveyance ceremony. The fabrication was probably intended to demonstrate Abingdon's title to Uffington, for which there was no direct documentation. There is no reason to suggest that it is based on a memory of some genuine transaction benefiting Abingdon, which evidently gained possession some time after 953 . . . There may, however, be a remote possibility that the forger knew of some document which linked Ealdorman

written in the year of our Lord 931, the fourth indiction, the authority of this resolute confirmation being with the witnesses recorded above in the first charter consenting to the largesse of this king.

23. (B52) *Charter of Æthelstan the 'senator' concerning Uffington.*[112] I, Æthelstan the 'senator', set down in writing this land of Uffington for the church of St Mary of Abingdon in the days of King Æthelstan. And this was by witness of Bishop Cynsige of Berkshire, and Archbishop Wulfhelm, and Bishop Hrothweard, and many other bishops, abbots, and nobles who had gathered here when that village was granted to the church of St Mary at Abingdon.[113] Also, Archbishop Wulfhelm and all the bishops and abbots who were present together there excommunicated from Christ and from all communion of Christ and from all Christianity anyone who ever changes this gift or diminishes that land, in pastures or boundaries, so that he be sent away and sunk in the lowest Hell, without end. And all the people who were present there said 'So be it, so be it, Amen.'

24. At that time,[114] a certain boy named Æthelwold, a mere youth in age but most mature in behaviour, was supported by King Æthelstan's very close friendship. Since the king perceived him to be a zealous practitioner of virtues, desirous of letters, and to excel in these matters with the highest intelligence, he commended Æthelwold to Bishop Ælfheah of Winchester, then a noteworthy man in God's affairs and sometimes honoured with the spirit of prophecy, to be instructed in spiritual exercises. He thought (which was true) that there would be a great future for him in the Church.[115] Not long after, that king was

Æthelstan with the estate.' For the Old English version, see also *Anglo-Saxon Charters*, ed. Robertson, no. 22; Stenton, *Early History*, pp. 34–5. The land concerned seems to have received the name Uffington only in the second half of the 10th c., presumably from a man called Uffa. Earlier it was part of an area called *Æscesbyrig*; EPNS, *Berkshire*, ii. 380; *Charters of Abingdon Abbey*, pp. 117–18, 199–200. Abingdon held Uffington for forty hides *TRE*; *DB*, i, fo. 59^{r}. Æthelstan was ealdorman of East Anglia, known as Æthelstan 'Half-king'; see C. R. Hart, 'Athelstan "Half King" and his family', *ASE*, ii (1973), 115–44.

[113] Wulfhelm was archbishop of Canterbury *c.*926–41; Hrothweard archbishop of York 904 × 928–31; *Handbook of British Chronology*, pp. 214, 224. On the basis of the Old English text in MS B, *Charters of Abingdon Abbey*, p. 117, argues that the first witness should be Wynsige bishop of Ramsbury rather than an assistant bishop Cynsige having special responsibility for Berkshire. The latter possibility was suggested in *Anglo-Saxon Charters*, ed. Robertson, p. 300.

[114] The period within Æthelstan's reign to which this passage refers cannot be defined with precision. Cf. the account in MS B, below, B83.

[115] Ælfheah was bishop of Winchester 934/5–51; *Handbook of British Chronology*, p. 223.

summamque rem fratri suo Eadmundo delegauit.[116] Post cuius obitum,[117] Abbendonense cenobium ad tantam est solitudinem redactum ut, omnibus sibi adiacentibus possessionibus regio subactis dominio, a monachis omnino destitueretur. Cuius infortunii malum quibus ex causis acciderit, nil ueri ad meam peruenit noticiam. Veruntamen testamentorum libri[118] possessiones ecclesie continentium, quanquam tam inopinatis irruentibus malis, Dei utique reseruati sunt prouidentia, quatinus reparatores earum et post ipsorum successores antiquitatum nosse indicia potuissent.[119] A tempore autem Ine regis, sub quo cenobium primo constructum est, ad hanc eius desolationem ducentorum et quadraginta reuolutio annorum fuisse reputatur.[120]

[i. 91] 25. *Carta Eadmundi regis de Culaham.*[121]

Ego Eadmund, desiderio regni celestis exardens, fauente superno numine basileos industris[a] Anglorum ceterarumque gentium in circuitu persistentium, cuidam regalis progeniei mee tipo[122] exorte matrone, que humanis nuncupatur fatibus Ælfhild, quindecim mansas cum optimatum consilio meorum perpetue tribuo ubi uulgus sedulis uocabulis nomen indidit Culanham, quatinus illa bene perfruatur ac perpetualiter possideat dum huius labentis eui cursum transeat inlesa atque uitalis spiritus in corruptibili carne inhereat, et post se cuicumque uoluerit perhenniter heredi derelinquat, sicuti prediximus.[123] Sit autem predictum rus liberum[b] ab omni mundiali obstaculo, cum omnibus que ad ipsum locum pertinere dinoscuntur, tam in magnis quam in modicis rebus, campis, pascuis, pratis, diriuatisque[c] cursibus aquarum, donans donabo libertatem.[124] Ideo scripsimus nouam cartulam quia antiquam non habebamus. Sed si quis

25 [a] *rectius* industrius? [b] *ending over erasure, followed erasure allowing space for about five letters MS* [c] dirauatisque *MS*

[116] Edmund was king of England 939–46; *Handbook of British Chronology*, p. 26. The remainder of this paragraph is closely related to, although more extended than, an equivalent passage in the Abingdon versions of the Worcester *Chronicle*; John of Worcester, *Chronicle*, ii. 610–11.

[117] It would appear most likely that this refers to Æthelstan's death; above, p. cxiii. This certainly was the opinion of the Abingdon versions of the Worcester *Chronicle*; John of Worcester, *Chronicle*, ii. 610. Cf. the closely related passage in MS B, below, p. 292.

[118] The phrase 'books of deeds' probably has the general sense of documents, rather than just land-books, as might be suggested by 'libri', or wills, as might be suggested by 'testamentorum'.

[119] Compare also below, p. 268, on the secret preservation of charters in the time of Danish attack.

allotted the end of his life and bequeathed the highest position to his brother Edmund.[116] After his death,[117] the monastery of Abingdon was reduced to such forlornness that all possessions belonging to it were subjected to royal lordship and it was utterly destitute of monks. As to what caused the evil of this misfortune, nothing true has come to my notice. Nevertheless, despite the impact of such unforeseen evils, the books of deeds[118] containing the possessions of the church were preserved—assuredly by God's foresight—so that the restorers of the possessions and afterwards their successors could have evidence of times of old.[119] Moreover, 240 years are reckoned to have passed from the time of King Ine, under whom the monastery had first been built, to this its desolation.[120]

25. *Charter of King Edmund concerning Culham.*[121]

I, Edmund, burning with desire of the heavenly kingdom, by the favour of the celestial power diligent emperor of the English and of the other peoples living round about, grant perpetually with the counsel of my leading men to a certain matron born as a pattern of my royal stock,[122] who is called Ælfhild in human words, fifteen hides where the common people with attentive words bestowed the name Culham, so that she may enjoy it well and possess it perpetually while she proceeds unharmed along the course of this fleeting life and the vital spirit abides in the corruptible flesh, and after her she may leave it for ever to whomsoever she wishes as heir, as we have said before.[123] Moreover, let that land be free from every worldly hindrance with everything known to pertain to that place, both in great things and small, fields, pastures, meadows, and channelled water-courses; I give and will give freedom.[124] We wrote a new charter as we had not the old one. But if anyone

[120] Ine had been king of Wessex 688–*c*.726, Æthelstan died and Edmund succeeded in 939, so 240 years is a reasonable estimate for the length of this phase of Abingdon's history.

[121] Sawyer, no. 460; *Charters of Abingdon Abbey*, no. 31; the charter appears to be authentic. The document appears only in MS C. The compiler of MS B may deliberately have omitted the charter, as Ælfhild's tenure challenged the idea that Culham had a long and continuous attachment to Abingdon; see above, p. xlvii. A boundary clause appearing in the quire of MS C devoted to such clauses, fos. 200^{v}–201^{r}, and in MS B, may well belong to this charter; below, B64; *Charters of Abingdon Abbey*, no. 31A, p. 588 (no. 40).

[122] The sense of 'tipo' is uncertain; another possibility could be that it means 'pride', hence a matron 'born of my proud royal stock'.

[123] Ælfhild's identity is uncertain.

[124] See *Charters of Abingdon Abbey*, p. 131, for the surprising lack of any clause reserving the *trinoda necessitas*.

in propatulo aliam cartulam produxerit, sciat se proculdubio cum sempiterno singrapho agie crucis ab omnibus fidelibus abdicandam et ad nichilum ualeat. Si quis autem (quod non optamus) hanc nostram
C fo. 111r diffinitionem, elationis | habitu incedens, infringere temptauerit, perpessus sit gelidis glatiarum flatibus et pennino exercitu malignorum spirituum, nisi prius irriguis penitentie gemitibus et pura emendatione emendauerit. Acta est hec prephata donatio anno ab incarnatione
[i. 92] Domini nostri Ihesu Christi .dccccxl., indictione tercia decima. Ego Eadmundus rex Anglorum prefatam donationem cum sigillo sancte crucis confirmaui +. Ego Eadred frater eiusdem regis consignaui +. Ego Wulfhelm Dorobernensis ecclesie archiepiscopus consignaui. Et multi alii consignauerunt et firmauerunt.

Eadem itaque matrona, ad finem uite perueniens, hanc ecclesiam de sua possessione fecit heredem.

[i. 119 n.] **26.** *De Eadredo rege.*[125]

Rex itaque Eadmundus, paucis annis regia functus potestate, uite edidit finem. Cui Eadredus in imperium succedens, et ipse duorum germanus predictorum regum, Eadwardo genitorum,[a] filio[b] Alfredi litteris liberalibus optime eruditi regis.[126]

[i. 121 n.] **27.** *De reparatione huius ecclesie tempore Eadredi regis.*[127]

Vir namque uite uenerabilis Æthelwoldus, de quo prelibauimus, artioris conuersationis uitam ob Dei amorem scandere ratus, Glestonie sub patre Dunstano sacre habitum religionis induit,[128] in quo, dum uirtutum forma in propatulo reluceret, a principe Eadredo et
[i. 122 n.] regni inclitis summe diligitur et ueneratur. Vnde suorum consilio optimatum et maxime sue matris Ædgiue commonitu,[129] seruum Dei accitum rex ipse abbatem canonice Abbendonie constituit, omnia monasterii loca precipiens a fundamentis extrui. Ille, monasterio a fundamentis extructo, prope ubi amnis Yche in flumen Tamesin influit, uiris uite laudabilis illud incolendum tradidit. Quorum usui

26 [a] geniti *MS* [b] filii *MS*

[125] Eadred was king of England 946–55; *Handbook of British Chronology*, p. 26. This section does not appear in MS B, but cf. below, B81, B82.

[126] In the later version of the *History*, the death of Edmund and the accession of Eadred mark the dividing point between its first two books; below, p. 294. The two sons of Edward are Æthelstan and Edmund.

[127] This section does not appear in MS B, but cf. below, B83, B84.

[128] Dunstan was archbishop of Canterbury 959–88; see N. Ramsay, M. Sparks, and T. Tatton-Brown, eds., *St Dunstan: His Life, Times, and Cult* (Woodbridge, 1992).

publicly produces the other charter, let him know beyond doubt that it is to be disavowed by all the faithful with the eternal sign of the holy cross and let it be worth nothing. Moreover, if (which we do not desire) anyone, proceeding in a state of pride, attempts to violate this our decree, let him suffer the freezing wind blasts of icy regions and a winged army of malign spirits, unless previously he makes amends with tearful groans of penance and with faultless emendation. This aforementioned gift was carried out in the year of our Lord Jesus Christ 940, the thirteenth indiction. I Edmund king of the English have confirmed this gift with the mark of the holy cross +. I Eadred, brother of that king, have joined in signing +. I Wulfhelm archbishop of the church of Canterbury have joined in signing. And many others have joined in signing and confirmed.

Therefore that matron, coming to the end of her life, made this church the heir of her possession.

26. *Concerning King Eadred.*[125]
And so when King Edmund had exercised royal power for a few years he reached the end of his life. Eadred succeeded him in dominion, and he was the brother of the two aforesaid kings, the children of Edward, son of Alfred the most learned king in liberal letters.[126]

27. *Concerning the restoration of this church in the time of King Eadred.*[127]
Now the man of venerable life, Æthelwold, whom we have already mentioned, thought about ascending to a more rigorous religious life for the love of God and took the habit of sacred religion at Glastonbury under father Dunstan.[128] The model of virtues shone openly in him and so he was loved to the utmost and venerated by prince Eadred and the renowned men of the realm. Therefore by the counsel of his leading men and especially the advice of his mother Eadgifu,[129] the king summoned the servant of God and canonically appointed him abbot of Abingdon, ordering that all the areas of the monastery be built up from the foundations. When the monastery had been built up from its foundations, close to where the river Ock flows into the river Thames, Æthelwold handed it over to men of praiseworthy life to occupy. To their use the king bestowed land amounting to one

[129] Eadgifu was daughter of Sigelhelm ealdorman of Kent, and third wife of Edward the Elder. She died in 966/7; *Edward the Elder*, ed. Higham and Hill, pp. 32, 122–5, 258–9; *Handbook of British Chronology*, p. 24.

rex centum cassatorum terras largitus est, pecuniaque ad acceleranda ecclesie opera copiose iuuit.

28. (B85) *Carta centum hidarum quas Eadredus rex huic ecclesie dedit, scilicet Abbendun uiginti hidarum, Gaing decem hidarum, Gosige decem* [i. 124] *hidarum, Wrthe triginta hidarum, Cumenora triginta hidarum.*[a] [130]

B fo. 33v Anno[b] Dominice incarnationis .dcccclv., ego[c] Eadred,[d] totius Albionis [i. 125] gubernator et rector, animaduertens (quodam [e]mihi abbate[e] per uetusta priuilegia narrante nomine[f] Æthelwoldo)[g] [131] uillam que uulgari onomate[h] Aebbandun[i] dicitur, cum suis appenditiis rusculis, priscis temporibus cenobio quod situm in eadem uillula constat fore subiugatam; uerum tempore quo archipirate[132] totam hanc insulam deuastantes peruagati sunt, ab auo meo, rege uidelicet Elfredo,[j] ipsam cum omnibus suis adiectiuis[k] a predicto cenobio fuisse abstractam, uictori Domino impares pro uictoria qua functus est reddens taliones.[133] Nunc igitur ob quam rem, cum consilio atque consensu meorum presulum obtimatumque quorum nomina caraxantur inferius, pro redemptione anime mee et pro expiatione scelerum meorum predecessorum,[l] eandem uillam prefato arcisterio ad usus predicti abbatis fratrumque inibi Deo seruientium uoti compos perpetualiter restituo. Terras uero appenditias que per loca diuersa ad eandem C fo. 111v uillam | pertinent, id est Gaincg decem,[m] Gosige decem, Weorðe triginta, Cumenoran triginta, cum licentia prenominati abbatis subiectorumque sibi fratrum, diebus uite mee ad necessarios perfruar usus. Decurso autem uite mee spacio, eedem[n] cum omnibus ipsarum suppellectilibus[o] ad prescriptam uillam redacte iugiter predicto monasterio subiugentur.[134] Si quis autem hanc nostre munificentie singrapham,[p] quam ego ab omni seculari iugo reddidi liberam tribus B fo. 34r exceptis, expeditione, pontis arcisue constructione, de|monica[q] instinctus philargiria[r] infringere immutareue aliorsum quam constituimus presumpserit, sit alienatus a consortio sancte Dei ecclesie et a

28 [a] *heading om. B* [b] *initial om. B* [c] *om. B* [d] Edredus *B* [e–e] abbate mihi *B* [f] scilicet *add. B* [g] Æþelwold *B* [h] *over erasure, presumably of a word such as* nominatur *or* appellatur *B* [i] Abbendun *B* [j] Aelfredo *B* [k] abiectiuis *B* [l] meorum *scored out B* [m] *the numerals appear above the place names* [n] *corr. from* eadem *B* [o] suppellectibbus *C* [p] singrafam *B* [q] *corr. from* demoniaca *B* [r] filargiria *B*

[130] Sawyer, no. 567; *Charters of Abingdon Abbey*, no. 51, which, at pp. 212, 214, sees this as 'almost certainly a forgery', probably from 'no earlier than the beginning of the 960s'; see also above, p. cxxxviii. Later in the medieval period the charter became very important to the abbey in relation to its rights in the town of Abingdon.

[131] See above, p. lxxxii, on Æthelwold's use of charters.

hundred hides and helped plentifully with money to speed up works relating to the church.

28. (B85) *Charter regarding one hundred hides which King Eadred gave to this church, namely Abingdon, amounting to twenty hides, Ginge amounting to ten hides, Goosey amounting to ten hides, Longworth amounting to thirty hides, Cumnor amounting to thirty hides.*[130]

In the year of our Lord 955, I, Eadred, governor and ruler of the whole of Albion, noted (as a certain abbot named Æthelwold informed me through old privileges)[131] that the village which is called by the vernacular name Abingdon, with its country appendages, in former times had been subject to a monastery which—it is agreed—was situated in that small village. However, at the time when the vikings[132] were roving widely and devastating this whole island, the village together with all its appurtenances was taken away from the aforesaid monastery by my grandfather, that is King Alfred, rendering inappropriate compensation to the victorious Lord for the victory that he had achieved.[133] Now, therefore, in connection with this matter, with the counsel and consent of my prelates and leading men whose names are spelt out below, for the redemption of my soul and for the expiation of my predecessors' sins, in full attainment of my wishes I perpetually restore that village to that monastery, for the use of the aforesaid abbot and the brethren serving God therein. But I am to have full enjoyment of the appended lands which pertain to that vill in diverse places, that is Ginge (ten hides), Goosey (ten hides), Longworth (thirty hides), Cumnor (thirty hides), with the permission of the aforenamed abbot and the brethren subjected to him, for necessary purposes through the days of my life.[134] When, though, the period of my life has passed, these with all their accessories are to be brought back perpetually to that village and subjected to the aforesaid monastery. Moreover, if anyone prompted by demonic love of money takes on himself to violate or alter in a fashion other than we have established this charter of our munificence, which I have given back free of all secular yoke except three—military service, bridge and fortress construction—let him be estranged from the fellowship of the

[132] Ælfric's glossary has the entry 'Archipirata yldest wicing'; London, British Library, Add. 32246, fo. 4r.

[133] Cf. above, p. 32.

[134] Eadred is thus promising Abingdon the reversion of these lands, although no such grant is mentioned in his will (*EHD*, i. no. 107); see *Charters of Abingdon Abbey*, pp. xxxvii, cii–ciii, and above, p. cxxxviii. *DB* i, fo 58v, gives the assessment of Cumnor at fifty hides *TRE*, thirty in 1086, but this includes lands at Seacourt and Wytham.

participatione corporis et sanguinis Ihesu Christi, eternisque baratri
[i. 126] lugubriter[s] deputatus incendiis cum Iuda Christi proditore iugiter crucietur, ni prius digna satisfactione emendauerit quod contra
[i. 127] nostrum deliquit decretum. [t]Hec autem sunt huiusce donationis seu libertatis testium nomina: Ego Eadred Christi suffragante gratia basileus hoc donum agie crucis taumate confirmaui. ⟨E⟩go Odo Dorobernice sedis archipresul consolidaui +. Ego Oscytel Eboracensis ecclesie primas consensi +.[135] Ego Ælfsinus Wentane cathedre pontifex roboraui. Ego Osulf episcopus huic regie dapsilitati affui. Ego Eadgiua eiusdem regis genitrix hanc donationem adquisiui +. Ego Æthelwold prefati cenobii abbas congaudens dictaui.[t][136]

[i. 128] **29.** *De Ælfstano monacho.*[137]

Operariorum prouidere alimenta Adelstanus monachus, precepto abbatis, curam acceperat.[138] Hunc, uno dierum dum qualiter se ageret ecclesiasticum esse specula Christi Æthelwoldus obiret, in coquina cibos coquentem forte solitarium et ipse solus repperit. Et cernens quicquid utensilium erat mundissimum, pauimentum domus uersum, ipsumque monachum excoquendis uultu hilari ignem sumministrantem,[139] ac eius experiri pio desiderio satagens deuotionem, 'A fundo lebetis' (aqua enim elixarum carnium iam bullitus emittebat) 'extrahe', inquit, 'nuda manu calidum frustum.' Nil moratus, simplicitatis siquidem magne ille uir erat, exerto in feruenti ac si in tepido brachio pro uelle iubentis agebat attrectatum. Miratus ipsius deuotionem,[a] abbas exegit quatinus se uiuente id tacitum foret.[140] Qui cum postea, ob uite meritum, pontificatus culmen apud Wiltonam adeptus fuisset, adueniente sui ab hac uita

[s] lugubiter *B* [t–t] *see Charters of Abingdon Abbey, pp. 210–11, for the witness list and boundaries in B. The boundaries also appear in the quire of C devoted to such clauses, fo. 196*[r]*, Charters of Abingdon Abbey, no. 51A, p. 585 (no. 1)*

29 [a] *corr., probably from* deuotionis *MS*

[135] Oscytel became archbishop of York only in 956, the year after the supposed granting of this charter. This is one of the grounds for condemning the charter as a forgery.

[136] On Æthelwold and charter production, see above, p. cxcvii–cxcviii.

[137] Ælfstan was later abbot of the Old Minster, Winchester, from 964, and then bishop of Ramsbury from 970 to 12 Feb. 981; Wulfstan, *Life of Æthelwold*, ed. Lapidge and Winterbottom, p. 28 n. 1. The bishopric had been moved from Wilton to Ramsbury, but the earlier name is used in the passage that follows; see F. Barlow, *The English Church 1000–1066* (2nd edn., London, 1979), p. 220.

[138] This sentence also appears in the Abingdon versions of the Worcester *Chronicle*; John of Worcester, *Chronicle*, ii. 611. However, the Worcester text thereafter follows the version of the miracle in Wulfstan, *Life of Æthelwold*, c. 14, ed. Lapidge and Winterbottom, pp. 26–

holy Church of God and from participation in the body and blood of Jesus Christ, and mournfully committed to the eternal fires of Hell and endlessly tormented with Judas the betrayer of Christ, unless previously he makes amends with worthy compensation for what he did wrong against our decision. Moreover, these are the names of the witnesses of this gift and liberty: I Eadred, emperor with the aid of Christ's grace, have confirmed this gift by the mark of the holy cross. I Oda archbishop of the see of Canterbury have made firm +. I Oscytel primate of the church of York have consented +.[135] I Ælfsige bishop of the cathedral of Winchester have strengthened. I Bishop Osulf was present at this royal munificence. I Eadgifu, the king's mother, procured this gift +. I Æthelwold, abbot of the aforementioned monastery, rejoicing, composed.[136]

29. *Concerning the monk Ælfstan.*[137]

At the abbot's order, the monk Ælfstan took care of providing the workmen's provisions.[138] One day when Æthelwold was making his visits as Christ's overseer regarding how church matters were performed, he by himself happened to discover this man, likewise alone, in the kitchen cooking food. He saw that all the utensils were sparkling, the paved floor of the room swept, and that Ælfstan, with a cheerful expression,[139] was heating what was to be cooked. Out of pious desire he strove to test Ælfstan's devotion, saying 'With your bare hand take a hot bit of food from the bottom of the cauldron' (for the water of the boiled meats was already bubbling). A man of great simplicity, Ælfstan without delay thrust his arm into the boiling water as if into lukewarm and carried out what the man giving the order wished regarding the object he touched. The abbot was amazed at his devotion and demanded that he be silent about this as long as he lived.[140] Afterwards this man, because of the merit of his life, acquired the eminence of a bishopric at Wilton. When his call from

8. The account of the miracle in William of Malmesbury, *Gesta Pontificum*, bk. ii, c. 83, ed. Hamilton, p. 181, is very largely copied from the *Life of Æthelwold*.

[139] In the version in the *Life*, it was Æthelwold who had the cheerful expression; Wulfstan, *Life of Æthelwold*, c. 14, ed. Lapidge and Winterbottom, p. 26.

[140] Wulfstan, *Life of Æthelwold*, ed. Lapidge and Winterbottom, pp. cvii–cviii, states that this 'injunction is based ultimately on Christ's command to the two blind men not to reveal who had healed them (Matt. 9: 30), but it occurs frequently in hagiography (for example, in Bede's prose *Vita S. Cuthberti*, c. 10)'.

uocatione, Abbendoniam deportatus atque sepultus est anno ab incarnatione Christi .dcccclxxx..[141]

30. *De Ædmero puero.*

Erat et puer in eodem monasterio, pure innocentie studii, nomine Ædmerus, quem abbas[142] ob morum uenustatem amoris sedulitate pie fouebat. Hic ad extrema perueniens, raptus et coram celi regina [i. 129] angelorum maxima frequentia circumsepta, claritate permirabili fulgida (ut postea abbati suo et fratribus retulit) ductus est. A qua iocunde quesitus utrum sibi an adhuc seculo coherere mallet, tante quam intendebat frui beatitudinis gestiens, respondit 'Nusquam, O dominatrix omnium, tantam dulcedinem, tantam bonitatem quam tecum esse constat. Ideoque si placitum excellenti tue fit misericordie, tibi amodo ut militare merear exopto.' At illa 'Voto', inquit,[a] 'ab hodie potieris tuo.' Cumque his aliisque celestibus tirunculus iam tante C fo. 112r domine edo|ceretur oraculis, insinuandum hec suis cohabitatoribus ad superiora paulisper remittitur. Quibus peroratis, spiritus eius (ut fas est credi) ad ipsius Dei genitricis curiam angelorum euehitur conductu.

31. *De Osgaro monacho.*[143]

Religionis morem sanctus pater nequaquam ab aliis melius ratus suos exequi quam a Floriaco monasterio, sancti Benedicti reliquiis decorato, de suis monachis unum Osgarum illuc instrui derexit. Isque reuersus ceteris commilitonibus, que didicerat edocendo benigne impertiit.

Vt[144] districtioris autem uite tramitem, cum e diuersis Anglie partibus uiri Dei, audita Æthelwoldi sanctitate, plurimi differenti more legendi canendique instituti, ad eum conuenirent atque reciperentur; uolens eos in ecclesia consona Deo uoce iubilare, ex Corbiensi

30 [a] inquid *MS*

---

[141] The passage describing Ælfstan's acquisition of the bishopric and his death also appears in the Abingdon versions of the Worcester *Chronicle*; John of Worcester, *Chronicle*, ii. 611. Their attribution of his death to 980 rather than 981 as given in the *Anglo-Saxon Chronicle* may arise from a scribal error in the source for the date, or from that source calculating the year from the Annunciation (25 Mar.), in this case taking 980 to start on 25 Mar. 980, 981 to start on 25 Mar. 981, and thus placing in 980 Ælfstan's death on 12 Feb. 981; see *Handbook of Dates*, p. 5.

[142] The sentence to this point appears in the Abingdon versions of the Worcester *Chronicle*; John of Worcester, *Chronicle*, ii. 611. The two accounts of the miracle then diverge. I have been unable to discover any more concerning Ædmer.

[143] Osgar's time at Fleury is also mentioned in Wulfstan, *Life of Æthelwold*, c. 14, ed. Lapidge and Winterbottom, p. 26, and in the Abingdon versions of the Worcester

this life came, he was taken to Abingdon and buried in the year 980 from the Incarnation of Christ.[141]

30. *Concerning the boy Ædmer.*

There was also in that monastery a boy named Ædmer, of pure innocence of zeal, whom the abbot[142] cherished with the assiduity of pious love because of the charm of his behaviour. When he came to his last moments he was seized and taken to the presence of the Queen of Heaven, who was surrounded by a great throng of angels and shone with a quite wonderful clarity (as he afterwards told his abbot and brethren). He was pleasantly asked by her whether he preferred still to remain in the world, and, desiring to enjoy the great beauty at which he was looking, he answered 'It is certain that nowhere, O Lady of all, is there such great sweetness, such great goodness as with you. So if it pleases your excellent mercy, I desire that I may henceforth deserve to fight for you.' Then she said 'From today you may possess your desire.' And once the little novice was instructed in these and other heavenly utterances of the great Lady, he was sent back for a short time to his previous life to make known these matters to his fellows. When they had been fully recounted, his spirit (as it is right to believe) was taken by a retinue of angels to the court of the mother of God.

31. *Concerning the monk Osgar.*[143]

The holy father considered that his monks could not imitate the custom of the religious life of anyone better than the monastery of Fleury, adorned with the relics of St Benedict, and sent one of his monks, Osgar, there to be instructed. He returned with other fellow soldiers and kindly imparted by teaching what he had learnt.

Moreover,[144] to follow the stricter way of life, very many men of God, from diverse parts of England and instructed in different manners of reading and singing, heard of the holiness of Æthelwold, came to him, and were received. Wishing them to sing praise to God in church with a harmonious voice, he summoned from the

chronicle; John of Worcester, *Chronicle*, ii. 612. The date of Osgar's visit to Fleury cannot be certain. The later version of the *History*, below, B207, places it in the reign of King Edgar. Robinson, *Times of St Dunstan*, p. 111, suggests that it may have been during Eadwig's reign. On Fleury and England, see e.g. D. Gremont and L. Donnay, 'Fleury, le Mont Saint-Michel et l'Angleterre à la fin du xe et au début du xie siècle', *Millénaire monastique du Mont Saint-Michel*, ed. J. Laporte *et al.* (4 vols., Paris, 1966–7), i. 751–93, esp. pp. 769–77.

[144] A near identical passage appears in the Abingdon versions of the Worcester *Chronicle*; John of Worcester, *Chronicle*, ii. 612.

cenobio (quod in Francia situm est, ecclesiastica ea tempestate disciplina opinatissimo) uiros accersiit sollertissimos quos in legendo psallendoque sui imitarentur.[145]

[i. 130] 32. *De ydromello.*[146]

Virtutum huiusmodi uirorum opinione uulgata, cum oportunitas iuuabat, ecclesiam rex adire seque patris ac Dei seruorum inibi degentium orationibus commendare sed et eorum[a] precatu apud eos cibari solebat. In quo, uice quadam, accidit mirabile, ut dum epulantibus cunctis ex uno uase ad sufficientiam pincerne miscerent, non nisi unius mensura palmi potus exhaustum sit, cum multitudo causa regalis presentie uel conuiuii interesset.[147]

33. *De Eadgiua regina.*

Mater quoque eiusdem regis, uocabulo Eadgiua, maximo abbatem cum monachis fouebat amore, et nunc eis suarum copias facultatum effundebat, nunc admonitu sedulo filii sui tantopere gratiam eis expetebat, ut in principio constituendi cenobii ipse fundamenta faciendi operis propria metiretur manu, deinde regia liberalitate illos optime donaret.[148] Gratia itaque Dei modernis se incolis sic innotescente beniuolam, cum rex hinc, cum matre sua supra memorata, potentes quoque plurimi locum donis frequentare et terras conferre sibi gauderent, tum illinc possessiones ad eundem locum antiquitus pertinentes abbas, partim ratione, partim dato pretio, conquireret, paucos ante annos cenobium ibi totum honorifice extructum et ubertim ditatum uideres.

32 [a] *written over an erasure MS*

[145] See M. Chibnall, 'Corbie et Angleterre', in L. Gaillard and J. Daoust, eds., *Corbie, Abbaye Royale: Volume du XIIIe centenaire* (Lille, 1963), pp. 223–9, esp. 225–6. Unfortunately no music book survives from 10th-c. Abingdon.; the monks were probably instructed orally. For Winchester, see Wulfstan, *Life of Æthelwold*, ed. Lapidge and Winterbottom, pp. lxxxiii–lxxxiv.

[146] On mead as a drink on feast days, see below, p. 342. Wulfstan, *Life of Æthelwold*, c. 12, ed. Lapidge and Winterbottom, pp. 22–4, gives a more circumstantial version of this miracle, which also appears in the Abingdon versions of the Worcester *Chronicle*; John of Worcester, *Chronicle*, ii. 611. King Eadred had come to oversee the Abingdon building works in person, and the abbot invited him and his followers to dine. 'Now it chanced that he had with him not a few of his Northumbrian thegns, and they all accompanied him to the party. The king was delighted, and ordered the guests to be served with lavish draughts of mead. The doors were carefully secured to make sure that no one should get out and be seen to be leaving the royal carousal. Well, the servants drew off drink all day to the hearts' content of the diners, but the level in the container could not be reduced below a palm's measure. The Northumbrians became drunk, as they tend to, and very cheerful they were when they left at evening.'

monastery of Corbie (situated in France and with a very high reputation for ecclesiastical discipline at that time) highly skilled men whom his own monks might imitate in reading and chanting.[145]

32. *Concerning mead.*[146]

After the reputation of men of such virtues had spread, and when circumstances were favourable, the king was accustomed to come to the church and to commend himself to the prayers of the father and of the servants of God living therein, and also at their request to eat with them. There, on one occasion, a miracle occurred, so that while the butlers were mixing from one container sufficient mead for all those feasting, only one hand's breadth of drink was used up, despite the great number in attendance because of the king's presence and the feast.[147]

33. *Concerning Queen Eadgifu.*

Also, that king's mother, named Eadgifu, cherished the abbot and monks with the greatest love. Sometimes she showered quantities of her wealth on them, at other times she sought her son's favour for them by assiduous persuasion, to the extent that at the start of the construction of the monastery he measured the foundations of the work with his own hand, and then in excellent fashion made gifts to them with royal generosity.[148] And so, with the grace of God revealing itself thus as favourable to the new inhabitants, on the one hand the king, with his afore-mentioned mother Eadgifu, and many powerful men rejoiced to shower the place with gifts and to confer lands for themselves, and on the other hand the abbot, partly by reasoned argument, partly by purchase, acquired the possessions which formerly pertained to Abingdon, and so within a few years you might see the whole monastery honourably built and richly endowed.

[147] For the nominal breadth of the palm of a hand as a measurement, see R. E. Zupko, *A Dictionary of Weights and Measures for the British Isles: The Middle Ages to the Twentieth Century* (Philadelphia, 1985), pp. 273–4.

[148] On the construction of the new church, see above, p. clxviii. Cf. Wulfstan, *Life of Æthelwold*, c. 12, ed. Lapidge and Winterbottom, p. 22, on the circumstances of the miracle which has just been recounted in the previous chapter of the *History*: 'One day the king visited the monastery to oversee the building-works in person. With his own hand he measured all the foundations of the monastery according to his plan for the erection of the walls.' There are only very limited verbal parallels between the two accounts, most notably the phrase 'mensusque est omnia fundamenta monasterii propria manu' in the *Life*, 'ipse fundamenta faciendi operis propria metiretur manu' in the *History*. The *Life*'s passage also appears in the Abingdon versions of the Worcester *Chronicle*; John of Worcester, *Chronicle*, ii. 611. On great men being described as doing works 'propria manu', see Dodwell, *Anglo-Saxon Art*, pp. 49–50.

[i. 151 n.] **34.** *De Ciuelea.*[149]

Idem rex concessit cuidam suorum ministro Wulfrico uocitato quinque et uiginti mansas apud Ciuenlea, cum pascuis in quodam monte ibi, libere tenendas et cuicumque uellet etiam libere donandas.[150]

[i. 151] **35. (B101)** [a]*Carta Eadredi regis de Ciuelea.*[a] [151]

B fo. 39^{r} In nomine Domini nostri Ihesu Christi. Omnibus quibus Christiani-
tatis censuram a [b]Deo arcipotenti[b] poli per suam largifluam miser-
icordiam concessum est quod huius instantis labentisque uite
[i. 152] prosperitas totis nisibus restaurare perditos[c] ac nefandos per illius
auxilium possumus, ceu psalmigrafus[d] ita fando dixit 'Initium
sapientie timor Domini'.[152] Quamobrem ego Eadred,[e] diuina indul-
gente clementia rex Anglorum, cuidam meo fideli ministro, uocitato
nomine Wlfrico,[f] quinque et uiginti mansas cum pascua que in
quodam monte habetur, quem a me impetrauit, eternaliter concedo,
in illo loco ubi iam dudum ruricole illius terre nomen indiderunt ad[g]
B fo. 39^{v} Cifanlea, quatinus[h] habeat ac pos|sideat[i] quamdiu | uitalis spiritus
C fo. 112^{v} aluerit corpus. Cum autem dissolutionis sue dies aduenerit, cuicum-
que uoluerit heredi[j] derelinquat, ceu supra diximus, in eternam
hereditatem. Maneat igitur meum hoc immobile donum, eterna
libertate iocundum, cum omnibus que ad ipsum locum pertinere
dinoscuntur, tam in magnis quam in modicis rebus, campis, pascuis,
pratis, siluis, excepto communi labore, expeditione, pontis arcisue
coedificatione. Si qui denique, mihi non optanti, hanc libertatis
cartam liuore depressi uiolari satagerint, agminibus tetre caliginis
lapsi, uocem audiant examinationis die arbitris sibi dicentis 'Discedite
a me, maledicti, in ignem eternum',[153] ubi cum demonibus ferreis
sartaginibus crudeli torqueantur in pena,[154] si non ante mortem digna
[i. 154] hoc emendauerint penitentia. [k]Acta est hec prefata donatio anno ab

35 [a–a] Carta regis Edredi de Chiuelea *B* [b–b] Dei arcipotentis *B C* [c] *corr. from* perditosis *B* [d] psalmigraphus *B* [e] Eadredus *B* [f] Wulfrico *B* [g] æt *B* [h] quatenus *B* [i] *first three letters appear at bottom of fo. 39^{r} and again at top of fo. 39^{v} B* [j] *corr. from* hereditatem *B* [k–k] *see Charters of Abingdon Abbey, pp. 186–7, for the boundaries, dating clause, and witness list in B. The boundaries also appear in the quire of C devoted to such clauses, fo. 198^{r}, Charters of Abingdon Abbey, p. 586 (no. 14)*

[149] MS B introduces the gift of Chieveley, Berkshire, with a different passage; below, B100.

[150] On Wulfric Cufing, see above, p. cxxiii. Following confiscation, Chieveley had been restored to Wulfric by King Edgar in 960; below, B186 (*Charters of Abingdon Abbey*, no. 86). According to B100, Wulfric had given Chieveley to Abingdon, but this has been questioned; *Charters of Abingdon Abbey*, p. 188. MS C does describe some lay beneficiaries

34. *Concerning Chieveley.*[149]
That king granted twenty-five hides at Chieveley, with pastures on a hill there, to a thegn of his named Wulfric, to be held freely and also to be given freely to whomsoever he wished.[150]

35. (B101) *Charter of King Eadred concerning Chieveley.*[151]
In the name of our Lord Jesus Christ. To all to whom has been granted the veneration of Christianity by God the all-powerful ruler of the heavens through his copious mercy that through his help by every endeavour we can restore the lost and wicked through the prosperity of this present and fleeting life, or as the writer of the Psalms said, speaking thus: 'The fear of the Lord is the beginning of wisdom.'[152] Therefore I, Eadred, by favour of divine clemency king of the English, grant eternally to a faithful thegn of mine, called by the name Wulfric, twenty-five hides with the pasture which it has on a certain hill, which he sought from me, in that place on which at this time the local inhabitants of that land have bestowed the name Chieveley, so that he may have and possess it as long as the vital spirit nourishes his body. Moreover, when the day of his death arrives, he may leave it to whatever heir he wishes, as we said above, in eternal inheritance. Therefore let this gift of mine remain immovable, happy in eternal liberty, with everything known to pertain to that place, both in great things and in small, in fields, pastures, meadows, woods, except common labour, military service, bridge and fortress building. Finally, if, against my will, any men afflicted with malice strive to violate this charter of liberty, having fallen with the hosts of foul darkness, on the Day of Judgement let them hear the Judge's voice say to them 'Depart from me, ye cursed, into everlasting fire',[153] where they are to be tormented in cruel punishment with demons and iron pans,[154] if they do not make amends for this with suitable penance before death. This aforementioned gift was carried out in the year of

themselves passing estates directly to Abingdon, so its silence here may be significant. Abingdon held twenty-seven hides in Chieveley *TRE*; *DB* i, fo. 58^{v}.

[151] Sawyer, no. 558; *Charters of Abingdon Abbey*, no. 45. This charter also survives in a 16th-c. copy of a lost single sheet, Cambridge, Corpus Christi College 111, pp. 155–8. The charter appears to be authentic.

[152] Ps. 110 (111): 10. The preceding sentence is clearly grammatically flawed, and caused confusion for the scribe of MS B, who had to correct himself at one point. I have sought to make sense of it in the translation. It would seem to mean that Christians can use worldly prosperity to help save the lost and wicked.

[153] Matt. 25: 41.

[154] *Charters of Abingdon Abbey*, p. 188, notes that 'the anathema is a standard formula in regular use from c. 940, which threatens an abstruse demonic torture apparently involving frying-pans'. The inspiration may derive from e.g. 2 Macc. 7: 3–5.

incarnatione Domini nostri Ihesu Christi .dccccli.. Ego Eadredus rex Anglorum prefatam donationem sub sigillo sancte crucis indeclinabiliter consensi atque roboraui +. Ego Eadgiua eiusdem regis mater cum sigillo sancte crucis confirmaui +. Ego Odo Dorobernensis ecclesie archiepiscopus conclusi. Et multi alii consenserunt et subscripserunt.[k]

[i. 168 n.] 36. *De Eadwio rege.*[155]

Eadredus igitur rex ad uite terminum ueniens, filio fratris sui Eadmundi, qui ap⟨p⟩ellabatur Eadwi, imperium dereliquit. Sanctus [i. 169 n.] ergo pater Æthelwoldus in ipso mox primordio eius imperii de libertate monasterii Abbendonensi et rerum sibi pertinentium priuilegium, ab eodem rege uniuersisque Anglie episcopis constabilitum et confirmatum, adquisiuit.

[i. 169] 37. (B114) [a]*Priuilegium Eadwii regis.*[a] [156]

B fo. 43r Ortodoxorum uigoris ecclesiastici monitu creberrime instruimur ut—illi oppido subiecti suppeditantes—famulemur, qui totius mundi fabricam miro ineffabilique serie disponens, microcosmum,[b] Adam uidelicet (tandem quadriformi plasmatum materia, almo ad sui similitudinem instinctum spiramine),[157] uniuersis que in infimis formauerat, uno probandi causa excepto uetitoque, preficiens, paradisiace amenitatis iocunditate, collaterana[c] Eua, scilicet comite, decentissime collocauit. Laruarica, proh[d] dolor, seductus cauillatione, uersipellis suasibilisque tergiuersatione uiraginis pellectus, anathematis alogio[e] ambro pomum momordit uetitum, et sibi ac posteris in hoc erumpnoso deiectus seculo letum promeruit perpetuum. Vaticinantibus siquidem prophetis et celitus superni regis diuturna clandestino presagia dogmate promentibus, nitide orthodoxis[f] eulogium ex supernis deferens, non ut Iudeorum seditiosa elingue fatetur loquacitas, sed priscorum atque modernorum lepidissimam ambiens facundiam, B fo. 43v Arrianas Sabellianasque[g] [158] prote|rendo nenias anagogico infrustrans

37 [a–a] Priuilegium Edwii regis de uilla Abbendonie et de abbate eligendo de propria congregatione *B* [b] micocrosmum *B C* [c] conlaterana *B* [d] pro *B* [e] alogia *B* [f] ortodoxis *B* [g] Scabellianasque *B*

[155] Eadwig, king 955–9, his authority from 957 being restricted to England south of the Thames; *Handbook of British Chronology*, p. 27. This passage is replaced by a longer equivalent in MS B, which draws on the present version; below, B113.

[156] Sawyer, no. 658; *Charters of Abingdon Abbey*, no. 83. See above, pp. cxcix–cciv, on the authenticity of this document.

[157] I follow the translation of the phrase 'almo spiramine' in Aldhelm's letter to Heahfrith; Aldhelm, *The Prose Works*, tr. Lapidge and Herren, p. 162.

our Lord Jesus Christ 951. I Eadred king of the English have unfailingly consented and strengthened the aforementioned gift under the mark of the holy cross +. I Eadgifu that king's mother have confirmed with the mark of the holy cross +. I Oda archbishop of the church of Canterbury have approved. And many others have consented and subscribed.

36. *Concerning King Eadwig.*[155]
Therefore when King Eadred was coming to the end of his life, he left dominion to his brother Edmund's son, who was called Eadwig. So, very early in his dominion, the holy father Æthelwold acquired a privilege concerning the liberty of the monastery of Abingdon and of the things pertaining to it, strengthened and confirmed by that king and all the bishops of England.

37. (B114) *King Eadwig's privilege.*[156]
We are frequently instructed by the advice of orthodox men of ecclesiastical vigour that we are to serve—as totally devoted subjects—Him who, setting down the fabric of the whole world in wonderful and ineffable sequence, most fittingly established the microcosm, that is Adam (who at length was created from the fourfold material, prompted by the Holy Spirit[157] to a likeness of himself), with a consort, Eve, that is, a companion; and He had set him over everything which He had formed in the world below, in the joy of paradisiac loveliness, with one thing excepted and forbidden as a test. Seduced, alas, by diabolical trickery, captivated by the apostasy of the self-metamorphosing and persuasive virago, with disregard of the anathema, the glutton bit the forbidden apple. Cast down in this wretched world he thoroughly merited perpetual death for himself and his posterity. While prophets warned by divine inspiration and set forth in secret doctrine the long-standing portents of the highest King in Heaven, an angel luminously bore good news to orthodox men from the heavens, not inarticulately like the seditious loquacity of the Jews, but embracing the most elegant eloquence of the ancients and moderns, bringing to nothing and crushing the Arian and Sabellian nonsenses[158] by anagogic utterance, and calling us from

[158] The Arian heresy asserted that Christ was not God as the Father was, but a creature brought forth by God's free will. Sabellius 'taught that the three Persons are three modes of God in the same sense that the sun is bright, hot and round'. The Arian and Sabellian heresies were sometimes treated together, for example by St Augustine. See D. Christie-Murray, *A History of Heresy* (Oxford, 1976), quotation at p. 41.

famine, nosque ab obtunsi cecitate umbraminis ad supernorum alacrimoniam patrimoniarum[h] aduocans, angelus, supernis elapsus liminibus in aurem intemerate uirginis, ut euuangelica promulgant
[i. 170] famina, stupenda[i] cecinisse uidetur carmina. Cui ecclesia tota, uidelicet catholica, consona uoce altiboando[j] proclamat, 'Beata es
C fo. 113r uirgo Maria, que credidisti; perficientur in te que dicta sunt tibi | a Domino.'[159] Mirum dictu, incarnatur uerbum et incorporatur, scilicet illud de quo euangelista[k] supereminens uniuersorum altitudine sensuum inquit: 'In principio erat uerbum, et uerbum erat apud Deum, et Deus erat uerbum', et reliqua.[160] Qua uidelicet sumpta de uirgine incarnatione, antique uirginis facinus demitur, et cunctis mulieribus nitidis precluens taumatibus decus irrogatur. Intacta igitur redolente Christi diuinitate, passaque ipsius humanitate, libertas addictis clementer contigit seruulis. Hinc ego [l]Eadwi, altithrono adminiculante[l] Anglorum ceterarumque gentium in circuitu triuiatim persistentium basileus, ut huius libertatis altithroni[m] moderatoris clementia merear optinere consortium, cenobio loco celebri qui ab huius prosapie solicolis Aebbandun[n] nobili [o]uocabulo nuncupatur[o] situm, genitricique Domini nostri semper uirgini Marie necnon beato Petro apostolorum principi eiusque coapostolo Paulo dedicatum habetur,[161] monachis regulariter degentibus monastici eternam priuilegii concedo libertatem; quatinus,[p] post decessum Æthelwoldi[q] abbatis egregii, cuius temporibus hec libertatis restauratio, Christo suffragante, concessa est, quem sibi uniuersa prefati cenobii congregatio apto elegerit consilio, secundum regularia beati Benedicti instituta, abbatem iuste ex eodem fratrum cuneo eligens constituat. Huius priuilegii[r] libertas deinceps usu perpetuo a cunctis teneatur catholicis, nec extraneorum quispiam tirannica fretus contumatia in predicto monasterio ius arripiens exerceat potestatis, sed
[i. 171] eiusdem cenobii collegium perpetue, ut predixi, libertatis glorietur priuilegio. Sit autem prefatum monasterium omni terrene seruitutis eodem tenore liberum quo a predecessoribus nostris catholicis, a

[h] patrominiorum *B* [i] *corr. from* stupendia *B* [j] altibohando *B*
[k] euuangelista *B* [l–l] Eadwig altitrono amminiculante *B* [m] altitroni *B*
[n] Æbbændun *B* [o–o] nuncupatur uocabulo *B* [p] quatenus *B* [q] Æþelwoldi *B*
[r] priuilegiis *B*

[159] Cf. Luke 1: 45: 'Et beata, quae credidisti, quoniam perficientur ea, quae dicta sunt tibi a Domino.' This sentence precedes the Magnificat in the Gospel. The charter's wording, 'perficientur in te', is that of the antiphon to the Magnificat, so the draftsman was thinking liturgically rather than biblically.

the blindness of deadened darkness to the joy of heavenly patrimonies. This angel slipped from the heavenly territories and is seen to have sung astonishing songs into the ear of the undefiled Virgin, as the words of the Gospel make known. The whole, that is Catholic, Church cries out to her, by proclaiming aloud with united voice, 'You are the blessed Virgin Mary, you have believed these things; there will be performed in you those things which were told to you from the Lord.'[159] Wonderful to say, the word was made flesh and took on bodily form, concerning which, of course, the evangelist—outstanding in the loftiness of all the senses—says: 'In the beginning was the Word, and the Word was with God, and the Word was God', etc.[160] It is clear that when this incarnation by the Virgin had been taken on, the sin of the ancient virgin [i.e. Eve] was taken away, and renowned honour is ascribed to all women with the shining marks of the cross. Therefore with the fragrant divinity of Christ intact, and His humanity having suffered, liberty mercifully befell the sentenced servants. Hence I Eadwig, with the support of the One enthroned on high emperor of the English and of the other peoples living round about, far and wide, so that I may deserve to obtain a share of this liberty by the mercy of the Judge enthroned on high, grant the eternal liberty of monastic privilege to the monastery situated in the well-known place called by the noble name of Abingdon by local inhabitants of this race, and is held to be dedicated to the mother of our Lord Mary, ever Virgin, and also to the blessed Peter prince of the apostles and to his fellow apostle Paul,[161] and to the monks living according to the Rule, that, after the death of the outstanding Abbot Æthelwold, in whose times, with Christ's aid, this restoration of liberty was granted, the entire congregation of the aforementioned monastery may by suitable counsel choose someone for themselves, according to the regular institutions of the blessed Benedict, and, choosing him from that body of brethren, justly appoint him abbot. The liberty of this privilege is to be held henceforth in perpetual use by all Catholics, and no outsider relying on tyrannical arrogance is to seize and exercise the right of power in the aforesaid monastery, but the community of that monastery is perpetually to be glorified by the privilege of liberty, as I have said before. Moreover, let the aforementioned monastery be free from all earthly servitude on the same terms on which it was freed by our Catholic predecessors, that is, by

[160] John I: I.

[161] On dedication to Peter and Paul, see above, p. clxv.

sancto Leone uidelicet papa et Cenulfo[s] rege catholico, uetusto continetur priuilegio Rhethuno[t] abbate optinente solutum.[162] Agri equidem ad usus monachorum Domino nostro Ihesu Christo eiusque genitrici Marie, priscis modernisque temporibus, a regibus et religiosis utriusque sexus hominibus et a me ipso meoque patruo Eadredo rege fidelissimo restituendo iure concessi sunt, eiusdem perpetualiter sint libertatis. Nam rex prefatus rus quod Abbandun[u] nuncupatur, quod rex Ceadwæla[v] Domino nostro eiusque genitrici Marie priscis temporibus deuoto concesserat animo, in quo prede-
B fo. 44r cessores nostri (diabolica decepti auaritia) edificium regale | sibi iniuste construxerant, ecclesie Dei restituens, interdixit ut regum nemo inibi pastum requireret nec edificium in sempiternum construeret. Quod ego Eadwig, Anglorum basileus, optimatum meorum usus consilio, tam meis quam meorum successorum temporibus fixum, in nomine Patris et Filii et Spiritus[w] Sancti, fieri in eternum precipio. Si quis uero tam epilempticus philargirie seductus amentia (quod non optamus) hanc nostre munificentie dapsilitatem ausu temerario infringere temptauerit, sit ipse alienatus a consortio sancte Dei ecclesie necnon et a participatione sacrosancti corporis et sanguinis Ihesu Christi filii Dei, per quem totus terrarum orbis ab antiquo[x] humani generis inimico liberatus est, et cum Iuda Christi[y] |
C fo. 113v proditore sinistra in parte deputatus, ni[z] prius hic digna satisfactione humilis penituerit quod contra sanctam Dei ecclesiam rebellis agere presumpsit, nec in uita hac practica ueniam nec in theorica requiem
[i. 172] apostata obtineat ullam, sed eternis baratri[a] incendiis trusus cum Anania et Saphira iugiter miserrimus crucietur.[163] Anno Dominice incarnationis .dcccclix., indictione secunda, regni autem mei quarto, sexto decimo kalendas Iunii, scripta est huius munificentie singrapha,[b] his testibus consentientibus quorum inferius nomina secundum uniuscuiusque dignitatem caraxantur. [c]+ Ego Eadwi Brittannie Anglorum monarchus preformatas propinquorum sed et regum donationes hoc taumate agie crucis + roboraui. Ego Eadgiua eius regis aua hanc donationem cum sigillo sancte crucis + confirmaui. Ego Osulf plebi Dei famulus firmaui +. Ego Æthelwold abbas hoc eulogium manu propria apicibus depinxi. Et multi alii consenserunt et confirmauerunt.[c]

[s] Coenulfo *B* [t] Rethuno *B* [u] Abbendun *B* [v] Ceadwala *B* [w] Spiritu *B*
[x] antico *B* [y] *interlin. B* [z] nisi *B* [a] *corr. by erasure from* baratris *C*
[b] singrafa *B* [c–c] *see Charters of Abingdon Abbey, pp. 339–41, for the witness list in B*

162 See above, p. 20.

St Leo the pope and by Coenwulf the Catholic king, as is contained in the old privilege obtained by Abbot Hræthhun.[162] Equally the lands granted in ancient and modern times to our Lord Jesus Christ and His mother Mary, for the use of the monks, by kings and religious people of both sexes, and rightly restored by myself and my uncle the most faithful King Eadred, are perpetually to have the same liberty. For that king, when he restored to the church of God the land called Abingdon—which King Ceadwalla had granted devoutly to our Lord and His mother Mary in former times, and on which our predecessors (deceived by diabolical avarice) had unjustly built themselves a royal building—forbade that any king seek hospitality therein or ever construct a building. I, Eadwig, emperor of the English, after taking counsel of my leading men, order this to be eternally fixed both for my time and my successors', in the name of the Father and the Son and the Holy Spirit. If indeed (which we do not desire) anyone, seduced by the madness of love of money, is so insane as to attempt by rash daring to infringe this bounty of our munificence, let him be estranged from the fellowship of the holy Church of God and also from participation in the sacrosanct body and blood of Jesus Christ son of God, through whom the whole world has been freed from the ancient enemy of the human race, and be assigned to the left hand side with Judas the betrayer of Christ, unless previously he humbly does penance here with worthy compensation for having presumed to act as a rebel against the holy Church of God; nor, as an apostate, is he to obtain any forgiveness in this active life nor any rest in the contemplative, but the most wretched man, thrust into the eternal fires of Hell with Ananias and Sapphira, is to be endlessly tortured.[163] In the year of our Lord 959, the second indiction, moreover the fourth of my reign, the sixteenth of the kalends of June, was written the charter of this munificence, with these witnesses consenting whose names are spelt out below according to the rank of each. + I Eadwig monarch of the English of Britain have strengthened the aforelisted gifts of relatives and of kings by this mark of the holy cross. + I Eadgifu, grandmother of this king, have confirmed this gift with the mark of the holy cross. + I Osulf servant of the people of God have strengthened. + I Abbot Æthelwold set down in letters this pronouncement with my own hand. And many others have consented and confirmed.

[163] For the story of Ananias and Sapphira, who laid at the feet of the apostles only a part of the price of a possession they sold, see Acts 5: 1–11.

[i. 172 n.] [d]Locus ubi monasterium situm est Abbendona dictus est, de quo istius regis edictum repperimus ita litteris commendatum:[d]

[i. 175] 38. **(B115)** *Carta regis Eadwi[a] de Abbendona.*[164]

B fo. 44v Anno Dominice incarnationis .dcccclv.,[b] indictione quarta decima,[165] ego Eadwi,[c] diuina allubescente gratia rex et primicerius Albionis, mox ut me Dominus celestis in regimen subthronizauit[d] terrestre, ruris quandam particulam uicenis ab accolis mansiunculis estimatam, Domino Ihesu Christo eiusque genitrici beate Marie semper uirgini, simulque beato Benedicto preclarissimo monachorum patrono, eiusque seruulo abbati Æthelwoldo[e] ad monasterium quod est in Abbanduna[f] prona admodum deuotione concedo, precipiens in nomine Domini nostri Ihesu Christi ut nostrorum nemo successorum—quamdiu Christianitas uigeat—hoc nostrum decretum uiolare audeat. Quod si[g] quisque (quod non[h] optamus) cupidinis liuore
B fo. 45r perculsus huiusce | priuilegium donationis infringere temptauerit, se in perpetuo sacrilegii reum noscat, ni prius in hoc seculo hoc inorme
[i. 177] scelus digna penitudine deterserit. [i]Huius doni testes extiterunt quorum inferius nomina annotata[j] uidentur: Ego Eadwi rex +. Ego Eadgar frater eiusdem regis +. Ego Odo archiepiscopus, et ego Wlfstanus archiepiscopus, et ego ⟨Æ⟩lfsius Wintoniensis episcopus, et ego Alfwold episcopus, et ego Osulfus episcopus, cum multis coepiscopis, et ego Dunstanus abbas subscripsimus et
[i. 178] corroborauimus.[i] | Sit[k] autem predictum rus quod ego cum consensu
B fo. 45v optimatum meorum[l] sancte ecclesie eternaliter restitui, olim ab ea[m] iniuste abstractum, ab omni terrene seruitutis iugo liberum excepta omnibus indicta necessitate,[n] rata uidelicet expeditione, pontis arcisue restauratione.[166]

[d–d] *om. B*

38 [a] Edwi *B* [b] .dcccclvi. *CCCC* [c] Eadwig *B* [d] subtronizauit *B* [e] Æþelwoldo *B* [f] Abbendune *B* [g] *interlin. B* [h] *interlin. B* [i–i] *see Charters of Abingdon Abbey, pp. 217–18, for the boundaries and witness list in B. The boundaries also appear in the quire of C devoted to such clauses, fo. 198v, Charters of Abingdon Abbey, p. 586 (no. 17)* [j] adnotata *B* [k] Ait *B* [l] eorum *B* [m] *followed by* hec *del. B* [n] neccessitate *B*

[164] Sawyer, no. 605; *Charters of Abingdon Abbey*, no. 52. This charter also survives in a 16th-c. copy of a lost single sheet, Cambridge, Corpus Christi College 111, pp. 147–8, 153–4. It is hard to be certain of the authenticity of this charter. Its formulation is acceptable, but the boundary clause which appears with the charter in MS B and the Corpus Christi manuscript, and in a separate quire in MS C, includes land which was probably acquired by

The place where the monastery is situated is called Abingdon, concerning which we have found an edict of that king committed to letters thus:

38. **(B115)** *Charter of King Eadwig concerning Abingdon.*[164]
In the year of our Lord 955, the fourteenth indiction,[165] I, Eadwig, by favourable divine grace king and ruler of Albion, shortly after the heavenly Lord enthroned me in terrestrial kingship, grant with very eager devotion a small portion of land reckoned at twenty small hides by the inhabitants, to the Lord Jesus Christ and His mother the blessed Mary, ever Virgin, and also to the blessed Benedict most famous patron of monks, and to his poor servant Abbot Æthelwold for the monastery at Abingdon, ordering in the name of our Lord Jesus Christ that none of our successors—so long as Christianity flourishes—may dare to violate this our decision. If anyone (which we do not desire) afflicted with the malice of greed attempts to infringe the privilege of this gift, let him know himself to be guilty of sacrilege in perpetuity unless previously in this world he wipes away this enormous crime with suitable penance. These were witnesses of this gift whose names are seen to be noted below: I King Eadwig +. I Edgar that king's brother +. I Archbishop Oda, and I Archbishop Wulfstan, and I Bishop Ælfsige of Winchester, and I Bishop Ælfwold, and I Bishop Osulf, with many fellow bishops, and I Abbot Dunstan have subscribed and corroborated. Moreover, let the aforesaid land, once unjustly taken from the holy church, which I have restored eternally to it with the consent of my leading men, be free of every yoke of earthly servitude except the necessity required of all, that is, fixed military service, and bridge and fortress repair.[166]

Abingdon only in the latter part of 956 or 957. A possibility is that a genuine charter has had its boundary clause amended soon after it was originally issued, to take into account the new acquisition; see *Charters of Abingdon Abbey*, pp. 219–20.

[165] The Corpus Christi manuscript gives the date 956, which fits better with the fourteenth indiction. Technically, that indiction began in Sept. 955, but in general Anglo-Saxon charters synchronize the incarnation and indiction year; *Charters of Abingdon Abbey*, p. 219.

[166] *Charters of Abingdon Abbey*, p. 219, suggests that the immunity clause may have appeared here because the draftsman's model lacked such a clause. Kelly also notes such a positioning of the immunity clause in MS B's version of Eadwig's Hawkridge charter, below, B119 (*Charters of Abingdon Abbey*, no. 57), and in Sawyer, no. 626.

[–] 39. *De Hermundeslea.*

Item idem rex testamento confirmauit eidem abbati Æthelwoldo quinque mansas in loco qui Earmundeslea uocatur, in usus monachorum Abbendonie.[167]

[i. 179 n.] 40. *De Hengestesige.*[168]

Item uiginti cassatorum tribus in locis, id est in Hengestesige et Seouecanwrthe et Wihtham, predicto abbati et monachis sub eo degentibus Abbendonie idem rex testamentum condidit.[169]

[i. 179] 41. (B117) [a]*Carta de Hengestesige, Seouecawrða, et Withham.*[a] [170]

C fo. 114r Regnante in perpetuum Domino nostro Ihesu | Christo. Cunctis sophie studium pene[171] meditantibus notum est quod, instantis uite periculis imminentibus et curis[b] euanescentium rerum crebrescentibus, humana cognitio quasi ros elabitur[172] et obliuioni traditur, nisi aliqua certa ratione prenotetur, quia non sunt eterna que hic conspiciuntur sed terrena,[173] ut imbutus sermone tonantis apostolus inquit, 'Nunc uelut umbra cito sic corporee fugiunt[c] res, sed decus eternum hoc uisu stat certius omni.'[174] Ideo ego Eadwi,[d] Anglorum ac totius Brittannice telluris gubernator et rector, uni meo abbati cui[e] uocabulum certa astipulatione profertur Æðelwold[f] necnon et humili
[i. 180] cohorti que sub eius regimine commoratur, aliquam[g] terre portionem id est secundum estimationem uiginti cassatorum concedo liberaliter in eternam possessionem, tamen tribus in locis illic, ubi uulgariter[h] prolatum est ad[i] Hengestesige [j]et ad Seouecanwrthe et ad Wihtham;[j] ut illud predictum territorium ad illud monasterium quod situm est in uilla que dicitur Abbandun eternaliter pertineat, cum his rebus que

41 [a–a] Carta regis Edwi de Hengstessie *B* [b] cuius *B* [c] fiunt *C* [d] Eadwig *B. Comparison with other charters suggests that the title* rex *is missing here* [e] *corr. from* cuidam *B* [f] Æþelwoldus *B* [g] aliquem *B* [h] uulgaliter *C* [i] æt *B* [j–j] and æt Seofecanwyrþe, and æt Wihtham *B*

[167] For the absence of a charter following this section, see above, p. lxvii n. 339.

[168] MS B introduces the gift of Hinksey with a different passage; below, B116.

[169] All in Berkshire. *DB* i, fo. 58v, treats Seacourt and Wytham as part of the larger unit of Cumnor. Seacourt was held by a man named Norman for five hides *TRE*, and by a knight, Anskill, for four hides in 1086; see also vol. ii. 52. The *History* mentions that in William the Conqueror's reign Abbot Adelelm gave to a knight named Hubert five hides in Wytham 'from the land of the peasants who were accustomed to do suit at the court of Cumnor'; see below, vol. ii. 8. *Domesday Book* does not mention Hinksey, but it had a continuing association with Cumnor; *VCH*, *Berkshire*, iv. 406. However, an administrative list in MS C has Roger Grim holding half a hide in Hinksey, in an entry concerned with lands associated with Barton; vol. ii. 387. Given the evidence for Wytham and Hinksey, the situation described in the present text must refer to the post-Conquest period, but no more precise date can be given.

39. *Concerning* Earmundesleah.
Likewise, that king confirmed by a deed five hides in the place called *Earmundesleah* to the same Abbot Æthelwold, for the use of the monks of Abingdon.[167]

40. *Concerning Hinksey.*[168]
Likewise, that king drew up a deed concerning twenty hides in three places, that is Hinksey and Seacourt and Wytham, for the aforesaid abbot and the monks living under him at Abingdon.[169]

41. (B117) *Charter concerning Hinksey, Seacourt, and Wytham.*[170]
With our Lord Jesus Christ reigning in perpetuity. It is known to all who even slightly[171] contemplate the study of wisdom that, as the dangers of the present life threaten and the cares of evanescent matters grow frequent, human knowledge vanishes like dew[172] and is given over to oblivion, unless it is set out in writing by some certain method, since the things that are seen here are not eternal but of this world,[173] as the apostle, imbued with the speech of the Thunderer, says, 'Now, like a shadow, corporeal things swiftly flee, but eternal glory stands more certain than all that is seen.'[174] So I, Eadwig, governor and ruler of the English and of all the British land, freely grant in eternal possession to one of my abbots to whom is given by reliable statement the name Æthelwold and also to the humble company which lives under his rule, a portion of land, reckoned at twenty hides but in three places, commonly called Hinksey and Seacourt and Wytham; so that the aforesaid territory may pertain eternally to that monastery situated in the village called Abingdon,

[170] Sawyer, no. 663; *Charters of Abingdon Abbey*, no. 59, which, at pp. 252–3, expresses some doubts about the authenticity of this charter, but finds no definite reason to reject it. In *Domesday Book*, the twenty hides mentioned here were included under Abingdon's fifty-hide manor at Cumnor. R. J. Faith, *The English Peasantry and the Growth of Lordship* (Leicestere, 1997), pp. 44–5, notes that this was the *geburland* of Abingdon's manor of Cumnor, and that 'there were then evidently scattered homesteads surrounded by their own land in this area, and there is no sign of the nucleated settlements which were there in the twelfth century'. It is possible that the lands mentioned in the present document, together with the twenty hides in Abingdon mentioned in the charters above, cc. 2, 38, formed the forty hides belonging to Abingdon when it was acquired by Æthelwold; see above, p. cxxxvii. On possible earlier links between Seacourt, Wytham, and Abingdon, see above, p. lxxxvi n. 419.

[171] Use of the word 'pene' here may be surprising, and could be an error; cf. below, p. 108.

[172] Cf. Mic. 5: 7.

[173] Cf. 2 Cor. 4: 18: 'Quae enim videntur, temporalia sunt: quae autem non videntur, aeterna sunt.'

[174] There is no clear source for this whole statement. Job 14: 2 includes the phrase 'Et fugit velut umbra'.

ad eandem terram pertinere dinoscuntur, tam in magnis quam in minimis, campis, pascuis, pratis, siluis. Prefatum rus omni seruitio careat preter expeditionem, pontis et arcis munimen. Si quis uero hominum hanc meam donationem, cum stultitie temeritate iactitando, infringere temptauerit,[k] sit ipse grauibus per[l] colla [m]depressus cathenis[m] inter flammiuomas tetrorum demonum cateruas, nisi prius
[i. 181] irriguis penitentie gemitibus et pura emendatione emendauerit. [n]Ego Eadwig rex Anglorum indeclinabiliter concessi +. Ego Eadgar eiusdem regis frater consensi +. Ego Odo archiepiscopus. Ego Alfsinus presul. Ego Kenwald episcopus. Ego Oscytel episcopus. Ego Osulf episcopus. Ego Dunstan abbas. Ego Athelwold abbas. Et multi alii consenserunt et subscripserunt.[n]

[i. 181 n.] [o]Eadem confirmatione ab eodem rege eodem abbate, ipsius loci tunc
[182 n.] maiore, roboratum est testamentum de Gaing decem mansarum.[o] [175]

[i. 186] **42. (B121)** [a]*Carta regis Eadwi de Gaing.*[a] [176]

B fo. 47r Regnante in perpetuum Domino nostro Ihesu[b] Christo, qui cuncta Patris imperio ac pariter Sancti Spiritus gratia uiuificante disponit. Plerumque, sicut notum est, contingere solet, pro incerta futurorum temporum uicissitudine,[c] ut ea que prius multarum fidelium personarum testimonio[d] roborata fuerunt fraudulenter per contumatiam posterorum[e] et machinamenta simulationis sine ulla consideratione rationis periculose dissipentur, nisi auctoritate litterarum et testimonio cirographorum eterne memorie inserantur. Quapropter ego Eadwi,[f] regali delibutus unguine sceptrigeraque[g] gentis Anglorum monarchia altithroni[h] fauente clementia sublimatus, celestis regni inflammatus desiderio, omnipotenti Christo eiusque beate[i] genitrici[j] semper uirgini[k] Marie gratulabundo corde largior et concedo possessionem decem mansarum in loco qui celebri uocabulo nuncupatur Gainge, cum omnibus ad se rite pertinentibus, campis, pascuis, pratis, aquis, Abbendonensi[l] cenobio ad usum
[i. 187] monachorum regulariter inibi degentium ut hec possessio perpetuo iure mancipata subiaceat. Igitur hanc mee munificentie donationem

[k] certauerit *B* [l] pre *B* [m–m] depresus catenis *B* [n–n] *see Charters of Abingdon Abbey, pp. 251–2, for the boundaries and witness list in B. The boundaries also appear in the quire of C devoted to such clauses, fos. 198v–199r, Charters of Abingdon Abbey, p. 587 (no. 19)* [o–o] *om. B*

42 [a–a] Carta regis Edwi de Gaing *B* [b] *om. B* [c] *abbreviation above final letter erased B C* [d] testmonio *B* [e] posterum *B* [f] Eadwig *B* [g] ceptrigeraque *B* [h] altitroni *B* [i] *followed by* et gloriose *B* [j] *corr. by erasure from* genitrice *C* [k] *corr. by erasure from* uirginis *C* [l] Abbandunensi *B*

with those things which we know to pertain to that land, both in great things and in the smallest, fields, pastures, meadows, woods. The aforementioned land is to be free of all service besides military service, and bridge and fortress fortification. If indeed any man, boasting with the rashness of stupidity, attempts to infringe this my gift, let him be pressed down with heavy chains around the neck amongst the flame-belching bands of foul demons, unless previously he makes amends with tearful groans of penance and with faultless emendation. I Eadwig king of the English have granted unfailingly +. I Edgar that king's brother have consented +. I Archbishop Oda. I Bishop Ælfsige. I Bishop Cenwold. I Bishop Oscytel. I Bishop Osulf. I Abbot Dunstan. I Abbot Æthelwold. And many others have consented and subscribed.

A deed concerning Ginge amounting to ten hides was strengthened with a similar confirmation by King Eadwig for Abbot Æthelwold, then head of that monastery.[175]

42. (B121) *Charter of King Eadwig concerning Ginge.*[176]
With our Lord Jesus Christ reigning in perpetuity, who disposes of all things by order of the Father and equally by the life-giving grace of the Holy Spirit. As is well known, it very commonly happens that, because of the uncertain vicissitude of future times, those things which earlier had been strengthened by the testimony of many faithful persons are dangerously brought to nothing fraudulently by the contumacy of later men and the devices of pretence without any consideration of reason, unless they are inserted into the eternal memory by the authority of letters and the testimony of written documents. Therefore I, Eadwig, anointed with royal oil and elevated with the sceptre-bearing monarchy of the people of the English by the favourable mercy of the One enthroned on high, inflamed with desire for the heavenly kingdom, with thankful heart bestow and grant to almighty Christ and his blessed mother Mary, ever Virgin, a possession amounting to ten hides in the place called by the well-known name of Ginge, with everything duly pertaining to it, fields, pastures, meadows, waters, so that the possession transferred may be subject by perpetual right to the monastery of Abingdon, for the use of the monks living according to the Rule therein. Therefore I set

[175] MS B introduces the gift of Ginge with a different passage; below, B120.

[176] Sawyer, no. 583; *Charters of Abingdon Abbey*, no. 58, which, at p. 248, sees this document as 'of uncertain authenticity.'

C fo. 114v eternaliter ceteris | scedulis[m] prescribo, propter contentionem[n] et minacem quorundam tirannidem qui eandem terram sibi usurpare moliti sunt. Et si quando[o] tempus oportunum illis suppeteret, se uiolenter hanc inuadere et a predicto cenobio penitus auferre comminati sunt. Et ut hoc mee donationis cirographum ueteri concordetur priuilegio, hoc quoque tam mea quam Dei omnipotentis auctoritate precipio, ut numquam ullius hominis altior aut inferior persona hanc mee donationis portionem a prefato cenobio occasione qualibet auferre temeraria audeat, sed hec eadem possessio
B fo. 47v ab omni terrene seruitutis iugo eternaliter libera permaneat | exceptis tribus, rata uidelicet expeditione, pontis arcisue restauratione. Qui hec benigna mentis intentione atque illesa[p] cogitatione custodierit eterna claritate cum omnibus sanctis in regno celorum sine fine letetur, coronetur, et glorificetur. Si quis autem (quod absit) tirannica cupiditate instinctus hoc mee beneficientie[q] munus, seculari potentia fretus, obuiare presumpserit,[r] eterne maledictioni subiaceat, cum Iuda [s]Christi proditore[s] in inferno inferiori cum diabolo et angelis eius eternaliter crucietur, nisi digna satisfactione emendauerit quod contra nostrum deliquit decretum, cum diuina
[i. 188] Dei omnipotentis auctoritate roboratum. [t]Anno Dominice incarnationis .dccccclvi. donatum. Ego Eadwi rex meum donum proprio sigillo roboraui. Ego Eadgar eiusdem regis frater. Ego Odo archiepiscopus. Ego Ælfsinus episcopus. Ego Kenwald episcopus. Et multi alii consenserunt et subscripserunt.[t]

[–] Nemus quoque quod ab incolis uocatur Heafochrycg idem rex domno Æthelwoldo abbati, cum suis campis, paulo plus sexaginta iugeribus, ad architectandum ecclesiam Abbendonensem, eterna donauit hereditate.[177]

[i. 183] **43. (B119)** [a]*Carta de nemore Heafochrig.*[a] [178]

B fo. 46r Nichil in hoc seculo prolixa felicitate fruitur, nichil diuturna
B fo. 46v dominatione | potitur, nichil quod non ad fatalem uite terminum ueloci cursu tendatur. Ideoque, ut orthodoxorum[b] demonstrant

[m] cedulis *B* [n] *corr. by erasure, possibly from* contentiosam *C;* contentiosam *B* [o] quandoque *B* [p] inlesa *B* [q] beneficentie *B* [r] presumserit *B* [s–s] proditore Christi et *B* [t–t] *see Charters of Abingdon Abbey, pp. 247–8, for the boundaries, dating clause, and witness list in B*

43 [a–a] Carta regis Edwii de Hafochrycg *B* [b] ortodoxorum *B*

down in writing this my munificent gift eternally with the other documents, because of the quarrelling and the threatening tyranny of certain men who have made efforts to seize that land for themselves. And they have threatened to invade this violently and take it away utterly from the aforesaid monastery, if ever an opportune time presents itself to them. And so that this document of my gift may agree with the old privilege, this too I order, both by my own and by almighty God's authority, that no higher- or lower-ranking man ever dare to take away this portion of my gift from the aforementioned monastery in any rash circumstance, but that this same possession is to remain eternally free of every yoke of earthly servitude except three, that is, fixed military service, and bridge and fortress repair. Whoever guards this with kind intent in their mind and with undiminished thought is without end to rejoice, to be crowned, and to be glorified with eternal brilliance with all the saints in the kingdom of Heaven. But if anyone (let it not be so) prompted by tyrannical greed takes on himself to go against this gift of my beneficence, relying on secular power, let him be subject to eternal malediction, let him be eternally tortured with Judas the betrayer of Christ in the lowest Hell with the devil and his angels, unless he make amends with worthy compensation for what he did wrong against our decision, strengthened with the divine authority of almighty God. Given in the year of our Lord 956. I King Eadwig have strengthened my gift with my own mark. I Edgar that king's brother. I Archbishop Oda. I Bishop Ælfsige. I Bishop Cenwold. And many others have consented and subscribed.

That king also gave to lord Abbot Æthelwold as eternal inheritance the woodland called Hawkridge by the inhabitants, with its fields, a little more than sixty yokes, for building the church of Abingdon.[177]

43. (B119) *Charter concerning the woodland of Hawkridge.*[178]
Nothing in this world is enjoyed with prolonged happiness, nothing is possessed with long-lasting lordship, there is nothing which does not proceed towards the fatal end of life with swift impetus. So, as the

[177] MS B introduces the gift of Hawkridge, Berkshire, with a different passage; below, B118. A *iugerum/iugum* or yoke was an area of approximately two-thirds of an acre, originally the area which could be ploughed in a day by one plough; *DMLBS*, fasc. v, *s.v.* *jugerum*, *jugum*. See also below, p. 108, for the word being used for strips in fields.

[178] Sawyer, no. 607; *Charters of Abingdon Abbey*, no. 57, which, at p. 244, accepts this charter as 'more likely than not to be genuine'. Note the doubts expressed by others as listed in the revised Sawyer, no. 607.

paradigmata, sic nobis mundanarum rerum patrimonie sunt perfruende ut tamen eterne patrie emolumentis numquam fraudemur. Quamobrem ego Eadwi,[c] annuente altithroni[d] moderatoris imperio totius Albionis triuiatim potitus[e] regimine, non inmemor ob hoc mihi recidua[f] fore concessa ut his strenue eterna dapsilis lucrarer, quoddam nemus cum suis campis, paulo [g]plus scilicet[g] sexaginta iugeribus, ad architectandum sanctam Dei genitricis ecclesiam que sita est in Abbandune, Æthelwoldo[h] abbati deuotissimo necnon monachorum collegio sub eius disciplina Benedicti abbatis egregii regulam seruantium prona admodum[i] deuotione in eternam largitus sum hereditatem. Cui uidelicet nemori ipsius diocesis solicole notum
B fo. 47r [i. 185] imposuerunt uocabulum Heafochrycg.[j] | Sit autem predictum nemus, quod ego cum consensu optimatum meorum prefato perpetualiter largitus sum abbati ad architectandum ecclesiam, ab omni terrene seruitutis iugo liberum, tribus his exceptis, rata uidelicet expeditione, pontis archisue[k] restauratione. Si quis autem, laruarico
C fo. 115r instinctus spiritu, hoc | donum uiolare immutareue presumptuosus temptauerit, nisi digna satisfactione ante obitum suum reus penituerit, eternis barathri[l] prostratus incendiis cum Iuda Christi proditore eternaliter lugubris puniatur. Scripta est hec munificentie singrapha[m] anno Dominice incarnationis .dcccclvi., indictione quarta decima, idus Februarii. [n]Ego Eadwi rex confirmaui. Ego Eadgar eiusdem regis frater consensi. Ego Odo archiepiscopus, et ego Daniel episcopus, et ego Athelwold abbas, et multi alii subscripserunt.[n]

[i. 216] B fo. 53v **44. (B141)** [a]*Carta regis Eadwi de Cenituna.*[a] [179]

Omnipotens rerum Creator insimul uniuersarum per sex dies distinxit formulas singulorum, statumque custodiuit[b] naturalem, excepto homine et angelo preuaricatore per quem omnis aduersitas irrepsit[c] in genus humanum. Quod miserando diuina gratia liberauit tandem in fine seculorum. Hoc audito et prelibato a multis peritioribus, ego Eadwi,[d] rex Dei gratia, tam pecuniis quamque[e] prediis honorare

[c] Eadwig *B* [d] altitroni *B* [e] *corr. from* poti *by interlin. B* [f] recidiua *B* [g–g] scilicet plus *B* [h] Aþelwuoldo *B* [i] *corr. from* ammodum *B* [j] *see Charters of Abingdon Abbey, pp. 242–3, for the boundaries and witness list included here in B. The boundaries also appear in the quire of C devoted to such clauses, fo. 199r, Charters of Abingdon Abbey, p. 587 (no. 20)* [k] arcisue *B* [l] baratri *B* [m] singrafa *B* [n–n] *om. B*

44 [a–a] Carta regis Edwii de Kenitune *B* [b] custodiunt *B* [c] inrepsit *B* [d] Eadwig *B* [e] quam, *corr. possibly from* quamque *B*

warnings of orthodox men demonstrate, the patrimonies of earthly things are for us to enjoy in such a fashion that nevertheless we may never be defrauded of the emoluments of the eternal fatherland. Therefore I, Eadwig, with the assent of the power of the Judge enthroned on high possessed of the kingship of the whole of Albion far and wide, not unmindful that fleeting things have been granted to me so that by them I, a bountiful man, may actively obtain eternal things, have with very eager devotion bestowed in eternal inheritance on the most devout Abbot Æthelwold, and also on the community of monks under his discipline and keeping the Rule of the outstanding Abbot Benedict, a certain woodland with its fields, that is a little more than sixty yokes, for building the holy church of the mother of God, situated at Abingdon. On this woodland, that is, the local inhabitants in that district have bestowed the well-known name Hawkridge. Moreover, let that woodland which, with the consent of my leading men, I have perpetually bestowed on the aforementioned abbot for building the church, be free of every yoke of earthly servitude except these three, that is, fixed military service, and bridge and fortress repair. Moreover, if any presumptuous man, prompted by diabolical spirit, attempts to violate or change this gift, unless the offender does penance with worthy compensation before his death, let the mournful man eternally be laid down and punished in the eternal fires of Hell with Judas the betrayer of Christ. This charter of munificence was written in the year of our Lord 956, the fourteenth indiction, on 13 February. I King Eadwig have confirmed. I Edgar that king's brother have consented. I Archbishop Oda, and I Bishop Daniel, and I Abbot Æthelwold, and many others have subscribed.

44. (B141) *Charter of King Eadwig concerning Kennington.*[179]

The almighty Creator of all things together distinguished the forms of each over a period of six days, and He protected the state of nature, except man and the transgressing angel through whom all adversity stole into the human race. However, at the end of time divine grace freed it by taking mercy. After hearing and having a foretaste of this from many more experienced men, I, Eadwig, king by the grace of God, am disposed to honour my faithful men both with money and with estates, and I grant in perpetual inheritance Kennington to this

[179] Sawyer, no. 614; *Charters of Abingdon Abbey*, no. 56, which, at p. 239, takes the charter to be 'probably fundamentally authentic, although it is certainly surprising that the text does not mention the hidage of the estate'.

dispono meos fideles, huic etiam meo fideli Brihthelmo[f][180] presbitero
B fo. 54^r Cenigtun in hereditatem concedo | perpetuam, cum omnibus ad se pertinentibus, possidendam et tradendam cui uult[g] heredi. Facta est autem hec prefati agelli libertas ab omni censu regali soluta exceptis tribus, expeditione uidelicet, pontis arcisque edificatione, que pernecessaria sunt omnibus regionibus. Anno .dcccclvi. incarnationis Dominice, indictione quarta decima, anno uero primo imperii
[i. 218] nostri.[h] Quicumque[i] amodo nostrum decretum muniendo seruauerit pascatur manna celesti; si quis autem (quod absit) contraire temptauerit, obstaculum patiatur gehenne, nisi cito emendare festinet.

[j]Domnus autem abbas Athelwoldus commutationem eiusdem terre, id est Cenintun, concedente eodem rege, egit aput Brihtelmum episcopum, in cuius uicissitudine ipse episcopus accepit illam uillam que appellatur Crydanbrigce.[181] Testes autem fuerunt huius commutationis Ælfgifa regis uxor et Æthelgefa mater eius, Ælfsige episcopus, Osulfus episcopus, Kenwald episcopus, et multi alii.[j][182]

[–] 45. *De Cudesduna.*[183]

De terris que sequuntur non ab eodem rege abbatie donatis, sed ab ipsis potius quibus ille optionem libere easdem donandis quibus liberet concesserat, hinc breuiter annotemus. De quibus est Codesdona quam Ælfhere principi rex ipse contulit.[184]

[i. 200] 46. (B131) [a]*Carta de Cudesduna.*[a][185]

B fo. 50^r In[b] nomine Creatricis omnium rerum et Dominatricis sancte Trinitatis omnipotentis, que sola regnum immutabile et incorruptibile

[f] Byrhtelmo *B* [g] uis *B* [h] *see Charters of Abingdon Abbey, pp. 238–9, for the boundaries and witness list in B. The boundaries also appear in the quire of C devoted to such clauses, fo. 199^r, Charters of Abingdon Abbey, p. 587 (no. 29)* [i] Cuicumque *B* [j–j] *om. B*

46 [a–a] Carta regis Edwii de Cuþenesdune, quomodo dedit comiti *B* [b] *preceded by chrismon symbol A*

[180] *Charters of Abingdon Abbey*, p. 240, argues that this is the man who was bishop of Wells from 956 until 973.

[181] Oxfordshire. This and the following sentence, not in MS B, are a Latin summary of an Old English document recording the transaction and included in MS B; see below, B142 (*Charters of Abingdon Abbey*, no. 76). The transaction must have taken place after Brihthelm had become a bishop and while Eadwig was still in control of Mercia, and can therefore be dated to 956 × 957; see *Charters of Abingdon Abbey*, p. 315. Ælfgifu and Eadwig were separated in 958 on account of their kinship.

[182] Queen Ælfgifu may have had a particularly close connection with Æthelwold, who—unlike Dunstan and Oda—seems to have accepted her marriage to Eadwig; see Yorke, 'Æthelwold and the politics of the tenth century', in *Bishop Aethelwold*, ed. Yorke, pp. 68–

faithful priest of mine Brihthelm,[180] with everything pertaining to it, to be possessed and handed over to whomsoever he wishes as heir. Moreover, this liberty of the aforementioned plot of land was made unburdened of all royal exaction except three, which are very necessary in any region, that is, military service, and bridge and fortress building. In the year of the Lord's Incarnation 956, the fourteenth indiction, indeed in the first year of our dominion. Whoever henceforth preserves our decision by defending it may feast on heavenly manna, but if anyone (let it not be so) attempts to go against it, let him suffer the difficulties of Hell, unless he swiftly hurries to make amends.

Moreover, with that king's permission, lord Abbot Æthelwold made an exchange with Bishop Brihthelm concerning the above land, that is Kennington, the bishop receiving in return the village called Curbridge.[181] Moreover, the witnesses of this exchange were Ælfgifu the king's wife and Æthelgifu her mother, Bishop Ælfsige, Bishop Osulf, Bishop Cenwold, and many others.[182]

45. *Concerning Cuddesdon.*[183]

From this point let us note briefly the following lands which were given not by that king to the abbey, but rather by those to whom he had granted the option of giving them freely to whomsoever they might wish. Amongst these is Cuddesdon which the king himself conferred on Ælfhere, a noble.[184]

46. (B131) *Charter concerning Cuddesdon.*[185]

In the name of the almighty Holy Trinity that created and governs all things, who alone possesses and retains a kingdom unchangeable and

88, at 80, and pp. 76–7 on Ælfgifu more generally. The Old English charter recording this transaction also names as witnesses Ealdorman Byrhtnoth (of Essex), Ælfheah the king's *discthegn*, and Eadric his brother; *Charters of Abingdon Abbey*, no. 76. The involvement of the royal women and of the laymen of importance in the area may indicate Æthelwold's desire to obtain Kennington, and something of the means he used to achieve his ends; see also *Charters of Abingdon Abbey*, pp. 315–16.

183 Oxfordshire. MS B introduces the gift of Cuddesdon with a different passage, which states that Ælfhere gave the land to Abingdon; below, B130. In *Domesday*, Abingdon's Cuddesdon holding was assessed at eighteen hides; *DB* i, fo. 156^{v}.

184 For Ealdorman Ælfhere of Mercia, see above, p. cxxii.

185 Sawyer, no. 587; *Charters of Abingdon Abbey*, no. 70. The charter also survives as a single-sheet copy, possibly datable to the 11th c. on palaeographical grounds; London, British Library, Cotton Augustus ii. 33, reproduced in *BM Facs.*, iii. 17. *Charters of Abingdon Abbey*, p. 296, suggests very tentatively that it may be a forgery modelled on King Eadwig's grant of land at Wormleighton, Warwickshire, to Ælfhere; below, B148 (*Charters of Abingdon Abbey*, no. 71). For suggestions that Abingdon acquired Cuddesdon rather

atque ineffabile perpetua potestate possidet ac continet. Ego Eadwi,[c] industris[d] Anglorum rex ceterarumque gentium in circuitu persistentium gubernator et rector, primo anno imperii mei litteratoriis [i. 201] apicibus hanc roboraui cartulam quam, cum consensu heroicorum uirorum, tradidi cuidam comiti, non solum mihi per omnia fideli subiectione obtemperanti, uerum etiam in omnibus meum uelle subicienti, a suis carissimis predecessoribus claro insignitus nomine Ælfhere, modicam in regno meo partem, id est uiginti mansos, perpetualiter impendo,[e] penes illum locum qui assertione B fo. 50v multorum | hominum profertur ita ad Cuthesdune.[f] Precipiens C fo. 115v itaque precipio ut | terram iam prefatam, meo scilicet ouanti concessu, in omni suo[g] curriculo possideat uite, deinceps namque sibi succedenti cuicumque uoluerit heredi derelinquat in perpetuam hereditatem. Maneat igitur meum hoc immobile donum perpetua libertate munitum, cum omnibus ad se pertinentibus, campis, pascuis, pratis, siluis, excepto communi labore, expeditione, pontis arcisue coedificatione. Si qui denique, me non optanti, hanc libertatis cartam, cupiditatis liuore depressi, uiolare satagerint, cum agminibus tetre caliginis lapsi, uocem audiant in examinationis die arbitris sic dicentis 'Discedite a me, maledicti, in ignem eternum',[186] ubi cum demonibus ferreis sartaginibus crudeli torqueantur in [i. 202] pena,[h] si non ante mortem hoc emendauerint penitentia.[i] [j]Hec carta scripta est anno Dominice incarnationis .dccccclvi., indictione quarta decima. Ego Eadwi rex Anglorum indeclinabiliter concessi. Ego Eadgar eiusdem regis frater, et ego Odo archiepiscopus, et multi alii consenserunt et subscripserunt.[j]

[–] [k]Hanc itaque terram sanctus pater Æthelwoldus, concedente rege, ab eodem comite adquisiuit, cum carta sibi a rege data, et sic terra ista ad ecclesiam istam peruenit.[k]

[c] Eadwig *A, B* [d] *rectius* industrius? [e] inpendo *A, B* [f] æt Cuþenesdune *A, B* [g] sue *B*; suae *A* [h] poena *A* [i] poenitentia *A* [j–j] *see Charters of Abingdon Abbey, pp. 294–5, for the boundaries, dating clause, and witness list in A and B. The boundaries also appear in the quire of C devoted to such clauses, fo. 198r–v, Charters of Abingdon Abbey, p. 586 (no. 16)* [k–k] *om. B*

incorruptible and ineffable in perpetual power. I, Eadwig, vigorous king of the English and governor and ruler of the other peoples living round about, in the first year of my dominion have strengthened with written characters this charter which, with the consent of heroic men, I handed over to a certain earl, by his most dear predecessors distinguished by the famous name Ælfhere, not only obedient to me in all respects with faithful subjection, but also subject to my will in everything; I bestow perpetually a moderate portion of land in my kingdom, that is twenty hides, in the place that by the assertion of many men is called thus, Cuddesdon. Therefore I command and order that he possess by my joyful concession the aforementioned land for the whole course of his life, and that thereafter he may leave it to whomsoever he wish as heir succeeding to him in perpetual inheritance. Therefore let this my gift remain immovable, defended with perpetual liberty, with everything pertaining to it, fields, pastures, meadows, woods, except common labour, military service, and bridge and fortress building. Finally, if, against my will, any men, afflicted by the malice of greed, strive to violate this charter of liberty, having fallen with the hosts of foul darkness, on the Day of Judgement let them hear the Judge's voice saying this, 'Depart from me, ye cursed, into everlasting fire',[186] where they are to be tormented in cruel punishment with demons and iron pans, if they do not make amends for this with penance before death. This charter was written in the year of our Lord 956, the fourteenth indiction. I Eadwig king of the English have granted unfailingly. I Edgar that king's brother, and I Archbishop Oda, and many others have consented and subscribed.

And so the holy father Æthelwold, with the king's permission, acquired this land from that earl, with the charter given to him by the king, and thus that land came to this church.

closer to 1066, see *Charters of Abingdon Abbey*, p. 296; on the other hand at p. cxxxiii, Kelly seems willing to accept that the compiler may have had some independent source for Æthelwold's acquisition of Cuddesdon. It is certainly interesting that in this case the statement is that Æthelwold obtained the land from Ælfhere and thus it passed to the church, rather than simply the routine statement that Ælfhere, the charter's beneficiary, gave the land to the church; see further, above, p. cxxxi.

[186] Matt. 25: 41.

[–] 47. *De duabus et uiginti mansionibus ad Weligford.*[187]
Item alteri cuidam ministro suo Eadrico idem rex contulit Weligford duarum et uiginti mansionum.[188]

[i. 207] 48. (B135) [a]*Carta regis Eadwi de Waligford.*[a] [189]
B fo. 52ʳ Intimo precordialis affectu caritatis,[b] ego Eadwi,[c] altitonantis prouidentia non solum gubernator et rector Angligene prosapie immo aliarum nationum circumquaque morantium, cuidam meo ministro, uocato nomine Eadrico, duas et uiginti mansas impendo, cum his utilitatibus que iure pertinere ad illum cernuntur locum, tam in pratis et campis quam in pascuis et siluis penes illum locum qui dicitur Weligford,[d] ut possideat cunctis diebus uite sue, cum omnibus ad se pertinentibus, tam in magnis quam in minimis. Cum uero dissolu-
[i. 208] tionis sue tempus accesserit, cuicumque uoluerit heredi derelinquat, ut ante caraxatum est, eternaliter. Maneat autem predictum rus defensum ab omni obstaculo et liberum a cuncto seruitio excepto communi labore, expeditione, pontis renouatione, arcisue constructione. Si quis uero,[e] tirannica inflatus potestate, infringere temptauerit huius nostri decreti cirographum, sciat se coram Christo et angelis eius in tremendo examine rationem redditurum, nisi hic prius
[i. 209] emendare satagerit. [f]⟨A⟩cta est hec supradicta donatio anno ab incarnatione Domini nostri Ihesu Christi .dcccclvi., indictione quarta decima. Ego Eadwi rex Anglorum confirmaui. Ego Eadgar eiusdem regis frater, et ego Odo archiepiscopus, et ego Ælfsinus episcopus, et multi alii subscripserunt.[f]

[–] [g]Moriens itaque, concedente rege, istam terram huic ecclesie Eadricus idem, quia antiquitus ad eam pertinebat, cum carta a rege sibi data concessit.[g]

[–] 49. *De Middeltuna.*[190]
Idem rex dedit cuidam ministro suo nomine Alfwino quindecim mansas apud Middeltune, et ipse huic ecclesie cum carta a rege data.

48 [a–a] Carta regis Eadwii duorum et uiginti cassatorum in Welliford *B* [b] caricatis *B* [c] Eadwig *B* [d] æt Weligforda *B* [e] uere *B* [f–f] *see Charters of Abingdon Abbey, pp. 271–2, for the boundaries, dating clause, and witness list in B. The boundaries also appear in the quire of C devoted to such clauses, fo. 199ʳ, Charters of Abingdon Abbey, p. 587 (no. 23)* [g–g] *om. B*

[187] MS B introduces the gift of Welford with a different passage, which states that Eadric gave the land to Abingdon; below, B134. Compared with a grant of eighteen hides in Welford to a thegn called Wulfric in 949, below B96–B97 (*Charters of Abingdon Abbey*, no. 44), the estate here appears to have been enlarged. It may be that Wulfric had granted Welford to Eadric, or someone else, by 956. Eadric may have wished for the following royal charter because of the increased hidage, or simply for greater security. Welford appears in

47. *Concerning twenty-two hides at Welford.*[187]
Likewise, on another thegn of his, Eadric, that king conferred Welford, amounting to twenty-two hides.[188]

48. (B135) *Charter of King Eadwig concerning Welford.*[189]
By the innermost impulse of heartfelt love, I, Eadwig, by the providence of the One thundering on high, governor and ruler not only of the English race but also of other nations living on every side, bestow on a thegn of mine, called by the name Eadric, twenty-two hides, with those appurtenances which are perceived to pertain to that place by right, both in meadows and fields and in pastures and woods belonging to that place which is called Welford, so that he may possess it for all the days of his life, with everything pertaining to it, both in great things and in the smallest. When, indeed, he comes to the time of his death, he may leave it eternally to whomsoever he wish as heir, as has been spelt out before. Moreover, let the aforesaid land remain protected from every hindrance and free from all service except common labour, military service, bridge repair, and fortress construction. If indeed anyone, puffed up with tyrannical power, attempts to infringe the document of this our decision, let him know that he will render account in the fearful trial before Christ and His angels, unless he previously strives to make amends for this. This above gift was carried out in the year of our Lord Jesus Christ 956, the fourteenth indiction. I Eadwig king of the English have confirmed. I Edgar that king's brother, and I Archbishop Oda, and I Bishop Ælfsige, and many others have subscribed.

And so, as he was dying, Eadric, with the king's permission, granted that land, together with the charter given to him by the king, to this church, since of old the land pertained to it.

49. *Concerning Milton.*[190]
That king gave fifteen hides at Milton to a thegn of his named Ælfwine, and he granted it to this church, with the charter given by the king.

King Coenwulf's supposed charter for Abingdon, above, c. 11, marking it as one of the claimed early possessions of the abbey.

[188] On Eadric, see above, p. cxxiii. He may also have been the grantee of Eadwig's grant of Pyrford, Surrey, below, B145–B146 (*Charters of Abingdon Abbey*, no. 63).

[189] Sawyer, no. 622; *Charters of Abingdon Abbey*, no. 64, which, at p. 273, accepts this charter as authentic.

[190] Berkshire. MS B introduces the gift of Milton with a different passage, which states that Ælfwine gave the land to Abingdon; below, B138. Abingdon held Milton *TRE* for twenty-eight hides, although the assessment was reduced to twenty-three by 1086; *DB* i, fo. 59^{r}. Ælfwine may have been a son of Ealhhelm ealdorman of Mercia; see above, p. cxxiii.

[i. 213] **50. (B139)** [a]*Carta de Middeltuna.*[a] [191]

B fo. 53r Creator[b] celi ac terre, per uerbum spiritui sancto coeternum, in
C fo. 116r principio carismata[c] per tempora | legis, nature, littere,[d] uel gratie distribuit gubernando generi humano. Sed ubi descendere dignatus est[e] Deus uerus et homo, amplexatus est iure hereditario septiformem spiritum quo repleuit orbem terrarum,[192] unicuique diuidens katacapta[f] [193] singulorum, ex quo preuenti ingenio fulgent, uiribus pollent, dominari iam audent uitiis suis, quippe peruncti nomine Christi. Proindeque[g] nonnulli minime hesitant dispertiri caduca, uilia deputantes comparando mansura.[194] Iccirco[h] ego Eadwi,[i] Dei largiente gratia rex Anglorum, adornari cupio quemque deuotum. Huic
B fo. 53v etiam meo familiarissimo | Ælfwine[j] uocitato quindecim mansas ad[k] Middeltune in hereditatem concedo perhennem,[l] cum omnibus ad se pertinentibus possidendam, et tradendam quandoque cuicumque uoluerit heredi. Acta est autem hec solutio agri ab omni censu regali libera, excepta expeditione, pontis arcisque constructione, anno .dcccclvi. ab incarnatione Dominica, indictione quarta decima,
[i. 214] primo[m] anno imperii mei, coram testibus idoneis: [n]Ego Eadwi rex, ego
[i. 215] Eadgar frater regis, ego Elfsige episcopus consensimus.[n] Hoc donum amodo seruanti[o] glorificetur a Christo; destruens uero conatum illum non impleat, sed precipitatus corruat in baratri[p] profundo.

[i. 242 n.] **51.** *De Bochelanda.*[195]

Idem rex dedit cuidam ministro suo Ælfehah nomine decem mansas apud Bochelande, et ipse huic ecclesie.[196]

50 [a–a] Carta regis Edwii de Middeltuna *B* [b] *preceded by cross A* [c] karismata *A* [d] litere *B* [e] *om. A, B* [f] catacapta *B* [g] que *interlin. C* [h] Idcirco *A, B* [i] Eadwig *A, B* [j] Ælfwine *A, B* [k] æt *A, B* [l] perennem *A* [m] uero *add. A, B* [n–n] *see Charters of Abingdon Abbey, pp. 226–7, for the boundaries and witness list in A and B. The boundaries also appear in the quire of C devoted to such clauses, fo. 199v, Charters of Abingdon Abbey, p. 587 (no. 26)* [o] seruaturus *A, B* [p] barathri *A*

[191] Sawyer, no. 594; *Charters of Abingdon Abbey*, no. 54. The original charter also survives; London, British Library, Cotton Augustus ii. 41, reproduced in *BM Facs.*, iii. 18. The authenticity of the charter, and most notably the original, is disputed. It is accepted, for example, by Dumville, *English Caroline Script*, p. 52, but rejected by P. Chaplais, review of Dumville, *English Caroline Script*, in *Journal of the Society of Archivists*, xvi (1995), 105–7, at pp. 105–6, on grounds of script, pre-existing holes in the parchment, and problems with the witness list. *Charters of Abingdon Abbey*, p. 229, concludes that it 'can probably be accepted as an original'.

[192] Cf. Wisd. 1: 7 'spiritus Domini replevit orbem terrarum'. For the seven spirits of God, see Rev. 3: 1, 4: 5, 5: 6.

[193] The sense and derivation of the obscure word *katacapta* is problematic, particularly regarding its second element; see *DMLBS*, fasc. ii. *s.v.* 'cata', for the suggestion that it should be read 'kata capita', 'according to heads'; *Charters of Abingdon Abbey*, p. 641, for the

50. (B139) *Charter concerning Milton.*[191]

The Creator of Heaven and earth, through the word coeternal with the Holy Spirit, in the beginning apportioned gifts of law, nature, letters, and grace throughout the ages for governing the human race. But when the true God and man deigned to descend, He embraced by hereditary right the seven-form spirit with which he filled the world,[192] dividing to each individual proportionately,[193] whereby those advanced in intellect shine, exert influence with strength, and now dare to master their vices, as they have been anointed in the name of Christ. And accordingly some hesitate not at all to distribute transitory things, assigning the worthless in acquiring what lasts.[194] Therefore I, Eadwig, by bestowal of God's grace king of the English, desire to honour a certain devoted man. So I grant to my very close supporter called Ælfwine fifteen hides at Milton in perennial inheritance, to possess with everything pertaining to it, and to hand over to anyone as heir when he wishes. Moreover, this remittal of land is carried out free of all royal due except military service, and bridge and fortress building, in the year of our Lord 956, the fourteenth indiction, the first year of my dominion, in the presence of suitable witnesses: I King Eadwig, I Edgar the king's brother, I Bishop Ælfsige have consented. He who preserves this gift is henceforth to be glorified by Christ; he indeed who destroys it is not to complete his effort, but is to be cast down and fall into deep Hell.

51. *Concerning Buckland.*[195]

The same king gave ten hides at Buckland to a thegn of his named Ælfheah, and he gave it to this church.[196]

suggestion that it derived 'from Greek *kata* "according to", and καπτος, "strength"', and meant '? According to the virtues'. Another possibility is that it is a corruption of the Greek 'κατα κοπον', i.e. according to work done, as in 1 Cor. 3: 8.

[194] For such sentiments, see S. D. White, *Custom, Kinship, and Gifts to Saints: The Laudatio Parentum in Western France, 1050–1150* (Chapel Hill, NC, 1988), pp. 154–5.

[195] Berkshire. MS B introduces the gift of Buckland with a different passage, which states that Ælfheah gave the land to Abingdon; below, B162.

[196] On Ælfheah, see above, p. cxxiii. In *Domesday Book*, Abingdon's holding at Buckland is assessed at five hides; *DB* i, fo. 59^{v}. However, the problematic list of knights appearing early in Book III of MS B records Hugh of Buckland owing one knight for ten hides at Buckland; vol. ii. 324. *Charters of Abingdon Abbey*, p. 313, suggests that the abbey may in the meantime have established its right to some of Bishop Osbern of Exeter's land at Buckland, which was disputed at the time of *Domesday Book*; *DB* i, fo. 58^{v}. It may be that Hugh of Buckland gained some of this land; *VCH*, *Berkshire*, iv. 453. However, none of the other 12th-c. Abingdon lists records an assessment of ten hides; vol. ii. 388, 391. It seems likely that, rather than the size of the estate having increased, the list of knights may be inaccurate or revive an earlier assessment. *DB* i, fo. 59^{v} has the *TRE* holder of Buckland as Ælmer. It does not specify that he held from Abingdon, but such information is not always recorded in *Domesday*.

[i. 242] B fo. 60r **52. (B163)** [a]*Carta de Bochelanda.*[a] [197]

Regnante Theo in perpetuum architectorio. Dum igitur secularia regimina rite creator omnium rerum ita decreuit,[b] ut nobis non solum [i. 243] que temporalia ac transitoria creauerat ad uictum largiendo cotidie distribuit, immo etiam eisdem[c] ipsis momentaneis ac labentibus eterna posse mercari permisit.[198] Quamobrem ego Eadwi, Dei gratia rex Anglorum, cuidam meo duci, mihi ualde fideli, qui ab huiusce patrie gnosticis[d] nobili Ælfheah appellatur uocabulo, pro obsequio eius deuotissimo, perpetua largitus sum hereditate decem mansas ubi ruricoli antiquo usu nomen imposuerunt Beclande,[e] ut ille bene perfruatur ac perpetualiter possideat quamdiu uiuat et post se cuicumque uoluerit heredi derelinquat, ceu supra diximus, in hereditatem eternam. Sit autem predicta terra cum omnibus ad se rite pertinentibus libera, campis, pascuis, pratis, exceptis[f] istis tribus, expeditione, pontis arcisue constructione. Si quis uero (quod non optamus) contra nostrum decretum machinari uel infringere aliquid uoluerit, sciat se rationem grauiter redditurum in die iudicii ante tribunal Domini, nisi prius hic digna emendauerit penitentia ante [i. 244] mortem. [g]Anno Dominice incarnationis .dcccclvii., indictione quinta decima. Ego Eadwi rex, ego Eadgar frater regis, ego Elfsie episcopus consensimus.[g]

[i. 219] B fo. 54v **53. (B144)** [a]*Carta de Bagenwrthe.*[a] [199]

Christi disponente gratia, ego Eadwi,[b] imperiali Angol[c] Saxonum diademate infulatus, ac bonorum regum exempla secutus, et populos mihi a Deo concessos regere pacifice obtans,[d] aliquam terre partem, id est mensuram quinque et uiginti cassatorum, uni meo ministro Ælfrico[200] concedo [e]in loco[e] ubi dicitur [f]ad Bagenwrde,[f] ut uita comite habeat et post obitum suum[g] derelinquat successori cui

52 [a–a] Carta regis Edgari de Bochelande *B* [b] decreuerit *B* [c] *corr. from* eiusdem *B* [d] gnoscis *B* [e] æt Boclande *B* [f] excepto *B* [g–g] *see Charters of Abingdon Abbey, p. 312, for the boundaries, dating clause, and witness list in B. The boundaries also appear in the quire of C devoted to such clauses, fo. 199v, Charters of Abingdon Abbey, p. 587 (no. 29)*

53 [a–a] Carta regis Edwii de Baenwurþe *B* [b] Eadwig *B* [c] Anglo *B* [d] optans *B* [e–e] *om. B* [f–f] æt Bægenweorðe *B* [g] sui *B*

[197] Sawyer, no. 639; *Charters of Abingdon Abbey*, no. 75. The charter is dated 957 but Ælfheah probably became an ealdorman only in 959. Notably, the preceding passage which introduces the gift describes him as a thegn. It is possible that the text was emended to take into account his new status, although the charter could also be a more complete forgery. See also below, B162.

52. (B163) *Charter concerning Buckland.*[197]

With God the Creator ruling in perpetuity. Since therefore the Creator of all things duly ordained as follows with regard to worldly regimes, that not only did He distribute daily to us in bestowing sustenance those temporal and transitory things that He had created, but He also permitted that eternal things could be purchased with these same short-lived and fleeting ones.[198] Therefore I, Eadwig, by the grace of God king of the English, have bestowed as perpetual inheritance on an ealdorman of mine, outstandingly faithful to me, who is called by the noble name of Ælfheah by the sages of this land, for his most devoted service, ten hides where the local inhabitants have imposed by ancient usage the name Buckland, so that he may enjoy it well and possess it perpetually as long as he lives and after him leave it to whomsoever he wishes as heir, as we have said above, in eternal inheritance. Moreover, let the aforesaid land be free with everything duly pertaining to it, fields, pastures, meadows, except these three, military service, and bridge and fortress building. Moreover, if anyone (which we do not desire) wishes to contrive or infringe anything against our decision, let him know that he will render account grievously on the Day of Judgement before the throne of the Lord, unless previously he makes amends here with suitable penance before death. In the year of our Lord 957, the fifteenth indiction. I King Eadwig, I Edgar the king's brother, I Bishop Ælfsige have consented.

53. (B144) *Charter concerning Bayworth.*[199]

By the disposition of Christ's grace, I, Eadwig, adorned with the imperial diadem of the Anglo-Saxons, and following the examples of good kings, and choosing to rule peacefully the peoples granted to me by God, grant a portion of land, that is the measure of twenty-five hides, to one of my thegns, Ælfric,[200] in the place called Bayworth, so that he may have it as long as he lives and after his death may leave it

[198] The grammar of this sentence is problematic, and this may explain the variant reading 'decreuit' and 'decreuerit'.

[199] Berkshire. Sawyer, no. 590; *Charters of Abingdon Abbey*, no. 60, which, at p. 257, accepts this charter as genuine.

[200] This bearer of the common name Ælfric may or may not be the same thegn who received land at Curridge, Berkshire, from King Eadred in 953, below, B102–B103 (*Charters of Abingdon Abbey*, no. 49); Ælfric Cild, who was probably the beneficiary of a grant of twenty hides in Hanney by King Eadwig in 956, below, B132–B133 (*Charters of Abingdon Abbey*, no. 55); and Ælfric, who received nine hides at *Ætheredingetune* from King Edgar in 961, below, B193 (*Charters of Abingdon Abbey*, no. 90). See also above, p. cxxiii.

uoluerit in eternam possessionem, cum campis, pascuis, pratis, siluis. Hec tellus a cuncto[h] sit immunis seruitute[i] nisi pontis et arcis
C fo. 116v expeditionisque[j] | iuuamine. Gloria consentientibus, tartarum nolen-
[i. 220] tibus. [k]Hec carta scripta est anno Dominice incarnationis .dcccclvi.,
[i. 221] indictione quarta decima. Ego Eadwi rex, et ego Eadgar frater regis, ego Odo archiepiscopus concessimus et subscripsimus.[k]

[l]Vir itaque ille hanc ecclesiam de Abbendona[m] de ista terra heredem post exitum sue uite fecit.[l] [201]

[i. 191] **54. (B125)** [a]*Carta decem cassatorum ad Tademertun.*[a] [202]
B fo. 48r Mundi terminum, ruinis crebrescentibus appropinquantibus,[b] etiam indicia manifesta et experimenta liquida declarant, et ad discutien-
B fo. 48v dum torpentes infidelium mentes illa dudum | dicta oracula incumbere noscuntur. Refrigescit[c] ardor summe (que Deus est) caritatis[d]
[i. 192] salutarisque sacri arescit limpha lauachri.[e] Querit quisque secundum sua desideria sibi magistros erroris; abicientes sententiam euuangelice ueritatis, quasi nausium nectar et cenose laticis fabulas uertunt aures.[203] Caueat quisque qui sapiens est sibi hec. Quamobrem ego Eadwi,[f] basileon totius Albionis Domino dispensante—dum mihi creator et conditor rerum a quo totius mundane machine rite gubernacula reguntur, posteritatis iure successionisque priores sequenti sceptra largire dignatus est—opere pretium reor futurorum temporum uicissitudinem preoccupans anticipari et incertum humane conditionis statum sagaci mentis intuitu preuidere, quatinus ex his inflictis facinorum uulneribus indulta superne pietatis remedia

[h] cunctis *C* [i] seruitu *B* [j] que *om. B* [k–k] *see Charters of Abingdon Abbey, pp. 256–7, for the boundaries, dating clause, and witness list in B. The boundaries also appear in the quire of C devoted to such clauses, fo. 200r, Charters of Abingdon Abbey, p. 588 (no. 33)* [l–l] *om. B* [m] *final* a *corr. from* e *C*

54 [a–a] Carta regis Edwi de Tademertuna *B* [b] adpropinquantibus *B* [c] Rifrigescit *C* [d] caritas *B* [e] lauacri *B* [f] Eadwig *B*

[201] MS B records Ælfric's gift of Bayworth with a different passage; below, B143. The lands granted to Ælfric were more extensive than the later manor of Bayworth, the charter boundaries including an area equivalent to the modern parishes of Sunningwell and Wootton, as well as two stretches of meadow. The estate then appears to have been broken up (see *Charters of Abingdon Abbey*, p. 258), but all to have come into Abingdon's hands. Wulfric held ten hides at Bayworth from the abbot of Abingdon *TRE*; *DB* i, fo. 58v. These are the only hides *Domesday* records for Bayworth, but the abbey also had five hides at Sunningwell, whilst ten in Wootton may have been included as part of Cumnor; *DB* i, fo. 58v.

[202] Oxfordshire. Sawyer, no. 617; *Charters of Abingdon Abbey*, no. 67, which, at p. 285, considers this charter 'probably authentic'; cf. e.g. the doubts expressed by C. R. Hart, *The Danelaw* (London, 1992), p. 132 n. 51. This and the following two charters grant a total of

to that successor he wishes, in eternal possession, with fields, pastures, meadows, woods. This estate is to be immune from all servitude except assistance of bridge and fortress and military service. Glory to those consenting, Hell for those objecting. This charter was written in the year of our Lord 956, the fourteenth indiction. I King Eadwig, and I Edgar the king's brother, I Archbishop Oda have granted and subscribed.

And so Ælfric made this church of Abingdon heir of that land after the end of his life.[201]

54. (B125) *Charter regarding ten hides at Tadmarton.*[202]
With ruins growing more common and closer at hand, manifest signs and clear experiences reveal the end of the world, and those utterances spoken some time before are known to be bearing down to shake the inert minds of faithless men. The ardour of the greatest love (which is God) cools and the salvation-giving water of sacred cleansing dries up. Everyone seeks, according to his own desires, masters of error for himself; rejecting the sentence of evangelical truth, they turn their ears to fables of filthy water, like nausea-inducing nectar.[203] Let anyone who is wise beware of these for himself. Therefore I, Eadwig, by the Lord's disposition emperor of the whole of Albion—since the Creator and Founder of physical things, by whom the governances of the whole worldly structure are duly ruled, has deigned to bestow the sceptres on me following earlier rulers by right of posterity and of succession—deem it worthwhile to seize in advance and anticipate the vicissitude of future times and to foresee with wise mental contemplation the uncertain state of the human condition, so that I may deserve to acquire forgiving remedies

twenty hides in Tadmarton, matching Abingdon's holding in *Domesday Book*; *DB* i, fo. 156^{v}. Another charter, preserved in a 16th-c. copy of a lost single sheet, records King Eadwig giving twenty hides in Tadmarton to Abingdon in 956; *Charters of Abingdon Abbey*, no. 68. It is a quite skilful fabrication, contradicted by the present three charters and notably absent from the *History*; see *Charters of Abingdon Abbey*, pp. 288–9.

[203] Part of this proem echoes a common west Frankish formula found in both the influential late 7th- or early 8th-c. formulary of Marculf and in private charters of the Carolingian period. See also P. Chaplais, 'Some early Anglo-Saxon diplomas on single sheets: Originals or copies?', in F. Ranger, ed., *Prisca Munimenta: Studies in Archival and Administrative History Presented to Dr A. E. J. Hollander* (London, 1973), pp. 63–87, at 79. Chaplais finds the use of a Continental formula not hard to explain, given Æthelwold's links to Fleury. *Charters of Abingdon Abbey*, p. 285, concludes that 'it seems reasonable to treat this diploma as the work of an unpractised draftsman (and therefore probably a member of a scriptorium where charter-production was not a regular occurrence) who decided to model his text on an unusual exemplar; this is more likely to have been a document based on one of Marculf's formulae than a copy of the formulary itself.'

merear adipisci. Quapropter ego Eadwi,[g] rex et primicerius istius insule, cum consensu meorum sapientium archontumque, libenti animo concedens, donaui Brithnodo[h] ministro meo aliquam terræ[i] partem, id est decem cassatorum in loco qui dicitur Tademertun, in hereditatem perpetuam sibi suisque heredibus;[204] ab omni tributo liberam donamus exceptis his, arcis pontisque et expeditionis,[j] ut
[i. 193] habeat et perfruatur cum omnibus ad eam pertinentibus.[k] Acta[l] est autem hec donatio anno ab incarnatione Domini .dcccclvi., indictione uero quarta decima, his testibus consentientibus et conscribentibus quorum nomina hic ponuntur.[m] Interdictum sit omni Christiano in nomine sancte Trinitatis hoc donum mutare uel fringere; alioquin anathema sit a Deo et hominibus, nisi prius emendat[n] digne. [o]Ego Eadwi rex, et ego Eadgar frater regis, et ego Odo archiepiscopus cum coepiscopis meis confirmauimus.[o]

[i. 194] 55. (B127) [a]*Carta quinque hidarum ad Tademertuna.*[a] [205]
B fo. 49[r] Christo tripudiante, sagaci prouidendo intuitu casus lapsusque nature[b] humane, de qua Ecclesiastes[c] 'Vanitas', inquit, 'vanitatum et omnia uanitas',[206] incessanter referre debitrices gratias oportet ei, scilicet cuius bonitate, dum non essemus, conditi sumus, dum periclitamur[d] beneficiis refocillamur, dum denique omnino eterna
[i. 195] perditi nece ipsius unigeniti liuore[207] nos esse credimus redintegratos ad uitam, et eandem mercando mutuari[e] conceditur eterna caducis, ueritate dicente 'Thesaurizate uobis thesauros in celo',[208] et cetera. Qua de re ego Eadwi,[f] rex et primicerius totius Albionis Deo opitulante, cuidam ministro nomine Brihtric quinque cassatos in loco qui dicitur Tadermertun,[g] in hereditatem perpetuam concedo cum omnibus ad se pertinentibus, ad possidendum atque tradendum

[g] Eadwig *B* [h] Byrhtnðo *B* [i] terre *B* [j] *a noun such as* iuuamine *appears to be missing here; cf. above, p. 86.* [k] *see Charters of Abingdon Abbey, p. 284, for the boundaries in B. The boundaries also appear in the quire of C devoted to such clauses, fo. 200[r–v], Charters of Abingdon Abbey, p. 588 (no. 34)* [l] Fcta, *the wrong initial having been inserted B* [m] postponuntur *B* [n] *clumsily corr. from* emendet *B* [o–o] *see Charters of Abingdon Abbey, p. 284, for the witness list in B*

55 [a–a] Carta regis Edwi de quinque cassatis in Tademertun *B* [b] *here and elsewhere the original uses the diphthong -æ for the ending* [c] Eclesiastes *A* [d] pereclitamur *A, B* [e] mutari *B* [f] Eadwig *A* [g] Tademærtun *A*, Tademertun *B*

[204] Byrhtnoth became ealdorman of Essex in 956, dying at Maldon in 991; for his career, see Hart, *Danelaw*, pp. 131–5. Byrhtnoth received another grant in Tadmarton, below, c. 56, and another at *Bragenfelda* in 967, below, B191 (*Charters of Abingdon Abbey*, no. 106).

[205] Sawyer, no. 618; *Charters of Abingdon Abbey*, no. 66. The charter also survives as a single sheet; London, British Library, Cotton Augustus ii. 43, reproduced in *BM Facs.*, iii.

of celestial mercy for these inflicted wounds of sins. Therefore I, Eadwig, king and ruler of this island, with the consent of my wise and ruling men, grant willingly and have given to Byrhtnoth my thegn a portion of land, that is amounting to ten hides in the place called Tadmarton, in perpetual inheritance for him and his heirs.[204] We give it free of all tribute except these, fortress and bridge and military service, so that he may have and enjoy it with everything pertaining to it. This grant moreover was carried out in the year of our Lord 956, the fourteenth indiction indeed, with these witnesses consenting and subscribing whose names are placed here. In the name of the Holy Trinity it is forbidden to every Christian to change or break this gift; rather let him be made anathema by God and men, unless previously he worthily makes amends. I King Eadwig, and I Edgar the king's brother, and I Archbishop Oda with my fellow bishops have confirmed.

55. (B127) *Charter regarding five hides at Tadmarton.*[205]
With Christ rejoicing, and with the acute and foreseeing consideration of the fall and lapse of human nature, about which Ecclesiastes says 'Vanity of vanities, all is vanity',[206] it is proper unceasingly to render due thanks to Him, namely that by His goodness, while we did not exist yet we have been created, while we are in danger yet we are comforted with benefits, and finally while we have been utterly lost in eternal death we believe that by the stripes of his only son[207] we have yet been restored to life, by purchasing this [life] it was granted to us to obtain eternal things in exchange for transitory ones, since as Truth says 'Lay up for yourselves treasures in Heaven',[208] etc. Therefore I, Eadwig, with God's assistance king and ruler of the whole of Albion, grant to a thegn named Beorhtric five hides in the place called Tadmarton, in perpetual inheritance with everything pertaining to it, to possess and hand over to

19. *Charters of Abingdon Abbey*, p. 281, states that the charter can 'be accepted as probably authentic'. The authenticity of the single sheet is disputed; D. N. Dumville, 'English square minuscule script: The mid-century phases', *ASE*, xxiii (1994), 133–64, at p. 146 n. 71, suggests that its script may belong to later in the 10th c., whereas Keynes, *Diplomas*, pp. 68–9, accepts it as authentic if reflecting a more 'adventurous' approach to charter writing.

[206] Eccles. 1: 2 'Vanitas vanitatum, dixit Ecclesiastes; Vanitas vanitatum, et omnia vanitas.'

[207] Cf. Isa. 53: 5 'livore eius sanati sumus'; 1 Pet. 2: 24 'cuius livore sanati estis'; the Authorized Version translates 'livore' as 'stripes'.

[208] Matt. 6: 20 'Thesaurizate autem vobis thesauros in caelo.'

cui sibi placuerit.[209] Solutum [h]autem idem hoc rus[h] permaneat omni
C fo. 117r iugo regali | preter expeditionem, pontis arcisque constructionem. Si quis uero huic donationi contrauenire nitatur penas[i] sustineat[j] auerni,
[i. 196] ubi[k] erit fletus et stridor dentium.[210] [l]⟨A⟩cta est autem hec donatio anno ab incarnatione Dominica .dcccclvi., indictione quarta decima, regni autem mei anno primo. Ego Eadwi rex, et ego Eadgar frater regis, et ego ⟨O⟩do archiepiscopus firmauimus.[l]

[i. 197] **56. (B126)** [a]*Carta aliarum quinque hidarum ad Tademertuna.*[a] [211]
B fo. 49v Regnante in perpetuum Domino nostro Ihesu Christo. Cunctis supernorum sacramenta donorum celitus perscrutantibus notum est quod non solum huius mundi status antiqui hostis fraude atque[b] molimine deficiendo corrumpitur, uerum etiam in presentis uite prope consummato curriculo humana prosperitas iniquorum hominum acri intentione et angore constringuntur. Nunc ergo dum nobis
[i. 198] tempus est uenie, festinemus laqueum totis nisibus deuitare mortis dumque carnale possidemus patrimonium spirituale[c] exerceatur mercimonium, quo inter angelicos choros mereamur adipisci gaudia sine fine mansura. Quapropter ego Eadwi,[d] rex Anglorum ceterarumque gentium in circuitu persistentium gubernator et rector, cuidam meo fideli, nomine Beorhtnoð, principi,[e] quinque mansas perpetualiter concedo in illo loco qui dicitur Tadmertun, quatinus[f] habeat ac possideat quamdiu uitalis spiritus aluerit corpus. Cum autem dissolutionis sue dies aduenerit, cuicumque uoluerit heredi derelinquat, ceu supradiximus, in eternam hereditatem. Sit autem predicta donatio ab omni mundiali obstaculo libera cum omnibus ad se rite pertinentibus, campis, pascuis, pratis, exceptis istis tribus, expeditione, pontis arcisque[g] constructione. Si quis uero hominum hanc meam donationem cum stultitie temeritate iactitando infringere certauerit, sit ipse grauibus per[h] colla depressus catenis[i] inter flammiuomas tetrorum demonum cateruas, nisi digne[j] prius hic ad
[i. 199] satisfactionem uenire maluerit. [k]Acta est hec prefata donatio anno ab

[h–h] etiam hoc idem rus *A, B* [i] poenas *A* [j] sentiat *A, B* [k] ibi *A, B*
[l–l] *see Charters of Abingdon Abbey, pp. 280–1, for the boundaries, dating clause, and witness list in A and B. The boundaries also appear in the quire of C devoted to such clauses, fo. 200r–v, Charters of Abingdon Abbey, p. 588 (no. 34)*

56 [a–a] Carta regis Edwii de quinque cassatis in Tademertuna *B* [b] adque *B* [c] spiritale *B* [d] Eadwig *B* [e] princeps *B* [f] quatenus *B* [g] arcisue *B* [h] pre *B* [i] cathenis *B* [j] *om. B* [k–k] *see Charters of Abingdon Abbey, pp. 306, 308, for the boundaries, dating clause, and witness list in B and CCCC. The boundaries also appear in the quire of C devoted to such clauses, fo. 200r–v, Charters of Abingdon Abbey, p. 588 (no. 34).*

whomsoever it pleases him.[209] Moreover, that land is to remain unburdened of all royal yoke besides military service, and bridge and fortress construction. Indeed if anyone strives to go against this gift let him sustain the punishments of Hell, where 'there shall be weeping and gnashing of teeth'.[210] Moreover, this gift was carried out in the year of our Lord 956, the fourteenth indiction, moreover the first year of my reign. I King Eadwig, and I Edgar the king's brother, and I Archbishop Oda have confirmed.

56. (B129) *Charter regarding another five hides at Tadmarton.*[211]
With our Lord Jesus Christ reigning in perpetuity. It is known to all studying the hidden truths of celestial gifts from heaven that not only is the state of this world failing and corrupted by the fraud and exertion of the ancient enemy, but also in the near completed course of the present life human prosperity is afflicted by the disagreeable attention and distress of unjust men. Now therefore, while there is time for pardon for us, let us hasten with every endeavour to avoid the noose of death and, while we possess the carnal patrimony, let a spiritual transaction be performed by which we may deserve to acquire joys enduring without end amidst the angelic choruses. Therefore I, Eadwig, king of the English and governor and ruler of the other peoples living round about, grant perpetually to a faithful noble of mine named Byrhtnoth five hides in the place called Tadmarton, so that he may have and possess it as long as the vital spirit nourishes his body. When, moreover, the day of his death comes, he may leave it to whomsoever he wishes as heir, as we said above, in eternal inheritance. Moreover, let the aforesaid gift be free of all worldly hindrance, with everything duly pertaining to it, fields, pastures, meadows, except these three, military service, and bridge and fortress construction. If indeed any man strives to infringe this my gift, boasting with the rashness of stupidity, let him be pressed down with heavy chains around the neck amidst the flame-spewing bands of foul demons, unless previously he prefers to come worthily

[209] Beorhtric may be the same man who received land in Hendred in 956, below, B122–B123 (*Charters of Abingdon Abbey*, no. 53). A thegn called Beorhtric witnessed another charter of King Eadwig, below, B170 (*Charters of Abingdon Abbey*, no. 79). *Charters of Abingdon Abbey*, p. 282, suggests very tentatively that the Beorhtric of the present charter may have been a relative of Byrhtnoth who received land in Tadmarton in the previous charter.

[210] See Matt. 8: 12; 13: 42, 50; 22: 13; 24: 51; 25: 30; Luke 13: 28.

[211] Sawyer, no. 611; *Charters of Abingdon Abbey*, no. 73. This charter also survives in a 16th-c. copy of a lost single sheet, Cambridge, Corpus Christi College 111, pp. 161–2. *Charters of Abingdon Abbey*, p. 307, accepts the charter as authentic.

incarnatione Domini nostri Ihesu Christi .dcccclvi., indictione quarta decima, et in palatio regis scripta est in Ceoddre, tertio kalendas Decembris.[212] Ego Eadwi rex et ego Odo archiepiscopus cum multis aliis subscripsimus.[k]

[i. 114n.] [l]Concedente uero rege, supradicti uiri cartas cum terra huic ecclesie Abbendonensi dederunt, sancto patre Æthelwoldo suggerente, atque huic ecclesie presidente.[l] [213]

57. *De Winechefeld.*[214]

Istius sancti patris nostri Æthelwoldi temporibus, quedam nobilis matrona nomine Sethriða possessionem quam a rege Ædmundo acceperat, id est Winecanfeld et Swinlea, cum carta sibi a rege concessa, huic ecclesie dimisit. Que carta ita se habet:

[i. 114] **58. (B78)** [a]*De Winecanfeld carta.*[a] [215]

B fo. 30v B fo. 31r Regnante in perpetuum | Domino nostro Ihesu Christo. Manifestum est cunctis quod omnia celestia et terrestria prouidentia Dei gubernantur,[b] que sollicitudo mortalis uite totis nisibus in carorum amicorumque amissione conqueritur ac defletur. Ideo certis astipulationibus[c] mellita oracula diuine clamationis nos frequentatiuis hortationibus[d] suadet ut cum his fugitiuis et sine dubio transitoriis possessiunculis iugiter mansura regna Dei suffragio adipiscenda sunt. Iccirco[e] ego Eadmund,[f] rex Anglorum ceterarumque gentium in
C fo. 117v circuitu per|sistentium, cuidam religiose femine uocitate nomine Sethride[g] modicam numinis mei partem, id est undecim mansas agelluli, eternaliter tradendo concessi, pro illius amore qui dixit 'Date, et dabitur uobis',[216] ubi turbarum collatione iam dudum
[i. 115] nomen illatum hoc adesse profertur Winecanfeld,[h] ut terram iam prefatam, meo scilicet ouante concessu, tramitibus sue possideat uite

[l–l] *om. B*

58 [a–a] Carta regis Eadmundi de Winkefeld et Swinlea *B* [b] *corr. from* gubernatorum *B* [c] adstipulationibus *B* [d] orationibus *B* [e] Idcirco *B* [f] Eadmundus *B* [g] Sæþryþe *B* [h] æt Winecanfelda and æt Swinlea *B*

[212] For Cheddar, see P. Rahtz, *The Saxon and Medieval Palaces at Cheddar* (British Archaeological Reports, British Series lxv, 1979); J. Blair, 'Palaces or minsters? Northampton and Cheddar reconsidered', *ASE*, xxv (1996), 97–121, at pp. 108–20.

[213] Cf. below, B124, B126, B128.

[214] MS B introduces the gift of Winkfield with a different passage, below, B77. Swinley and Winkfield are both in Berkshire. Note that in MS C, the charter only mentions Winkfield; in MS B, it mentions Winkfield and Swinley. *Charters of Abingdon Abbey*, p. 147, suggests that MS B's addition of Swinley came when that name began 'to be used to refer to a significant section of the Winkfield estate'. However, both place-names are included in the

to compensation here. This aforementioned gift was carried out in the year of our Lord Jesus Christ 956, the fourteenth indiction, and was written in the king's palace at Cheddar on 29 November.[212] I King Eadwig and I Archbishop Oda with many others have subscribed.

With the king's permission, indeed, the above men gave the charters with the land to this church of Abingdon, at the suggestion of the holy father Æthelwold, who was presiding over this church.[213]

57. *Concerning Winkfield.*[214]
In the times of this our holy father Æthelwold, a noble matron named Sæthryth bestowed on this church a possession which she had received from King Edmund, that is Winkfield and Swinley, with the charter granted to her by the king. This charter is as follows:

58. (B78) *Charter concerning Winkfield.*[215]
With our Lord Jesus Christ reigning in perpetuity. It is manifest to everyone that all heavenly and earthly things (which the anxiety of mortal life in all its struggles laments and bewails in the loss of loved ones and friends) are governed by God's providence. So the honeyed oracle of the divine pronouncement urges us with frequent exhortations and with assured assertions that with these fleeting and no doubt transitory little possessions eternally lasting kingdoms are to be acquired with God's help. Therefore I, Edmund, king of the English and of the other peoples living round about, have granted by handing over eternally to a certain woman of religious life, called by the name Sæthryth, a moderate part of my property, that is eleven hides of a tiny plot of land, for love of him who said 'Give, and it shall be given unto you',[216] where the name bestowed some time before by the conferment of multitudes is pronounced to be this, Winkfield, so that she may possess the already aforementioned land, that is by my joyful

introductory narrative in MS C. The scribe of MS B may have noticed this inconsistency and changed the charter accordingly. Alternatively, it is possible that the scribe of MS C made an error in omitting Swinley, and that the original charter would provide the first instance of the place-name. I have been unable to discover any more concerning Sæthryth.

[215] Sawyer, no. 482; *Charters of Abingdon Abbey*, no. 35, which, at p. 146, states that it is likely that the charter is authentic. As a charter of Edmund, this is out of chronological order in MS C. It may appear here because the compiler believed Sæthryth gave the land to Abingdon in Eadwig's time. In MS B, the charter appears among those of Edmund, below, B78. Possibly Winkfield passed to Abingdon rather later; see below, c. 107, for a certain Eadflæd giving lands in Winkfield and elsewhere to Abingdon. The positioning of the passage suggests that her gift may well have been in Æthelred's reign, although *De abbatibus* dates it to the time of Abbot Ordric (1052–66); *CMA* ii. 282.

[216] Luke 6: 38.

et post se cuicumque uoluerit heredi derelinquat in eternam hereditatem, [i]maiori minoriue[i] persone. Sit autem predicta terra libera, cum omnibus que rite ad ipsam[j] pertinere dinoscuntur, campis, pascuis, siluis, et undecim segetes prati[k] in loco ubi dicitur Hocesham[l] [217] excepto istis tribus, expeditione, pontis arcisue constructione. Si quis uero (quod non optamus) contra nostrum hoc decretum machinari uel infringere aliquid uoluerit, sciat se rationem grauiter redditurum in die iudicii ante tribunal Domini, nisi prius hic digna[m] emendauerit
[i. 116] penitentia ante mortem. [n]Acta[o] est hec[p] donatio anno ab incarnatione
B f. 31v Domini nostri Ihesu Christi .dcccxlii..[q] Ego Eadmundus rex et ego Odo archiepiscopus confirmauimus.[n]

[i. 255 n.] 59. *De rege Eadgaro.*[218]

[i. 256 n.] Defuncto itaque rege Ædwio, frater eius Eadgarus a cunctis regni primoribus rex constituitur. De regis uero huius munificis liberalitatibus circa hunc locum, et libertate eius rerumque illic pertinentium, sua auctoritate roborata, breuiter hic perstringamus.

[i. 256] 60. (B175) [a]*Priuilegium Eadgari regis de Abbendona.*[a] [219]

B fo. 63r B fo. 63v Ego[b] Eadgar, [c]altithrono adminiculante[c] Anglorum ceterarumque
[i. 257] gentium in circuitu triuiatim persistentium basileus, ut huius libertatis altithroni[d] moderatoris clementia merear optinere consortium,[220] rura que olim a predecessoribus nostris largita sunt, iniuste ab infidelibus quondam abstracta, in Gaing[e] uidelicet decem mansas, in Gosige[f] quindecim, in Weorthe[g] triginta, in Earmundesleah quinque,[221] Abbendonensi[h] ecclesie restituens, Domino nostro eiusque genitrici Marie ad usum monachorum inibi degentium eterna largitus sum hereditate. Gratuita itidem Domini gratia instinctus, monachis in[i] prefato Abbendonensi[j] monasterio[k] regulariter degentibus monastici eternam priuilegii (ut predecessores nostri) concedo

[i–i] maiore minoreue *C*, maiore minoriue *B* [j] ipsum *B* [k] prate *B* [l] Hoceshamm *B* [m] *corr. by erasure, probably from* digne *C* [n–n] *see Charters of Abingdon Abbey, pp. 145–6, for the boundaries, dating clause, and witness list in B. The boundaries also appear in the quire of C devoted to such clauses, fo. 199v, Charters of Abingdon Abbey, p. 587 (no. 25)* [o] Fcta *B* [p] prefata *B* [q] indiccione quinta decima *add. B*

60 [a–a] Priuilegium Edgari regis *B* [b] *see Charters of Abingdon Abbey, pp. 341–2, for the preceding proem and exposition in B* [c–c] altitrono amminiculante *B* [d] altitroni *B* [e] Gæging *B* [f] Gosie *B* [g] Weorþe *B* [h] Abbandunensi *B* [i] *om. B* [j] Abbendunensi *B* [k] *om. B*

---

[217] This place has not been identified, although Gelling, *Early Charters of the Thames Valley*, p. 35, suggests that it may have been near the Thames.

[218] Eadwig died on 1 Oct. 959; *ASC*, 'A', *s.a.* 959. Edgar was king of the Mercians and

concession, for the course of her life and after her may leave it to whomsoever she wishes as heir, in eternal inheritance, to a greater or lesser person. Moreover, let the aforesaid land be free, with everything known duly to pertain to it, fields, pastures, woods, and eleven fields of meadow in the place called *Hocesham*,[217] except these three, military service, and bridge and fortress construction. If indeed anyone (which we do not desire) wishes to contrive or infringe anything against this our decision, let him know that he will render account grievously on the Day of Judgement before the throne of the Lord, unless previously he make amends here with fitting penance before his death. This gift was carried out in the year of our Lord Jesus Christ 942. I King Edmund and I Archbishop Oda have confirmed.

59. *Concerning King Edgar.*[218]
And so when King Eadwig died, his brother Edgar was made king by all the leading men of the realm. Upon, indeed, the bountiful generosities of this king in relation to this monastery, and the liberty of it and of the possessions pertaining to it, strengthened by his authority, let us here briefly touch.

60. (B175) *Privilege of King Edgar concerning Abingdon.*[219]
I, Edgar, with the support of the One enthroned on high, emperor of the English and of the other peoples living round about, far and wide, so that I may deserve to obtain a share of this liberty[220] by the mercy of the Judge enthroned on high, have restored to the church of Abingdon and have bestowed as eternal inheritance on our Lord and His mother Mary, for the use of the monks living therein, lands which once were bestowed by our predecessors and were formerly taken away by faithless men, that is ten hides in Ginge, fifteen hides in Goosey, thirty hides in Longworth, five hides in *Earmundesleah*.[221] Inspired in like manner by the Lord's freely given grace, I (like our predecessors) grant the eternal liberty of monastic privilege to the monks living according to the Rule in the aforementioned monastery of Abingdon, that, after the death of the outstanding Abbot

Northumbrians from 957, of England 959–75; *Handbook of British Chronology*, p. 27. This section does not appear in MS B, but cf. below, B173.

[219] Sawyer, no. 673; *Charters of Abingdon Abbey*, no. 84. On the authenticity of this charter, see above, pp. cxcix–cciv.

[220] The introduction in the charter had ended 'Intacta igitur redolente Christi diuinitate, passaque ipsius humanitate, libertas addictis clementer contigit seruulis'; *Charters of Abingdon Abbey*, p. 342.

[221] On the history of these estates, and for the suggestion that the clause mentioning them may be an interpolation, see above, pp. cxxxiii, cxcix.

libertatem, quatinus,[l] post decessum Æthelwoldi[m] abbatis egregii, cuius temporibus hec libertatis restauratio, Christo suffragante, concessa est, quem[n] sibi uniuersa prefati cenobii congregatio apto elegerit consilio, secundum regularia beati Benedicti instituta, abbatem iuste ex eodem fratrum cuneo eligens constituat. Huius [o]libertas B fo. 64r priuilegii[o] deinceps usu per|petuo a cunctis teneatur catholicis, nec extraneorum quispiam tirannica fretus contumatia in predicto mon- [i. 258] asterio ius arripiens exerceat potestatis, sed eiusdem cenobii collegium perpetue, ut predixi, [p]glorietur libertatis[p] priuilegio. Sit autem prefatum monasterium omni terrene seruitutis eodem tenore liberum quo a predecessoribus nostris catholicis, a sancto [q]uidelicet Leone[q] papa et Kenulfo[r] rege catholico, uetusto continetur priuilegio Rethuno abbate optinente solutum.[222] Agri equidem ad usus monachorum Domino nostro Ihesu Christo eiusque genitrici Marie priscis modernisque temporibus a regibus et religiosis utriusque sexus hominibus et a meipso meoque patruo Eadredo rege fidelissimo C fo. 118r restituendo | iure concessi sunt, eiusdem perpetualiter sint libertatis. Nam rex prefatus rus quod Abbendun[s] nuncupatur, quod Ceadwalla[t] Domino nostro eiusque genitrici Marie priscis temporibus deuoto concesserat animo, in quo predecessores nostri (diabolica decepti auaritia) edificium [u]sibi regale[u] iniuste construxerant, ecclesie Dei restituens, interdixit ut regum nemo inibi pastum requireret nec edificium in sempiternum construeret.[223] Quod ego Eadgar Anglorum basileus, optimatum meorum usus consilio, tam meis quam meorum successorum temporibus fixum, in nomine Patris et Filii et Spiritus Sancti, fieri in eternum precipio. Tempore siquidem quo rura, que Domino deuoto concessi animo, iniuste a sancta Dei ecclesia ablata fuerant, perfidi quique nouas sibi hereditarias cartas[v] usurpantes ediderunt. Sed in nomine[w] Patris et Filii et Spiritus Sancti precipimus ut catholicorum nemo easdem recipiat, sed a cunctis repudiate fidelibus in anathemate deputentur, ueteri iugiter uigente priuilegio. Si quis uero tam epilempticus[x] philargirie seductus amentia (quod non optamus) hanc nostre munificentie dapsilitatem [i. 259] ausu temerario infringere temptauerit, sit ipse alienatus a consortio sancte Dei ecclesie necnon et a participatione sacrosancti corporis et sanguinis Ihesu Christi filii Dei, per quem totus terrarum orbis ab

[l] quatenus *B*   [m] Æþelwoldi *B*   [n] que *B*   [o–o] priuilegii libertas *B*
[p–p] libertatis glorietur *B*   [q–q] Leone uidelicet *B*   [r] Coenulfo *B*   [s] Abbandun *B*
[t] *preceded by* rex *B*   [u–u] regale sibi *B*   [v] kartas *B*   [w] *follows* Spiritus Sancti *B*
[x] epylempticus *B*

Æthelwold, in whose times, with Christ's aid, this restoration of liberty was granted, the entire congregation of the aforementioned monastery may by suitable counsel choose someone for themselves, according to the regular institutions of the blessed Benedict, and, choosing him from that body of brethren, justly appoint him abbot. The liberty of this privilege is to be held henceforth in perpetual use by all Catholics, and no outsider relying on tyrannical arrogance is to seize and exercise the right of power in the aforesaid monastery, but the community of that monastery is to glory perpetually in the privilege of liberty, as I have said before. Moreover, let the aforementioned monastery be free from all earthly servitude on the same terms on which it was freed by our Catholic predecessors, that is by St Leo the pope and by Coenwulf the Catholic king, as is contained in the old privilege obtained by Abbot Hræthhun.[222] Equally the lands granted in ancient and modern times to our Lord Jesus Christ and His mother Mary, for the use of the monks, by kings and religious people of both sexes, and rightly restored by myself and my uncle the most faithful King Eadred, are perpetually to have the same liberty. For that king, when he restored to the church of God the land called Abingdon—which Ceadwalla had granted devoutly to our Lord and His mother Mary in former times, and on which our predecessors (deceived by diabolical avarice) had unjustly built themselves a royal building—forbade that any king seek hospitality therein or ever construct a building.[223] I, Edgar, emperor of the English, after taking counsel of my leading men, order this to be eternally fixed both for my time and my successors', in the name of the Father and the Son and the Holy Spirit. Since, at the time when the lands, which I have devoutly granted to the Lord, had been unjustly taken from the holy church of God, some perfidious men seized the hereditary charters and issued new ones for themselves. In the name of the Father and the Son and the Holy Spirit we order that no Catholic accept these new charters, but—repudiated by all faithful men—they are to be considered anathema and the old privilege is to flourish perpetually. If indeed (which we do not desire) anyone, seduced by the madness of love of money, is so insane as to attempt by rash daring to infringe this bounty of our munificence, let him be estranged from the fellowship of the holy Church of God and also from participation in the sacrosanct body and blood of Jesus Christ son of God, through whom the whole world has been freed from the ancient enemy of the human

[222] See above, p. 20.
[223] See above, p. 64.

antiquo[y] humani generis inimico liberatus est, et cum Iuda traditore[z] sinistra in parte deputatus, ni[a] prius hic digna satisfactione humilis penituerit quod sanctam contra[b] Dei ecclesiam rebellis agere presumpsit, nec in uita hac practica ueniam nec in theorica requiem apostata obtineat ullam, sed eternis baratri incendiis trusus iugiter
B fo. 64v miserrimus crucietur.[c] | Anno Dominice incarnationis .dcccclviii.,[224]
[i. 261] indictione secunda, scripta est huius munificentie singrapha, his aliisque[d] testibus consentientibus quorum inferius nomina secundum uniuscuiusque dignitatem utriusque ordinis decusatim, Deo[e] disponente, caraxantur.[f] [g]Ego Eadgar Brittannie Anglorum monarchus hoc taumate agie crucis roboraui. Ego Dunstan Dorobernensis ecclesie archiepiscopus eiusdem regis beniuolentiam consensi. Ego Oscytellus Eboracensis basilice primas insegnis hoc donum regale confirmaui. Ego Osulfus, et ego Brithtelmus, et ego Odulfus, et ego Alfwoldus, et ego Ælfstanus, et ego Daniel episcopi canonica subscriptione manu propria hilariter subscripsimus. Ego Eadiua,[h] eiusdem regis aua, hanc
[i. 262] largitionem firmaui. Ego Æthelwold abbas Abbendonensis cenobii hoc sintagma triumphans dictaui. Ego Alfwoldus abbas et ego Aldredus abbas consensimus. Ego Alferus dux et ego Alfheah dux annuimus.[g]

[i. 313] [i]In donationibus autem quas ipse rex Eadgarus huic ecclesie Abbendonensi sub sancto patre Æthelwoldo contulit datur conici quantum
[i. 314] illum reuerentie et amori penes se tenuerit, cum locum quo deguerit sic honorauerit. Siquidem Bedwidan duorum et septuaginta cassatorum illic largitus est.[i] [225]

B fo. 77r **61. (B197)** [a]*Carta regis Eadgari de Bedwidan.*[a] [226]

Ego Eadgar, altithrono[b] adminiculante Anglorum ceterarumque gentium in circuitu triuiatim persistentium basileus, ut huius

[y] antico *B* [z] Christi proditore *B* [a] nisi *B* [b] contra sanctam *B* [c] *see Charters of Abingdon Abbey, pp. 343–4, for the boundaries in B. The boundaries also appear in the quire of C devoted to such clauses, fos. 196v–197r, 198v, Charters of Abingdon Abbey, p. 585 (no. 3)* [d] *om. B* [e] domino *B* [f] karaxantur *B* [g–g] *see Charters of Abingdon Abbey, pp. 344–6, for the witness list in B* [h] E *over erasure, the wrong initial having been added C* [i–i] *om. B*

61 [a–a] Carta regis Edgari de Bedewinde *B* [b] altitrono *B*

[224] This date is incompatible with the indiction, whereas 959 would fit. The latter date also appears to be acceptable in terms of the witness list and of Edgar being described as ruler of all the English; *Charters of Abingdon Abbey*, pp. xcviii–xcix.

[225] Wiltshire. There was clearly uncertainty over the hidage. The narrative in MS C

race, and be assigned to the left-hand side with Judas the betrayer of Christ, unless previously he humbly does penance here with suitable compensation for having presumed to act as a rebel against the holy Church of God; nor as an apostate is he to obtain any forgiveness in this active life nor any rest in the contemplative, but the most wretched man is to be endlessly tortured, thrust into the eternal fires of Hell. In the year of our Lord 958,[224] the second indiction, was written the charter of this munificence, with these and other witnesses consenting whose names are spelt out below according to the rank of each of both orders, by God's disposition. I Edgar monarch of the English of Britain have strengthened this by this mark of the holy cross. I Dunstan archbishop of the church of Canterbury have consented to the benevolence of this king. I Oscytel diligent primate of the cathedral of York confirmed this royal gift. I Osulf, and I Brihthelm, and I Athulf, and I Ælfwold, and I Ælfstan, and I Daniel, bishops, cheerfully have subscribed with canonical subscription by our own hand. I Eadgifu, grandmother of this king, have confirmed this largesse. I Æthelwold abbot of the monastery of Abingdon, exulting, composed this document. I Abbot Ælfwold and I Abbot Ealdred have consented. I Ealdorman Ælfhere and I Ealdorman Ælfheah have agreed.

Moreover from the gifts which King Edgar himself conferred on this church of Abingdon under the holy father Æthelwold is to be inferred how much he revered and loved that man, since he honoured thus the place where he resided. So, indeed, Bedwyn amounting to seventy-two hides was bestowed on it.[225]

61. (B197) *Charter of King Edgar concerning Bedwyn.*[226]

I, Edgar, with the support of the One enthroned on high, emperor of the English and of the other peoples living round about, far and wide,

gives the figure seventy-two, but the charter seventy-three. In MS B there is no narrative but the figure in the charter was altered from seventy-three to seventy-two.

[226] Sawyer, no. 756; *Charters of Abingdon Abbey*, no. 108, which, at p. 427, states that this 'is a very suspicious diploma', almost certainly based on the charter in the previous chapter; cf. other opinions noted at the revised Sawyer, no. 756. Edgar did give land at Bedwyn to Abingdon, but it—and other lands—were taken back by Edward the martyr. Finally, Æthelred gave other lands to Abingdon in compensation; see below, c. 99. Æthelred's charter probably dates from 999, and given that it probably brought Abingdon interest in Bedwyn to a satisfactory end, it is likely that the present charter was put together before that date. The area covered by this grant seems to be approximately the same as that in the charter concerning Burbage, below, c. 69. The relationship of these two charters is uncertain; *Charters of Abingdon Abbey*, p. 428. See also D. N. Dumville, 'The Anglo-Saxon Chronicle and the origins of English square minuscule script', *Wessex and England from Alfred to Edgar* (Woodbridge, 1992), pp. 55–129, at 107–12, esp. 109.

dapsilitatis altithroni[c] moderatoris clementia merear optinere consortium,[227] quandam rusculi particulam in locis diremptam,[d] trium et
C fo. 118v septuaginta[e] cassatorum | quod solicole huiusce prouincie Bedwindan[f] uocitant,[g] cum omnibus utilitatibus ad eam rite pertinentibus, campis, siluis, pratis, pascuis, piscuariis, Abbendonensi ecclesie designans, Domino nostro eiusque genitrici Marie, Æthelwoldo,[h] optinente abbate, ad usum monachorum inibi degentium eterna largitus sum hereditate. Sit autem prefatum rus, quod ego cum consensu optimatum meorum deuote concessi, omni terrene seruitutis iugo solutum, tribus uidelicet exceptis, expeditione, pontis arcisue restauratione. Si quis uero tam epilempticus philargirie[i] seductus amentia (quod non optamus) hanc nostre munificentie dapsilitatem ausu temerario infringere temptauerit, sit ipse alienatus a consortio sancte Dei ecclesie necnon et a participatione corporis sacrosancti et sanguinis Ihesu Christi filii Dei, per quem totus terrarum orbis ab antiquo humani generis inimico liberatus est, et cum Iuda proditore
[i. 315] Christi sinistra in parte deputatus, ni[j] prius hic digna satisfactione humilis penituerit quod contra sanctam Dei ecclesiam rebellis agere presumpsit, nec in uita hac practica ueniam, nec in theorica requiem apostata optineat ullam, sed eternis baratri incendiis trusus iugiter
[i. 316 n.] miserrimus crucietur. [k]Anno Dominice incarnationis .dcccclviii. scripta est huius munificentie singrapha. Ego Eadgar rex donaui. Ego Dunstanus archiepiscopus consensi, cum ceteris episcopis et principibus gentis nostre. Ego Æthelwold Abbendonensis cenobii archimandrita, iuuante Theo, hoc donum adquisiui. Ego Eadgiua, eiusdem regis aua, hanc dapsilitatem hilaris fore concessi.[k]

[l]Item aput Draigtun uiginti cassatos loco eidem largitus est sub eodem abbate.[l] [228]

[i. 270] **62. (B179)** [a]*Carta regis Eadgari de Draigtun.*[a] [229]
B fo. 66v Confirmat nos sacre auctoritatis scriptura, dicens 'Nudus egressus sum ex utero matris mee, et nudus reuertar illuc', et iterum, 'Nichil

[c] altitroni *B* [d] direptam *B* [e] *final minim of* .lxxiii. *erased, B* [f] Bedewindan *B* [g] uocitan *B* [h] Aþelwoldo *B* [i] phirargirie *B* [j] nisi *B* [k–k] *see Charters of Abingdon Abbey, pp. 425–7, for boundaries, dating clause, and witness list in B. The boundaries also appear in the quire of C devoted to such clauses, fo. 197r, Charters of Abingdon Abbey, p. 585 (no. 4)* [l–l] *om. B*

62 [a–a] Carta regis Eadgari de uiginti hidis in Draitun *B*

[227] This appears to be a reference to the proem of the charter, which neither MS C nor MS B included; see *Charters of Abingdon Abbey*, pp. 427–8.

so that I may deserve to obtain a share of this munificence by the mercy of the Judge enthroned on high,[227] designate to the church of Abingdon and bestow as eternal inheritance on our Lord and His mother Mary, for the use of the monks living there, under the charge of Abbot Æthelwold, a small portion of land drawn from various places, amounting to seventy-three hides, which the local inhabitants of this region call Bedwyn, with all appurtenances duly pertaining to it, fields, woods, meadows, pastures, fisheries. Moreover, let the aforesaid land, which I have devoutly granted with the consent of my leading men, be unburdened of every yoke of earthly servitude except three, that is, military service, and bridge and fortress repair. If indeed (which we do not desire) anyone, seduced by the madness of love of money, is so insane as to attempt by rash daring to infringe this bounty of our munificence, let him be estranged from the fellowship of the holy Church of God and also from participation in the sacrosanct body and blood of Jesus Christ the son of God, through whom the whole world has been freed from the ancient enemy of the human race, and be assigned to the left-hand side with Judas the betrayer of Christ, unless previously he humbly does penance here with suitable compensation for having presumed to act as a rebel against the holy Church of God, nor as an apostate is he to obtain any forgiveness in this active life, nor any rest in the contemplative, but the most wretched man is to be endlessly tortured, thrust into the eternal fires of Hell. In the year of our Lord 958 was written the charter of this munificence. I King Edgar have given. I Archbishop Dunstan have consented, with the other bishops and nobles of our people. I Æthelwold archimandrite of the monastery of Abingdon have acquired this gift, with God's aid. I Eadgifu, grandmother of this king, have happily granted that this munificence take place.

Likewise, he bestowed twenty hides at Drayton on that monastery under the same abbot.[228]

62. (B179) *Charter of King Edgar concerning Drayton.*[229]

The writing of sacred authority strengthens us, saying 'Naked came I out of my mother's womb and naked shall I return thither', and again

[228] Berkshire.

[229] Sawyer, no. 682; *Charters of Abingdon Abbey*, no. 85, which, at p. 350, accepts this document as 'probably authentic', and suggests that its formulation may have been the basis of other forged documents.

intulimus in hunc mundum, [b]nec ab eo uerum[b] auferre quid
B fo. 67r poterimus'.[230] Quapropter lubrici poten|tatus non inmemor, ego
[i. 271] Eadgar, Christo conferente rex et primicerius totius Albionis, regni fastigium humili presidens animo, ob remunerationem maioris premii, aliquantulam ruris particulam uicenis comparatam cassatis, cui uocabulum certa astipulatione Draigtun[c] profertur, ad ecclesiam beate Marie genitricis Dei ac Domini nostri Ihesu Christi in loco qui dicitur Abbendun[d] ad usus ibidem fratrum Deo seruientium libenter concedo, obsecrans et precipiens in nomine Christi ut nemo successorum nostrorum superioris uel inferioris gradus hoc nostre deuotionis donum aliquo temeritatis aliquatenus instinctu dirumpat.[e] Predictarum enim [f]mansarum decem[f] scilicet patruus meus Eadredus rex uni pridem militi,[g] [231] Eadwold[h] nomine, in eternam largitus est hereditatem,[232] et postea, ipso iam ex hac uita migrante, eidem restituit cenobio. Sit autem predicta tellus, quam ego cum consensu optimatum meorum prefato[i] largitus sum cenobio, ab omni terrene seruitutis iugo libera, tribus his exceptis, rata uidelicet expeditione, pontis arcisue restauratione. Si quis autem, laruarico instinctus spiritu, hoc donum uiolare immutareue[j] presumpserit,[k] nisi digna
C fo. 119[r] satisfactione ante obitum suum reus pe|nituerit, eternis baratri prostratus incendiis cum Iuda Christi proditore eternaliter lugubris
[i. 272] puniatur. [l]Anno Dominice incarnationis .dcccclx. scripta est hec carta, his testibus consentientibus quorum nomina in precedentibus intitulata sunt.[l] [233]

[i. 317] **63.** *De Hysseburna.*[234]

Item apud Hisseburnan quinquaginta cassatos rex ipse illic, sub eodem abbate, largitus est, cum tredecim prediis apud Wintoniam urbem sitis, ad predictum rus Hisseburnan pertinentibus.

[b–b] uerum nec ab eo *B* [c] Drægtun *B* [d] Abbandun *B* [e] disrumpat *B* [f–f] mansurarum uiginti *B* [g] *followed by* deuoto *B* [h] Eadwoldo *B* [i] prefato *rep. C* [j] *corr. by erasure from* immutare uere *C, by interlin. from* immutaue *B* [k] presumptuosus temptauerit *B* [l–l] *see Charters of Abingdon Abbey, pp. 349–50, for the boundaries, dating clause, and witness list in B. The boundaries also appear in the quire of C devoted to such clauses, fo. 197*[r]*, Charters of Abingdon Abbey, p. 585 (no. 5)*

[230] Job 1: 21, 1 Tim. 6: 7.

[231] On this rendering of *miles*, see above, p. cxciii.

[232] See below, B167 (*Charters of Abingdon Abbey*, no. 78), a charter of King Eadwig (not Eadred) granting ten hides at Drayton to Eadwold. The statement in the present charter that Eadwold restored (*restituit*) the land to Abingdon suggests that the monastery believed it had a prior claim to Drayton, perhaps as part of its early endowment. Gelling, *Early Charters of the Thames Valley*, p. 53, says that 'such an account [of the earlier history of the

'We brought nothing into this world, and it is certain we can carry nothing out from it.'[230] Therefore, not unmindful of the transitoriness of power, I, Edgar, by Christ's appointing king and ruler of the whole of Albion, exercising this eminence of kingship humbly, with a view to payment of a greater reward, willingly grant a small portion of land totalling twenty hides, called by reliable statement Drayton, to the church of the blessed Mary mother of God and of our Lord Jesus Christ in the place called Abingdon, for the use of the brethren serving God there, entreating and ordering in the name of Christ that none of our successors, of higher or lower rank, prompted by any rashness break to any degree this gift of our devotion. For ten of the aforementioned hides my uncle King Eadred formerly bestowed on one of his knights[231] named Eadwold in eternal inheritance,[232] and afterwards, when he was on the point of leaving this life he restored it to this monastery. Moreover, let the aforesaid estate, which I have bestowed on the aforementioned monastery with the consent of my leading men, be free of every yoke of earthly servitude except these three, that is, fixed military service, and bridge and fortress repair. Moreover, if anyone, prompted by diabolical spirit, takes on himself to violate or change this gift, unless the offender does penance with worthy compensation before his death, let the mournful man eternally be laid down and punished in the eternal fires of Hell with Judas the betrayer of Christ. This charter was written in the year of our Lord 960, with the witnesses consenting whose names are recorded in what precedes this.[233]

63. *Concerning Hurstbourne*.[234]

Likewise, the king himself bestowed on the monastery, under the same abbot, fifty hides at Hurstbourne, with thirteen holdings situated at the town of Winchester, pertaining to the aforesaid land of Hurstbourne.

land] is, however, unusual in a charter of Edgar, and it may be an interpolation intended to reconcile the evidence of this charter with that of the earlier one'. *Charters of Abingdon Abbey*, p. 351, does not appear to find this suggestion convincing. For other charters concerning Drayton, see below, B224, B231 (*Charters of Abingdon Abbey*, nos. 120, 130). *Domesday* does not explicitly mention any Abingdon estates at Drayton, but Abingdon holdings there are revealed in 12th-c. documents, vol. ii. 387 (eighteen hides), *CMA* ii. 310 (twenty hides). *Domesday* may conceal these holdings, or—alternatively or additionally—lands may have been lost by the abbey before 1066 and regained after 1086; see vol. ii. 198 n. 486, *Charters of Abingdon Abbey*, pp. 322, 467.

[233] *Charters of Abingdon Abbey*, p. 351, takes this as 'scribal laziness', as the witness lists given in MS B for this and the preceding document differ greatly.

[234] Hurstbourne Tarrant, Hampshire.

B fo. 77v **64. (B198)** [a]*Carta regis Eadgari de Hysseburna.*[a] [235]

Vniversa sacri eloquii oracula crebris nos instruunt ammonitionibus ut ei deuoti toto famulemur annisu,[b] qui, diuino omnia fundans uerbo, microcosmum,[c] hominem scilicet, quadriformi plasmatum materia omnigene totius cosmi prefecit creature. Nam diuine auctoritas scripture multifido nos[d] exhortatur[e] monitu, dicens 'Nudus egressus sum ex utero matris mee, et nudus reuertar illuc', et iterum, 'Nichil intulimus in hunc mundum, uerum nec ab eo auferre
[i. 318] quid poterimus'.[236] Quapropter, lubrici potentatus non inme|mor, ego
B fo. 78r Eadgar, Christo conferente totius Albionis basileus, regni fastigio humili presidens animo, ob remunerationem premii maioris, aliquantulam ruris particulam, quinquaginta uidelicet cassatos, loco qui celebri Hysseburna nuncupatur onomate, Abbendonensi[f] ecclesie beate Dei genitrici semperque uirgini Marie honorifice[g] dicate ad monachorum usus inibi regulariter degentium Dominoque nostro deuote seruientium, cum omnibus utensilibus que Deus celorum in ipsa telluris edidit superficie, pratis uidelicet, pascuis, siluis siluarumque nemoribus, eterna largitus sum hereditate. Predia utique tredecim que Wintoniensi sita sunt urbe ad rus prefatum pertinentia, eadem libertate prefate Dei ecclesie, admodum deuoto[h] [i]Æthelwoldo optinente[i] eiusdem loci abbate,[237] plaudat. Sit autem predictum rus omni terrene seruitutis iugo liberum, tribus exceptis, rata uidelicet expeditione, pontis arcisue recuperatione. Si quis autem prescriptis statutis noluerit consentire aut obedire, sciat se alienum esse a consortio sancte Dei ecclesie et a corpore et sanguine Domini nostri Ihesu Christi, per auctoritatem beati Petri apostoli sociorumque eius, nisi prius emendauerit[j] hic digna penitentia[k] ante
[i. 319] mortem.[l] Anno Dominice incarnati|onis .dcccclxi. scripta est hec
B fo. 78v carta, [m]prefatis testibus consentientibus et auctorizantibus.[m]

64 [a–a] Carta regis Edgari de Hisseburna *B* [b] ad nisu *B* [c] micocrosmum *B C* [d] *corr. from* uos *C*; uos *B* [e] exortatur *B* [f] Abbadunensi *B* [g] onorifice *B* [h] deuoti *C* [i–i] Aþelwoldo obtinente *B* [j] *follows* hic digna *B* [k] *corr. from* penitentiam *by erasure of abbreviation mark B* [l] *see Charters of Abingdon Abbey, p. 365, for the boundaries in B. The boundaries also appear in the quire of C devoted to such clauses, fo. 197r, Charters of Abingdon Abbey, p. 586 (no. 6)* [m–m] *see Charters of Abingdon Abbey, pp. 365–6, for the witness list in B*

[235] Sawyer, no. 689; *Charters of Abingdon Abbey*, no. 89, which, at pp. 366–7, states of this charter that its authenticity 'is uncertain, but it is perhaps more likely than not to be genuine'; however, 'we should probably be aware of the possibility that, even if [it] is basically authentic, the details of the property may have been interfered with and revised'. The estate history of Hurstbourne is like that of Bedwyn, discussed above, p. 99 n. 226, in

64. (B198) *Charter of King Edgar concerning Hurstbourne.*[235]

Every oracle of sacred eloquence reminds us with frequent warnings that we devout men are to serve Him with every effort, who, creating everything by divine word, set above every type of created thing of the whole world a microcosm, that is man, fashioned of the material of the four elements. For the authority of divine Scripture urges us with manifold warnings, saying 'Naked came I out of my mother's womb and naked shall I return thither', and again 'We brought nothing into this world, and it is certain we can carry nothing out from it.'[236] Therefore, not unmindful of the transitoriness of power, I, Edgar, by Christ's appointing emperor of the whole of Albion, exercising this eminence of kingship humbly, with a view to payment of a greater reward, have bestowed as eternal inheritance a small portion of land, that is fifty hides, in the place called by the well-known name Hurstbourne to the church of Abingdon, honourably dedicated to the blessed mother of God Mary, ever Virgin, for the use of the monks living according to the Rule therein and devoutly serving our Lord, with all associated resources which the God of Heaven has brought forth on the surface of that estate, that is meadows, pastures, woods, and forests. He particularly approves thirteen holdings that are situated in the town of Winchester, pertaining to the aforementioned land, with the same liberty, for the aforementioned church of God, still under the charge of the devout Abbot Æthelwold as abbot of that monastery.[237] Moreover, let the aforesaid land be free of every yoke of earthly servitude except three, that is, fixed military service, and bridge and fortress restoration. Moreover, if anyone is unwilling to consent to or obey the aforewritten provisions, let him know that he is estranged from the fellowship of the holy Church of God and from the body and blood of our Lord Jesus Christ, by authority of St Peter the apostle and his fellows, unless previously he make amends here with fitting penance before his death. This charter was written in the year of our Lord 961, with the aforementioned witnesses consenting and authorizing.

that it was given to Abingdon by Edgar and removed by Edward the martyr, before Æthelred gave the abbey other land in compensation. For possible earlier Abingdon interest in Hurstbourne, see below, B13, B14 (*Charters of Abingdon Abbey*, no. 7), B19, B20 (*Charters of Abingdon Abbey*, no. 6).

[236] Job 1: 21, 1 Tim. 6: 7.

[237] The verb 'plaudat' is very unusual for a charter, and its form, in the third person, does not connect easily to what has gone before. *Charters of Abingdon Abbey*, p. 367, suggests that this sentence 'could be a later addition or interpolation'.

[i. 321] **65. (B199)** [a]*Carta regis Eadgari de Suðhamtuna.*[a] [238]

In onomate alme et indiuidue Trinitatis. Cuncta seculorum patrimonia incertis nepotum heredibus relinquuntur,[b] et omnis mundi gloria, appropinquante[c] uite huius termino, ad nichilum reducta fatescit. Iccirco[d] terrenis caducarum possessionibus semper mansura superne patrie emolumenta adipiscentes, Domino patricinante,[e] lucranda decernimus.[f] Quamobrem ego Eadgar, totius Brittannie basileus, instinctu Dei monitus, magno animi conamine procuraui ut omnia presentis uite commoda Abbendonensi[g] monasterio, quod ego, Creatoris nostri iuuamine, regulari uite restauraui, per nostram largifluam donationem[h] largirentur. Vnde[i] uineam Wecet[j] sitam cum uinitoribus,[239] rusque sibi pertinens suis giratum terminis; censum quoque regale ad cenobium prefatum per singulos annos decorandum C fo. 119v [k]apud | Suthamtunam;[k] [240] unius eque[l] na|uis piscationem et regale B fo. 79r uectigal [m]ad Hwitancliue,[m] alterius autem [n]ad portmanna hythe;[n] [241] unam capturam[242] et salinum, unamque terre mansam, et ex regis nemore capture restaurationem que Brunwicwer[o] nuncupatur,[243] Domino nostro Ihesu Christo eiusque genitrici Marie ad usus monachorum inibi degentium, ob facinorum meorum[p] ueniam et [i. 322] eterne beatitudinis premium, Æthelwoldo[q] abbate optinente,[r] eterna largitus sum hereditate. His monachorum cuneus[s] communiter locupletatus donis regularem tripudians seruando custodiam, in Domino iugiter uoti compos hilarescat, crebraque Dominum supplicatione pro nostris intercedendo excessibus ueniam impetrans sedulo deprecetur. Qui autem hanc nostram munificentie dapsilitatem augere uoluerit, augeat Dominus uitam et prosperitatem eius hic et in euum. Si quis igitur hanc nostram donationem in aliud quam constituimus transferre uoluerit, priuatus a[t] consortio sancte Dei

65 [a–a] Carta regis Edgari de Suthhamtuna *B* [b] *changed to* relinquntur *by erasure of abbreviation mark B* [c] adpropinquante *B* [d] Idcirco *B* [e] patrocinante *B* [f] decreuimus *B* [g] Abbendunensi *B* [h] deuote *add. B* [i] *om. B* [j] circa Wæcet *B* [k–k] æt Suðhamtune *B* [l] æque *B* [m–m] æt Hwitan clife *B* [n–n] æt port monna hyðe *B* [o] Brunwic wer *B* [p] nostrorum *B* [q] Aþelwoldo, *with final* o *corr. from* e *B* [r] obtinente *B* [s] *clumsily corr. to* cuneis *B* [t] *om. B*

[238] Hampshire. Sawyer, no. 701, *Charters of Abingdon Abbey*, no. 93, according to which, at p. 379, this document is very unconventional but there are grounds for accepting it as genuine.

[239] Watchet, Somerset. The *ASC*, *s.a.* 988, mentions Watchet being ravaged, *s.a.* 997 it being much damaged and burnt by the Danes. Such destruction may explain why Abingdon allowed its interest in the land to be lost.

[240] The exact nature of these payments is uncertain. *Charters of Abingdon Abbey*, p. 380, suggests that they may have included payments in kind exacted from merchants, thereby bringing the monastery 'a supply of useful goods such as wax and oil (used for lighting),

65. (B199) *Charter of King Edgar concerning Southampton.*[238]
In the name of the blessed and indivisible Trinity. All patrimonies of this life are left to uncertain heirs of descendants, and all glory of the world fails and is reduced to nothing with the approaching end of this life. For that reason, under the Lord's protection, we decide to gain and acquire with earthly possessions of transitory things the everlasting advantages of the heavenly land. Therefore I, Edgar, emperor of the whole of Britain, warned by the prompting of God, with great effort of mind have procured that all the conveniences of the present life be bestowed by our generous gift on the monastery of Abingdon, which I, with the help of our Creator, have restored to the regular life. Wherefore I have bestowed as eternal inheritance on our Lord Jesus Christ and His mother Mary, for the use of the monks living therein, for the forgiveness of my sins and the reward of eternal blessedness, under the charge of Abbot Æthelwold, a vineyard situated at Watchet with vineyard workers,[239] and the land pertaining to it surrounded with its own boundaries; also the royal payment each year at Southampton, for glorifying the aforementioned monastery;[240] in like manner the fishing and royal toll of one ship at White Cliff and of another at the haven of the townsmen;[241] a trap[242] and salt pan, and one hide of land, and restoration of the trap out of the king's woodland called *Brunwic* weir.[243] Let the body of monks, enriched with these gifts, communally celebrate by maintaining regular observance and, having what they desire, perpetually grow cheerful in the Lord, and let them assiduously entreat the Lord with frequent supplication and seek pardon by interceding regarding our sins. Moreover, whoever wishes to increase this bounty of munificence, let the Lord increase his life and prosperity here and forever. If, therefore, anyone wishes to change this our gift into something other than we have established, let the mournful man be removed from the

ivory, furs and textiles'. Later evidence for Abingdon receiving these payments from Southampton is lacking.

[241] This may by Hythe, on Southampton Water, or the area around Portchester and Portsmouth Harbour; *Charters of Abingdon Abbey*, p. 380. If so, White Cliff may be on the Solent, and could relate to Whitecliff Bay on the Isle of Wight, although there is no strong supporting place-name evidence for this. The translation of this clause is somewhat problematic. *Charters of Abingdon Abbey*, p. 380, suggests taking 'eque' as an adjective in agreement with 'nauis'.

[242] i.e. a fish-trap; see C. R. Salisbury, 'Primitive British fishweirs', in G. L. Good, R. H. Jones, and M. W. Ponsford, eds., *Waterfront Archaeology* (Council for British Archaeology Research Report, lxxiv, 1991), pp. 76–87.

[243] This may be associated with Brownwich in Hook, close to the 11th-c. royal estate of Titchfield; *Charters of Abingdon Abbey*, p. 381.

ecclesie,[u] baratri incendiis lugubris iugiter cum Iuda[v] proditore eiusque complicibus puniatur, si non satisfactione emendauerit congrua quod contra nostrum deliquit decretum. [w]Scripta uero hec carta fuit anno .dcccclxii. ab incarnatione Dominica, prescriptis in prima carta testibus consentientibus huius regis largitati.[w]

[i. 329] [x]Item eodem anno et hoc in dono adiecit rex ipsi ecclesie, scilicet tres cassatos ad Henneride, quorum mete non in continenti sed sparsim mixta iugera cum aliorum habentur.[x] [244]

B fo. 80v **66. (B202)** [a]*Carta de Henneriðe.*[a] [245]

Altithrono[b] in eternum[c] regnante. Vniuersis sophie studium intento mentis conamine sedulo rimantibus liquido patescit quod, huius uite periculis nimio ingruentibus terrore, recidiui terminus cosmi appropinquare dinoscitur, ut ueridica Christi promulgat sententia, qua dicit 'Surget gens contra gentem et regnum aduersus regnum'.[d] [246] Quamobrem ego Eadgar, totius Brittannie basileus, quandam ruris particulam, tres uidelicet cassatos, loco qui celebri [e]ad Hennenriðe[e] nuncupatur uocabulo, sancte Dei ecclesie beate Dei genitrice[f] semperque uirgini Marie in Abbendune dicate, perpetua largitus sum hereditate, cum omnibus utensilibus, pratis uidelicet, pascuis, [i. 330] siluis. Sit autem predictum rus omni terrene seruitutis iugo liberum tribus exceptis, rata uidelicet expeditione, pontis arcisue restauratione. Si quis igitur hanc nostram donationem in aliud quam constituimus transferre uoluerit, priuatus consortio sancte Dei ecclesie, eternis barathri[g] incendiis lugubris iugiter cum Iuda Christi proditore eiusque complicibus puniatur, si non satisfactione emendauerit congrua quod contra nostrum deliquit decretum.[h]

[u] eternis *add. B* [v] Christi *add. B* [w–w] *see Charters of Abingdon Abbey, p. 378, for the dating clause and witness list in B* [x–x] *om. B*

66 [a–a] Carta Edgari regis de tribus hidis in Henneriþe *B* [b] altitrono *B* [c] æternum *B* [d] et reliqua *add. B* [e–e] æt Henneriþe *B* [f] genitrici *B* [g] baratri *B* [h] *see Charters of Abingdon Abbey, pp. 375–6, for the boundaries, dating clause, and witness list in B. The boundaries also appear in the quire of C devoted to such clauses, fo. 197r, Charters of Abingdon Abbey, p. 586 (no. 7)*

[244] Berkshire. The last clause of this sentence derives from the boundary clause in the charter: 'þises landes gemære synd gemære sua þæt lið æfre æcer under æcer'. It seems likely that *iugerum* here means strip rather than a specific land unit, the yoke; cf. above, p. 72. On such intermixed holding, see D. Hooke, *The Landscape of Anglo-Saxon England* (London, 1998), pp. 113–30. B123 (*Charters of Abingdon Abbey*, no. 53), a charter of King Eadwig, records his grant of ten hides in Hendred to his thegn Beorhtric. A dubious charter of King Edgar, below, c. 73, grants ten hides at Hendred to Abingdon. *Domesday* makes no

fellowship of the holy Church of God and endlessly punished in the fires of Hell with Judas the betrayer and his accomplices, if he will not make amends with fitting compensation for what he did wrong against our decision. This charter indeed was written in the year of our Lord 962, with the witnesses aforewritten in the first charter consenting to this king's largesse.

Likewise, in the same year, the king added the following as a gift to this church, that is three hides in Hendred, of which the boundaries are not in a block, but scattered here and there among the strips of others.[244]

66. (B202) *Charter concerning Hendred.*[245]
With the One enthroned on high reigning for ever. It grows plainly clear to all zealously examining the study of wisdom with intent mental effort that, with the dangers of this life pressing with exceeding terror, the end of the changeable world is seen to be approaching, as the truthful statement of Christ makes known, in which he says 'Nation shall rise against nation, and kingdom against kingdom'.[246] Therefore I, Edgar, emperor of the whole of Britain, have bestowed as perpetual inheritance a small portion of land, that is three hides, in the place called by the well-known name Hendred, on the holy church of God dedicated in Abingdon to the blessed mother of God Mary, ever Virgin, with all associated resources, that is meadows, pastures, woods. Moreover, let the aforesaid land be free of every yoke of earthly servitude except three, that is, fixed military service, and bridge and fortress repair. If, therefore, anyone wishes to change this our gift into something other than we have established, let the mournful man be removed from the fellowship of the holy Church of God and endlessly punished in the fires of Hell with Judas the betrayer of Christ and his accomplices, if he will not make amends with fitting compensation for what he did wrong against our decision.

mention of Abingdon holdings in Hendred (for the complexity of land-holding at Hendred in *Domesday*, see *Charters of Abingdon Abbey*, pp. 224–5), but later documents do reveal at least a small estate there; vol. ii. 322, 388. That small estate may be much the same land which the present charter records Edgar giving.

[245] Sawyer, no. 700; *Charters of Abingdon Abbey*, no. 92, according to which, at p. 376, this document 'appears to be authentic'. The date given in the version of the charter in MS B is 962.

[246] Luke 21: 10.

[i. 340] **67. (B206)** [a]*Carta regis Eadgari de Rimecuda.*[a] [247]

B fo. 83r Almus[b] totius cosmi fabrice conditor superna infimaque miro ineffabilique ordine collocans, hominem tantundem quadriformi plasmatum materia, sancto ad sui similitudinem inspiratum flamine, cunctis que in infimis creauerat, uno probandi causa excepto uetitoque, preficiens, paradisiace iocunditatis amenitate, cum sua coniuge, luculentissime constituit. Qui, proh dolor, demoniaco instinctus spiramine, sibi ac posteris in hoc erumpnoso deiectus seculo [c]promeruit mortem[c] perpetuam. Quamobrem ego Eadgar, totius Brittannie gubernator et rector, ut huius miserie repagulum (quam
C fo. 120r [d]prothoplastus | irretitus[d] promeruit), Domini nostri Ihesu Christi gratia redemptus euadere queam, quandam ruris particulam, duos et uiginti uidelicet cassatos loco qui celebri Rimecuda[e] nuncupatur onomate, Abbendonensi[f] ecclesie beate Dei genitrici semperque uirgini Marie honorifice dicate ad monachorum usus inibi regulariter degentium Dominoque nostro deuote seruientium, cum omnibus utensilibus que Deus celorum in ipsa telluris edidit superficie, pratis uidelicet, pascuis, siluis siluarumque nemorum,[g] eterna largitus sum hereditate. Sit autem predictum rus omni terrene seruitutis iugo liberum tribus exceptis, rata uidelicet expeditione, pontis arcisue restauratione. Si quis autem nostram donationem in aliud quam constituimus transferre uoluerit, priuatus consortio sancte Dei eccle-
[i. 341] sie, eternis barathri incendiis lugubris iugiter cum Iuda Christi proditore eiusque complicibus puniatur, si non satisfactione emen-
[i. 342] dauerit congrua quod contra nostrum deliquit[h] decretum. [i]Scripta est hec carta anno ab incarnatione Dominica .dcccclxi., prescriptis in prima carta testibus consentientibus huius regis largitati.[i]

[i. 334] **68.** *De Burhbece.*[248]

Eodem anno et eisdem testibus, concessit idem rex huic ecclesie terram de Burhbece, uiginti scilicet cassatos.

67 [a–a] Carta regis Edgari regis de Rimecunda *B* [b] *preceded by chrismon symbol A* [c–c] mortem promeruit *A, B* [d–d] protoplastus inretitus *A, B* [e] Rimecunda *B* [f] Abbandunensi *A*, Abbendunensi *B* [g] *for* nemoribus*?* [h] deliquid *A* [i–i] *see Charters of Abingdon Abbey, pp. 356–7, for the boundaries, dating clause, and witness list in A and B*

[247] Hampshire. Sawyer, no. 690; *Charters of Abingdon Abbey*, no. 87. The original charter also survives; London, British Library, Cotton Aug. ii. 39, reproduced in *BM Facs.*, iii. 23. The charter is genuine. It is a very unusual charter in that the text and bounds were the work of one scribe, the dating clause and witnesses added by another; see *Charters of Abingdon Abbey*, pp. lxxix, 357–8. Dumville, *English Caroline Script*, pp. 52–3, suggests that Bishop Oswald may himself have composed and written the eight attestations which follow the main text of the charter; for words of caution, see *Charters of Abingdon Abbey*, p. 358.

67. (B206) *Charter of Edgar concerning Ringwood.*[247]

The holy Founder of the fabric of the whole world placed the heavens and the world below in wonderful and ineffable order and, in the loveliness of the pleasures of paradise, most splendidly established man, equally fashioned from the four-element matter, inspired with the holy breath to likeness of Himself, setting him—together with his wife—in charge of everything that He had created in the world below, except a single forbidden one for the sake of testing. Alas, by demonic inspiration, he was cast down in this wretched world and thoroughly deserved for himself and his posterity perpetual death. Therefore I, Edgar, governor and ruler of the whole of Britain, so that I can escape the restraints of this misery (which the first-created man deserved after he had been ensnared), redeemed by the grace of our Lord Jesus Christ, have bestowed as eternal inheritance a small portion of land, that is twenty-two hides in the place called by the well-known name Ringwood, on the church of Abingdon honourably dedicated to the blessed mother of God Mary, ever Virgin, for the use of the monks living therein according to the Rule and devoutly serving our Lord, with all associated resources which the God of Heaven bestowed on the surface of that estate, that is meadows, pastures, woods, and forests. Moreover, let the aforesaid land be free of all yoke of earthly servitude except three, that is, fixed military service, and bridge and fortress repair. If, moreover, anyone wishes to change this our gift into something other than we have established, let the mournful man be removed from the fellowship of the holy Church of God and endlessly punished in the fires of Hell with Judas the betrayer of Christ and his accomplices, if he will not make amends with fitting compensation for what he did wrong against our decision. This charter was written in the year of our Lord 961, with the witnesses aforewritten in the first charter consenting to this king's largesse.

68. *Concerning Burbage.*[248]

In the same year and with the same witnesses, the same king granted the land of Burbage, that is twenty hides, to this church.

The history of the estate and its relationship to Abingdon is somewhat obscure. It seems to be the estate at Ringwood bequeathed by Bishop Ælfsige of Winchester to the Old Minster; Sawyer, no. 1491; *Anglo-Saxon Wills*, ed. Whitelock, no. 4. Ælfsige died in 959; *Handbook of British Chronology*, p. 214. It is surprising therefore that the estate passed so soon to Abingdon. It was held by Earl Tostig *TRE*, and by 1086 the king held it; *DB* i, fo. 39^{r}.

[248] Wiltshire. The history of the land at Burbage is similar to that at Bedwyn and Hurstbourne; see above, p. 99 n. 226.

[249] Sawyer, no. 688; *Charters of Abingdon Abbey*, no. 88, which, at p. 363, is uncertain of

B fo. 81v **69. (B204)** [a]*Carta de Burhbece.*[a] [249]

[i. 335] Ego[b] Eadgar, totius Brittannie gubernator et rector, ut huius miserie repagulum (quam [c]prothoplastus irretitus[c] promeruit), Domini nostri Ihesu Christi gratia redemptus euadere queam,[d] quandam ruris particulam, uiginti uidelicet cassatos loco qui celebri Burhbece nuncupatur onomate, Abbendonensi[e] ecclesie beate Dei genitricis semperque uirgini Marie honorifice dicate ad monachorum usus inibi regulariter degentium Dominoque [f]seruientium deuote,[f] cum omnibus utensilibus que Deus celorum in ipsa telluris edidit superficie, pratis uidelicet, pascuis, siluis siluarumque nemorum,[g] eterna largitus sum hereditate. Sit autem predictum rus omni terrene
B fo. 82r seruitutis iugo | liberum tribus exceptis, rata uidelicet expeditione, pontis arcisue restauratione. Si quis autem nostram donationem in aliud quam constituimus transferre[h] uoluerit, priuatus consortio sancte ecclesie, eternis baratri incendiis lugubris iugiter cum Iuda Christi proditore eiusque complicibus puniatur, si non satisfactione emendauerit congrua quod contra nostrum deliquit decretum.[i] [250]

[i. 327] **70. (B201)** [a]*Carta regis Eadgari de Easthealle.*[a] [251]

B fo. 80r Cuncta seculorum patrimonia incertis nepotum heredibus relinquuntur, et omnis mundi gloria appropinquante debite mortis termino ad nichilum reducta fatescit. Huius rei gratia, terrenis caducarum rerum possessionibus semper mansura superne patrie emolumenta[b] adipiscentes, Domino iuuante, lucremur. Quapropter, lubrici potentatus non inmemor, ego Eadgar, Christo conferente rex et primicerius totius Albionis, regni fastigium humili presidens animo, ob remunerationem[c] maioris premii, aliquantulam ruris particulam, quatuor uidelicet cassatos loco qui celebri ad[d] Easthealle profertur, ad ecclesiam beate Marie genitricis Dei ac Domini nostri Ihesu Christi in loco qui dicitur Abbendun ad usus ibidem fratrum Deo

69 [a–a] Carta regis Edgari de Burgbeche *B* [b] *see Charters of Abingdon Abbey, p. 361, for the preceding proem in B* [c–c] protoplastus inretitus *B* [d] quem *B* [e] Abbandunensi *B* [f–f] nostro deuote seruientium *B* [g] *for* nemoribus? [h] tranferre *C* [i] *see Charters of Abingdon Abbey, pp. 361–3, for the boundaries, dating clause, and witness list in B*

70 [a–a] Carta regis Edgari de Esthalla *B* [b] emulumenta *B* [c] remuneratione *B* [d] æt *B*

---

the authenticity of this charter, which is in essence identical to that concerning Ringwood, above, c. 67. Kelly writes that it 'could be an Abingdon forgery', based on the Ringwood charter, or 'it might be an authentic near-duplicate', produced on the same occasion. The date given in the version of the charter in MS B is 961.

69. (B204) *Charter concerning Burbage.*[249]
I, Edgar, governor and ruler of the whole of Britain, so that I can escape the restraints of this misery (which the first-created man deserved after he had been ensnared), redeemed by the grace of our Lord Jesus Christ, have bestowed as eternal inheritance a small portion of land, that is twenty hides in the place called by the well-known name Burbage, on the church of Abingdon honourably dedicated to the blessed mother of God Mary, ever Virgin, for the use of the monks living according to the Rule therein and devoutly serving our Lord, with all associated resources which the God of Heaven bestowed on the surface of that estate, that is meadows, pastures, woods, and forests. Moreover, let the aforesaid land be free of every yoke of earthly servitude except three, that is, fixed military service, and bridge and fortress repair. If, moreover, anyone wishes to change this our gift into something other than we have established, let the mournful man be removed from the fellowship of the holy Church and endlessly punished in the eternal fires of Hell with Judas the betrayer of Christ and his accomplices, if he will not make amends with fitting compensation for what he did wrong against our decision.[250]

70. (B201) *Charter of King Edgar concerning Easthall.*[251]
All patrimonies of this life are left to uncertain heirs of descendants, and all glory of the world fails and is reduced to nothing with the approaching end of due death. Because of this, may we, with the Lord's help, acquire and gain with earthly possessions of transitory things the ever-lasting advantages of the heavenly land. Therefore, not unmindful of the transitoriness of power, I Edgar, by Christ's appointing king and ruler of the whole of Albion, exercising this eminence of kingship humbly, with a view to payment of a greater reward, willingly grant a small portion of land, that is four hides at the place commonly called Easthall, to the church of the blessed Mary mother of God and of our Lord Jesus Christ in the place called Abingdon, for the use of the brethren serving God there, entreating

[250] The boundaries recorded in MS B are closely related to those for Bedwyn, above, c. 61; see also Dumville, 'Origins of English square minuscule', pp. 109–10.

[251] Sussex. Sawyer, no. 708; *Charters of Abingdon Abbey*, no. 96; trans. E. E. Barker, 'Sussex Anglo-Saxon Charters: Part III', *Sussex Archaeological Collections*, lxxxviii (1949), 93–5. *Charters of Abingdon Abbey*, p. 389, accepts this charter as 'probably authentic'. The place-name can be associated with the present-day East Hale Bottom, south-west of Eastbourne; EPNS, *Sussex*, ii. 429. Apart from this charter, there is no other evidence of Abingdon interest in Easthall, or indeed in the surrounding area.

seruientium libenter concedo, obsecrans et precipiens in nomine Christi ut nemo successorum nostrorum superioris[e] uel inferioris
C fo. 120v gradus hoc nostre deuotionis donum aliquo temeritatis aliquatenus | instinctu dirumpat.[f] Sit autem predictum rus omni terrene seruitutis iugo liberum tribus exceptis, rata uidelicet expeditione, pontis arcisue restauratione.[g] Si quis igitur hanc nostram donationem in aliud quam constituimus transferre uoluerit, priuatus consortio sancte Dei ecclesie, eternis barathri incendiis lugubris iugiter cum Iuda Christi proditore eiusque complicibus puniatur, si non satisfactione emen-
[i. 328] dauerit congrua quod [h]nostrum contra decretum deliquit.[h] [i]⟨S⟩cripta est hec carta anno ab incarnatione Dominica .dcccclxiii., prescriptis in prima carta testibus consentientibus huius regis largitati.[i]

[i. 348] **71. (B209)** [a]*De Osgaro abbate.*[a] [252]
B fo. 85r Interea dum uiri[b] Dei Æthelwoldi[c] abbatis uita et Deo acceptabilis et hominibus predicabilem in dies se exhiberet, a predicto rege Eadgaro eligitur Wintoniensi urbi antistes, anno a Dominica incarnatione .dcccclxiii..[253] Huius uice Abbendonie abbas constituitur Osgarus,
B fo. 85v eiusdem ecclesie monachus.[254] | Et quanquam patriarchatum conscenderit presulatus, non tamen a monachice iugo discipline aliquatenus se relaxauit. Vnde clerici, qui tunc temporis apud illius episcopatus sedem in ecclesia conuiuere canonice debuerant, religionis rigorem in suo presule negligentes, loco cedere quam districtius uiuere maluerunt.[d] Quapropter, predicti regis et beati Dunstani tunc archiepiscopi consiliis et auctoritate, eos expulit monachosque de Abbendonia intromisit illuc, qui usque hodie Deo regulariter in eadem ecclesia deseruiunt. Similiter[e] et de ecclesia ubi abbatia est in eadem ciuitate fecit, nam in ea monachos et abbatem eis primus ipse instituit.[255] Siquidem et apud Orientales Anglos in insula Heliensi unum, in loco uero qui Burch appellatur aliud, et apud Torneium tercium monasteria cenobitarum constituit.[256] Que cuncta
[i. 349] ex Abbendonensium sumpsere collegio cultum et fundamina, ubi

[e] supioris *B* [f] disrumpat *B* [g] restaurationem *C* [h–h] contra nostrum deliquit decretum *B* [i–i] *see Charters of Abingdon Abbey, p. 388, for the boundaries, dating clause, and witness list in B*

71 [a–a] Sanctus Adelwoldus factus est episcopus ab Adgaro rege *B* [b] *final* i *interlin. B* [c] Aþelwoldi *B* [d] moluerunt *C, corr. from* moluerunt *B, suggesting that B derives from C* [e] *initial om. at start of line C*

[252] This is the first narrative shared by the two manuscripts; see above, p. xxxviii. For the unusual arrangement of the text on MS B fo. 81r, see above, p. clxxxvi.

[253] Consecrated 29 Nov. 963; *Handbook of British Chronology*, p. 223.

and ordering in Christ's name that none of our successors, of higher or lower rank, prompted by any rashness break to any degree this gift of our devotion. Moreover, let the aforesaid land be free of every yoke of earthly servitude except three, that is, fixed military service, and bridge and fortress repair. If, therefore, anyone wishes to change this our gift into something other than we have established, let the mournful man be removed from the fellowship of the holy Church of God and endlessly punished in the eternal fires of Hell with Judas the betrayer of Christ and his accomplices, if he will not make amends with fitting compensation for what he did wrong against our decision. This charter was written in the year of our Lord 963, with the witnesses recorded above in the first charter consenting to the king's largesse.

71. (B209) *Concerning Abbot Osgar.*[252]

Meanwhile, since the life of the man of God Abbot Æthelwold was both acceptable to God and continually showed itself praiseworthy to men, he was chosen as bishop for the town of Winchester by the aforesaid King Edgar, in the year of our Lord 963.[253] In his place was constituted as abbot of Abingdon Osgar, a monk of that church.[254] And although, after his episcopal election Æthelwold ascended to the bishopric, he did not, however, relax at all from the yoke of monastic discipline. Therefore the clerics, who ought then to have been living together canonically in the church at that episcopal see, disdained the rigour of their prelate's religion and preferred to leave the place rather than live more strictly. Therefore by the advice and authority of the aforesaid king and the blessed Dunstan, then archbishop, he expelled them and introduced there monks from Abingdon, who to this day serve God according to the Rule in that church. He did likewise concerning the church where the abbey is in that city, for he was the first to establish monks in it, and an abbot for them.[255] Also, among the East Angles he set up one monastery of monks on the Isle of Ely, another indeed in the place that is called Peterborough, and a third at Thorney.[256] All these took their form of worship and their foundations from the community of the monks of Abingdon, where that cultivator

[254] A similar sentence appears in the Abingdon versions of the Worcester *Chronicle*; John of Worcester, *Chronicle*, ii. 613.

[255] This refers to New Minster, Winchester; see also Wulfstan, *Life of Æthelwold*, c. 20, ed. Lapidge and Winterbottom, p. 36.

[256] On these East Anglian foundations, see also Wulfstan, *Life of Æthelwold*, cc. 23–4, ed. Lapidge and Winterbottom, pp. 38–42, and xlviii–l.

pietatis iusticieque cultor ille uineam plantauerat tam fertilem, de qua per loca plurima tot propagines propagaret. Sed quia ecclesiam Abbendonensem[f] ante susceptum episcopatum dedicandam reliquerat, post sui consecrationem et ipsam una cum beato Dunstano et aliis nonnullis coepiscopis suis in honorem Dei genitricis consecrauit, die quinto kalendarum Ianuariarum.[257]

[i. 331] 72. *De Henritha decem mansarum.*[258]

Posteaquam in pontificali ipse uenerabilis abbas Æthelwoldus constitutus est cathedra, rex Eadgarus circa hunc locum non destitit sue munificentie impendere operam. Siquidem anno qui est a natiuitate Christi .dcccclxiiii. eiusdem regis testamentum ita scriptum comperimus:

B fo. 81r 73. (B203) [a]*Carta regi⟨s⟩ Eadgari de Henriða.*[a] [259]

In nomine Domini nostri Ihesu Christi saluatoris. Quoniam quidem transeuntis mundi uicissitudo cotidie per incrementa temporum crescendo decrescit[b] et ampliando minuatur, crebrescentibusque repentinis uariorum incursuum[c] ruinis, uicinus finis terminus esse cunctis in proximo cernitur. Iccirco[d] uanis ac transibilibus rebus [i. 332] mansura celestis patrie premia mercanda sunt. Quapropter ego Eadgar, rex Anglorum ceterarumque gentium in circuitu persistentium gubernator et rector, sancte ecclesie Dei genitrici semperque uirgini | C fo. 121r Marie honorifice in Abbendune dedicate decem optime ruris mansas, in loco qui celebri Henneriðe nuncupatur uocabulo, ad usus monachorum inibi degentium, eterna largitus sum hereditate. Sit autem predictum rus, quod ego Domino[e] Ihesu Christo eiusque genitrici semperque uirgini Marie deuotus concessi, omni terrene seruitutis iugo cum omnibus utensilibus eidem ruri pertinentibus, pratis uidelicet, pascuis ceterisque rebus necessariis perpetua solutum libertate tribus exceptis, rata uidelicet expeditione, pontis arcisue constructione.

[f] Abbendunensem *B*

73 [a–a] Carta regis Edgari de decem hidis in Henneriþe *B* [b] decreuit *B* [c] incursum *B* [d] Idcirco *B* [e] nostro *add. B*

[257] An almost identical sentence appears in the Abingdon versions of the Worcester *Chronicle*; John of Worcester, *Chronicle*, ii. 613. Wulfstan, *Life of Æthelwold*, ed. Lapidge and Winterbottom, p. 30 n. 1, takes this text to imply that the dedication took place in 963, the year when Æthelwold became bishop of Winchester. They point out, however, that churches were normally dedicated on Sundays, and 28 Dec. was not a Sunday in 963—or in 964 or 965—and conclude that 'the date of the consecration of the church cannot be determined on present evidence'. In 963, 27 Dec. (.vi. kal. Ian.) was a Sunday, so it seems plausible that a minim had been accidentally omitted, giving '.v. kal. Ian.' for '.vi. kal. Ian.'.

of piety and justice had planted a very fertile vine, from which he propagated so many offshoots in a multiplicity of places. But since, before he took up his bishopric he had left the church of Abingdon needing to be dedicated, after his own consecration he, together with the blessed Dunstan and some other of their fellow bishops, consecrated it in honour of the mother of God, on 28 December.[257]

72. *Concerning Hendred amounting to ten hides.*[258]

After that venerable Abbot Æthelwold was established in his episcopal see, King Edgar did not cease to exercise his munificence regarding this place. Indeed from the year which is 964 from the birth of Christ we find a deed of that king written thus:

73. (B203) *Charter of King Edgar concerning Hendred.*[259]

In the name of our Lord Jesus Christ the saviour. Since indeed the vicissitude of the transitory world daily through the advance of time declines in its growing and is diminished in its expanding, and with the sudden ruins of various assaults growing common, the imminent finish is perceived close at hand to be the end for all. For that reason, lasting rewards of the heavenly land are to be purchased with empty and transitory things. Therefore I, Edgar, king of the English and governor and ruler of the other peoples living round about, have bestowed as eternal inheritance on the holy church honourably dedicated to the mother of God Mary, ever Virgin, in Abingdon ten hides of the best land in the place called by the well-known name Hendred, for the use of the monks living therein. Moreover, let the aforesaid land, which I as a devout man have granted to the Lord Jesus Christ and His mother Mary, ever Virgin, with all associated resources pertaining to that land, that is meadows, pastures, and other necessary things, be unburdened with perpetual liberty of every yoke of earthly servitude except three, that is, fixed military service, and

In a later context, MS B again mentions Dunstan and Æthelwold dedicating the altar of St Mary; vol. ii. 328.

[258] See above, c. 66, for Edgar giving Abingdon three hides in Hendred. The ten hides mentioned here may be same as those granted by King Eadwig to his thegn, Beorhtric, in the mid-950s; see below, B123 (*Charters of Abingdon Abbey*, no. 53). It is impossible to be certain what *Domesday* holding is equivalent to these ten hides, and indeed *Charters of Abingdon Abbey*, p. 225, suggests they could even have been 'reckoned under a different Abingdon manor'. For similar silences of *Domesday*, see above, pp. 20 n. 59, 102 n. 232, on Drayton, Wickham, and Wootton; note also *Charters of Abingdon Abbey*, p. clix.

[259] Sawyer, no. 724; *Charters of Abingdon Abbey*, no. 100, which, at p. 401, expresses 'a high level of suspicion' concerning this charter, primarily on linguistic grounds regarding the boundary clause, but 'there is no decisive diplomatic argument against [its] authenticity'.

Si quis autem cartam hanc iure meo conscriptam inimicali zelo corrumpere desiderauerit, se non dubitet a cunctis regni mei seruientibus Deo nunc et tunc et usque in sempiternum abdicatum et excommunicatum, sine fine cruciandus. Vnde post mortem, a tartareis raptus ministris, in profundum pestifere mortis infernum flammigera concludetur in domo, et ibidem in quandam ollam Vulcani ligatis proicietur[f] membris, que assidue bulliente pice repleta esse testatur, et a talibus[g] frangentibus seu minuentibus intolerantissime atrociterque absque ulla misericordia sentitur, nisi[h] ante mortem penitentie lamentis
[i. 333 n.] emendauerit.[260] [i]Et hii testes consenserunt regio dono. Ego Dunstanus Dorobernensis ecclesie policrates crucis + taumate consolidaui. Ego Oscytel Eboracensis ecclesie archipresul confirmaui. Ego Ædelwold Wentane ecclesie presul hoc regium donum signo dominico solidaui +. Ego Ælfstan Lundonie episcopus confirmaui. Cum his et plures alii confirmandum idem susceperunt.[i]

[i. 264 n.] 74. *De Mercham.*

Item apud Mercham quinquaginta cassatos ad Abbandonam rex ipse concessit, anno Dominice incarnationis .dccccclxv., predictis testibus consentientibus.

[i. 264] B fo. 65^v 75. (B176) [a]*Carta quinquaginta hidarum de Mercham.*[a] [261]

Confirmat nos sacre auctoritatis scriptura, dicens 'Nudus egressus sum ex utero matris mee, et nudus reuertar illuc', et iterum 'Nichil intulimus in hunc mundum, uerum nec ab eo auferre quid poterimus'.[262] Quapropter, lubrici potentatus non inmemor, ego Eadgar, Christo conferente rex et primicerius totius Albionis, regni fastigium

[f] prospicietur *B* [g] talia *B C* [h] hoc *add. B* [i–i] *see Charters of Abingdon Abbey, pp. 400–1, for the boundaries, dating clause, and witness list in B. The boundaries also appear in the quire of C devoted to such clauses, fo. 197^{r–v}, Charters of Abingdon Abbey, p. 586 (no.8)*

75 [a–a] Carta regis Edgari de Mercham *B*

[260] On the anathema, see *Charters of Abingdon Abbey*, p. 401; cf. Gregory the Great, *Dialogues*, iv. 31, ed. A de Vogüé (3 vols., Sources Chrétiennes, ccli, cclx, cclxv; Paris, 1978–80), iii. 104: 'uinctis manibus deductus in hac uicina uulcani olla iactatus est'. The date given in the version of the charter in MS B is 964.

[261] Sawyer, no. 734; *Charters of Abingdon Abbey*, no. 102, which, at pp. 412–13, discusses this charter, the next one concerning Denchworth, and the one concerning Beedon, below, p. 86, and concludes that 'these are dubious texts, but it is impossible to dismiss them as obvious forgeries'. They may be Abingdon products, at the time they claim, or very soon after. The date given in the version of the charter in MS B is 965. See above, p. 22 n. 66, for a Winchester charter in the name of King Ecgberht of Wessex giving fifty hides at Marcham to Abingdon. In MS B, Edgar's charter is followed by the statement that 'Frilford,

bridge and fortress construction. Moreover, if anyone desires with antagonistic zeal to violate this charter written with my authority, let him not doubt that he should be tortured without end, banished and excommunicated from all the men of my kingdom serving God now and in future and ever more. Wherefore after death, seized by infernal servants, let him be shut in a fiery house in deepest Hell of pestiferous death, and there, with his limbs bound, thrown into a pot of Vulcan's, reported to be filled with constantly boiling pitch, and he is to suffer such destruction and reduction unendurably and savagely without any mercy, unless he makes amends before death with the laments of penance.[260] And these witnesses have consented to the royal gift. I Dunstan ruler of the church of Canterbury have made it firm with the mark of the cross +. I Oscytel archbishop of the church of York have confirmed. I Æthelwold bishop of Winchester have strengthened this royal gift with the Lordly sign +. I Ælfstan bishop of London have confirmed. With these many others also undertook to confirm this.

74. *Concerning Marcham.*

Likewise, the king himself granted fifty hides at Marcham to Abingdon, in the year of our Lord 965, with the aforewritten witnesses consenting.

75. **(B176)** *Charter regarding fifty hides in Marcham.*[261]

The writing of sacred authority strengthens us, saying 'Naked came I out of my mother's womb and naked shall I return thither', and again 'We brought nothing into this world, and it is certain we can carry nothing out from it.'[262] Therefore, not unmindful of the transitoriness of power, I, Edgar, by Christ's appointing king and ruler of the

Appleton, and Bessels Leigh were in King Edgar's time members of Marcham, the bounds of which are partly defined here, partly elsewhere'; see below, p. 330. *Charters of Abingdon Abbey*, pp. 413–14, notes that the bounds of Edgar's charter cover the modern parishes of Marcham, Frilford, and Tubney. *DB* i, fo. 58^{v}, records Abingdon as having twenty hides in Marcham *TRE*, as opposed to the fifty mentioned in the charters. The difference of hidage may reflect the detachment of lands which the charters in Ecgberht and Edgar's names had taken as part of Marcham. Frilford and Bessels Leigh were recorded separately in *Domesday* as Abingdon holdings, Appleton was held by others; *DB* i, fos. 58^{v}, 61^{v}, 63^{v}. Abingdon also held on hide at Tubney; *DB* i, fo. 58^{v}. *Charters of Abingdon Abbey*, p. 414, argues that Edgar may not have been in a position to give the entirety of the earlier land unit which would also have included the 'members' mentioned here and was assessed at fifty hides, 'but it may well have been the case that Æthelwold and his successors made an attempt, on the basis of ancient claims, to reconstitute the full area of fifty hides. If [Edgar's charter] is authentic, or was drawn up with some sort of official permission, it may reflect a partial triumph on these lines; if it is a later production, it may have been intended to legitimize piecemeal acquisition (or re-acquisition) of land in the Marcham area.'

[262] Job 1: 21, 1 Tim. 6: 7.

humili presidens animo, ob remunerationem maioris premii, aliquantulam ruris particulam quinquaginta comparatam cassatis, cui uocabulum certa astipulatione Mercham profertur, ad ecclesiam beate Marie genitricis Dei ac Domini nostri Ihesu Christi in loco qui dicitur Abbendon[b] ad usus ibidem fratrum Deo seruientium libenter concedo, obsecrans et precipiens in nomine Domini[c] ut nemo successorum nostrorum superioris uel inferioris gradus hoc nostre deuotionis donum aliquo temeritatis aliquatenus instinctu dirumpat.[d] Sit autem predicta tellus, quam ego cum consensu optimatum meorum prefato largitus sum cenobio, ab omni terrene seruitutis iugo liberum,[e] tribus
[i. 265] his exceptis, rata uidelicet expeditione, pontis arcisue restauratione. Si quis autem, laruarico instinctus spiritu, hoc donum uiolare immutareue presumptuosus temptauerit, nisi digna satisfactione ante obitum suum reus penituerit, eternis baratri prostratus incendiis cum Iuda [f]Christi proditore[f] eternaliter lugubris puniatur.[g]

[i. 281] 76. *De Denceswrðe.*[263]

C fo. 121v Item rex ipse dedit ad Abbendoniam | duos cassatos terre apud Deniceswrðe, eodem anno predicto a natiuitate Domini, et eisdem consultoribus fauentibus.

B fo. 69r 77. (B183) [a]*Carta de Denceswrðe.*[a] [264]

Ego[b] Eadgar, Christo conferente rex et primicerius totius Albionis, regni fastigium humili presidens animo, ob remunerationem maioris premii, aliquantulam ruris particulam duobus comparatam cassatis cui uocabulum certa astipulatione Denceswrðe[c] profertur, ad ecclesiam beate Marie genitricis Dei ac Domini nostri Ihesu Christi in loco qui dicitur Abbandun ad usus ibidem fratrum Deo seruientium libenter concedo, obsecrans et precipiens in nomine Christi ut nemo succes-
[i. 282] sorum nostrorum, superioris uel inferioris gradus hoc nostre deuotionis donum aliquo temeritatis aliquatenus instinctu dirumpat.[d] Sit autem predicta tellus, quam ego cum consensu optimatum meorum prefato largitus sum cenobio, ab omni terrene seruitutis iugo libera,

[b] Abbandun *B* [c] Christi *B* [d] disrumpat *B* [e] libera *B* [f-f] proditore Christi *B* [g] *see Charters of Abingdon Abbey, pp. 407–8, for the boundaries, dating clause, and witness list in B. The boundaries also appear in the quire of C devoted to such clauses, fo. 197v, Charters of Abingdon Abbey, p. 586 (no. 9)*

77 [a–a] Carta regis Edgari de Dencheswrþe *B* [b] *see Charters of Abingdon Abbey, p. 411, for the preceding proem in B* [c] Denceswurðe *B* [d] disrumpat *B*

[263] Two charters in the name of King Coenwulf, above, cc. 10, 11, include Denchworth among his gifts to Abingdon. These are fabrications, but do show that Abingdon was claiming

whole of Albion, exercising this eminence of kingship humbly, with a view to payment of a greater reward, willingly grant a small portion of land totalling fifty hides, called by reliable statement Marcham, to the church of the blessed Mary mother of God and of our Lord Jesus Christ in the place called Abingdon, for the use of the brethren serving God there, entreating and ordering in the Lord's name that none of our successors, of higher or lower rank, prompted by any rashness break to any degree this gift of our devotion. Moreover, let the aforesaid estate, which I have bestowed on the aforementioned monastery with the consent of my leading men, be free of every yoke of earthly servitude except these three, that is, fixed military service, and bridge and fortress repair. Moreover, if any presumptuous man, prompted by diabolical spirit, attempts to violate or change this gift, unless the offender does penance with worthy compensation before his death, let the mournful man eternally be laid down and punished in the eternal fires of Hell with Judas the betrayer of Christ.

76. *Concerning Denchworth.*[263]
Likewise, the king gave two hides of land at Denchworth to Abingdon, in the same aforesaid year from the birth of Christ, and with the same counsellors approving.

77. **(B183)** *Charter concerning Denchworth.*[264]
I, Edgar, by Christ's appointing king and ruler of the whole of Albion, exercising this eminence of kingship humbly, with a view to payment of a greater reward, willingly grant a small portion of land totalling two hides, called by reliable statement Denchworth, to the church of the blessed Mary mother of God and of our Lord Jesus Christ in the place called Abingdon, for the use of the brethren serving God there, entreating and ordering in the name of Christ that none of our successors, of higher or lower rank, prompted by any rashness break to any degree this gift of our devotion. Moreover, let the aforesaid estate, which I have bestowed on the aforementioned monastery with the consent of my leading men, be free of every yoke

the land as part of its early endowment. Two further charters, of King Eadred and Eadwig, which appear only in MS B record the grant of five hides in Denchworth to Wulfric Cufing; B91, B172 (*Charters of Abingdon Abbey*, nos. 41, 81). In 1086, the mutilated knight Hermer held seven hides entered in *Domesday Book* under Goosey, but described by the *History* as in Denchworth; *DB* i, fo. 59^{r}, vol. ii. 8. It seems likely that these seven hides were composed of Wulfric's five hides and the two mentioned in the present section.

[264] Sawyer, no. 733; *Charters of Abingdon Abbey*, no. 104. On the authenticity of this charter, see the comments above on the preceding charter concerning Marcham. The date given in the version of the charter in MS B is 965.

tribus his[e] exceptis, rata uidelicet expeditione, pontis arcisue restau-
B fo. 69v ratione. Si quis | autem, laruarico instinctus spiritu, hoc donum uiolare immutareue presumptuosus temptauerit, nisi digna satisfactione ante obitum suum reus penituerit, eternis barathri prostratus incendiis cum Iuda Christi proditore eternaliter lugubris puniatur.[f]

[i. 323] 78. *De Fifhida.*[265]

Item apud Fifhidam quinque et uiginti cassatos ad Abbendoniam ipse rex largitus est, Osgaro abbate ab eo optinente. Hoc constitutum est sub anno a natiuitate Christi .dcccclxviii., astipulantibus predictis episcopis et ceteris probis testibus quod concessum est.

B fo. 79r 79. **(B200)** *Carta regis Eadgari[a] de Fifhida.*[266]

Regnante in perpetuum Domino nostro Ihesu Christo, qui imperio Patris cuncta, simul Sancti Spiritus gratia uiuificante, disponit.
[i. 324] Quamuis enim uerba sacerdotum et decreta iudicum in robore firmitatis iugiter perseuerent, attamen pro incerta futurorum mutabil-
B fo. 79v itate annorum cirographorum | testamento sunt roboranda. Quapropter ego Eadgar, totius Brittannie basileus, quandam telluris particulam, quinque et uiginti uidelicet cassatos loco qui celebri[b] Fifhidan nuncupatur uocabulo, Domino nostro Ihesu Christo sancteque eius [c]genitrice Marie ecclesie[c] dicate loco qui celebri Abbendone[d] nuncupatur onomate ad usus monachorum Dei inibi degentium, cum omnibus utensilibus, pratis uidelicet, pascuis, siluis, Osgaro optinente abbate, eterna largitus sum hereditate. Sit autem predictum rus omni terrene seruitutis iugo liberum tribus exceptis, rata uidelicet expeditione, pontis arcisue restauratione. Si quis igitur hanc nostram donationem in aliud quam constituimus transferre uoluerit, priuatus consortio sancte Dei ecclesie eternis baratri incendiis lugubris iugiter cum Iuda Christi proditore eiusque complicibus puniatur, si non satisfactione emendauerit congrua quod contra nostrum deliquit decretum.[e]

[e] is *B* [f] *see Charters of Abingdon Abbey, pp. 411–12, for reference to the boundaries, the dating clause, and witness list in B*

79 [a] Edgari *B* [b] *followed by* æt *B* [c–c] ecclesie beate Dei genitrice Marie *B* [d] æt Abbendune *B* [e] *see Charters of Abingdon Abbey, pp. 433–4, for the boundaries, dating clause, and witness list in B. The boundaries also appear in the quire of C devoted to such clauses, fo. 197v, Charters of Abingdon Abbey, p. 586 (no. 10)*

[265] Berkshire. *DB* i, fo. 60v, records Fyfield among the lands of Henry de Ferrers in 1086, but states of ten hides that Godric the sheriff had held from the abbot.

[266] Sawyer, no. 758; *Charters of Abingdon Abbey*, no. 110. This charter also survives in a 16th-c. copy of a lost single sheet, Cambridge, Corpus Christi College 111, pp. 167–8.

of earthly servitude except these three, that is, fixed military service, and bridge and fortress repair. Moreover, if any presumptuous man, prompted by diabolical spirit, attempts to violate or change this gift, unless the offender does penance with worthy compensation before his death, let the mournful man eternally be laid down and punished in the eternal fires of Hell with Judas the betrayer of Christ.

78. *Concerning Fyfield.*[265]

Likewise, the king himself bestowed twenty-five hides at Fyfield on Abingdon, which Abbot Osgar obtained from him. This was established in the year from the birth of Christ 968, with the aforesaid bishops and other trustworthy witnesses affirming what was granted.

79. **(B200)** *Charter of King Edgar concerning Fyfield.*[266]

With our Lord Jesus Christ reigning in perpetuity, who by the order of the Father disposes of all things, with the grace of the Holy Spirit at the same time giving life. For, however much the words of priests and the decisions of judges constantly persist in the strength of security, nevertheless because of the uncertain changeableness of future years they should be strengthened by the testimony of written documents. Therefore I, Edgar, emperor of the whole of Britain, have bestowed as eternal inheritance a small portion of an estate, that is twenty-five hides in the place which is called by the well-known name of Fyfield, on our Lord Jesus Christ and on His holy church dedicated to the honour of His mother Mary, in the place which is called by the well-known name of Abingdon, for the use of the monks of God living therein, with all associated resources, that is meadows, pastures, and woods, under the charge of Abbot Osgar. Moreover, let the aforesaid land be free of every yoke of earthly servitude except three, that is, fixed military service, and bridge and fortress repair. If, therefore, anyone wishes to change this our gift into something other than we have established, let the mournful man be removed from the fellowship of the holy Church of God and be endlessly punished in the eternal fires of Hell with Judas the betrayer of Christ and his accomplices, if he does not make amends with fitting compensation for what he did wrong against our decision.

Charters of Abingdon Abbey, pp. 435–6, is tentative about the authenticity of this charter. It could be an authentic document drawn up at Abingdon, and the language of the boundary clause is 'linguistically credible for the 960s'. Alternatively, it may be a fabrication, possibly put together in the context of a dispute with Godric, the sheriff in 1066, or with Henry de Ferrers after the Conquest; below, p. 224. The date given in the version of the charter in MS B is 968.

[i. 267 n.] **80.** *De Cumenora.*

Item hoc eodem anno ipse rex largitus est apud Cumenora triginta mansas Abbendonensi ecclesie, [a]ea qua et alia constitutione,[a] [267] et eisdem consultoribus testibus.

[i. 267] **81. (B177)** *Carta [a]Eadgari regis[a] de Cumenora.*[268]

B fo. 66r Ego[b] Eadgar, totius Brittannie basileus, quandam telluris particulam, triginta uidelicet cassatos loco qui celebri[c] Cumenoran nuncupatur uocabulo, Domino nostro Ihesu Christo sancteque eius ecclesie beate
C fo. 122r Dei genitrice Marie dicate[d] loco qui celebri[e] Abbendune nun|cupatur[f] onomate ad usus monachorum Dei inibi degentium, cum omnibus utensilibus, pratis uidelicet, pascuis, siluis, Osgaro obtinente abbate, eterna largitus sum hereditate. Sit autem predictum rus omni terrene[g] seruitutis iugo liberum tribus exceptis, rata uidelicet expeditione, pontis arcisue restauratione. Si quis igitur hanc nostram donationem in aliud quam constituimus transferre uoluerit, priuatus consortio sancte Dei ecclesie eternis baratri incendiis lugubris iugiter cum Iuda Christi proditore eiusque complicibus puniatur, si non satisfactione emendauerit congrua quod contra nostrum deliquit decretum.[h]

[i. 273 n.] **82.** *De Hannie.*[269]

Item apud Hannie decem mansas rex idem, uti alia, concessit ecclesie Abbendonensi, eodem anno et eisdem fautoribus.

[i. 273] **83. (B180)** *[a]Carta Eadgari regis de Hannie.*[a] [270]

B fo. 67v Ego[b] Eadgar, totius Brittannie basileus, quandam telluris particulam, decem[c] uidelicet cassatos[271] loco qui celebri Hannie[d] nuncupatur uocabulo, Domino nostro Ihesu Christo sancteque eius ecclesie

80 [a] *the text may be corrupt here*

81 [a–a] regis Edgari *B* [b] *see Charters of Abingdon Abbey, p. 437, for the preceding invocation and proem in B* [c] *followed by* æt *B* [d] dedicate *B* [e] *followed by* æt *B* [f] *the side of the MS is damaged at top of page in C, so the text is here completed from B* [g] *C here has a hole in the parchment leading to omissions; the text is completed from B* [h] *see Charters of Abingdon Abbey, pp. 437–8, for the boundaries, dating clause, and witness list in B. The boundaries also appear in the quire of C devoted to such clauses, fo. 197v, Charters of Abingdon Abbey, p. 586 (no. 12)*

83 [a–a] Carta regis Edgari de Hannie uiginti cassatarum *B* [b] *see Charters of Abingdon Abbey, p. 440, for the preceding invocation and proem in B* [c] uiginti *over erasure*; .xx. *in margin B* [d] æt Hanige *B*

---

[267] The precise sense of this phrase must be uncertain because of the probable problems with the text.

[268] Sawyer, no. 757; *Charters of Abingdon Abbey*, no. 111, which, at pp. 435–6, is

80. *Concerning Cumnor.*
Likewise, in the same year, the king himself bestowed thirty hides at Cumnor on the church of Abingdon, by this as by the other decree,[267] and with the same counsellors as witnesses.

81. (B177) *Charter of King Edgar concerning Cumnor.*[268]
I, Edgar, emperor of the whole of Britain, have bestowed as eternal inheritance a small portion of an estate, that is thirty hides in the place called by the well-known name of Cumnor, on our Lord Jesus Christ and on His holy church dedicated to the blessed Mary mother of God in the place called by the well-known name of Abingdon, for the use of the monks of God living therein, with all associated resources, that is meadows, pastures, and woods, under the charge of Abbot Osgar. Moreover, let the aforesaid land be free of every yoke of earthly servitude except three, that is, fixed military service, and bridge and fortress repair. If, therefore, anyone wishes to change this our gift into something other than we have established, let the mournful man be removed from the fellowship of the holy Church of God and be endlessly punished in the eternal fires of Hell with Judas the betrayer of Christ and his accomplices, if he does not make amends with fitting compensation for what he did wrong against our decision.

82. *Concerning Hanney.*[269]
Likewise, the same king granted ten hides at Hanney to the church of Abingdon, as the others, in the same year and with the same witnesses.

83. (B180) *Charter of King Edgar concerning Hanney.*[270]
I, Edgar, emperor of the whole of Britain, have bestowed as eternal inheritance a small portion of an estate, that is ten hides[271] in the place called by the well-known name of Hanney, on our Lord Jesus Christ

suspicious of this charter, like the previous one, but does not rule out the possibility that it is a genuine Abingdon product. The date given in the version of the charter in MS B is 968.

[269] Berkshire.

[270] Sawyer, no. 759; *Charters of Abingdon Abbey*, no. 112, which, at p. 435, is suspicious of this charter, like the previous one, but does not rule out the possibility that it is a genuine Abingdon product, and notes that linguistically the boundary clause is credible for the 960s. The date given in the version of the charter in MS B is 968.

[271] MS B's emendation of the text to twenty hides may have been to bring it in line with King Eadwig's charter granting twenty hides at Hanney to his adoptive kinsman Ælfric; below, B133 (*Charters of Abingdon Abbey*, no. 55). *DB* i, fo. 59^r, records Abingdon holding ten hides in (East) Hanney. It may be that these ten formed only part of the land given to Ælfric. *DB* i, fos. 60^r, 61^v, record two other manors at (East) Hanney, amounting to a further twelve hides *TRE*.

beate Dei genitrice[e] Marie dicate loco qui celebri[f] Abbendune nuncupatur onomate ad usus monachorum Dei inibi[g] degentium, cum omnibus utensilibus, pratis uidelicet, pascuis, siluis, Osgaro obtinente abbate, eterna largitus sum hereditate. Sit autem predictum rus omni terrene seruitutis iugo liberum tribus exceptis, rata uidelicet
[i. 274] expeditione, pontis arcisue restauratione. Si quis igitur hanc nostram donationem in aliud quam constituimus transferre uoluerit, priuatus consortio sancte Dei ecclesie eternis baratri incendiis lugubris iugiter cum Iuda Christi proditore eiusque complicibus puniatur, si non satisfactione emendauerit congrua quod contra[h] nostrum deliquit decretum.[i]

[i. 276] 84. *De Ora.*[272]

Item apud Oran decem cassatos idem rex simili donatione ecclesie Abbendonensi, eodem anno et eisdem fautoribus, concessit.

B fo. 68r 85. (B181) [a]*Carta regis Eadgari de Ora.*[a] [273]

Ego[b] Eadgar, totius Brittannie basileus, quandam telluris particulam, decem uidelicet cassatos loco qui celebri[c] Oran nuncupatur uocabulo, Domino nostro Ihesu Christo sancteque eius ecclesie beate Dei genitrice[d] Marie dicate loco qui celebri[e] Abbendune nuncupatur onomate[f] ad usus monachorum Dei inibi degentium, cum omnibus utensilibus, pratis uidelicet, pascuis, siluis, Osgaro obtinente abbate,
[i. 277] eterna largitus sum hereditate. Sit autem predictum rus omni terrene seruitutis iugo liberum tribus exceptis, rata uidelicet expeditione, pontis arcisue restauratione. Si quis igitur hanc nostram donationem in aliud quam constituimus transferre uoluerit, priuatus consortio sancte Dei ecclesie eternis baratri incendiis lugubris iugiter[g] cum Iuda Christi proditore eiusque complicibus puniatur, si non satisfactione emendauerit congrua quod contra nostrum deliquit decretum.[h]

[e] genitriceque *B* [f] *followed by* æt *B* [g] ibidem *B* [h] *interlin. B* [i] *see Charters of Abingdon Abbey, pp. 440–1, for the boundaries, dating clause, and witness list in B. The boundaries also appear in the quire of C devoted to such clauses, fo. 197v, Charters of Abingdon Abbey, p. 586 (no. 11)*

85 [a–a] Carta regis Edgari de Ora decem cassatarum *B* [b] *see Charters of Abingdon Abbey, p. 443, for the preceding invocation and proem in B* [c] *followed by* æt *B* [d] genitrici, *corr. by erasure from* genitrice *B* [e] *followed by* æt *B* [f] onomante *B* [g] *om., but in dry point in margin B* [h] *see Charters of Abingdon Abbey, pp. 443–4, for the boundaries, dating clause, and witness list in B. The boundaries also appear in the quire of C devoted to such clauses, fo. 197v*

and on His holy church dedicated to the blessed Mary mother of God, in the place called by the well-known name of Abingdon, for the use of the monks of God living therein, with all associated resources, that is meadows, pastures, and woods, under the charge of Abbot Osgar. Moreover, let the aforesaid land be free of every yoke of earthly servitude except three, that is, fixed military service, and bridge and fortress repair. If, therefore, anyone wishes to change this our gift into something other than we have established, let the mournful man be removed from the fellowship of the holy Church of God and be endlessly punished in the eternal fires of Hell with Judas the betrayer of Christ and his accomplices, if he does not make amends with fitting compensation for what he did wrong against our decision.

84. *Concerning Oare.*[272]

Likewise, the same king granted ten hides at Oare by a similar gift to the church of Abingdon, in the same year and with the same supporters.

85. (B181) *Charter of King Edgar concerning Oare.*[273]

I, Edgar, emperor of the whole of Britain, have bestowed as eternal inheritance a small portion of an estate, that is ten hides in the place called by the well-known name of Oare, on our Lord Jesus Christ and on His holy church dedicated to the blessed Mary mother of God in the place called by the well-known name of Abingdon, for the use of the monks of God living therein, with all associated resources, that is meadows, pastures, and woods, under the charge of Abbot Osgar. Moreover, let the aforesaid land be free of every yoke of earthly servitude except three, that is, fixed military service, and bridge and fortress repair. If, therefore, anyone wishes to change this our gift into something other than we have established, let the mournful man be removed from the fellowship of the holy Church of God and be endlessly punished in the eternal fires of Hell with Judas the betrayer of Christ and his accomplices, if he does not make amends with fitting compensation for what he did wrong against our decision.

[272] These lands, in Berkshire, were probably included in *Domesday Book* within the abbey's manor of Chieveley; *DB* i, fo. 58^{v}.

[273] Sawyer, no. 760; *Charters of Abingdon Abbey*, no. 113, which, at p. 435, is suspicious of this charter, like the previous three, but does not rule out the possibility that it is a genuine Abingdon product. The date given in the version of the charter in MS B is 968.

[i. 279] **86. (B182)** [a]*Carta Eadgari regis de Bydene.*[a] [274]

B fo. 68v Confirmat nos sacre auctoritatis scriptura, dicens 'Nudus egressus sum ex utero matris mee, et nudus reuertar illuc', et iterum 'Nichil intulimus in hunc mundum, uerum nec ab eo auferre quid poterimus'.[275] Quapropter, lubrici potentatus non inmemor, ego Eadgar, Christo conferente rex et primicerius totius Albionis, regni fastigium humili presidens animo, ob remunerationem maioris premii, aliquantulam ruris particulam quinque comparatam[b] cassatis cui uocabulum C fo. 122v certa astipulatione Bydene | profertur ad ecclesiam beate Marie genitricis Dei ac Domini nostri Ihesu Christi in loco qui dicitur Abbendun[c] ad usus ibidem fratrum Deo seruientium libenter concedo, obsecrans et precipiens in nomine Domini[d] ut nemo successorum nostrorum superioris uel inferioris gradus hoc nostre deuotionis donum aliquo temeritatis aliquatenus instinctu dirumpat.[e] B fo. 69r Sit autem | predictum[f] tellus, quam ego cum consensu optimatum meorum prefato largitus sum cenobio, ab omni terrene seruitutis iugo libera, tribus his exceptis, rata uidelicet expeditione, pontis arcisue restauratione. Si quis autem, laruarico instinctus spiritu, hoc donum [i. 280] uiolare immutareue presumptuosus temptauerit, nisi digna satisfactione ante obitum suum reus penituerit, eternis baratri prostratus incendiis cum Iuda Christi proditore eternaliter lugubris puniatur.[g] Anno Dominice incarnationis .dcccclxv. scripta est hec carta, [h]supradictis testibus consentientibus.[h]

[i. 291] 87. *De Wiscelea.*[276]

Idem rex concessit cuidam suo ministro, uocabulo Wlfstan, decem mansas apud Wisclea, eo tenore, ut cuicumque post suum decessum heredi uellet donare libertatem donationis regia auctoritate inde haberet.[277] Vnde ille hanc ecclesiam de Abbendona heredem post exitum sue uite fecit, predictis fautoribus consentientibus, anno ab incarnatione Dominica .dcccclxviii..

86 [a–a] Carta regis Edgari de Bedene *B* [b] compatam *B* [c] Abbandun *B* [d] Christi *B* [e] disrumpat *B* [f] predicta *B* [g] Termini uero huius libri iacent in libro Ciuenlea *add. B, perhaps a reference to Charters of Abingdon Abbey, no. 45; see Kelly's comments at pp. 174, 188, 414* [h–h] *see Charters of Abingdon Abbey, pp. 409–10, for the witness list in B*

[274] Berkshire. Sawyer, no. 732; *Charters of Abingdon Abbey*, no. 103, which, at pp. 412–13, concludes of this charter and those concerning Marcham and Denchworth, above cc. 75, 77, that 'these are dubious texts, but it is impossible to dismiss them as obvious forgeries'. They may be Abingdon products, at the time they claim, or very soon after. However, Kelly is particularly doubtful concerning the authenticity of this charter; *Charters of Abingdon*

86. (B182) *Charter of King Edgar concerning Beedon.*[274]

The writing of sacred authority strengthens us, saying 'Naked came I out of my mother's womb and naked shall I return thither', and again 'We brought nothing into this world, and it is certain we can carry nothing out from it.'[275] Therefore, not unmindful of the transitoriness of power, I, Edgar, by Christ's appointing king and ruler of the whole of Albion, exercising this eminence of kingship humbly, with a view to payment of a greater reward, willingly grant a small portion of land totalling five hides, called by reliable statement Beedon, to the church of the blessed Mary mother of God and of our Lord Jesus Christ in the place called Abingdon, for the use of the brethren serving God there, entreating and ordering in the Lord's name that none of our successors, of higher or lower rank, prompted by any rashness break to any degree this gift of our devotion. Moreover, let the aforesaid estate, which I have bestowed on the aforementioned monastery with the consent of my leading men, be free of every yoke of earthly service except these three, that is, fixed military service, and bridge and fortress repair. Moreover, if any presumptuous man, prompted by diabolical spirit, attempts to violate or change this gift, unless the offender does penance with worthy compensation before his death, let the mournful man eternally be laid down and punished in the eternal fires of Hell with Judas the betrayer of Christ. This charter was written in the year of our Lord 965, with the above-written witnesses consenting.

87. *Concerning Whistley.*[276]

The same king granted ten hides at Whistley to a thegn of his named Wulfstan, on the following terms, that he would have by royal authority the freedom of gift concerning this, to give it to whomsoever he might wish as heir after his death.[277] Hence he made this church of Abingdon heir after the end of his life, with the aforesaid supporters consenting, in the year of our Lord 968.

Abbey, p. 414. She suggests that the bequest by Ealdorman Eadwine of Sussex, who died in 982, may well be the point at which Abingdon obtained the main estate at Beedon; see below, c. 108. *DB* i, fo. 58^{v}, records that Edward the Confessor had reduced Beedon's assessment from fifteen to eleven hides, and that it was assessed at ten hides *TRE*, eight in 1086.

275 Job 1: 21, 1 Tim. 6: 7.

276 Berkshire. It is uncertain whether in fact the estate did pass directly to Abingdon; see above, p. cxxvii. *DB* i, fo. 59^{r}, records that Abingdon held Whistley for ten hides *TRE*, for seven in 1086.

277 The identity of this thegn is not certain.

[i. 292] **88. (B187)** [a]*Carta de Wiscelea.*[a] [278]

B fo. 71v Regnante in perpetuum Domino nostro Ihesu Christo. Cunctis supernorum sacramenta donorum celitus perscrutantibus notum est quod non solum huius mundi status antiqui hostis fraude atque molimine deficiendo corrumpitur, uerum etiam in presentis uite prope consummato curriculo[b] humana prosperitas iniquorum hominum acri intentione et angore constringuntur.[c] Nunc ergo, dum nobis [d]est tempus[d] uenie, festinemus laqueum totis nisibus deuitare mortis dumque carnale possidemus[e] patrimonium spiritale exerceatur mercimonium, quo inter angelicos choros mereamur adipisci gaudia sine fine mansura. Quapropter ego Eadgar, rex Anglorum[f] ceterarumque gentium in circuitu persistentium gubernator et rector, cuidam[g] fideli ministro uocitato nomine Wlfstan decem mansas perpetualiter concedo in illo loco ubi iam dudum ruricole illius terre nomen indiderunt[h] Wisclea, quatinus habeat ac possideat quamdiu uitalis spiritus aluerit corpus. Cum autem dissolutionis sue dies aduenerit, cuicumque uoluerit heredi derelinquat, ceu supradiximus, in eternam hereditatem. Sit autem predicta donatio ab omni mundiali obstaculo
B fo. 72r libera, cum omnibus ad se rite pertinentibus, campis, | pascuis, pratis, siluis, exceptis istis tribus, expeditione, pontis arcisue constructione. Si quis uero hominum hanc meam donationem cum stultitie temeritate iactitando infringere certauerit, sit ipse grauibus per colla depressus catenis inter flammiuomas tetrorum demonum[i] cateruas, nisi prius hic ad satisfactionem uenire maluerit.[j]

[i. 310] **89.** *De Boxora.*[279]

Item idem rex concessit alteri sui ministro, uocabulo Ælfwino, decem mansas apud Boxoran, predicto tenore (et ita ad hanc ecclesiam ius illius peruenit), eodem anno et eisdem ut predictum est testibus confirmantibus.

88 [a–a] Carta regis Edgari de Wissele *B* [b] *the side of the MS is damaged at top of page in C, so the text is here completed from B* [c] constnguntur *B* [d–d] tempus est *B* [e] possedemus *C* [f] *C here has a hole in the parchment leading to omissions; the text is completed from B* [g] meo *add. B* [h] æt Wiscelea, quatenus *B* [i] *last three letters om., at end of line B* [j] *see Charters of Abingdon Abbey, pp. 431–2, for the dating clause and witness list in B*

[278] Sawyer, no. 769; *Charters of Abingdon Abbey*, no. 109, which, at p. 432, accepts the charter as 'probably authentic'. Neither manuscript provides boundaries. The date given in the version of the charter in MS B is 968.

[279] For the possibility that Ælfwine may have been a son of Ealhhelm ealdorman of Mercia, see above, p. cxxiii. This land had earlier been granted to Wulfric Cufing; see below, B107, B186 (*Charters of Abingdon Abbey*, nos. 77, 86). Boxford also appears in the

88. (B187) *Charter concerning Whistley.*[278]

With our Lord Jesus Christ reigning in perpetuity. It is known to all studying the hidden truths of celestial gifts from heaven that not only is the state of this world failing and corrupted by the fraud and exertion of the ancient enemy, but also in the near-completed course of the present life human prosperity is afflicted by the disagreeable attention and vexation of unjust men. Now therefore, while we have time to gain pardon, let us hasten with every endeavour to avoid the noose of death and, while we possess the carnal patrimony, let a spiritual transaction be performed by which we may deserve to acquire joys enduring without end amidst the angelic choruses. Therefore I, Edgar, king of the English and governor and ruler of the other peoples living round about, grant perpetually to a faithful thegn of mine, called by the name Wulfstan, ten hides in that place where the local inhabitants of that land have bestowed the name Whistley, so that he may have and possess it as long as the vital spirit nourishes his body. When, moreover, the day of his death comes, he may leave it to whomsoever he wishes as heir, as we said above, in eternal inheritance. Moreover, let the aforesaid gift be free of all worldly hindrance, with everything duly pertaining to it, fields, pastures, meadows, woods, except these three, military service, and bridge and fortress construction. If indeed any man strives to infringe this my gift, boasting with the rashness of stupidity, let him be pressed down with heavy chains around his neck amidst the flame-spewing bands of foul demons, unless previously he prefers to come to compensation here.

89. *Concerning Boxford.*[279]

Likewise, the same king granted ten hides at Boxford to another thegn of his, named Ælfwine, on the aforesaid terms (and hence his property came to this church), in the same year and with the same witnesses confirming as aforesaid.

charter for Abingdon in the name of King Coenwulf, above, c. 11, which may have been constructed in Æthelwold's time. *DB* i, fo. 58^{v}, under Abingdon's large manor of Welford, records the knight Berner holding two hides at Boxford from the abbey in 1086. *DB* i, fo. 63^{r}, records Humphrey Visdeloup having four hides there, once held 'in alodio' by three brothers from King Edward for nine hides, but this may long have been a separate manor; *Charters of Abingdon Abbey*, p. 319. It is possible that *Domesday* conceals the extent of Abingdon's holding in Boxford, only mentioning Berner's tenancy. A list dating from around the second quarter of the 12th c., and copied into MS C in the same hand as the *History*, states that there were ten hides in Boxford, of which Hugh son of Berner held two, 'men' held five and a quarter, and two and three-quarters were in demesne; vol. ii. 389.

[i. 311] **90. (B196)** [a]*Carta regis Eadgari de Boxora.*[a] [280]

B fo. 76r Omnium conditor creaturarum, cum in constitutione uergentis C fo. 123r mundi cuncta creasset ex nichilo, ceptamque[b] sui operis | perfectionem sexto die complesset, adiuncto sancte Trinitatis uocabulo inquit 'Faciamus hominem ad imaginem et similitudinem nostram'.[281] De | B fo. 76v cuius dormientis latere cum subtractam costam procreasset in feminam eamque in adiutorium eidem adduxisset, uocauit nomen eius Virago, quoniam sumpta est de uiro suo.[282] Quapropter quicquid adquiritur desudando fragilitas uiri, datur fecunde coniugi[c] procreandisque filiis et fidelibus seruis. Et si in tantum diligitur dilectio carnis, multo magis amari debetur amor eterni regis, qui dat cui uult filios, seruos, ac liberos, cunctosque suo nutu alit[d] et crescere[e] permittit. Vnde ego Eadgar, gratia Dei Anglorum rex pacificus, meo cuidam ministro nuncupato nomine Ælfwine,[f] pro suo fideli seruitio, tradens trado decem uidelicet mansas in loco cui antecessores ruricole imposuerunt nomen Boxoran, tali uidelicet tenore ut post sui dissolutionem corporis cuicumque placuerit amico in perpetuam concedat hereditatem. Predicta igitur uilla ab omni seculari seruitio permaneat absoluta, cum omnibus sibi impositis, exceptis tribus, populari expeditione, uiatici pontis restauratione, regie arcis constructione. Si quis ergo, inuidie stimulis stimulatus, hoc meum [g]inuadere temptauerit donum,[g] sit anathema, hoc est alienatus[h] a consortio Christianorum, nisi ad satisfactionem cum fructu penitentie uenire festinauerit.[i]

[i. 349 n.] **91.** *De temporibus Eadwardi regis.*[283]

Defuncto itaque rege Eadgaro, filius eius Eadwardus successit in regnum. Is[a] enim dum regnaret, de Kigestuna[b] [284] Abbendonensi[c] ecclesie septem hidas concessit, et de concessu his litteris roborauit:

90 [a–a] Carta Edgari regis de Boxora *B* [b] cœptamque *B* [c] coniugii *C;* coniugii *with final* i *interlin. B* [d] *corr. from* alio *C* [e] *corr., probably from* crescit *C* [f] Ælfwino *B* [g–g] donum inuadere temptauerit *B* [h] alienatio *B* [i] *see Charters of Abingdon Abbey, pp. 422–3, for the boundaries, dating clause, and witness list in B. The boundaries also appear in the quire of C devoted to such clauses, fos. 197v–198r, Charters of Abingdon Abbey, p. 586 (no. 13)*

91 [a] His *B C* [b] Kingestuna *B* [c] Abbendunensi *B*

[280] Sawyer, no. 761; *Charters of Abingdon Abbey*, no. 107, which, on grounds of the witness list (appearing only in MS B) and of various diplomatic aspects, states at p. 423 that this charter 'is unlikely to be authentic in its present form, although it may be based on an

90. (B196) *Charter of King Edgar concerning Boxford.*[280]

The Creator of all creatures, when He had created all things from nothing in the establishment of the finite world, and had on the sixth day accomplished the completion of His work as undertaken, having added the name of the Holy Trinity, said 'Let us make man in our image, after our likeness'.[281] When He had formed into a woman a rib taken from the man's side whilst sleeping and had brought her forward as a helper for him, He gave her the name Virago, since she was taken from her man.[282] Therefore whatever the weakness of man acquires by toiling is given to his fecund wife, and to his children who are to be begotten, and to his faithful servants. And if carnal affection is so greatly held in affection, much more should love of the eternal King be loved, who gives to whom He wishes children, slaves, and free men, and nourishes them all at his will, and allows them to grow. Wherefore I, Edgar, by the grace of God peaceable king of the English, hand over to a thegn of mine, called by the name Ælfwine, for his faithful service, ten hides, that is, in the place on which local forebears imposed the name Boxford, that is on the condition that he may grant it after the dissolution of his body to whatever friend he pleases in perpetual inheritance. Therefore the aforesaid village is to remain exempt from all secular service, with everything attached to it, except three, common military service, road bridge repair, royal fortress construction. If anyone, therefore, pricked by goads of envy, attempts to invade this my gift, let him be anathema, that is estranged from the fellowship of Christians, unless he hastens to come to compensation with the fruit of penance.

91. *Concerning the times of King Edward.*[283]

When therefore King Edgar died, his son Edward succeeded to the kingdom. While he was reigning, he granted seven hides at Kingston[284] to the church of Abingdon, and strengthened this grant with these letters:

authentic document and record a genuine transaction'. The date given in the version of the charter in MS B is 968. Ælfwine may be a thegn who was a regular witness of Edgar's charters from 958 to *c.*970; see *Charters of Abingdon Abbey*, p. 424.

281 Gen. 1: 26.

282 In the Latin, this statement links the form of the words 'virago' and 'vir' (cf. in English woman and man).

283 This section does not appear in MS B, but cf. below B210.

284 Kingston Bagpuize, Berkshire.

[i. 349] **92. (B211)** [a]*Carta septem cassatorum de Kingestun.*[a] [285]
B fo. 85v Confirmat nos sacre auctoritatis scriptura, dicens 'Nudus egressus
[i. 350] sum ex utero matris mee, et nudus reuertar illuc', et iterum 'Nichil
intulimus in hunc mundum, uerum nec ab eo auferre quid poter-
imus'.[286] Quapropter, lubrici potentatus non inmemor, ego Eadward,[b]
rex et primicerius totius Albionis, regni fastigium humili presidens
animo, ob remunerationem maioris premii, aliquantulam ruris parti-
B fo. 86r culam septem comparatam cassatis, cui uocabulum cer|ta astipula-
tione Kingestun[c] profertur, ad ecclesiam beate Marie genitricis Dei ac
Domini nostri Ihesu Christi in loco qui dicitur Abbendun[d] ad usus
ibidem fratrum Deo seruientium libenter concedo, obsecrans et
precipiens in nomine Christi ut nemo successorum nostrorum super-
ioris uel inferioris gradus hoc nostre deuotionis donum aliquo
temeritatis aliquatenus instinctu dirumpat.[e] Sit autem predicta
tellus, quam ego cum consensu optimatum meorum prefato largitus
sum cenobio, ab omni terrene seruitutis iugo libera, tribus his
exceptis, rata uidelicet expeditione, pontis arcisue restauratione. Si
quis autem, laruarico instinctus spiritu, hoc donum uiolare immutar-
eue presumptuosus temptauerit, nisi digna satisfactione ante obitum
suum reus penituerit, eternis baratri prostratus incendiis cum Iuda
[i. 351] Christi proditore eternaliter lugubris puniatur. [f]Anno Dominice
incarnationis .dccccclxv.[287] scripta est hec carta, his testibus: Ego
Eadwardus rex Anglorum prefatam donationem concessi. Ego Dun-
stanus archiepiscopus cum signo sancte crucis + roboraui. Ego
C fo. 123v Oswaldus archipresul | signum sancte crucis + impressi. Ego
Adelwoldus episcopus consignaui. Ego Alfstanus episcopus acquieui.
Ego Osgarus abbas, ego Escwi abbas, ego Adelgarus abbas consensi-
mus. Ego Alfhere dux, et Æthelwine dux, et Brithnodus dux
subscripsimus.[f]

92 [a–a] Carta Sancti Edwardi martiris de septem hidis in Kingestune *B* [b] Eadweard Christo conferente *B* [c] Cingestune *B* [d] Abbandun *B* [e] disrumpat *B* [f–f] *see Charters of Abingdon Abbey, pp. 451–2, for the boundaries, dating clause, and witness list in B*

[285] Sawyer, no. 829; *Charters of Abingdon Abbey*, no. 116, which, at p. 456, states of this charter and B212 (*Charters of Abingdon Abbey*, no. 117) that 'it is not easy to decide the status of these texts'. They could be classified as Abingdon forgeries made very soon after the purported grants, or they may be 'official and genuine (if incompetent) royal diplomas, drawn up at Abingdon between 975 and 978 with King Edward's permission'; note also the

92. (B211) *Charter regarding seven hides at Kingston.*[285]

The writing of sacred authority strengthens us, saying 'Naked came I out of my mother's womb and naked shall I return thither', and again 'We brought nothing into this world, and it is certain we can carry nothing out from it.'[286] Therefore, not unmindful of the transitoriness of power, I, Edward, king and ruler of the whole of Albion, exercising this eminence of kingship humbly, with a view to payment of a greater reward, willingly grant a small portion of land totalling seven hides, called by reliable statement Kingston, to the church of the blessed Mary mother of God and of our Lord Jesus Christ in the place called Abingdon, for the use of the brethren serving God there, entreating and ordering in Christ's name that none of our successors, of higher or lower rank, prompted by any rashness break to any degree this gift of our devotion. Moreover, let the aforesaid estate, which I have bestowed on the aforementioned monastery with the consent of my leading men, be free of every yoke of earthly service except these three, that is, fixed military service and bridge and fortress repair. Moreover, if any presumptuous man, prompted by diabolical spirit, attempts to violate or change this gift, unless the offender does penance with worthy compensation before his death, let the mournful man eternally be laid down and punished in the eternal fires of Hell with Judas the betrayer of Christ. In the year of our Lord 965[287] was written this charter, with these witnesses. I Edward king of the English have granted the aforementioned gift. I Archbishop Dunstan have strengthened with the sign of the holy cross +. I Archbishop Oswald have applied the sign of the holy cross +. I Bishop Æthelwold have joined in signing. I Bishop Ælfstan have agreed. I Abbot Osgar, I Abbot Æscwig, I Abbot Æthelgar have consented. I Ealdorman Ælfhere, and Ealdorman Æthelwine, and Ealdorman Byrhtnoth have subscribed.

opinions listed at the revised Sawyer, no. 829. The next chapter states that Abbot Osgar bought twenty hides at Kingston from Ealdorman Ælfhere. A charter in Edgar's name records him giving seven hides in Kingston (probably Kingston Bagpuize) to Brihtheah, a deacon, in 970; below, B190 (*Charters of Abingdon Abbey*, no. 114). The present charter may have been composed in the context of a reorganization of the twenty hides, which allowed thirteen of them to Bishop Ælfstan, probably the bishop of Ramsbury; see below, B212 (*Charters of Abingdon Abbey*, no. 117).

[286] Job 1: 21, 1 Tim. 6: 7.

[287] If this is a charter of Edward the martyr, this date is clearly an error.

[i. 354] **93. (B213)** [a]*De Kingestuna.*[a]

B fo. 87r [b]Item[288] de hac eadem terra in uetustissimis et pene consumptis litteris ita Anglice scriptum repperimus:[b][289]

[i. 355] Alfheagus[c] princeps hereditauit Alferum principem de uiginti hidis apud Kingestuna.[d] Tunc rogauit Osgarus abbas ipsum Alferum principem quatinus sibi permitteretur propriari pretio [e]ipsa terra.[e] Cui annuit idem princeps, et ipse[f] abbas[g] dedit centum mancosas auri.[290] Et contigit illo tempore, circa Paschale tempus, haberi concilium[h] apud locum qui Ædelwaraburh[i] dicitur,[291] et illic senioribus qui intererant de[j] hoc relatum est, scilicet Athelwoldo[k] episcopo, et Ædelstano[l] episcopo,[292] et Ædelgaro[m] abbati,[293] Eadwino[294] et Alfrico cognomento puer,[295] et alio Alfrico filio Siraui, et Brithrico[n] illius fratri,[o] cum his et multis aliis. Et istud factum est in plurimorum testimonio. Huius etiam scripti diuisionem recepit ipse princeps iam predictus pro ostensione.

[i. 356] **94.** *De Sidemanno episcopo.*[296]

Anno tercio huius regis, concilio apud Kyrtlincgtun Paschali tempore constituto,[297] Sidemannus (unus eorum qui intererant) Defnescire episcopus, subitanea arreptus egritudine, ibidem defungitur. Cuius

93 [a–a] Quomodo Osgarus abbas emit uiginti hidas in Kingestune *B* [b–b] *om. B* [c] Alfhegus *B* [d] Gingestun *B* [e–e] ipsam terram *B* [f] *om. B* [g] illi *add. B* [h] *om. B* [i] Adelwareburh *B* [j] *erased B* [k] Aþelwoldo *B* [l] Aþelstano *B* [m] Aþelgaro *B* [n] Brihtrico *B* [o] *corr. from* fratre *by erasure C,* fratre *B*

[288] Gelling, *Early Charters of the Thames Valley*, p. 59, suggests that the land concerned may be Kingston Lisle. She rejects Kingston Bagpuize because of the discrepancy with the *Domesday* record of the latter as consisting of two estates of five hides each, both in lay hands *TRE*. However, she does not consider the combination of the thirteen and seven hides grants mentioned above, p. 134 n. 285, nor take into account the frequency of hidage reductions between the 10th-c. charters and *Domesday Book* or the possibility that the hidage has been tampered with in the present document. It may only be the compiler's own interpretation that Ælfheah's grant concerned land in the same Kingston as King Edward's. However, the other documents suggest that the compiler's interpretation was correct.

[289] The present text is a Latin translation of a vernacular record included in the quire of MS C devoted to charter boundaries; MS C, fo. 202r; Sawyer, no. 1216; *Charters of Abingdon Abbey*, no. 115; *Anglo-Saxon Charters*, ed. Robertson, no. 51; also trans. Stenton, *Early History*, pp. 36–7. *Charters of Abingdon Abbey*, p. 450, suggests that the original vernacular version may have been the Abingdon half of a cirograph. It is plausible that the hidage has been tampered with in copying, perhaps in the context of later disputes over the land; *Charters of Abingdon Abbey*, p. 450. Kingston does not appear in the will of Ælfheah, who died in 971 (Sawyer, no. 1485; *Anglo-Saxon Wills*, ed. Whitelock, no. 9). Stenton, *Early History*, p. 37, and Gelling, *Early Charters of the*

93. (B213) *Concerning Kingston.*

Likewise,[288] concerning the same land, we have found what follows written in English in very old and almost worn-away letters:[289]

Ealdorman Ælfheah made Ealdorman Ælfhere heir concerning twenty hides at Kingston. Then Abbot Osgar asked Ealdorman Ælfhere himself that he be permitted to acquire ownership of that land by payment. That ealdorman agreed to this, and the abbot himself gave one hundred mancuses of gold.[290] And it happened at that time, around the time of Easter, that a council was held at the place called Alderbury,[291] and there this matter was recounted to those high-ranking men who were present, that is Bishop Æthelwold, and Bishop Æthelstan,[292] and Abbot Æthelgar,[293] and Eadwine,[294] and Ælfric surnamed 'Cild',[295] and another Ælfric the son of Siraf, and Beorhtric his brother, with these and many others. And this was done in the witness of very many. Also the aforesaid ealdorman received a portion of this document as evidence.

94. *Concerning Bishop Sidemann.*[296]

In the third year of this king, a council was held at Kirtlington at Easter time,[297] and Bishop Sidemann of Devonshire (one of those who was present) was seized by a sudden illness and died there. By order of the

Thames Valley, p. 59, raise the possibility that Kingston was associated with one of the places mentioned in the will, most likely Faringdon, Berkshire, but *Charters of Abingdon Abbey*, p. 449, rejects this idea on the grounds that all the evidence points to Kingston being a separate estate. Kelly suggests instead that Ælfheah may have acquired the estate after his will was drawn up.

290 A *mancus* was worth 30 silver pence.

291 Wiltshire. On the basis of the witness list and on the OE text's reference to the meeting as a 'micel gemot', Stenton, *Early History*, p. 37, comments that this was a special assembly, similar in kind to meetings of several shires in one place after the Norman Conquest.

292 Bishop Ælfstan in the Old English version.

293 Abbot of New Minster, Winchester, 964–?988, and also bishop of Selsey 980–8; *Heads of Religious Houses*, pp. 80–1, 258. His promotion to the bishopric probably provides a *terminus ante quem* for the present document. He was archbishop of Canterbury 988–90.

294 *Charters of Abingdon Abbey*, p. 450, suggests this may be the ealdorman of Sussex mentioned below, c. 108, or the brother of Ælfric Cild who became abbot of Abingdon, below, c. 96.

295 Ælfhere's brother-in-law, and successor as earl of Mercia.

296 See above, pp. lxi–lxii, for its relationship to an extremely similar passage in *ASC*, 'B' and 'C', *s.a.* 977. Sidemann was bishop of Crediton between 973 and 977; *Handbook of British Chronology*, p. 215.

297 Kirtlington, Oxfordshire. Easter fell on 8 Apr. 977, and Sidemann died on 30 Apr. according to *ASC*, 'C'.

corpus iussu regis ac Dunstani archiepiscopi Abbendonam defertur et in porticu sancti Pauli apostoli illic decenter humatur.[298]

95. (cf. B214) *De interfectione Eadwardi regis.*[299]

Nec multo post rex Ædwardus, nil mali erga quemlibet sua pro simplici conuersatione autumans, nefandorum insidiis Quadragesimalibus diebus immerito perimitur. Diuulgato per Anglie populos de regis nece uero indicio, in unum coadunati Ædelredum eiusdem germanum in regnum substituunt. Qui, ubi imperitandi iubendique nactus est potestatem, religioni minus intendere, prauorum consultui se committere, pro libitu multa facere. Adeo ecclesie Abbendonie prauorum commonitu infestus extitit, ut queque pater eius de suis dominiis possessionibus illic deuote contulerat ipse irreuerenter[a] suis restitueret usibus.

Hec dum in regno mouentur, ecclesiarum ualde necessarius defensor, Adelwoldus[b] episcopus sanctissimus, e seculo rapitur.[300] Sed et pie memorie domnus Osgarus, pro eo Abbendonie abbas substitutus, illo uite ultima sortitur.[301] In huiusmodi infortunio locus iste sine defensionis fit obstaculo.

[i. 357] **96. (cf. B215)** [a]*De Eadwio abbate.*[a] [302]

Erat tunc maior regie domus Ælfricus[b] quidam prepotens,[c] fratrem habens Eadwinum nomine,[303] monachum[d] institutione. Hic apud regem pretio egit[e] ut is[f] frater eius Abbendonie abbas preficeretur.[304] In quo distrahitur rerum abbatie copia, tepescit deintus ac deforis predicande [g]fame gratia.[g] Qua etiam tempestate gens Danorum, multa cum classe, in Angliam appulsa, incursare ubique, incendere, diripere omnia, multos necare, alios in captionem mittere cepit.[305] Cui rex inbellis, non armis sed pecunia obuiare optimum ratus, uectigal

95 [a] irreuerentur *B* [b] Aþelwoldus *B*

96 [a–a] De Edwino abbate *B* [b] Edricus *B* [c] prepotes, filius Ælferi ducis Merciorum, *B* [d] monacum *B* [e] exegit *B* [f] his *B* [g–g] gratie fama *B*

[298] A similar sentence, but omitting mention of the king and Dunstan, appears in the Abingdon version of the Worcester *Chronicle* preserved in Lambeth Palace Library; John of Worcester, *Chronicle*, ii. 613. *ASC*, 'B' and 'C', *s.a.* 977, specify that Sidemann was buried on the north side of the chapel. On burials at Abingdon, see above, p. cxxi.

[299] The beginning of this section, up to 'When he acquired . . .', does not appear in MS B; for that manuscript's different treatment of these matters, see below, B214.

[300] Æthelwold died on 1 Aug. 984; Wulfstan, *Life of Æthelwold*, c. 41, ed. Lapidge and Winterbottom, p. 62; Cambridge, University Library, Kk. i 22, fo. 5[r].

[301] Osgar's death is also mentioned in the Abingdon versions of the Worcester *Chronicle*; John of Worcester, *Chronicle*, ii. 613. An Abingdon obit list, Oxford, Bodleian Library, Digby 227, dates Osgar's death to 24 May; *Heads of Religious Houses*, pp. 23, 240.

king and Archbishop Dunstan his body was taken to Abingdon and fittingly buried there in the chapel of St Paul the Apostle.[298]

95. (cf. B 214) *Concerning the death of King Edward.*[299]
Not long after, King Edward, asserting no evil towards anyone on account of his own simple way of life, was undeservedly killed by the treachery of wicked men during the days of Lent. When information concerning the death of the king spread among the peoples of England, united as one they substituted his brother Æthelred into the kingship. When he acquired the power of ruling and ordering, he paid too little attention to religion, entrusted himself to the counsel of evil men, and did many deeds at will. He was so hostile to the church of Abingdon on the evil men's advice that he irreverently restored to his own use whatever his father had devoutly conferred on it from his own demesne possessions.

While these events were going on in the kingdom, the greatly needed defender of churches, the most holy Bishop Æthelwold, was seized from the world.[300] Also lord Osgar, of pious memory, who had been substituted for Æthelwold as abbot of Abingdon, was allotted the end of his life.[301] Amidst misfortune of this sort that monastery came to be without defensive protection.

96. (cf. B215) *Concerning Abbot Eadwine.*[302]
There was then a leading man of the royal household, Ælfric, a very powerful man, who had a brother, Eadwine by name,[303] a monk by rule.[304] Ælfric by bribing the king arranged that his brother be appointed abbot of Abingdon.[305] Under him, much of the abbey's property was taken away and the grace of its praiseworthy reputation cooled within and without. Also at that time the people of the Danes, with a great fleet, came ashore in England and began to attack everywhere, to burn, to ravage everywhere, to kill many, and to send others into captivity.[305] The unwarlike king considered it best to meet this not with arms but money and imposed a very heavy tribute

[302] MS B contains a very similar section, but replaces the passage 'Also at that time . . . for payment' with a different one; below, B215.

[303] On Abbot Eadwine and the identification of Ælfric, see above, p. cxxiii. Cf. also below, B215.

[304] Two almost identical sentences appear in the Abingdon versions of the Worcester *Chronicle*, followed by 'Quod et factum est'; John of Worcester, *Chronicle*, ii. 613.

[305] On the limited evidence for Viking attacks on England in the 980s, see S. Keynes, 'The historical context of the Battle of Maldon', in D. G. Scragg, ed., *The Battle of Maldon, AD 991* (Oxford, 1991), pp. 81–113, at 85–6. It could be that the *History* wrongly associates losses in Eadwine's abbacy and those due to Viking attacks.

B fo. 87v populo Anglorum satis ad persoluendum graue iniungit.[306] | His uniuersis calamitatibus, Abbendonense cenobium, paulo ante ditissimum, plurimarum iam incurrit suarum rerum in[h] periculum.[307]

97. (B216) [a]*De Wulfgaro abbate.*[a]

Sed qui Petro apostolo inter marinos fluctus labanti porrexit manus, C fo. 124r ipse dignatur ecclesie sue | discrimina releuare.[308] Nam fere sexennio predictis ingruentibus aduersis exacto, Eadwinus abbatie prepositus defungitur ac domnus Wlgarus substituitur, uir maxima probitate perspicuus et imminenti articulo temporis ad ecclesie libertatis restitutionem necessarius.[309] Regis etiam animus, hactenus ergo[b] cenobium istud obstinatus, in melius conuertitur ac pro hoc abbatem [i. 358] pro bonitate quam in eo didicerat diligere, uenerari, et admonitis ipsius se subdere cepit.[310] Quare Abbendonense cenobium iterum a cunctis ueneratur et colitur, et qui apud regem excellentius erant ipsum de honore eiusdem loci cotidie suggerebant. Huiusmodi frequenti commonitu adeo erga Dei timorem et ecclesie uenerationem rex commutatur ut in multitudinis frequentia fateretur[c] in his que ad se deferebantur[d] grauiter se errasse. Deinde prouidit que pro rebus ecclesie hactenus detentis condigna forent solutioni. Super hoc et libertatis libellum edidit, in quo omnem circa hunc[e] locum simoniacam sectam fieri,[311] tam se uiuente[f] quam successoribus suis in reliquum regnantibus, anathemate perpetuo interdixit. Cuius seriei talis fuit prosecutio:

98. (B217) [a]*Priuilegium Æthelredi regis.*[a] [312]

[i. 359] Ego,[b] inquit,[c] Æthelredus,[d] altithrono[e] adminiculante[f] Anglorum ceterarum[g] gentium in circuitu triuiatim persistentium basileus, [i. 360] non inmemor angustiarum mihi[h] meeque[i] nationi septimo regni mei

[h] *erased B*

97 [a–a] De morte Edwini abbatis *B* [b] erga *B* [c] *followed by* ut *B* [d] deferbantur *B* [e] huc *B* [f] seuiente, *corr. from* seuientem *B*

98 [a–a] De priuilegio Adelredi regis *B* [b] *see Charters of Abingdon Abbey, pp. 477–8, for the preceding proem and exposition in A and B* [c] *om. A* [d] Æþelræd *A;* Aþelredus *B* [e] altitrono *B* [f] aminiculante *A* [g] ceterarumque *A* [h] michi *A* [i] *here and elsewhere A uses the diphthong -æ for the ending*

[306] The *Anglo-Saxon Chronicle* records the first payment of tribute under the year 991; the *History* appears to be accumulating disasters within the abbacy of Eadwine.

[307] A charter restoring Moredon, Wiltshire, to Abingdon, below, c. 102, specifies that the land had been unjustly acquired from the abbey in the time of Abbot Eadwine.

[308] See Matt. 14: 30–3.

on the English people for payment.[306] Amidst all these calamities, the monastery of Abingdon, which had been extremely rich a little before, now met with loss of a great many of its possessions.[307]

97. (B216) *Concerning Abbot Wulfgar.*

But He who stretched out a hand to Peter the apostle floundering amidst the waves of the sea, deigned to relieve the crises of His church.[308] For when nearly six years had passed with these threatening misfortunes, Eadwine, overseer of the abbey, died and lord Wulfgar replaced him, a perspicuous man of the greatest probity and needed for the restoration of the church's liberty in that threatening crisis.[309] For the king's mind, hitherto inflexible towards that monastery, was changed for the better and correspondingly began to love and venerate this abbot, and subject himself to his advice, on account of the goodness which he had learnt to love in him.[310] Therefore the monastery of Abingdon was again venerated and revered by all, and those who were pre-eminent around the king daily prompted him about the honour of that monastery. By frequent advice of this type the king was so transformed to fear of God and veneration of the Church that he admitted amidst a great crowd of people that he had erred grievously in those matters of which he was accused. Then he provided what would be suitable payment for those possessions of the church that hitherto had been withheld. In addition, he issued a charter of liberty, in which he forbade by perpetual anathema, both during his own lifetime and during the reigns of his successors in future, all simoniacal suit concerning this monastery.[311] The following was the wording of the contents of this:

98. (B217) *Privilege of King Æthelred.*[312]

I, he said, Æthelred, with the support of the One enthroned on high emperor of the English and of the other peoples living round about, far and wide, not unmindful of the afflictions frequently and manifoldly befalling me and my nation in the seventh year of my

[309] For the dating of Eadwine's death to 17 Apr. 990, and for Abbot Wulfgar, see above, p. xcix.

[310] For Æthelred's change of attitude to the Church and to Abingdon, see Keynes, *Diplomas*, pp. 186–93, esp. p. 191 for Wulfgar.

[311] 'Simoniacal suit' probably refers to the purchase of the abbacy for Eadwine, referred to in the preceding chapter and in the charter which follows.

[312] Sawyer, no. 876; *Charters of Abingdon Abbey*, no. 124. The original charter also survives; London, British Library, Cotton Aug. ii. 38, reproduced in *BM Facs.*, iii. 36. On the authenticity of this document and its relationship to earlier diplomas, see above, p. cxcix–cciv.

anno et deinceps frequenter ac multipliciter accidentium, post decessum uidelicet beate memorie mihique[j] interno amore dilectissimi Æthelwoldi[k] episcopi, cuius industria ac pastoralis cura non solum mee uerum etiam uniuersorum huius patrie, tam prelatorum quam subditorum, utilitati, superno plasmatore inspirante, consuluit, mecum plurima uoluere tacitus cepi et que tantorum causa periculorum existeret studiose percunctari sollicitus curaui. Tanto igitur talique studio magnopere[l] incitatus, et archana queque diligenti cura | B fo. 88r mecum examinans, tandem Domini compunctus[m] gratia, ad memoriam reduxi partim hec infortunia pro mee iuuentutis ignorantia—que diuersis [n]uti solet[n] moribus—partim etiam pro quorundam illorum detestanda philargiria qui mee utilitati consulere debebant,[o] accidisse. Siquidem inter cetera memorie occurrit, me rogatu quorundam (talium Wlfgari scilicet episcopi defuncti atque ducis Alfrici[p] qui adhuc superest), sacri Abbendonensis[q] cenobii[r] libertatem pro munere in seruitutem redegisse,[313] quod prefatus beate memorie episcopus Æthelwoldus[s] a predecessoribus meis, Eadredo scilicet rege patruo patris mei, necnon et a patruo meo rege Eadwio,[t] nec minus et a patre meo rege uidelicet Eadgaro, ad usum monachorum, Domino[u] Ihesu Christo eiusque genitrici Marie, humilitatis et obedientie ceterarumque uirtutum meritis in eternam promeruit hereditatem, et in perhennem adquisiuit libertatem. Hec igitur mecum uigilanti pectore uoluens et citius a tanto tamque exhorrendo anathemate liberari [i. 361] cupiens, anno Dominice incarnationis .dccccxciii., mei autem regni septimo decimo,[314] sinodale concilium Wintonie in die sancto Pentecosten fieri iussi, illucque episcopis et abbatibus ac ceteris optimatum C fo. 124v meorum primoribus uerba salutaria[v] | et pacifica benignissime destinaui, cunctosque, Christi inspirante gratia, monui ut queque superno creatori digna, queque spirituali[w] anime mee saluti, seu regali mee dignitati congrua, queque etiam omni Anglorum populo oportuna ualerent, Domino consulente in commune tractarent, uouens [x]me etiam,[x] uita comite, et retro actas ad purum cohercere negligentias et, iuxta predecessorum meorum decreta, Ihesu Christo Domino

[j] michique *A* [k] Adelwoldi *A*, Aþelwoldi *B* [l] magno opere *B* [m] conpunctus *A* [n–n] solet uti *A; corrected by erasure from* uti solet uti *C* [o] debeant *B* [p] Ælfrici *A* [q] Æbbandunensis *A;* Abbendunensis *B* [r] coenobii *A* [s] Adelwold *A*, Aþelwoldus *B* [t] Eadwige *A* [u] *followed by* nostro *interlin. B* [v] salutatoria *A* [w] spiritali *A* [x–x] etiam me *A*

[313] See above, p. 138, and below, p. 144, on Ealdorman Ælfric obtaining Abingdon for his brother Eadwine. Wulfgar was bishop of Ramsbury 981–85/6; *Handbook of British*

reign and thereafter, that is following the death of Bishop Æthelwold of blessed memory and most beloved to me with the deepest love, whose industry and pastoral care counselled not only for my benefit but also that of all of this land, both dignitaries and subjects, inspired by the heavenly Creator, have begun silently to turn over many matters in my mind and anxiously have taken care to investigate studiously what is the cause of such great dangers. So, having been thoroughly aroused to such great study and, examining certain mysteries with diligent care, at length having my conscience pricked by the Lord's grace, I have recalled to my memory that these misfortunes happened partly because of the ignorance of my youth—which is accustomed to practise different behaviour—partly also because of the detestable covetousness of those men who ought to counsel me for my benefit. Amongst other things, indeed, it came to my memory that, at the request of certain such men (Bishop Wulfgar, now deceased, and Ealdorman Ælfric, who is still alive), for payment I had reduced to servitude the liberty of the sacred monastery of Abingdon,[313] which the aforementioned Bishop Æthelwold of blessed memory had deserved in eternal inheritance by the qualities of humility and obedience and other virtues, and acquired in perennial liberty from my predecessors, that is King Eadred my father's uncle, and also from my uncle King Eadwig, and not less from my father, that is King Edgar, for the use of the monks, for our Lord Jesus Christ and His mother Mary. Therefore wakefully pondering these matters and desiring to be more swiftly freed from so great and so fearsome an anathema, in the year of our Lord 993, moreover the seventeenth of my reign,[314] I ordered a synodal council to be held at Winchester on the day of holy Pentecost [4 June 993], and I most kindly sent salutary and peaceful words thither to the bishops and abbots and other leading men amongst my nobles, and inspired by Christ's grace I advised all that together they discuss by the Lord's counsel all things that may be worthy for the heavenly Creator, all such as may be fitting for the spiritual salvation of my soul, or for my royal dignity, also what may be advantageous for the whole people of the English, vowing also that I, as long as I live, will both purge past neglectful acts and, according to the decisions of my predecessors,

Chronology, p. 220. He was diocesan bishop of Abingdon, and hence may have had an interest in reduction of the monastery's liberty.

[314] The correct regnal year would be the sixteenth. It could be that the scribe of the original has simply written an extra minim; Keynes, *Diplomas*, p. 251; *Charters of Abingdon*, p. cxii.

nostro eiusque genitrici priscum restituere libertatis cirographum.[y] Hoc illi meo, immo Christi, monitu simul et hortatu magnopere[z] delectati, uoti compotes saluatori Christo gratias egerunt et queque condigna salubriter instituta sanxerunt pacto spirituali[a] confirmauerunt.

Nunc autem ego Æthelred,[b] Anglorum Christo opitulante basileus, quo debitum uoti mei factis adimpleam, et ut eterne libertatis altithroni[c] moderatoris clementia merear obtinere consortium, pretium quod mihi[d] dux prefatus Ælfric[e] pro fratris sui Eadwini prioratu contulit,[315] quo prefata Christi sancteque eius genitricis hereditas iniqua seruitute est uenundata, perpetualiter anathematizando reicio, et, gratuita Domini inspirante gratia meorumque optimatum tam laicorum quam ordinatorum rogatus simul et usus consilio, eiusdem[f] sancte Christi genitricis ecclesie[g] monachisque inibi degentibus eternam priuilegii ut predecessores mei renouandam concedo libertatem.
B fo. 88v [i. 362] Huius et enim renouande libertatis auctoritas Christi | auctoritate nostraque largitate concessa et corroborata est die sexto decimo kalendarum Augustarum in oratorio uici qui usitato Gillingaham nominari solet,[316] misseque celebratione peracta sub horum testium presentia me assensum prebente confirmata est, abbatis scilicet Ælfsini, consanguinei[h] mei Ædelmari,[i] necnon et auunculi mei Ordulfi;[317] ac prioratum prefati Abbendonensis[j] cenobii[k] in manu ac[l] potestate Wlfgari abbatis, mihi[m] humillima deuotione subiecti, gratis sine pretio uoluntarie renouando commisi.[n] [318] Hancque priuilegii libertatem, tam sibi quam cuncte simul eiusdem sancte ecclesie congregationi, pro mille quingentis missarum sollempniis[o] ac mille ducentis psalteriorum melodiis quas spontanea deuotione pro eterna anime mee redemptione decantauerunt, eternaliter renouandam cum sancte crucis impressione concessi; quatinus post decessum eiusdem prefati abbatis Wlfgari, cuius temporibus hec ipsa libertatis restauratio,

[y] cyrographum *A* [z] magno opere *B* [a] spiritali *A* [b] Æþelræd *A;* Aþelred *B*
[c] altitroni *B* [d] michi *A* [e] Alfric *B* [f] eidem *A* [g] aeclesiae *A*
[h] consanguineique *A*, que *interlin.* *B* [i] Æþlmæri *A*, Aþelmari *B*
[j] Æbbandunensis *A*, Abbendunensis *B* [k] coenobii *A* [l] et *A* [m] michi *A*
[n] *corr. from* commissi *B* [o] sollemniis *A*

[315] i.e. the abbacy. Note *Regularis Concordia*, Prooem. 7, 10, ed. Symons, pp. 4, 7, for uses of *prioratus* in relation to spiritual and secular authority respectively.

[316] Keynes, *Diplomas*, p. 101, states that is impossible to decide whether this is the Gillingham in Dorset, Kent, or Norfolk, but proposes the Dorset Gillingham, as it was a royal manor in *Domesday Book*; *DB* i, fo. 75r.

[317] Abbot Ælfsige is almost certainly Ælfsige abbot of New Minster, Winchester, ?988–

restore the old cirograph of liberty to Jesus Christ our Lord and His mother. Greatly pleased with this my, or rather Christ's, advice and exhortation, those who had obtained what they desired gave thanks to Christ the saviour and whatever they ratified as worthily and profitably instituted they confirmed by spiritual agreement.

Now moreover, I, Æthelred, with Christ's assistance emperor of the English, in order that I may fulfil in actions the debt of my vow, and so that I may deserve to obtain a share of eternal liberty by the mercy of the Judge enthroned on high, reject with perpetual anathematizing the payment that the aforementioned Ealdorman Ælfric conferred on me for the office of authority[315] of his brother Eadwine, whereby the aforementioned inheritance of Christ and His holy mother was sold in unjust servitude, and, inspired by the freely given grace of the Lord and having asked and taken the counsel of my leading men, both lay and ordained, like my predecessors I grant the eternal liberty of privilege that needs to be renewed to the church of that holy mother of Christ and the monks living therein. And indeed the authority of this liberty that needed to be renewed was granted and strengthened by the authority of Christ and by our own bestowal on 17 July in the church of the place that is accustomed by usage to be called Gillingham.[316] And when the celebration of mass had been completed, it was confirmed with my assent in the presence of these witnesses, that is Abbot Ælfsige, my kinsman Æthelmar, and also my uncle Ordulf.[317] I freely, without the payment needing to be renewed, and willingly entrusted the office of authority of the aforementioned monastery of Abingdon to the hand and power of Abbot Wulfgar, subject to me with humble devotion.[318] And with the mark of the holy cross I have granted that this liberty of privilege ought eternally to be renewed, both for himself and at the same time for the whole congregation of that holy church, for 1,500 solemn masses and 1,200 singings of psalters which they have sung with spontaneous devotion for the eternal redemption of my soul; inasmuch as after the death of that aforementioned Abbot Wulfgar, in whose times, with Christ's aid, this restoration of liberty was granted the entire

1007; *Heads of Religious Houses*, pp. 81, 225, 298. Æthelmaer was son of Æthelweard ealdorman of the western provinces. He was probably King Æthelred's *discthegn*. He founded the abbeys of Cerne and Eynsham, and was a patron of Ælfric. Ordulf founded Tavistock abbey. Their appearances as witnesses in royal diplomas suggests that they were leading associates of the king in the 990s and early 1000s; see Keynes, *Diplomas*, p. 192.

[318] The emphasis on the freedom from payment, and in the subsequent passage on free election, relates to the previous sale of office to Eadwine.

Christo suffragante, concessa est, quem sibi uniuersa prefati cenobii[p] congregatio apto elegerit consilio, secundum regularia beati Benedicti instituta, abbatem iuste[q] [r]ex eodem[r] fratrum cuneo eligens constituat.

Huius[s] priuilegii libertas deinceps [t]perpetuo usu[t] a cunctis teneatur catholicis, nec extraneorum quispiam tirannica[u] fretus contumatia in predicto monasterio ius arripiens exerceat potestatis, sed eiusdem cenobii[v] collegium perpetue, ut predixi, libertatis glorietur priuilegio. Sit autem prefatum monasterium omni terrene seruitutis iugo[w] eodem tenore liberum quo a predecessoribus nostris catholicis, a sancto Leone uidelicet papa et Kenulfo[x] rege catholico, uetusto
[i. 363] continetur priuilegio Rethuno[y] abbate optinente[z] solutum.[319] Agri equidem ad usus monachorum [a]Ihesu Christo Domino[a] eiusque genitrici Marie priscis modernisque temporibus a regibus et religiosis
C fo. 125r utriusque sexus ho|minibus et a meipso meoque patre Eadgaro rege fratreque[b] eius meo patruo rege Eadwio[c] eorumque patruo scilicet rege Eadredo fidelissimo restituendo iure concessi sunt, eiusdem perpetue sint libertatis.[320] Nam reges prefati rus[d] Abbendun[e] nuncupatur, quod rex Ceadwalla[f] Domino nostro eiusque genitrici Marie priscis temporibus deuoto concesserat animo, in quo predecessores nostri (diabolica decepti auaritia) edificium sibi regale iniuste construxerant, ecclesie[g] Dei restituentes, interdixerunt ut regum nemo inibi pastum requireret nec edificium in sempiternum construeret.[321] Quod ego Æthelred[h] Anglorum basileus, optimatum meorum usus consilio, tam meis quam meorum successorum temporibus, fixum in nomine Patris et Filii et Spiritus Sancti fieri in eternum precipio. Tempore siquidem quo rura, que Domino deuote per hoc modernum |
B fo. 89r priuilegium restauraui animo, iniuste a sancta Dei ecclesia[i] ablata fuerant, perfidi quique nouas sibi hereditarias cartas[j] usurpantes ediderunt. Sed in Patris et Filii et Spiritus Sancti nomine precipimus ut catholicorum nemo easdem recipiat, sed a cunctis repudiate fidelibus in anathemate deputentur, ueteri iugiter uigente priuilegio. Si quis uero tam [k]epilempticus philargirie[k] seductus amentia (quod non optamus) hanc nostre munificentie renouatam libertatem ausu temerario infringere temptauerit, sit ipse alienatus a consortio sancte

[p] coenobii *A* [q] iusta *C*, iusta *corr. to* iuste *B* [r–r] exodem *A* [s] Euius *B* [t–t] usu perpetuo *A* [u] tyrannica *A* [v] coenobii *A* [w] *om. A* [x] Coenulfo *A* [y] Hrethuno *A*, Retuno *B* [z] obtinente *B* [a–a] domino nostro Ihesu Christo *A*; *followed by* nostro *B* [b] *corr. from* fratremque *B* [c] Eadwigo *A* [d] *followed by* quod *A*, *B* [e] Abbandun *A* [f] Ceadwealla *A* [g] aeclesiae *A* [h] Æþelred *A*, Aþelred *B* [i] aeclesia *A* [j] kartas *A* [k–k] epylempticus phylargiriae *A*

congregation of the aforementioned monastery may by suitable counsel choose someone for themselves, according to the regular institutions of the blessed Benedict, and, choosing him from that body of brethren, justly appoint him abbot.

The liberty of this privilege is to be held henceforth in perpetual use by all Catholics, and no outsider relying on tyrannical arrogance is to seize and exercise the right of power in the aforesaid monastery, but the community of that monastery is perpetually to glory in the privilege of liberty, as I have said before. Moreover, let the aforementioned monastery be free from every yoke of earthly servitude on the same terms on which it was freed by our Catholic predecessors, that is by St Leo the pope and by Coenwulf the Catholic king, as is contained in the old privilege obtained by Abbot Hræthhun.[319] Equally the lands granted in ancient and modern times to the Lord Jesus Christ and His mother Mary, for the use of the monks, by kings and religious people of both sexes, and rightly restored by myself and my father King Edgar, and his brother my uncle King Eadwig, and their uncle, that is the most faithful King Eadred, are perpetually to have the same liberty.[320] For those kings, when they restored to the church of God the land called Abingdon—which Ceadwalla had granted devoutly to our Lord and His mother Mary in former times, and on which our predecessors (deceived by diabolical avarice) had unjustly built themselves a royal building—forbade that any king seek hospitality therein or ever construct a building.[321] I, Æthelred, emperor of the English, after taking counsel of my leading men, order this to be eternally fixed both for my time and my successors', in the name of the Father and the Son and the Holy Spirit. Since, at that time when the lands, which I have devoutly restored to the Lord through this new privilege, had been unjustly taken from the holy church of God, some perfidious men seized the hereditary charters and issued new ones for themselves. In the name of the Father and the Son and the Holy Spirit we order that no Catholic accept these new charters, but—repudiated by all faithful men—they are to be considered anathema and the old privilege is to flourish perpetually. If indeed (which we do not desire) anyone, seduced by the madness of love of money, is so insane as to attempt by rash daring to infringe this renewed liberty of our munificence, let him be estranged from the

319 See above, p. 20.
320 See above, pp. 64, 96.
321 See above, pp. 64, 96.

[i. 364] Dei ecclesie[l] necnon et a participatione sacrosancti corporis et sanguinis Domini nostri Ihesu Christi, per quem totus terrarum orbis ab antiquo humani generis inimico liberatus est, et cum Iuda Christi proditore [m]sinistra in[m] parte deputatus, ni prius hic digna satisfactione humilis penituerit quod contra sanctam Dei ecclesiam[n] rebellis agere presumpsit, nec in uita hac practica ueniam nec in theorica requiem apostata optineat ullam, sed eternis baratri[o] incendiis trusus iugiter miserrimus crucietur. Anno [p]incarnationis Domini, ut prediximus,[p] .dccccxciii., indictione sexta, humillimo rogatu prefati et deuoti abbatis Wlfgari, scriptum est huius renouande[q] libertatis priuilegium, his testibus consentientibus quorum[r] inferius nomina secundum uniuscuiusque dignitatem utriusque ordinis decusatim, Domino dispensante, caraxantur:[s] [t]Ego Æthelredus Brittannie Anglorum monarchus hoc taumate agie crucis[u] roboraui. Ego Sigeric Dorobernensis ecclesie archiepiscopus + eiusdem regis beniuolentiam subscripsi. Ego Elfstan Lundoniensis ecclesie episcopus hanc regis munificentiam confirmaui. Ego Ælfheah Wintoniensis ecclesie episcopus hanc renouationis libertatem corroboraui +. Ego Alfric Coruinensis[322] parrochie episcopus qua prefatum adiacet monasterium huic dono sanctam crucem + impressi. Ego Ælfehah[v] Licetfeldensis
[i. 365] ecclesie episcopus testitudinem sancte crucis + depinxi. Ego Oswigus Dorccensis ecclesie episcopus + hoc regale donum consolidaui. Ego + Heodredus orientalium Anglorum episcopus[323] huic largitati assensum prebui. Ego Alfstan Hrofensis ecclesie episcopus huic dapsilitati + crucem imposui. Ego Ordbrith australium Saxonum episcopus signum sancte crucis annotaui. Ego Wlsie[w]
C fo. 125v Scireburnensis ecclesie episcopus gaudenter | consensi. Ego Ealdulf Wigornensis ecclesie episcopus hilari uultu + subscripsi. Ego Athuf Herefordensis ecclesie episcopus mihi placere respondi +. Ego Sigar Willensis ecclesie episcopus ita posse fieri dignum duxi. Ego Alfwold Cridiænsis ecclesie episcopus huic statuto non contradixi. Ego Ealdred Cornubiensis ecclesie episcopus hoc decretum[x] consentiendo laudaui +. Ego Ælfdrith mater eiusdem regis huius doni fautrix extiti. Ego Æthelstan et Ecgbyrth et Eadmund et Eadred filii eiusdem regis

[l] aeclesiae *A* [m–m] in sinistra *A* [n] aeclesiam *A* [o] barathri *A* [p–p] Dominice incarnationis, ut predixi, *A* [q] renouate *A*, renouate, *corr. from* renouande *B* [r] *followed by erasure C* [s] karaxantur *A* [t–t] *see Charters of Abingdon Abbey, pp. 480–2, for the witness list in A and B* [u] *a gap has been left for a cross here, but none was supplied by the rubricator C* [v] *initial om. at start of line C* [w] Elsie, *the rubricator having added the wrong initial C; see also Charters of Abingdon Abbey, p. cxiv* [x] drecretum *C*

fellowship of the holy Church of God and also from participation in the sacrosanct body and blood of our Lord Jesus Christ, through whom the whole world has been freed from the ancient enemy of the human race, and be assigned to the left-hand side with Judas the betrayer of Christ, unless previously he humbly does penance here with suitable compensation for having presumed to act as a rebel against the holy Church of God; nor as an apostate is he to obtain any forgiveness in this active life nor any rest in the contemplative, but the most wretched man is to be endlessly tortured, thrust into the eternal fires of Hell. In the year of our Lord, as we have said above, 993, the sixth indiction, at the very humble request of the aforementioned and devout Abbot Wulfgar was written the privilege of this liberty needing renewal, with these witnesses consenting, whose names are spelt out below according to the rank of each of both orders, by God's disposition: I Æthelred monarch of the English of Britain have strengthened this by this mark of the holy cross. I Sigeric archbishop of the church of Canterbury + have subscribed the benevolence of this same king. I Ælfstan bishop of the church of London have confirmed the munificence of the king. I Ælfheah bishop of the church of Winchester have strengthened the liberty of this renewal +. I Ælfric bishop of the diocese of Ramsbury[322] which includes the aforementioned monastery have applied the holy cross + to this gift. I Ælfheah bishop of the church of Lichfield have depicted the protective sign of the holy cross +. I Æscwig bishop of the church of Dorchester + have made firm this royal gift. I + Theodred bishop of the East Saxons[323] have provided assent for this bestowal. I Ælfstan bishop of the church of Rochester have applied a cross + to this munificence. I Ordbriht bishop of the South Saxons have recorded the sign of the holy cross. I Wulfsige bishop of the church of Sherborne have rejoicingly consented. I Ealdulf bishop of the church of Worcester have subscribed + with cheerful face. I Athulf bishop of the church of Hereford have answered that it pleases me +. I Sigegar bishop of the church of Wells have considered that it can be fitting thus. I Ælfwold bishop of the church of Crediton have not contradicted this edict. I Ealdred bishop of the church of Cornwall have praised this decision by consenting +. I Ælfthryth this king's mother have acted as a supporter of this gift. I Æthelstan and Ecgberht and Edmund and Eadred this king's sons have assented.

[322] For *Coruinensis* as Ramsbury, see Keynes, *Diplomas*, p. 119 n. 114.
[323] i.e. Elmham.

assenserunt. Ego Wlfgar abbas Abbendonensis cenobii hoc sintagma
[i. 366] + triumphans dictaui. Ego Ælfward[y] Gleston' abbas, et ego Ælfsie Niwem' abbas, et ego Liuinc Ceort' abbas, et ego Alfric Meal' abbas, et ego Alfere Bathon' abbas, et ego Leofric Micel' abbas, et ego Ælfhun Middel' abbas, et ego Brithelm Eaxc' abbas, et ego Æthelric Ethel' abbas, et ego Wlfsie[z] West' abbas, et ego Germanus Ram' abbas, et ego Kenulf Burch abbas, et ego Godeman Torn' abbas, et ego Alfwold Winch' abbas consensimus. Et Leofric abbas Alban' assentio. Ego Ethelward dux, et Alfric dux, et Ælfhelm dux consensimus.[t]

[i. 367] B fo. 89v **99. (B218)** *Hucusque de ecclesie libertate. Nunc uero de terrarum restitutione subinferendum.*[324]

Regnante in perpetuum Domino[a] nostro Ihesu Christo omniumque regna seculorum magni moderaminis imperio gubernante. Ego Ethelred,[b] ipsius opitulante gratia rex Anglorum, inter uarias huius labentis seculi uicissitudines, ad memoriam reduxi qualiter in tempore pueritie mee erga me gestum fuerit, dum pater meus rex Eadgar, uniuerse terre uiam ingrediens, senex et plenus dierum migrauit ad Dominum, quod uidelicet omnes utriusque ordinis optimates ad regni gubernacula moderanda fratrem meum Eadwardum unanimiter elegerunt, mihique terras ad regios pertinentes filios in meos usus tradiderunt.[325] Ex quibus scilicet terris, quasdam pater meus, dum regnaret, omnipotenti Christo eiusque genitrici sancte Marie ad monasterium quod Abbandun nuncupatur, pro redemptione anime sue, concessit, hoc est Bedewide[c] cum omnibus ad se pertinentibus, Hisseburna cum uniuersis suis appenditibus, Burhbec omnesque sibi adiacentes redditus.[326] Que statim terre iuxta decretum et preceptionem cunctorum optimatum de prefato sancto cenobio uiolenter abstracte, meeque ditioni hisdem precipientibus sunt subacte.
B fo. 90r Quam rem si iuste aut | iniuste fecerint, ipsi sciant. Deinde cum frater meus hoc erumpnosum deseruit seculum et sibi a Deo predestinatum percepit interminabilis uite emolumentum, ego,

[y] *initial om. at start of line C* [z] Ælfsie, *the rubricator having entered the wrong initial C*

99 [a] *interlin. B* [b] Aþelred *B* [c] Bedewinde *B*

[324] Sawyer, no. 937; *Charters of Abingdon Abbey*, no. 129; trans. *EHD*, i. 123; calendared in Wormald, 'Lawsuits', nos. 63–4. *Charters of Abingdon Abbey*, p. 506, and Keynes, *Diplomas*, p. 96 n. 42, agree that there is no decisive reason not to accept the document, although its form and content are 'anomalous'. Keynes, *Diplomas*, p. 256, states that this document 'can probably be assigned to 999' because of its connection with the charter

I Wulfgar abbot of the monastery of Abingdon, exulting, composed this document +. I Ælfweard abbot of Glastonbury, and I Ælfsige abbot of the New Minster, and I Lyfing abbot of Chertsey, and I Ælfric abbot of Malmesbury, and I Ælfhere abbot of Bath, and I Leofric abbot of Muchelney, and I Ælfhun abbot of Milton, and I Brihthelm abbot of Exeter, and I Æthelric abbot of Athelney, and I Wulfsige abbot of Westminster, and I Germanus abbot of Ramsey, and I Coenwulf abbot of Peterborough, and I Godeman abbot of Thorney, and I Ælfwold abbot of Winchcombe have consented. And I Leofric abbot of St Albans assent. I Ealdorman Æthelweard, and Ealdorman Ælfric, and Ealdorman Ælfhelm have consented.

99. (B218) *Up to here concerns the liberty of the church. The following now concerns the restitution of lands.*[324]

With our Lord Jesus Christ reigning in perpetuity and governing with the power of great control the kingdoms of all ages. I, Æthelred, with the assistance of His grace king of the English, amidst the various vicissitudes of this fleeting world, have recalled to my memory conduct in relation to myself in the time of my childhood, when my father King Edgar was entering the way of all the earth, and old and full of days departed to the Lord; that is, that all leading men of both orders unanimously chose my brother Edward to guide the governance of the realm, and handed over to me for my use the lands pertaining to kings' sons.[325] My father, whilst he was reigning, granted some of the lands to almighty Christ and His mother St Mary for the monastery which is called Abingdon, for the redemption of his soul, that is Bedwyn with everything pertaining to it, Hurstbourne with all its appendages, Burbage and all the revenues belonging to it.[326] These lands were forthwith violently taken away from the aforementioned holy monastery according to the decision and order of all the leading men, and at their command were subjected to my power. Whether they did this justly or unjustly, they themselves may know. Then, when my brother left this wretched world and received the reward of never-ending life predestined for him by God, I, with Christ's assent, received lordship

concerning South Cerney, Gloucestershire, below, c. 101. *Charters of Abingdon Abbey*, p. 506, suggests that 'the text does give some grounds for thinking that the charter was drawn up some time after the lands had been ceded'.

[325] See Wormald, 'Kingship and royal property', in *Edward the Elder*, ed. Higham and Hill, esp. pp. 271, 274; Maitland, *Domesday Book and Beyond*, pp. 254–5. 'Universe terre uiam ingrediens' is from Josh. 23: 14, 3 Kgs. (1 Kgs.) 2: 2.

[326] See above, cc. 61, 64, 69.

annuente Christo, et regalium simul et ad regios filios pertinentium terrarum suscepi dominium.

Nunc autem quia mihi uidetur esse ualde molestum patris mei [i. 368] incurrere et portare maledictum retinendo hoc quod ipse pro sue anime redemptione Deo contulit donarium, et quia gratia Dei me ad intelligibilem perducere dignata est etatem mihique per meorum optimatum decreta affluentem et copiosam terrarum largita est portionem, iccirco et ego ex mea propria hereditate prefatum sanctum cenobium munere congruo honorare et oportuna possessionum largitione ditare[d] dispono, primum pro Dei omnipotentis eiusque sancte genitricis amore, ut ipsa pro me pia interuentrix[e] esse dignetur C fo. 126r ad Dominum Deum | nostrum, deinde pro anime genitoris mei dilectione meeque proprie anime eterna redemptione, necnon et pro meorum causa liberorum qui easdem prefatas sibi attrahere sueque ditioni cogitant subicere terras. Nomina uero terrarum quas ad prefatum libenti animo concedo monasterium hec sunt: unum scilicet apud Feornebeorh, alterum apud Wilmaleahtun, tercium apud Cyrne.[327] Has terrarum portiones Alfric cognomento Puer a quadam uidua Eadfled appellata[328] uiolenter abstraxit, ac deinde, cum in ducatu suo contra me et contra omnem gentem meam reus existeret, et he quas prenominaui portiones et uniuerse quas posse-derat terrarum possessiones mee subacte sunt ditioni, quando ad sinodale concilium ad Cyrneceastre uniuersi optimates mei simul in unum conuenerunt, et eundem Alfricum maiestatis reum de hac patria profugum expulerunt, et uniuersa ab illo possessa mihi[f] iure possidenda omnes unanimo consensu decreuerunt.[329] Deinde prefatam uiduam, pro amore optimatum meorum qui eius apud me extiterant aduocati, suam hereditatem possidere clementi benignitate permisi,[g] et ipsa tandem in extrema sue migrationis sententia mihi rursus earundem terrarum possessionem benigno et libenti animo in perhennem dereliquit hereditatem.

[i. 369] Tellurem uero ad Pyrian, quam etiam ad idem prefatum concedo monasterium, unam illarum constat esse terrarum quas Adelward

[d] *interlin. B* [e] inuentrix *B* [f] michi *B* [g] *corr. from* permissi *B*

[327] A charter granting Wormleighton to Ealdorman Ælfhere in 956 appears in MS B; below, B148 (*Charters of Abingdon Abbey*, no. 71). It probably came into Abingdon's possession when King Æthelred gave the estate to the monastery. By 1066, the land was no longer in Abingdon's possession; *DB* i, fos. 240v, 241v, 243v. The place-name form, in the singular, suggests that the Farnborough mentioned in the charter is the one in Warwickshire, rather than the one in Berkshire, although there is no other secure evidence linking

both of the royal lands and at the same time those pertaining to kings' sons.

Now, moreover, since it seems to me very vexing to incur and bear the curse of my father by retaining this which he conferred on God as an endowment for the redemption of his soul, and since the grace of God has deigned to bring me to the age of understanding and has bestowed on me through the decisions of my leading men a lavish and plentiful portion of lands, therefore I too am disposed to honour the aforementioned holy monastery from my own inheritance with a fitting gift and to enrich it with advantageous bestowal of possessions; first for the love of almighty God and His holy mother, that she may deign to be a pious intercessor for me with our Lord God; secondly, for the love of the soul of my father and for the eternal redemption of my own soul, and also for the sake of my children who consider taking these aforesaid lands for themselves and subjecting them to their control. Indeed the names of the lands that I grant willingly to the aforementioned monastery are these: namely, one at Farnborough, another at Wormleighton, a third at Cerney.[327] Ælfric surnamed 'Cild' violently took these portions of lands from a widow named Eadflæd.[328] Then he was guilty in his ealdormanship of an offence against me and all my people, and these portions which I named above and all the possessions of lands which he had possessed were subjected to my control, when all my leading men gathered together at a synodal council at Cirencester and expelled that Ælfric, guilty of treason, as a fugitive from this country, and all decreed by unanimous consent that rightly I should possess everything he had possessed.[329] Then, for love of my leading men who acted as her advocates before me, with merciful kindness I allowed that widow to possess her inheritance, and finally in her last decision at her departure from life she kindly and willingly left possession of these lands to me again in perennial inheritance.

Moreover, it is agreed that the estate at Perry, which I also grant to that monastery, is one of those lands that Æthelweard son of Ceolflæd

the Warwickshire Farnborough to Abingdon; see *Charters of Abingdon Abbey*, pp. 88, 506; Gelling, *Early Charters of the Thames Valley*, p. 136. If so, the estate had passed from the abbey's hands by 1066; *DB* i, fo. 238^{v}. Abingdon held the Berkshire Farnborough for ten hides *TRE*, for four and a half in 1086; *DB* i, fo. 59^{r}. For South Cerney, Gloucestershire, see below, c. 101.

[328] Probably the widow of Ealdorman Ælfhere of Mercia; see *Charters of Abingdon Abbey*, p. 506.

[329] See *ASC*, *s.a.* 985: 'In this year Ealdorman Ælfric was driven out of the land.'

Ceolflede filius mihi eternaliter possidendas pro mea donauit amicitia.[330] Omni uulgo, longe lateque, satis est cognitum qualiter ipse et frater eius contra me rei extiterint qualiterque ambo meam inimicitiam exigentibus suis reatibus incurrerint. Hec prefatarum descriptio terrarum facta est per admonitionem Ordulfi auunculi mei, atque Adelmari[h] consanguinitate mihi conglutinati, et Wlfgeati[i] ministri mei dilecti,[331] necnon et abbatis mei Wlfgari, tota mihi deuotione benigni, qui me frequenti suggestione cum ceterorum fidelium B fo. 90v commonuit suasione quati|nus Dei omnipotentis hereditatem ex aliqua parte innouare et augere curarem. Quod et feci propter Christi qui me in regno sublimauit amorem et eorum qui me amica assiduitate ad meam exhortantur[j] necessariam et eternam salutem, et propter humilem et benignam quam mihi prefatus abba fideliter et gratanter exhibere[k] solet obedientiam.

Hoc quoque uoluntatis mee beneficium palam cunctis innotesco, quod earundem possessionum terras, in unaquaque cui adiacent prouincia, cum omnibus ad se pertinentibus, siue in prediorum municipiis[332] siue in tributo siue in theloneo siue in quocumque negotio quod in unoquoque rure diuerso modo solet exigi, plena libertate ab omni terrene seruitutis iugo liberas esse concedo, quemadmodum pater meus supra nominatarum portionem terrarum ab uniuersa mundanarum rerum seruitute liberas esse concessit exceptis tribus, rata uidelicet expeditione, pontis arcisue restauratione. Illud etiam, cum sancte Trinitatis et indiuidue Vnitatis et beate Marie semper uirginis auctoritate, precipio, ut nullus hominum presumat hanc donationem occasione qualibet immutare, nec [i. 370] territorii[l] | codicem uel cirographi[m] dictatum contra mee munificentie C fo. 126v scripta in | medium proferre; sed uniuersa illa antiqua territoria, supradicto exigente reatu, semper in posterum pro nichilo computentur, et ad nichilum redacta omnium sputis obnoxia conculcentur, et huius priuilegii decreta stabili et inconcussa soliditate roborentur.[333] Si quis autem, instigante diabolo, hec consulta, tam mea quam diuina auctoritate corroborata, uiolare presumpserit, siue meus sit

[h] Aþelmari *B* [i] Wlgati *B* [j] exortantur *B* [k] exibere *B* [l] terriori *B* [m] cirografi *B*

[330] For this place, see above, p. cxlvii. I have not been able to identify Æthelweard with any certainty.

[331] Wulfgeat witnessed royal documents from the mid-980s, but really came to prominence in 993. Thereafter, he was close to the king until his fall—assuming it is the same Wulfgeat—in 1006; Keynes, *Diplomas*, pp. 188–9, 192, 210–11. He may also have

gave to me to be possessed eternally, for my friendship.[330] It is well known to all and sundry, far and wide, how he and his brother were guilty of an offence against me and how they both incurred my enmity as their crimes demanded. This document concerning the aforementioned lands was made at the admonition of Ordulf my uncle, and of Æthelmaer who is bonded to me by kinship, and of Wulfgeat my beloved thegn,[331] and also of Wulfgar my abbot who, well disposed to me with complete devotion, urged and frequently suggested to me, while other faithful men exhorted the same, that I take care to replenish and increase the inheritance of almighty God to some degree. This also I did because of the love of Christ who raised me in the kingship and of those who exhort me with friendly perseverance for my necessary and eternal salvation, and because of the humble and kind obedience which the aforementioned abbot is accustomed to show me faithfully and cordially.

Also I make known openly to all this favour of my good will, that I grant that the lands of these possessions, in whatever province they belong, with everything pertaining to them, whether in town holdings[332] of the estates, or in tribute, or in toll, or in any imposition which is accustomed to be demanded in diverse manner in any land, be free with full liberty of every yoke of earthly servitude, as my father granted a portion of those above-named lands to be free from all servitude of worldly things except three, that is, fixed military service, and bridge and fortress repair. With the authority of the Holy Trinity and of the indivisible Unity and of the blessed Mary, ever Virgin, I also order this, that no man take on himself to change this gift in any circumstance, nor put forward in public a land-book or the text of a cirograph against the written record of my munificence; but all those old land-deeds, as the above offence demands, are always and forever to be reckoned null, and reduced to nothing are to be trampled under foot, subject to be spat on by all, and the decisions of this privilege are to be strengthened by stable and resolute security.[333] Moreover, if anyone at the devil's instigation takes on himself to violate these decisions, strengthened both by my and divine authority, whether it be my son or an ealdorman or a bishop or

been a Berkshire landowner, but there are difficulties in assuming that all references to a Wulfgeat at this time are to one man; see *Charters of Abingdon Abbey*, pp. 506, 530.

[332] *Municipium* is a very rare word in Anglo-Saxon charters and its sense here is not clear; Whitelock, in *EHD*, i. no. 123, translates it 'town-properties'.

[333] On such clauses, which seem to have developed in the early 980s, see Keynes, *Diplomas*, p. 88. This is the first instance in the text of the *History*.

filius siue dux siue episcopus siue minister aut cuiuscumque dignitatis extiterit, omnipotens Deus sanctaque eius genitrix semperque uirgo Maria et omnis supernorum sancta uirtus exercituum maiestatem diuinam incessabili uoce laudantium, hunc in uita ista despiciat et despectum in futuro seculo sine fine disperdat illum, nisi congrua satisfactione ante exitum suum emendauerit quod contra Deum sanctamque Mariam deliquit. Amen. Huius priuilegii descriptio iugiter in prenominato conseruetur monasterio, ut sit libertas eterna[n] librorum ad uniuersas supradictarum possessiones terrarum, quas omnipotenti Deo eiusque sancte genitrici Marie ad idem cenobium benigno et libenti animo concessi et concessas eterna stabilitate commendaui.

[i. 373] **100.** *De Cyrna.*[334]

Preterea et singulariter de Cyrne sue auctoritatis testamentum huiusmodi condidit:

B fo. 91r **101. (B220)** [a]*Carta Æthelredi regis de Cyrna.*[a] [335] |

B fo. 91v Regnante in perpetuum Domino nostro Ihesu Christo, qui imperio Patris cuncta, simul Sancti Spiritus gratia uiuificante, disponit. Quamuis enim uerba[b] sacerdotum et decreta iudicum in robore firmitatis iugiter perseuerent, attamen pro incerta futurorum mutabilitate annorum cirographorum[c] testamento sunt roboranda. Quapropter ego Æthelred[d] totius Brittannie basileus quandam telluris particulam, quindecim uidelicet cassatos, loco qui celebri[e] Cyrne nuncupatur uocabulo, Domino nostro Ihesu Christo sancteque eius ecclesie beate[f] Dei genitrice[g] Marie[h] dicate,[i] qui celebri Abbandun[j] nuncupatur onomate ad usus[k] monachorum Dei inibi degentium, cum omnibus utensilibus, pratis uidelicet, pascuis, aquarumque cursibus, Wlfgaro obtinente abbate, eterna largitus sum hereditate. Sit autem predictum rus omni terrene seruitutis iugo liberum tribus
[i. 374] exceptis, rata uidelicet expeditione, pontis arcisue restauratione. Est sane prefata terra Cyrne de illis uillulis quas pridem quidam comes

[n] externa *B; the error may derive from C's tailed* e. *There is a very faint line through the additional letter in B, perhaps indicating that the scribe had realized his mistake, but no real effort at deletion has been made*

101 [a–a] Carta regis Adelredi de Cerne *B* [b] ueba *B* [c] cyrographorum *B* [d] Æþelred *B* [e] *followed by* æt *B* [f] beata *C* [g] genitricis *corr. from* genitrice *B* [h] Maria *C* [i] *om. B* [j] Abbend' *B* [k] ad usus *rep., then del. B*

[334] The land concerned is again South Cerney, for later developments concerning which see below, p. 196. For a charter probably concerned with nearby lands at North Cerney, preserved in the Abingdon archive but not recording a grant to Abingdon, see below, B22 (*Charters of Abingdon Abbey*, no. 13).

a thegn or of whatever dignity he may be, let almighty God and His holy mother Mary, ever Virgin, and all the holy strength of the heavenly hosts that praise the divine majesty with unceasing voice, despise him in this life and destroy him, despised, without end in the world to come, unless he makes amends with fitting compensation before his death for what he did wrong against God and holy Mary. Amen. The document of this privilege is to be constantly preserved in the aforenamed monastery, so that the liberty of the books may be eternal for all the possessions of the above-said lands, which I have kindly and willingly granted to almighty God and His holy mother Mary for that monastery and have commended with eternal stability what I granted.

100. *Concerning Cerney.*[334]
Besides he also composed a deed of his authority specifically concerning Cerney, as follows:

101. (B220) *Charter of King Æthelred concerning Cerney.*[335]
With our Lord Jesus Christ reigning in perpetuity, who by order of the Father, together with the life-giving grace of the Holy Spirit, disposes of all things. For however much the words of priests and the decisions of judges constantly persist in the strength of security, nevertheless because of the uncertain changeableness of future years they should be strengthened by the testimony of written documents. Therefore I, Æthelred, emperor of the whole of Britain, have bestowed as eternal inheritance a small portion of an estate, that is fifteen hides, in the place called by the well-known name of Cerney, to our Lord Jesus Christ and to His holy church dedicated to the blessed Mary mother of God, which is called by the well-known name of Abingdon, for the use of the monks of God living therein, with all associated resources, that is meadows, pastures, and watercourse, under the charge of Abbot Wulfgar. Moreover, let the aforesaid land be free of every yoke of earthly servitude except three, that is, fixed military service, and bridge and fortress repair. The aforementioned land of Cerney is indeed from those small villages which previously

[335] Sawyer, no. 896; *Charters of Abingdon Abbey*, no. 128; calendared in Wormald, 'Lawsuits', no. 63. This charter also survives in a 16th-c. copy of a lost single sheet, Cambridge, Corpus Christi College 111, pp. 169–70. *Charters of Abingdon Abbey*, p. 500, describes this as 'a difficult document, but a case can be made for its probable authenticity', suggesting, p. 501, that it was an '"in-house" production'. *DB* i, fo. 169^{r}, gives the hidage of South Cerney as fourteen hides and one virgate.

uocitamine Ælfric a quadam[l] matrona[m] Eatfled nomine diripuit et sibi in propriam hereditatem usurpauit.[336] Ac deinde, temporum uariante uice, necne instigante humani generis peruersissimo temptatore diabolo, contra Deum meumque regale imperium multa et inaudita miserabiliter committens piacula, episcoporum, ducum, omniumque huius regni optimatum unanimo legali consilio equissimoque iudicio, in uilla regia que Anglica appellatione Cyrneceaster[n] dicitur, ipso extra[o] patriam in exilium addicto, non solum ille que a prefata muliere abstraxit sed et cetere omnes quas iure possidebat hereditario, sibi ac omni sue posteritati interdicte fuerunt, mihique in proprium ius habendi donandique firmiter et immobiliter[p] sunt eternaliter deputate. Ego quoque, post hec, cum consilio et precatu optimatum meorum, concessi quatinus prefata uidua[337] sua direpta[q] resumeret ac uita comite possideret. Que humiliter suscipiens et rationabiliter fruens, et in ultimo huius labilis uite termino omnia[r] mihi beniuola mente in proprium ius restituit. Si autem tempore contigerit aliquo quempiam hominum aliquem libellum ob istarum apicum adnichilationem in palam producere, omnimodo in nomine sancte Trinitatis ab
[i. 375] omnibus Christianis interdico, ita ut meum donum corroboratum sit cum signaculo sancte crucis ut nec sibi nec aliis proficiat, sed in sempiterno graphio[338] deleatur. Denique uero si quis nostre dapsilitatis donum uiolari fraudulenter temptauerit, sciat se die ultima iudicii coram Deo rationem redditurum atque cum reprobis quibus dicitur 'Discedite a me maledicti in ignem eternum',[339] penis atrocibus se esse passurum, si non antea corporea lamentatione emendauerit.[s]

[text of MS C cannot be reconstructed here]

[l] *corr. from* ad quandam *B* [m] matrone *B* [n] Cirneceastre *B* [o] *interlin. B* [p] inmobiliter *B* [q] *folio missing after* direp *C* [r] omnia *MS. CCCC leaves a small gap where the word should appear* [s] *B goes on to give boundaries, which would not have appeared here in C; B and CCCC a dating clause for 999, which almost certainly would have appeared in some form in C; and B and CCCC a witness list, which probably appeared in a different and shorter form in C; see Charters of Abingdon Abbey, pp. 499–500. The boundaries also appear in the quire of C devoted to such clauses, fo. 201ᵛ, Charters of Abingdon Abbey, p. 589 (no. 45)*

an earl called Ælfric seized from a matron named Eadflæd and usurped for himself into his own inheritance.[336] And then, with the changing vicissitude of time, and at the instigation of the devil, the most perverse tempter of the human race, he wretchedly committed many and unheard of sins against God and my royal dominion. By the unanimous lawful opinion and most equitable judgement of the bishops, ealdormen, and all the leading men of this realm, in the royal vill called by the English name Cirencester, he was sentenced to exile outside this country, and not only those possessions that he had taken from the aforementioned woman but also all the others which he possessed by hereditary right, were forbidden to him and all his posterity and were eternally assigned to me in full ownership to have and give firmly and immovably. Then, at the counsel and request of my leading men, I granted that the aforementioned widow[337] might take back her property which had been plundered and possess it as long as she lived. Humbly receiving and reasonably enjoying these possessions, at the final end of this fleeting life, with good will she restored them all to me in full ownership. If, however, at any time it happens that any man produces in the open any document for the rendering null of these words, in the name of the Holy Trinity I ban him from all Christians in every way, in such a way that my gift may be strengthened with the sign of the holy cross so that it profit neither him nor others, but let him be deleted from the Everlasting Charter.[338] Finally, then, if anyone attempts fraudulently to violate the gift of our munificence, let him know that he will render account of this in God's presence on the Last Day of Judgement, and will suffer with awful punishments with those wicked men to whom it is said 'Depart from me, ye cursed, into eternal fire',[339] if he does not previously make amends with bodily lamentation.

[text of MS C cannot be reconstructed here]

[336] See above, p. 153 n. 328.

[337] MS C here is missing a folio. Completion from MS B of the charters that here appear in part in MS C allows us to reconstruct something of the text, but other material too must have been included, presumably including a section introducing the gift of Moredon. What further material is missing must remain uncertain.

[338] i.e. the Book of Life, the record of the names of those who are to inherit eternal life; *DMLBS*, fasc. iv, *s.v. graphium*.

[339] Matt. 25: 41.

[i. 377] **102. (B221)** *Carta regis Adelred de Mordune.*[340]

B fo. 92^r^ Scimus quia in multis offendimus omnes. Si uero in rebus aliquando ecclesiasticis offendimus, ea[a] que, Deo adiuuante, emendare conamur [i. 378] firmissimo litterarum libro munire debemus ne iterum (quod absit) res ecclesiastica a manibus possideatur alienis cupiditatis causa. Qua de re ego Aþelredus Dei nutu Anglorum basileus[b] notum uolo adesse omnibus meo subiectis imperio quod quidam miles Ælfgarus nomine,[341] meus uidelicet prepositus atque preciosus, quandam iniuste adquisiuit uillam sanctissime genitricis Marie Abbendonensis B fo. 92^v^ cenobii ab | incolis Mordun nominatam uiginti mansos tempore uidelicet Eadwini abbatis, me tamen consentiente quamuis iniuste, deditque coniugi sue Ælfgife sub hereditario datalicii dono.[342] Quo mortuo predicta mulier Ælfgifu alii copulata est marito Wulgæt uocabulo. Qui ambo crimine pessimo iuste ab omni incusati sunt populo causa sue machinationis proprie de qua modo non est dicendum per singula.[343] Propter quam uero machinationem que iniuste adquisierunt omnia iuste perdiderunt. Quo audito Wulfgarus predicti pastor monasterii de predicta statim admonuit me uillula quam ipsi iniuste possidebant. Ego autem, memor illorum iniuste adquisitionis et mee non bone consensionis cum omni cordis C fo. 127^r^ desiderio | prefatam[c] reddidi uillam beate Dei genitrici Marie. Sed et unum prediolum in Crocgelade[d] ciuitate situm, quod dudum meo prefato dederam preposito, trado et concedo eidem sancte Marie perpetua hereditate. Si quis alium libellulum, false cupiditatis atramento,[e] pretitulatum contra istum in palam protulerit, nec sibi nec sue proficiat auaritie, sed a diuino sit in perpetuum perforatus graphiolo,[f][344] et ipse meo atque meorum interdictu pontificum permaneat anathematizatus, et a Christianorum consortio alienatus,

102 [a] *wrongly corr. by interlin. to* eae *MS* [b] *corr. from* basileo *MS* [c] *C resumes with this word* [d] Crocelade *B* [e] attramento *B* [f] grafiolo *B*

[340] Sawyer, no. 918; *Charters of Abingdon Abbey*, no. 135; calendared in Wormald, 'Lawsuits', no. 72. Details of witnessing and diplomatic lead *Charters of Abingdon Abbey*, p. 529, to conclude that the document should be treated 'with suspicion: it was certainly drawn up at Abingdon, but whether at a much later date or as a contemporary but "unofficial" product is uncertain. There does, however, seem to be some reason to accept the details of the estate history which it obtains.' The charter concerns lands in Moredon and Cricklade, both Wiltshire. For Edgar granting twenty hides at Moredon to his thegn, Eadwine, see below, B194 (*Charters of Abingdon Abbey*, no. 94). *Charters of Abingdon Abbey*, pp. 383–4, 530–1, argues persuasively that Abingdon had only a short-lasting connection with these lands.

102. (B221) *Charter of King Æthelred concerning Moredon.*[340]

We know that we all do wrong in many matters. But if at some point we have done wrong with regard to church property, we ought to fortify with a very strong book of letters those things which we strive to make good with God's help, lest again (let it not be so) church property is possessed by outsiders' hands through greed. Therefore I, Æthelred, by the will of God emperor of the English, wish it to be known to all those subject to my dominion that a certain knight named Ælfgar,[341] my reeve and favourite, unjustly acquired a village of the most holy mother Mary of the monastery of Abingdon, named by the inhabitants Moredon, twenty hides, in the time, that is, of Abbot Eadwine, with my consent although unjustly, and he gave it to his wife Ælfgifu as a hereditary gift of dower.[342] When he was dead, the aforesaid woman Ælfgifu was joined to another husband, Wulfgeat by name. They were both justly accused by all the people of a terrible crime, in the matter of their own plot of which we cannot now speak in detail.[343] So because of this plot, they justly lost everything that they had unjustly acquired. When he heard this, Wulfgar, the shepherd of the aforesaid monastery, immediately warned me about the aforesaid small village, which they unjustly possessed. Mindful, moreover, of their unjust acquisition and my wrongful consent, with the desire of my whole heart I have restored the aforementioned village to the blessed Mary mother of God. Also I hand over and grant to the same St Mary as perpetual inheritance one small estate situated in the city of Cricklade, which I had given some time ago to my aforementioned reeve. If anyone brings forward into the open any document previously drawn up with the ink of false greed against this one drawn up above, let it profit neither him nor his avarice, but be pierced in perpetuity by a divine sword,[344] and let him remain anathematized by the interdict of myself and my bishops, and estranged from the fellowship of Christians, and in addition cut off

[341] For Ælfgar, see Keynes, *Diplomas*, pp. 183–4; *Charters of Abingdon Abbey*, p. 530. He may be the Ælfgar who is a common witness of royal charters between 982 and 990, and possibly also the beneficiary of royal grants at that time. It is conceivable that he is also the Ælfgar son of Ealdorman Ælfric who was blinded in 993. He may have been one of those laymen who turned Æthelred against monasteries following the death of Æthelwold. A woman who may have been his mother is commemorated in *Liber Vitae*, ed. Keynes, p. 95 and fo 26^{r}: 'Wulfgyð mater Ælfgaris procuratoris'.

[342] 'Ælfgyfu coniunx Ælfgari presidis' appears in the *Liber Vitae*, ed. Keynes, fo. 26^{r}.

[343] Cf. Heb. 9: 5: 'de quibus non est modo dicendum per singula'.

[344] *Charters of Abingdon Abbey*, p. 640, persuasively suggests this as the translation, developed from the term for a sharp writing instrument or stylus.

[i. 379] insuper a corpore et sanguine Domini sequestratus, usque dum sancte reddat Dei genitrici Marie bis binas in quadruplum uillas[345] cum corporali penitentia, calliditate sue machinationis relicta. Et ut[g] prefate telluris ruricole inuiolabile robur libertatis semper obtinere[h] ualeant, regali liberati sunt precepto ab omni seculari iugo exceptis trium rerum obsequiis, expeditione scilicet populari, uiatici funda-
[i. 380] B fo. 93r tione pontis, arcis conditione regalis.[i] [346] Acta[j] est hec pre|fata donatio anno ab incarnatione Christi[k] .mviii., indictione sexta. Vt iterum hec presentis nostre donationis cartula ab omnium stimulis inuidorum inconcussa[l] et incontaminata perpetuo iure possit persistere, [m]ego primus Æthelred rex eandem circumquaque pretitulo et corroboro sancte crucis signaculo +, quod omnes mei proceres hoc idem ut faciant euidenter precipio. ⟨E⟩go[n] Alfgiua eiusdem regis collaterana predictum donum confirmo. ⟨E⟩go Æthelstan, et ⟨e⟩go Eadmun, et ⟨e⟩go Eadred, et ⟨e⟩go Eadwi, et ⟨e⟩go Eadgar, et ⟨e⟩go Eadward filii regis consensimus. ⟨E⟩go Alfheah Dorouernensis archiepiscopus laudo. ⟨E⟩go Wlfstan Eboracensis archiepiscopus consentio. Et multi alii episcopi, abbates, et duces subscripserunt.[m]

[i. 411 n.] **103.** ⟨I⟩n dono autem perpetuo possidendo, suis aut episcopis aut ministris, que secuntur concessit, que etiam illi ecclesie Abbendonensi libertate et potestate sibi ab eodem rege libere permissa concesserunt; et quidem quedam ab antiquis regibus illi loco collata fuerant sed a posterioribus ut supra retulimus retracta, sic de Domeltun actum est. Que uilla ab Ethelstano rege ad ipsum cenobium data fuit, sed, ut prediximus, postea ab aliis ablata.[347] Qualiter uero iuri ecclesie redierit, monimentum litterarum Ethelredi istius regis sic prodit:[a]

[g] *corr. from* cum *B* [h] optinere *B* [i] *see Charters of Abingdon Abbey, p. 527, for the boundaries in B* [j] *initial om., possibly by rubricator C* [k] domini nostri Ihesu Christi *B* [l] inconuulsa *B* [m–m] *see Charters of Abingdon Abbey, pp. 527–8, for the witness list in B* [n] *the rubricator failed to add the initial* E *in this and the following cases*

103 [a] produnt *MS*

[345] *Charters of Abingdon Abbey*, p. 529, comments that 'this [phrase] is unparalleled in Anglo-Saxon diplomatic, and very difficult indeed to understand'.

[346] The boundaries from this charter as it appears in MS B may also appear in the quire of MS C devoted to such clauses, fo. 202r, *Charters of Abingdon Abbey*, p. 589 (no. 51),

from the body and blood of the Lord, until he abandons the craftiness of his trickery and renders to holy Mary mother of God twice two multiplied by four villages[345] with corporeal penance. And so that the local inhabitants of the aforementioned estate can always hold the inviolable strength of liberty, by royal order they have been freed from every secular yoke except services of three things, that is, common military service, road bridge strengthening, and royal fortress building.[345] This aforementioned gift was carried out in the year 1008 from the Incarnation of Christ, the sixth indiction. Moreover, so that this charter of our present gift can remain by perpetual right unshaken and not infringed by the goads of all envious men, I, first of all, King Æthelred sign and strengthen it in all directions with the sign of the holy cross +, and I order all my leading men that they manifestly do the same. I Ælfgifu the king's consort confirm the aforesaid gift. I Æthelstan, and I Edmund, and I Eadred, and I Eadwig, and I Edgar, and I Edward the king's sons consent. I Ælfheah archbishop of Canterbury praise. I Wulfstan archbishop of York consent. And many other bishops, abbots, and ealdormen have subscribed.

103. Moreover, he granted as gifts these following things to be possessed perpetually, either to his bishops or thegns, which they also granted to that church of Abingdon with the liberty and power freely permitted to them by that king; also indeed certain possessions conferred on that monastery by kings of old but taken back by later men as we recounted above, as in the case of Dumbleton. This village was given by King Æthelstan to that monastery but, as we have said above, was afterwards taken away by others.[347] How, indeed, it returned to the property of the church, King Æthelred's written document records thus:

although they may belong to the charter concerning Moredon which appears only in MS B, below, B194. This latter possibility is suggested by the absence of the clause concerning Cricklade, which ends the boundaries in the present charter in MS B. However, orthography, and the very presence of the charter in the *History* in MS C, may suggest that the detached boundary clause derives from the present document.

[347] For Æthelstan's gift, see above, c. 19. MS B, below B233, attributes to the predecessors of Wulfric Spot the taking of the vill of Dumbleton, although in fact Wulfric seems to have possessed only a small portion of Dumbleton; *Charters of Abingdon Abbey*, p. 517. No specific reference to the loss of Dumbleton occurs in MS C, but it may have appeared on the lost folio between cc. 101 and 102 above. *Charters of Abingdon Abbey*, p. 98, considers it much more likely that Archbishop Ælfric's grant was the first time Dumbleton passed into Abingdon's hands.

B fo. 100v **104. (B234)** [a]*Carta regis Æthelredi de Dumeltuna.*[a] [348]

Largitori[b] bonitatis totius in sue maiestatis stellato super cherubin[c] [i. 412] residente solio, omniaque que sub trifaria rerum machina ab ipso facta continentur sue diuinitatis moderante monarchia. Nos miserrimi, pauperes, pusilli, terra peregrinique, cinis puluisque fauilla, et ineuitabili mortis obnoxii cirographo,[349] primo nostro Ade uicissitudine sue obiecto preuaricationis,[350] nudi hinc lacrimabilibus exire B fo. 101r compellimur casibus, nichil | nobiscum huius seculi preter peccata portantes, nisi quis Dei solummodo saluatus miseratione, fideique, spei, et caritatis,[d] [351] armis premunitus inexpugnabilibus, multiplici proborum preualente qualitate meritorum, dignius ad tanti tribunal iudicis, ut retributionem proprii laboris sortiatur inmortalem, representari ab angelicis mereatur spiritibus, secundum quod noster patientissimus Iob hora sui orbitatis[e] promulgat uaticinando 'Nudus egressus sum de utero matris mee, et[f] nudus reuertar illuc', C fo. 127v rursumque 'Dominus dedit, Dominus abstulit; sicut | Domino placuit, ita factum est; sit nomen Domini benedictum'.[352] Si ergo ille sanctissimus uir, in artiori uite[g] sue dampno anxietatis, tam honorificas suo factori exsoluere non est cunctatus gratias, quid obstat[h] mihi, ab ipso omnium distributori dignitatum sat redundanti collata potestate, a plebibus quoque que nostre regali circumquaque subiacent ditioni Athelredo[i] agnominato? Si et supradicti norma uatis ipsius nomen digna extollere laude non differam, promptissima deuotione ea que ab ipso mihi de die in diem proueniunt suis, prout cuiusque necessitas poposcerit, distribuendo fidelibus. Verum ut sermonis initium ad certum perducatur finem, quandam possessionis proprie tellurem, uiginti scilicet ac quatuor mansarum ab indigenis Dumeltun[j] appellatam, tribusque in locis disiacentem, meo admodum fideli largior archipresuli Ælfrico,[k] quam ipse a me [i. 413] cum quinquaginta talentis exigebat, ponderosa trutinationis publice probatis libratione. Que portio terre cuiusdam femine fornicaria

104 [a–a] Carta Adelredi regis de Dummeltun *B* [b] *initial om. C* [c] cherubim *B* [d] karitatis *B* [e] orbitatus *B C* [f] *om. B* [g] *om. B* [h] ostat *corr. from* constat *B* [i] Æþelred *B* [j] æt Dumoltun *B* [k] Alfrico *B*

[348] Sawyer, no. 901; *Charters of Abingdon Abbey*, no. 132; calendared in Wormald, 'Lawsuits', no. 68. *Charters of Abingdon Abbey*, p. 515, states that this document 'is probably authentic, although there is a problem in the witness list'. The problem is that the witness list in MS B seems to include two successive bishops of Dorchester, Æscwig and Ælfhelm. This may be explicable by the charter being produced around the time of Æscwig's death; Keynes, *Diplomas*, pp. 258–9. The document appears to draw on the charter in King Æthelstan's name, confirming Abbot Cynath's grant of Dumbleton to Bishop Osulf of

104. (B234) *Charter of King Æthelred concerning Dumbleton.*[348]
With the Bestower of all goodness sitting on the throne of His majesty adorned with stars above the Cherubim, and with the monarchy of His divinity governing everything that is contained under the tripartite system of things made by him. Most wretched, poor, faint-hearted, wanderers on earth, ash and dust from embers, and subject to the contract of inevitable death,[349] as our first forebear Adam was charged on the occasion of his sin,[350] we are compelled to go out naked from here in mournful circumstances, taking with us nothing of this world except sins, unless anyone, saved by God's mercy and fortified with the undefeatable weapons of faith, hope, and love,[351] with the manifold quality of good merits prevailing, more worthily deserves to be represented by angelic spirits at the throne of so great a judge, so that he may acquire the immortal recompense of his own labour, according to what our most patient Job at the hour of his bereavement promulgated by prophesying 'Naked came I out of my mother's womb, and naked shall I return thither', and again 'The Lord gave, and the Lord hath taken away; as it pleased the Lord, so hath it been done; blessed be the name of the Lord.'[352] If therefore that most holy man, amidst the most difficult loss of his life of tribulation, did not hesitate to pay such honourable thanks to his maker, what prevents me, named Æthelred also by the peoples on every side which are subject to our royal power, very copiously overflowing with the power conferred by that Creator of all dignities? If also I am not to postpone extolling with fitting praise His name according to the example of the aforesaid prophet, by distributing with most prompt devotion to His faithful those things which come to me from Him from day to day, as the need of each demands. But to bring the beginning of this speech to a definite end, I bestow a certain estate of my own possession, amounting to twenty-four hides, that is, Dumbleton as it is called by the locally born, lying separately in three places, to my very faithful Archbishop Ælfric, which he acquired from me with fifty talents, tested by the mighty measure of public weighing. This portion of land was subjected to me, according to

Ramsbury; see above, p. 35 n. 94. For Archbishop Ælfric being given further land in Dumbleton by Wulfric Spot, see below, B233.

349 Cf. Col. 2: 13–14.

350 Note Rom. 5: 14 'Sed regnavit mors ab Adam usque ad Moysen etiam in eos qui non peccaverunt in similitudinem praevaricationis Adae, qui est forma futuri.'

351 See 1 Cor. 13: 13.

352 Both quotations are from Job 1: 21.

preuaricatione mihimet uulgari subacta est traditione.[353] Itaque, ut diximus, ternis diuiditur in locis, decem et septem in occidentali parte fluminis Esingburnan continens mansas, ac duas in orientali eiusdem torrentis climate, sorte communes populari ad[l] Eastune, necnon et quinque locis siluaticis in utraque parte riuuli qui Pidwella appellatur, huiusque agnomen loci [m]ad Fleferth[m] dicitur.[354] Et hoc definimus, ut predictus pontifex hoc donum sibi quamdiu uixerit, cum omnibus ad se rite pertinentibus, campis, siluis, pratis, pascuis, confiniisque siluaticis, omni mundiali seruitio possideat liberrimum tribus exceptis, expeditione, arcis seu pontis constructione. Qui uero hoc augmentare uoluerit, augeatur ei benedictio superna. Qui autem minuere temptauerit uel aliud quid adinuenerit[n] contrarietatis, seu antiquiorem[o] forsan produxerit scedulam, a Christianismo anathematizetur latrociniique crimine obiurgetur, ni quantocius resipiscat.[p]
[i. 414] B fo. 101v Acta annotataque est hec donatio anno ab[q] incarnatione Christi .mii., indictione quinta decima, [r]his testibus consentientibus: Ego Æthelredus rex Anglorum hanc munificentiam largitus sum. Ego Ædelstan, et Egbrith, et Eadmund, et Eadward,[355] et Eadwi, et Eadgar filii regis. Ego Alfricus archiepiscopus pretio adquisiui. Ego Ælfheah, et Wlfstan, et Edulf, et Alfwold, et Eswic, et Liuinc, et
[i. 415] Æthelric episcopi, et plures alii coepiscopi. Ego Wlfgar abbas, et Alfward, et Kenulf, et Godwine, et Elfsie, et Germanus, et Eadnothus, et Leofricus abbates cum aliis abbatibus. Ego Alfric dux, et Alfhelm dux, et Leofwine dux.[r]

Ita regis donum ad archiepiscopum de Dumeltun processit. At ipse cum ad ultima uite perueniret, Abbendonensem[s] ecclesiam unde monachus extiterat inde heredem substituit, suam auctoritatem
[i. 416] intendendo ne quis presumptor suum testamentum irritum faceret.
B fo. 102r Cuius exemplar tali Anglico ca|ractere conditum fuit:[356]

[l] æt *B* [m–m] æt Fleferht *B* [n] *corr. by interlin. from* aduenerit *C* [o] antiquorem *B* [p] *see Charters of Abingdon Abbey, p. 514, for the boundaries in B* [q] *om. B* [r–r] *see Charters of Abingdon Abbey, pp. 514–15, for the witness list in B* [s] Abbendunensem *B*

[353] It is possible that this was the direct or indirect heiress of Bishop Osulf; see above, p. 35 n. 94.

common tradition, by a certain woman's transgression of fornication.[353] And so, as we have said, it is divided between three places, containing seventeen hides on the west side of the river Isbourne, and two on the east side of the same torrent, delegated by popular allocation to Aston; and also with five wooded places on either side of the river called the Piddle, the name of which place is *Fleferth*.[354] And we lay this down, that the aforesaid pontiff is to possess this gift for himself as long as he lives, with everything duly pertaining to it, fields, woods, meadows, pastures, and wooded regions, completely free of all worldly service except three, military service, and fortress and bridge construction. Whoever indeed wishes to augment this, let heavenly blessing be increased for him. But whosoever attempts to diminish it or devise anything else antagonistic, or perhaps produces an older document, is to be anathematized from Christianity and punished for the crime of theft, unless he recovers his senses at once. This gift was carried out and written down in the year 1002 from the Incarnation of Christ, the fifteenth indiction, with these witnesses consenting. I Æthelred king of the English have bestowed this munificence. I Æthelstan, and Ecgberht, and Edmund, and Edward,[355] and Eadwig, and Edgar the king's sons. I Archbishop Ælfric have acquired it with a payment. I Ælfheah, and Wulfstan, and Athulf, and Ælfwold, and Æscwig, and Lyfing, and Æthelric bishops, and many other fellow bishops. I Abbot Wulfgar, and Ælfweard, and Coenwulf, and Godwine, and Ælfsige, and Germanus, and Eadnoth, and Leofric abbots, with other abbots. I Ealdorman Ælfric, and Ealdorman Ælfhelm, and Ealdorman Leofwine.

Thus the king's gift of Dumbleton passed to the archbishop. But when he came to the end of his life, he made heir of it the church of Abingdon, where he had been a monk, by exerting his authority lest any presumptuous man make void his testament. An exemplar of this was drawn up in the following English writing:[356]

[354] Cf. above, p. 36.

[355] Almost certainly a mistake for Eadred, who appears here in the witness list in MS B.

[356] The Abingdon versions of the Worcester *Chronicle* specify that Ælfric was buried at Abingdon, but translated to his own see [Canterbury] in the reign of Cnut; John of Worcester, *Chronicle*, ii. 613.

105. (B236) *Testamentum Ælfrici archiepiscopi.*[a] [357]

[i. 417] Hic notificatur quomodo Ælfricus[b] archiepiscopus suarum rerum testamentum in extremo condidit. In primo[358] ecclesie Christi Cantuarie terram apud Wellam et apud Burnam et Hrisenburgam[c] [i. 418] B fo. 102v C fo. 128r contulit.[359] Domino suo me|liorem suarum nauium unam, | cum[d] sibi pertinentibus armamentis, et sexaginta galeas cum totidem loricis.[360] Et hoc apud ipsum [e]dominum suum[e] erat interueniens,[361] ut concederet loco Sancti Albani terram apud Chingesbiri[f] et ipse in commutationem reciperet Eadulfingtun.[362] Abbendonensi ecclesie terram apud Dumeltun, ubi Alfnodo[g] cuidam tres hidas concessit tenere tantum suis diebus, et postea rediret cum reliqua terra Abbendonensis ecclesie potestati; insuper et decem boues cum duobus hominibus.[363] Cuidam[h] quoque uiro nomine Celewardo terram quam emerat apud Walingaford, ut quamdiu uiueret possideret,[364] et post eius decessum ecclesia de Ceolsiga ipsius [i]dominatu terre[i] potiretur.[365] Ecclesie Sancti Albani terram apud Tiwan et Osanig, cum terra de Lundonia quam emerat idem archiepiscopus.[366] Que omnia quidam Ceolricus tunc tenebat, sed secundum quod archiepiscopo in conuentione habebat, post uite illius uiri finem ad predictam ecclesiam martiris uniuersa redirent. Libros etiam suos uniuersos illic delegauit. Precepitque ut de suis propriis expensis quicquid in mutuo ab aliquo acceptum erat restitueretur, et cetera in eius exequiis expenderentur.[367] Populo Cantie unam nauem, et alteram genti Wiltescire, iussit largiri.[368] Reliqua uniuersa que sua

105 [a] *following Old English version,* Quod Latine sic interpretatur *B* [b] Alfricus *B* [c] Hrisenbeorgam *B* [d] *followed by* eius *del. B* [e–e] suum dominum *B* [f] Cingesbiri *B* [g] Alfnoð primo *B* [h] Quidam *B* [i–i] terre dominatum *B*

[357] This is a Latin translation of an Old English original; the Old English is Sawyer, no. 1488; *Charters of Abingdon Abbey*, no. 133; *Anglo-Saxon Wills*, ed. Whitelock, no. 18, whose translation also appears in *EHD*, i. no. 126. *Anglo-Saxon Wills*, ed. Whitelock, pp. 160–3, provides extensive notes on the will. *Charters of Abingdon Abbey*, p. 519, states that 'there can be little doubt that [the will] is authentic'. MS B gives the Old English version, followed by the Latin. It is probably reproduced in full because of its use in the post-Conquest dispute concerning Dumbleton; vol. ii. 50. It is the only Anglo-Saxon will to appear in the *History*, even though other sections seem to draw on such wills; see above, p. xxxi, *Charters of Abingdon Abbey*, pp. 579–83.

[358] The Old English version specifies this was 'saulsceat', or burial due, on which see *Anglo-Saxon Wills*, ed. Whitelock, pp. 109–10.

[359] Westwell and probably Bishopsbourne, Kent; Monks Risborough, Buckinghamshire.

[360] On King Æthelred's desire for such bequests of military equipment, see N. P. Brooks, 'Arms, status and warfare in late-Saxon England', in D. Hill, ed., *Ethelred the Unready: Papers from the Millenary Conference* (British Archaeological Reports, British Series lix; 1978), pp. 81–103, at 90. *Anglo-Saxon Wills*, ed. Whitelock, p. 161, states that 'this is not a payment of heriot, as the Archbishop leaves instructions about this later in his

105. (B236) *Archbishop Ælfric's will.*[357]

Here it is made known how Archbishop Ælfric at the last drew up a testament of his possessions. First,[358] he conferred on Christ Church Canterbury land at Well and at Bourne and Risborough.[359] To his lord the best of his ships, with the tackle pertaining to it, and sixty helmets with as many mail coats.[360] And he was in his lord's presence, pleading this,[361] that he would grant land at Kingsbury to the monastery of St Alban and himself receive in exchange *Eadulfington*.[362] To the church of Abingdon land at Dumbleton, where he granted to a certain Ælfnoth three hides to hold only for life, and afterwards it would return with the rest of the land to the power of the church of Abingdon; in addition ten oxen with two men.[363] Also to a man named Ceolweard land that he had bought at Wallingford, that he might possess as long as he lives,[364] and after his death the church of Cholsey is to control the lordship of that land.[365] To the church of St Alban land at Tew and Osney, with land at London which that archbishop had bought.[366] All these a certain Ceolric was then holding, but according to the terms of agreement he had with the archbishop, after the end of that man's life the entirety would return to the aforesaid church of the martyr. Also he bequeathed to there all his books. And he ordered that whatever had been received as a loan from anyone should be restored from his own funds, and the remainder was to be spent on his funeral.[367] He ordered one ship to be bestowed on the folk of Kent, another on the people of Wiltshire.[368]

will'; see below, n. 367. However, the later provision of money could be in addition to this payment of military equipment to provide for his heriot.

361 Cf. the Old English version 'he wilnode gif hit his lafordes willa wære', 'he wishes, if it were his lord's will'; *Charters of Abingdon Abbey*, pp. 518–19.

362 Kingsbury, Middlesex. *Eadulfington* was probably close to Edmonton, Hertfordshire; *Charters of Abingdon Abbey*, p. 521.

363 See below, B225 (*Charters of Abingdon Abbey*, no. 126). For comment on the status of the two men, see D. A. E. Pelteret, *Slavery in Early Medieval England* (Woodbridge, 1995), p. 122.

364 This point is not spelt out in the Old English version.

365 Wallingford, Berkshire. Also in Berkshire, the church of Cholsey had been founded by King Æthelred and was in Ælfric's former diocese of Ramsbury; *Charters of Abingdon Abbey*, p. 521.

366 Tew and Osney are both in Oxfordshire. Instead of this and the following sentence, the Old English version has a fuller description of the arrangements concerning Tew, as well as recording the gift of land in Osney and London.

367 In the Old English version, this is referred to as his heriot, rather than expenditure on his funeral.

368 Previous to being archbishop of Canterbury, Ælfric had been bishop of Ramsbury, hence his connection with the people of Wiltshire as well as Kent.

uidebantur esse[j] domnum Wlfstanum episcopum et Leofricum abbatem rogauit quatinus sua prouidentia quo melius consulerent dispertirent.[369] Sororibus suis et earum filiis terram de Fittinctune et[k] Niwentune contulit,[370] et terram que erat Alfeagi[l] filii Esni restituit iis[m] quibus proprie pertinuerat habere.[371] Domno[n] Wlfstano archiepiscopo unum philacterium[372] cum uno anulo et codice psalterii, sed
[i. 419] et Alfheago[o] episcopo unam crucem in suam memoriam dedit.[373] Debita que sibi debebantur a multis passim condonauit.[374] Si quis uero, secundum patrie Anglie morem, in aliquam incurrisset seruitutem tempore sue potestatis, libertate sibi penitus contributa, relaxatus eius iussu est.[375] De his quicumque aliter quam ut dictata[p] sunt peruerterit, inde cum Deo concertamen habeat. Amen.

B fo. 105r **106. (B240)** [a]*Quomodo Cealgraua et Bulteswrða ad hanc ecclesiam uenerunt.*[a] [376]

[i. 428] Matrona temporibus his quedam nomine Alfgifa terram de Cealgraue et de Bulteswrðe[b] ecclesie isti concessit Abbendonensi.[c] Cuius
[i. 429] concessionis testes fuerunt Oswold[d] archiepiscopus, et Alfheah episcopus, et Æscwi[e] episcopus, et Ædelsi[f] episcopus, et Odulf[g] episcopus;[377] dux quoque Thured,[378] et multi primatuum, rege etiam fauente, et abbate Eadwino inibi presidente.

[j] *om. B* [k] *followed by* de *B* [l] Alfheagi *B* [m] hiis *B* [n] Homno *B* [o] Alfego *B* [p] *corr. from* dicta *by interlin. C*

106 [a–a] *heading in right-hand margin C;* De Alfifa que reddidit Chelgraue et Bulteswurþ *B* [b] Bulteswrþe *B* [c] Abbendunensi *B* [d] *each name preceded by a cross B* [e] Aeswig *B* [f] Aþelsige *B* [g] *rectius* Ædulf *or* Adulf

[369] Wulfstan was bishop of London 996–1002, bishop of Worcester 1002–16, and archbishop of York 1002–23; *Handbook of British Chronology*, pp. 220, 224. It is curious that he is here referred to as bishop, later in the document as archbishop. *Charters of Abingdon Abbey*, p. 520, suggests that the first reference may simply be a scribal error, or that the will was first composed when Wulfstan was bishop of London but revised after his promotion to York. Leofric was abbot of St Albans from *c.*990 to an uncertain date, and was Archbishop Ælfric's brother; *Heads of Religious Houses*, pp. 65, 254.

[370] Both Gloucestershire. The Old English version specifies that these lands were in the west ['be westan'].

[371] The Old English version specifies rather that the land was to remain in Ælfheah son of Esne's family.

[372] The Old English version specifies a 'sweorrode', a pectoral cross.

[373] Ælfheah was bishop of Winchester 984–1005, and archbishop of Canterbury 1006–12; *Handbook of British Chronology*, pp. 214, 223.

[374] *Anglo-Saxon Wills*, ed. Whitelock, p. 163, speculates that 'probably these debts were incurred during the Danish raids, in order to bribe the invaders'. The Old English version

Everything else that appeared to be his he asked lord Bishop Wulfstan and Abbot Leofric that they distribute by their own provision as they considered best.[369] On his sisters and their children he bestowed the land of Fiddington and Newton,[370] and the land of Ælfheah son of Esne he restored to those to whom it properly pertained to have.[371] To lord Archbishop Wulfstan he gave in memory of himself a phylactery[372] with one ring and a codex of the Psalter, and also to Bishop Ælfheah a cross.[373] He pardoned everywhere debts that were owed to him by many men.[374] If anyone, indeed, according to the custom of the land of England, incurred any servitude in the time of his power, that person was released by his order and liberty completely rendered him.[375] Whoever corrupts these arrangements contrary to what has been dictated is to have a conflict with God concerning this. Amen.

106. (B240) *How Chalgrave and* Bulthesworthe *came to this church.*[376] At this time a certain matron named Ælfgifu granted land at Chalgrave and *Bulthesworthe* to this church of Abingdon. Witnesses of this grant were Archbishop Oswald, and Bishop Ælfheah, and Bishop Æscwig, and Bishop Æthelsige, and Bishop Athulf;[377] also Ealdorman Thored[378] and many other of the leading men, by the king's favour too, when Abbot Eadwine was in charge there.

specifies that, in accordance with God's will, he forgave the people of Kent the debts that they owed him and the people of Middlesex and Kent the money he had advanced them.

375 The synod held at Chelsea in 816 ordered that every Englishman subjected to slavery in a bishop's lifetime should be freed at the bishop's death; *Councils and Ecclesiastical Documents relating to Great Britain and Ireland*, ed. A. W. Haddan and W. Stubbs (3 vols., Oxford, 1869–78), iii. 583; Pelteret, *Slavery*, pp. 83, 120. The Old English version specifies that after his day all penally enslaved men ['*witefæstne*'] condemned in his time were to be freed, but does not use the phrase 'according to the custom of the land of England'.

376 *Charters of Abingdon Abbey*, p. 580 (iv), suggests that this section was 'probably based on a witnessed private charter'. King Æthelstan had granted Chalgrave, probably the Chalgrave in Bedfordshire, to his thegn Ealdred, and *Bulthesworthe* to his thegn Wulfnoth; below, B55, B59 (*Charters of Abingdon Abbey*, nos. 21, 24). *Bulthesworthe* cannot be identified with any certainty. Abingdon had no interest in these lands by the time of *Domesday Book*, when Albert of Lorraine held eight hides and half a virgate there; *DB* i, fo. 216^{v}. From this section onwards, the proportion of the *History* made up of charters drops markedly; see above, p. lxxii.

377 Oswald was archbishop of York 971–92; Æscwig probably bishop of Dorchester 975 × 979–1002; Æthelsige bishop of Sherborne 978 × 979–991/3; Athulf bishop of Hereford *c.*971–*c.*1013; *Handbook of British Chronology*, pp. 215, 217, 222, 224.

378 Thored was an ealdorman in Northumbria, last heard of in 992; Keynes, *Diplomas*, p. 197.

107. (B241) [a]*Quomodo Winecafeld et Wicham et Hildesduna ad istam ecclesiam peruenerint.*[a] [379]

Item nobilis alia matrona nomine Eadfled terram de Winekefeld[b] et de Wicham et de Hisdesduna Abbendonensi ecclesie largita est, cum scrinio sanctarum reliquiarum et textu euuangeliorum, argento et auro redimitis, cum calice quoque argenteo[c] et uestimento sacerdotali.[380]

108. (B242) [a]*De Bydena et Hordwille.*[a]

Item princeps[b] australium Saxonum[c] Eadwinus[d] nomine obiens,
B fo. 105v Ab|bendonensi loco sepelitur. Cuius testamenti concessu terre de Budene et de Hordewilla eidem derelicte sunt.[381]

[i. 430] **109.** Duxit[382] autem rex Æthelredus Normannorum comitis Ricardi filiam in coniugium, nomine Emmam, quam Angli Elfgiuam Immam cognominarunt, de qua Eadwardum et alios liberos genuit, magne
[i. 431] pietatis hominem.[383] Frater uero eiusdem regine Ricardus iunior dicebatur, de quo natus est Robertus, Willelmi pater qui Angliam
C fo. 128v postea aggressus regnum | illic sibi usurpauit. Interea tanta ecclesiasticarum et secularium rerum his temporibus, tamque frequens fieri hac in patria permutatio, quanta hactenus apud Anglos quisquam non audierat. Nam eodem rege regnante, Cantuariensis cathedre apicem quinque, sibi inuicem succedentes, patriarche morte commutarunt, scilicet Dunstanus, Ælfgarus, Sigericus, Alfricus, Ælfegus, Liuingus.[384] At in secularium personarum maiores, diuersi anfractus

107 [a–a] *heading in right hand margin C;* De Alfled que reddidit Winkefeld *B* [b] Winkefeld *B* [c] argento *B*

108 [a–a] De Edwio qui reddidit Bedene *B* [b] *corr. from* principes *B* [c] Westsaxonum, *corr. by another hand to* australium *by expunction and interlineation C* [d] Eadwius *B*

---

[379] See *Charters of Abingdon Abbey*, pp. 580–1 (v), which suggests that this passage was probably derived from an undated Old English will. Eadflæd may have been the widow of Ealdorman Ælfhere of Mercia; see above, p. cxxiii. *De abbatibus* states that a woman named 'Elfleda' gave the church Winkfield, Wickham, Ginge, and Hillesden, during the abbacy of Ordric (1052–66); *CMA* ii. 282. However, the compiler of *De abbatibus* may have been guessing, and the position in the *History* certainly suggests a date in Æthelred's reign. If the donor is Ælfhere's widow, the gift would have been made at the end of the 10th c. See *Charters of Abingdon Abbey*, no. 43, for a grant by King Eadred to Æthelmær *praeses* that included Hillesden, Buckinghamshire. It is notable that *Charters of Abingdon Abbey*, no. 43, does not appear in the *History*; see above, p. cxcvi. Abingdon had no interest in Hillesden at the time of *Domesday*; *DB* i, fos. 146v, 147v.

[380] On reliquaries in lay hands, particularly women's, see Dodwell, *Anglo-Saxon Art*, p. 197.

107. (B241) *How Winkfield and Wickham and Hillesden came to this church.*[379]

Likewise, another matron named Eadflæd bestowed the land of Winkfield and of Wickham and of Hillesden on the church of Abingdon, with a reliquary of holy relics and a Gospel book cased in silver and gold, together with a silver chalice and a priestly vestment.[380]

108. (B242) *Concerning Beedon and Hardwell.*

Likewise, a noble of the South Saxons named Eadwine died, and was buried at the monastery of Abingdon. By grant of his testament lands at Beedon and Hardwell were bequeathed to it.[381]

109. Moreover[382] King Æthelred took in marriage the daughter of Richard, count of the Normans, Emma by name, whom the English called Ælfgifu Imma, with whom he had Edward, a man of great piety, and other children.[383] That queen's brother, indeed, was called Richard the younger, from whom was born Robert the father of the William who later attacked England and seized for himself the kingship there. Meanwhile at this time there was so great and so frequent change of ecclesiastical and secular affairs in this country as no one had hitherto heard of amongst the English. For during the king's reign five patriarchs exchanged at death the crowning dignity of the see of Canterbury, succeeding one another in turn, that is Dunstan, Æthelgar, Sigeric, Ælfric, Ælfheah, Lyfing.[384] Also amongst the greater secular persons, affairs took a contrary turn. For the people of the

[381] *Charters of Abingdon Abbey*, p. 581 (vi), suggests that the details probably come from an undated Old English will which does not survive. The donor is probably Eadwine ealdorman of Sussex, who died in 982. See also above, c. 86, on Beedon, and below, B44–B45 (*Charters of Abingdon Abbey*, no. 19), on Hardwell, Berkshire. *De abbatibus* states that a man named 'Edwi' gave Hardwell and Beedon to the church of Abingdon, again dating the gift to Abbot Ordric's time (1052–66); *CMA* ii. 282. Again, however, the compiler of *De abbatibus* may have been guessing, and the position in the *History* certainly supports a date in Æthelred's reign. Hardwell does not have a separate *Domesday* entry, but land there may be the three hides one virgate held by Gilbert de Colombières entered under Watchfield; see *DB* i, fo. 59^r, vol. ii. 324. The name survives in Hardwell Farm, Compton Beauchamp; EPNS, *Berkshire*, ii. 360–1.

[382] MS B, below B243, contains a different section, although with some verbal parallels to MS C.

[383] Æthelred married Emma in 1002. The Edward mentioned here is the future King Edward the Confessor. Æthelred and Emma's other children were a son named Alfred and a daughter named Godgifu; P. Stafford, *Queen Emma and Queen Edith* (Oxford, 1997), p. 3.

[384] The five deaths in Æthelred's reign were Dunstan in 988, Æthelgar 990, Sigeric 994, Ælfric 1005, and Ælfheah 1012. Lyfing lived until 1020; *Handbook of British Chronology*, p. 214.

incussio. Siquidem gens Danorum cum rege suo Sueino, in Angliam appulsa, adeo ferocitatem ubique locorum et impietatem suam uiritim infudit ut prede, crematui, necique uniuersa dederent. Non dignitati, non etati, non sexui, ulla tunc reuerentie delatio seruata. Peruersus quisque iusticieque proditor ad hostes diffugium habere, idem metu alii facere. Ita rex Ethelredus, a suis diatim destitutus, Normanniam una cum uxore petiit comitique Normannorum Ricardo iuniori, cuius sororem habebat in matrimonium, sese credidit.[385] Verum Sueinus regnum usurpans Anglie, recipitur pro domino. Sed non diu inde letari permissus, quia et regno et uita in proximo priuatur Dei arbitrio. Post cuius interitum, a transmarinis rex Anglorum remeans oris,[a] regno potitur prius habito.[386]

B fo. 105ᵛ **110. (B244)** [a]*De temporibus Cnut regis.*[a]

Interim[b] Danis Sueini defuncti complicibus una cum Anglis contra genuinum dominum conspirantibus, Canutoni filio eiusdem regis [i. 432] sese summittunt, dant fidem, ad que liberet prompte se pergere spondent. Talibus iterum circumuentionibus, rex sollicitus morbo corripitur ac triginta et sex exactis in regno annis uario periculorum euentu implicitis moritur.[387] Nec mora Eadmundus filius eius ab his qui patri adheserant coronatur.[388] Qui temptans partes Cnutonis fundere bello, multorum mentes consciuit ferre iuuamen, quatinus barbare gentis dominatum uiuida a se repellerent manu. Multitudine ergo sibi adunata, quinquies eodem anno suis intulit bellum aduersariis.[389] Nec tamen fieri superior eis ualuit, immo augeri illos et se deorsum iri, tum et maximam nobilium copiam hinc et inde cesam fuisse contigit. Quare utriusque principis exercitus id consilii equi B fo. 106ʳ fore decernunt, quo | pax[c] sacramento fideque utrimque constatuatur, ne uidelicet amplius suorum tanti sanguinis regnandi illectu[d] proueniat effusio. Consultus ad ipsam rem usque deducitur, itaque regibus ad inuicem conciliatis, Eadmundus[e] occidentalibus,[390] Cnuto

109 [a] horis *C*

110 [a–a] De morte Adelredi regis et de regno Edmundi regis filii sui *B* [b] Item *B* [c] *followed by* et *B* [d] intellectu *B* [e] Aþelredus *B*

[385] Emma in fact went to Normandy before Æthelred in 1013. He joined her there after Christmas of that year; *ASC*, *s.a.* 1013. William of Malmesbury, *Gesta regum*, bk. ii, c. 178, ed. Mynors *et al.*, i. 304, places his crossing in Jan. 1014. See also S. Keynes, 'The Æthelings in Normandy', *ANS*, xiii (1991), 173–205, at pp. 175–6.

[386] Swein died 3 Feb. 1014. After some negotiation, Æthelred returned, having agreed that he would rule more justly than before; *ASC*, *s.a.* 1014.

[387] Æthelred died on 23 Apr. 1016; *ASC*, *s.a.* 1016. Whilst he succeeded in Mar. 978,

Danes with their King Swein landed in England and each spilt out such ferocity and impiety everywhere that they gave everything over to booty, burning, and death. No delay on account of reverence then paid heed to rank or age or sex. Every depraved man and betrayer of justice made his escape to the enemies, and others did the same out of fear. So King Æthelred, daily abandoned by his men, went together with his wife to Normandy and entrusted himself to Richard the younger, count of the Normans, whose sister he had in marriage.[385] Swein, seizing the realm of England, was accepted as lord. However, he was not allowed to rejoice about this for long, since he was soon deprived both of the kingdom and of life by the judgement of God. After his death, the king of the English returned from overseas shores and possessed the kingdom he had previously had.[386]

110. (B244) *Concerning the times of King Cnut.*

Meanwhile the Danish associates of the deceased Swein conspired together with Englishmen against the genuine lord and submitted to Cnut, Swein's son, pledged their faith to him, and promised that they would readily pursue those things he might desire. Amidst such plots again, the troubled king was seized by illness and died after completing in his reign thirty-six years embroiled in diverse dangerous events.[387] Without delay his son Edmund was crowned by those who had adhered to his father.[388] He tried to rout Cnut's side in battle, directing the minds of many to bring help so that with spirited force they might drive back from themselves the lordship of a barbarous people. Therefore, when he had gathered a multitude for himself, he took battle to his opponents five times in the same year.[389] However, he could not prevail over them and gain the upper hand, but rather they increased and he declined, a great mass of nobles on both sides being slain. Therefore the armies of both princes decided that the following plan would be just: that peace be established by oath and pledge of faith by both sides, lest, that is, the streaming forth of so much of their men's blood proceeded in greater quantity with the enticement of ruling. Counsel brought this about, and so, when the kings had been reconciled, Edmund ruled the western peoples,[390]

according to the *ASC*, 'C', he was only consecrated on 4 May 979. In that case, only thirty-six years were completed between his consecration and his death.

[388] On the events of Edmund Ironside's reign mentioned in the following sentences, see Lawson, *Cnut*, pp. 19–20.

[389] *ASC*, *s.a.* 1016, refers to Edmund's preparations for the battle of *Assundun* in 1016 as the fifth time he gathered the people of England.

Merciorum, populis imperarunt. His taliter[f] peractis, Eadmundus hominem exiuit, non plusquam sex mensium transcurso curriculo ex quo regni sumpserat moderamina.[391] Inde totius Brittannie Cnuto monarchiam, quin et Datie et Norweie dominatum, adipiscitur triuiatim. Inter quos tam dissidentes in Anglia motus, hinc Dei miseratione protegente, illic abbatis Wlfgari industria uigilante, cenobium Abbendonense a Danorum deuastatione permansit immune, cum dextra leuaque hostium incursio passim loca uniuersa subrueret aut, si beniuolentior fieret, maximo sese pretio habitatores eorum redimere sineret.

[i. 433] 111. *De morte Wlfgari abbatis.*[392]

Circa idem tempus domnus Wlfgarus pastor defecit.[393] Deflendo funera fecit quem pie tractauit deuotus grex et amauit.[394] Cui in pastoralitate domnus Æthelwinus successit, equitatis comprobatus C fo. 129r assertor, et plurime apud Cnutonem familiaritatis iccirco | consecutus usum.[a] Vnde loco Abbendonensi se rex priuatum[b] gerebat, uenerationem suam illic sedulo conferendo.[395] Quod adhuc celebri predicatur indicio, quo tecam de argento et auro decenter ornatam honori martiris ac leuite Vincentii Hispaniensis fieri fecit,[396] quatinus in ea eiusdem martiris reliquie locarentur, summa ab uniuersis suffragium eo diuinum petentibus ueneratione in palam colende. In qua etiam apices sculpte erant quorum forma hec est:

Rex[c] Cnut hanc thecam necnon Ælfgiua regina
Cudere iusserunt. Bis centum necne decemque,
Coctos igne chrison[397] mancosos atque uiginti,
Necne duas libras argenti pondere magno.

[f] itaque *B*

111 [a] ausum *MS* [b] rex *rep. MS* [c] *the initials starting the lines of the reliquary inscription are set slightly into the margin*

[390] i.e. Wessex; see also *ASC*, *s.a.* 1016.

[391] Edmund died 30 Nov. 1016; *ASC*, *s.a.* 1016.

[392] This section does not appear in MS B, which provides a much shorter passage, the opening of which contains some verbal parallels to MS C; see below, B245.

[393] Wulfgar died 18 Sept. 1016; *ASC*, 'C', Cambridge, University Library, Kk. i 22, fo. 5v. The Abingdon version of the Worcester *Chronicle* preserved in Lambeth Palace Library states that 'Pius pastor Abbendonie Wulgarus obiit anno .xxviii. ex quo illum diuina pietas eidem ecclesie prefecit.' It then includes a passage similar to that at the end of c. 110, followed by mention of Æthelwine's succession. Of Æthelwine, it states 'Quem rex

Cnut those of the Mercians. When these events had been completed thus, Edmund departed human life, following the passage of not more than six months from when he had undertaken the governance of the kingdom.[391] And so Cnut attained the monarchy of the whole of Britain, far and wide, and also lordship of Denmark and Norway. Amidst such dissensions in England, sometimes by the protection of God's mercy, sometimes by the alertness of Abbot Wulfgar's industry, the monastery of Abingdon remained unharmed by the devastation of the Danes, while the enemies' incursions were everywhere, right and left, undermining all places or, if more merciful, allowing their inhabitants to ransom themselves at a very great price.

111. *Concerning the death of Abbot Wulfgar.*[392]

Around that time lord Wulfgar the shepherd died.[393] The devoted flock that piously treated and loved him performed his funeral rites in mourning.[394] Lord Æthelwine succeeded him in the pastorship, a proven assertor of justice, and therefore he enjoyed the closest familiarity with Cnut. Whence the king conducted himself like an ordinary man towards the monastery of Abingdon, by earnestly conferring his veneration on it.[395] This is still proclaimed by a famous sign, in that he had made from silver and gold a reliquary fittingly decorated in honour of the martyr and levite Vincent of Spain,[396] so that the relics of this martyr might be placed in it, to be openly honoured with the highest veneration by all seeking divine help through this. Also on it letters were engraved, of which this is the form:

King Cnut and also Queen Ælfgifu ordered the casting of this reliquary.
Twice a hundred and also ten and twenty
gold[397] mancuses smelted with fire,
and two pounds in great weight of silver.

Kanutus pro laudabilis uite merito secretorum suorum conscium efficiens a noxiis sese retrahere ac recta appetere eius suasionibus studebat. Hinc et cenobium Abbendonense a rege diligitur et muneribus eius cumulatur, nam inter alia sua donaria capsam de argento et auro parari fecit in qua sancti Vincentii leuite et martiris reliquie collocarentur'; John of Worcester, *Chronicle*, ii. 614.

[394] For this metrical epitaph, see above, p. xxxvi. On the problem of abbatial succession at this point, see above, p. c.

[395] Cf. below, B249. The text here is corrupt, and its sense somewhat uncertain.

[396] On St Vincent, see above, p. clxxiv.

[397] Interestingly, an Abingdon charter of 1007 uses a related form of this Greek-derived word, below, B237 (*Charters of Abingdon Abbey*, no. 134): 'pro trecentis criseis adpreciauit mancusis'.

[i. 434] Hec in superiori parte, et ista inferius continebantur, scripta:

Istud Ædelwini patris sub tempore domni
Martiris est Vincentii sub honore peractum.

Hec uero nominata regina binomia quidem, scilicet Ælfgiua Imma, Ædelredo regi conubio primum copulata, quam iste Cnuto regno confirmato in coniugem duxit, Hardecnutonemque ex ea genuit.[398] Addidit huic pio rex Cnuto beneficio ut duo grossioris soni signa tunc quidem laudabilis istic donaret. Abbas autem Ædelwinus capsam alteram, ad formam illius que per regem facta fuit, pari pene magnitudine, condidit, ubi reliquias sanctorum a se exquisitas intulit.

112. *De Siwardo abbate.*[399]

His ergo uita decedens, successorem Siwardum, ex Glestoniensi quidem cenobio monachum, accepit, tam secularium quam ecclesiasticarum uigore admodum suffultum.[400] Cuius mentio in quadam eiusdem regis cartula sic continetur.

113. *Carta regis Cnut de Mytuna.*[401]

In nomine Dei et Domini nostri Ihesu Christi. Anno Dominice incarnationis .mxxxiiii., indictione secunda, ego Cnut, rex Anglorum totiusque Brittannice orbis gubernator et rector, superna annuente gratia, ab eodem Deo et Domino nostro Ihesu Christo populis et tribubus preelectus in regem, anno imperii mei undeuicensimo, fui rogatus a uenerabili abbate Abbendonensis ecclesie, uocitato nomine Siwardo, ut quandam terram trium manentium in loco qui dicitur ab accolis Mytun ad monasterium beatissime Dei genitricis semperque
[i. 435] uirginis Marie, quod situm est ad Abbandune, libenter concedo, eius gratia amoris qui dicit 'Petite, et dabitur uobis'.[402] Maneat igitur hoc nostrum immobile donum, eterna libertate iocundum, cum omnibus ad se rite pertinentibus, tam in notis causis quam ignotis, in modicis et in magnis, campis, pratis, pascuis, aquarumque cursibus, excepto istis tribus, expeditione, pontis arcisue restauratione. Et mandamus in

[398] For Emma's marriage to Cnut in 1017, see Stafford, *Queen Emma and Queen Edith*, esp. pp. 226–30. The marriage also produced a daughter named Gunnhild.

[399] MS B contains a different passage, but with some verbal parallels; below, B251.

[400] The Abingdon version of the Worcester *Chronicle* preserved in Lambeth Palace Library contains a similar sentence concerning Siward, preceded by the statement that Æthelwine had died; John of Worcester, *Chronicle*, ii. 614. Æthelwine died on 25 Feb. 1030.

[401] Warwickshire. Sawyer, no. 973; *Charters of Abingdon Abbey*, no. 140. This is an unusual instance of a charter appearing only in MS C. MS B has a different charter concerning Myton, below, B246 (*Charters of Abingdon Abbey*, no. 139). *Charters of Abingdon*

These words were written on the top, and the following were stated below:

> This was done in the time of lord father Æthelwine
> In honour of the martyr Vincent.

This queen with two names, that is Ælfgifu Imma, who had first been joined in marriage to King Æthelred, Cnut took as his wife once he had been confirmed in the kingship, and from her he had a son Harthacnut.[398] King Cnut added to this pious favour that he would then praiseworthily give two very resonant bells in this place. Moreover, Abbot Æthelwine constructed another reliquary of almost equal size, on the model of that which had been made on the king's behalf, where he put saints' relics that he had sought out.

112. *Concerning Abbot Siward.*[399]

When he departed life, he had as successor Siward, a monk indeed from the monastery of Glastonbury, well buttressed with vigour in both worldly and ecclesiastical matters.[400] He is mentioned as follows in a charter of the same king:

113. *Charter of King Cnut concerning Myton.*[401]

In the name of God and our Lord Jesus Christ. In the year of our Lord 1034, the second indiction, I, Cnut, king of the English and governor and ruler of the whole British world, with the assent of heavenly grace, chosen by that God and our Lord Jesus Christ as king for the peoples and tribes, in the nineteenth year of my dominion, have been asked by the venerable abbot of the church of Abingdon, called by the name Siward, that I willingly grant certain land amounting to three hides in the place called Myton by the inhabitants to the monastery of the most blessed mother of God Mary, ever Virgin, situated at Abingdon, by grace of the love of Him who says 'Ask, and it shall be given you'.[402] Therefore let this gift of ours remain immovable, happy in eternal liberty, with everything duly pertaining to it, both in known and unknown affairs, in small things and in great, fields, meadows, pastures, and watercourses, except these three, military service, and bridge and fortress repair. And we

Abbey, pp. 547–9, examines the difficulties of accepting both charters as genuine, although there is no certain reason for condemning either. Abingdon did not hold land in Myton in *Domesday*; *DB* i, fos. 239^{v}, 241^{v}. For speculation that the estate may have been exchanged with Earl Eadwine for lands at Barford St Michael, Oxfordshire, see *Charters of Abingdon Abbey*, pp. 548–9.

[402] Matt. 7: 7, Luke 11: 9.

nomine Dei Patris omnipotentis et Filii et Spiritus Sancti ut nullus superueniat hominum, superbia inflatus aut aliqua maliuola instigatione, hanc prefatam donationem atque libertatem in alicuius honeris molestia mutare audeat. Et si prescriptis litteris noluerit consentiens esse, sit ipse in profundum chaos igneis nexibus mancipatus et eius memoria caligine mortis obtecta. Sciatque se alienum a consortio sancte Dei ecclesie per auctoritatem beati Petri apostoli omniumque sociorum eius, nisi hic digna satisfactione emendauerit ante mortem quod contra nostrum decretum maliuola machinatione peregit. Si autem aliquis hoc adaugere uoluerit, augeat Deus partem illius in terra uiuentium. Ego Cnut rex Anglorum concessi. Ego Ælfgiua regina hanc libertatem libentissime a prefato rege domino meo adquisiui. Ego Æthelnotus archipresul et ego Ælfricus, cum ceteris omnibus, confirmauimus.[403] |

C fo. 129^{v} **114. (B247)** [a]*Carta duorum manentium de Linford.*[a] [404]

[i. 439] B fo. 106^{v} Pax et uictoria apostolice fidei[b] cultoribus. Ecclesie uero catholice auctoritas iugis et indefessa obtamus ut permaneat. Ad sacra autem B fo. 107^{r} sanctuaria | in Domini gazophilatio[c] diuersa iubentur iactari ac offerri munuscula, quia Regi nato celorum, ut scriptum est, reges terre [d]munera obtulerunt.[d] [405] Vnde ego Cnut, eius gratuita miseratione et inolita benignitate totius Albionis basileus, paruam ruris particulam quod ab huius patrie incolis Linford nuncupatur, duorum uidelicet manentium quantitatem, quoddamque monasteriolum in honore sancti Martini presulis consecratum, cum adiacenti prediolo in urbe que famoso nomine Oxanaford[e] nuncupatur,[406] Domino nostro Ihesu Christo eiusque genitrici semperque uirgini Marie ad usus monachorum loco qui celebri Abbandun uocitatur onomate eterna largitus sum hereditate; in nomine sancte Trinitatis et indiuidue Vnitatis precipiens ut nullus alicuius persone hominum prefatam donationem a predicto cenobio auferre presumat. Hec autem ruris particula libera ut maneat precipio, causis tribus segregatis, expeditione scilicet

114 [a–a] Carta regis Cnut de Linford *B* [b] *followed by* in perpetuum *B* [c] gazofilatio *B* [d–d] optulerunt munera *B* [e] Oxnaford *B*

[403] See *Charters of Abingdon Abbey*, no. 140A, for the boundary clause preserved in the quire of charter bounds at the end of MS C (fo. 202^{v}), in the main scribe's hand.

[404] Sawyer, no. 964; *Charters of Abingdon Abbey*, no. 138, which, at p. 542, states that this charter 'can probably be considered authentic', most likely 'drawn up in the abbey'; see also the other comments noted in the revised Sawyer, no. 964. The estate mentioned in this charter may be included with the smaller of Abingdon's two *Domesday* holdings at Lyford,

order in the name of almighty God the Father and Son and Holy Spirit that no man, puffed up with pride or at any malevolent instigation, shall come up and dare to change this aforementioned gift and liberty by the infliction of any burden. And if he is unwilling to consent to the aforewritten letters, let him be assigned to deep chaos with fiery bonds and his memory concealed by the darkness of death. And let him know that he is outside the fellowship of the holy Church of God by the authority of the blessed apostle Peter and all his associates, unless he makes amends here with fitting compensation before death for having gone against our decision by malevolent plotting. If, moreover, anyone wishes to augment this, let God increase his share in the land of the living. I Cnut king of the English have granted. I Queen Ælfgifu have acquired this liberty most willingly from the aforementioned king my husband. I Archbishop Æthelnoth and I Ælfric, with all others, have confirmed.[403]

114. (B247) *Charter regarding two hides in Lyford.*[404]

Peace and victory to worshippers of the apostolic faith. We truly desire that the authority of the Catholic Church remain endless and constant. Moreover, diverse small gifts are ordered to be set down and offered to the sacred sanctuaries in the treasury of the Lord, since, as it has been written, the kings of earth brought gifts to the King of Heaven when he was born.[405] Wherefore I, Cnut, by His freely given mercy and accustomed kindness emperor of the whole of Albion, have bestowed as eternal inheritance a very small portion of land called Lyford by the inhabitants of the land, that is the quantity of two hides, and a little minster consecrated in honour of St Martin the bishop, with the adjacent small estate in the town called by the famous name Oxford,[406] on our Lord Jesus Christ and His mother Mary, ever Virgin, for the use of the monks at the monastery which is called by the well-known name Abingdon; ordering in the name of the Holy Trinity and the indivisible Unity that no man of any rank may presume to take away the aforementioned gift from the aforesaid monastery. Moreover, I order that this small portion of land remain free, with three matters set aside, namely war service, royal fortress

Berkshire, amounting to three hides, which had been held from the abbey by a monk called Lindbald *TRE*; *DB* i, fo. 59^r; *Charters of Abingdon Abbey*, p. 160.

[405] Cf. Ps. 67 (68): 30 'Tibi offerent reges munera'; Ps. 71 (72): 10–11 'Reges Tharsis et insulae munera offerent; reges Arabum et Saba dona adducent; et adorabunt eum omnes reges terrae, omnes gentes seruient ei'; Matt. 2: 11.

[406] St Martin's at Carfax, with land probably between Queen Street and Shoe Lane; Blair, *Anglo-Saxon Oxfordshire*, pp. 151, 156.

hostili, fundatione arcis regie, pontisque restauratione. Si quis uero inuidus, ignicomis philargirie flammis accensus, huic ueridico libellulo alium circumatramentatum[f] cupiditatis fallacia libellum superimponere conatus fuerit, sit anathema marathana,[g][407] hoc est alienatio a consortio Christianorum, donec resipiscens peniteat quod in inuidie
[i. 440] fallacis liuore probarat.[h] [i]Tantillum terre huius Adelwinus testamento hereditauit Abbendonam et curiam apud Oxonofordam in qua ipsemet commanebat.[i][408] Et hoc fecit multorum testimonio. [j]Acta est hec cartula anno Dominice incarnationis duo et triginta post mille. Et ut hoc inuiolabilis firmitas soliditatem obtinere possit, ego Cnut regali dextera eandem uexillo sancte crucis + corroboro, manibusque
[i. 441] omnium mihi subiectorum confirmare precipio. Ego Ælfgiua predicti regis collatera istud donum crucis uexillo + consolidaui. Ego Æthelnodus Dorobernensis ecclesie archiepiscopus regium munus gabulo sancte crucis confirmo. Idem ego Ælfricus Eboracensis ecclesie archiepiscopus facio. ⟨I⟩dem[k] Wlfsius episcopus cum multis aliis facio.[j]

[i. 442] **115. (cf. B248)** In his et tempora predicti abbatis sed et confirmationes Cnutonis regis harum ecclesie Abbendonensis possessionum intelligi dantur quibus tunc eadem ecclesia aucta est.

B fo. 107v Illis[a] diebus uir prepotens, nomine Adelwardus,[b] ad nouissimum uite terminum ueniens, octo hidas et dimidiam apud Sandford[c] et scrinia tria cum uno grandi cristallo huic[d] cenobio largitus est.[409]

Temporibus[410] etiam huius regis, reliquie sancti Ædwardi regis et martiris sunt Abbendone delate. Dumque portitor inde eas postea referre deliberasset, non longe ab ecclesia Dei nutu in itinere uestigio solo tenus hesit nec ultra progredi quiuit. Ita sacra pignora ad ecclesiam reuecta hucusque inibi conseruantur.

[f] circumattramentatum *B* [g] maratana *B* [h] *see Charters of Abingdon Abbey, p. 541, for the boundaries in B* [i–i] þisne lansplot becwæþ Æþelwine in to Abbendune 7 þone hagan on Oxnaford þe he sylf onsæt on mycelre gewitnysse *B* [j–j] *see Charters of Abingdon Abbey, pp. 541–2, for the dating clause and witness list in B* [k] *initial om. at start of line, and perhaps because of large capital* I *starting the next section C*

115 [a] *rubricator failed to provide coloured initial C;* Testamentum Adelredi regis *as rubricated heading B* [b] Aþelwardus *B* [c] Samford *B* [d] huius *C; changed almost certainly from* huius *B, suggesting that B derives from C*

[407] See 1 Cor. 16: 22.

strengthening, and bridge repair. If indeed any envious man, set on fire with the fiery radiant flames of covetousness, tries to set in place of this truthful document another document soiled with the deceit of greed, let him be anathema maranatha,[407] that is estrangement from the fellowship of Christians, until he comes to his senses and repents that which he approved in the malice of envious falsity. By his testament, Æthelwine made Abingdon heir of a very small quantity of this land and of the messuage at Oxford in which he lived.[408] And he did this by the testimony of many. This charter was carried out in the year of our Lord 1032. And so that this inviolable confirmation can acquire security, I Cnut, with the royal right hand, strengthen it with the mark of the cross + and order confirmation by the hands of all those subject to me. I Ælfgifu, spouse of the aforesaid king, have made firm this gift with the mark of the cross +. I Æthelnoth archbishop of the church of Canterbury confirm the royal gift with the sign of the holy cross. I Ælfric archbishop of the church of York do the same. I Bishop Wulfsige with many others do the same.

115. (cf. B248) In these matters, both the aforesaid abbot's times and King Cnut's confirmations of these possessions of the church of Abingdon are given that it be understood by whom that church was then enhanced.

In those days a very powerful man named Æthelweard, coming to the end of his life, bestowed on this monastery eight and a half hides at Sandford and three reliquaries with one large crystal.[409]

Also[410] in the time of that king, the relics of St Edward, king and martyr, were moved to Abingdon. And when their carrier afterwards resolved to take them away from there, not far from the church on his journey, by God's will he was stopped in his tracks and could go no further. Thus the sacred relics were brought back to the church and are preserved therein to this day.

[408] Æthelwine's identity is obscure. Lawson, *Cnut*, pp. 151–2, states that Æthelwine was 'probably the Abingdon abbot who died in 1030', but *Charters of Abingdon Abbey*, p. 543, disagrees, primarily on account of the lack of reference to his position in the charter.

[409] The donor cannot be identified with certainty. The land was at either Dry Sandford, Berkshire, or Sandford-on-Thames, Oxfordshire.

[410] Cf. the passage below, B250, which has limited verbal parallels to that in MS C. Abingdon is presenting a claim to rival that of Shaftesbury, which was recorded in various sources as the resting place of Edward; J. Blair, 'A handlist of Anglo-Saxon saints', in A. T. Thacker and R. Sharpe, eds., *Local Saints and Local Churches in the Early Medieval West* (Oxford, 2002), pp. 495–565, at 529. See also above, p. clxxv.

116. Rex autem Cnuto, Datiam, Norweiam, et Angliam imperialiter equa et ualida manu moderans,[411] summorum apostolorum Petri ac Pauli expetitis apud Romanas arces suffragiis, legibus hinc quibus nationes sibi subacte in causarum controuersiis unirentur, seniorum prudentumque consultu, sancitis, in pace diem obiuit.[412]

[i. 446 n.] Post[413] eum in regem constituitur Haroldus, | filius, ut ferebatur,
C fo. 130r ipsius Cnutonis ex concubina progenitus, quinquennioque emenso moritur.[414] Hinc Hardecnuto, ex Cnutone rege et Emma regina progenitus, imperium Anglie sumpsit.

B fo. 108v **117. (B254)** [a]*Carta regis Hardecnut de Ferneburga.*[a] [415]

[i. 446] Cuncta seculorum patrimonia incertis nepotum heredibus relinquuntur, et omnis mundi gloria appropinquante[b] debite mortis termino ad nichilum reducta fatescit. Huius rei[c] gratia, terrenis caducarum rerum possessionibus semper mansura superne patrie emolumenta[d] adipiscentes, Domino iuuante, lucremur. Quapropter, lubrici potentatus non immemor, ego Hardacnut, Christo conferente rex et primicerius Anglorum atque Danorum, ob remuneratione[e] celestis premii, aliquantulam ruris particulam, decem scilicet mansas loco qui celebri Fernbeorgan[f] profertur, ad ecclesiam beate Marie genitricis Dei ac
[i. 447] Domini nostri Ihesu Christi illo in locello qui dicitur Abbendun[g] ad usus ibidem fratrum Deo seruientium libenter concedo, obsecrans et precipiens in nomine Christi ut nemo successorum nostrorum superioris inferiorisue gradus hoc nostre deuotionis donum aliquo temeritatis aliquatenus instinctu dirumpat.[h] Si quis ergo alium libellulum, false cupiditatis atramento,[i] pretitulatum contra istum in palam protulerit, nec sibi nec sue proficiat auaritie, sed a diuino sit in perpetuum perforatus graphiolo, et ipse meo atque meorum interdictu pontificum permaneat anathematizatus et a Christianorum consortio alienatus, insuper a corpore et[j] sanguine Domini

117 [a–a] Carta Hardecnuti de Fernburga *B* [b] *corr. from* approprinquanto *C;* adpropinquante *B* [c] regi *B* [d] emulumenta *B* [e] remunerationem *B* [f] æt Feornbergan *B* [g] Abbandun *B* [h] disrumpat *B* [i] attramento *B* [j] *followed by* a *B*

[411] See above, p. xxxiii.

[412] Cnut visited Rome in 1027 and perhaps again in 1031. The laws to which the text here refers are a letter he sent on his departure from Rome, preserved in the Worcester *Chronicle* and William of Malmesbury's *Gesta regum*; see John of Worcester, *Chronicle*, ii. 512–18; William of Malmesbury, *Gesta regum*, bk. ii, cc. 182–3, ed. Mynors *et al.*, i. 324–8, ii. 173–5; *Gesetze*, ed. Liebermann, i. 276–7; P. Wormald, *The Making of English Law: King Alfred to the Twelfth Century*, i: *Legislation and its Limits* (Oxford, 1999), pp. 348–9.

[413] Cf. below, B253. Cnut died at Shaftesbury on 12 Nov. 1035; Lawson, *Cnut*, p. 113 and n. 110.

116. Moreover, King Cnut, who ruled Denmark, Norway, and England with a just and strong hand as becomes an emperor,[411] after he had sought the aid of the greatest apostles, Peter and Paul, at the Roman citadels, and from there, by the advice of high-ranking and prudent men, ordained laws whereby the nations subjected to him might be reconciled in disputes, died in peace.[412]

After[413] him Harold was instituted as king, the son, as they said, of that Cnut born of a concubine. He died after five years had passed.[414] Harthacnut, born of King Cnut and Queen Emma, took up dominion in England.

117. (B254) *Charter of King Harthacnut concerning Farnborough.*[415] All patrimonies of this life are left to uncertain heirs of descendants, and all glory of the world fails and is reduced to nothing with the approaching end of due death. Because of this, we, with the Lord's help, acquire and gain with earthly possessions of transitory things the ever-lasting advantages of the heavenly land. Therefore, not unmindful of the transitoriness of power, I, Harthacnut, by Christ's appointing king and ruler of the English and Danes, with a view to payment of a heavenly reward, willingly grant a small portion of land, that is ten hides, at the place commonly called Farnborough, to the church of the blessed Mary mother of God and of our Lord Jesus Christ in that small place called Abingdon, for the use of the brethren serving God there, entreating and ordering in Christ's name that none of our successors, of higher or lower rank, prompted by any rashness break to any degree this gift of our devotion. If therefore anyone brings forward into the open any document previously drawn up with the ink of false greed against this one drawn up above, let it profit neither him nor his avarice, but be pierced in perpetuity by a divine sword, and let him remain anathematized by the interdict of myself and my bishops, and estranged from the fellowship of Christians, and in addition cut off from the body and blood of the Lord, and miserably damned after his death in infernal punishments.

[414] Harold died on 17 Mar. 1040; *Handbook of British Chronology*, p. 28.

[415] Farnborough, Berkshire. Sawyer, no. 993; *Charters of Abingdon Abbey*, no. 141, which, at pp. 552–3, states that 'the authenticity of [this document] is uncertain, but there seems to be a good chance that it [is] at least based on a contemporary diploma. . . . There can be little doubt that, in its present form, [the document] was drawn up at Abingdon (as claimed in Abbot Siward's subscription).' See above, p. 152, for Æthelred granting Farnborough to Abingdon. B57 (*Charters of Abingdon Abbey*, no. 29) records King Æthelstan granting ten hides in Farnborough to his thegn Ælfheah. Ælfheah may have been a future ealdorman in central Wessex; see above, p. cxxiii.

sequestratus, et in penis infernalibus post obitum miserabiliter
dampnatus. Et ut prefate telluris ruricole inuiolabile robur libertatis
semper obtinere ualeant, regali liberati sunt precepto ab omni seculari
iugo exceptis trium rerum obsequiis, expeditione scilicet populari,
[i. 448] uiatici fundatione pontis, arcis conditione regalis. [k]⟨A⟩cta est ergo
huius donationis cartula anno Dominice incarnationis duo et quad-
raginta post mille, anno imperii mei secundo, in regali uilla que
Suðtun nuncupatur, his testibus: Ego[l] Heardecnut rex meum donum
[i. 449] corroboro sancte crucis + signaculo. Ego Ælfgiua eiusdem regis mater
collaudo.[416] Ego Eadward predicti regis frater assentio. Ego Eadsie
archipresul Dorobernensis consigno. Ego Alfric archiepiscopus Ebor-
acensis consentio, cum multis aliis episcopis et abbatibus et laicis. Ego
Siward abbas presentem scedulam gaudens composui.[k]

[i. 450] 118. *De morte Hardecnut regis.*[417]

Rex itaque Heardacnut uectigal pene importabile passim a popular-
ibus Anglie exegit.[418] Cadauer quoque Haroldi ante se regnantis,
causa nimii odii quod pre se regnum anticiparit, effossum iussit in
locum profundissimi ceni demergi.[419] Vnde in singulorum ore
hominum de eo haberi imprecatus ut tante crudelitatis non diu
[i. 451] abesset animaduersio. Et id contigit. Siquidem ipso in regia hilariter
epulante, improuise humi decidit et expirauit, uerbum uel unum
suarum rerum alicui non indicens.[420] His ita compositis, Eadwardus
filius Ædelredi regis ab omnibus cum leticia in dominum suscipitur,
fauor effunditur, et diadema ei imponitur.[421]

[i. 451 n] 119. *De temporibus Eadwardi regis.*[422]

Regnante itaque hoc rege, secundo anno regni eius Cantuariensis
metropolis archiepiscopus, Eadsius nomine, accitum Siwardum abba-
tem, quem prudentia plurimum uigere nouerat,[423] regis consensu et
regni primorum pontificatus decorauit apice ac patriarchatus sui uice
C fo. 130v ipsum fungi in|stituit. Nam priuatis ipse uti uolebat, quia egritudine

[k–k] *see Charters of Abingdon Abbey, pp. 550–2, for the boundaries, dating clause and witness list in B* [l] *the* E *at the start of each* Ego *appears in the centre margin C*

[416] On Emma, mother of Harthcnut, also being called Ælfgifu Imma, see above, p. 172.

[417] The events with which this passage deals appear in B255.

[418] This is presumably the geld of 1040, recorded in the *Anglo-Saxon Chronicle* and elsewhere.

[419] *ASC*, 'C', records this event *s.a.* 1040.

[420] John of Worcester, *Chronicle*, ii. 532–4, states that Harthacnut collapsed at the wedding feast of Tofi the Proud and Gytha, daughter of Osgod Clapa, held at Lambeth. Following his collapse he remained speechless until his death on 8 June 1042.

And so that the local inhabitants of the aforementioned estate can always hold the inviolable strength of liberty, by royal order they are freed from every secular yoke except services of three things, that is common military service, road bridge building, and royal fortress building. So the charter of this gift was carried out in the year of our Lord 1042, the second year of my dominion, in the royal vill called Sutton, with these witnesses: I King Harthacnut strengthen my gift with the sign of the holy cross +. I Ælfgifu mother of that king join in praising.[416] I Edward brother of the aforesaid king assent. I Eadsige archbishop of Canterbury join in signing. I Ælfric archbishop of York consent, with many other bishops and abbots and laymen. I Abbot Siward, rejoicing, have composed the present document.

118. *Concerning the death of King Harthacnut.*[417]
And so King Harthacnut demanded an almost unbearable tax everywhere from the populace of England.[418] Also, he ordered the corpse of Harold who reigned before him to be dug up and sunk in a place of deepest filth, because of his excessive hatred arising from Harold having taken the kingship before him.[419] Therefore, every man's mouth prayed concerning him that such great cruelty would not long go unpunished. And this happened, inasmuch as, while he was happily feasting in a royal palace, he fell down and expired without warning, not proclaiming even one word concerning his affairs to anyone.[420] When these matters had taken place thus, Edward son of King Æthelred was joyously adopted as lord by everyone, approval was poured forth, and the diadem placed on him.[421]

119. *Concerning the times of King Edward.*[422]
And so with this king reigning, in the second year of his reign the archbishop of the metropolitan see of Canterbury, Eadsige by name, summoned Abbot Siward, whom he knew to flourish greatly in prudence.[423] With the consent of the king and the leading men of the realm Eadsige honoured Siward with the eminence of a bishopric and instituted him to perform as a substitute in his patriarchal position. For he was wishing to spend his time on private matters

[421] Edward was crowned on 3 Apr. 1043; see Barlow, *Edward the Confessor*, p. 61.

[422] MS B deals with Siward and Canterbury in B256. The present section closely resembles a passage in the Abingdon version of the Worcester *Chronicle* which is preserved in Lambeth Palace Library; John of Worcester, *Chronicle*, ii. 614. On Siward and Canterbury, see above, pp. ci–ciii.

[423] Eadsige was archbishop of Canterbury 1038–50; *Handbook of British Chronology*, p. 214.

laborabat. ⟨A⟩bbendonensi autem ecclesie Ædelstanus eiusdem loci sacrista abbas constitutus est.

[i. 457] **120. (B259–60)** [a]*De Lechamstede.*[a] [424]

B fo. 111r De uilla quadam[b] Lechamstede appellata tunc Abbendonie agitabatur questio. Dicebat enim quidam diues, Brichwinus[c] nomine, quod Siwardi dono ipsam in ius suum hereditarie possidendam acceperit, dum pro potestate dominatus que liberet disponeret.[425] Sed id falso imposuit. Nam Cnutonis tempore regis, pater huius—Brithmundus[d] uocatus—a conuentu cenobitarum Abbendonensium eandem impet-
[i. 458] ratu acquisiuit,[e] eo dictatu ut trium hominum uita, ipsiusmet scilicet et duorum quos ipse Brithmundus[f] prospiceret, inde frueretur. Hoc tempore euoluto, monachorum manui libere restitueretur. Defuncto ergo illo, ad uxorem ipsius transfertur terre fruendi secundaria permissio, tercia ad Brithnodum[g] filium horum. Cuius post mortem Siwardus, uolens usui monachorum eandem terram delegare, cum iam trium manutenentium numerositas defecisset, predictus Brithwinus[h] frater Brithnodi[i] cum nobilium quorundam comitatu Abbendoniam requisitum abbatem ueniunt,[j] quatinus et iste quoad uiueret inde tenens foret. Diu rogatum et tandem id impetratum est. Cumque is abbas iam alias frena direxisset,[426] quicquid antea pactum fuerat preuertere ille homo sategit, protestando sibi suisque de terra ipsa ius hereditarium concessum. Quo contra episcopus Siwardus Godwino comiti litteras dirigens, falso eundem prosecutum ostendit, ita scribens:[k] [427]

Siwardus episcopus Godwino comiti, et Hermanno episcopo, et Kinewardo, et ceteris omnibus nobilibus de Bearrucscira, salutem.[428] Audiui Brithwinum[l] terram de Lechamstede sibi omnino appropriare.

120 [a–a] De contentione Lechamstede *B* [b] *corr. from* quedam *B* [c] Brihtwinus *B* [d] Brihtmundus *B* [e] adquisiuit *B* [f] Brihtmundus *B* [g] Brihtnodum *B* [h] Brihtwinus *B* [i] Brihtnodi *B* [j] *rectius* uenit [k] Responsio Siwardi episcopi de Lechamstede *as rubricated heading B* [l] Brihtwinum *B*

[424] For this case, see also above, pp. clxiii–clxv. The dispute is calendared as Wormald, 'Lawsuits', no. 86. It is uncertain when Abingdon first obtained Leckhampstead, although it was claimed as part of the early endowment; above, cc. 10–11. See below, c. 137, B71–B72, for it being granted to the thegn Eadric in the mid-10th c.

[425] Note that the evidence of *DB* i, fo. 58v, suggests that 'Bricstuinus', i.e. Brihtwine, was one of Abingdon's tenants at Leckhampstead *TRE*.

[426] i.e. taken on Eadsige's duties at Canterbury.

[427] Sawyer, no. 1404; *Charters of Abingdon Abbey*, no. 143; *Anglo-Saxon Writs*, ed. Harmer, no. 3. *Charters of Abingdon Abbey*, p. 558, states that the writ which follows 'is

since he was struggling with illness. Æthelstan sacrist of this monastery was made abbot of the church of Abingdon.

120. (B259–60) *Concerning Leckhampstead.*[424]
A dispute was then under way concerning a village of Abingdon's called Leckhampstead. For a certain rich man named Brihtwine was saying that he received that land by gift of Siward to be possessed hereditarily as his own property, in that he might dispose what he wished according to the power of lordship.[425] But he claimed this falsely. For in the time of King Cnut, his father—called Brihtmund—acquired this from the convent of the Abingdon monks by request, on this specification, that thereafter it be enjoyed for the lives of three people, that is of Brihtmund himself and of two whom he would specify. When this time had passed, it would be freely restored into the monks' hands. So when he died, the second permission to enjoy the land passed to his wife, the third to their son Brihtnoth. After his death Siward wished to assign that land to the monks' use, since now the total of three holders was exhausted, but the aforesaid Brihtwine brother of Brihtnoth came to Abingdon with a band of noblemen and asked the abbot that he might be tenant of that land as long as he lived. After a long period of asking, at length this was obtained. And when this abbot had taken up the reins elsewhere,[426] Brihtwine strove to exceed whatever had been previously agreed by protesting that the hereditary right of that land had been granted to him and his. Against this Bishop Siward sent letters to Earl Godwine and showed that man was pursuing the case falsely, writing thus:[427]

Bishop Siward to Earl Godwine, and Bishop Hereman, and Kineweard, and all other noble men of Berkshire, greeting.[428] I have heard that Brihtwine is entirely appropriating the land of Leckhampstead to

almost certainly a Latin translation of a genuine Old English writ'; see also *Anglo-Saxon Writs*, ed. Harmer, p. 123. The writ can be dated to 1045 × 1048.

[428] Godwine's earldom of Wessex included Berkshire. Godwine was earl from possibly 1018 until his death in 1053; Barlow, *The Godwins*, pp. 22, 48. Hereman was bishop of Ramsbury 1045–55 and of Sherborne 1058–78; *Handbook of British Chronology*, pp. 220, 222. Kineweard was probably the sheriff of Berkshire, witnessing various charters as *prepositus* or *prefectus*; see below, c. 132, B43, B254, B257, B258, B273 (*Charters of Abingdon Abbey*, nos. 141–2, 145–7). The writ must date from 1045 × 1048, after the consecration of Bishop Hereman and before the death of Siward. It is one of only three episcopal writs surviving from Anglo-Saxon England; *Charters of Abingdon Abbey*, p. 558. It may have been necessary for Siward to submit his evidence in writing because his episcopal duties kept him in Kent. Alternatively, written testimony may have been more common than the surviving evidence allows us to know.

Sed iniuste id agit. Nam, me permittente, ea potitus est eo tenore, ut post suum decessum monachorum libere in manum redeat. Quod conuentione dispositum est illustrium uirorum plurimorum presentia, eo die quo Brithnodus,[m] eius frater[n] defunctus, Abbendonie sepultus fuit. Qui tercius a patre, nam mater eius inter se et patrem [i. 459] media eiusdem terre possessione functus est, quibus tantummodo Cnutonis regis tempore trino uite spacio hominum possessores fieri [B fo. 111v] inde a monachis Abbendonensibus concessum fuerat. Hec | haud aliter haberi fide quam Deo et regi meo domino debeo interposita iuro. Sed et si adhuc his quis discrederit, iudicio quo censura uestra potuerit iure definiri, inueritare[o] que protestatus sum ero paratus.

Hec quanquam ab episcopo sint testimonio prolata, uir ille tamen tanto calluit ingenio[p] ut ad Ordrici abbatis, de quo inferius tractabitur, illius inde dominatus excuti nequiuerit tempora.[429]

121. (B261) [a]*De Luuechenora.*[a] [430]

Matrona quedam, Ælfgiua nomine, de genere regali nobilissima—Ædiue scilicet regine regis Ædwardi[b] consanguinea—uillam quandam que Luuechenora dicitur de matrimonio suo habebat, in qua frequentius degebat.[431] Hec uite presentis cursu peracto cum ad finem appropinquaret, quod in forensibus rebus carius habebat, cognate sue predicte quam et pre ceteris diligebat—quamuis absenti—uillam de Luuechenora habendam dereliquit. Que cum uite finem sortita esset, procurator domus eius in uilla, quasi sibi donata esset, dominium exercere cepit, prorsus ignorante regina, quoniam absens erat, quia ei donata fuisset. Predictus uero[c] procurator subiectos sibi non medio- [C fo. 131r] criter affligebat, modis omnibus eis gra|uis existens et honerosus. Res namque eorum diripiebat et unicuique ultra modum exactor auarus [i. 460] imminebat. Inter quos cuidam Eadwino cognomento Ramere mala multa inferebat, et quamuis omnes odio haberet, hunc tamen pre

[m] Brihtnodus *B* [n] eius *rep. C* [o] ueritate *changed from* ueritare *B* [p] *followed by* prolata *del. B*

121 [a–a] De uilla Leuekenore *B* [b] Eadwardi *B* [c] *om. B*

[429] See below, p. 208.

[430] Oxfordshire. Calendared *Charters of Abingdon Abbey*, p. 582 (ix); Wormald, 'Lawsuits', no. 134. The events must have taken place between 1045 and Mar. 1052, that is between Edward's marriage to Edith and the death of his mother Emma. Note, however, that *De abbatibus* dates the gift to the time of Abbot Ealdred (1066–71); *CMA* ii. 283. In 1086 Abingdon had seventeen hides at Lewknor; *DB* i, fo. 156v. *Accounts of the Obedientiars*, pp. 36–7, has income from Lewknor in the kitchener's account.

himself. However, he does this unjustly. For, with my permission, he gained possession of it on this condition, that after his death it is to return freely to the hands of the monks. This was set down by agreement in the presence of very many illustrious men, on the day on which Brihtnoth, his late brother, was buried at Abingdon. Brihtnoth was the third from the father (for in between himself and his father his mother enjoyed possession of that land) to whom alone it had, in the time of King Cnut, been granted by the monks of Abingdon to be possessors thereof for the space of the lives of three men. Having pledged the faith that I owe to God and my lord king, I swear that these things did not happen in any other fashion. But if anyone still disbelieves these things, I will be prepared to prove what I have testified, by a judicial method whereby your judgment can rightly be determined.

Although these things were put forward by the bishop as testimony, Brihtwine, however, was so skilled in trickery that his lordship of the land could not be shaken off until the times of Abbot Ordric (about whom it shall be treated below).[429]

121. (B261) *Concerning Lewknor.*[430]

A most noble matron named Ælfgifu, of the royal family—that is a kinswoman of Edith queen of King Edward—had from her marriage a village called Lewknor, in which she very frequently resided.[431] When the course of the present life was run and she was approaching her end, she left the village of Lewknor, which she held particularly dear among her worldly possessions, for her aforesaid kinswoman to have, whom she loved beyond others, although she was not there. When she was allotted the end of her life, the guardian of her house in the village began to exercise lordship, as if it had been given to him. The queen, since she was not there, was altogether unaware that it had been given to her. Moreover, the aforesaid guardian to no small extent afflicted those subject to him, in every way acting in an oppressive and burdensome fashion to them. An avaricious official, he used to take away their possessions and threatened everyone beyond measure. Amongst those people he inflicted many evils on a certain Eadwine, surnamed Ramere, and, although he hated everyone,

[431] Ælfgifu's identity cannot be established for certain, although Queen Edith did have a sister of that name; see Barlow, *The Godwins*, p. 26 n. 32. Edith, daughter of Earl Godwine, married King Edward in 1045 and lived until Dec. 1075; *ASC*, *s.a.* 1045, 1075.

ceteris laboribus fatigabat.[432] Ædwinus[d] autem, tantis malis prouocatus grauiterque de illata sibi ferens iniuria, cogitabat aliquando tam nequam hominis a suo et cohabitantium collo iugum inhumanum excutere. Veniensque ad prenominatam reginam, uiri tirannidem et suorum grauem oppressionem ostendit, et enarrans qualiter a cognata sua defuncta ei uilla eadem donata esset, querebat quare, sicut suis, non eis melius prouideret. Regina uero quia ei uilla donata esset se nescire dicebat et usque ad tempus illud neminem sibi hoc indicasse asserebat. Et Ædwinus[e] 'ego,' inquit, 'quocumque modo iusseris, et uillam tuam esse et ipsum eam iniuste tenere probabo'. Vocatus deinde predictus procurator ad curiam uenit et, ne multis morer, manifesta ueritate conuictus, ita esse ut Ædwinus[f] asserebat negare minime potuit. Villam postea regine, quamuis inuitus, tradidit pro commisso quoque in eiusdem[g] misericordia cum rebus omnibus incidit.

His ita gestis, contigit regem Ædwardum[h] cum matre et uxore hospitandi gratia ad Abbendoniam uenire. Cumque officina fratrum omnia uidendi[i] gratia lustrassent, inuenerunt in refectorio pueros monachos, ut moris est puerorum, propter etatis[j] infirmitatem ante
B fo. 112[r] refectionem fratrum cibum sumentes. | Propiusque uenientes nichilque excepto pane appositum eis inspicientes, quesiuit regina utpote urbana quare tam prope mensam comederent et preter panem ad gustandum nil[k] haberent. Quibus respondentibus se uix aliquando aliud habere, commota est regina ad pietatem pro eorum uictus exiguitate. Et aduocans regem, qui aderat, obnixe petebat ut pueris aliquid redditus concederet, quo scilicet eis exinde melius esset, quod ipsi (ut ita dicam) ad eorum conuiuium uenissent. Rege autem cum hilaritate dicente se eis libenter daturum si terram aut possessionem
[i. 461] in promptu[l] deliberatam haberet, 'ego', ait regina, 'uillam unam que Luuechenora dicitur nuper adquisiui. Hanc, si tibi placet, pro honore beate Marie dono perpetuo illis concedo.' Qui cum respondisset hoc sibi magnifice gratum esse, sub specie refectionis matutinalis puerorum, attitulata est uilla de Luuechenora in dominium abbatie Abbendonensis a rege Ædwardo[m] et regina Ædgiða[n] donatione perpetua.[433]

[d] Eadwinus *B* [e] Eadwinus *B* [f] Eadwinus *B* [g] eius *B* [h] Eadwardum *B* [i] *corr. from* uidenda *B* [j] propter etatis *rep. and del. B* [k] nichil *B* [l] impromptu *B* [m] Eadwardo *B* [n] Eadgiþa *B*

this man beyond others he wore out with burdens.[432] But Eadwine, provoked by such great evils and taking hard the wrong done to him, at length considered how to shake off from his own and his fellow inhabitants' necks the inhuman yoke of so depraved a man. He came to the aforenamed queen and demonstrated that man's tyranny and the heavy oppression of his men. He told how that village had been given to her by her late kinswoman, and inquired why she did not provide better for these people, as for her own. The queen, indeed, said that she did not know that the village had been given to her and asserted that hitherto no one had indicated this to her. And Eadwine said, 'I will prove, in whatever way you order, both that the village is yours and that he holds it unjustly'. Then the aforesaid guardian was summoned and came to court, and (lest I delay with many details), convicted by manifest truth, he could not deny at all that it was as Eadwine asserted. Afterwards, although unwilling, he handed over the vill to the queen and also fell into her mercy with all his possessions for his misdeed.

Following these events, it happened that King Edward with his mother and wife came to stay at Abingdon. When they had gone round to see all the domestic buildings of the brethren, in the refectory they found boy-monks who, as is the custom of boys, were taking food before the brethren's meal, because of the weakness of their age. Coming closer and seeing nothing but bread placed before them, the queen asked, politely as one might expect, why they ate so close to the meal and why they had nothing but bread of which to partake. When they answered that they scarcely ever had anything else, the queen was moved to compassion for the meagreness of their provisions. She appealed to the king, who was there, seeking resolutely, on the grounds that they themselves had (as one might say) come to their feast, that Edward grant some rent for the boys whereby they would be better off in future. The king, however, cheerfully said that he would willingly give to them if he had any land or possessions ready for disposal. The queen said 'I have recently acquired a village called Lewknor. If it pleases you, I grant this to them by perpetual gift for the honour of the blessed Mary'. When he answered that this was splendidly agreeable to him, the village of Lewknor was consigned to the demesne of the abbey of Abingdon by King Edward and Queen Edith by perpetual gift, for the specific purpose of the boys' morning repast.[433]

[432] I have been unable to establish any more with certainty concerning Eadwine.

[433] In the later 13th c. the abbey had a charter in King Edward's name that was produced as evidence of its right to Lewknor; see Lyell, no. 538, *Placita de Quo Warranto*, pp. 664–5.

Inuenimus preterea[o] hanc eandem uillam priscis temporibus a quodam Danorum nobilissimo Nouitoui nominato, una cum membris suis (id est Hachamstede et ceteris), huic ecclesie cum obiret donatam,[434] sed postmodum per aduersitates que contra ecclesiam oriri solent a dominio ecclesie fuisse ad tempus alienatam, et ut prediximus succedente tempore iterum recuperatam, immo iterum donatam, et ore regio confirmatam. Cessabit ergo merito omnis obiectio prioris et, uolente Deo, ultime perditionis, cum manifesta sit ratio secunde reuersionis.

122. (B262) Transactis[a] aliquot reuerendus episcopus Siwardus in episcopatu annis, dum languore deprimeretur, quorum monitu episcopalem indeptus[b] fuerat dignitatem, eorum quoque ad Abbendoniam gratia regreditur, ibique decedens, sepulture honorifice commendatur,[435] posteris illic[c] degentibus munificum sui monimentum derelin-
C fo. 131ᵛ quens, cum uillam Witteham | eius dono hucusque monachi in dominio habuerint, in ciuitatis Walingaford[d] contermino sitam;[436] cunctum etiam sue capelle paratum, in qua continebantur scrinium
[i. 462] sanctarum reliquiarum, euuangeliorum duo codices non granditate sed uenustate decenter argenti et auri parati; calix laudabilis operis permaximus;[437] pecten eburneus et decorus;[e] alba;[438] super humerale;[439] stola cum fanone et casula albi coloris,[440] de pallio aurifrixo singula perlucida; pluraque alia que breuitatis studio preterimus.

123. (B263) *De morte Æthelstani[a] abbatis.*

Obierat[b] anno precedenti domni Siwardi transitus et pie memorie domnus Adelstanus[c] abbas, elemosinarum et pietatis precipuus cultor.[441] Vt enim huiusmodi in eo probaretur efficientia, instante tante inedia famis, qua tunc frumenti sextarius solidis quinque

[o] pretea *B*

122 [a] *preceded by* De morte Siwardi episcopi *as rubricated heading B* [b] ineptus *B* [c] *over erasure B* [d] Walingford *B* [e] *add. at end of line B*

123 [a] Adelstani *B* [b] Abierat, *the wrong initial having been added by rubricator C* [c] Aþelstanus *B*

[434] See *Charters of Abingdon Abbey*, p. 582 (viii). Ackhamstead is a lost village site, formerly in Oxfordshire, now in Buckinghamshire; A. Morley Davies, 'Abefeld and Ackhamstead: Two lost places', *Records of Buckinghamshire*, xv (1947–52), 166–71. On it being a member of Lewknor, see also vol. ii. 292. Nefetofi 'minister' witnessed B271, B273, B275 (*Charters of Abingdon Abbey*, nos. 144, 145, 147). His identity is uncertain.

[435] Siward died on 23 Oct. 1048. His illness, return to Abingdon, and death after two months of being confined to bed are also mentioned in the Abingdon versions of the Worcester *Chronicle*; John of Worcester, *Chronicle*, ii. 614.

We have found besides that this same village, together with its members (that is Ackhamstead and others) had in former times been given to this church by a certain very noble Dane named Nefetofi when he was dying.[434] However, it had afterwards been for a time alienated from the church's demesne by adversities that were accustomed to arise against the church. Then, as we have said, it was later recovered again, or rather given again and confirmed by the king's mouth. Therefore every reproach concerning the earlier and, God willing, final loss will deservedly cease, since the correctness of the second reversion is obvious.

122. (B262) When some years had passed in his episcopate, the reverend Bishop Siward, as he was pressed down by illness, returned to Abingdon by the grace of those same men by whose advice he had attained episcopal dignity, died there, and was honourably handed over for burial.[435] He left a generous reminder of himself for those living there in future, since the monks still have in demesne by his gift the village of Wittenham, situated next to the city of Wallingford;[436] also all the furnishings of his chapel, in which were contained a reliquary of holy relics, two gospel books fittingly produced not with large quantity but with elegant quality of silver and gold; a very large chalice of praiseworthy work;[437] a beautiful ivory comb; an alb;[438] a superhumeral;[439] a stole with a maniple and a white chasuble,[440] each one radiant from gold embroidered cloth; and many other things we pass over in eagerness for brevity.

123. (B263) *Concerning the death of Abbot Æthelstan.*
In the year preceding the passing away of lord Siward had also died lord Abbot Æthelstan of pious memory, an outstanding devotee of alms and compassion.[441] The influence of this upon him is shown by the fact that, when starvation through a great famine was at hand,

[436] See *Charters of Abingdon Abbey*, pp. 582–3 (x), where it is suggested that the details may come from a lost will or a more general account of Siward. On Little Wittenham, see also above, c. 16.

[437] A chalice is a cup for consecrated eucharist wine. For liturgical vessels and vestments, see e.g. *A New Dictionary of Liturgy and Worship*, ed. J. G. Davies (London, 1986).

[438] A white vestment, reaching to the ankles, with tight-fitting sleeves and held in by a girdle at the waist. It was worn at celebration of mass.

[439] A vestment worn over the shoulders, like an amice or pallium.

[440] A stole is a vestment consisting of a narrow strip of silk or linen, worn over the shoulders and hanging down to the knee or below. A maniple is a eucharistic vestment consisting of a strip of cloth worn over the left wrist and hanging down. A chasuble is a sleeveless mantle, the outermost vestment worn by the celebrant at the eucharist.

[441] Æthelstan died on 29 Mar., probably in 1048; see above, p. ciii.

uenundabatur,[442] in nulla circum se posita regione tam suis quam
B fo. 112v alienis ab eo stipem queritan|tibus alimonie nemo studiosius et copiosius[d] ipso subuenit.[443]

124. (B264) *De Sperauoc abbate.*

Talibus ergo patribus ad requiem, ut credimus, hinc profectis, rex quendam monachum de ecclesia sancti Ædmundi[a] regis et martiris, aurificis arte peritissimum, nomine Spearhauoc, Abbendonie abbatem constituit.[444] A quo Stigandus Wentane ciuitatis episcopus, tunc uero archiepiscopatus Cantie curam gerens (nam inde defuncto gubernatore locus uacuus manebat regimine), uti callidus perorator, extorsit terram Cyrne uocatam in Gloecestrensi scira sitam, sibi ad tempus
[i. 463] determinatum commendari;[445] ea retributionis [b]mercede, ut restitutionis tempore sui proprii iuris[b] Eastun,[446] quandam uillam contiguam Leuechenore ecclesie Abbendonensi perpetua coniungeret donatione. Sed eo quesito iam potito, nec commendatum reddidit, nec commendati remunerationem exsoluit.[447] Siquidem rex Willelmus senior, triumphata Anglia, ipsum Stigandum captioni deditum ad mortem usque in ea detinuit.[448] Spearhauoc autem a rege ciuitati Lundonensi, eodem predicte pactionis anno, in episcopum promotus,[449] dum auri gemmarumque electarum pro corona imperiali cudenda, regis eiusdem assignatione, receptam haberet copiam, hinc et ex episcopii pecunia marsupiorum farsisset plurimum receptacula, clanculo Anglia secedens, ultra non apparuit. Huiusmodi exitus Dei

[d] *corr. from* copiosus *by interlin. B*

124 [a] Eadmundi *B* [b–b] tempore sui proprii iuris mercede ut restitutionis *B; these and the following two words are over an erasure. Marginalia in dry-point and brown ink also refer to the correction*

---

[442] A sester of grain was probably eight bushels, also referred to as a seam or a quarter; Zupko, *Dictionary of Weights and Measures*, p. 374. There are not accurate figures for the price of grain in the Anglo-Saxon period, but later prices make the *History*'s figure seem reasonable. The price of a quarter of wheat was under 2*s*. in the 1160s, rising towards 6*s*. in the first decade of the 13th c., then fluctuating around 4*s*. for the next forty years; *The Agrarian History of England and Wales*, ii: *1042–1350*, ed. H. E. Hallam (Cambridge, 1988), p. 734.

[443] The *Anglo-Saxon Chronicle* does not mention famine at this time, but it does record a pestilence, earthquake, and wildfire; *ASC*, 'C', *s.a.* 1047, 'D', *s.a.* 1048–9.

[444] Spearhafoc's succession is also mentioned in the Abingdon versions of the Worcester *Chronicle*, *s.a.* 1048, but in a form with only very limited verbal connection to the *History*; John of Worcester, *Chronicle*, ii. 614. On his career, see the entry by J. Blair in the *Oxford Dictionary of National Biography*; also Dodwell, *Anglo-Saxon Art*, pp. 46–7, 55, 58, 213.

[445] Stigand became bishop of Winchester in 1047, and he retained that see following his appointment to Canterbury in 1052 until his deposition in 1070; *Handbook of British Chronology*, pp. 214, 223; M. F. Smith, 'Archbishop Stigand and the eye of the needle',

whereby a sester of corn was put up for sale at 5 shillings,[442] no one anywhere around him was more zealous or more lavish than he in providing help both for his own men and for others who sought from him an offering of nourishment.[443]

124. (B264) *Concerning Abbot Spearhafoc.*
So when such fathers, as we believe, had departed from here to rest, the king appointed as abbot of Abingdon a certain monk of the church of St Edmund king and martyr, most skilled in the goldsmith's art, Spearhafoc by name.[444] Stigand, bishop of the city of Winchester, who then indeed had care of the archbishopric of Canterbury (for with its ruler dead that place lacked governance), as a crafty pleader extracted from Spearhafoc the land called Cerney, situated in Gloucestershire, to be entrusted to him for a set time.[445] As repayment, at the time of the restitution he would add as a perpetual gift to the church of Abingdon his own property of Aston, a village neighbouring Lewknor.[446] But when he had acquired what he sought, he neither restored what had been entrusted to him, nor discharged the payment for what had been entrusted.[447] King William the elder indeed, when he had conquered England, placed Stigand in captivity and kept him there until death.[448] But Spearhafoc, in the year of the aforesaid agreement, was promoted by the king to be bishop for the city of London.[449] Then, at a time when he had, by the king's allocation, plenty of gold and chosen gems acquired for fashioning the imperial crown, he stuffed money-bags full with riches from the bishopric, left England in secret, and did not appear again. God's

ANS, xvi (1994), 199–219. The dating of these events and the description of Stigand's position raises difficulties. Archbishop Eadsige had died at the end of Oct. 1050. He was succeeded in Mar. 1051 by Robert of Jumièges, who in turn was expelled in Sept. 1052, to be succeeded by Stigand. The *History*'s dating of the agreement concerning Cerney to the year in which Spearhafoc was appointed to London indicates 1051, when Stigand was not archbishop of Canterbury. One possibility is that this is otherwise unsupported evidence for Stigand having a custodial role at Canterbury before the appointment of Robert; another is confusion on the part of the composer of the *History*.

[446] Aston is presumably Aston Rowant, Oxfordshire, about a mile from Lewknor.

[447] *DB* i, fo. 169^r, states that Walter son of Roger held South Cerney, and that Archbishop Stigand had held it. It goes on: 'this manor has been claimed for the church of St Mary of Abingdon, but the whole county witnessed that Archbishop Stigand had held it for ten years in King Edward's lifetime. Earl William [fitzOsbern] gave this manor to Roger the sheriff, Walter's father.' For Abingdon holding or claiming Cerney in the mid-12th c., see vol. ii. 266, 274.

[448] Stigand died on 21 or 22 Feb. 1072; *Handbook of British Chronology*, p. 214.

[449] Spearhafoc was appointed to London in succession to Robert of Jumièges; *Handbook of British Chronology*, p. 220.

uindicta tulere, quorum machinatione suis diminuta est ecclesia augmentis. Secundum itaque predictam definitionem, sub presentia et testimonio regis Ædwardi[c] sic de manerio deliberatum fuit.

125. (B265) *De Rodulfo episcopo [a]et abbate.[a]*

Inde Rodulfum quendam longeuum abbatis loco ponendum rex transmisit, qui episcopatum apud Norweiam gentem diu moderans, et tandem ab huiusmodi fasce priuatum se agere malens, ad regem ipsum suum, ut ferebatur, cognatum uenit, a quo et susceptus est. Vt uero tam Dei quam sui respectu eum monachi reciperent honorifi-
[i. 464] ceque tractarent, utpote summa canicie iam maturum, eo discedente,[b] licere eis dedit quem de suis uellent potius successorem eligere. Paretur regi. Reuerentie subiectio[c] debite a fratribus uiro competenter impenditur. At ipsos regia nequaquam fefellit in posterum promissio.

126. (B266) *De Ordrico abbate [a]ecclesie huius.[a]*

Siquidem sene predicto annis haud[b] duobus integris transactis obeunte, Ordricus, etatis medie, affabilitatis gratiose homo, monachus
C fo. 132r Abbendonensis | ecclesie ingenti omnium gaudio, fauente rege, abbas ab eis suscipitur.[450] Qui, quia a rege non mediocriter diligebatur, eius edicto[c] plura sanciri[d] ecclesie ad libertatis necessaria impetrauit. Quorum hucusque ad formam, ceteri post eum successores abbates ipsius abbatie inuestitura se potiri usualiter, cum primo initiantur, expetunt. Que huiusmodi habent modum:

B fo. 113r **127. (B267)** *Carta regis Eadwardi Anglice.*[451]

Eadward king gret his bisceopas and his abbodas[a] and his heorlas and þeignas þe on þam scyran syndon þe Ordric abbud hæfð[b] land inne. And ic[c] kyþe eow ꝥ ic hæbbe geunnon him into sancta Mariam
[i. 465] mynstre sace[d] and socne, toll and team, and infangeneþeof,[e] binnan burgon and butan burgon, hamsocne and griðbrice[f] and foresteal, ofer

[c] Eadwardi *B*

125 [a–a] *om. B* [b] discedende *C* [c] *second* i *interlin. B*

126 [a–a] *om. B* [b] haut *B* [c] *corr. from* edictio *B* [d] sancciri *B*

127 [a] abbotes *B* [b] hæf *C* [c] hic *B* [d] sake *B. In C, the legal terms are numbered i–viii in both this English writ and the Latin one that follows; in B, such numbers only appear in the Latin text, and only over the first five terms. The numbers are in the main hand, above the specific term* [e] infangueneþeof *B, perhaps misled by the numeral* v *above the word in C* [f] griðbryce *B*

[450] Rodulf's death in 1052 and Ordric's succession are also mentioned in the Abingdon versions of the Worcester *Chronicle*; John of Worcester, *Chronicle*, ii. 615.

[451] Sawyer, no. 1065; *Charters of Abingdon Abbey*, no. 148; *Anglo-Saxon Writs*, ed.

vengeance brought such ends for those by whose trickery the Church was diminished for their own profit. And so according to the aforesaid decision, in the presence and by witness of King Edward, it was settled thus concerning the manor.

125. (B265) *Concerning Rodulf, bishop and abbot.*
Then the king sent a certain aged man, Rodulf, to be put in the abbot's place. He had long been governing a bishopric among the Norwegian people, and finally preferring to free himself from such office he went to King Edward, his kinsman so they said, by whom he was received. So that the monks would, out of respect both for God and himself, receive and treat honourably Rodulf, inasmuch as he was already of ripe old age, the king gave them permission rather to elect as his successor whomsoever they wished from amongst themselves when Rodulf died. The king was obeyed. Submission of due reverence was fittingly paid by the brethren to Rodulf. But the royal promise by no means deceived them thereafter.

126. (B266) *Concerning Ordric, abbot of this church.*
The aforesaid old man died without two whole years having passed, and Ordric, a man of middle age and charming affability, a monk of the church of Abingdon, was received by them as abbot, with the king's approval, and to the immense joy of everyone.[450] Since he was greatly loved by the king, he obtained affirmation by his edict of very many things necessary for the liberty of the church. Other abbots succeeding after him still usually seek to possess an edict of similar form at their installation in the abbacy when they are first admitted to office. These have the following form:

127. (B267) *Charter of King Edward in English.*[451]
King Edward greets his bishops and his abbots and his earls and thegns who are in those shires within which Abbot Ordric has land. And I inform you that I have granted him for St Mary's monastery sake and soke, toll and team, and infangentheof, inside borough and outside borough, hamsocn and grithbreach and foresteal over his own

Harmer, no. 4, with translation. The writ also appears in one of the later Abingdon cartularies, Lyell, no. 70. *Charters of Abingdon Abbey*, p. 573, states that the authenticity of the writ is uncertain, but also notes a similar grant to St Augustine's, Canterbury, and argues that 'it is not difficult to believe that the abbot of Abingdon was granted such privileges'. The writ, if authentic, can be dated no more precisely than to 1052 × 1066, the abbacy of Ordric. On this writ, and the Latin translation which follows, see also above, p. clviii.

his agen land. And ic nelle nanu⟨m⟩ men geþafian ꝥ him ænig[g] þara þinga of anime þe ic him geunnen hebbe.[h]

128. (B268) *Interpretatio in Latinum.*

Eadwardus rex salutat suos episcopos et suos abbates et suos comites et barones qui in illis uicecomitatibus sunt ubi Ordricus abbas habet terram infra. Et ego ostendo uobis quia ego habeo permissum sibi ad sancte Marie monasterium litigium, exquisitionem, teloneum et appropriationem, et infra captum latronem, infra burgum et extra burgum, domus assaltum, et pacis infractionem, obuiationem, super suam propriam terram. Et ego nolo ulli homini permittere ut ei aliqua harum rerum auferat que ego sibi concessi habere.

129. (B269) *Carta regis Eadwardi[a] de hundredo de Hornimere.*[452]

Eadward cyninge[b] gret Hereman bisceop[c] and Harold eorl and Godric and ealle his[d] þegenas on Bearrucscyre freondlic.[453] And ic cyðe eow ꝥ Ordric abbud and eal ꝥ hired on Abbendunes mynstre, be minre unne [i. 466] and gife, frigelice habban and wealdan Hornemeres hundred,[e] on hyre agenre andwealde on ecere worulde. And swa ꝥ nan scyrgerefe oððe[f] motgerefe þar habban æni socne oððe[g] gemot[h] buton þes abbudes[i] agen hæse and unne.

130. (B270) *Interpretatio in Latinum.*

Eadwardus rex salutat Hermannum episcopum et Haroldum comitem et Godricum et omnes suos[a] barones de Bearrucscira[b] amicabiliter. Et ego ostendo uobis quod Ordricus[c] abbas et omnis congregatio[d] Abbendonensis monasterii, meo concessu et dono, libere habeant et possideant hundredum de Hornemere, in sua propria potestate in sempiterna secula. Et sic ut nullus uicecomes uel prepositus ibi habeant aliquam appropriationem seu placitum sine abbatis proprio iussu et concessu.

[g] æng *B* [h] hæbbe *B*

129 [a] Edwardi *B* [b] king *B* [c] biscop *B* [d] *corr., almost certainly from* mine *C* [e] hunred *B* [f] odðe *B* [g] odðe *B* [h] mot *B* [i] *corr. from* abbutes *B*

130 [a] *corr., possibly from* meos *C* [b] Bearcscira *B* [c] Ordicus *C* [d] n *erased at end of word C*

[452] Sawyer, no. 1066; *Charters of Abingdon Abbey*, no. 149; *Anglo-Saxon Writs*, ed. Harmer, no. 5, with translation. *Charters of Abingdon Abbey*, p. 575, concludes that 'it is impossible to establish whether [this document] is a genuine writ to which an exclusionary clause has been added, or whether it is a later fabrication perhaps based in part on a genuine writ of the Confessor concerned with some other transaction'. If authentic, the writ dates from 1053 × 1055 or 1058 × 1066. Hormer is the Berkshire hundred in which Abingdon lies. The abbey held all the *Domesday* estates therein. On this writ, and the Latin translation that follows, see also above, p. clix.

land. And I will permit no one to take away from him any of the things which I have granted him.

128. (B268) *Translation into Latin.*
King Edward greets his bishops and his abbots and his earls and barons who are in those shires within which Abbot Ordric has land. And I show you that I have permitted to him for St Mary's monastery lawsuit, investigation, toll and appropriation, and thief captured within, inside borough and outside borough, house assault, and breach of the peace, confrontation, over his own land. And I am not willing to permit any man that he take away from him any of those things which I have granted to him to have.

129. (B269) *Charter of King Edward concerning the hundred of Hormer.*[452]
King Edward greets in friendly fashion Bishop Hereman and Earl Harold and Godric and all his thegns in Berkshire.[453] And I inform you that Abbot Ordric and all the congregation in the monastery of Abingdon, by my grant and gift, are to have and possess freely Hormer hundred, in their own power for ever more. And thus that no sheriff or court-reeve may have any soke or court there without the abbot's own order and grant.

130. (B270) *Translation into Latin.*
King Edward greets in friendly fashion Bishop Hereman and Earl Harold and Godric and all his barons of Berkshire. And I show you that Abbot Ordric and all the congregation of the monastery of Abingdon, by my grant and gift, are to have and possess freely the hundred of Hormer, in their own power for ever more. And thus that no sheriff or reeve may have any appropriation or plea without the abbot's own order and grant.

[453] Godric was the sheriff probably of Berkshire and possibly of Buckinghamshire before 1066; J. A. Green, *English Sheriffs to 1154* (HMSO, 1990), pp. 26, 28; see also Clarke, *English Nobility*, pp. 135–8, 309–10. See below, p. 224, for the *History* stating that he fell at Hastings. *DB* i, fo. 60^{v}, has a Godric unjustly taking lands at Sparsholt after Hastings, which has led to suggestions that the sheriff may have survived Hastings. However, the preceding *Domesday Book* entry mentions Godric 'a free man [*unus liber homo*]' holding land there, perhaps to distinguish the Sparsholt Godric from Godric the sheriff, who appears in the next entry but one with reference to holding *TRE*; see also below, p. 212, on Godric Cild holding land at Sparsholt. This may be to distinguish two Godrics. Otherwise either the hundred jurors in 1086 or the *History* have made a mistake. For other discrepancies between the *History* and *Domesday*, see Hudson, 'Abbey of Abingdon', pp. 189–90. Harold, who became Harold II king of England in 1066, here appears as earl of Wessex. He succeeded to the earldom following the death of his father, Godwine, in 1053.

[i. 469 n.] **131.** *De Haroldo comite.*[454]

Rex autem Eadwardus dederat comiti Haroldo terre portionem quandam transflumen Tamisie quatuor hidarum, que Sandford uulgo uocitatur. Sed postea, eiusdem comitis suggestione, abbate Ordrico optinente, ecclesie Abbendonensi eandem terram concessit. De quo ita cartula inscripta est:

[i. 469] **132. (B273)** *Carta quatuor hidarum de Sandford.*[a] [455]

B fo. 114r Cuncta seculorum patrimonia incertis nepotum heredibus relinquuntur,[b] [i. 470] et omnis mundi gloria appropinquante[c] debite mortis termino ad nichilum reducta fatescit. Huius rei[d] gratia, terrenis caducarum rerum possessionibus semper mansura superne patrie emolumenta adipiscentes, Domino iuuante, lucremur. Quapropter, lubrici potentatus non inmemor, ego Eadwardus,[e] Christo conferente rex et primicerius C fo. 132v Anglorum,[456] | ob[f] remunerationem[g] celestis premii, aliquantulam ruris particulam, quatuor mansas in communi terra loco qui celebri Sandford[h] profertur, ad ecclesiam beate Marie genitricis Dei ac Domini nostri Ihesu Christi illo in locello qui dicitur Abbandun ad usus ibidem fratrum Deo seruientium libenter concedo, obsecrans et precipiens in nomine Christi ut nemo successorum nostrorum superioris inferiorisue gradus hoc nostre deuotionis donum aliquo temeritatis aliquatenus instinctu dirumpat.[i] Si quis ergo alium libellulum, false cupiditatis atramento,[j] pretitulatum contra istum in palam protulerit,[k] nec sibi nec sue proficiat auaritie, sed a diuino sit in perpetuum perforatus graphiolo, et ipse meo atque meorum interdictu pontificum permaneat anathematizatus, et a Christianorum consortio alienatus, insuper a corpore et sanguine Domini sequestratus, et in penis infernalibus post obitum miserabiliter[l] dampnatus. Et ut prefate telluris ruricole inuiolabile robur libertatis semper obtinere ualeant, regali liberati sunt precepto ab omni seculari iugo exceptis trium rerum obsequiis, expeditione scilicet populari, uiatici

132 [a] Samford *B* [b] relinquuntur *B* [c] adpropinquante *B* [d] regi *B* [e] Eadward *B* [f] *preceded by* atque Danorum *struck out C;* atque Donorum *B* [g] remuneratione *B* [h] æt Sandfordan *B* [i] disrumpat *B* [j] attramento *B* [k] protulererit *C* [l] misabiliter *B*

[454] This section does not appear in MS B, although there are some verbal parallels in the latter's introduction to this gift of Sandford-on-Thames; below, B272.

[455] Sawyer, no. 1025; *Charters of Abingdon Abbey*, no. 147, which, at p. 571, states that this charter 'would appear to be a fabrication'. The main problem is the witness list in MS B, whereas that in MS C is more acceptable. However, the latter still refers to Stigand as a

131. *Concerning Earl Harold.*[454]
Moreover, King Edward had given to Earl Harold a portion of land amounting to four hides across the Thames, which is commonly called Sandford. But afterwards, at the suggestion of that earl, he granted that land to the church of Abingdon, under the charge of Abbot Ordric. Concerning this a charter was written thus:

132. (B273) *Charter regarding four hides in Sandford.*[455]
All patrimonies of this life are left to uncertain heirs of descendants, and all glory of the world fails and is reduced to nothing with the approaching end of due death. Because of this, we, with the Lord's help, acquire and gain with earthly possessions of transitory things the ever-lasting advantages of the heavenly land. Therefore, not unmindful of the transitoriness of power, I, Edward, by Christ's appointing king and ruler of the English,[456] with a view to payment of a greater reward, willingly grant a small portion of land, four hides in the common land in the place commonly called Sandford, to the church of the blessed Mary mother of God and of our Lord Jesus Christ in that small place called Abingdon, for the use of the brethren serving God there, entreating and ordering in Christ's name that none of our successors, of higher or lower rank, prompted by any rashness break to any degree this gift of our devotion. If therefore anyone brings forward into the open any document previously drawn up with the ink of false greed against this one drawn up above, let it profit neither him nor his avarice, but be pierced in perpetuity by a divine sword, and let him remain anathematized by the interdict of myself and my bishops, and in addition estranged from the fellowship of Christians, and in addition cut off from the body and blood of the Lord, and miserably damned after his death in infernal punishments. And so that the local inhabitants of the aforementioned estate can always hold the inviolable strength of liberty, by royal order they are freed from every secular yoke except services of three things, that is, common military service, road bridge strengthening, and royal

bishop, whereas he had become archbishop by the time of the charter; see also above, p. 196 n. 445. On the possible circumstances of fabrication, see above, p. ccvi. The four hides separately specified in *Domesday* as being held from the abbot by Wenric in 1086 may correspond to the four mentioned in this charter, and in the grant to Earl Godwine, recorded in an apparently authentic charter of 1050; *DB* i, fo. 156^{v}, below, B271 (*Charters of Abingdon Abbey*, no. 144).

[456] *Charters of Abingdon Abbey*, p. 572, suggests that the deletion of 'atque Danorum' may 'reflect a belated realization that this was not such an appropriate component of a royal style for Edward the Confessor'.

[i. 471] fundatione pontis, arcis conditione regalis. [m]Acta est hec donatio anno ab incarnatione Christi .mliiii., his subscribentibus testibus: Ego Eadward rex Anglorum prefatam donationem sub signo sancte crucis [i. 472] indeclinabiliter consensi atque roboraui. Ego Stigandus episcopus subscripsi. Ego Hermannus episcopus, ego Ældredus episcopus, ego Duduca episcopus, ego Leofric episcopus subscripsimus. Ego Ordricus abbas, ego Alfwardus[n] abbas,[457] ego Alfwinus abbas concessimus. Ego Siwardus dux,[458] ego Haroldus dux, ego Leofric dux concessimus. Ego Kinewardus prepositus, ego Ælfwi prepositus annuimus.[m]

[i. 488] B fo. 117ᵛ Idem[o] rex, sub eodem abbate, quinque hidarum portionem terre apud Cildatun[p] concessit huic ecclesie, quam portionem[q] Ædelredus[r] rex, pater huius Ædwardi[s] regis, Beorhtwaldo episcopo Wiltoniensi donauerat.[459]

133. (B288) *Carta regis Eadwardi[a] de Cildatun.*[460]

Confirmat nos sacre auctoritatis scriptura, dicens 'Nudus egressus sum ex utero matris mee, et nudus reuertar illuc', et iterum 'Nichil intulimus in hunc mundum, uerum nec ab eo auferre quid poterimus'.[461] Quapropter, lubrici potentatus non inmemor, ego Eadward,[b] Christo conferente rex et primicerius totius Albionis, regni fastigium humili presidens animo, ob remunerationem maioris premii, aliquantulam ruris particulam quinque comparatam cassatis, cui uocabulum certa astipulatione Cildatun[c] profertur, ad ecclesiam beate Marie genitricis Dei ac Domini nostri Ihesu Christi in loco qui dicitur Abbandun ad usus ibidem fratrum Deo seruientium libenter concedo, obsecrans et precipiens in nomine Christi ut nemo successorum meorum superioris uel inferioris gradus hoc nostre deuotionis donum aliquo temeritatis aliquatenus instinctu dirumpat. [i. 489] Sit autem predicta[d] quam ego cum consensu optimatum meorum prefato largitus sum cenobio ab omni terrene seruitutis iugo libera, tribus his exceptis, rata uidelicet expeditione, pontis arcisue

m–m *see Charters of Abingdon Abbey, pp. 570–1, for the boundaries, dating clause, and witness list in B* n *rectius* Wlwardus, *the rubricator having entered the wrong intial C* o Item idem *B* p Childatun *B* q potionem *B* r Adelredus *B* s Edwardi *B*

133 a Edwardi *B* b Edward *B* c Childatun *B* d terra *add. B*

457 Abbot Ælfweard of Evesham had died in 1044; *Heads of Religious Houses*, p. 47. It is possible that the rubricator had entered the wrong initial in MS C and that MS B's reading of 'Wulfweard' is correct. If so, his abbey cannot be identified.

458 On this rendering of 'dux', see above, p. cxciii.

459 This sentence concerning Chilton, Berkshire, does not appear at this point in MS B, but rather on the second appearance of the charter, below, B288. Byrhtwold was bishop of

fortress building. This gift was carried out in the year 1054 from the Incarnation of Christ, with these witnesses subscribing: I Edward king of the English have consented to and strengthened unfailingly the aforementioned gift under the sign of the holy cross. I Bishop Stigand have subscribed. I Bishop Hereman, I Bishop Ealdred, I Bishop Duduca, I Bishop Leofric, have subscribed. I Abbot Ordric, I Abbot Ælfweard,[457] I Abbot Ælfwine have granted. I Ealdorman[458] Siward, I Ealdorman Harold, I Ealdorman Leofric have granted. I Kineweard the reeve, I Ælfwig the reeve have agreed.

The same king, under the same abbot, granted to this church a portion of land amounting to five hides at Chilton, which portion King Æthelred, father of this King Edward, had given to Byrhtwold bishop of Wilton.[459]

133. (B288) *Charter of King Edward concerning Chilton.*[460]
The writing of sacred authority strengthens us, saying 'Naked came I out of my mother's womb and naked shall I return thither', and again 'We brought nothing into this world, and it is certain we can carry nothing out from it.'[461] Therefore, not unmindful of the transitoriness of power, I, Edward, by Christ's appointing king and ruler of the whole of Albion, exercising this eminence of kingship humbly, with a view to payment of a greater reward, willingly grant a small portion of land totalling five hides, called by reliable statement Chilton, to the church of the blessed Mary mother of God and of our Lord Jesus Christ in the place called Abingdon, for the use of the brethren serving God there, entreating and ordering in Christ's name that none of my successors, of higher or lower rank, prompted by any rashness break to any degree this gift of our devotion. Moreover, let the aforesaid land, which I have bestowed on the aforementioned monastery with the consent of my leading men, be free of every yoke of earthly servitude except these three, that is, fixed military service,

Ramsbury 1005–45; *Handbook of British Chronology*, p. 220. The bishopric had been moved from Wilton to Ramsbury, but the earlier name is here used; see Barlow, *English Church 1000–1066*, p. 220.

[460] Sawyer, no. 1023; *Charters of Abingdon Abbey*, no. 146. MS B had also already contained a fuller version, below, B258. *Charters of Abingdon Abbey*, p. 568, states that the document 'was evidently drawn up at Abingdon, and is likely to be spurious', primarily on grounds of problems in the witness list. On the possible circumstances of fabrication, see above, p. ccvi. A charter only in MS B records King Æthelred granting five hides in Chilton to Byrhtwold bishop of Ramsbury in 1015; below, B239 (*Charters of Abingdon Abbey*, no. 137). *DB* i, fo. 59^r, records that Abingdon had five hides in Chilton in 1086; *TRE* Blæcmann had held it from Earl Harold 'in alodio'.

[461] Job 1: 21, 1 Tim. 6: 7.

restauratione. Si quis autem, laruarico instinctus spiritu, hoc donum
B fo. 118r uiolare | immutareue presumptuosus temptauerit, nisi digna satisfactione ante obitum suum reus penituerit, eternis barathri[e] prostratus incendiis cum Iuda[f] Christi proditore eternaliter lugubris puniatur. Acta est hec prefata donatio anno ab incarnatione
C fo. 133r Domini .mlii., | his testibus quorum nomina in superiori carta nominantur.

[i. 473] **134. (B274)** [a]*De Leowartun.*[a]
B fo. 114v Idem rex, sub eodem abbate, adiecit in dono octo hidas apud flumen Cynete, terre portionem que Leowartun[b] uocatur, quam Ædelredus[c] rex Brithrico[d] ministro suo donauerat.[462]

135. (B275) [a]*Carta regis Eadwardi de Leowartun.*[a] [463]
Ego Eadward, Christo conferente rex et primicerius totius Albionis regni fastigium humili presidens animo, ob remunerationem maioris premii, aliquantulam ruris particulam octo mansas iuxta flumen quod Cynete uocatur, illud uidelicet rus quod Eðeric[b] quidam rusticus habuisse cognoscitur, largiendo libenter concedens perdonabo ad ecclesiam beate Marie genitricis Dei ac Domini nostri Ihesu Christi in loco qui dicitur Abbendun ad usus ibidem fratrum Deo seruientium libenter concedo,[464] obsecrans et precipiens in nomine Christi ut nemo successorum nostrorum superioris uel inferioris gradus hoc nostre [c]deuotionis donum[c] aliquo temeritatis aliquatenus instinctu dirumpat. Sit autem predicta tellus quam ego cum consensu optimatum meorum prefato largitus sum cenobio ab omni terrene seruitutis
B fo. 115r iugo libera, tribus his exceptis, rata uidelicet expeditione, | pontis arcisue restauratione. Si quis autem, laruarico instinctus spiritu, hoc
[i. 474] donum uiolare immutareue presumptuosus temptauerit, nisi digna satisfactione ante obitum suum reus penituerit,[d] eternis barathri[e]

[e] baratri *B* [f] *interlin. B*

134 [a–a] Rex Edwardus dedit Leofwartun *B* [b] Leofwartun *B* [c] Aþelredus *B* [d] Brihtrico *B*

135 [a–a] Carta regis Edwardi *B* [b] *corr. from* Eðerec *B* [c–c] donum deuotionis *B* [d] petuerit *B* [e] baratri *B*

[462] Æthelred's charter recording his gift of eight hides in Leverton, Berkshire, to his thegn Beorhtric in 984 appears only in MS B; B228 (*Charters of Abingdon Abbey*, no. 122). That the compiler of the earlier version of the *History* knows of the earlier gift presumably indicates that he knew of the Æthelred charter but chose to omit it, although a possible alternative is that he learnt of Æthelred's gift from a note connected to the present charter.

and bridge and fortress repair. Moreover, if any presumptuous man, prompted by diabolical spirit, attempts to violate or change this gift, unless the offender does penance with worthy compensation before his death, let the mournful man eternally be laid down and punished in the eternal fires of Hell with Judas the betrayer of Christ. This aforementioned gift was carried out in the year of our Lord 1052, with those witnesses whose names are named in the charter above.

134. (B274) *Concerning Leverton.*

The same king, under the same abbot, added as a gift eight hides by the river Kennet, a portion of land that is called Leverton, which King Æthelred had given to Beorhtric his thegn.[462]

135. (B275) *Charter of King Edward concerning Leverton.*[463]

I, Edward, by Christ's appointing king and ruler of the whole of Albion, exercising this eminence of kingship humbly, with a view to payment of a greater reward, willingly grant by bestowing and will remit a small portion of land, eight hides next to the river called the Kennet, specifically that land which a certain rustic Ætheric is known to have had, to the church of the blessed Mary mother of God and of our Lord Jesus Christ in the place called Abingdon, I grant willingly[464] for the use of the brethren serving God there, entreating and ordering in Christ's name that none of our successors, of higher or lower rank, prompted by any rashness break to any degree this gift of our devotion. Moreover, let the aforesaid estate, which I have bestowed on the aforementioned monastery with the consent of my leading men, be free of every yoke of earthly servitude except these three, that is, fixed military service, and bridge and fortress repair. Moreover, if any presumptuous man, prompted by diabolical spirit, attempts to violate or change this gift, unless the offender does penance with worthy compensation before his death, let the mournful

[463] Sawyer, no. 1020; *Charters of Abingdon Abbey*, no. 145. MS B has again already included a full version, below B257. *Charters of Abingdon Abbey*, p. 566, states that the document 'was certainly drawn up at Abingdon', and 'is likely to be a fabrication, though probably an early one'. The present charter draws on Æthelred's charter to Beorhtric. In addition it has inconsistencies in its witness list. However, it is notable that the care taken to insert the name of Kineweard, reeve of Berkshire, in the witness list in MS B may indicate that the document 'came into existence not very long after the given date'. For further discussion of the circumstances of fabrication, see above, p. ccvi. *DB* i, fo. 59^{r}, records Abingdon having lands in Leverton in 1086. *TRE* it had been held by Blæcmann 'in feudo'. The *TRE* assessment was six and a half hides, the 1086 assessment four and a half.

[464] The possibly redundant proliferation of dispositive phrases in this charter may be related to partial copying from King Æthelred's charter concerning the same lands.

prostratus incendiis cum Iuda Christi proditore eternaliter lugubris puniatur. Acta est hec donatio anno ab incarnatione Domini .ml. Ego[f] Eadward[g] rex Anglorum consensi et roboraui. Ego Stigandus episcopus confirmaui. Ego Hermannus episcopus conclusi. Ego Vlfo[h] episcopus consensi. Ego Ordricus abbas quieui. Ego Godwine dux, cum multis aliis, subscripsi.

136. (B276) Per idem tempus[a] presbiter nomine Blacheman pecuniosus, abbatis et monachorum permissu, ecclesiam ob uenerationem apostoli Andree in insula ad australem monasterii locum sita fabricauit.[465] Cuius in lateribus dextrorsum[b] et sinistrorsum claustralibus, ad monachorum[c] formam habitaculorum, cum domibus edendi uictusque coquendi, quiescendi quoque,[d] et ceteris conuersationi uirorum necessariis mirifice coaptatis, picturis celeturisque[e] infra et extra ubique locorum delectabile uisu subhornatis, singulorum tecta plumbi laminis edificiorum texit. Cui insule a uocabulo Andree Andresia insitum est nomen. Tali ibi parata mansione, priuatim se monachis ingerendo, tum auri argentique ostentu, tum facundi oris profusione, ad hoc processum sui emolumenti perduxit, ut predictarum terrarum, id est Sandford,[466] Cildatun,[f] et Leowartun,[g]
[i. 475] possessor haberetur. Ceterum quod emolumenti de edificatis mansionibus in insula sibi prouenerit, postea dicemus.[467] Interim huius temporis euentus prosequamur.

Brichwinus, de quo in[h] domni Siwardi episcopi tractatu intulimus,[i][468] terra Lechamstede hucusque absque monachorum permissu potiebatur, agebatque se loquatius cum landboc, id est telluris descripte libellum, secum haberet.[469] Poterat enim quis illo fiducialius pro qualibet terra disceptare, in cuius manu huiuscemodi scriptura haberetur. Quare abbas primum prudenti sategit argumento quatinus eadem scriptura sibi restitueretur. Quod postquam factum est, per

[f] *preceded by heading* Testes, *and with a cross preceding each witness B* [g] Eadwardus *B* [h] *initial om. C*

136 [a] temporis *C*; temporis *corr. from* tempus *B* [b] dextrosum *B* [c] monacorum *B* [d] *interlin. B* [e] celaturisque, *the first four letters being over an erasure B* [f] Childatun *B* [g] Leofwartun *B* [h] *interlin. B* [i] *followed by* in, *struck out, B*

---

[465] The island of Andersey lies between two branches of the Thames, near Abingdon. The *History* suggests that Blæcmann was seeking to found a substantial minster church or monastery at Andersey. For this, and for Andersey's earlier connection to kings and to the abbey, see above, p. cviii. For later developments including the removal of the lead from the roofs of the buildings on Andersey, see vol. ii. 72–4. Blæcmann was clearly a rich priest, probably with a close connection to the Godwine family.

man eternally be laid down and punished in the eternal fires of Hell with Judas the betrayer of Christ. This gift was carried out in the year of our Lord 1050. I Edward king of the English have consented and strengthened. I Bishop Stigand have confirmed. I Bishop Hereman have approved. I Bishop Ulf have consented. I Abbot Ordric have agreed. I Ealdorman Godwine, with many others, have subscribed.

136. (B276) During this period a wealthy priest named Blæcmann, out of reverence for the Apostle Andrew, built a church on the island situated to the south of the monastery, with the permission of the abbot and monks.[465] To left and right were cloistered sides, after the pattern of monks' dwellings, with rooms for eating and cooking food, also for resting, and with the other necessities made marvellously suitable for the religious life of men, and decorated with paintings and carvings everywhere inside and out in a fashion delightful to the sight, and he covered the roof of each building with lead sheets. To this island was attached the name Andersey, from the word Andrew. When he had built such a house there, by privately presenting himself to the monks, both with a display of gold and silver and with a pouring forth of eloquent speech, he furthered his own advantage thus that he might be the possessor of the aforesaid lands, that is Sandford,[466] Chilton, and Leverton. For the rest, we shall speak later of what advantage came to him from the houses built on the island.[467] Meanwhile let us pursue events of this time.

Brihtwine, about whom we told in the discussion of lord Abbot Siward,[468] had hitherto possessed the land at Leckhampstead without the monks' permission, and he was behaving in particularly loud-mouthed fashion since he had the land-book, that is the document of the estate described.[469] For he who had in his possession such writing could thereby dispute more confidently for any land. Therefore the abbot first strove by prudent argument to have the document returned to him. This afterwards happened, through Earl Harold, whose favour the abbot enjoyed in this matter. It was decreed that, when the opposing pleas brought by the

[466] i.e. Sandford-on-Thames.

[467] See below, p. 222.

[468] See above, c. 120.

[469] The document which Brihtwine had in his possession was probably the charter which follows this section. It may never have passed to Abingdon, or Brihtwine may have obtained it from the monastery, directly or indirectly, by some unrecorded means. *Charters of Abingdon Abbey*, p. 559, suggests as an alternative possibility 'that Brihtwine simply approached the king (? Harold Harefoot or Harthacnut) and acquired a landbook for the property'.

Haroldum comitem,[j] cuius gratia in id abbas utebatur. Edicitur ut, in consistorio seniorum[470] ratiociniis de predicta terra ex diuersa ill-
C fo. 133v atione disceptantium | pensatis, cui rectius in reliquum ipsius terre proprietas competeret decerneretur. Itaque cum die denominato inde disceptaretur, causidici quibus illic ius equum disponere fuerat delegatum, cognito alternarum disputationum uero indicio, abbatis causam decernunt iustiorem. Vnde ipsi et monachis terra libere restituitur.[471] Nec multo post, dedicante huius loci parrochiano
B fo. 115v episcopo Hermanno ecclesiam tunc tem|poris in cimiterio[k] introitu constructam, inter cetera que episcopali officio admitti uel excludi eo habebantur, uniuersos qui ullo modo predicte terre extractum a uictualitate monachorum Abbendonie degentium ab illo tempore satagerent a communitate Christianitatis exclusit et perpetuo perculit anathemate. Videant posteri quid inde cauendum sit.[472]

[i. 476] **137. (B277)** *Carta decem cassatorum de Lecamstede.*[473]

In nomine Dei summi et altithroni,[a] qui omnia de summo celi apice uisibilia et inuisibilia ordinabiliter gubernans atque moderans. Presentisque uite curriculo cotidie temporales possessiones et uniuerse diuitiarum facultates nostris humanis obtutibus cernimus deficientes ac decrescentes. Sic mutando fragilitas mortalis uite marcessit, et rotunda seculorum uolubilitas inanescit, ac in carorum propinquorum amicorumque amissione conqueritur ac defletur. Quapropter ego Eadwi, Angligenarum rex ceterarumque gentium in circuitu persistentium, fideli meo ministro uocitato nomine Eadrico, ob illius amabile obsequium eiusque placabili fidelitate, decem mansas largiendo libenter concedens perdonabo illic, ubi uulgus prisca relatione uocitat Lechamstede;[474] quatinus ille bene perfruatur ac perpetualiter possideat dum huius labentis eui cursum transeat illesus atque uitalis spiritus in corruptibili carne inhereat, et post se cuicumque uoluerit perhenniter heredi derelinquat, sicuti predixi. Sit autem predictum rus liber ab omni mundiali obstaculo, cum omnibus que rite ad ipsum

[j] comtem *B* [k] cimiterii, *altered from* cimiterio *B*

137 [a] altitroni *B*

[470] The nature of this assembly cannot be known for certain; see above, p. clx.

[471] Nevertheless, the evidence of *DB* i, fo. 58v, suggests that Brihtwine was the abbot's tenant for Leckhampstead *TRE*; see also above, p. clxiii.

[472] For the church at the cemetery entrance, see above, p. clxix. For later dispute concerning Leckhampstead, see vol. ii. 56–8, 196–8.

[473] Sawyer, no. 665; *Charters of Abingdon Abbey*, no. 37. MS B had again already included a different version, which has King Edmund as the grantor, below, B72. *Charters*

disputants concerning that land had been weighed in an assembly of high-ranking men,[470] it would be decided to whom the ownership of that land belonged more justly for the future. And so when the matter was debated on the specified day, the pleaders, to whom in that place it had been delegated to set down the equitable right, got to know the facts in both sides' arguments and decided that the abbot's case was the more just. Therefore the land was freely restored to him and the monks.[471] Not long afterwards, when Hereman the diocesan bishop of this place was dedicating the church then constructed at the cemetery entrance, amongst the rest of the things which were there held to be admitted or excluded by episcopal office, he excluded from the community of Christianity and struck with perpetual anathema all who from that time strove in any way for the extraction of the aforesaid land from the sustenance of the monks living at Abingdon. Let men in future see what should be guarded against concerning this.[472]

137. (B277) *Charter regarding ten hides in Leckhampstead.*[473]
In the name of the highest and high-enthroned God, who governs and rules in orderly fashion everything visible and invisible from the highest apex of Heaven. And with our human gazes we perceive the temporal possessions and all the wealth of riches daily failing and decreasing in the course of the present life. Thus the mortal fragility of life grows feeble in changing, and the circular mutability of the ages becomes nothing, and is lamented and bewailed in the loss of dear relatives and friends. Therefore I, Eadwig, king of the English and of the other peoples living round about, willingly grant by bestowing and will remit to my faithful thegn, called by the name Eadric, on account of his beloved service and by his pleasing loyalty, ten hides in the place which the common people call Leckhampstead by ancient naming,[474] so that he may enjoy it well and possess it perpetually while he proceeds unharmed along the course of this fleeting life and the vital spirit abides in the corruptible flesh, and after him he may leave it for ever to whomsoever he wishes as heir, as I have said before. Moreover, let that land be free from every worldly hindrance, with everything known to pertain duly to that place, both

of Abingdon Abbey, p. 156, states of the full version that the charter 'seems to be authentic'. The full version is dated 943.

[474] It is impossible to identify Eadric with certainty as there was more than one thegn of that name in the mid-9th c. *Charters of Abingdon Abbey*, p. 273, comments that the Eadric who received Welford from King Eadwig, above, cc. 47–8, 'can probably be identified as the son of Ealdorman Ealhhelm and brother of Ealdormen Ælfheah and Ælfhere', and that Leckhampstead is immediately north of Welford.

locum pertinere dinoscuntur, tam in magnis quam in modicis rebus, campis, pascuis,[b] siluis, excepto istis, expeditione, pontis arcisue coedificatione. Insuper ad augmentum predicte donationis gratia [c]unam molinam[c] iuxta diriuatiuis cursibus aquarum Lamburnam[d] [475]
[i. 477] perpetuali donatione dedi predicto ministro. Hoc tempore cachinnantes nenias subdolosi huius seculi [e]dinoscuntur interdum inchoasse, alienum[e] lucrum sibi usurpatiue cum ambitione iniquitatis uendicare. Sed torpentes auaritie incessus omni modo in nomine sancte Trinitatis ab omnibus Christianis interdico, ita ut meum donum corroboratum sit cum signaculo sancte crucis. Etiam si quis alium antiquum librum in propatulo protulerit, nec sibi nec aliis proficiat, sed in sempiterno graphio[476] deleatur, et cum iustis non scribatur[f] nec audiatur.[g] Denique uero si quis (nobis non obtantibus) nostrum hoc donum uiolari fraudulenter perpetrando consenserit, consideret hinc se die ultima iudicii coram Deo rationem redditurum, atque cum reprobis quibus dicitur 'Discedite a me, maledicti, in ignem eternum',[477] penis atrocibus se esse passurum, si non antea corporea lamentatione emendauerit.

B fo. 116ʳ Hanc igitur cartulam cum terra moriens idem Eadricus | ecclesie Abbendonensi dereliquit, quam cartulam cum terra abbas Ordricus a predicto Brithwino extorsit.

C fo. 134ʳ **138. (B278)** Consuetudinis apud Anglos tunc erat ut monachi qui uellent pecuniarum patrimoniorumque forent susceptibiles, ipsisque fruentes quomodo placeret dispensarent.[478] Vnde et in Abbendonia duo Leofricus et Godricus Cild appellati, quorum unus Godricus Speresholt iuxta locum qui uulgo mons Albi Equi nuncupatur, alter Leofricus Hwitceorce super flumen Tamisie maneria sita patrimoniali iure obtinebant.[479] Quorum unum, id est Speresholt, usque hodie

[b] pratis *add.* B [c–c] *redundant abbreviation marks over* unam molinam B [d] Lamburniam B [e–e] *over erasure* B [f] scribantur C; *corr. from* scribantur B [g] *corr. from* audiantur B

[475] The Lambourn is a tributary of the river Kennet, and passes to the south of Leckhampstead. The mill on the Lambourn must have been outside the estate; EPNS, *Berkshire*, iii. 657.

[476] See above, n. 338.

[477] Matt. 25: 41.

[478] See above, p. clxxii.

[479] The first of the pieces of land concerned seems to be the manor of 'Spersold', Berkshire, assessed at ten hides, which appears as a 1086 Abingdon holding in *DB* i, fo. 59ʳ. This is the manor later known as Fawler; see vol. ii. 52, 182–4. *Domesday* provides more

in great things and in small, fields, pastures, woods, except these, military service, and bridge and fortress building. In addition, to increase the aforesaid gift, I have given as a favour to the aforesaid thegn as a perpetual gift one mill, beside the channelled currents of the waters of the Lambourn.[475] At this time deceitful men of this world, desirous of injustice, are known sometimes to begin guffawing complaints, to claim another's income improperly for themselves. But in the name of the Holy Trinity I forbid the paralysing attacks of avarice by all Christians in every way, thus that my gift may be strengthened by the sign of the holy cross. Also if anyone publicly brings forth another old land-book, let it profit neither him nor others, but let him be deleted from the Everlasting Charter[476] and not be written or heard with the just. Finally, then, if anyone (which we do not choose) agrees to violate this our gift by acting fraudulently, let him consider that he will render account of this in God's presence on the Last Day of Judgement, and will suffer with awful punishments with those wicked men to whom it is said 'Depart from me, ye cursed, into eternal fire',[477] if he does not previously make amends with bodily lamentation.

Therefore, when that Eadric was dying, he left this charter with the land to the church of Abingdon, which charter Abbot Ordric extorted with the land from the aforesaid Brihtwine.

138. **(B278)** It was then the custom among the English that those monks who wished might receive goods and patrimonies, enjoy them, and do with them as they pleased.[478] Therefore in Abingdon, two monks called Leofric and Godric Cild obtained manors by patrimonial right, Godric Sparsholt next to the place commonly called the hill of the White Horse, Leofric Whitchurch, situated on the river Thames.[479] One of these, i.e. Sparsholt, has remained to this day in

detail about the descent of the land at Sparsholt. A man named Eadric had held it 'in alodio' from King Edward. He conveyed it to his son, presumably Godric Cild, who was a monk of Abingdon; see also above, p. 201 n. 453. From it the son was to support his father while he lived, and have the manor after Eadric died. However, the men of the shire did not know what belonged to the abbey, as they had not seen the king's writ or seal which might have signified the conveyance of the land. The abbot, backed by the monks, stated that the son had transferred the lands to the church in the time of King Edward, and that he had the king's writ and seal concerning this. As to the second of the pieces of land, *DB* i, fo. 159^{r}, records that Leofric and Alwin held Whitchurch, Oxfordshire, *TRE*; see also below, p. 217 n. 486. In 1086 Miles Crispin held it. It was assessed at ten hides. Miles Crispin was one of the successors of Wigod of Wallingford, whose granddaughter he married; Blair, *Anglo-Saxon Oxfordshire*, p. 174.

ecclesie feudo[a] remansit, aliud[b] uero Wigodus oppidanorum Walin-
[i. 478] gafordensium dominus possedit, uelle monachorum predictorum hinc et inde de eisdem terris sic se referente.[480] Nec accidisset de una secus quam de altera, si uiro[c] secundum morem gentis necdum austeriora edocto ferre remissius blandiretur, domno Adelelmo[d] abbate dominatum loci huius optinente.[481]

139. (B279) *Carta de Speresholt decem cassatorum.*[482]

Quecumque enim secundum decreta canonum atque ecclesiastica instituta salubri consilio definiuntur, quanquam sermo tantum absque[a] textu sufficeret, tamen quoniam plerumque nostris temporibus tempestates et turbines secularium rerum etiam portas[b] ecclesie pulsa⟨n⟩t, iccirco opere pretium censuimus ob cautelam futurorum ea que definita sunt paginis[c] scripturarum annectere, ne in posterum obliuione tradita ignorentur. Quapropter ego Eadgar, regali fretus a Domino dignitate, quandam ruris particulam, decem uidelicet mansas in loco qui dicitur Speresholt, et unam mansam cum duodecim agrorum quantitate qui sunt in loco qui Baðalacyng[d] dicitur, et etiam unum molendinum ad Hirdegraue[e] cum duodecim agrorum portione pertinente[f] ad ipsum molendinum,[484] camerario meo uocitato Æþelsie[g] [483] perpetua largitus sum[h] hereditate. Tali autem tenore tradendo concessi ut possideat usque ad ultimum uite sue cum omnibus ad se rite pertinentibus, campis, pratis, pascuis, siluis, et post se cuicumque uoluerit heredi in perpetuum ius derelinquat. Sit autem predicta terra libera ab omni regali tributo preter expeditionem et pontis arcisue
[i. 479] constructionem.[i] Si quis uero, cupiditate illectus, temptauerit irritam facere aut frangere huius decreti diffinitionem, sciat se in tremendo examine rationem redditurum. Scripta est hec scedula anno ab incarnatione Domini .dcccclxiii., his testibus: Ego[j] Eadgar rex. Ego Dunstan archiepiscopus. Ego Kynsie[k] episcopus. Et multis aliis.

138 [a] ecclesie *interlin. after instead of before* feudo *B* [b] aliut *B* [c] uero *B* [d] Aþelelmo *B*

139 [a] abque *B* [b] *corr. from* portans *B* [c] *corr. from* paganis *B* [d] Baþalacyng *B* [e] Hyrdegraue *B* [f] pertinentem, *on account of redundant final abbreviation mark B C* [g] Aþelsige in *B* [h] sunt *C*; *corr. from* sunt *B* [i] constructione *C* [j] *a cross precedes each witness B* [k] Kinsie *B*

[480] Wigod was a kinsman of Edward the Confessor and a prominent landholder, with possessions in at least seven counties. He was dead by 1086. For his lands, see Clarke, *English Nobility*, pp. 144–5, 356–7. His daughter, Ealdgyth, married Robert d'Oilly, and their daughter married Miles Crispin; Blair, *Anglo-Saxon Oxfordshire*, p. 174; K. S. B. Keats-Rohan, 'The devolution of the Honour of Wallingford, 1066–1148', *Oxoniensia*, liv (1989), 311–18.

[481] Adelelm was abbot 1071–84.

the fee of the church, but of the other Wigod lord of the garrison of Wallingford took possession, thus in every way going back on the wishes of the aforesaid monks concerning those lands.[480] And the outcome for the two estates would not have differed one from the other, if, when lord Abbot Adelelm held lordship of this monastery, he had more indulgently flattered the man according to the custom of his people, when he had not yet learnt to bear harsher circumstances.[481]

139. (B279) *Charter concerning Sparsholt amounting to ten hides.*[482] For whatever is laid down according to the decrees of the canons and ecclesiastical institutes by beneficial counsel, although speech alone without text would suffice, nevertheless, since in our times storms and whirlwinds of secular matters beat even the doors of the Church very frequently, therefore we have decided it to be worthwhile, out of circumspection concerning the future, to attach in pages of writing those things which have been laid down, lest in future they might not be known, having passed into oblivion. Therefore I, Edgar, strengthened by the Lord with the royal dignity, have bestowed as perpetual inheritance on my chamberlain called Æthelsige[483] a small portion of land, that is ten hides in the place called Sparsholt, and one hide with the quantity of twelve fields that are in the place called Balking, and also a mill at *Hirdegrave*, with a portion of twelve fields pertaining to that mill.[484] Moreover, I have granted it by handing over, with the following condition, that he may possess it to the end of his life with everything duly pertaining to it, fields, meadows, pastures, woods, and after him may leave it in perpetual right to whomsoever he wishes as heir. Moreover, let the aforesaid land be free of all royal tribute besides military service, and bridge and fortress construction. If anyone indeed, enticed by greed, attempts to make null or to breach the decree of this decision, let him know that he will render account at the awe-inspiring trial. This document was written in the year of our Lord 963, with these witnesses: I King Edgar. I Archbishop Dunstan. I Bishop Cynsige. And with many others.

[482] Sawyer, no. 713; *Charters of Abingdon Abbey*, no. 97, which, at p. 392, states that the document 'appears to be genuine'. MS B had already included fuller version of this charter in the chronologically appropriate place, below, B184.

[483] There are several thegns named Æthelsige in witness lists of Edgar's charters. This one may be identical to the Æthelsige *pedisecus* who witnessed Sawyer, no. 768; *Charters of Abingdon Abbey*, p. 392.

[484] Balking, Berkshire, north-west of Sparsholt; see also below, B92, B93. *Hirdegrave* seems to be the lost Hurgrove, in the north of Steventon parish; EPNS, *Berkshire*, ii. 418; *Charters of Abingdon Abbey*, p. 394. Neither place is named in *Domesday Book*.

140. (B280) *Carta de Hwitcyrce.*[485]

Aurea, ut fertur, quondam secula haud hominum toxicatis infecta nequitiis, sed pura simplicitate, remotis simultatibus, ubique uigente, nullis territoriis usa noscuntur. At nostra etas, liuida mortalium malignitate fuscata ac multimodis cladibus obsessa, causa B fo. 116v uitandarum | litium terminis telluris proprie exoptat[a] perfrui, que tamen iusticia emendanda, prudentia gubernanda, temperantia tenenda, fortitudine corroboranda est, et in hac uita labili summis studiis eterna mortalibus mercanda est. Vnde ego Ædelredus,[b] basileus totius Albionis, omnipotentis Dei nutu regente, cuidam ministro meo mihimet[c] fideliter obsequenti, Leofrico uocamine,[486] quoddam ruris amminiculum, scilicet decem cassatos proprio iure possidendum largiter tribuo in uilla que famose a ruricolis[d] Hwitcyrce[e] dicitur, in prouincia Oxnafordnensi[f] sita[g] iuxta ripam fluminis C fo. 134v Tamesis, ut libere uoti compos, uita comite, possideat, et | cui heredi libuerit derelinquat. Sit hec tellus cum appenditiis suis libera ab omni [i. 480] secularis seruitutis honere exceptis que omnibus communia sunt, uidelicet procinctu pontis arcisue recuperatione, nostra auctoritate sibimet et heredibus per tempora cuncta permansura. Et si forte quispiam hanc nostram donationem (quod absit) annullare satagerit, et impie proprio dominio subdi maluerit, sciat se reum fore iustissimi iudicis Christi examinis, nisi forte ante suppremum diem semet neuo huius piaculi emaculet. Hoc denique rus cuiusdam possessoris Leofricus onomate quondam et[h] etiam nostris diebus paterne hereditatis iure fuerat,[487] sed ipse impie uiuendo, hoc est rebellando meis militibus in mea expeditione, ac rapinis insuetis et adulteriis, multisque aliis nefariis sceleribus, semetipsum condempnauit simul et possessiones. Ideoque uolumus ut hec cartula nostra potestate antiquiora territoria, si inuenta fuerint, omnimodis condempnet, ut

140 [a] *corr. from* optat *by interlin. B* [b] Aþelredus *B* [c] michimet *B* [d] ruriculis *B* [e] Hwitcirce *B* [f] Oxnafordensi *B* [g] *interlin. following erasure B* [h] *interlin. B*

[485] Sawyer, no. 927; *Charters of Abingdon Abbey*, no. 136; calendared in Wormald, 'Lawsuits', no. 76. MS B had already included a fuller version of this charter in the chronologically appropriate place, below, B238. *Charters of Abingdon Abbey*, p. 533, comments that 'the authenticity of [the document] is a matter of uncertainty, largely due to dating difficulties', especially regarding the compatibility of the witness list in the full version with the date 1012; see also Keynes, *Diplomas*, p. 265. A Bishop Æthelstan witnessed the charter, but he is most likely the bishop of Hereford, and cannot have been appointed before 1013. It is possible that the charter should be dated to that year. *Charters of Abingdon Abbey*, p. 534, concludes that 'the problem of the witness-list . . . really comes down to the attestation of Bishop Æthelstan: either his subscription represents an error of

140. (B280) *Charter concerning Whitchurch.*[485]

Golden ages, so it is said, not infected with the poisoned wickedness of men, are known once to have existed without units of land, with pure simplicity flourishing everywhere and disputes removed. But our age, blackened with the malicious malignity of mortal men and besieged with many kinds of disaster, for the sake of avoiding law cases greatly desires to enjoy boundaries to its estates, which, however, should be emended with justice, governed with prudence, held with temperance, strengthened with courage, and in this fleeting life eternal things should with the greatest efforts be purchased with mortal ones. Wherefore I, Æthelred, emperor of the whole of Albion, with the will of almighty God ruling, generously assign to be possessed by proprietary right to a thegn of mine, faithfully obedient to me, Leofric by name,[486] a certain provision of land, that is ten hides, in the village famously called by the local inhabitants Whitchurch, in Oxfordshire situated next to the bank of the river Thames, so that he may freely possess it in full attainment of his wishes as long as he lives, and may leave it to which heir he pleases. Let this estate with its appendages be free from all burden of secular servitude except those which are common to all, that is battle service, and bridge and fortress restoration; by our authority all are to remain to him and his heirs throughout all times. And if anyone (let it not be so) strives to annul this our gift, and prefers to subject it impiously to his own lordship, let him know that he will be guilty at the trial of the most just judge Christ, unless by chance before the final day he cleanses himself from the blemish of this sin. In conclusion, this land once and also in our days belonged to a certain possessor named Leofric by right of paternal inheritance.[487] But he condemned himself and also his possessions by living impiously, that is by rebelling against my soldiers in my service, by extraordinary plunderings and adulteries, and by many other wicked crimes. And so we wish that this charter, by our power, may condemn in every way older land-books, if they

some kind, or the date of the diploma is incorrect. Whether this inconsistency is enough to condemn the diploma is a matter of opinion. None of the formulation gives reason for concern.'

[486] A Leofric of Whitchurch witnessed the settlement of a Berkshire land dispute in 990 × 992; Sawyer, no. 1454; *Anglo-Saxon Charters*, ed. Robertson, no. 66. *ASC*, 'A', *s.a.* 1001, records a Leofric of Whitchurch being slain in battle. It is impossible to tell whether these are references to the same or different men. If they were not the same man, the former could be the beneficiary of the present gift.

[487] Again this could be one of the Leofrics of Whitchurch mentioned in the previous note.

nil usquam preualeant contra nostram auctoritatem. Scripta est hec nostra donatio anno .mxii. post incarnationem Domini nostri Ihesu Christi, indictione decem, mense Iulio, his testibus: [i]Ego Ædelredus[j] rex. Ego Æthelstanus[k] filius regis. Ego Wulfstanus[l] archiepiscopus,[i] cum multis aliis.

141. (B281–3) Monasterium autem Abbendonense Tamisie flumen ex australi parte habet sui preterfluum, per quod hac illacque deducitur nauigium.[488] Verum tempore abbatis Ordrici, ultra ecclesie aream que
[i. 481] illic ab habitantibus Bertun[a] dicitur, iuxta uiculum nomine ad Tropam, alueus eiusdem amnis porrectus, perinde remigantibus difficultatem non minimam[b] prestabat. Nam tellus inferius longe quam superius altior subrecta ipsum alueum sepe aque indigum faciebat.[489] Vnde Oxenefordensis urbis ciues,[490] nam illorum nauigium sepius transitum illic habebat, perorant quatinus per pratum ecclesie quod inferius ad austrum patet fluuii cursus eo tenore diriuetur, ut in reliquum[c] euum exinde de unaquaque naui sua centum allecia cellarario monachorum de more persoluentur.[491]
B fo. 117r Quorum uotum dum procederet ad effectum, ut pacta est, ho|die usque sponsio predicta exigitur.

Per idem tempus, dum Dominice natiuitatis diei nocturnale sollenniter officium a fratribus celebraretur, contractus quidam coram multis qui aderant subito diuinitus est curatus.

Preterea[d] mos illis diebus futurum ad dampnum[e] non parum insoleuerat,[f] ut offerente quolibet auri uel argenti copiam, trium aut quinque terre portionem hidarum, siue uillam integram, diuersis

[i–i] *heading* Testes, *with a cross preceding each witness B* [j] Aþelredus *B* [k] Aþelstanus *B* [l] Wlfstanus *B*

141 [a] *erasure at start and end of this word B* [b] miniman *C* [c] reliqum, *with erasure at end B* [d] Peterea *C* [e] damnum *B* [f] insoluerat, *involving correction B*

[488] J. Blair, 'Transport and canal-building on the Upper Thames, 1000–1300', in id., ed., *Water Transport and Canal-Building in Medieval England* (Oxford, forthcoming), explains that 'the difficult stretch of the Thames . . . must . . . be identified with the modern main channel, sweeping in a large bend around the south edge of the Abbey precinct. If Orderic's diversion went "through the church's meadow . . . below it to the south", it is unlikely (in the absence of any relevant earthwork or cropmark) to have bisected the flat gravel island of Andersey, and certainly did not traverse Culham Hill. The only possible candidate is the rivulet, now called Swift Ditch, which runs along a strip of alluvium between them. . . . Both courses are in fact natural versions of the Thames at different stages of prehistory. What Abbot Orderic did in the 1050s or early 1060s was to enlarge the lesser but more direct course, diverting river-traffic from the north to the south side of Andersey Island: his

are found, so that they may nowhere prevail at all against our authority. This our gift was written in the year 1012 after the Incarnation of our Lord Jesus Christ, the tenth indiction, in the month of July, with these witness: I King Æthelred. I Æthelstan the king's son. I Archbishop Wulfstan, with many others.

141. (B281–3) Moreover, the monastery of Abingdon has the river Thames flowing past on its southern side, through which shipping passes in both directions.[488] But in the time of Abbot Ordric, the channel of that river lay beyond the church's plot of land which is called Barton by those living there, next to the hamlet named Thrupp, thereby presenting considerable difficulty for those rowing. For often, when the river-bed downstream stood considerably higher than that upstream, it made that channel devoid of water.[489] Therefore the citizens of the town of Oxford,[490] as their shipping very often had passage there, pleaded that the course of the river be channelled through the church's meadow which extended below to the south of the river, on the following terms, that for the rest of time one hundred herrings be customarily paid from each of their ships to the monks' cellarer.[491] As their petition was fulfilled, the said undertaking is exacted, as agreed, to this day.

At that same time, when the night office of the day of the Lord's birth was being solemnly celebrated by the brethren, a certain cripple was suddenly cured by God, in the presence of the many who were there.

Besides, a custom in those days got out of control, to considerable future damage: anyone offering plenty of gold or silver would receive by purchase a portion of land amounting to three or five hides, or a

workmen laboured through silt, not gravel. Over the centuries since then, the main flow has reverted once again to its "natural" Anglo-Saxon course beside the late Iron Age valley-fort, and the abbey and town which succeeded it.' See also R. H. C. Davis, 'The ford, the river, and the city', *Oxoniensia*, xxxviii (1973), 258–67, at pp. 263–4; and the map in C. J. Bond, 'The reconstruction of the medieval landscape: The estates of Abingdon Abbey', *Landscape History*, i (1979), 59–75, at p. 70.

[489] The large manor of Barton, Berkshire, contained Abingdon. Barton is rarely named in the *History*; see also below, B178, vol. ii, 202, 266 (papal privilege), 274 (papal privilege), 292. Thrupp, Berkshire, is just east of Abingdon/Barton. The Latin in the text is somewhat unclear, and the present translation requires *tellus* to be translatable as 'river-bed', i.e. ground under the water. What is clear, though, is that the sentence is describing blocking of the channel with silt.

[490] *De abbatibus* attributes the action to the citizens of London as well as Oxford; *CMA* ii. 282.

[491] See also vol. ii. 174, for this render. *De abbatibus* specifies that the render was to be paid between the feast of Purification of the Virgin (2 Feb.) and Easter; *CMA* ii. 282.

abbatie locis reciperet emptione, quodam subornatu id palliantes, quatinus trium uel duorum uita hominum inde possidendi protenderetur permissio.[492] Quo ex facto contigit ut, Anglorum non longum post principatu ad Normannos traducto, loca eadem singula illorum militibus dispertirent.[493] Nec de his cuiquam mirandum. Nam post nimias Danorum et diuturnas importunitates, indulta iam in proximo earum quiete, oblitis erumpnis, quisque ad illicitos ausus prosiliit.

[i. 482] **142. (B284)** *De morte Eadwardi[a] regis.*

Tot[b] rerum nouitatibus per dies regnum fedantibus, natalitium Christi geniture instabat. Qua tempestate in presentia regis optimatumque eius apud Westmonasterium, dedicatio ecclesie illic ab ipso rege in sancti apostoli Petri titulo constructe celebrata est.[494] Cum C fo. 135r ecce, | in septimane ipsius festo, cunctis gaudio intendentibus, rex morbo corripitur ac in uigilia Epiphaniorum diem clausit ultimum.[495] Cui in regem successit Haroldus comes, filius Godwini comitis.[496]

143. (B285) [a]*De Ælaldredo abbate.*[a]

Abbas etiam Ordricus, postquam domum sibi commissam honorifice gubernasset et a memoria principum apostolorum (quo deuotionis gratia perrexerat) ad sua remeasset, diutina egritudine decoctus diem sortitur ultimum.[b] [497] [c]Ealdredus uero, in eodem monasterio prepositure officium exibens, abbatie dominatum post illum adipiscitur.[c] [498]

In proximo autem Paschali festo sidus insolitum, quod cometem [i. 483] uocant, unius continuatione septimane apparuit,[499] et[d] mense Septembrio instante rex Norweie, eodem denominatus uocabulo quo rex Anglie, scilicet Haroldus, Angliam appulit, regnum illic sibi uendicare pro lucro reputans, suffragium ferente fratre nostri regis Haroldi

142 [a] Edwardi *B* [b] Pot *C*

143 [a–a] *second and third words of heading erased C;* De Ordrico abbate *B* [b] circa sollempnitatem sancti Vincentii martiris *add. B, and also in dry-point in margin of C* [c–c] *see below, p. 368, for the version in B* [d] *om. B; see below, p. 368, for the version in B*

[492] See above, p. clxii, on leases. [493] See vol. ii, pp. lix, 6.

[494] The dedication took place on 28 Dec. 1065. *The Life of King Edward*, ed. F. Barlow (2nd edn., OMT, 1992), pp. 110–12, indicates that Edward was not present in person at the dedication; see also Barlow, *Edward the Confessor*, p. 247. The *ASC, s.a.* 1065, and John of Worcester, *Chronicle*, ii. 598, state that he made it be dedicated, phraseology that the *History* could quite easily take to indicate Edward's personal presence.

[495] 5 Jan. 1066; see also Barlow, *Edward the Confessor*, p. 250.

[496] Edward was buried on 6 Jan. 1066, and Harold crowned on the same day; Barlow, *Edward the Confessor*, pp. 253–4.

[497] Abbot Ordric died on 23 Jan. 1066; see above, p. cvi.

whole village, in various places of the abbey, under the cover that permission to possess this land was to extend for the lives of three, or two, men.[492] It thereby happened that when the governance of the English was not long afterwards transferred to the Normans, each of these places was disposed of to their knights.[493] Nor should anyone wonder at this. For now peace was bestowed following the excessive and long-lasting oppressions of the Danes, those distresses were forgotten and everyone rushed to commit improper and presumptuous deeds.

142. (B284) *Concerning the death of King Edward.*

With so many novelties continually befouling the kingdom, the day of Christ's birth was at hand. At that time, in the presence of the king and his leading men at Westminster, the dedication was celebrated of the church built there by the king himself in the honour of the holy apostle Peter.[494] When behold, during the feast of that week when everyone was devoted to joyfulness, the king was seized by illness and passed away on the vigil of Epiphany.[495] To him succeeded as king Earl Harold, son of Earl Godwine.[496]

143. (B285) *Concerning Abbot Ealdred.*

Abbot Ordric too, after he had honourably governed the house entrusted to him and had returned home from the shrine of the princes of the apostles (to which he had gone for the sake of devotion), was worn out by a long-lasting illness and allotted his final day.[497] So Ealdred, who was performing the office of provost in that monastery, acquired the lordship of the abbey after him.[498]

Moreover, at the next festival of Easter an unusual star, which they call a comet, appeared for the duration of one week,[499] and with the month of September upon them, the king of Norway, called by the same name as the king of England, that is Harold, landed in England, thinking to claim the realm there for his own benefit. He was aided by

[498] The Abingdon version of the Worcester *Chronicle* preserved in Lambeth Palace Library contains two very similar sentences; John of Worcester, *Chronicle*, ii. 615. MS B, below, p. 368, states that Ealdred was provost for external matters, and I here translate *prepositure officium* as 'office of provost'. However, *prepositure officium* could mean the priorship; for *prepositus* meaning prior, see vol. ii, p. xlv; *The Monastic Constitutions of Lanfranc*, rev. edn., ed. D. Knowles and C. N. L. Brooke (OMT, 2002), p. 112. Symeon of Durham, *Libellus de exordio atque procursu istius, hoc est Dunhelmensis, ecclesie*, bk. iv, c. 8, ed. D. Rollason (OMT, 2000), p. 246, wrote that Cuthbert 'successit in prepositi (id est prioris) officium. Nam qui nunc prior, a beato Benedicto prepositus monasterii appellatur.'

[499] Easter fell on 16 Apr. 1066. *ASC*, 'C' and 'D', *s.a.* 1066, report that the 'star'—which we know as Halley's comet—first appeared on 24 Apr. and shone all week.

Tosti comite.[500] Quibus [e]ultra Eboracum[e] rex Anglorum occurrens utrumque [f]cum auxiliatoriis[f] eorum bello extinxit.[501]

Cuius[g] uix soluto fine uictorie, ecce, comitem Normannie Willelmum sibi imminere apud Hastingas bellumque paratum inferre [h]ex nuntio discit.[h] [502] Ille [i]nimium suis[i] uiribus fidens, minus prouide quam decuerat [j]comitem aggressus,[j] sensit superiorem.[k] Itaque bello deuictus,[l] tam ipse quam cuncti eius socii[m] interiere.[n] [503] [o]Willelmus uero Anglie diadema optinuit.[504] Cui dum quidam subiectionis fidelitatem sponderent, nonnulli exteras sibi sedes per alia regna [i. 484] consulti rati petere sese subducerent. Abbas Ealdredus, primorum[505] sese sententie dedens, regi fidelitatis sacramenta persoluit. At in posteriorum numero, cum multi diuerterent, tum et perempti regis mater, secum in comitu suo una cum plurimis aliis presbiterum Blachemannum habens, Angliam deseruit.[506] His presbiter, sicut in cronicis Ordrici abbatis meminimus, ecclesie homo effectus de ea tenuerat Sandford, Cildestun, et Leowardestun.[507] Verum ipso, ut dixi, ab Anglia discedente, quecumque illius fuerant in manum regis, utputa profugi, redacta sunt. Quare abbas magno cum labore predictarum terrarum apud regem optinuit restitutionem.[o]

B fo. 118r **(B290)** Vt de his terris ipse abbas explicauerat, in ceteris quoque
B fo. 118v que tum ab | ecclesie dominio alienum in ius transierunt forte explicasset, si non ad[p] infortunium suum et ecclesie regis[q] incurrisset indignationem, de quo post edocebimus.[508] Nam quidam diues, Turkillus nomine, sub Haroldi comitis testimonio et consultu, de se cum sua terra que Kingestun dicitur[509] ecclesie Abbendonensi et abbati Ordrico homagium fecit. Licitum quippe libero cuique illo in tempore sic agere erat, quatinus predicte uille dominatio sub huius ecclesie perpetuo iure penderet. Hic cum in bello memorato

[e–e] Eboracem ultra urbem *B* [f–f] una cum auxiliariis *B* [g] Huius *B* [h–h] *see below, p. 368, for the version in B* [i–i] suis nimium *B* [j–j] aggressus comitem *B* [k] *for an addition here in B, see below, p. 368* [l] corruens *B* [m] secum *add. B* [n] interire *B* [o–o] *om. B* [p] *interlin. B* [q] regie *B C, suggesting that B derives from C*

[500] Harold, or Harald, Hardrada was king of Norway 1046–66. For Tostig, see Barlow, *The Godwins*.

[501] The battle of Stamford Bridge, 25 Sept. 1066.

[502] Henry of Huntingdon, *Historia Anglorum*, bk. vi, c. 28, ed. Greenway, pp. 388–9, mentions that Harold learnt of William's landing from a messenger, whilst dining at York on the same day as Stamford Bridge. See further D. C. Douglas, *William the Conqueror* (London, 1964), pp. 398–9. William had landed in England on 28 Sept. 1066. The battle of Hastings took place on 14 Oct. 1066.

[503] The present paragraph ends here in MS B.

[504] William was crowned on 25 Dec. 1066.

Earl Tostig, brother of our King Harold.[500] The king of England hurried to meet them beyond York and in battle killed them both with their supporters.[501]

With this victory scarcely complete, behold, he learnt from a messenger that William count of Normandy was threatening him and prepared to join battle at Hastings.[502] Harold put too much trust in his strength and attacked the count less prudently than was fitting, but discovered William was the superior. And so defeated in battle, both Harold and all his allies died.[503] William, then, obtained the diadem of England.[504] While certain men were promising him the loyalty of subjection, others were withdrawing, thinking themselves well advised to seek foreign dwelling-places for themselves in other kingdoms. Abbot Ealdred submitted himself to the opinion of the former[505] and paid oaths of loyalty to the king. But among the latter, as many were departing, the mother of the slain king too quit England, who had with her in her company the priest Blæcmann, together with many others.[506] This priest, as we recorded in the chronicles of Abbot Ordric, had become the man of the church and held from it Sandford, Chilton, and Leverton.[507] But, as I said, he left England, and whatever had been his was taken back into the king's hand, as a fugitive's. Therefore with great effort the abbot obtained restitution of these aforesaid lands from the king.

(B290) When this abbot had extricated these lands, he might also perhaps have extricated others which had passed from the lordship of the church to the right of another, had he not incurred the king's anger, to his own and the church's misfortune (concerning this we will speak later).[508] For a certain rich man named Thorkell, by the witness and advice of Earl Harold, did homage to the church of Abingdon and Abbot Ordric concerning himself together with his land which is called Kingston.[509] Indeed, it was then permitted to any free man to do so, so that the lordship of the aforesaid village would be dependent on the perpetual right of this church. When this man died in the battle mentioned earlier, Henry de Ferrers seized for

[505] The context makes it likely that this is the sense of 'primorum', which would normally mean 'leading men'; the word 'priorum' would fit better.

[506] For the flight of Blæcmann and Gytha, mother of Harold, in 1068, see Barlow, *The Godwins*, p. 119. Cf. MS B's treatment of Blæcmann, below, p. 372.

[507] See above, p. 208.

[508] See below, p. 226.

[509] Kingston Bagpuize. Thorkell's identity cannot be established with certainty. On 'homage', see above, pp. clvii–clviii.

occubuisset, terram, cuius dominationis inuestituram[510] multo ante tempore quam bellum foret ecclesia in manus habebat, Henricus de Ferrariis sibi usurpauit, abbate inualido obstare.[511] Similiter et de terra que Fifhide dicitur actum est. Nam Godricus quidam uicecomes eo tenore ab ecclesia eandem terram tenendam acceperat, ut trium hominum uita hereditario iure ipsa possideretur; quicquid tamen offensionis possessoribus forte accideret, ecclesia inde iac-
[i. 485] turam nullam incurreret. Itaque ipso cum predicto uiro pariter in bello occiso, idem Henricus de Ferrariis hanc uillam cum altera sue ditioni adiecit.[512]

Nec tantum deforis per hos dies huiusmodi incommoda, sed et de ornamentis ecclesie dispendia infra ipsum sanctuarium prouenerunt. Siquidem regine imperio eorumdem pretiosiora sibi deferri mandauit. Quid facto opus esset in his abbate cum fratribus consulentibus,
C fo. 135ᵛ regine de | electioribus[r] transmittere ornamentis deliberant. Que ut sibi exhibita[s] sunt respuit, ac ornatiora requirit. Illi, quibus undique peregrinus incumbebat metus nouorum principum, quod cautius seruare debuerant pro uoto imperantis domine ad medium deferunt, id est casulam aurifrixo per totum mirifice consutam, cum cappa choreali ualde optima, alba quoque cum stola,[513] et textu euangeliorum,[t] singulis auro gemmisque laudabili[u] opere redimitis.

B fo. 119ʳ **144. (B292)** *De captione Aldredi abbatis.*

Interim[a] ceperunt multa in regno Anglico machinari molimina, satagentibus id iis[b] quibus transmarinorum dominatum ferre nunc erat necessarium, quanquam hactenus sibi insolitum. Horum pars siluarum, quidam in locis insularum sese abdere, piratarum more raptim uiuere, quosque obuios obtruncare. Pars gentem Danorum ut

[r] electoribus *B* [s] exibita *B* [t] euuangeliorum *B* [u] laudabi *B*

144 [a] Hinc non multo post *B* [b] his *B*

[510] The word 'inuestitura' is also used at vol. ii. 10 and 88, at the latter of which it is glossed 'saisiatio'.

[511] *DB* i, fo. 60ᵛ, records Henry de Ferrers holding Kingston, assessed at five hides. It states that Stankell had held it *TRE*. *DB* i, fo. 61ʳ, attributes another four hides (five hides *TRE*) at Kingston to William son of Ansculf. These had been held *TRE* by Thorkell from King Edward. Most likely either the *History* or *Domesday* has confused the estates or their holders' names, although conceivably Thorkell had had some relationship to Stankell's lands which *Domesday* does not record. See also Hudson, 'Abbey of Abingdon', p. 190. Henry de Ferrers was a very substantial *Domesday* lord, and a *Domesday* commissioner in the west Midlands; see J. C. Holt, '1086', *Domesday Studies* (Woodbridge, 1987), pp. 46, 58.

himself the land, seisin[510] of the lordship of which the church had had in its hands a long time before that battle, and the abbot was unable to resist.[511] It happened similarly concerning the land called Fyfield. For a certain sheriff Godric had received that land from the church to hold on these terms, that it be possessed by hereditary right for the lives of three men; however, whatever harm by chance happened to the possessors, the church was to incur no loss thereby. And so when he, with Thorkell, was killed in battle, the same Henry de Ferrers added this village with the other to his lordship.[512]

Nor at this time was it only in external affairs that troubles of this sort occurred, but losses also entered the sanctuary itself with respect to the church ornaments. The queen by her order instructed that the more precious of them be brought to her. When the abbot consulted the brethren concerning what should be done in these matters, they decided to send some of the more choice ornaments to the queen. She rejected those that were shown to her, and sought more magnificent ones. Pressed on all sides by fear of the foreign and of their new rulers, the monks followed the imperious queen's wishes and brought into the open what they ought to have preserved more carefully, that is a chasuble marvellously sewn all over with orphrey, with quite the very best choir cope, also an alb with a stole,[513] and a gospel text, each bordered with gold and gems in magnificent work.

144. (B292) *Concerning the capture of Abbot Ealdred.*

Meanwhile many plots began to be hatched in the English kingdom. At such plots worked away those now compelled to bear the lordship of men from overseas, to which they had hitherto not been accustomed. Some hid themselves away in woods, some in islands, living by plunder like pirates, slaughtering those who came their way. Some enticed the

[512] *DB* i, fo. 60^{v}, records two manors at Fyfield, both held by Henry de Ferrers in 1086. The first was held by Godric the sheriff *TRE* (*uicec'* being interlined above his name by the main scribe), the second by Godric, almost certainly Godric the sheriff. Of the first, assessed at ten hides, it states that Godric held of the abbot and could not go wherever he wished with land. Clarke, *English Nobility*, p. 66, takes this contrast with the *History* as 'showing that on occasion Domesday was quite capable of omitting such information'. Alternatively, the *History* may here have been seeking to establish a clearer limit to Godric's hold on the land. Of the second manor, assessed at ten hides *TRE* but now five hides because King Edward so remitted, *Domesday* simply states that Godric had held from King Edward. For Godric, see also above, p. 201 n. 453. Fyfield and Kingston Bagpuize are adjacent to one another. Abingdon did not succeed in re-establishing its claims to them; see vol. ii. 42, 176–8, on Kingston church.

[513] This phrase could also be translated 'with a white stole'; Dodwell, *Anglo-Saxon Art*, p. 182; Blair, *Anglo-Saxon Oxfordshire*, p. 173.

Angliam appetant illicere.[c] [514] Illi Angliam pro uoto dum aduenissent, predam tantum agere, ignibus quedam absumere, quosdam captioni summittere. Ceterum nec armis comminus rem[d] agere nec regnum[e] deuincere[f] ualentes, infecto negotio ad propria[g] remearunt.

Talibus temptatis[h] cum diuersi ordinis et dignitatis uiri se commiscuissent,[i] tum episcopus Dunelmensis quoque, Ægelwinus
[i. 486] nomine, inter eos qui capti sunt inuentus, et Abbendoniam missus in captione ibi ad sue mortis degens diem obiuit.[j] [515] Sed et homines abbatie Abbendonensis, dum regis parti fauere Willelmi[k] debuerant, animo et consultu mutati, armati, quo hostes regis ipsius consistere acceperant, gressum contenderunt.[516] Circumuenti in itinere, captique incarcerantur, et satis misere affliguntur. [l]In illorum etiam dominum, id est abbatem Ealdredum (qui et Brichwinus dictus est, binomius enim erat) regis inimicitia est perlata adeo ut absque dilatione eius precepto apud castellum Walingafordense in captione poneretur.[517] Aliquanto autem post tempore a predicto loco eductus, in manu Wintoniensis episcopi Walchelini seruandus committitur, apud quem mansit quoad uixit.[l] [518]

Ea tempestate, recenter commutati status regni causa, cum plurimorum plurime in monasterio Abbendonensi recule reposite essent, ne domi direptoribus raptum tutore cariture irent, delatorum illatione
B fo. 119v aulicis officia|libus id intimatum, ac proinde illuc transmissum, et quicquid huiusmodi reperitur, adimitur. Supra[m] hoc, et que infra septa monachorum pretiosiora inueniri poterant—[n]auri argentique, uestium, librorum, uasorumque[o] diuersi generis copia[n] usibus ecclesie honorique computata—multa indiscrete distracta[p] sunt.[519] [q]Nullius

[c] *followed by* si uenerint regnum posse adipisci inualida manu obstante *B* [d] *corr. from* regem *B* [e] *followed by* quod autumatum leue *B* [f] *followed by* duxerant uendicare *B* [g] *followed by* maximo suorum detrimento *B* [h] temtatis *B* [i] comiscuissent *B* [j] obiit *B* [k] *followed by* ut pote cui iam fides ubique regionum Anglie seruari iurata fuerat *B* [l–l] Quo infortunii casu Ealdredus, qui et Brithwinus, abbas, (binomius enim erat), pastorali non multo post potestate nudatus, Wincestrem ad urbem dirigi iubetur ibique custodie quamdiu uitales carpsit auras mancipatur *B* [m] Super *B* [n–n] etiam *B* [o] *corr. from* vasarumque *C* [p] distractata *B* [q–q] *om. B*

[514] This passage refers to the Danish expedition which began in 1069; see Douglas, *William the Conqueror*, pp. 218–22.

[515] Æthelwine was bishop of Durham 1056–71; *Handbook of British Chronology*, p. 216. The form 'Ægelwinus' used by the *History* suggests the 12th-c. vernacular, but I here give the form appropriate to the 11th c. For Æthelwine's fall, see also *ASC*, 'E', *s.a.* 1069; Symeon of Durham, *Libellus de Exordio*, ed. Rollason, pp. 192–4. *ASC*, 'E', *s.a.* 1071, places his death in the winter following his capture in 1071. It is unclear whether Æthelwine was held in the monastery at Abingdon or perhaps in the royal buildings nearby.

people of the Danes to claim England.[514] When they came to England in response to the request, all they did was plunder, destroy certain things with fire, subject certain people to capture. But they were not strong enough to fight hand to hand nor to conquer the kingdom, but went home with their task incomplete.

While men of various orders and ranks had involved themselves in these attempts, the bishop of Durham, Æthelwine by name, was also found amongst those captured, was sent to Abingdon, and died, having lived in captivity there until the day of his death.[515] In addition the men of the abbey of Abingdon, while they ought to have favoured King William's side, changed their minds and opinions and hastened armed to where they had learnt that the king's enemies were situated.[516] En route they were surrounded, captured, imprisoned, and very wretchedly afflicted. The king's anger was so directed against their lord, that is Abbot Ealdred (who was also called Brihtwine, for he had two names), that by the king's order he was immediately placed in captivity at Wallingford castle.[517] A little while later he was taken from that place and for safekeeping committed into the hands of Bishop Walkelin of Winchester, with whom he remained as long as he lived.[518]

At this time, because of the recently changed state of the realm, very many possessions of numerous people had been deposited in the monastery of Abingdon, lest at home they lack a protector and become booty for plunderers. Informers intimated this to court officials, and the information was likewise passed on, so whatever possessions of this sort were found were taken away. In addition, many very precious goods which could be found within the monks' precinct—a wealth of gold and silver, vestments, books, and vessels of diverse types, assigned to the use and honour of the church—were indiscriminately taken away.[519] There was no reverence for the sight

[516] Æthelwine was seized at Ely, but the destination of the men of Abingdon cannot be known for certain.

[517] Wallingford castle is mentioned in *DB* i, fo. 56^{r}. It would appear that Ealdred was placed in captivity in 1071, the same year as Bishop Æthelwine. Ealdred seems to have been one of those churchmen who had a double name, like, for example, Lyfing, who was also known as Æthelstan, bishop of Wells and archbishop of Canterbury in the early 11th c.; see G. Tengvik, *Old English Bynames* (Nomina Germanica, 4; Uppsala, 1938), pp. 397–8.

[518] Walkelin was nominated bishop of Winchester on 23 May 1070 and consecrated on 30 May. He died on 3 Jan. 1098; *Handbook of British Chronology*, p. 276.

[519] See Dodwell, *Anglo-Saxon Art*, pp. 216–18, for other instances of Norman spoliation of churches.

sacrorum liminum prospectus reuerentia, nulla fratrum desolatorum compassio.[q] Extra per uillas, posthabito cuiuslibet respectu, passim impensa uastatio. Itaque temporis illius rerum abbatie amissarum, uel insinuatio uel computatio non facile dictu. Quarum executioni Frogerus tunc Berchescire[r] uicecomes precipuus efferebatur.[s] [520] Sed eiusdem illo potentis hominis immoderatum super homines depressos progressum, Moderantis uniuersa, postea Dei[t] uindicta cohercuit, ut et ius quo efferebatur[u] tirannicum regia sibi iusticia auferretur, et in despectum omnium inopia et stoliditate quoad uixit
[i. 487] uerteretur, suis in his[v] miseriis patulam prebens formam sequacibus quia locus tutele celi regine deditus, tum et sanctorum qui et fundarunt et incoluerunt uirorum memoria consecratus, reuereri potius quam depredari debeat.

[w]*Explicit liber primus terrarum huius ecclesie Abbendonensis, continens in se annos .ccccxiiii. a Ceadwalla rege usque ad Willelmum regem.*[w] [521]

[r] Berkescire *B* [s] efferrebatur *B* [t] *om. B* [u] offerebatur *B* [v] hiis B
[w–w] *om. B*

of sacred precincts, no compassion for the ravaged brethren. Outside, with no respect for anyone, devastation was dispensed indiscriminately throughout the villages. And so it is not easy to give either record or reckoning of the abbey's possessions lost at that time. Froger, then sheriff of Berkshire, was said to be the leading participant in carrying out these deeds.[520] But afterwards the vengeance of God, the Governor of all things, punished the ungoverned advances of that powerful man over those whom he had oppressed, so that royal justice took away from him the tyrannical right by which he was raised up, and as long as he lived it was changed into universal contempt by his neediness and stupidity. In these his afflictions, he presents a clear model for those to come that a place dedicated to the guardianship of the Queen of Heaven, and consecrated in memory of the holy men who founded it and inhabited it, should be revered rather than ravaged.

Here ends the first book of the lands of this church of Abingdon, containing in it 414 years from King Ceadwalla to King William.[521]

[520] Froger's shrievalty cannot be precisely dated, but was most likely in the early post-Conquest years; Green, *English Sheriffs*, p. 26. For Froger, see also *DB* i, fos. 57^{r}, 58^{r}.

[521] Ceadwalla was king of Wessex 685–8, William king of England 1066–87; the calculation therefore is incorrect.

APPENDIX

APPENDIX: MS B

[i. 1] **B1**. . . . -lam inhabitantibus nouo usus uocabulo, a nomine suo Bruto,
fo. 4r insulam Britanniam sociosque suos Britones nuncupauit.[1] De carn⟨i⟩s exuto ergastulo sine fide catholica, successerunt ei reges multi usque ad tempus regis Lucii fidei Christiane similiter ignari.[2] Hic autem Lucius, audita fama et sanctitate predicatorum in ciuitate Romana tunc temporis degentium, nuntios suos cum litteris suis patentibus[3] ad uenerabilem papam Eleutherium destinauit, quantocius rogans deuotissime et supplicans attencius quatinus per mandatum et uoluntatem eius Christianus efficeretur. Huius itaque comperta deuotione, ad precum suarum instantiam, misit uir uenerabilis Eleutherius papa ad Lucium regem illustrem nuntios suos, Faganum uidelicet et Diuianum, uiros religiosos necnon fide catholica sufficienter instructos.[4] Hii uero, cum celebri deuocione, regem ipsum et populum suum unanimi assensu et pari concordia baptizauerunt, destruentes ydola et ecclesias fideliter construentes. Quid multa? Hii duo uiri, sincere in omnibus et per omnia Deo deuoti, Christianitatis
[i. 2] executores effecti, constituere decreuerunt per loca singula singulos ministros Dei omnipotentis, et ubi archiflamines secundum legem gentilium inuenerunt, loco eorum archipresules, similiter ubi flamines, episcopos subrogauerunt. Fuerunt autem tunc temporis archipresules tres tribus in locis famosissimis, uidelicet Londonia, Eboraci, et apud Vrbem Legionum.[5]

[1] This sentence is drawn from Geoffrey of Monmouth; see *The Historia regum Britannie of Geoffrey of Monmouth*, i: *Bern, Burgerbibliothek, MS 568*, ed. N. Wright (Cambridge, 1985), p. 13. See above, p. clxxxvi, on what may have preceded this passage. According to Geoffrey, Brutus was the great-grandson of Aeneas.

[2] The story of Lucius's letter to Pope Eleutherius appears in *Historia regum*, ed. Wright, p. 46, and in Bede, *Ecclesiastical History*, bk. i, c. 4, ed. Colgrave and Mynors, p. 24. Bede derives it from the *Liber Pontificalis*, and perhaps some other source; J. M. Wallace-Hadrill, *Bede's Ecclesiastical History of the English People: A Historical Commentary* (Oxford, 1988), p. 11; A. Harnack, 'Der Brief des britischen Königs Lucius an den Papst Eleutherus', *Sitzungsberichte der preussischen Akademie der Wissenschaften zu Berlin* (1904), 909–16. The *Anglo-Saxon Chronicle* mentions it briefly *s.a.* 167, the year in which it says Eleutherius became pope. Eleutherius was in fact pope *c.*174–89; *Oxford Dictionary of Popes*, pp. 11–12.

[3] Both Bede and Geoffrey use the noun *epistola/epistula*; the compiler of the *History* presumably changed this to *littere patentes* to emphasize that the letter was a solemn royal communication.

APPENDIX: MS B

B1. . . . by a new name used by the inhabitants, he called the island Britain and his associates Britons, from his name Brutus.[1] After he had left the prison of the flesh without the Catholic faith, many kings likewise ignorant of the Christian faith succeeded him, up to King Lucius's time.[2] Lucius, however, had heard of the reputation and holiness of the preachers then living in the city of Rome, and he sent his messengers, with his letters patent,[3] to the venerable Pope Eleutherius, asking most devotedly and begging very earnestly that he be made a Christian as soon as possible by the pope's instruction and will. So, in response to these prayers, once he had discovered the king's devotion, the venerable man Pope Eleutherius sent to the illustrious king, Lucius, his own messengers, that is Faganus and Divianus, religious men appropriately trained in the Catholic faith.[4] With renowned devotion, they baptized the king himself and his people with unanimous assent and shared agreement, destroying idols and building churches in accordance with the faith. What's more, these two men, sincerely devoted to God in everything and every way, who had been made the agents of Christianity, ordered that individual ministers of almighty God be appointed for each place, and where they found high priests according to the law of heathens, in their place they substituted archbishops, where they found priests, they substituted bishops. At that time, moreover, there were three archbishops in three very famous places, that is London, York, and the City of the Legions.[5]

[4] On Faganus, Divianus, and their place in Geoffrey's version of the story of Lucius and Eleutherius, see J. S. P. Tatlock, *The Legendary History of Britain* (Berkeley and Los Angeles, 1950), pp. 230–5. Note also parallels to the story in *De antiquitate Glastonie ecclesie*, c. 2, Scott, *Early History of Glastonbury*, pp. 46–50.

[5] Cf. *Historia regum*, ed. Wright, p. 46: 'ubi erant flamines episcopos, ubi archiflamines archiepiscopos posuerunt. Sedes autem archiflaminum in nobilibus tribus ciuitatibus fuerant, Lundoniis uidelicet atque Eboraci et in Urbe Legionum, quam super Oscam fluuium in Glamorgancia ueteres muri et edificia sitam fuisse testantur.' The City of the Legions is identified with Caerleon, Monmouthshire; for the tradition concerning the archbishopric, see C. N. L. Brooke, 'Geoffrey of Monmouth as historian', in C. N. L. Brooke *et al.*, eds., *Church and Government in the Middle Ages* (Cambridge, 1976), pp. 77–91, at 80–2.

B2. *Per quantum tempus durauit Christianitas in Brittannia postquam Lucius rex suscepit Christianitatem.*

Interea, rege Lucio uiam uniuerse carnis ingresso, corpus ipsius in uilla Gloucestrie honorifice humatum est, ut regiam decebat sepulturam.[6] Post huius uero decessum, ut multa paucis perstringamus, usque ad tempus Diocliciani imperatoris sub tranquilla deuotione et sancta conuersatione in Brittannia durauit Christianitas.[7] Floruit etiam his temporibus in Brittannie finibus, Deo disponente, feruentissima monachorum religio et sanctitatis multis in locis memoranda deuotio. Verumptamen tunc temporis fuit quidam religiosus monachus, Abbennus nomine, qui ex Hibernia Brittanniam ueniens uerbum Dei, prout Spiritus Sanctus dabat eloquium illi, fideliter predicabat.[8] Hic uero post temporis processum, illustrissimi regis Brittonum curiam adiens ubi, laudabiliter receptus et magnifice ab omnibus honoratus, ipsi regi amoris priuilegio in tantum specialis est effectus ut in ipso se gauderet alterum repperisse Ioseph.[9] Optinuit autem memoratus Abbennus a rege Brittonum, ad precum suarum instantiam, maximam partem Berroccensis prouincie, in qua, de consensu regis et consilio regni, monasterium feliciter fundauit cui nomen Abbendoniam, uel a nomine suo uel a loci uocabulo alluden-
[i. 3] ter, imposuit. Secundum enim idioma Hibernensium, ut ex relatione modernorum accepimus, Abbendon mansio Abenni interpretatur;
fo. 4v secundum uero idioma Anglorum Abbendun mons Abenni | uulgariter nuncupatur. Est autem locus ille in planitie montis, uisu desiderabilis, paulisper ultra uillam que nunc uocatur Suniggewelle, inter duos riuulos amenissimos qui, locum ipsum quasi quendam sinum inter se concludentes, gratum cernentibus prebent spectaculum et oportunum habitantibus subsidium. Congregauit etiam ibi uenerabilis uir Abbennus copiosam monachorum multitudinem, uidelicet trecentos monachos uel eo amplius iugi deuotione ibidem Deo famulantes, quibus prior et abbas non tantum prefuit sed, secundum regulam beati Benedicti plus studens amari quam timeri omnibus,[10] per omnia profuit. Nouissimis uero diebus suis, cum esset cani capitis, sanctus uir Abbennus, Christi uestigia sequens et pro eius

[6] See *Historia regum*, ed. Wright, p. 47; Geoffrey dates his death to 156. The phrase 'ingredi viam universe carnis' is quite common in medieval writings. It has biblical roots, although it is not a quotation from the Bible: note esp. Gen. 6: 13 'finis universae carnis'; Josh. 23: 14 'ingredior viam universae terrae'; 3 Kgs. (1 Kgs.) 2: 2 'ingredior viam universae terrae'. For its use by the compiler of MS B, see above, p. liv.

[7] See Bede, *Ecclesiastical History*, bk. i, c. 4, ed. Colgrave and Mynors, p. 24; *Historia regum*, ed. Wright, pp. 49–50. Diocletian was emperor 284–305.

B2. *How long Christianity lasted in Britain after King Lucius adopted Christianity.*

Meanwhile, when King Lucius had gone the way of all flesh, his body was honourably interred at Gloucester, as befitted a royal burial.[6] After his death, indeed, to pass briefly over many matters, Christianity in Britain endured until Emperor Diocletian's time, in a state of peaceful devotion and holy religious life.[7] For then, by God's disposition, there flourished within the borders of Britain a most fervent monastic life and a noteworthy devotion to holiness in many places. At that time there was a devout monk named Abben, who came to Britain from Ireland and in accordance with the faith preached the word of God, as the Holy Spirit used to give him eloquence.[8] After some time passed, moreover, this man came to the court of the most distinguished king of the Britons, where he was received in praiseworthy fashion and magnificently honoured by everyone, and he became so privileged in the king's love that the latter rejoiced that he had discovered in Abben another Joseph.[9] Furthermore, in response to his prayers, that Abben obtained from the king of the Britons most of the region of Berkshire, within which, by the consent of the king and the counsel of the kingdom, he happily founded a monastery on which he conferred the name Abingdon, alluding either to his own name or that of the place. For we have learnt from our contemporaries that, according to the language of the Irish, Abingdon is interpreted 'house of Aben'; but according to the language of the English, Abingdon commonly means 'the hill of Aben'. Moreover, that place is on the plateau of a hill, pleasing to the eye, a little beyond the village now called Sunningwell, between two lovely streams which enclose that place between them like a promontory and provide an agreeable view for onlookers and suitable support for those living there. The venerable man Abben gathered there a plentiful multitude of monks, that is three hundred monks or more who served God there in constant devotion; he was not merely in charge of them as prior and abbot but rather benefited them all in every respect, striving according to the Rule of St Benedict rather to be loved than feared.[10] Indeed in his final days, when he was white-haired, the holy man Abben followed in the footsteps of Christ, and,

[8] For Abben and the following version of the foundation story, see above, p. lxxxvii.

[9] An allusion to the story of Joseph and Pharaoh; see Gen. 39–50.

[10] *Rule of St Benedict*, c. 64: 'et studeat plus amari quam timeri'. The Rule of St Benedict of course had not been composed at the time when Abben supposedly lived.

amore gloriam mundi spernens captusque dulcedine natalis soli, Hiberniam petiit; ibique, diuina disponente clementia, in sancta conuersatione uitam suam finiuit. Mansit autem monasterium Abbandonie in Catholica fide et monastica religione usque ad aduentum Anglorum. Et quia de Anglis a nobis est mentio facta, uirtus nobis assit angelica, ut nichil preter ueritatem de Anglis proferamus.[11]

B3. *De aduentu Saxonum in Brittanniam.*

Anno itaque Dominice incarnationis .ccccxlix., regnante Vortegerno in Brittannia, ut ex tenore ueritatis uenerabilis Bede presbiteri accepimus, uenerunt in Brittanniam nauali uehiculo de partibus Germanie Saxones, Angli, et Iuti.[12] Qui, licet diuersarum essent
[i. 4] prouinciarum, maxima tamen eos concatinauit dileccionis integritas pariter et federis confederatio. Hii ad peticionem regis Vortegerni Brittannie applicuerunt ad insulam, pollicentes contra inimicos ipsius regis, Scottos uidelicet et Pictos qui Brittanniam atrociter debellauerant, auxilium se fore prestaturos. Verumptamen quibus succedentibus ad uotum his que in animo auide conceperant, inito certamine cum Scottis et Pictis, Saxones sumpsere uictoriam.[13] Verum quod cum Saxonie prospero euentu renuntiatum,[a] pariter et insule fertilitas denuntiata et Brittonum segnities fuisset expressa, itidem retransmittitur illo ueloci cursu classis prolixior armatorum manum deferens forciorem, que, formidinem formidini Brittonum exaggerans et uires uiribus accumulans, inexpugnabilem reddidit exercitum. Hii itaque in Brittannia degentes, inito consilio cum Scottis et Pictis, post temporis protelacionem neminem qui eis in aliquo resisteret aut iuridictioni eorum perfunctorie uel ⟨h⟩orarie contradiceret inuenerunt. Hiis ita gestis, disponente iusto mundi iudice cuius prouidentia in sui dispositione non fallitur, gens memorata ciuitates muratas pariter et agros, arboribus extirpatis, depopulantes, suum ubique continuauerunt incendium ita ut totam insule superficiem funere et fumo obtexisse uiderentur.[14] Sed ad quid . . .[15]

B3 [a] *followed by* et, *expunged*

[11] The play on the words 'Angli' and 'angeli' appears in Bede, *Ecclesiastical History*, bk. ii, c. 1, ed. Colgrave and Mynors, p. 134.

[12] See Bede, *Ecclesiastical History*, bk. i, c. 15, ed. Colgrave and Mynors, pp. 48–52. For the British leader Vortigern, see Wallace-Hadrill, *Bede's Ecclesiastical History: A Historical Commentary*, pp. 20–1.

spurning the glory of the world for the love of Him and taken by the sweetness of his native soil, sought Ireland. There, by the disposition of divine clemency, he ended his life in holy religious living. The monastery of Abingdon, moreover, remained in the Catholic faith and monastic religion until the coming of the English. And since we have mentioned the English, let angelic virtue be present with us, lest we state anything but the truth about the English.[11]

B3. *Concerning the coming of the Saxons into Britain.*

Therefore in the year of our Lord 449, when Vortigern was reigning in Britain, as we have learnt from the venerable priest Bede's statements of truth, Saxons, Angles, and Jutes came into Britain on sea transport from areas of Germany.[12] Although from diverse regions, nevertheless an immense unity of love and also a compact of agreement bound them together. At the request of Vortigern king of Britain, these men landed on the island, promising that they would furnish help against the king's enemies, that is the Scots and the Picts who had savagely waged war on Britain. Nevertheless, with the matters reaching the desired conclusion that they had greedily conceived in their minds, the Saxons joined battle with the Scots and Picts and claimed victory.[13] When this, with its favourable outcome, was reported back to Saxony, and also the island's fertility was made known and the sloth of the Britons recounted, a larger fleet bearing a stronger force of armed men was in similar fashion sent rapidly back from there. Heaping fear on the Britons' fear, and piling strength on strength, it made up an indestructible army. Therefore those living in Britain took counsel with the Scots and Picts, but, after a delay, found no one who would resist the invaders in any way or perfunctorily or briefly contest their authority. So, following these events, by the disposition of the just Judge of the world whose foresight does not err in its arrangements, the Saxon people devastated walled cities and also fields, uprooted trees, and extended their arson everywhere so that they were seen to cover the entire surface of the island with death and smoke.[14] But to this . . .[15]

[13] This sentence and the following one draw on the wording of Bede, *Ecclesiastical History*, bk. i, c. 15, ed. Colgrave and Mynors, p. 50.

[14] This sentence has some verbal parallels to Bede, *Ecclesiastical History*, bk. i, c. 15, ed. Colgrave and Mynors, p. 52.

[15] See above, p. clxxxvii, on what may have followed this passage.

fo. 5r **B4.** . . . annis iuuentutis sue,[16] tam nature quam industrie, et cum se inuenisset longe recessisse a creatore suo, oculis cum manibus in celum erectis, longa tra⟨h⟩ens suspiria, in hunc modum prorupit in uocem: 'Creator creaturarum, Deus, miserere mei super omnes homines miseri. Peccaui, erraui, et scienter te[a] negaui. Sed tu, mitissime Domine, qui non uis mortem peccatoris sed ut magis conuertatur et uiuat,[17] uerte uultus ad singultus, uerte ad suspiria
[i. 5] mea oculos misericordie tue, et concede mihi spacium emendationis uite mee, ut sufficienter doleam et deleam ea que ab ineunte etate scienter et ignoranter contra uoluntatem tuam perpetraui.' Nec mora potauit eum uino compunctionis Deus, cui omne cor patet et omnis uoluntas loquitur ut fugeret a facie arcus.[18] Inspiratus itaque rex Cedwalla gratuito et repentino instinctu Spiritus Sancti, qui quando uult et 'ubi uult spirat',[19] qui quem uult et quantum uult inspirat, qui 'cui uult miseretur, et quem uult indurat',[20] dixit se uelle ad baptismum[b] cum omni festinantia properare et errori gentilitatis penitus renuntiare. Quod ut fieret cum maiori sollempnitate, quamuis sacramentum in se non minus ⟨h⟩abeat efficatie in baptizatis propter personas baptizantium, exclusa necessitate, rebus tamen domi bene dispositis Romam, festinanti gressu peciit.[21] Vbi a Sergio papa honorifice susceptus et ab eo in die sancti sabbati Paschalis anno Dominice incarnationis .dclxxxix. gloriosissime est baptizatus, et a beato Petro Petrus feliciter est appellatus.[22] Vbi etiam, dum adhuc in albis esset, carnis exutus ergastulo duodecimo kalendas [c]Maiarum feria tercia[c] [23] sepultus in basilica beatorum apostolorum Petri et Pauli, quieuit in pace pectoris pacem prestolans eternitatis.[24] Fecit autem Sergius papa epitaphium ipsius regis metrice et in sarcofago ipsius exarari decreuit. Cuius epitaphii tenor hic est:

B4 [a] *interlin.* [b] baptissmum *MS* [c–c] Marciarum feria sexta *MS*

[16] The person referred to is Ceadwalla king of the West Saxons.
[17] Cf. Ezek. 18: 23, 33: 11, which was widely quoted, for example in patristic literature, in the form in the text.
[18] See Ps. 59 (60): 6; Isa. 21: 15.
[19] Cf. John 3: 8: 'Spiritus ubi vult spirat.'
[20] Cf. Rom. 9: 18: 'Ergo cuius vult miseretur, et quem vult indurat.'
[21] This passage derives from Bede, *Ecclesiastical History*, bk. v, c. 7, ed. Colgrave and Mynors, p. 470.

B4. . . . in the years of his[16] youth, both of nature and diligence, and when he found that he had withdrawn far from his Creator, he raised his eyes and his hands to Heaven, and, taking a deep breath, burst into speech in the following way: 'Creator of the creatures, God, pity me pitiful above all men. I have sinned, I have erred, and knowingly I have denied You. But You, gentlest Lord, who do not wish a sinner to die but rather that he be converted and live,[17] turn Your face to my sobs, turn the eyes of Your mercy to my sighs, and grant me the time to correct my life, so that I may sufficiently grieve and may expunge those deeds which from an early age I knowingly and unknowingly perpetrated against Your will.' And without delay God, to whom every heart opens and every will speaks so that it may flee from the face of the bow,[18] made him drink the wine of remorse. Inspired, therefore, by the graciously given and sudden instigation of the Holy Spirit, which blows when it wishes and 'where it wishes',[19] inspires whom it wishes and as much as it wishes, 'which hath mercy on whom it will hath mercy, and whom it will it hardeneth',[20] King Ceadwalla said that he wished to make all haste to baptism and renounce entirely the error of heathenism. Although the sacrament in itself does not have less efficacy on the baptized because of the persons of those baptizing, nevertheless that this might be done with greater solemnity, he put matters of necessity aside, set in order affairs at home, and travelled swiftly to Rome.[21] There he was honourably received by Pope Sergius and most gloriously baptized by him on the holy Saturday before Easter in the year of our Lord 689, and happily called Peter, after the blessed Peter.[22] There, while still in his white robes, he left the prison of the flesh on Tuesday 20 April,[23] was buried in the basilica of the blessed apostles Peter and Paul, and rested with peaceful heart awaiting the peace of eternity.[24] Moreover, Pope Sergius made an epitaph for that king in metre and decreed that it should be inscribed on his tomb. The text of that epitaph is as follows:

[22] Sergius I was pope 687–701; *Oxford Dictionary of Popes*, pp. 82–3. Easter fell on 11 Apr. 689.

[23] The date given in the manuscript is 18 Feb., the day of the week Friday. 18 Feb. 689 was in fact a Thursday, and of course was before Easter. Given the obvious error, and the ease with which it could have been made in copying, I have emended the text. Bede, *Ecclesiastical History*, bk. v, c. 7, ed. Colgrave and Mynors, p. 470, gives 'duodecimo kalendarum Maiarum die', but does not specify the day of the week.

[24] The final phrase is also used of Abbot Hugh; below, p. 360.

B5. *Epitaphium regis Cedwalle.*[25]

Culmen, opes, sobolem, pollentia regna,
Triumphos, exuuias, proceres, menia, castra, lares;
Queque patrum uirtus et que congesserat ipse,
Cedwalla regnipotens[a] liquit amore Dei,
[i. 6] Vt Petrum sedemque Petri rex cerneret hospes,
Cuius fonte meras sumeret almus aquas,
Splendificumque iubar radianti carperet haustu,
Ex quo uiuificus fulgur ubique fluit,
Precipiensque alacer rediuiue premia uite.
Barbaricam rabiem, nomen et inde suum
Conuersus, conuertit ouans, Petrumque uocari
Sergius antistes iussit, ut ipse pater,
Fonte renascentis quem Christi gratia purgans,
Protinus albatum uexit in arce poli.
Mira fides regis, clementia maxima Christi,
Cuius consilium nullus adire potest,
Sospes enim ueniens supremo[b] ex orbe Britanni,
Per uarias gentes, per freta perque uias,
Vrbem Romuleam uidit templumque uerendum
Aspexit Petri, mistica dona gerens.
fo. 5v Candidus inter oues Christi sociabilis | ibit,
Corpore nam tumulum, mente superna, tenet.
Commutasse magis sceptrorum insignia credas
Quem regnum Christi promeruisse uides.

B6. *Descriptio uille Seuekesham, postea Abbendoniam appellate.*

Verum ne sub silentio nobilitatem uille Seouechesham pretereamus, quasi rei ueritatis ignari, aliquid de ea probabili relatione et fide digna ad presens in medium proferamus. Fuit itaque Seouechesham ciuitas famosa, aspectu desiderabilis, diuiciis plena, agris circumdata uberrimis, uernantibus pratis, diffusis campis, et gregibus lactifluis. Hic sedes regia, huc cum de regni precipuis et arduis tractaretur negociis, [i. 7] concursus fiebat populi.[26] Vbi etiam a primis Britonum temporibus locus fuit religionis, tam tempore religionis fanatice quam tempore

B5 [a] uel armipotens *interlin. above* regnipo [b] subpremo *MS*

[25] The epitaph appears in Bede, *Ecclesiastical History*, bk. v, c. 7, ed. Colgrave and Mynors, pp. 470–2. See further R. Sharpe, 'King Ceadwalla's Roman epitaph', in K. O'Brien O'Keeffe and A. Orchard, eds., *Latin Learning and English Lore: Papers for Michael Lapidge* (2 vols, Toronto, 2005), i. 171–93.

[26] See above, p. cvii.

B5. *Epitaph of King Ceadwalla.*[25]

Eminence, wealth, kindred, powerful kingdoms,
Triumphs, spoils, great men, fortified cities, strongholds, homes;
And those qualities of his fathers and those he had assembled himself,
Powerful-ruling Ceadwalla abandoned for love of God,
So that as a visitor the king might look on Peter and the see of Peter,
Blessed he might take the pure waters from his fount,
Gather a brilliant radiance from the shining draught,
From which flows everywhere a life-giving brightness,
Swiftly taking the rewards of reborn life.
Rejoicing he changed his barbarous rage and, following that, his own name:
The Archbishop Sergius, as his father, ordered that he be called Peter,
Purifying him at the font the grace of reborn Christ
Immediately carried him, clad in white, to the height of Heaven.
Remarkable the king's faith, greatest the mercy of Christ,
Whose counsel no one can approach,
For coming safe from Britain, the endmost part of the world,
Through diverse peoples, through seas and roads,
He saw the town of Romulus, and, bearing mystic gifts,
Gazed upon Peter's awe-inspiring temple.
White-clad he will go as an intimate among the sheep of Christ,
He occupies a tomb with his body, the heavens with his soul.
You should believe to have exchanged for something better the insignia of sceptres
Him whom you see to have deserved the kingdom of Christ.

B6. *Description of the village of* Seuekesham, *afterwards called Abingdon.*

Lest we pass over in silence the nobility of the village of *Seuekesham*, as if ignorant of the truth of the matter, we now make generally known something about it with a credible and trustworthy account. So, *Seuekesham* was a renowned city, of desirable appearance, full of riches, surrounded with the richest farmlands, flourishing meadows, abundant fields, and milk-giving herds. Here was a royal seat, to this place people gathered when the important and difficult business of the realm was discussed.[26] From the earliest times of the Britons it was also a place of religion, in the time both of pagan religion and of religionis Christiane. In hac etiam ciuitate plura fuerunt indicia Christianitatis ex antiquorum[a] conuersatione Britonum, ut supra dictum est, cruces etenim et imagines, que in uilla ipsa nunc hic nunc illic effosse reperiebantur, huius rei prebent experimentum.

B7. *De inuentione nigre crucis.*

Inter alias etiam cruces inuenta fuit crux illa sancta que nigra crux appellatur. Sancta enim adeo est ut nullus, iuramento super eam prestito, impune et sine periculo uite sue possit affirmare mendacium; creditur etenim ex clauis Domini ex magna parte conflata et facta. Nec tamen a Constantino magno, qui in ea regione imperator creatus fuit,[27] ibi reposita, ut quidam dicunt; sed credibilius quidem a beniuolis suis Britannis quos secum Romam profecturus deduxerat transmissa illuc, ut memoria sanctitatis et meriti utrorumque—scilicet matris et filii—insignius appareret, ubi et corporalis presentie ip⟨s⟩orum conuersatio habita magnificabatur.[28] Vel certe transmittente[a] Cesare ipso uel matre eius ad honorem et tuicionem patrie de qua ad imperium assumptus fuerat, ut prediximus, a quibus propter merita et sanctitatem eorum crucem Domini constat fuisse inuentam. Tempore Anglorum edificata ibi capellula ipsius sancte Helene, que aliquando ibi tempore uiri siue filii conuersata fuerat, crucem illam repertam fuisse asserunt, per quam, multa signa indicens, sanctuarii illius uirtutes monstrate sunt. Quot rei periurio super eam deprehensi
[i. 8] sint? Non est numerus miraculorum. Vnde[b] (cum tot uirtutibus quas enumerare non possumus mendacia et asserciones false detegerentur) reuerentia qua debebat honorabiliter tractabatur; et uolentibus fratribus eam auro et argento ornare, quicquid ei in una die circa adaptabatur, totum altera decidisse et dissolutum esse uidebant, nec potuit aliqua parte aliquando aurum uel argentum circa eam con-
fo. 6r firma|ri, sindone tantum exterius per totum inuoluta est.

B6 [a] anticorum *MS*

B7 [a] transtmittente *MS* [b] Vnus *MS*

[27] Constantine the Great, son of Constantius and Helena, was emperor 306–37. See also *Historia regum*, ed. Wright, p. 51, from which the compiler of the *History*'s knowledge of Constantine presumably derives.

[28] The narrative could be clearer here, with the sudden mention of Constantine's

Christian. Also in this city was considerable evidence of Christianity from the religious life of the ancient Britons, as mentioned above, for crosses and images, which were found buried in various places in this village, provide proof of this.

B7. *Concerning the finding of the Black Cross.*

Among the other crosses found was, indeed, that holy cross which is called 'the Black Cross'. It is so holy that no one who has taken an oath on it can affirm a lie without punishment and mortal danger, for it is believed to have been smelted and made in large part from nails of the Lord. However, it was not, as some say, deposited there by Constantine the great, who was made emperor in that area.[27] It is more plausible that it was sent there by his well-wishers, the Britons, whom he had taken with him when setting out for Rome, to make clearer the memory of the holiness and merit of both—that is mother and son—at the place where the sojourn of their corporeal presence was also extolled.[28] Certainly, whether sent by the Caesar or his mother to the honour and protection of the homeland from which he was raised to dominion, as we have said above, it is agreed that the cross of the Lord was found by those people because of their merits and holiness. It is asserted that the cross was discovered at a small chapel (built there in the time of the Angles) of that Saint Helen who had lived the religious life there at some point in the time of her husband or son, and through it, as many signs demonstrate, the powers of that holy relic have been revealed. How many wrongdoers have been caught by perjury on it? Those miracles cannot be numbered. As a result (since lies and false assertions are revealed by so many miracles which we cannot number) it was honourably treated with the reverence due; the brethren wished to decorate the cross with gold and silver, but they saw that whatever was one day added to it, the next day entirely fell off and was shed, and that gold or silver could never be fixed anywhere around it, but it could only be wrapped all round with muslin on the outside.

mother, Helen. It is possible that this lack of clarity results from a lapse by the compiler or/ and the scribe of MS B. For Helen, see A. Harbus, *Helena of Britain in Medieval Legend* (Cambridge, 2002), which unfortunately does not consider the incorporation of Helen into the Abingdon legend.

Verumptamen rex Cedwalla—cuius anime propitietur Deus[29]—non tamen bona supra enumerata Abbendonie contulit,[30] uerum etiam de propria uoluntate sua Cille, sorori Heani patricii, dedit licentiam construendi monasterium in loco qui nunc dicitur Helnestoue, iuxta Thamisiam, ubi uirgo Deo sacrata et sacro uelamine uelata quam plurimas choadunauit sanctimoniales, quarum in posterum mater extitit et abbatissa. Post huius decessum succedente te⟨m⟩poris interuallo quam plurimo,[31] translate sunt sanctimoniales prefate ab illo loco ad uillam que dicitur Witham.[32] Succedentibus uero nonnullis annis, cum graue bellum et a seculo inauditum ortum fuisse inter Offam regem Merciorum et Kinewlfum regem Westsaxonum, tunc temporis factum erat castellum super montem de Witham, ob cuius rei causam recesserunt sanctimoniales ille a loco illo nec ulterius redire perhibentur.[33]

[i. 9] **B8**. *De morte Cedwalle*[a] *et Ina rege.*

Nunc restat ut ad successores regis Cedwalle et eorum tam maleficia quam beneficia succincte[b] describenda, pro modulo scientie nostre, stilum uertamus reciprocum. Itaque audito decessu regis Cedwalle in Westsaxonia, fama uolitante (qua nihil uelocius),[34] successit ei in hereditatem[c] Ina rex, affinis illi lineari propinquitate.[35] Hic autem primo donationes et beneficia predecessorum suorum Cisse[36] et Cedwalle necnon maximam portionem hereditatis Heani abbatis precipue erga monasterium Abbendonie[d] irrita fieri decreuit, sed postmodum ad cor suum rediens et facti penitens, perspicaciterque intelligens illas duas partes iusticie quibus dicitur 'Declina a malo et fac bonum',[37] non solum a malo declinauit uerum etiam faciens bonum, de suis maneriis et licitis donationibus ipsius domus beneficia auxit uberius. Primo etenim ablatis in integrum restitutis, .ccl. cassatorum descriptionem, prout carta ipsius subsequens testatur, prefate domui et monachis ibidem Deo seruientibus, abbate Heano

B8 [a] *corr., in black ink, from* Cedwalla [b] sucstincte *MS* [c] *possibly corr. to* hereditate, *although the deletion of the abbreviation mark may be accidental* [d] *followed by a redundant second use of the word* primo

---

[29] Cf. Exod. 30: 16. Similar phrases were used in the liturgical commemoration of the dead.

[30] Presumably in the section which has been lost; see above, p. xlvi. For gifts by Ceadwalla, see also above, cc. 2–3.

[31] Ceadwalla died 689; Offa was king of Mercia 757–96, Cynewulf king of Wessex 757–86.

[32] Either Wytham or Wittenham; see above, p. lxxxvi.

To continue, King Ceadwalla—to whose soul may God be rendered favourable[29]—not only conferred on Abingdon the goods enumerated above,[30] but also of his own will gave Cilla, sister of Hæha the nobleman, permission to build a monastery in the place now called *Helenstou*, next to the Thames, where the virgin, consecrated to God and veiled with the sacred veil, gathered together a large number of nuns, of whom she thereafter was mother and abbess. A very considerable time after her death,[31] those nuns were moved from there to the village called *Witham*.[32] But after a few years, when a serious and unprecedented war had arisen between Offa king of the Mercians and Cynewulf king of the West Saxons, a fort was then built on the hill at *Witham*, on account of which the nuns withdrew from that place and are reputed never to have returned.[33]

B8. *Concerning the death of Ceadwalla, and King Ine.*

Now it remains for us to turn our pen, which moves back and forth, to King Ceadwalla's successors, and to describe succinctly both their bad and their good deeds, according to the extent of our knowledge. And so, when King Ceadwalla's death [689] had been heard of in Wessex, and rumour (than which nothing is swifter)[34] was flying about, King Ine, who was related to him by genealogical line, succeeded him in his inheritance.[35] At first he decreed to make void the gifts and endowments of his predecessors Cissa[36] and Ceadwalla and also the greatest part of the inheritance of Hæha the abbot particularly to the monastery of Abingdon, but afterwards he returned to his senses and repented his deed. Perceptively understanding those two elements of justice about which it is said 'Depart from evil and do good',[37] not only did he depart from evil but also he did good, increasing the endowments of that house in greater abundance from his own manors and legitimate gifts. After first fully restoring what had been taken away, he gave and granted and by his charter confirmed to the aforementioned house and the monks serving God there, with Abbot Hæha present in person and watching,

[33] See Stenton, *Early History*, pp. 23–5.

[34] Cf. Vergil, *Aeneid*, iv. 174: 'Fama, malum qua non aliud uelocius ullum'.

[35] According to the genealogies in *ASC*, *s.a.* 685, 688, their closest common ancestor was their great-great-grandfather, Ceawlin.

[36] This is the first mention of Cissa in the surviving part of MS B, but it seems very likely that he had appeared in the missing folios.

[37] Ps. 36 (37): 27.

uiuente et uidente, dedit et concessit et carta sua confirmauit.[38] Cuius carte subscriptio hec est:

B9. *Carta Ine regis.*[a]
Charters of Abingdon Abbey, no. 4; above, cc. 3, 4.

[i. 13] fo. 6[v] **B10.** *Testamentum Heani antequam abbas efficeretur.*
Charters of Abingdon Abbey, no. 3; above, c. 7.

[i. 14] fo. 7[r] **B11.** *De donatione uille que appellatur Suttun.*
Iste uero Ina primo dedit et concessit Deo et beate Marie et domui Abbendonie et monachis ibidem Deo seruientibus uillam de Suttune in puram et perpetuam elemosinam, cum omnibus ad illam integre pertinentibus, quam uillam monachi libere et quiete in pace possederunt usque ad tempus Kenulfi regis et Retuni abbatis, utputa inferius dicemus enucleatius.

B12. *Qualiter rex Ina Romam petiit et ibi obiit.*[39]
Postquam uero supradicta bona rex Ina fecerat, Deo acceptabilia, perpendens sollicite quod nudus intrauit in mundum et quod nudus reuerteretur ad humum,[40] homo ad humum properans, disponens sibi prouide ne morsu mortis corrueret corporis et anime, quod bene inceperat fine pociori consummauit. Relicto namque imperio suo ad Adelardo consanguineo suo commendato, anno Dominice incarnationis .dccxxviii. Romam profectus est, ubi, ne conuersionis sue pompam faceret, quasi ad populum falerans, non in publico comam deposuit sed, ut solius Dei placeret oculis qui iudicat uerba, cor, renes hominum,[41] amictu tectus plebeio clam uixit clamque consenuit. Remansit itaque Adelardus in regno. Quo mortuo, successit ei Cuthredus, cui Sigebertus, cui Kinewlfus.[42] Quo ab Offa rege Merciorum in bello uicto, omnia que iuridictioni sue subdita fuerant, ab oppido Walingefordie in australi parte ab Ichenildestrete usque ad Esseburiam et in aquilonali parte usque ad Tamisiam,[43] rex Offa sibi usurpauit. Iste uero Offa Deo et beate Marie et domui Abbendonie et

B9 [a] *an illustration of the king appears at the start of this charter*

[38] The use of 'descriptio' is not typical of the *History*, and could perhaps reflect the peculiar nature of the 'charter' that follows. The arithmetic whereby the figure 250 was reached is obscure.

[39] Cf. MS C's brief statement above, p. 10.

[40] Cf. Job 1: 21 'nudus egressus sum de utero matris mee, et nudus revertar illuc', a passage used in several Abingdon charters; see p. 387.

[41] Cf. e.g. Rev. 2: 23. The 'renes', translated in the Authorized Version of the Bible as 'reins', are the kidneys or the loins, and following biblical usage the term was used to refer to the seat of feelings, affections, or appetites.

a delineation of 250 hides, as his following charter witnesses.[38] This is the text of that charter:

B9. *Charter of King Ine.*
Charters of Abingdon Abbey, no. 4; above, cc. 3, 4.

B10. *Testament of Hæha before he was made abbot.*
Charters of Abingdon Abbey, no. 3; above, c. 7.

B11. *Concerning the gift of the village called Sutton.*
This Ine, indeed, first gave and granted to God and the blessed Mary and the house of Abingdon and the monks serving God there the village of Sutton in pure and perpetual alms, with everything entirely pertaining to it, which village the monks possessed freely and undisturbed in peace up to the time of King Coenwulf and Abbot Hræthhun, as we will tell more plainly below.

B12. *How King Ine sought Rome and died there.*[39]
Indeed, after King Ine had done these good deeds, which were welcome to God, he anxiously contemplated that he entered the world naked and that he would return naked to the earth.[40] As a man hastening to the earth, he made prudent dispositions for himself lest he be brought down by the bite of the death of body and soul, and what he had begun well he completed in even better fashion. So he left his dominion entrusted to his kinsman Æthelheard, and in the year of our Lord 728 set out for Rome. There, lest he make a display of his conversion, as it were showing off to the people, he accepted the tonsure not in public, but in such a way that he might please the eyes of God alone, who judges men's words, hearts, and feelings,[41] and he lived secretly clad in a common man's garment and grew old secretly. Æthelheard therefore remained in the kingdom. When he died, Cuthred succeeded him, to whom Sigeberht succeeded, to whom Cynewulf.[42] When he had been defeated in battle by Offa king of the Mercians, the latter seized for himself everything which had been subjected to Cynewulf's authority, from the Icknield Way between the town of Wallingford and Ashbury in the south to the river Thames in the north.[43] That Offa, indeed, conferred the village called

[42] Cuthred reigned 740–56, Sigeberht 756–?757, Cynewulf 757–86; *Handbook of British Chronology*, p. 23.

[43] Ashbury, Berkshire. For Offa's victory and capture of Benson, Oxfordshire, see *ASC*, *s.a.* 779. Note the comments of Stenton, *Early History*, pp. 23–5, who suggests that Mercian dominance may have stretched further south in Berkshire than the present Abingdon account allows.

[i. 15] monachis ibidem Deo seruientibus uillam que Gosi appellatur in puram et perpetuam contulit elemosinam.[a] [44] Tempore etiam istius Offe regis quidam episcopus nomine Rethunus, de regno Merciorum contumeliis et ui hostilitatis coactus, episcopatui suo renuntiauit et in monasterio Abbendonie monachatum suscipiens, abbas et pater postea est effectus.

B13. *De Brihtrico rege Westsaxonum.*

fo. 7v Interfecto Kinewlfo Westsaxonum rege a Kinewardo, Sige|berti predecessoris sui fratre, successit ei Brihtricus frater eius.[45] Iste uero Brihtricus uillam de Estun cuidam principi suo Lullan nomine dedit, et concessit ei et carta sua confirmauit ut memoratus Lullan prefatam[a] uillam cum omnibus appendiciis suis cuicumque uellet daret pariter et assignaret.[46] Cuius carte memoratus Lullan[b] fretus munimine, ante mortem suam, de consensu regis Brihtrici et consilio uirorum autenticorum, desiderans Christum sibi facere heredem, uillam predictam, scilicet Estune, Deo et sancte Marie[c] et domui Abbendonie et monachis ibidem Deo seruientibus dedit et concessit, et cartam illam, qua rex Brihtricus terram memoratam illi confir-
[i. 16] mauerat, que tunc temporis plus efficatie et confirmationis habebat quam aliqua alia quam de eadem terra facere posset, super altare beate Marie Abbendonie posuit. Et in signum maioris federis protulit Anglice 'Al mine rihte þat ic hædde in Estun ic gife sæinte Marie in Abbendun.'

B14. *Hec est carta Brihtrici regis.*
Charters of Abingdon Abbey, no. 7.[47]

B12 [a] *corr. from* helemosinam *by expunction*

B13 [a] *corr. from* prefatas *by erasure* [b] *corr. from* Lullam *by erasure* [c] *interlin.*

[44] Offa's gift of Goosey is not mentioned in any charter. The compiler of MS B may have read of Offa's gift in *De abbatibus*, which states that the king gave it in return for Andersey; *CMA* ii. 273. Alternatively, he may have worked backwards from the charter in King Coenwulf's name restoring, amongst other properties, Goosey, and have guessed that Offa was the original donor; see above, c. 10.

[45] These events are recorded in the *ASC*, *s.a.* 786, and note also the entry *s.a.* 757. See further S. D. White, 'Kinship and lordship in early medieval England: The story of Sigeberht, Cynewulf, and Cyneheard', *Viator*, xx (1989), 1–18. Beorhtric was king of Wessex 786–802; *Handbook of British Chronology*, p. 23.

Goosey on God and the blessed Mary and the house of Abingdon and the monks serving God there, in pure and perpetual alms.[44] Also in that King Offa's time a certain bishop named Hræthhun, driven from the kingdom of the Mercians by indignities and force of enmity, renounced his bishopric and became a monk in the monastery of Abingdon, afterwards being made abbot and father.

B13. *Concerning Beorhtric king of the West Saxons.*

After Cynewulf king of the West Saxons was killed by Cyneheard, brother of his predecessor Sigeberht, his own brother Beorhtric succeeded him.[45] Beorhtric, indeed, gave the village of Easton to a noble of his named Lulla, and granted to him and confirmed by his charter that Lulla might equally give and assign that village with all its appendages to whomsoever he wished.[46] Strengthened by the protection of this charter, Lulla, desiring before his death to make Christ his heir, with the consent of King Beorhtric and the counsel of authoritative men, gave and granted to God and St Mary and the house of Abingdon and the monks serving God there the aforesaid village, that is Easton, and placed on the altar of the blessed Mary at Abingdon that charter whereby King Beorhtric had confirmed that land to him. At that time this had greater efficacy and confirmatory power than anything else that he could do concerning that land. And as a sign of complete agreement he pronounced in English 'All my right which I had in Easton I give to St Mary in Abingdon'.

B14. *This is the charter of King Beorhtric.*

Charters of Abingdon Abbey, no. 7.[47]

[46] Crux Easton, Hampshire. Lulla may be the same man as the *prefectus* Lulla who witnessed a charter for Glastonbury; *Charters of Abingdon Abbey*, p. 35. It may be that Abingdon did have an early interest in Crux Easton and associated lands at Hurstbourne, but surrendered it in an exchange with King Ecgberht of Wessex. The lands may have passed to Abingdon under Edgar, but were no longer in the abbey's hands in 1066; see *Charters of Abingdon Abbey*, no. 89, pp. clxvi, ccvii, 30–1, 367; *Charters of the Early West Saxon Kingdom*, ed. Edwards, p. 184.

[47] Sawyer, no. 268. This charter records Beorhtric granting the above ten hides to Lulla. It is dated 801. *Charters of the Abbey of Abingdon*, p. 33, states that the charter 'is a very difficult document to evaluate, in part because there are relatively few reliable West Saxon texts from the eighth and early ninth centuries with which to compare it'. Edwards, in *Charters of the Early West Saxon Kingdom*, p. 183, states that 'there is good reason to argue that the charter is basically genuine and it may be that the whole text is authentic'.

[i. 18] **B15.** *De morte Offe regis Merciorum et successione Kenulfi.*
fo. 8r Interea Offa rege Merciorum uiam uniuerse carnis ingresso, successit ei in regnum filius eius Egbertus, qui paucis diebus post patrem suum regnauit et statim cessit in fatum.[48] Cui successit Kenulfus.

B16. *De sororibus Kenulfi.*[49]

Iste uero Kenulfus duas habuit sorores uterinas, non solum facie decoras uerum etiam elegantia morum bonorum insignitas et—quod est longe melius—in omnibus et per omnia omnipotenti Deo deuotas. Has uero nonnulli proceres potentissimi, tum propter regiam dignitatem, tum propter earum famam memoria dignam, in copulam adoptauerunt sibi maritalem. Quas cum rex puta[a] (de cuius consensu et uoluntate huiuscemodi penderet negocium) quadam die affabili uultu interrogaret cuiusmodi uitam actitare, quosue sponsos in hac mortali tunica habere desiderassent, demissis in terram paulolum uultibus earumque mentibus in celum iugiter erectis, quasi desuper
[i. 19] eis datum et celitus prouisum, regi huiuscemodi dedere responsum: 'Rex piissime, bene nouit sanctitas uestra nos ex regali prosapia esse propagatas. Nouit etiam benignitas uestra, frater amantissime, quod ab ineunte etate Deo seruire eique soli placere finaliter, tota mente totisque uiribus nostris, desiderauimus. Nunc ergo benignitatem
fo. 8v uestram, capitibus demis|sis, iunctis manibus, flexis poplicibus, uoce lugubri, petimus habere exoratam, quatinus, pro amore illius qui de uirgine nasci dignatus est uirgines nos permanere et in integritate mentis et corporis ei iugiter famulari cui seruire regnare est pacifice permittatis. Hunc etenim, pre omnibus mortalibus, ut decet sponsum habere preadoptauimus, nec alium quempiam habebimus, licet in continenti capitalem subire deberemus sententiam.' Quibus rex, plenus pietate et uisceribus misericordie,[50] hec uerba respondit: 'Quid ergo, dilectissime sorores et famule Dei deuote, sedet animis uestris? Petite quod iustum fuerit[51] nec repulsam paciemini.' Cui uirgines 'Volumus et desideramus insuper beniuolentiam uestram omni qua possumus deuocione deprecamur quatinus nobis aliquam porciunculam terre, liberam ab omni humano seruitio et seculari

B16 [a] *followed by* id est *erased*

[48] Offa's son was in fact called Ecgfrith, and he ruled in the latter part of 796; the mistake derives from John of Worcester, *Chronicle*, ii. 226. For the duration of his reign, see also *Handbook of British Chronology*, p. 16.

[49] For the relationship of this section to a late forged charter, *Charters of Abingdon Abbey*, no. 10, see above, p. lxviii.

B15. *Concerning the death of Offa king of the Mercians, and the succession of Coenwulf.*

Meanwhile, when Offa king of Mercians had gone the way of all flesh, his son Ecgberht succeeded him in the kingdom, who reigned for a few days after his father and immediately yielded to death.[48] Coenwulf succeeded him.

B16. *Concerning Coenwulf's sisters.*[49]

That Coenwulf, indeed, had two uterine sisters, who were not only beautiful in appearance but also distinguished in the elegance of their good conduct, and—which is far better—devoted in everything and every way to almighty God. Moreover, some very powerful great men selected these sisters to join with themselves in marriage, both because of their royal status and because of their noteworthy reputation. When one day the king (on whose consent and will business of this type rested) with a kind expression asked the sisters what sort of life they would desire to live, and what husbands they would desire to have in this mortal garb, they lowered their faces somewhat to the ground and raised their minds constantly to Heaven, and gave to the king the following answer, as if it had been given to them from above and provided from Heaven: 'Most pious king, your holiness knows well that we are sprung from royal stock. Also, your goodness knows, most beloved brother, that from an early age we have desired to serve God and please Him alone for ever, with all our minds and all our strength. Therefore now, with heads bowed, hands clasped, knees bent, voices mournful, we seek to entreat your goodness that, for love of Him who deigned to be born of a virgin, you peacefully allow us to remain virgins and constantly, in wholeness of mind and body, to serve Him to serve whom is to reign. For as is fitting we have chosen to have Him as a husband, before all mortals, and we will not have anyone else at all, even were we obliged to undergo immediately a capital sentence.' The king, full of compassion and 'the bowels of mercy',[50] answered them in these words: 'What, therefore, most beloved sisters and devoted servants of God, resides in your souls? Seek what is just[51] and you will not suffer rebuff.' The virgins replied to him: 'We wish and desire and in addition beseech your good will with all the devotion of which we are capable that you grant us a small portion of land, free of all human service and worldly

[50] The phrase 'uiscera misericordie' appears in Luke 1: 78, Col. 3: 12; note also vol. ii. 344; Wulfstan, *Life of Æthelwold*, c. 33, ed. Lapidge and Winterbottom, p. 50.

[51] See Matt. 20: 4.

exaccione, ubi in Dei seruitio manere possimus, nobis concedatis. Petimus etiam ut illam terram Deo et beate Marie Abbendonie monachisque ibidem Deo seruientibus, ubi corpora nostra temporalem habebunt sepulturam, libere et quiete cum omni libertate prescripta post decessum nostrum in perpetuam dare possimus elemosinam.' Tunc rex cum magna deliberatione, conuocatis archiepiscopis et episcopis et comitibus et baronibus regni ipsius, uillam que Culeham appellatur, cum omnibus ad illam integre pertinentibus, eis in uita earum concessit, et post earum decessum ecclesie sancte Marie Abbendonie et conuentui ibidem Deo seruienti,[b] liberam et [i. 20] quietam ab omni seculari exaccione, sub omnium episcoporum anathemate firmiter confirmauit, ita ut nec regi nec regiis ministris homines uillam inhabitantes aut alterius precepto pareant aut iuridiccioni, preterquam abbatis principaliter aut illius uel illorum quem uel quos abbas Abbendonie custodem[c] ibi constituerit aut custodes.[d] Impetrauit etiam rex Kenulfus a papa Leone tercio priuilegium de ecclesiastico beneficio in eadem uilla, sub anathematis interminatione, ne quis mortalium, siue archiepiscopus siue episcopus siue archidiaconus siue decanus aut eorum officiales siue homines eorum, ab ipsa ecclesia uel persona ecclesie uel uicario, uel ab alio annua pensione ipsam tenente ecclesiam, aut in ius uocare aut aliquid ab ea exigere presumat, unde in posterum alicui iuridiccioni episcopali uel alii subici posset et sic libertatis sue pati detrimentum. Solus autem abbas ex beneficio priuilegii aliquem iuris peritum quemcumque uoluerit constituet qui querimonias et placita tam de criminalibus quam de aliis ad ius ecclesiasticum pertinentibus diligenter audiat et fine canonico decidat.[52] Ex illo etiam tempore sacerdos uel clericus ecclesie de Culeham crisma in uigilia Pasche per manum sacriste in ecclesia Abbendonie ad usum baptismi et infirmorum accipiet. Persona uero uel uicario ipsius ecclesie in fatum cedente, abbas Abbendonie, auctoritate propria non de consensu uel consilio archiepiscopi uel episcopi uel archidiaconi uel decani uel alicuius officialis fo. 9r ecclesiastici, personatum uel uicariam cui uoluerit dabit, | nulla facta presentacione ad diocesanum uel ad alium. Quod si de abbate ipsius ecclesie humanitas contigerit, et ecclesia nominata uacauerit, prior et conuentus de consilio communi personatum uel uicariam cui uoluerint et dabunt et assignabunt et carta sua confirmabunt. Istam uero uillam cum omni libertate prescripta non solum uenerabilis papa Leo

[b] *corr. from* seruientibus [c] custodere *MS* [d] *corr. from* custodies.

exaction, where we can live in the service of God. We also seek that after our death we can give that land freely and undisturbed with all the above liberty in perpetual alms to God and blessed Mary of Abingdon and the monks serving God there, where our bodies will have earthly burial.' Then, when he had called together the archbishops and bishops and earls and barons of that realm, with great deliberation the king granted to them for their lives the village called Culham, with everything entirely pertaining to it, and he confirmed it after their deaths to the church of St Mary of Abingdon and the convent serving God there, free and quit of all secular exaction, firmly under the anathema of all the bishops, in such a way that the men living in that village were to obey neither the king nor royal officials, nor the order or jurisdiction of anyone else, except of the abbot in person or of him or those whom the abbot of Abingdon appointed guardian or guardians there. King Coenwulf also obtained from Pope Leo III a privilege concerning the ecclesiastical benefice in that village, under threat of anathema, that no mortal man, whether archbishop or bishop or archdeacon or dean or their officials or their men, presume to summon to justice or demand anything therefrom, from that church or its parson or vicar, or from another holding that church by annual pension, whereby it could for the future be subjected to any episcopal or other jurisdiction and thus suffer harm to its liberty. Moreover, the abbot alone according to the favour of the privilege may choose and constitute a man experienced in law to hear diligently and bring to a canonical decision complaints and pleas concerning both criminal and other matters pertaining to ecclesiastical law.[52] From that time, too, the priest or cleric of the church of Culham was to receive the chrism on the vigil of Easter by the hand of the sacrist in the church of Abingdon, to use for baptism and the sick. Moreover, when the parson or vicar of that church yields to death, the abbot of Abingdon, by his own authority and not by the consent or counsel of the archbishop or bishop or archdeacon or dean or any ecclesiastical official, shall give the parsonage or vicarage to whom he wishes, without presentment being made to the diocesan or another. But if the abbot of that church suffer the fate of mankind, and the named church is vacant, the prior and convent by common counsel will give and assign and by their charter confirm the parsonage or vicarage to whom they wish. Not only did the venerable Pope Leo by his privilege confirm that village, with all the above

[52] On the privileges of Culham, see above, p. clx.

[i. 21] domui abbatie Abbendonie priuilegio suo confirmauit, sed et litteras suas regi Kenulfo misit petitorias, rogans[e] attentius quatinus memoratam uillam cum omnibus appendiciis suis et libertatibus prescriptis, sicut et ipse summus pontifex priuilegiauerat, ut et ipse rex eandem uillam Abbendonie priuilegio suo confirmaret. Cuius peticioni licet rex non in continenti adquieuerit, tamen pro loco et tempore multo melius et consulcius, utputa inferius dicetur, summi pontificis salubri adquieuit consilio.

B17. *De temporibus Rethuni episcopi et abbatis.*[53]

Succedentibus itaque annis circiter[a] septem, uenatores et aucupes regis Kenulfi, prout illa gens assolet absque uerecundia aliena uiuere quadra,[54] nunc in expensis prodigis et exaccionibus indebitis, nunc in
[i. 22] contumeliis uariis et dilapidationibus patrimonii crucifixi superfluis, domum Abbendonie aggrauare presumebant, nec a tali presumptione et tam detestabili aut prece uel precio aliquatenus desistere uolebant. Verumptamen quod cum abbas Abbendonie, nomine Rethunus, et unanimis eiusdem loci conuentus egritudine tulissent, ne quid in preiudicium domus sue super huiuscemodi iniuriis fieret in posterum, multiplici ammonitione pretaxata tam regi quam regiis ministris[b] ut ab huiusmodi desisterent iniuriis, nec aliqua suscepta, abbas et conuentus pro statu suo et domus sue ad sedem appellauerunt apostolicam. Nec mora memoratus abbas curiam adiit Romanam ubi a uenerabili papa Leone laudabiliter susceptus, ipsum pontificem super negotio suo quoad cautius potuit propensius consuluit. Quem conquerentem seruus seruorum Dei, affabili lenitate consultum, puta ex inolita bonitate (de cuius pectore semper exuberabat tam pietatis quam dulcedinis immensitas), cum sue tuicionis apicibus insimul et auctoritatis apostolice priuilegiis, perpropere remisit ad propria. Sane quod cum rex iam accepisset tum ex tenore literarum summi pontificis tum ex uiua uoce portitoris uel se debere Anglicane ecclesie libertati diligenter intendere, et maxime defensioni domus Abbendonie uigilanter insistere et ab indebitis exaccionibus pariter et uexationibus ipsius domus penitus desistere, uel indignationem sedis apostolice maturius incurrere, nunc blandiciis cauillatoriis, nunc

[e] regans *MS*

B17 [a] scirciter *MS* [b] *interlin.*

[53] Cf. c. 9 above, dealing with the same matters. The content of this chapter probably derives from Coenwulf's privilege which follows it. [54] See Juvenal, *Satires*, v. 2.

liberty, to the house of the abbey of Abingdon but he also sent his petitory letters to King Coenwulf, asking very earnestly with regard that village with all its above appendages and liberties, that the king also would confirm that village to Abingdon by his own privilege, just as the highest pontiff had granted in his privilege. Although the king would not immediately agree to his request, afterwards, however, much more appropriately and advisedly taking into account the circumstance, he did agree to the highest pontiff's beneficial plan, as will be told below.

B17. *Concerning the times of Hræthhun, bishop and abbot.*[53]
Then, after about seven years had passed, King Coenwulf's huntsmen and fowlers, being a breed who are accustomed without restraint 'to live at another man's board',[54] presumed to oppress the house of Abingdon, now with wasteful charges and undue exactions, now with various affronts and excessive waste of the patrimony of the crucified Christ, and they were unwilling to desist in the least from such detestable effrontery either for prayer or payment. Nevertheless, when the abbot of Abingdon, named Hræthhun, and the like-minded convent of that place had endured this with suffering, and when both the king and the royal officers had received manifold warnings that they desist from such wrongs and they had made no such undertaking, the abbot and convent appealed to the apostolic see regarding their own situation and that of their house, lest any further wrongs of this type be done in future to the prejudice of their house. Without delay, that abbot went to the Roman Curia where he was received in praiseworthy fashion by the venerable Pope Leo, and very eagerly took counsel with that pontiff concerning his business, as prudently as he could. With good-natured mildness, as from habitual goodness, the servant of the servants of God (from whose breast an immensity both of piety and of sweetness always abundantly flowed) advised the complainant and then sent him very swiftly home, with letters of his protection and privileges of apostolic authority. When, indeed, the king learnt both from the terms of the highest pontiff's letters and from their bearer's own words that he ought either to pay attention diligently to the liberty of the English Church, and especially apply himself vigilantly to the defence of the house of Abingdon and utterly desist from undue exactions and similarly from vexations of that house, or incur very promptly the indignation of the apostolic see, he strung out that business now with quibbling flattery,

fulminantibus minis, quasi exceptionibus dilatoriis, sic ipsum elongauit negocium ut uel minimo uel penitus nulli rex iam procurasset
[i. 23] effectui mancipare.[55] Interea cum iam de summo pontifice humanitus
fo. 9v contigisset, littere ipsius abbatis de negotio suo | exequendo, quoad[c] usum penitus sunt quassate, attestante lege qua dicitur mortuo mandatore, respirat mandatum. Quo uiso, abbas Retunus et conuentus domus Abbendonie, uehementer timentes ne illis in posterum ad culpam et detrimentum domus sue imputaretur quod litteras prefatas contra regiam dignitatem, ut asserebat rex, impetrassent. Memoratus abbas Rethunus de consilio fratrum suorum regem adiit super negotio suo cum ipso pacifice locuturus. Quod ut securius faceret, aurum et argentum secum deportauit ad summam .cxx. librarum, diiudicans hoc sibi fore potissimum consilium de regis amore optinendo et ultimum remedium. Quod cum factum esset, regi illud tantillulum argenti et auri pro bono pacis optulit,[56] et preterea centum manentes ad uillam regalem Suttun prope Abbendoniam sitam. Quorum donorum gratia adeo animum regis ad beniuolentiam uir Dei Rethunus sibi et domui sue captauerat ut decretum publice sanctiretur ne quisquam domus regie officialium uel prefectorum aut episcoporum in possessionibus ecclesie[d] Abbendonensi pertinentibus ultra iam aliquid lucri siue seruitutis uel indebite exaccionis requireret, immo libertas ex integro omnibus ipsis perpetuaretur. Nacta itaque occasione ab huiusmodi concordia, abbas Rethunus ea que inter regem et ipsum iam fuerant sopita, ne in rediuiuam litem resurgere possent, utile sibi decreuit et domui sue in scriptum redigere et ad noticiam posterorum transmittere. Quo libenter a rege concesso, priuilegium suum fecit rex domui Abbendonie de uillis ad ipsam domum pertinentibus similiter et de propriis donationibus suis, que in priuilegio suo sequenti singillatim specificantur. Tenor uero priuilegii hic est:

[i. 25] B18. *Priuilegium Kenulfi.*[a]
Charters of Abingdon Abbey, no. 9; above, c. 11.

[c] *corr. from* ad *by interlin. of* quo [d] *partially corr. from* ecclesia

B18 [a] *an illustration of the king appears at the start of this charter* now with fulminating threats, dilatory exceptions as it were, thereby taking care that the order had either only very little or absolutely no impact.[55] Meanwhile, when the highest pontiff had suffered the fate of mankind, the abbot's letters concerning the business he had to pursue were rendered completely useless, in accordance with the law whereby it is said that with the death of the one ordering, the order breathes its last. When this was apparent, Abbot Hræthhun and the convent of the house of Abingdon feared tremendously that in future they would be accused, as a crime and to the loss of their house, of having sought those letters against the royal dignity, as the king was asserting. Therefore, the aforementioned Abbot Hræthhun on his brethren's advice went to the king to speak with him peacefully concerning their business. To do this more confidently, he took with him gold and silver to the value of £120, judging that this would provide for him the most powerful persuasion and the greatest salve in obtaining the king's love. When this was done, he offered the king for the good of peace that tiny amount of silver and gold,[56] and in addition one hundred hides at the royal vill of Sutton, situated close to Abingdon. By grace of these gifts, the man of God Hræthhun made the king's mind so favourable to himself and his house that a decree was publicly ordained that in future no official of the king's household or reeve or bishop should seek any money or servitude or undue exaction in the possessions pertaining to the church of Abingdon, but instead freedom was wholly to be perpetuated for them all. Having obtained opportunity from an agreement of this sort, Abbot Hræthhun decided that it would be useful for himself and his house to have drawn up in writing, and conveyed to the notice of men in future, those matters now settled between the king and himself, lest they could arise again in a revived dispute. The king willingly granted this and made his privilege for the house of Abingdon concerning the villages pertaining to that house and likewise concerning his own gifts, which are individually specified in his privilege which follows. The terms of the privilege are, indeed, as follows:

B18. *Privilege of Coenwulf.*
Charters of Abingdon Abbey, no. 9; above, c. 11.

[55] The *libertas ecclesie Anglicane* is very much a concept of the compiler's own time; cf. *Magna Carta*, c. 1 'Anglicana ecclesia libera sit'. On the emergence of the phrase *ecclesia Anglicana*, see Z. N. Brooke, *The English Church and the Papacy* (Cambridge, 1952), ch. 1. For the style of this and the following sentence, see above, p. liii.

[56] The author is here, of course, playing down a very substantial payment.

[i. 27] **B19.** *De Brihtrico rege West Saxonum.*

fo. 10r His diebus memoratus rex Westsaxonum Brihtricus, de quo superius prelibauimus, dedit cuidam principi suo, nomine Hemele, uillam que Mene uocatur, et carta sua confirmauit et concessit ei omni eodem
[i. 28] modo quo supradicto principi suo Lullan, ut et ipse post decessum suum quemcumque uellet de eadem terra heredem sibi faceret.[57] Dedit itaque memoratus Hemele uillam de Mene de consensu regis Brihtrici Deo et beate Marie et domui Abbendonie et monachis ibidem Deo seruientibus, cum omnibus ad illam pertinentibus.
fo. 10v Optulit etiam cartam ipsius | regis Brithrici super altare sancte Marie, quam habuit de eadem uilla. Cuius carte tenor hic est:

B20. *Carta Brihtrici de Hisseburna.*
Charters of Abingdon Abbey, no. 6.[58]

[i. 29] **B21.** *De morte Kenulfi regis.*

Post discessum Kenulfi regis Merciorum regnauit sanctus Kenelmus filius eius paucis diebus,[59] cui successit Ceolwlfus frater Kenulfi, cui Bertulfus.[60] Iste uero Bertulfus dedit Alfeo principi duodecim cassatos iuxta flumen quod appellatur Cirne et Kalemundesdene.[61] Ipse autem Alfeus de consensu regis Bertulfi dedit Deo et sancte Marie et domui Abbendonie et monachis ibidem Deo seruientibus eandem uillam cum duodecim cassatis terre supradictis, omni eodem modo quo supra de Lullan principe dictum est.[62] Et hec est karta regis Bertulphi:

[57] Hemele was probably an important ealdorman; see *Charters of Abingdon Abbey*, p. 29. On Hurstbourne, see above, p. 22 n. 66; for Lulla, above, B13. The charter which follows in fact leaves the land by the Bourne rivulet, Hampshire, not that by the Meon, in Hemele's hands; the compiler of the later version of the *History* appears to have misunderstood the charter.

[58] Sawyer, no. 269. This charter records Beorhtric granting thirty-six hides, in part by the Bourne rivulet, to Hemele, in exchange for thirty-four on the river Meon, Hampshire, previously granted to Hemele by King Cynewulf. The charter is datable to 786 × 794. *Charters of Abingdon Abbey*, p. 28, states that the charter 'is more likely than not to be an authentic document, although it is possible that the various hidages have been corrupted in transmission'. See also Stenton, *Early History*, pp. 29–30, who takes it as genuine, with an added phrase in the witness list; also *Charters of the Early West Saxon Kingdom*, ed. Edwards, pp. 179–83.

[59] i.e. St Kenelm, on whom see e.g. John of Worcester, *Chronicle*, ii. 238–40; *Three*

B19. *Concerning Beorhtric king of the West Saxons.*
In these days, that Beorhtric king of the West Saxons, whom we mentioned above, gave the village called Meon to a noble of his named Hemele, and by his charter confirmed and granted to him in entirely the same way as to his aforesaid noble Lulla, that after his death he might make whomsoever he wished his heir concerning that land.[57] Therefore that Hemele, by King Beorhtric's consent, gave the village of Meon to God and the blessed Mary and the house of Abingdon and the monks serving God there, with everything pertaining to it. He also offered on the altar of St Mary the charter of that King Beorhtric, which he had concerning that village. The terms of his charter are as follows:

B20. *Charter of Beorhtric concerning Hurstbourne.*
Charters of Abingdon Abbey, no. 6.[58]

B21. *Concerning the death of King Coenwulf.*
After the demise of Coenwulf king of the Mercians [821], his son St Cenelm reigned for a few days,[59] to whom succeeded Ceolwulf, brother of Coenwulf, and to him Berhtwulf.[60] This Berhtwulf indeed gave twelve hides next to the river that is called the Churn, and Calmesden, to Ælfheah, a noble.[61] Moreover, that Ælfheah by the consent of King Berhtwulf gave that village with those twelve hides of land to God and St Mary and the house of Abingdon and the monks serving God there, in entirely the same way as was said above concerning Lulla, the noble.[62] And this is King Berhtwulf's charter:

Eleventh-Century Anglo-Latin Saints' Lives, ed. R. C. Love (OMT, 1996); W. Levison, *England and the Continent in the Eighth Century* (Oxford, 1946), pp. 249–51; *Oxford Dictionary of Saints*, p. 231.

[60] Ceolwulf was king of Mercia from 821 until his expulsion by Beornwulf in 823. Berhtwulf came to the throne in 840 and died in ?852; *Handbook of British Chronology*, p. 17. Berhtwulf therefore was not Ceolwulf's direct successor, as the text implies. Conceivably the compiler was led into error by some similarities between the names Beornwulf and Berhtwulf.

[61] Calmesden, Gloucestershire; see further *Charters of Abingdon Abbey*, p. 63. The introduction to the boundary clause of the charter that follows states that King Berhtwulf booked the land to Ælfheah 'his fæder sune'. The exact relationship indicated by this phrase is uncertain. *Charters of Abingdon Abbey*, p. 63, takes it to mean that Ælfheah was Berhtwulf's nephew. Another possibility is that Ælfheah was Berhtwulf's half-brother, i.e. his father's son, not his mother's.

[62] See above, p. 248. Such routine statements in MS B that beneficiaries of royal gifts passed the grant to Abingdon are not to be trusted; see above, pp. cxxvi–cxxviii.

B22. *Carta Bertulfi regis.*
Charters of Abingdon Abbey, no. 13.[63]

[i. 31] fo. 11r **B23.**[a] Eidem Berthulfo Merciorum regi dedit Ceolredus antistes quatuordecim cassatos iuxta flumen Tamisie pro libertate quorumdam monasteriorum, et ipse rex Beorthulfus dedit Ethelwlfo principi eodem modo quo supra.[64] Et ipse Ethelwlfus princeps dedit Deo et beate Marie et domui Abbendonie et monachis ibidem Deo seruientibus eosdem duodecim cassatos, cum carta regis. Cuius descriptio carte hec est:

B24. *Carta regis Berthulfi.*
Charters of Abingdon Abbey, no. 12.[65]

[i. 32] **B25.** *De morte Brihtrici regis*[a] *West⟨saxonum⟩.*
fo. 11v Brihtrico rege Westsaxonum cedente in fatum, successit ei Egbrihtus nepos eius, filius Kinewlfi ab Offa rege Merciorum uicti.[b] [66] Iste uero Egbrihtus omnes reges tocius Albionis in dedicionem suscepit. Qui [i. 33] cum audisset famam bonitatis domus Abbendonie et uidisset donationes et beneficia que predecessores sui supradicti ipsi domui intuitu caritatis contulere, domum ipsam sincere dilexit, quem amorem euidentissime probauit ipsius operis exibitio. Videns etenim beneficia predecessorum suorum quam plurima, sua uero parua uel nulla, timens in se radices ficus fatue succidi si nullos fructus afferret,[67] ad se reuersus ac iugi meditatione mortem pre occulis habens suspectam, secum multociens deliberauit quid beneficii in remissionem peccatorum suorum domui Abbendonie dare posset in puram et perpetuam helemosinam. Quid multa? Ad hoc

B23 [a] *the rubricator failed to provide a heading, although the appropriate space had been left*

B25 [a] *corr. from* Brihtrico rege [b] *crudely written over erasure*

[63] Sawyer, no. 202. This charter records Berhtwulf granting the above twelve hides to Ælfheah. It is dated 852, although this may be a slip for 842. *Charters of Abingdon Abbey*, p. 61, states that 'the authenticity of [the document] is uncertain', and concludes, p. 62, that it is probably best to believe that it is 'a forgery, or at least a technical fabrication'. Apart from the presence of this charter in the archive, there is no other evidence of Abingdon interest in this land; note, however, *Charters of Abingdon Abbey*, pp. 63–4, for Abingdon interests in the vicinity.

[64] Ceolred was bishop of Leicester from the early 840s until perhaps as late as 888; *Handbook of British Chronology*, p. 218. This introductory passage is unusual in not specifying where the lands were situated. According to *Charters of Abingdon Abbey*, p. 56, the lands 'were probably located somewhere on the river Pang, not necessarily in the close vicinity of modern Pangbourne'. The variation in the hidage may simply be a scribal error.

[65] Sawyer, no. 1271; trans. *EHD*, i. no. 87. This charter records Bishop Ceolred granting

B22. *Charter of King Berhtwulf.*
Charters of Abingdon Abbey, no. 13.[63]

B23. Ceolred the bishop gave fourteen hides next to the river Thames to that Berhtwulf king of the Mercians in return for the freedom of certain monasteries, and King Berhtwulf gave it to Æthelwulf, a noble, in the same way as above.[64] And Æthelwulf, the noble, gave those twelve hides to God and the blessed Mary and the house of Abingdon and the monks serving God there, with the king's charter. This is the text of his charter:

B24. *Charter of King Berhtwulf.*
Charters of Abingdon Abbey, no. 12.[65]

B25. *Concerning the death of Beorhtric king of the West Saxons.* When Beorhtric king of the West Saxons yielded to death [802], there succeeded to him Ecgberht his nephew, son of the Cynewulf who was conquered by Offa king of the Mercians.[66] That Ecgberht, indeed, received in submission all the kings of the whole of Albion. When he heard report of the goodness of the house of Abingdon and saw the gifts and endowments that his predecessors mentioned above had charitably conferred on it, he sincerely loved that house, a love most clearly proved by the action he performed. For seeing that his predecessors' endowments were very many but his own few or none, and fearing that the roots of the sycomore would be cut if it bore no fruit,[67] he turned again to himself and, constantly meditating upon death held up before his eyes, he often deliberated internally what endowment he could give in pure and perpetual alms to the house of Abingdon for the remission of his sins. What's more, it

the fourteen hides on the river Pang to Berhtwulf, in return for freedoms, and Berhtwulf then granting the land to Æthelwulf. The charter is dated 844, although 843 may be correct. *Charters of Abingdon Abbey*, p. 55, states that the document 'seems to be authentic', at p. 59 that 'it is impossible to be certain whether [the document] is acceptable as it stands, or whether it has undergone some . . . interpolation or revision; what is clear is that it is based on genuine ninth-century documentation'. Kelly also suggests, at p. 57, that this may have been one of the documents from a minster at Bradfield, close to Pangbourne, which passed into the Abingdon archive. See Stenton, *Early History* pp. 25–6, for the charter's significance concerning Mercian control of Berkshire into the mid-9th c.

[66] Ecgberht was not, in fact, son of Cynewulf; *Handbook of British Chronology*, p. 23.

[67] Sycomore here is a species of fig tree, not the species of maple familiar in Britain (commonly spelt sycamore); see *DMLBS*, fasc. iv *s.v. fatuus*. The allusion is probably to Luke 13: 6–9, where Christ tells in a parable of a man who had planted a fig tree [*arborem fici*] in his vineyard, but then found no fruit upon it. He complained of this to the dresser of his vineyard, and the dresser answered that he would tend it for a year; if it then bore fruit, it was to be left, if it did not, it was to be cut down [*succides eam*].

tandem peruenit quod de consilio magnatuum regni ipsius uillam que Mercham appellatur, cum omnibus ad illam integre pertinentibus, Deo et beate Marie et domui Abbendonie et monachis ibidem Deo seruientibus dedit et concessit et carta sua confirmauit. Cuius carta hec est:

B26. *Carta Egbrihti regis Westsaxonum de Mercham.*[a]
Charters of Abingdon Abbey, no. 11; above, c. 12.

[i. 35] **B27**. *De morte Egbrithti regis.*
fo. 12v Egbrihto rege Westsaxonum carnis exuto ergastulo et hac luce communi priuato, successit ei Hathewlfus filius eius, qui cuidam principi suo, nomine Alcmundo, uillam que Essebiri appellatur dedit, et ut carta sua testatur concessit ei ut quemcumque uellet sibi faceret heredem.[68] Ipse uero Alcmundus hanc uillam domui Abbendonie in puram[a] et perpetuam helemosinam dedit, cum carta ipsius regis. Fecit etiam rex Hathewlfus generale priuilegium omnibus ecclesiis
[i. 36] regni sui, quibus decimam partem terrarum regni sui in puram et perpetuam helemosinam per partes distribuerat. E quibus prima et precipua fuit domus Abbendonie. Forma autem priuilegie eius hec est:

B28. *Quomodo Aðelwlfus rex dedit decimam partem regni sui ecclesiis.*
Charters of Abingdon Abbey, no. 14; above, c. 13.

[i. 38] **B29**. *De morte Adelwlfi regis et quomodo Aðelbaldus filius eius confirmauit ecclesie Abbendonie omnes donationes Cisse et Cedwalle et Ine.*
Hæthelwlfo mortuo, successit ei Æthelbaldus filius eius. Iste uero Æthelbaldus inter ceteras regni sui ecclesias domum Abbendonie
fo. 13r quasi quadam speciali prerogatiua in tantum dilexit, | ut non solum de propriis beneficiis suis illam dotaret, uerum etiam terras quas primi fundatores Abbendonensis cenobii, scilicet Cissa, Cedwalla, Hina, eidem cenobio dederant et confirmauerant, ipse eidem Ædelbaldus ipsas easdem terras cum donatione propria sua carta confirmauit, et eas singillatim specificauit. Tenor autem carte hic est:

B26 [a] *an illustration of the king appears at the start of this charter*

B27 [a] peruram, *because of unnecessary abbreviation mark MS*

[68] Calendared in *Charters of Abingdon Abbey*, p. 579 (i). No charter recording the king's gift to Ealhmund survives. If it survived until the time of the compilation of MS B, it is hard to understand why the compiler did not include it here; if it did not survive until his

finally came at length to this, that by the counsel of the magnates of that realm he gave and granted and by his charter confirmed the village called Marcham, with everything entirely pertaining to it, to God and the blessed Mary and the house of Abingdon and the monks serving God there. This is his charter:

B26. *Charter of Ecgberht king of the West Saxons concerning Marcham.* *Charters of Abingdon Abbey*, no. 11; above, c. 12.

B27. *Concerning the death of King Ecgberht.*
When Ecgberht king of the West Saxons had left the prison of the flesh and been deprived of this common light, Æthelwulf his son succeeded him [839]. Æthelwulf gave the village called *Ashbury* to a noble of his named Ealhmund, and as his charter witnesses granted to him that he might make whomsoever he wished his heir.[68] That Ealhmund, indeed, gave this village to the house of Abingdon in pure and perpetual alms, with that king's charter. King Æthelwulf also made a general privilege for all the churches of his realm, to whom he had distributed by shares the tenth part of the lands of his realm in pure and perpetual alms. The first and foremost of them was the house of Abingdon. Moreover, the form of his privilege is this:

B28. *How King Æthelwulf gave the tenth part of his realm to churches.* *Charters of Abingdon Abbey*, no. 14; above, c. 13.

B29. *Concerning the death of King Æthelwulf and how Æthelbald his son confirmed to the church of Abingdon all the gifts of Cissa and Ceadwalla and Ine.*
After Æthelwulf died, his son Æthelbald succeeded him [855]. Amongst the other churches of his realm, indeed, Æthelbald loved the house of Abingdon as if by a special precedence, so much so that not only did he endow it regarding his own benefactions, but also the lands which the first founders of the monastery of Abingdon, that is Cissa, Ceadwalla, Ine, had given and confirmed to that monastery, those lands too Æthelbald confirmed by his charter to the monastery with his own gift, and specified them individually. Moreover the terms of the charter are as follows:

compilation, it is unclear how he knew of the gift. 'Essebiri' is the *History*'s version of the Old English *Æscesbyrig*/*Æscesburh* (translatable as *Ashbury*), that is the area of Uffington and Woolstone, Berkshire; EPNS, *Berkshire*, ii. 380, *Charters of Abingdon Abbey*, pp. 118–19. A man or men named Ealhmund 'princeps' witnessed B14 (*Charters of Abingdon Abbey*, no. 7) and *Charters of Abingdon Abbey*, no. 10.

B30. *Carta Aðelbaldi regis Westsaxonum de Wachenesfeld.*[a] [69]
Charters of Abingdon Abbey, no. 5; above, c. 8.

[i. 40] fo. 13v **B31.**[a] Post decessum Athelbaldi successit ei frater eius Adthelbrihtus. Qui, licet paruo tempore regnasset, uidelicet quinque annis, et in largitione beneficiorum non ad sufficientiam salutis anime salubriter sibi prouidisset, nichilominus tamen proteccioni ecclesiastice incessanter studuit curam impendere. Quo cedente in fatum, regnauit frater eius Athelredus. Iste uero Athelredus, tenens regni gubernacula, dedit ac concessit uenerabili et familiari principi suo Athelwlfo terram decem cassatorum in uilla que dicitur Witham, omni eodem modo quo carta regis subsequens testatur, scilicet ut quemcumque uellet heredem post decessum suum sibi faceret. Ipse, uero non factus inmemor prescripti beneficii, domui Abbendonie uillam ipsam cum omnibus ad illam integre pertinentibus, de
[i. 41] consensu et uoluntate regis, cum carta regis ipsam donationem et modum donandi exprimente, dedit et firmiter concessit, et ipsam cartam regis ad maiorem munitionem in honore Dei et beate Marie super altare Abbendonie deuocione optulit reuerentissima. Et hec est carta regis:

B32. *Carta Adelredi regis de Witthenham.*
Charters of Abingdon Abbey, no. 15; above, c. 16, and cf. below, B89.

[i. 42] **B33.** *De Lakinge.*
His temporibus princeps Cufwlffus, minister Ethelswiþe regine Merciorum, dedit Deo et beate Marie et domui Abbendonie et monachis ibidem Deo seruientibus terram quindecim manentium in uilla que dicitur Lakinge, de consensu et uoluntate memorate regine,
fo. 14r in puram et | perpetuam helemosinam. Cartam etiam ipsius regine posuit super altare sancte Marie in testimonium donationis sue. Cuius carte subscriptio hec est:

B34. *Carta Adelsuið regine de Lakinge.*[a]
Charters of Abingdon Abbey, no. 17; above, c. 15.

B30 [a] *an illustration of the king appears at the start of this charter*

B31 [a] *the rubricator failed to provide a heading, although the appropriate space had been left at the end of the previous passage, at the bottom of the column*

B34 [a] *this heading appears at the top of the column, rather than at the start of the charter. An illustration of the queen appears at the start of the charter*

B30. *Charter of Æthelbald king of the West Saxons concerning Watchfield.*[69]

Charters of Abingdon Abbey, no. 5; above, c. 8.

B31. After Æthelbald's death his brother Æthelberht succeeded him [860]. Although he reigned for little time, that is five years, and in the generous giving of endowments did not provide sufficiently profitably for his soul's salvation, nevertheless, he did strive incessantly to take care of the protection of the Church. When he yielded to death [865], his brother Æthelred reigned. When Æthelred was holding the reins of the realm, he gave and granted land amounting to ten hides in the village called Wittenham to his venerable and intimate noble Æthelwulf, in entirely the same way as the following charter of the king witnesses, that is, that he might make whomsoever he wished his heir after his death. Not forgetful of the above favour, Æthelwulf gave and firmly granted that village to the house of Abingdon, with everything entirely pertaining to it, by the consent and will of the king, together with the king's charter expressing that gift and the manner of giving, and in most reverent devotion he offered the king's charter on the altar of Abingdon, for greater protection, in honour of God and the blessed Mary. And this is the king's charter:

B32. *Charter of King Æthelred concerning Wittenham.*

Charters of Abingdon Abbey, no. 15; above, c. 16, and below, B89.

B33. *Concerning Lockinge.*

At that time the noble Cuthwulf, a thegn of Æthelswith queen of the Mercians, gave land amounting to fifteen hides in the village called Lockinge to God and the blessed Mary and the house of Abingdon and the monks serving God there, by that queen's consent and will, in pure and perpetual alms. He also placed that queen's charter on the altar of St Mary in testimony of his gift. This is the text of her charter:

B34. *Charter of Queen Æthelswith concerning Lockinge.*

Charters of Abingdon Abbey, no. 17; above, c. 15.

[69] For MS B's mistaken positioning of this document of King Æthelbald of Mercia (716–57), see above, p. 12 n. 41.

[i. 44] **B35.** *De Feornberga.*[70]

Omni eodem modo princeps Edricus, familiaris Ælflede regine Merciorum, dedit Deo et beate Marie et domui Abbendonie et monachis ibidem Deo seruientibus uillam que Feornberga appellatur, per consensum et uoluntatem memorate regine et per carte auctoritatem quam prefata regina ei fecerat de supradicta uilla.[71] Posuit etiam cartam ipsam super altare domus Abbendonie, insignans omni iure suo quod habuit in eadem terra per carte ipsius regine attestationem. Cuius carte hec est notificatio:

B36. *Carta Elflede regine de Ferberga.*[a]
Charters of Abingdon Abbey, no. 20.[72]

[i. 46] fo. 14v **B37.** *De aduentu Danorum in Angliam et destructione de Abbendonia.*[73]

Tempore uero Æþelredi regis, utputa ex serie gestorum accepimus Anglorum,[a] gens quam plurima de Danubia nauali uehiculo in Angliam aduentasse peribetur.[74] Cuius sane duces principales et ductores uiri sanguinum Yngwar et Hubba extitisse commemorantur.[75] Applicuerunt autem Dani isti sub brumali emisperio in regno Norhanhimbrorum.[76] Quibus, tum propter loci amenitatem, tum propter insule fertilitatem, pariter et omnium bonorum affluentiam, tantus appetitus regnandi in ipsa fuisse comprobatur, ut nulli iam parcerent terrigenarum condicioni, aut etati, uel sexui, cuiuspiam etiam in mortis discrimine deferrent. Enimuero interfectis uiris et mulieribus pariter cum paruulis ad ubera matrum adhuc pendentibus, urbibus hinc inde subuersis, uicis passim suc⟨c⟩ensis, adiacentes

B36 [a] *an illustration of the Æthelflæd appears at the start of this charter*

B37 [a] *interlin.*

[70] *Charters of Abingdon Abbey*, pp. 87–8, argues that the Mercian character of the charter and the transaction would suggest Farnborough in Warwickshire, but that the place-name evidence seems to point to Farnborough in Berkshire. Abingdon may have had interests in both; see above, cc. 99 (p. 152), 117, below, B56, B57 (*Charters of Abingdon Abbey*, no. 29), B253, B254. This appears to be a 10th-c. gift, wrongly positioned here because the charter includes the date 878. Æthelflæd was the daughter of King Alfred of Wessex and wife of Æthelred II of Mercia.

[71] Eadric is a common name, and his identity cannot be established with certainty.

[72] Sawyer, no. 225. This charter records Æthelflæd confirming the above ten hides to Eadric her thegn, after an earlier document concerning the land had been lost. The charter, wrongly dated 878, is probably from 915 × 916. The charter appears to be acceptable as authentic, except for the date; *Charters of Abingdon Abbey*, pp. 86–8.

[73] Cf. the account in MS C, above, c. 14.

[74] This is the great army the arrival of which the *Anglo-Saxon Chronicle* dates to 866. Asser, *Life of King Alfred*, c. 21, ed. Stevenson, p. 19, and John of Worcester, *Chronicle*, ii.

B35. *Concerning Farnborough.*[70]

In exactly the same way the noble Eadric, a trusted man of Æthelflæd queen of the Mercians, gave the village called Farnborough to God and the blessed Mary and the house of Abingdon and the monks serving God there, by that queen's consent and will and by authority of the charter which the aforesaid queen had made for him concerning that village.[71] He also placed that charter on the altar of the house of Abingdon, recording all his right which he had in that land by attestation of the queen's charter. This is the message of her charter:

B36. *Charter of Queen Æthelflæd concerning Farnborough.*
Charters of Abingdon Abbey, no. 20.[72]

B37. *Concerning the coming of the Danes to England and the destruction of Abingdon.*[73]

In King Æthelred's time, indeed, as we have learnt from the account of the deeds of the English, a very numerous people from the Danube are reported to have come to England by sea transport.[74] Their principal leaders and leading men are recorded as being the bloodthirsty men Hinguar and Ubba.[75] Moreover, those Danes landed in the kingdom of the Northumbrians under the wintry heavens.[76] They proved to have such a desire to rule there, because of the loveliness of the place, the fertility of the island, and equally the abundance of all goods, that they then spared none of the inhabitants by reason of their standing, or age, or sex, but did away with them by any manner of death. Having killed the men and women and also the little children still on their mothers' breasts, toppled towns on all sides, and set alight settlements everywhere, they laid waste the neighbouring regions, which had been so happy,

280, but not the *Anglo-Saxon Chronicle*, state that the fleet came from the Danube. John of Worcester is probably the *History*'s source. S. Keynes and M. Lapidge, *Alfred the Great* (Harmondsworth, 1983), p. 238, comment that Asser's statement 'makes no sense; it is possible that he was simply recording his belief or assumption that it came from Denmark, and made a mistaken connection between Danes and the Danube'.

[75] Neither the *Anglo-Saxon Chronicle* nor John of Worcester mention the leaders' names at this point, but they do appear in Henry of Huntingdon, *Historia Anglorum*, bk. v, c. 5, ed. Greenway, p. 280, and William of Malmesbury, *Gesta pontificum*, bk. ii, c. 74, ed. Hamilton, p. 153. Hinguar may be identified with Ivar the Boneless, and Ubba may have been his brother; see Keynes and Lapidge, *Alfred*, pp. 238–9. The phrase 'viri sanguinum' appears in Ps. 54: 24, Ps. 138: 19, and Prov. 29: 10.

[76] The *ASC*, *s.a.* 866, 867, and John of Worcester, *Chronicle*, ii. 280, have the army land in East Anglia and then move to Northumbria. 'Brumali' could mean northern, rather than winter, but Symeon of Durham, *Historia Dunelmensis ecclesie*, bk. ii, c. vi, *Opera omnia*, ed. T. Arnold (2 vols., London, 1882–5), i. 55, has the Danes take York on 1 Nov. 867.

prouincias tam felices tam infelici deuastatione depopulauerant, ut nec
fo. 15r etiam manus mittere ad sancta sanctorum aliquatenus for|midarent.[77] Euertebat itaque domum Gedeonis[78] gens extera, agni fedus edus rapuit,[79] cornu Dauid flagellabat gens misera,[80] uiolente plena gente sola sedit ciuitas.[81] Vrbes itaque cum monasteriis subuertebantur, quorum etiam monimenta adhuc plurimis in locis prestant indicia, utputa ubi parietum ac murorum reliquie hucusque spectantur semidirute.[82] Quid multa? Dani isti de regno ad regnum et de
[i. 47] populo transeuntes ad populum alterum, quasi pro signo uictorie animi extollentes insolentiam, tandem ad Westsaxoniam infelici gressu peruenerunt ubi consimili modo quo ceteris in locis debacantes, ultimo sacrosanctam ac uenerabilem domum Abbendonie, quam tot reges sancti et uiri tam autentici supradicti fundauerant et dotis uariis ditauerant, tam inimica manu tamque leonina ferocitate necnon tam detestabili auiditate, monachis penitus effugatis destruxerant, ut nihil ibi preter parietes reliquisse periberentur. Hoc tamen diuinitus prouiso quod reliquie sanctorum cum cartis ipsius domus, [b]quasi superius in hoc libro annotauimus et inferius sunt annotate, clamdestine sunt res[b]eruate, ad hoc forte, quatinus recuperatores simul et reparatores eiusdem cenobii de terris ad ipsam ecclesiam [c]de iure[c] pertinentibus per easdem cartas imposterum fierent certiores.[83] O quis dolor et que anxietas! Et quis tam dure ceruicis,[84] tam ferrei pectoris, tam adamantini cordis, ut hec audiat et se a lacrimis abstineat? Expulsis itaque theofilis a gremio matris sue, locum ipsum tam sanctum et tam honestum non solum presumtuose sed et irreuerenter allophili[d][85] occupauerunt, et hii Dani immo pagani fuere. E quorum collegio dum plerique, inflati spiritu superbie, die quadam in refectorio de more monachorum residerent et tam scuriliter quam incomposite in omnibus se haberent, accidit huiuscemodi miraculum quod non est sub silentio pretereundum.

[b–b] *over erasure* [c–c] *interlin.* [d] *this word continued the line into margin. It is probably in a different pen although the same hand. The word also appears in dry point*

[77] The phrase 'sancta sanctorum' appears at various points in the Bible; see e.g. Num. 4: 19; Heb. 9: 3.

[78] For Gideon, see Judg. 6–9.

[79] The allusion, like the sentence more generally, is somewhat unclear. Some reference is being made to the distinction between good sheep and bad goats in Matt. 25: 33. In addition, the lamb here must refer to Christ.

[80] See Ps. 131: 17.

[81] Cf. Lam. 1: 1: 'Quomodo sedet sola civitas plena populo', 'How doth the city sit solitary, that was full of people'. The place of the word 'uiolente' within the sense of the sentence is somewhat unclear, and the word indeed could be corrupt.

with such unhappy devastation, not even fearing in the least to place their hands upon things most holy.[77] So the foreign people overturned the house of Gideon,[78] the young goat seized the covenant of the lamb,[79] the pitiful people were scourging the horn of David,[80] and with the whole people engaged in violence, the city sat solitary.[81] So towns together with monasteries were overthrown, reminders of which still provide evidence in very many places where the partially ruined remains of walls and buildings are to this day observed.[82] What's more, those Danes passed from kingdom to kingdom and from people to people, raising insolence of spirit like a mark of victory, and at length they made their evil entry into Wessex, where they vented their fury just as elsewhere. Finally, they entirely drove out the monks and destroyed with hostile hand, leonine ferocity, and detestable greed the sacrosanct and venerable house of Abingdon, which so many holy kings and such authoritative men, of whom we have spoken above, had founded and endowed with various endowments, so that nothing is reported to have remained there besides the walls. However, it was divinely provided that the relics of saints with the charters of that house, as we have recorded above in this book and also as recorded below, were secretly preserved, for this possibility, that in future through those charters the restorers and also repairers of that monastery would be more certain of the lands pertaining by right to that church.[83] Oh what grief and what anxiety! And who is so stiff-necked,[84] so steely spirited, so very hard-hearted, that he may hear these matters and refrain from tears? So when the lovers of God had been expelled from their mother's bosom, the Philistines[85] not only presumptuously but also irreverently occupied that place, which is so holy and honourable, and these Danes moreover were pagans. While one day very many of their company, puffed up with the spirit of pride, were sitting like monks in the refectory and were behaving themselves in all respects in a manner both scurrilous and disorderly, there occurred the following miracle which should not be passed over in silence.

[82] Cf. a similar sentence with some variations above, p. 28.

[83] See above, p. cxxxiii.

[84] See Exod. 32: 9, 33: 3, 5, 34: 9; Deut. 9: 13.

[85] The word 'allophilus' is used by Aldhelm, *De Virginitate* (prose), LIII, in *Aldhelmi Opera Omnia*, ed. R. Ehwald (MGH, Auctores Antiquissimi, xv; Berlin, 1919), p. 311, with reference to the 'giant of the Philistines [*alliphilorum*]', that is, Goliath.

B38. *Quomodo imago Danos expulit de refectorio.*[86]

Imago etenim affixa cruci, que in medio mense edicioris fuit posita,
[i. 48] imago quasi moleste ferens paganorum ingluuiem discumbentium, motu mirabili et brachio mobili necnon digito flexibili, lapides de maceria refectorii potenti uirtute et admirabili fortitudine extraxisse narratur, quibus mediantibus inaudita terribili turbine in ipsam seuiebat multitudinem paganorum. Verumptamen nec a tali lapidatione imago citra destitit donec uniuersos Satani satellites, [a]non pedetentim aut more testudinum[a] incedentes, extra refectorium penitus expulisset. Hec sunt Christi opera, omni laude digna, cui nichil est difficile. Qui licet naturas singulas certis astringi regulis statuerit, et sic prouiderit ut a prescriptis formulis nature eedem nullo possint conatu ultra naturam progredi uel per se citra regredi, tamen
fo. 15v earum auctor, quando uult et ubi uult | et sicut uult,[87] per quamlibet naturam, tam rationalem quam irrationalem, animatam et inanimatam, mirabilia sua mirifice dilucidat, ut cognoscatur ab omnibus quod quotiens factus superbit in factorem, aut plasmatus in figulum, uel creatura contra creatorem suum erigit calcaneum,[88] iusto Dei iudicio sciat se labi in profundum dum minus circumspecte tendit in altum. Discat itaque homo condicionis misere ex istius miraculi explanatione quam periculosum sit superbire et quam perniciosum aliquid arrogare, uel etiam cuiquam derogare, aut dilapidationi abrogare.[89] Intendat etiam quam tutum est humilitatis gradum sectari, necnon Deum timere, cui genuflectitur omne,[90] insimul et quam honestum ipsam legem naturalem qua nulla lex equior aut iustior firmiter obseruare, qua dicitur: 'Quod tibi non uis fieri, alii ne feceris.'[91]

B39. *De alio miraculo.*

Aliut etiam miraculum, non post multi[a] temporis elapsum, per
[i. 49] eandem imaginem, nec minus admiratione dignum, accidisse perhibetur.[b] Frater etenim quidam cum refectorium intrasset sitim leuaturus quam diutius sustinebat, nullo secum comite sui ordinis,

B38 [a–a] *this line is written over an erasure*

B39 [a] *corr. from* multum [b] *corr. from* peribetur *by interlin.*

[86] The miracle is also briefly mentioned in the late medieval Abingdon chronicle roll; Salter, 'Chronicle roll', 728.

[87] Cf. above, p. 238.

[88] i.e. rebel; note John 13: 18, 'levabit contra me calcaneum suum'.

[89] The sense of this sentence, which gives the morals of the preceding story, is slightly unclear, and it is possible that the text is corrupt.

B38. *How an image expelled the Danes from the refectory.*[86]

An image fixed to a cross, placed on the middle of the most distinguished table, an image as it were bearing ill the gluttony of the dining pagans, is said to have pulled out with powerful force and admirable strength the stones from the refectory wall, with a wondrous movement, a moving arm, and also a bending finger. By these means it vented its rage on the multitude of pagans with an unheard of and terrifying storm. Furthermore, the image did not cease such a stoning until it had entirely expelled all the followers of Satan from the refectory who did not go at a slow walking pace or like a tortoise. These are the works, worthy of all praise, of Christ, for whom nothing is difficult. Although He has decreed that each nature be bound by certain rules, and thus provides that by such regulations these natures cannot through any effort move beyond their nature or of themselves move back from it, however their Author, when He wishes and where He wishes and as He wishes,[87] may wondrously elucidate His marvels through any nature, both rational and irrational, animate and inanimate, so that everyone may learn that as often as the made disdains the maker, or the fashioned disdains the designer, or the creature raises its heel against its creator,[88] it is to know that by the just judgement of God it will slip into the depths as long as it stretches for the heights with insufficient caution. Therefore let man, of pitiful condition, learn from the exegesis of this miracle how dangerous it is to be proud, and how ruinous to claim anything as one's own, or even to detract from anything, or to give it up to wastefulness.[89] Let him direct his mind to how safe it is to follow the steps of humility, and also to fear God, to whom everything kneels,[90] and at the same time how honourable it is to observe firmly that natural law than which no law is more equitable or just, by which it is said: 'Do not do to another what you do not wish to be done to yourself.'[91]

B39. *Concerning another miracle.*

After not long had passed, another miracle, no less worthy of admiration, is also reported to have happened through that image. When one of the brethren, accompanied by no fellow monk, entered the refectory to slake his long-endured thirst and, before he tasted the

[90] Cf. Rom. 14: 11, Phil. 2: 10.

[91] Cf. Tob. 4: 16 'Quod ab alio oderis fieri tibi, vide ne tu aliquando alteri facias'; see also Matt. 7: 12 'Omnia ergo quaecumque vultis ut faciant vobis homines, et vos facite illis. Haec est enim lex, et prophetae'; Luke 6: 31 'Et prout vultis ut faciant vobis homines, et vos facite illis similiter.'

non factus inmemor priusquam quippiam gustasset de liquore signo crucis poculum signauit et more solito benedictionem proferens,[92] respondit imago uiua uoce ac ore rotundo, distincte et aperte dicens. Verum quod cum frater audisset, factus quasi in extasi quia neminem uidit, et inconsueti[c] uocis representationem perpendisset, sedit solitarius ac quidnam hoc esse posset secum propensius deliberauit. Quid multa? Tandem ad memoriam reuocans quod in dubiis benignius et sanccius est interpretandum, oculos attollit ad imaginem et, recolens quam magna et quam mirabilia Deus per illam subiectam creaturam fieri dignatus est, cruci neccessario duxit asscribendum quod fantasma sibi assolet preiudicare. Non est ergo dubium quin imago loqueretur, nec admiratione dignum si Deus, qui retrahit et tribuit, qui omnia creauit ex nichilo (id est non ex preiacenti materia), ex creatura inanimata uocem protulerit sonoram et quasi ex arteriis prolatam, qui quondam asino Balam mirabiliter contulit ut primo contra prophetam recalcitraret, deinde uoce uiua admoneret ne ulterius in uia pregrederetur.[93] Hec sunt tua, bone Ihesu, opera, cui laus et gloria.

B40. *De reedificatione Abbendonie.*

Nunc uero restat ut ad reedificationem domus Abbendonie stilum uertamus reciprocum. Adelredo[a] itaque Westsaxonum rege uiam
[i. 50] uniuerse carnis ingresso, pius ac misericors Dominus noster Ihesus Christus, cuius uniuerse uie misericordia et ueritas,[94] qui pios pati et impios regnare permittit, orphanis sancte matris ecclesie Abbendonie in tribulationibus factus est adiutor oportunus sui gratia qui cum seruis suis tantam nouit misericordiam. Suscitauit enim successores regis Adelredi, qui pio desiderio (utpote declarabitur inferius)
fo. 16r repara|tioni ipsius domus certatim curam impendebant, inter quos fuit predictus rex Ælfredus, Adelredi frater regis, qui primus post Adelredum regni suscepit gubernacula.[95] Hic uero mala malis accumulans, quasi Iudas inter duodecim, uillam in qua cenobium situm est, que uulgari onomate[b] Abbendonia appellatur, cum omnibus

[c] inconsuetis *MS*

B40 [a] *corr. to* Adelfredo *by interlin., not necessarily by main hand* [b] *altered in a later hand to* ydiomate

[92] On such observances, see e.g. R. J. Bartlett, *England under the Norman and Angevin Kings* (Oxford, 2000), p. 444; note also William of Malmesbury, *Gesta pontificum*, bk. iv, c. 140, ed. Hamilton, p. 282, stating that Wulfstan II of Worcester 'would never omit the benedictions that the English used to make over their drink'.

[93] See Num. 22: 21–30.

[94] Ps. 24 (25): 10 'Universae viae Domini, misericordia et veritas'.

drink, did not forget to mark the cup with the sign of the cross and set forth a blessing as usual,[92] the image replied with a living voice and polished speech, talking distinctly and openly. When indeed the brother had heard this, he was, as it were, stupefied because he saw no one; he assessed this manifestation of a strange voice, and then he sat down by himself and considered very eagerly what this could be. What's more, finally remembering at length that interpretation in doubtful matters should tend to the kinder and the more holy, he raised his eyes to the image and recalled how great and how wondrous things God deemed it worthy to be done through that subject creation, and he therefore thought it necessary to ascribe to the cross what ordinarily he would assume to be an illusion. For it is not to be doubted that an image may speak, nor does it merit wonder if God, who takes back and bestows, who created everything from nothing (that is, not from pre-existing matter), should bring forth from an inanimate creation a ringing voice, as if brought forth from the windpipe, who once wondrously assigned Balaam to an ass so that at first it kicked back against the prophet and then with a living voice admonished him not to go further on the way.[93] These are your works, good Jesus, to whom praise and glory.

B40. *Concerning the rebuilding of Abingdon.*

Now indeed it remains for us to turn our pen, which moves back and forth, to the rebuilding of the house of Abingdon. Therefore, when Æthelred king of the West Saxons had gone the way of all flesh, our compassionate and merciful Lord Jesus Christ, all of whose ways are mercy and truth,[94] who allows the pious to suffer and the impious to reign, became the advantageous supporter of the orphans of the holy mother church of Abingdon in their tribulations by the grace of Him who knows such mercy in relation to His servants. For He aroused King Æthelred's successors, who by pious desire gradually devoted care to the restoration of this house (as will be set out below), amongst whom was the aforesaid King Alfred, brother of King Æthelred, who first took up the reins of the kingdom after Æthelred.[95] He indeed piled evils on evils, like Judas amongst the twelve, and violently took away from that monastery the village in which the monastery is

[95] See above, p. cxii, on the *History*'s treatment of Alfred. There is confusion in the text in this and the preceding sentence, indicated by the change of 'Adelredo' to 'Adelfredo' and the use of 'predictus' with reference to Alfred, even though he had probably not been referred to earlier. The very logic of the present sentence is obscure, given what the *History* goes on to say about Alfred.

suis appendiciis, a predicto cenobio uiolenter abstraxit, uictori Domino pro uictoria qua functus est de Danis super Essedune uictis inparem reddens talionem.[96]

Tempore suo memoratus rex Alfredus uillam que Appelford appellatur cuidam fideli suo pro seruitio et homagio suo,[97] nomine Deormodo, dedit et, ut carta ipsius regis testatur, concessit ei ut quemcumque sibi uellet heredem constitueret. Constituit itaque predictus Deormodus heredem sibi Deum et beatam Mariam et ecclesiam Abbendonie post decessum[c] ipsius regis donationem ipsam ratam attestante et inconcussam. Cuius carte tenor hic est:

[i. 51] **B41.** *Carta Alfredi regis West Saxonum de Appelford.*
Charters of Abingdon Abbey, no. 18; above, c. 18.

[i. 52] fo. 16[v] **B42.** *De morte Alfredi regis West Saxonum et successione Edwardi filii sui.*

Mortuo Ælfredo rege, successit ei Ædwardus filius eius. Iste uero Ædwardus cuidam ministro suo, Ælfstano nomine, uillam que dicitur Sefouenhamtune[a] dedit et carta sua confirmauit, insuper et ei
[i. 53] concessit ut quemcumque sibi uellet post decessum suum heredem facere[b] de eadem terra, sine ulla contradiccione facere posset, et hoc idem carta regis testatur.[98] Cuius carte memoratus Ælfstanus fretus munimine ipsam terram dedit Deo et beate Marie et domui Abbendonie et monachis ibidem Deo seruientibus, in puram et perpetuam helemosinam, et in signum huius donationis, sicut tunc temporis consuetudo fuit, cartam regis (per quam totum[c] ius suum in memorata terra habebat) super altare beate Marie Abbendonie, coram ipso rege et magnatibus suis, nemine donationi sue contradicente, posuit. Cuius carte tenor hic est:

B43. *Carta regis Edwardi de Seuenhantun.*
Charters of Abingdon Abbey, no. 142.[99]

[c] *it seems likely that the word* suum *followed by another such as* auctoritate *or* carta *is missing here*

B42 [a] *final* e *interlin.* [b] *corr. from* faceret [c] totum *rep. MS*

[96] Cf. above, pp. 32, 50. For the battle of Ashdown, see *ASC*, *s.a.* 871, which makes clear that the battle took place before Æthelred's death following Easter, 15 Apr. 871.

[97] On such anachronisms concerning Anglo-Saxon lordship, see above, p. clvii.

[98] Sevington in Leigh Delamere, Wiltshire. The charter below, in fact, is one of Edward the Confessor's and the compiler of this version of the *History* has wrongly placed it in Edward the Elder's time.

situated, commonly called Abingdon, with all its appendages, rendering inappropriate compensation to the victorious Lord for the victory which he had enjoyed against the defeated Danes at Ashdown.[96]

In his time King Alfred gave the village called Appleford to a loyal man of his named Deormod, for his service and homage,[97] and, as that king's charter witnesses, he granted to him that he might appoint whomsoever he wished as his heir. Therefore the aforesaid Deormod appointed as his heir after his death God and the blessed Mary and the church of Abingdon, with the authority of that king witnessing his gift strong and unshakeable. The terms of his charter are as follows:

B41. *Charter of Alfred king of the West Saxons concerning Appleford.*
Charters of Abingdon Abbey, no. 18; above, c. 18.

B42. *Concerning the death of Alfred king of the West Saxons, and the succession of Edward his son.*
After King Alfred died, his son Edward succeeded him [899]. This Edward, indeed, gave and by his charter confirmed the village called Sevington to a thegn of his named Ælfstan, and in addition granted to him that he might make whomsoever he wished to make his heir concerning that land after his death, without any contradiction, as witnessed by the king's charter.[98] Strengthened by that charter's protection, Ælfstan gave the land to God and the blessed Mary and the house of Abingdon and the monks serving God there, in pure and perpetual alms, and, as was then the custom, as a symbol of this gift placed the king's charter (through which he had all his right in that land) on the altar of the blessed Mary at Abingdon, in the presence of the king himself and his magnates, with no one contradicting his gift. The terms of his charter are as follows:

B43. *Charter of King Edward concerning Sevington.*
Charters of Abingdon Abbey, no. 142.[99]

[99] Sawyer, no. 999. This charter records Edward the Confessor granting ten hides in Sevington to Ælfstan. It is dated 1043. *Charters of Abingdon Abbey*, p. 556, states that 'there seem good reasons to think that [the document] is essentially authentic, although the confused order of the subscriptions raises some problems'. The beneficiary was almost certainly the substantial landholder Ælfstan of Boscombe, whom *Domesday* records as holding the land *TRE*; see *DB* i, fo. 71^{v}; Clarke, *English Nobility*, pp. 46, 64, 126, 229–31. Apart from the presence of this charter in the archive, there is no other evidence of Abingdon interest in this land.

[i. 56] **B44.** *Quomodo rex dedit Aþelhuni f⟨i⟩l⟨i⟩o Hordwella.*[100]

fo. 17r Iste uero Eadwardus rex tocius Anglie, dum adhuc uitales carperet
fo. 17v auras,[101] cuidam fasallo[102] suo Tata Aeðelhuni f⟨i⟩l⟨i⟩o[a] | dedit Hordwelle trium manensium in puram et perpetuam helemosinam et carta sua confirmauit. Insuper et ei concessit ut quemcumque sibi uellet post decessum suum heredem facere de eadem terra, sine ulla contradictione, facere posset, et hoc idem carta regis testatur. Cuius carte memoratus Tata Æðelhuni f⟨i⟩l⟨i⟩us fretus munimine ipsam terram dedit Deo ⟨et⟩ beate Marie et domui Abbendonie et monachis ibidem Deo seruientibus, in puram et perpetuam helemosinam, et in signum huius donationis, sicut tunc temporis consuetudo fuit, cartam regis (per quam totum ius suum[b] in memorata terra habebat) super altare beate Marie Abbendonie coram ipso rege et magnatibus suis, nemine donationi sue contradicente, posuit.[103] Cuius carte tenor hic est:

B45. *Carta regis Edwardi de Hordwella.*
Charters of Abingdon Abbey, no. 19.[104]

[i. 59] **B46.** *De morte Edwardi regis et successione Adelstani filii sui.*[105]

fo. 18r Postquam uero Eadwardus rex Anglie Domino disponente uiam uniuerse carnis ingressus est, successit ei Athelstanus filius eius. Iste uero Athelstanus, post suscepta regni gubernacula subito,[106] tante pietatis ac uite sanctitatis extitisse peribetur ut granum sinapis quod in cordis eius orto bonus ortolanus, Dominus ac redemptor noster Ihesus, seminauerat mature radicatum ilico crescere cepisset in arborem magnam firmissime fidei et sancte spei insuper et caritatis inmense, que nec inuidet nec agit perperam.[107] Opera etenim que Deo sunt placabilia libenter uidit per discretionem, audiuit per obedientiam,

B44 [a] *this word is below the normal end of the column* [b] *followed by* quod *interlin. in different hand*

[100] The name of the recipient is problematic now, and perhaps was for the compiler of MS B. I follow Kelly in taking the peculiar name Æthelhuniflo to be a conflation of 'Æthelhuni' and 'filio'. The recipient of the charter would then be Æthelhun's son, Tata, who was probably a thegn; *Charters of Abingdon Abbey*, p. 84. Cf. Keynes, 'West Saxon charters', pp. 1146–7, and S. Keynes, 'Edward, king of the Anglo-Saxons', in Higham and Hill, eds., *Edward the Elder*, pp. 40–66, at 54, who argues that he was probably a Winchester priest.

[101] Vergil, *Aeneid*, i. 387–8; see also below, vol. ii. 332, 354.

[102] The word 'fasallus' is drawn from the charter which follows. For uses of the word, or near equivalents, to mean retainer, see above, p. 21 n. 63. Probably out of habit, the reviser has included the phrase 'in pure and perpetual alms' in a gift to a lay person, where it is inappropriate.

B44. *How the king gave Hardwell to the son of Æthelhun.* [100]
Moreover, that Edward, king of the whole of England, while he was still 'drawing the breath of life',[101] gave in pure and perpetual alms and by his charter confirmed Hardwell amounting to three hides to a retainer of his, Tata, son of Æthelhun.[102] In addition, he granted to him that he might make whomsoever he wished his heir concerning that land after his death, without any contradiction, as witnessed by the king's charter. Strengthened by the protection of this charter, Tata, son of Æthelhun, gave that land to God and the blessed Mary and the house of Abingdon and the monks serving God there, in pure and perpetual alms, and, as was then the custom, as a symbol of this gift placed the king's charter (through which he had all his right in that land) on the altar of the blessed Mary at Abingdon, in the presence of the king himself and his magnates, with no one contradicting his gift.[103] The terms of his charter are as follows:

B45. *Charter of King Edward concerning Hardwell.*
Charters of Abingdon Abbey, no. 19.[104]

B46. *Concerning the death of King Edward and the succession of Æthelstan his son.*[105]
After Edward king of the English by the Lord's disposition had gone the way of all flesh, his son Æthelstan succeeded him [924]. After he had taken up the reins of the kingdom suddenly,[106] this Æthelstan is reported to have been of such piety and holiness of life that the mustard seed which the good gardener, our Lord and redeemer Jesus, had sown in the garden of his heart became maturely rooted and began to grow there into a great tree of the strongest faith and holy hope and also of immense love, which neither is envious nor acts wrongly.[107] For works pleasing to God, he willingly saw through discernment, he heard through obedience, he tasted through love, he

[103] It seems more likely that Hardwell passed to Abingdon in the time of Æthelred the Unready; see above, c. 108.

[104] Sawyer, no. 369. This charter records Edward the Elder confirming the above three hides to Tata, which Edward's grandfather Æthelwulf had originally given (probably to Æthelhun), but whose charter had been rendered almost completely illegible by submersion in water. It is dated 903. *Charters of Abingdon Abbey*, p. 83, states that 'there is no particular reason to question its authenticity'.

[105] Cf. the passage in MS C, above, p. 34.

[106] This may refer to the death of Edward's son Ælfweard very soon after Edward's own demise; *ASC*, 'D', *s.a.* 924; John of Worcester, *Chronicle*, ii. 384.

[107] See Matt. 13: 31–2; Mark 4: 31–2; Luke 13: 19. The three theological virtues of faith, hope, and love go back to 1 Cor. 13: 13.

gustauit per caritatem, olfecit per spem et fidem, necnon tetigit pariter et consummauit per bonam operationem. In ecclesiis etenim quam plurimis destructis iterum reedificandis summam curam ac diligentissimam diligentiam incessanter impendere satagebat. Inter quas cen-
[i. 60] obium Abbendonie, Chinato abbate locum ipsum tunc temporis gubernante, tanta sinceritate tantoque amoris priuilegio est amplexatus ut non solum illud uariis ditaret ornamentis uerum etiam amplis eam dotaret possessionibus. Quibus possessionibus carte ipsius regis subsequentes ueritatis peribent testimonium, quarum prima hec est:

B47. *Carta Aþelstani regis de Dumeltuna.*[a]
Charters of Abingdon Abbey, no. 22; above, c. 19.

[i. 64] fo. 19ʳ B48. *Carta regis Aþelstani de Xalingeforda.*
Charters of Abingdon Abbey, no. 25; above, c. 20.

[i. 66] fo. 19ᵛ B49. *Carta regis Aþelstani de Swinford.*[108]
Charters of Abingdon Abbey, no. 26; above, c. 22.

[i. 68] fo. 20ʳ B50. *Carta regis Aþelstani de Sanford.*
Charters of Abingdon Abbey, no. 27; above, c. 21.

[i. 69] fo. 20ᵛ B51. *Quomodo Aþelstanus senator dedit Offentuna.*
Temporibus etiam Æthelstani regis fuit quidam uir nobilis, Æthelstanus senator, qui primo domui Abbendonie et monachis ibidem Deo seruientibus uillam que Vffentuna appellatur, cum omnibus ad
[i. 70] illam integre pertinentibus, sicut carta ipsi Æthelstani senatoris testatur, dedit et concessit in puram et perpetuam elemosinam. Cuius carte hec est notificatio:

B52. *Carta Aþelstani senatoris de Offentuna.*
Charters of Abingdon Abbey, no. 28; above, c. 23.

[i. 72] fo. 21ʳ B53. *Adelstanus rex dedit Alfrico ministro suo Wachenesfeld.*[109]
Eodem etiam tempore prefatus rex Athelstanus cuidam ministro suo, nomine Elfrico, dedit Wachenesfeld uiginti cassatorum, eo tenore ut, cuicumque post suum decessum heredi uellet donare, libertatem donationis regia auctoritate inde haberet. Sic enim carta regis testatur, unde memoratus Elfricus, in remissionem peccatorum suorum et pro animabus predecessorum suorum, eandem uillam, cum omnibus ad illam pertinentibus, de consensu et uoluntate regis

B47 [a] *an illustration of the king appears at the start of this charter* smelt through hope and faith, and also he touched and likewise completed through good deeds. For he strove unceasingly to expend the utmost care and the greatest diligence in rebuilding again numerous destroyed churches. Amongst these he embraced with such great sincerity and so great a privilege of love the monastery of Abingdon, then governed by Abbot Cynath, that not only did he enrich it with various ornaments but also endowed it with extensive possessions. The following charters of this king present the testament of truth for these possessions, of which charters this is the first:

B47. *Charter of King Æthelstan concerning Dumbleton.*
Charters of Abingdon Abbey, no. 22; above, c. 19.

B48. *Charter of King Æthelstan concerning Shellingford.*
Charters of Abingdon Abbey, no. 25; above, c. 20.

B49. *Charter of King Æthelstan concerning Swinford.*[108]
Charters of Abingdon Abbey, no. 26; above, c. 22.

B50. *Charter of King Æthelstan concerning Sandford.*
Charters of Abingdon Abbey, no. 27; above, c. 21.

B51. *How Æthelstan 'the senator' gave Uffington.*
Also in King Æthelstan's times there was a noble man, Æthelstan 'the senator', who first gave and granted the village called Uffington, with everything entirely pertaining to it, in pure and perpetual alms to the house of Abingdon and the monks serving God there, as the charter of Æthelstan 'the senator' himself witnesses. This is the message of his charter:

B52. *Charter of Æthelstan 'the senator' concerning Uffington.*
Charters of Abingdon Abbey, no. 28; above, c. 23.

B53. *King Æthelstan gave Ælfric his thegn Watchfield.*[109]
Also at that time the aforementioned King Æthelstan gave Watchfield amounting to twenty hides to a thegn of his named Ælfric, on the terms that, to whomsoever he wished to give it as heir after his death, he would by royal authority have the freedom of giving. For so the king's charter witnesses, whence that Ælfric, for the remission of his sins and for his predecessors' souls, made this most sacred house of

[108] See above, p. xlv n. 188, for problems arising from the compiler of MS B reversing the order of appearance of this and the next charter, and from the forms of the texts he gives.

[109] Watchfield is listed in a diploma of King Æthelbald as an Abingdon estate, above, p. 12. Ælfric is too common a name for the grantee to be confidently identified.

hanc sacratissimam domum Abbendonie, nullo donationi sue contradicente, fecit heredem.[110] Et hec est subscriptio carte regis hanc donationem confirmantis:

[i. 73] B54. *Carta regis Adelstani de Wachenesfeld.*
Charters of Abingdon Abbey, no. 23.[111]

[i. 76] B55.[a]
fo. 22r *Charters of Abingdon Abbey*, no. 24.[112]

[i. 78] B56.[a] Consimili etiam modo rex Æthelstanus concessit alteri ministro
fo. 22v suo, nomine Ælfeah, Fearnbornþæn decem cassatorum, et ille similiter huic domui Abbendonie contulit. Et hec est carta regis subsequens:[113]

[i. 79] B57. *Carta regis Athelstani de Ferberga.*
Charters of Abingdon Abbey, no. 29.[114]

[i. 82] B58. *De Cealhgræfan, quomodo Adelstanus rex dedit Ealdredo ministro*
fo. 23v *suo.*

Idem etiam rex Æthelstanus concessit Ealdredo ministro suo Cealhgræfan quinque manentium, et ipse ipsam uillam domui Abbendonie contulit eodem modo quo supra.[115] Et hec est carta regis hanc donationem confirmantis:

[i. 83] B59. *Carta regis Adelstani de Chelegraue.*
Charters of Abingdon Abbey, no. 21.[116]

B55 [a] *the rubricator failed to provide a heading, although the appropriate space had been left*

B56 [a] *the rubricator failed to provide a heading, although the appropriate space had been left*

[110] *Charters of Abingdon Abbey*, p. 103, takes B64 below—which mentions King Edmund confirming Watchfield to Abingdon—as a possible indication that the statement that Ælfric gave the land to Abingdon was, for once, correct. The passage inserted by the compiler of the later version of the *History* 'probably has some genuine foundation, and may be based on a contemporary record of some kind'. However, the possibility remains that the compiler simply derived his story of Ælfric's gift from Abingdon's later possession of the land.

[111] Sawyer, no. 413. This charter records Æthelstan granting the above twenty hides to Ælfric. It is dated 931. *Charters of Abingdon Abbey*, p. 102, describes this charter as 'an example of the very elaborate and standardised diplomas which were produced in the name of King Æthelstan between 928 and 934/5'. Note that D. N. Dumville, 'Ecclesiastical lands and the defence of Wessex in the first Viking-Age', in *Wessex and England from Alfred to Edgar* (Woodbridge, 1992), pp. 29–54, at 40 n. 55, describes it as 'genuine (but corrupt)', although he does not elaborate.

[112] Sawyer, no. 1604. This text records Æthelstan granting six hides in *Bulthesworthe* to his thegn Wulfnoth. It is dated 931. The *History* gives only a highly abbreviated version of the dispositive clause of this charter, no doubt because it so resembled the preceding elaborate document. Boundary, sanction, and date clauses are given in full. *Charters of*

Abingdon heir of that village, with everything pertaining to it, by the king's consent and will, with no one contradicting his gift.[110] And this is the text of the king's charter confirming this gift:

B54. *Charter of King Æthelstan concerning Watchfield.*
Charters of Abingdon Abbey, no. 23.[111]

B55.
Charters of Abingdon Abbey, no. 24.[112]

B56. Also, in a similar way King Æthelstan granted Farnborough amounting to twenty hides to another thegn of his named Ælfheah, and he likewise conferred it on this house of Abingdon. And the following is the king's charter:[113]

B57. *Charter of King Æthelstan concerning Farnborough.*
Charters of Abingdon Abbey, no. 29.[114]

B58. *Concerning Chalgrave, how King Æthelstan gave it to Ealdred his thegn.*
The same King Æthelstan also granted Chalgrave amounting to five hides to Ealdred his thegn, and the latter conferred that village on the house of Abingdon in the same way as above.[115] And this is the king's charter confirming this gift:

B59. *Charter of King Æthelstan concerning Chalgrave.*
Charters of Abingdon Abbey, no. 21.[116]

Abingdon Abbey, p. 106, states that 'there is no reason to think that the full text of [the document] available to the scribe of [MS B] was not authentic'. See above, c. 106, for the land passing to Abingdon.

[113] Ælfheah's identity cannot be established with certainty, but he may be the future ealdorman of Wessex; *Charters of Abingdon Abbey*, p. 124. The statement that Ælfheah gave the land to Abingdon may be doubted; King Harthacnut and perhaps Æthelred the Unready granted Farnborough, Berkshire, to Abingdon, above cc. 99 (p. 152), 117.

[114] Sawyer, no. 411. This charter also survives in a 16th-c. copy of a lost single sheet, Cambridge, Corpus Christi College 111, pp. 139–41. It records Æthelstan granting the above ten hides to Ælfheah, following Ælfheah's request for a grant of some land 'in eternal inheritance'. It is dateable to 934/5 × 938. *Charters of Abingdon Abbey*, p. 123, states that 'it seems likely that the charter . . . can be accepted as fundamentally authentic'. For an earlier charter possibly concerning the same ten hides, see above, B36.

[115] However, see above, c. 106, for the *History*'s account of a woman called Ælfgifu giving Chalgrave and *Bulthesworthe* to Abingdon at the end of the 10th c.

[116] Sawyer, no. 396; trans. *EHD*, i. no. 103. This charter records Æthelstan granting five hides at Chalgrave and Tebworth to Ealdred, which Ealdred had bought from the Danes for ten pounds of gold and silver, on the orders of Edward the Elder and Ealdorman Æthelred of Mercia. He has now paid Æthelstan 150 *mancuses*, it would seem for freeing the land from all secular burden except the *trinoda necessitas*. The charter is dated 926. *Charters of Abingdon Abbey*, pp. 90–1, takes the charter as authentic.

[i. 85] **B60.** *Quomodo Aþelstanus rex dedit Beorthwaldingtun.*[117]

fo. 24r Predictus rex Æþels⟨t⟩anus dedit cuidam religiose femine, nomine Eadulfu Eadlufa, Beorhtwaldingtun quindecim manentium eodem modo quo supra, et ipsa illam uillam domui Abbendonie contulit.[118] Et hec est carta regis:

B61. *Karta regis Aþelstani de Beorthwaldingtun.*
Charters of Abingdon Abbey, no. 30.[119]

[i. 88] fo. 24v **B62.** *De muneribus que misit Hugo Capet rex Francie Aþelstano regi Anglie.*[120]

Eodem tempore, rege illustri Anglorum Æþelstano tempore paschali apud Abbendoniam cum comitibus et baronibus suis curiam suam tenente plenariam, prout regio conuenit honori, aduenerunt nuntii regis Francie Hugonis, cognomento Capet, offerentes regi uaria
fo. 25r exenia aurea et argentea, necnon et alia super aurum et argentum | et lapidem preciosum dulciora,[121] reliquias uidelicet preciosas cum omni reuerentia tractandas pariter et uenerandas, scilicet partem spinee corone et partem claui Domini, uexillum etiam sancti Mauricii gloriossisimi martiris et Tebee legionis principis, cum precioso digito sancti Dionisii martiris.[122] Quibus a rege gratanter susceptis, peticioni nuntiorum de sorore sua regi Francie nubenda benignum prebuit assensum. Dedit etiam predictus rex A. memorata sanctuaria, in teca argentea cum omni honore recondita, huic sacratissime domui Abbendonie, quorum munimenta super uariis egritudinibus, diuina opitulante clementia, multis adhuc prebent subsidia.[123]

[117] Berkshire.

[118] The charter simply calls this woman 'Eadulfu'. It seems most likely that 'Eadlufa' is a product of confusion over an unfamiliar name; perhaps significantly 'Eadulfu' appears at the end of one line, 'Eadlufa' at the start of the next.

[119] Sawyer, no. 448. This charter records Æthelstan granting the above fifteen hides to Eadulfu. It is dated 939. *Charters of Abingdon Abbey*, p. 127, states that this charter 'is typical of the royal diplomas which were issued in the last five years of Æthelstan's reign . . . and there is no reason to question its authenticity'. Apart from the presence of this charter in the archive, there is no other evidence of Abingdon interest in this land.

[120] *ASC*, 'D', and Flodoard of Reims (trans. *EHD*, i. 344), place the marriage of Æthelstan's sister *s.a.* 926. It was in fact not the king of France, but Hugh, duke of the Franks and count of Paris, who married Æthelstan's sister. This is the first reference in the narratives in MS B to a 'king of England/the English'. On the meeting at Abingdon, see also Stenton, *Anglo-Saxon England*, p. 345; M. Wood, 'The making of King Æthelstan's empire: An English Charlemagne?', in P. Wormald *et al.*, eds., *Ideal and Reality in Frankish and Anglo-Saxon Society: Studies Presented to J. M. Wallace-Hadrill* (Oxford, 1983), pp. 250–72, at 266–7; S. Sharp, 'The West Saxon tradition of dynastic marriage: With

B60. *How King Æthelstan gave Brightwalton.*[117]
The aforesaid King Æthelstan gave Brightwalton amounting to fifteen hides to a woman of religious life, named Eadwulfu Eadlufa, in the same way as above, and she conferred that village on the house of Abingdon.[118] And this is the king's charter:

B61. *Charter of King Æthelstan concerning Brightwalton.*
Charters of Abingdon Abbey, no. 30.[119]

B62. *Concerning the gifts that Hugh Capet, king of France, sent to Æthelstan, king of England.*[120]
At that time, at Easter when the illustrious king of the English Æthelstan was holding his full court at Abingdon with his earls and barons, as befits royal honour, messengers of the king of France, Hugh, surnamed Capet, arrived, offering the king various gold and silver gifts, and others sweeter than gold and silver and precious stone,[121] that is, precious relics to be treated with all reverence and also to be venerated, specifically part of a thorn of the crown and part of a nail of the Lord, and the standard of St Maurice the most glorious martyr and commander of the Theban legion, with a precious finger of St Denis the martyr.[122] When the king had accepted these with thanks, he gave his cordial assent to the messengers' request that his sister be married to the king of France. The aforesaid King Æthelstan gave those relics, concealed with all honour in a silver reliquary, to this most sacred house of Abingdon, and, helped by divine clemency, the relics' defences against diverse sufferings still provide aid for many.[123]

special reference to Edward the Elder', in Higham and Hill, eds., *Edward the Elder*, pp. 79–88, at 85–6.

[121] Cf. Ps. 18: 11 (19: 10) 'Desiderabilia super aurum et lapidem pretiosum multum; et dulciora super mel et favum.'

[122] For St Maurice and his Theban legion, martyred in *c.*287, see *Oxford Dictionary of Saints*, pp. 272–3; for his standard, see L. H. Loomis, 'The holy relics of Charlemagne and King Athelstan: The lances of Longinus and St Mauricius', *Speculum*, xxv (1950), 437–56, at pp. 444–6. For Denis, bishop of Paris, martyred *c.*250, see *Oxford Dictionary of Saints*, pp. 105–6.

[123] The relic list compiled on Abbot Faritius's orders in the early 12th c. included a small piece of a nail from the crucifixion and the finger of St Denis but not the standard of St Maurice or part of the crown of thorns. According to William of Malmesbury, *Gesta regum*, bk. ii, c. 135, ed. Mynors *et al.*, i. 220, Æthelstan gave the piece of the crown of thorns, along with a piece of the Cross, to Malmesbury. See also L. H. Loomis, 'The Æthelstan gift story: Its influence on English chronicles and Carolingian romances', *Publications of the Modern Language Association of America*, lxvii(i) (1952), 521–37, and Loomis, 'Holy relics of Charlemagne'. On relics, see also above, p. clxxiii.

B63. *De morte Aþelstani regis.*

His itaque feliciter peractis non post multum temporis, memoratus rex Æþelstanus uiam uniuerse carnis ingressus est, cui[a] frater eius scilicet Eadmundus successit. Tempore uero istius Eadmundi orta est
[i. 89] controuersia inter abbatem et monac⟨h⟩os Abbendonie ex una parte et comprouinciales Oxenefordensis pagi ex altera parte, super quodam prato nomine Beri ecclesie Abbendonie de iure pertinente.[124] De cuius iure insimul et Dei clementia abbas et monachi plus presumentes quam de aliquibus exceptionibus dilatoriis aut cauillatoriis[125] uel obscuris placitis subterfugiis, de assensu communi et uoluntate pari, indictis sibi tribus diebus ieiuniis et orationibus, diuinam deuotissime implorabant clementiam, quatinus eorum ius merum de memorato prato cunctis mortalibus per eius omnipotentiam enucleatius claresceret. Quod dum serui Dei propensius actitarent, inspiratum est eis salubre consilium et (ut pium est credere) diuinitus prouisum. Die etenim statuto, mane surgentes monachi sumpserunt scutum rotundum cui imponebant manipulum frumenti et super manipulum cereum circumspecte quantitatis et grossitudinis. Quo accenso, scutum cum manipulo et cereo fluuio ecclesiam pretercurrenti committunt, paucis in nauiculo[b] fratribus subsequentibus. Precedebat itaque eos scutum et, quasi digito, demonstrans possessiones domui Abbendonie de iure adiacentes, nunc huc, nunc illuc, diuertens, nunc in dextra, nunc in sinistra parte fiducialiter eos prehibat, usque dum ueniret ad riuum prope pratum quod Beri uocatur, in quo cereus medium cursum Tamisie miraculose deserens se declinauit; et circumdedit pratum inter Tamisiam et Gifteleia,[126] quod hieme et multociens estate ex redundatione Tamisie in modum insule aqua circumdatur. Quo uiso miraculo ab astantibus et concurrentibus tam Berrocensis pagi quam Oxenefordensis nonnullis comprouincialibus, insimul et monachis cereum sequentibus, memoratum pratum domui Abbendonie est redditum, populo acclamante 'Ius Abbendonie, ius Abbendonie.' Ex hoc etiam miraculo omnes qui

B63 [a] *followed by* scilicet, *del. by expunction* [b] *possibly corr. from* nauicula*; the reading is not entirely clear*

[124] For this incident, see above, p. clxiv. According to EPNS, *Berkshire*, ii. 454, the name 'Berige' must mean barley island. It lay between the two arms of the river Thames east and south of New Hinksey; see also the boundary contained in *Charters of Abingdon Abbey*, nos. 51A, 56, 60, and commentaries.

B63. *Concerning the death of King Æthelstan.*

Not long after these matters had been happily concluded, King Æthelstan went the way of all flesh, and to him succeeded his brother Edmund [939]. In this Edmund's time, indeed, a controversy arose between the abbot and monks of Abingdon on one side and the locals of the county of Oxford on the other, concerning a certain meadow named Berry that pertained by right to the church of Abingdon.[124] The abbot and monks, setting greater store on their right and the clemency of God than on certain dilatory exceptions or quibblings[125] or obscure pleaded subterfuges, when three days of fasting and prayer had been imposed on them, by common consent and shared will most devoutly implored the divine clemency that by His omnipotence He very plainly clarify to all mortals their undiluted right concerning that meadow. While the servants of God were very eagerly carrying this out, they were inspired by beneficial and (as it is pious to believe) divinely provided counsel. For on the set day, as they were rising in the morning, the monks took up a round shield on which they placed a sheaf of wheat and on that sheaf a wax candle of prudent size and thickness. When this had been set alight, they committed the shield with the sheaf and the candle to the river flowing past the church, with a few brethren following in a small boat. And so the shield preceded them and, like a finger, pointed out the possessions belonging by right to the house of Abingdon, turning now this way, now that, confidently leading them now to the right, now to the left, until it reached the stream next to the meadow called Berry, to which the candle deviated, miraculously forsaking the middle of the Thames. It went round the meadow between the Thames and Iffley,[126] which through the flooding of the Thames is in winter and often in summer surrounded by water like an island. When this miracle had been seen by those standing there and the gathering of many locals of the counties both of Berkshire and Oxfordshire, as well as by the monks following the candle, that meadow was given back to the house of Abingdon, with the people acclaiming 'Abingdon's property, Abingdon's property'. Also, from

[125] For similar phraseology, see above, p. 256.

[126] A. Orchard, *A Critical Companion to 'Beowulf'* (Woodbridge, 2003), p. 103, comments that 'Gifteleia' is an early form of the place-name Iffley, suggesting an early origin for the story in the present text. However, EPNS, *Oxfordshire*, i. 32, notes the form 'Givetelei' in *Domesday Book*, and later use of 'Gyftelai'. The place-name form, in particular the presence of the letter 'G' at its start, therefore need not be evidence for an early origin for this story.

illud audierant tantus stupor inuaserat ut ab illo tempore usque ad
[i. 90] presens tempus non esset inuentus quispiam, rex uel dux[127] uel
fo. 25v princeps | uel aliquis alius prepotens, qui de eodem prato contra domum Abbendonie causam mouere aliquatenus auderet.

[i. 92] **B64.** *Carta regis Edmundi de Culeham.*[128]
Eadmundus, Æþelstano fratri succedens, confirmauit ecclesie Abbendonie Wachenesfeld, cum omnibus ad illam integre pertinentibus, quam predictus Aelfricus de consensu domini sui regis Æþelstani domui Abbendonie in puram et perpetuam contulerat elemosinam,[129] hac tamen condicione, ut Godescallus abbas Abbendonie et conuentus eiusdem loci concederent cuidam matrone regalis progeniei, nomine Ælfildæ, Culeham omnibus diebus uite sue, liberam et quietam, in ea forma[a] et omni eodem tenore quo rex Kenulfus concessit sororibus suis, que eandem uillam huic domui Abbendonie contulerunt, ut predictum est.[130] Et post decessum ipsius Ælfild, uilla memorata omni eodem modo ad proprios monachorum usus reuertetur. Quod utique sic factum est, memorata Ælfilda cedente in fatum. Sepulta est Ælfida matrona ista in capella quam in honore sancti Vincentii edificauerat.[131]

[i. 93] *Mete de Culeham.*
Charters of Abingdon Abbey, no. 31A.[132]

B65. *Dedit rex Eadmundus Wulfrico ministro suo Gareford.*[133]
Dedit etiam rex Eadmundus Wulfrico ministro suo Gareford quindecim manent⟨i⟩um, eo tenore, ut post decessum suum cuicumque uellet heredi daret. Et hec est carta regis donationem eius confirmantis:

B66. *Carta regis Eadmundi de Gareford.*
Charters of Abingdon Abbey, no. 33.[134]

B64 [a] *interlin.*

---

[127] It is uncertain whether *dux* should here be translated 'ealdorman', which is its meaning particularly in Anglo-Saxon charters, or more generally as 'leading noble', given that the passage deals with time up to the point of its composition.

[128] Despite this heading, the compiler of the later version of the *History* omitted the charter concerning Culham that appears above, c. 25. It seems that he attempted, probably deliberately, to hide any suggestion that there might have been a break in Abingdon's tenure of Culham. The royal grant of the land to Ælfhild 'perpetue', as recorded in the charter in MS C, would imply such a break. Instead, the present version states that Ælfhild had only a life tenure. See also above, pp. xlvii, lxxviii.

[129] See above, B53–B54 (*Charters of Abingdon Abbey*, no. 23).

[130] See above, B16.

[131] It is unclear whether this chapel was at Culham or at Abingdon; see *VCH, Oxfordshire*, vii. 35; Biddle *et al.*, 'Early history', pp. 47 n. 66, 64 n. 157.

this miracle such bewilderment seized all who had heard it that from that time to the present no one, king or ealdorman[127] or noble or any other very powerful man, has been found who has dared to move a case in any fashion against the house of Abingdon concerning that meadow.

B64. *Charter of King Edmund concerning Culham.*[128]
When Edmund succeeded his brother Æthelstan, he confirmed Watchfield to the church of Abingdon, with everything entirely pertaining to it, which the aforesaid Ælfric by the consent of his lord King Æthelstan had conferred on the house of Abingdon in pure and perpetual alms,[129] on this condition, however, that Godescealc abbot of Abingdon and the convent of that monastery grant Culham to a matron of royal lineage named Ælfhild, for all the days of her life, free and quit, in that form and on all the same terms as King Coenwulf granted to his sisters, who conferred that village on this house of Abingdon, as has been said earlier.[130] And after Ælfhild's death, that village was to revert in every way to the monks' own use. And thus it happened when Ælfhild yielded to death. That matron Ælfhild was buried in the chapel which had been built in honour of St Vincent.[131]

The bounds of Culham.
Charters of Abingdon Abbey, no. 31A.[132]

B65. *King Edmund gave Garford to his thegn Wulfric.*[133]
King Edmund also gave Garford amounting to fifteen hides to Wulfric his thegn, on these terms, that after his death he might give it to whomsoever he wish as his heir. And this is the charter of the king confirming his gift:

B66. *Charter of King Edmund concerning Garford.*
Charters of Abingdon Abbey, no. 33.[134]

[132] Sawyer, no. 1567. These bounds also appear in MS C, fos. 200^{v}–201^{r}, in the quire of charter bounds at the end of that manuscript, in the main scribe's hand; see also *Charters of Abingdon Abbey*, p. 588 (no. 40).

[133] i.e. Wulfric Cufing, on whom see above, p. cxxiii. Unusually this section does not specify that the lay beneficiary went on to grant the land to Abingdon. However, *DB* i, fo. 59^{r}, states that Abingdon held Garford in 1086, and had always done so. It answered for ten hides *TRE*, six in 1086.

[134] Sawyer, no. 471. This charter records Edmund granting the above fifteen hides to Wulfric, 'for his loving obedience and his pleasing money'. 943, rather than the stated date of 940, seems more likely. *Charters of Abingdon Abbey*, p. 139, states that the document 'is probably authentic, although the dating clause would appear to have been mis-copied'.

[i. 96] **B67.** *De Wealtham quomodo data erat.*

fo. 26v Idem rex Eadmundus dedit Ælfsige ministro suo Wealtham triginta mansarum. Et hec est carta regis per quam donatio ipsius Ælfsige de eadem terra huic domui, sicut tunc temporis consuetudo fuit, est confirmata:[135]

B68. *Carta regis Eadmundi de Wealtham.*
Charters of Abingdon Abbey, no. 32.[136]

[i. 99] **B69.** *De Earmundeslea et Appeltun.*[137]

fo. 27r Eodem anno[138] rex Eadmundus concessit Æþelstano ministro suo[139] Ermundeslea et Appeltun, eodem modo quo supra. Et hec est carta regis per quam donatio ipsius Æþelstani de eadem terra huic domui, sicut tunc temporis consuetudo fuit, est confirmata:

[i. 100] **B70.** *Carta regis Eadmundi de Ermundesleia.*
Charters of Abingdon Abbey, no. 34.[140]

[i. 103] **B71.** *De Lechamsteda quomodo data erat.*

fo. 28r Sequenti anno idem rex Eadmundus dedit Edrico ministro suo Lechamstede decem mansarum, eodem modo quo supra. Et hec est carta regis per quam donatio ipsius Edrici de eadem terra huic domui, sicut tunc consuetudo fuit, est confirmata:

B72. *Carta regis Eadmundi de Lechamstede.*
Charters of Abingdon Abbey, no. 37;[141] cf. above, c. 137, and below, B277.

[i. 106] **B73.** *De Linford quomodo data erat.*

fo. 29r Tercio anno concessit idem rex Eadmundus Ælfego ministro suo Linford sex manentium, eodem modo quo supra. Et hec est carta

[135] For various mentions of men called Ælfsige, none of which is certain to refer to this grantee, see *Charters of Abingdon Abbey*, p. 135. The land concerned may well be the equivalent of the modern parishes of Shottesbrooke, Waltham St Lawrence, and White Waltham, Berkshire; EPNS, *Berkshire*, iii. 635–8.

[136] Sawyer, no. 461. This charter records Edmund granting the above thirty hides to Ælfsige. It is dated 940. *Charters of Abingdon Abbey*, p. 134, states that this document 'seems likely to be authentic'. See below, B237 (*Charters of Abingdon Abbey*, no. 134), for a later charter probably concerning a portion of this land. It seems probable that the present charter entered the Abingdon archive only after the later grant (1007), and the statement that Ælfsige gave the land to Abingdon should not be believed. Apart from the presence of these two charters in the archive, there is no other evidence of Abingdon interest in this land. Eastern Berkshire was not an area where Abingdon held extensive lands, although it did have holdings at Whistley and Winkfield.

[137] *Charters of Abingdon Abbey*, p. 143, suggests that Appleton is introduced here and in

B67. *Concerning Waltham, how it was given.*
The same king Edmund gave Waltham amounting to thirty hides to Ælfsige his thegn. And this is the king's charter whereby Ælfsige's donation of that land to this house was confirmed, as was then the custom:[135]

B68. *Charter of King Edmund concerning Waltham.*
Charters of Abingdon Abbey, no. 32.[136]

B69. *Concerning* Earmundesleah *and Appleton.*[137]
In the same year,[138] King Edmund granted *Earmundesleah* and Appleton to Æthelstan his thegn,[139] in the same way as above. And this is the king's charter whereby Æthelstan's donation of that land to this house was confirmed, as was then the custom:

B70. *Charter of King Edmund concerning* Earmundesleah.
Charters of Abingdon Abbey, no. 34.[140]

B71. *Concerning Leckhampstead, how it was given.*
In the following year [943], the same King Edmund gave Leckhampstead amounting to ten hides to Eadric his thegn, in the same way as above. And this is the king's charter whereby Eadric's donation of that land to this house was confirmed, as was then the custom:

B72. *Charter of King Edmund concerning Leckhampstead.*
Charters of Abingdon Abbey, no. 37;[141] cf. above, c. 137, and below, B277.

B73. *Concerning Lyford, how it was given.*
In the next year [944], the same King Edmund granted Lyford amounting to six hides to Ælfheah his thegn, in the same way as

the charter as a gloss on an early place-name, to make the grant more comprehensible, or more precise.

[138] In fact the previous charter is dated 940, the one concerning *Earmundesleah* is dated 942.

[139] i.e. Æthelstan 'Half-king', ealdorman of East Anglia.

[140] Sawyer, no. 480. This charter records Edmund granting ten hides at *Earmundesleah* and Appleton to Ealdorman Æthelstan ('adoptiuo fideli meo comiti'). It is dated 942. *Charters of Abingdon Abbey*, p. 143, states that the document 'seems to be essentially authentic'.

[141] Sawyer, no. 491. This charter records Edmund granting the above ten hides, and a mill on the River Lambourn, to Eadric. It is dated 943. *Charters of Abingdon Abbey*, p. 156, states that the document 'seems to be authentic'. For a shortened version in King Eadwig's name, which appears in both MSS of the *History* in the context of the 11th-c. dispute over Leckhampstead, see above, c. 137, below, B277. The compiler of MS B presumably assumed they were two different charters because of the different kings named. The non-chronological positioning of the charter in MS C may also have led to confusion.

regis per quam donatio ipsius Ælfegi de eadem terra huic domui, sicut tunc temporis consuetudo fuit, est confirmata:[142]

B74. *Carta regis Edmundi de Linford.*
Charters of Abingdon Abbey, no. 38.[143]

[i. 109] fo. 29^v^ B75. *De Bleobirg,[a] quomodo Eadmundus rex dedit.*[144]
Eodem anno Eadmundus rex dedit Ælfrico ministro suo Bleobirg centum mansarum, eodem modo quo supra. Et hec est carta regis per quam donatio ipsius Ælfrici de eadem terra huic domui, sicut tunc consuetudo fuit, est confirmata:[145]

B76. *Carta regis Eadmundi de Bleobirg.*
Charters of Abingdon Abbey, no. 36.[146]

[i. 113] fo. 30^v^ B77. *Quomodo rex Eadmundus dedit Winkefeld et Swileie.*
Item eodem anno[147] dedit rex Eadmundus Sæþriþe, religiose femine, Winchefeld et Swinleie undecim cassatorum, et ipse de consensu regis Deo et beate Marie et domui Abbendonie et monachis ibidem
[i. 114] Deo seruientibus, in puram et perpetuam elemosinam. Et hec est carta regis hanc donationem confirmans:

B78. *Carta regis Eadmundi de Winkefeld et Swinlea.*
Charters of Abingdon Abbey, no. 35; above, c. 58.

[i. 117] fo. 31^v^ B79. *De Brinnigetuna,*[148] *quomodo data erat.*
Concessit idem rex Eadmundus e⟨o⟩dem anno Ordulfo ministro suo Brinniggetune uiginti mansarum, eodem modo quo supra.[149] Et hec est carta regis per quam donatio[a] ipsius Ordulfi de eadem terra huic domui, sicut tunc consuetudo fuit, est confirmata:

B75 [a] *corr. from* Beobirg *by interlin.*

B79 [a] *partially corr. from* donationem

---

[142] Ælfheah may be the future ealdorman of Wessex; see above, p. cxxiii.

[143] Sawyer, no. 494. This charter records Edmund granting the above six hides to Ælfheah. It is dated 944. *Charters of Abingdon Abbey*, p. 159, states that the document 'appears to be authentic'.

[144] Blewbury, Berkshire.

[145] Although this introduction refers to the beneficiary as 'minister', which is normally used to mean 'thegn', the charter indicates that he was a bishop, and this is almost certainly Ælfric bishop of Ramsbury, in whose diocese the grant lay. The composer of the introduction probably refers to the grantee as thegn out of habit formed over the previous repetitive sections. The very large grant probably was Blewbury hundred, mentioned, for example, in *Domesday Book*. By 1066 the large estate here granted had been broken up, and in the 12th c. a new hundred would be formed; *Charters of Abingdon Abbey*, p. 153. Abingdon had no lands in Blewbury hundred in 1066, although charters concerning Aston Upthorpe, part of the hundred hides here granted, did enter the Abingdon archive; see

above. And this is the king's charter whereby Ælfheah's donation of that land to this house was confirmed, as was then the custom:[142]

B74. *Charter of King Edmund concerning Lyford.*
Charters of Abingdon Abbey, no. 38.[143]

B75. *Concerning Blewbury, how King Edmund gave it.*[144]
In the same year, King Edmund gave Blewbury amounting to one hundred hides to Ælfric his thegn, in the same way as above. And this is the king's charter whereby Ælfric's donation of that land to this house was confirmed, as was then the custom:[145]

B76. *Charter of King Edmund concerning Blewbury.*
Charters of Abingdon Abbey, no. 36.[146]

B77. *How King Edmund gave Winkfield and Swinley.*
Likewise, in the same year,[147] King Edmund gave Winkfield and Swinley amounting to eleven hides to Sæthryth, a woman of religious life, and by the king's consent she gave them to God and the blessed Mary and the house of Abingdon and the monks serving God there, in pure and perpetual alms. And this is the king's charter confirming this gift:

B78. *Charter of King Edmund concerning Winkfield and Swinley.*
Charters of Abingdon Abbey, no. 35; above, c. 58.

B79. *Concerning Brimpton,*[148] *how it was given.*
The same King Edmund in the same year granted Brimpton amounting to twenty hides to Ordulf his thegn, in the same way as above.[149] And this is the king's charter whereby Ordulf's donation of that land to this house was confirmed, as was then the custom:

Charters of Abingdon Abbey, pp. 153, 406. Apart from the presence of these charters in the archive, there is no other evidence of Abingdon interest in this land.

146 Sawyer, no. 496. This charter records Edmund granting the above hundred hides to Bishop Ælfric. The charter gives the incarnation date of 944, but the indiction fits 942, not 944. *Charters of Abingdon Abbey*, p. 151, states that the document 'is probably authentic, although there is some difficulty with the date', and notes that 'the witness-list would be more compatible with 942 than with 944'. The preceding section, introducing the gift, says that it was in the same year as the grant of Blewbury, but the compiler was presumably just working from the incarnation dates contained within the charters.

147 The following charter shares the indiction but not the incarnation date with the preceding charter; both are probably from 942. MS C introduces the gift of Winkfield with a different passage, above, c. 57.

148 Berkshire.

149 The charter is dated 944. Ordulf's identity cannot be established with certainty. It is unclear why this passage states that Edmund gave twenty hides in Brimpton when the charter only records the gift of eight.

B80. *Carta regis Edmundi de Brinniggetune.*
Charters of Abingdon Abbey, no. 39.[150]

[i. 119] **B81.** *De morte Edmundi regis et successione Edredi fratris sui.*

fo. 32^{v} Iste uero rex Eadmundus, cum in die festiuitatis sancti Augustini Anglorum doctoris, in regia uilla que Anglice Pichile Chirche[151] nuncupatur curiam suam cum magnatibus suis festiue teneret, accidit ut coram eo pincerna suus primo conuiciis, deinde letaliter, in suum insurget[a] dapiferum.[152] Quod cum rex moleste tulisset, uolens [i. 120] dapiferum suum ex mortis eripere confinio, hictu detestabili et euentu flebili a pincerna suo nomine Leofwine interfectus, diem clausit suppremum. Post cuius obitum,[153] ut ex antiquorum librorum accepimus attestatione, Abbendonense cenobium ad tantam est solitudinem redactum ut, omnibus eiusdem cenobii possessionibus ceptrigera[154] potestate regio subactis dominio, monachis penitus destitueretur. Verum cuius infortunii malum ac talis euentus lapsus inopinati quibus ex causis acciderint nil ueri aut relatione dignum ad nostram peruenit noticiam. Qua de re utilius pariter et honestius fore diiudicauimus super huiuscemodi desolatione ad presens sapienter tacere, quam quicquam in medium producere quod nec uerum esse nec uerisimile de facili possit comprobari. Sane testamentorum libri possessiones ecclesie continentium, quamquam eidem cenobio tam inopinatum immineret dispendium, Dei tamen sunt reseruati prouidentia quatinus reparatores et restitutores eiusdem cenobii, cum eorum successoribus, per ipsos libros fierent certiores ac per processum temporis per eosdem antiquitatum indicia enucliatius nosse potuissent.

A temporibus uero Cisse et Cedwalle insuper et Hine regum Westsaxonum, per quorum patrocinia ipsum cenobium primo fuit erectum et constructum, usque ad hanc terciam eiusdem cenobii desolationem, ducentorum et quadraginta reuolutio annorum fuisse computatur.[155]

B81 [a] *corr. from* surget *by interlin.*

---

[150] Sawyer, no. 500. This charter records Edmund granting eight hides at Brimpton to Ordulf, in return for 90 *mancuses* of purest gold. It is dated 944. *Charters of Abingdon Abbey*, p. 162, states that 'there is no reason to question the authenticity of [the document]'. *DB* i, fos. 62^{r}, 62^{v}, records two manors at Brimpton, with a total assessment of eight hides *TRE*. Apart from the presence of this charter in the archive, there is no other evidence of Abingdon interest in this land.

[151] Gloucestershire.

[152] The killing of Edmund is also mentioned in e.g. *ASC*, 'D', *s.a.* 946; John of Worcester, *Chronicle*, ii. 398; William of Malmesbury, *Gesta regum*, bk. ii, c. 144, ed.

B80. *Charter of King Edmund concerning Brimpton.*
Charters of Abingdon Abbey, no. 39.[150]

B81. *Concerning the death of King Edmund and the succession of Eadred his brother.*

When that King Edmund, on the feast day of St Augustine teacher of the English [26 May 946], was in festive fashion holding his court with his magnates in the royal vill which in English is called Pucklechurch,[151] it happened that in Edmund's presence his butler attacked the king's steward first with insults and then fatally.[152] Angered by this, the king wished to snatch his steward from the verge of death, but instead he himself passed away, killed by his own butler named Leofwine with a detestable blow and in a lamentable outcome. After his death,[153] as we have learnt from the testimony of ancient books, the monastery of Abingdon was reduced to such a forsaken state that it was entirely destitute of monks, with all its possessions subjected to royal lordship by the sceptre-bearing power.[154] However, nothing true or worthy of recounting has come to our notice as to the causes of this evil misfortune and the occurrence of so unexpected a downfall. Concerning this matter we judge it more useful and also more honourable to remain for the moment wisely silent on such desolation, rather than to make something public which cannot easily be proved to be true or plausible. Yet despite such an unexpected loss threatening that monastery, nevertheless the books of records containing the church's possessions were certainly preserved by God's foresight, so that through those books the repairers and restorers of this monastery, with their successors, were better informed and could with the passing of time know through them more clearly evidence of times past.

From the time, indeed, of Cissa and Ceadwalla and also Ine, kings of the West Saxons, through whose patronage that monastery was first raised and constructed, right up to this third destruction of that monastery, 240 years are calculated to have passed.[155]

Mynors *et al.*, i. 232. On officials such as the steward and butler, see Keynes, *Diplomas*, pp. 158–62, L. M. Larson, *The King's Household in England before the Norman Conquest* (Madison, Wis., 1904).

[153] The remainder of this section has distinct parallels with the equivalent section in MS C, above, c. 24.

[154] The word *[s]ceptrigera* also appears above c. 42, and below, B223 (*Charters of Abingdon Abbey*, no. 118).

[155] Cf. above, c. 24.

Explicit liber primus.

[i. 121] **B82.** *Incipit secundus, de tercia reparatione domus Abbendonie.*

Itaque, Eadmundo rege Westsaxonum uiam uniuerse carnis ingresso, successit ei in imperium frater eius, memorande memorie, rex illustris Edredus, qui per sanctos admonitus matris sue Edgithe regine tercio domus Abbendonie extitit reparator ac possessionum eiusdem ablatarum fidelissimus restitutor. Sed antequam ad ipsius regis dotes pariter et donationes accedamus describendas, opere precium nobis fore diiudicamus ad presens mentionem de ipso facere, cum sit locus competens et congruus,[a] qui domui Abbendonie post desolationem
fo. 33r operis fidelissimus exsecutor, post merorem et dolo|rem gratulabundus consolator, sacri ordinis circumspectus constitutor, necnon et omnium bonarum ipsius domus consuetudinum felicissimus institutor, pater et pastor extitit precipuus.

B83. *De sancto Adelwoldo.*

Tempore itaque Eadmundi regis, de quo paulo superius in precedenti[a] libro prelibauimus, fuit quidam iuuenis in Wentana
[i. 122] ciuitate, ex illustri prosapia oriundus, nomine Æþelwoldus. Iste uero Æþelwoldus non solum genere illustrem uerum etiam titulo[b] spectabilem et omni sanctitate plenam lineam traxit nobilitatis. Vigebant autem in ipso ingenii pariter et industrie bona acceptabilia, adeptaque in puerilibus annis plena litterarum scientia, nature institucionum bona uenustissime accumulauit honestas. Inueniebantur etiam in eo corporis miranda uenustas, morum acceptissima gratia, eloquiorum gratissima luculentia, adeo ut et species et mores et gratia in adolesce⟨n⟩te Æþelwuoldo uiderentur ad inuicem emula sibi probitate certare.[156] Cuius etiam mentis mansuetudinem, animi constantiam, uultus hilaritatem, oris eloquentiam, manus largitatem, uite sanctitatem, hiis longe preciosorem, etsi feruentissime desideremus ad presens—at tamen ad plenum nequaquam possumus—dilucidare. Hic autem Aeþelwuoldus, cum iam adholeuisset et ad annos discretionis feliciter iam peruenisset, ad memoriam reuocans uerbum illud Dominicum, quo dicitur 'Non possunt mihi uiuere qui non sunt mundo mortui';[157]

B82 [a] *wrongly altered to* congruum *MS*

B83 [a] precidenti *MS* [b] *corr. from* titulos *by erasure*

[156] On the possible source for this description of Æthelwold, see above, p. liv n. 255.

[157] This is a frequently expressed monastic sentiment rather than a biblical quotation;

Here ends Book I.

B82. *Book II begins, concerning the third repair of the house of Abingdon.* Therefore, when Edmund king of the West Saxons had gone the way of all flesh, his brother, the illustrious King Eadred, whose memory should be commemorated, succeeded him in dominion [946]. By the holy admonitions of his mother Queen Eadgifu, he was on this third occasion the repairer of the house of Abingdon and most faithful restorer of its stolen possessions. But before we move on to that king's endowments and also the gifts to be described, we have judged it worth our while to mention now, since it is a suitable and proper place, the man who after the desolation was the most faithful executor of the work of the house of Abingdon, the joyful consoler after the sorrow and grief, the circumspect constitutor of sacred order, and also the happiest institutor of the good customs of that house, the outstanding father and shepherd.

B83. *Concerning St Æthelwold.*
In the time, therefore, of King Edmund, whom we have mentioned a little earlier in the preceding book, there was a certain young man in the city of Winchester, descended from illustrious stock, named Æthelwold. That Æthelwold, indeed, had behind him a noble line, not only illustrious by birth but also noteworthy in repute and filled with all holiness.[156] Moreover, in him flourished the welcome qualities of natural disposition and likewise of application, and having acquired full knowledge of letters in his boyhood years, qualities of education most pleasingly enhanced integrity of nature. For in him were found wonderful attractiveness of body, most welcome grace of behaviour, most agreeable splendour of eloquence, so much so that appearance and behaviour and grace seemed in the adolescent Æthelwold to be vying with one another by turns in competing probity. We have also desired to elucidate most fervently for the present day—but have been quite unable fully to do so—his mildness of mind, his constancy of soul, his cheerfulness of face, his eloquence of mouth, his generosity of hand, and his holiness of life which is far more precious than these. Moreover, this Æthelwold, when he had already grown up and now happily reached the years of discretion, recalled to his memory the Lord's word wherein it is said 'They cannot live with me who are not dead to the world'.[157] After

the scriptural basis appears to be Col. 3: 3, 'Mortui enim estis, et vita vestra est abscondita cum Christo in Deo.'

mundi retibus perpropere reiectis,[158] semetipsum abnegando, Christum ducem imitando, crucem eius eleuando, factus chore filius Glastonie sub uenerabili patre Dunstano, eiusdem loci abbate, sacre habitum felicissime induit religionis. Vbi uero sacratissime degens
[i. 123] uir uenerabilis Æþelwaldus per septemnium,[159] diligenter ad memoriam reuocans illud euuangelicum quo dicitur 'Cum iudex uenerit et cum uentilauerit triticum in area fructum, qui non fecerit decultoris in uinea palmes abscidetur',[160] iterumque diligenter attendens quod cinis est origine, cinis imitatione, cinis resolutione, necnon quid extiterit per originalis peccati contagionem, quid per baptismi gratiam, quid per naufragium, quid etiam per secundam tabulam post naufragium,[161] quid erit per mortis dissolutionem et glorie remunerationem, ad tantam peruenit sanctitatis perfectionem ut, in terra positus, ab hom⟨i⟩nibus[c] uitam actitare in terris uideretur angelicam.[162]

B84. *Qualiter enim cepit diligere rex Edredus.*

Huius itaque sanctitate pariter et bonitate comperta,[a] rex Edredus sanctum Æþelwaldum speciali quadam prerogatiua dileccionis [b]in tantum[b] eum est amplexatus ut iam placeret ei ipsum de monasterio accitum habere sibi familiarem. Placuit[163] etiam regi, suadente matre sua Edgiua, dare sancto uiro quendam locum uocabulo Abbendoniam, in quo quondam florebat monastica religio, sed tunc erat neglectum[c]
fo. 33v ac destructum, uilibus edificiis consistens et quadraginta tan|tum
[i. 124] mansas[d] possidens; reliquam uero prefati loci terram, que centum cassatorum lustris hinc inde giratur, regali dominio subiectam rex ipse possidebat.[164] Factumque[165] est, consentiente Dunstano abbate, secundum regis uoluntatem, ut uir Dei Æþelwoldus prenotati loci susciperet curam, quatinus in eo monachos ordinaret regulariter Deo

[c] *corr. from* omnibus *by interlin.*

B84 [a] *interlin.* [b–b] *interlin.* [c] negelctum *MS* [d] massas *MS*

[158] The allusion is not entirely clear, but see Matt. 4: 20, 22; Mark 1: 18, for Christ's disciples abandoning their nets.

[159] Wulfstan, *Life of Æthelwold*, c. 9, ed. Lapidge and Winterbottom, pp. 14–16, does not give any indication of the length of time Æthelwold spent at Glastonbury; Lapidge and Winterbottom, pp. xliii–xliv, suggest that 'Æthelwold spent a quite considerable period of his life studying at Glastonbury: from the late 930s until, probably, the early 950s (when he himself was aged between his early thirties and his mid-forties).'

[160] The allusions are to Matt. 3: 12, Luke 3: 17, John 15: 2.

most readily casting away the world's nets,[158] by denying himself, by imitating Christ his guide, by raising his cross, he was made a son of the choir of Glastonbury under the venerable father Dunstan, abbot of that monastery, and most happily assumed the habit of sacred religion. Living there, indeed, for seven years in a most sacred fashion,[159] the venerable man Æthelwold earnestly recalled to his memory the Gospel where it is said 'When the judge will come and when he will winnow the wheat on the threshing floor, and the cultivator's vine branch which does not produce fruit will be cut off'.[160] And again, earnestly considering that there is ash by origin, ash by imitation, and ash by disintegration, and also what exists by contagion of original sin, what by grace of baptism, what by shipwreck, what through a second plank after shipwreck,[161] what will be through the dissolution of death and the remuneration of glory, he reached such perfection of holiness that, placed on earth, he was seen by men to live in this world the angelic life.[162]

B84. *How King Eadred began to love him.*

Therefore when he had discovered this man's holiness and likewise his goodness, King Eadred embraced St Æthelwold with a special precedence of love to such a degree that, after summoning him from the monastery, he was now pleased to have him as his intimate. So,[163] swayed by his mother Eadgifu, the king decided to give the holy man a place called Abingdon. Here monastic religion had once flourished, but by now it was neglected and ruined, its buildings poor, and its estate consisted of only forty hides of land. The remainder of the estate, which lies adjacent to it and consists of a further hundred hides, was the king's possession and under his royal control.[164] At[165] the king's wish, and with Dunstan's consent, it came about that the man of God Æthelwold took charge of this place, with the aim of establishing monks there to serve God according to the Rule. The servant of God accordingly came to the place with which he had been

[161] See Jerome, *Commentary on Ezekiel*, concerning Ezek. 16: 52 (*PL* xxv. 155C): 'Secunda post naufragium tabula est, cum peccaveris, erubescere.' The phrase was used notably in the context of baptism and penance.

[162] A phrase also used below, B210, concerning Edward the Martyr.

[163] The text of the remainder of this section is closely based on Wulfstan, *Life of Æthelwold*, c. 11, ed. Lapidge and Winterbottom, pp. 18–22, and my translation deliberately follows that of Lapidge and Winterbottom.

[164] For these lands, see above, p. cxxxvii.

[165] The Abingdon versions of the Worcester *Chronicle* also incorporate the passage 'Factumque . . . sibi commissum' from Wulfstan, *Life of Æthelwold*; John of Worcester, *Chronicle*, ii. 611.

seruientes. Venit ergo seruus Dei ad locum sibi commissum: quem protinus secuti sunt quidam clerici de Glestonia, scilicet Osgarus, Flobbritus, Fridegarus, et Orbrintus de Wintonia, et Eadricus de Lundonia, eius discipulatui se subdentes.[166] Congregauitque[167] sibi in breui spatio gregem monachorum, quibus ipse abbas, iubente rege, ordinatus est. Dedit etiam rex possessionem regalem quam in Abbendonia possederat, sicut carta regis ipsius subsequens testatur,[168] hoc est centum cassatos, cum optimis edifitiis, abbati et fratribus ad augmentum cotidiani uictus, et de regio thesauro suo multum eos in pecuniis iuuit; sed mater eius largius solatia munerum eis direxit. Tantamque gratiam Dominus sibi seruientibus contulit ut ad prefatum cenobium, quod ante erat pauperimum, omnes simul diuitie putarentur affluere, et sic cuncta prosperis successibus occurrere ut palam sententia[e] Dominice promissionis impleri uidetur qua dicitur: 'Primum querite regnum Dei et iustitiam eius, et omnia aditientur uobis.'[169] Tenor carte regis hic est:

B85.[a]

Charters of Abingdon Abbey, no. 51; above, c. 28.[170]

[i. 131] fo. 34v **B86.** *Quomodo rex Edredus dedit Wulfrico Stanmere.*[171]

Dedit etiam predictus rex Edredus Wulfrico ministro suo Stanmere, cum omnibus que ad ipsum locum dinoscuntur pertinere, tam in magnis quam in modicis rebus, campis, pascuis, siluis, liberaliter ac eternaliter quamdiu uiuat habeat, et post generalem qui omnibus certus incertusque homunculis constat transitum,[172] cuicumque successionis heredi uoluerit in perpetuum derelinquat. Sic enim carta regis testatur, unde memoratus Wulfricus eandem uillam de consensu et uoluntate regis hanc sacratissimam domum Abbendonie fecit heredem. Et hec est subscriptio carte regis hanc donationem confirmantis:

[e] sententiam *MS*

B85 [a] *an illustration of the king appears at the start of the charter*

[166] On these monks, see above, p. cvii.

[167] The Abingdon versions of the Worcester *Chronicle* also incorporate the passages 'Congregauitque . . . possederat' and 'cum optimis . . . direxit' from Wulfstan, *Life of Æthelwold*; John of Worcester, *Chronicle*, ii. 611.

charged. He was immediately followed by certain clerics in minor orders from Glastonbury, namely Osgar, Foldbriht, and Frithegar, together with Ordbriht from Winchester, and Eadric from London, all of whom submitted themselves to his teaching.[166] Soon[167] he had assembled a flock of monks, and at the king's behest he was ordained their abbot. The king also gave his royal estates in Abingdon, as his charter which follows witnesses,[168] the hundred hides, with excellent buildings, to the abbot and monks to increase their everyday provisions, and he gave them much monetary help from his royal treasury. His mother sent them presents on an even more lavish scale. The Lord so bestowed His grace on His servants that men thought all riches were flowing at once into a monastery that had previously been very poor. All seemed to be going so well that it looked as if what the Lord promised was being manifestly fulfilled: 'Seek ye first the kingdom of God, and His righteousness; and all things should be added unto you.'[169] The terms of the king's charter are as follows:

B85.
Charters of Abingdon Abbey, no. 51; above, c. 28.[170]

B86. *How King Eadred gave Stanmore to Wulfric.*[171]
The aforesaid King Eadred also gave Stanmore, with everything which was known to pertain to that place, both in great things and in small, fields, pastures, woods, to Wulfric his thegn to have freely and eternally as long as he lived, and after the common passing which is agreed to be both certain and uncertain for all mere men,[172] he might leave it in perpetuity to whomsoever he wished as heir of succession. For so the king's charter witnesses, whereby that Wulfric made this most sacred house of Abingdon heir of that village by the king's consent and will. And this is the text of the charter of the king confirming this gift:

[168] This phrase concerning the charter does not appear in Wulfstan, *Life of Æthelwold.*

[169] Matt. 6: 33; Luke 12: 31.

[170] For the boundary clause and additional vernacular passage associated with the charter of Eadred for Abingdon, see above, p. 2 n. 5.

[171] Stanmore, Berkshire, is in the parish of Beedon and almost certainly was included in Abingdon's *Domesday* holding at Beedon; *DB* i, fo. 58^v. *Domesday Book* notes that Beedon had been assessed at fifteen hides; this may have been composed of the present ten hides and another five mentioned above, p. 128. The grantee is Wulfric Cufing.

[172] i.e. all know that death is certain, but none know when and how it will occur.

B87. *Carta regis Edredi de Stanmere.*
Charters of Abingdon Abbey, no. 42.[173]

[i. 134] fo. 35r **B88**. *Quomodo rex Edredus dedit Aþelwulfo Wittenham.*[174]

Consimili modo dedit rex Edredus Æþelwulfo principi Witthenham decem cassatorum, et ipse Æþelwulfus de consensu regis memoratam uillam, eodem tenore quo rex illi concesserat, Deo et beate Marie et huic domui Abbendonie et monachis ibidem Deo seruientibus in puram et perpetuam contulit helemosinam. Carta uero regis hanc donationem confirmans hec est:

B89. *Carta regis de Wittenham.*
Charters of Abingdon Abbey, no. 15; above, c. 16, B32.[175]

[i. 136] fo. 35v **B90**. *De Dencheswrþe.*

Similiter concessit Wlfrico[176] militi Denchewurþe quinque cassatorum, et ipse Wlfricus de consensu regis memoratam uillam, eodem tenore quo rex illi concesserat, Deo et beate Marie et huic domui Abbendonie et monachis ibidem Deo seruientibus in puram et perpetuam contulit helemosinam. Carta uero regis hanc donationem confirmans hec est:

B91. *Carta de Dencheswrþe.*
Charters of Abingdon Abbey, no. 41.[177]

[i. 139] fo. 36v **B92**. *Edredus dedit Cuthredo ministro suo Bedelakinges.*

Item rex Edredus dedit Cuthredo ministro suo Bedelachinges quinque cassatorum, et ipse Cuthredus de consensu regis memoratam[a] uillam, eodem tenore quo rex illi concesserat, Deo et beate Marie et huic domui Abbendonie et monachis ibidem Deo seruientibus in puram et perpetuam contulit elemosinam.[178] Carta uero regis hanc donationem confirmans hec est:

B92 [a] *followed by* terram *del. by expunction*

---

[173] Sawyer, no. 542. This charter records Eadred granting the above ten hides to Wulfric. The figure for the indiction (five) and the incarnation date (948) are incompatible, probably through scribal error; the charter may be from 947 or 948. *Charters of Abingdon Abbey*, p. 174, states that the charter 'is probably authentic, although the date may have been slightly miscopied'.

[174] This is in fact a gift by King Æthelred of Wessex; see above, c. 16.

B87. *Charter of King Eadred concerning Stanmore.*
Charters of Abingdon Abbey, no. 42.[173]

B88. *How King Eadred gave Wittenham to Æthelwulf.*[174]
In a similar fashion, King Eadred gave Wittenham amounting to ten hides to Æthelwulf, a noble, and Æthelwulf himself by the king's consent conferred that village, on the same terms as the king had granted it to him, on God and the blessed Mary and this house of Abingdon and the monks serving God there, in pure and perpetual alms. This indeed is the king's charter confirming this gift:

B89. *The king's charter concerning Wittenham.*
Charters of Abingdon Abbey, no. 15; above, c. 16, B32.[175]

B90. *Concerning Denchworth.*
He likewise granted Denchworth amounting to five hides to Wulfric, a knight,[176] and Wulfric himself by the king's consent conferred that village, on the same terms as the king had granted it to him, on God and the blessed Mary and this house of Abingdon and the monks serving God there, in pure and perpetual alms. This indeed is the king's charter confirming this gift:

B91. *Charter concerning Denchworth.*
Charters of Abingdon Abbey, no. 41.[177]

B92. *Eadred gave Balking to Cuthred, his thegn.*
Likewise, King Eadred gave Balking amounting to five hides to Cuthred his thegn, and Cuthred himself by the king's consent conferred that village, on the same terms as the king had granted it to him, on God and the blessed Mary and this house of Abingdon and the monks serving God there, in pure and perpetual alms.[178] This indeed is the king's charter confirming this gift:

[175] On the repetition of this charter in MS B, see above, p. xlvi n. 193. *Charters of Abingdon Abbey*, p. 68, notes that 'the exemplar of [this document] may have been in poor condition, for the scribe has left three short spaces in the bounds, as if these sections were not legible'.

[176] Most likely Wulfric Cufing.

[177] Sawyer, no. 529. This charter records Eadred granting the above five hides to Wulfric. It is dated 947. *Charters of Abingdon Abbey*, p. 170, states that it 'seems entirely acceptable'. A charter of King Eadwig, below, B172 (*Charters of Abingdon Abbey*, no. 81), also grants these five hides to Wulfric; it could be a confirmation.

[178] This statement is probably not to be trusted, particularly given the compiler's confusion over the king involved. For King Edgar giving one hide at Balking to Abingdon, see above, c. 139.

B93. *Carta de Bedelakinges.*
Charters of Abingdon Abbey, no. 16.[179]

[i. 141] fo. 37r **B94.** *Edredus dedit Eadrico Wasingetune.*[180]
Idem rex Edredus concessit Eadrico comiti Wasingetune uiginti cassatorum, et ipse Eadricus de consensu regis memoratam uillam, eodem tenore quo rex Eadredus illi concesserat, Deo et beate Marie et huic domui Abbendonie et monachis ibidem Deo seruientibus in puram et perpetuam contulit elemosinam. Carta uero regis hanc donationem confirmans et hec est:

B95. *Carta de Wasingetune.*
Charters of Abingdon Abbey, no. 40.[181]

[i. 145] fo. 37v fo. 38r **B96.** *De Welliford, quomodo rex Eadredus dedit Wulfrico.*[182]
Consimili modo dedit rex Eadredus Wulfrico ministro | suo Weligforda tredecim mansarum,[183] et ipse de consensu regis memoratam uillam, eo tenore quo rex illi concesserat, Deo et beate Marie et huic domui Abbendonie et monachis ibidem Deo seruientibus in puram et perpetuam contulit elemosinam.[184] Carta uero regis hanc donationem confirmans hec est:

B97. *Carta regis de Welliford.*
Charters of Abingdon Abbey, no. 44.[185]

[i. 149] fo. 38v **B98.** *De Escesburh, quomo⟨do⟩ rex Edredus dedit.*
Similiter rex Edredus concessit Elfsio ministro suo et coniugi[a] sue Eadgife Escesburh trium et triginta cassatorum, et ipse de consensu regis memoratam uillam, eo tenore quo rex illi concesserat, Deo et beate Marie et huic domui Abbendonie et monachis ibidem Deo

B98 [a] *corr. from* coniuge

[179] Sawyer, no. 539/338a. This in fact is a charter of King Æthelred of Wessex, probably originally dated 868, although the date as it currently appears is 948; *Charters of Abingdon Abbey*, p. 71. See above, B89, for a similar mistake. It records Æthelred granting the above five hides to a thegn named Cuthred, who may be the same man as Ealdorman Cuthred who appears as a witness in Alfred's reign. *Charters of Abingdon Abbey*, p. 71, states that in all respects apart from the alteration to the date, the document 'seems to be authentic'. Balking is not mentioned in *Domesday*, although the lands mentioned in this charter may have been included in their entirety or in part under other Abingdon entries; see *Charters of Abingdon Abbey*, p. 72.

[180] Washington, Sussex. Eadric was the brother of Æthelstan Half-king, ealdorman of East Anglia, and Æthelwold, an ealdorman in Wessex. His own ealdordom was probably in central Wessex; see C. R. Hart, 'Athelstan "Half King" and his family', *ASE*, ii (1973), 115–44, at p. 120. For his witnessing of royal charters, see Keynes, *Atlas of Attestations*,

B93. *Charter concerning Balking.*
Charters of Abingdon Abbey, no. 16.[179]

B94. *Eadred gave Washington to Eadric.*[180]
The same king gave Washington amounting to twenty hides to Eadric, an earl, and Eadric himself by the king's consent conferred that village, on the same terms as King Eadred had granted it to him, on God and the blessed Mary and this house of Abingdon and the monks serving God there, in pure and perpetual alms. This indeed is the king's charter confirming this gift:

B95. *Charter concerning Washington.*
Charters of Abingdon Abbey, no. 40.[181]

B96. *Concerning Welford, how King Eadred gave it to Wulfric.*[182]
In a similar fashion, King Eadred gave Welford amounting to thirteen hides[183] to Wulfric his thegn, and he himself by the king's consent conferred that village, on the same terms as the king had granted it to him, on God and the blessed Mary and this house of Abingdon and the monks serving God there, in pure and perpetual alms.[184] This indeed is the king's charter confirming this gift:

B97. *The king's charter concerning Welford.*
Charters of Abingdon Abbey, no. 44.[185]

B98. *Concerning* Æscesburh, *how King Eadred gave it.*
Likewise, King Eadred granted *Æscesburh* amounting to thirty-three hides to Ælfsige his thegn and Ælfsige's wife Eadgifu, and he himself by the king's consent conferred that village, on the same terms as the king had granted it to him, on God and the blessed Mary and this

table XXXII. In 963 King Edgar granted Bishop Æthelwold twenty-four hides in Washington; below, B205 (*Charters of Abingdon Abbey*, no. 98). The Æthelwold connection may explain why these charters appear in the Abingdon archive; see above, p. cxxx.

181 Sawyer, no. 525. This charter records Eadred granting the above twenty hides to Eadric. It is dated 947. *Charters of Abingdon Abbey*, p. 166, states that it 'is clearly authentic'.

182 The beneficiary may be Wulfric Cufing.

183 The charter that follows specifies eighteen hides. Given that the charter survives in the original, the error is almost certainly in the present passage, and arises from simple miscopying of the figure as 'xiii' instead of 'xviii'.

184 See also above, p. 80 n. 187.

185 Sawyer, no. 552. The original charter also survives; London, British Library, Cotton Augustus ii. 44, reproduced in *BM Facs.*, iii. 16. The charter records Eadred granting eighteen hides in Welford to Wulfric, in exchange for land in Pendavey, Cornwall. It is dated 949. *Charters of Abingdon Abbey*, pp. 182–3, accepts the charter as genuine.

seruientibus in puram et perpetuam elemosinam contulit.[186] Carta regis hanc donationem confirmans hec est:

B99. *Carta regis Eadredi de Escesbeurh.*
Charters of Abingdon Abbey, no. 48.[187]

[i. 151] fo. 39r **B100**. *De Chiuelea, quomodo data erat Wulfrico.*[188]
Idem rex Edredus dedit Wulfrico ministro suo Ciueleam quinque et uiginti mansarum, et ipse de consensu regis memoratam uillam, eo tenore quo rex illi concesserat, Deo et beate Marie et huic domui Abbendonie et monachis ibidem Deo seruientibus in puram et perpetuam contulit elemosinam. Carta uero regis hanc donationem confirmans hec est:

B101. *Carta regis Edredi de Chiuelea.*
Charters of Abingdon Abbey, no. 45; above, c. 35.

[i. 155] fo. 40r **B102**. *De Cusenricge, quomodo data erat ministro regis Eadredi.*[189]
Dedit etiam rex Eadredus Alfrico ministro suo Cusenricge quinque cassatorum, et ipse de consensu regis memoratam uillam, eo tenore [i. 156] quo rex illi concesserat, Deo et beate Marie et huic domui Abbendonie et monachis ibidem Deo seruientibus in puram et perpetuam helemosinam contulit.[190] Carta uero regis hanc donationem confirmans hec est:

B103. *Carta regis de Cusanricge*
Charters of Abingdon Abbey, no. 49.[191]

[i. 157] fo. 40v **B104**. *Quomodo rex Eadredus dedit Alfeo ministro suo Cumtune.*[192]
Consimili modo concessit rex Eadredus Alfeo ministro suo Cumtune iuxta Eccesdune[193] octo cassatorum, et ipse de consensu regis memoratam uillam, eo tenore quo rex illi concesserat, Deo et beate Marie et huic domui Abbendonie et monachis ibidem Deo seruientibus in puram et perpetuam contulit elemosinam. Carta uero regis hanc donationem confirmans hec est:

[186] Ælfsige cannot be identified with certainty; he may be the same man who received land at Waltham, above, B67–B68 (*Charters of Abingdon Abbey*, no. 32), and at Benham, below, B136–B137 (*Charters of Abingdon Abbey*, no. 72). For *Æscesburh*, and its correspondence with Uffington, see above, p. 44 n. 112.

[187] Sawyer, no. 561. This charter records Eadred granting the above thirty-three hides to Ælfsige and Eadgifu. It is dated 953. *Charters of Abingdon Abbey*, p. 199, states that it is 'entirely acceptable'.

[188] Wulfric Cufing. The equivalent section in MS C does not specifically state that Wulfric gave the land to Abingdon; above, c. 34.

[189] Curridge, Berkshire.

[190] Ælfric is too common a name to allow certain identification.

house of Abingdon and the monks serving God there, in pure and perpetual alms.[186] This is the king's charter confirming this gift:

B99. *Charter of King Eadred concerning* Æscesburh.
Charters of Abingdon Abbey, no. 48.[187]

B100. *Concerning Chieveley, how it was given to Wulfric.*[188]
The same King Eadred gave Chieveley amounting to twenty-five hides to Wulfric his thegn, and he himself by the king's consent conferred that village, on the same terms as the king had granted it to him, on God and the blessed Mary and this house of Abingdon and the monks serving God there, in pure and perpetual alms. This indeed is the king's charter confirming this gift:

B101. *Charter of King Eadred concerning Chieveley.*
Charters of Abingdon Abbey, no. 45; above, c. 35.

B102. *Concerning Curridge, how it was given to a thegn of King Eadred.*[189]
King Eadred also gave Curridge amounting to five hides to Ælfric his thegn, and he himself by the king's consent conferred that village, on the same terms as the king had granted it to him, on God and the blessed Mary and this house of Abingdon and the monks serving God there, in pure and perpetual alms.[190] This indeed is the king's charter confirming this gift:

B103. *Charter concerning Curridge.*
Charters of Abingdon Abbey, no. 49.[191]

B104. *How King Eadred gave Compton to Ælfheah his thegn.*[192]
In a similar fashion, King Eadred granted Compton next to *Æscesdune* amounting to eight hides to Ælfheah his thegn,[193] and he himself by the king's consent conferred that village, on the same terms as the king had granted it to him, on God and the blessed Mary and this house of Abingdon and the monks serving God there, in pure and perpetual alms. This indeed is the king's charter confirming this gift:

[191] Sawyer, no. 560. This charter records Eadred granting the above five hides to Ælfric. It is dated 953. *Charters of Abingdon Abbey*, p. 202, states that it 'is probably authentic'. Apart from the presence of this charter in the archive, there is no other evidence of Abingdon interest in this land, although Curridge did adjoin Abingdon lands at Chieveley.

[192] Compton Beauchamp, Berkshire. On Ælfheah, see above, p. cxxiii.

[193] From the context it would seem that *Æscesdune* here refers to a specific hill; see *Charters of Abingdon Abbey*, pp. 203–5; cf. EPNS, *Berkshire*, i. 2–4. The name probably survives in the present-day Ashdown Park, in Ashbury.

[i. 158] **B105.** *Carta regis Eadredi de Cumtune.*
Charters of Abingdon Abbey, no. 50.[194]

[i. 159] **B106.** *Quomodo rex Eadredus dedit Wulfrico ministro suo Boxora.*[195]
fo. 41r Similiter rex Edredus dedit Wulfrico ministro suo Boxora decem mansarum, et ipse de consensu regis memoratam uillam, eo tenore quo rex illi concesserat, Deo et beate Marie et huic domui Abbendo-
[i. 160] nie et monachis ibidem Deo seruientibus in puram et perpetuam contulit elemosinam. Carta uero regis hanc donationem confirmans hec est:

B107. *Carta regis Eadredi de Boxora.*
Charters of Abingdon Abbey, no. 77.[196]

[i. 162] **B108.** *Quomodo rex Eadredus dedit Beorcham Ælfwino ministro suo.*[197]
fo. 41v Idem rex Eadredus concessit Ælfwino ministro suo Beorcham trium cassatorum, et ipse de consensu regis memoratam uillam, eo tenore quo rex illi concesserat, Deo et beate Marie et huic domui Abbendonie et monachis ibidem Deo seruientibus in puram et perpetuam contulit elemosinam. Carta uero regis hanc donationem confirmans hec est:

B109. *Carta regis Eadredi de Beorcham.*
Charters of Abingdon Abbey, no. 47.[198]

[i. 165] **B110.** *Quomodo rex Edredus dedit Alfgaro ministro suo Weoufeld.*[199]
fo. 42r Item rex Edredus dedit Alfgaro ministro suo ac militi Weoufelde trium mansarum, et ipse de consensu regis memoratam uillam, eo

[194] Sawyer, no. 564. This charter records Eadred granting the above eight hides to his thegn and kinsman Ælfheah. It is dated 955. *Charters of Abingdon Abbey*, p. 204, states that 'there is no reason to suspect [its] authenticity'. Apart from the presence of this charter in the archive, there is no other evidence of Abingdon interest in this land. *DB* i, fo. 61r, records that Ælmer held it 'in alodio' from King Edward *TRE*.

[195] The grantee is Wulfric Cufing. The charter in the following section is dated 958, but is in the name of King Eadred (946–55); either date or name must be wrong. The compiler of MS B was here simply following the name in the charter.

[196] Sawyer, no. 577. This charter records the king granting the above ten hides to Wulfric. It is dated 958 although it is in the name of Eadred, who died in 955. Because of the problems of reconciling king's name and date, *Charters of Abingdon Abbey*, p. 318, states that 'it is difficult to come to a firm decision about the authenticity of [this document]'. See also C. Hart, 'The *Codex Wintoniensis* and the king's *haligdom*', *Agricultural History Review*, xviii (1970), supplement, 7–38, at p. 14, who suggests that such substitutions of Eadred's name for Eadwig's result from the fact that 'the titles of many charters issued in the troubled years of King Eadwig's reign were suspect in the generation after his death, and it appears to have been a common practice of the Benedictine reformers to amend them'.

[197] Barkham, Berkshire. Ælfwine may be the beneficiary of two other charters preserved in the *History*, above, cc. 50, 90; see further *Charters of Abingdon Abbey*, p. 196. Apart from

B105. *Charter of King Eadred concerning Compton.*
Charters of Abingdon Abbey, no. 50.[194]

B106. *How King Eadred gave Boxford to Wulfric his thegn.*[195]
Likewise King Eadred gave Boxford amounting to ten hides to Wulfric his thegn, and he himself by the king's consent conferred that village, on the same terms as the king had granted it to him, on God and the blessed Mary and this house of Abingdon and the monks serving God there, in pure and perpetual alms. This indeed is the king's charter confirming this gift:

B107. *Charter of King Eadred concerning Boxford.*
Charters of Abingdon Abbey, no. 77.[196]

B108. *How King Eadred gave Barkham to Ælfwine his thegn.*[197]
The same King Eadred granted Barkham amounting to three hides to Ælfwine his thegn, and he himself by the king's consent conferred that village, on the same terms as the king had granted it to him, on God and the blessed Mary and this house of Abingdon and the monks serving God there, in pure and perpetual alms. This indeed is the king's charter confirming this gift:

B109. *Charter of King Eadred concerning Barkham.*
Charters of Abingdon Abbey, no. 47.[198]

B110. *How King Eadred gave* Weonfelda *to Ælfgar his thegn.*[199]
Likewise, King Eadred gave *Weonfelda* amounting to three hides to Ælfgar his thegn and knight, and he himself by the king's consent

the presence of this charter in the archive, there is no other evidence of Abingdon interest in this land.

[198] Sawyer, no. 559. This charter also survives in a 16th-c. copy of a lost single sheet, Cambridge, Corpus Christi College 111, pp. 145–6. It records Eadred granting the above three hides to 'a vassal [*cuidam uasallo*]' called Ælfwine. It is dated 952, although the witness list would point to 953 × 955. *Charters of Abingdon Abbey*, p. 196, states that 'it seems best to treat [the document] as suspicious, and a possible forgery'.

[199] An Ælfgar is prominent in witness lists from 951; by 959–62, when witnessing, he usually appears first amongst the thegns. In 958 he witnesses B170 (*Charters of Abingdon Abbey*, no. 79) not as 'minister' but as 'regis propinquus'. *ASC*, *s.a.* 962 records that 'in this year Ælfgar, the king's kinsman in Devon, died, and his body rests in Wilton'. However, it is uncertain whether this man is the same Ælfgar who received *Weonfelda*. The boundary clause makes it clear that the land *Weonfelda* coincides significantly with Wokefield, Berkshire. Whether *Weonfelda* is etymologically linked to Wokefield is disputed; see EPNS, *Berkshire*, i. 227–8 and R. Forsberg, review article, 'An edition of the Anglo-Saxon charter boundaries of Berkshire', *Studia Neophilologica*, li (1979), 139–51, at p. 140. Apart from the presence of this charter in the archive, there is no other evidence of Abingdon interest in this land.

tenore quo rex illi concesserat, Deo et beate Marie et huic domui Abbendonie et monachis ibidem Deo seruientibus in puram et perpetuam contulit elemosinam. Carta uero regis hanc donationem confirmans hec est:

B111. *Carta regis Edredi de Weoufelde.*
Charters of Abingdon Abbey, no. 46.[200]

[i. 167] **B112.** *De morte Edredi regis.*
fo. 42v Iste uero rex Eadredus, letali morbo correptus, decidit in lectum
fo. 43r egritudinis, a quo non antea[a] disces|sit donec, disponente iusto mundi
[i. 168] iudice, spiritum exhalaret nouissimum. Cuius uero finis beatitudinem uox celitus elapsa beato Dunstano abbati Glastonie, itineranti ac quamtocius properanti ut ipsum gregem maturius inuiseret, quam humanitus de eo contigisset innotuit, dicens 'Rex Edredus obdormiuit in Domino'. O quam felix uita regis que tam felici commendatur attestatione!

B113. *De Edwio rege.*[201]
Successit Edredo regi in imperium Edwius, filius Edmundi regis fratris sui, in cuius conspectu uir uenerabilis Adþelwoldus abbas Abbendonie (de quo in anteis prelibauimus) tantam inuenit gratiam ut omni sue peticioni memoratus rex quantum ad promotionem domus Abbendonie, tam effectiuum quam affectiuum, preberet assensum. Cuius gratie uir uenerabilis Æþelwoldus non factus inmemor, mox in ipso primordio eius imperii de libertate monasterii Abbendonensis insuper et possessionum ad idem monasterium pertinentium priuilegium ab eodem rege, uniuersisque Anglie archiepiscopis et episcopis constabilitum et confirmatum, impetrauit, archiepiscopis et episcopis necnon et abbatibus sub anathematis interminatione firmiter inhibentibus ne quis mortalium aut quicquam libertati priuilegii contrarium impetrare aut etiam aliquo alio modo malitiose[a] contra ipsum agere inposterum presumeret. Tenor uero priuilegii hic est:

B112 [a] *final* a *interlin.*

B113 [a] *corr. from* malitiosie

conferred that village, on the same terms as the king had granted it to him, on God and the blessed Mary and this house of Abingdon and the monks serving God there, in pure and perpetual alms. This indeed is the king's charter confirming this gift:

B111. *Charter of King Eadred concerning* Weonfelda.
Charters of Abingdon Abbey, no. 46.[200]

B112. *Concerning the death of King Eadred.*
Seized by a deadly illness, King Eadred fell into his sickbed, which he did not leave until, by disposition of the just Judge of the world, he breathed out his final breath [955]. Indeed, there slipped from Heaven a voice which notified the blessed Dunstan abbot of Glastonbury—who was travelling and hurrying as quickly as possible the sooner to see that flock—of the blessedness of Eadred's death and how he had suffered the fate of mankind, saying 'King Eadred sleeps in the Lord'. Oh how happy the life of a king which is commended by such a happy attestation!

B113. *Concerning King Eadwig.*[201]
To King Eadred succeeded in dominion Eadwig, son of his brother King Edmund, in whose sight the venerable man Æthelwold abbot of Abingdon (mentioned in earlier passages) found such grace that the aforementioned king provided his assent, both effective and affectionate, to all his requests for the promotion of the house of Abingdon. Not forgetting this grace, the venerable man Æthelwold sought from that king, right at the start of his dominion, a privilege concerning the liberty of the monastery of Abingdon and also of the possessions pertaining to that monastery, supported and confirmed by all the archbishops and bishops of England, and with the archbishops and bishops and also abbots firmly prohibiting under penalty of anathema that any mortal in future presume either to seek anything contrary to the liberty of the privilege or to act maliciously against it in any way. The terms of the privilege are, indeed, as follows:

[200] Sawyer, no. 578. This charter records Eadred granting the above three hides to Ælfgar. It was issued between 946 (Eadred's accession) and 12 Mar. 951 (the death of Ælfheah bishop of Winchester, who witnessed the charter). *Charters of Abingdon Abbey*, p. 191, states that it 'is probably authentic, although it lacks a dating clause'.
[201] Cf. above, c. 36.

[i. 169] **B114.** *Priuilegium Edwii regis de uilla Abbendonie et de abbate eligendo de propria congregatione.*[a]
Charters of Abingdon Abbey, no. 83; above, c. 37.

[i. 175] fo. 44v **B115.** *Carta regis Edwi de Abbendonia.*
Charters of Abingdon Abbey, no. 52; above, c. 38.

[i. 179] fo. 45v **B116.** *Quomodo rex ecclesiam dedit de Hengestesige.*[202]
Item eodem anno dedit rex Edwius Deo et beate Marie et huic domui Abbendonie et monachis ibidem Deo in perpetuum seruientibus Hengesige, Seofecan Wyrþe, Wihtham, et carta sua confirmauit. Cuius carte tenor hic est:

B117. *Carta regis Edwi de Hengstessie.*
Charters of Abingdon Abbey, no. 59; above, c. 41.

[i. 182] fo. 46r **B118.** *De nemore quod dedit rex Edwius ecclesie Abbendonie.*[203]
Item anno primo regni sui dedit rex Eadwius Deo et beate Marie et domui Abbendonie et monachis ibidem Deo in perpetuum seruientibus quoddam nemus ad Heafochrycg, ⟨ad architec⟩tandum[a] ecclesiam sancte Marie Abbendonie, peticione Æþelwoldi eiusdem loci abbatis, et carta sua confirmauit. Cuius carte tenor hic est:

[i. 183] **B119.** *Carta regis Edwii de Hafochrycg.*
Charters of Abingdon Abbey, no. 57; above, c. 43.

[i. 186] fo. 47r **B120.** *Quomodo rex Edwius dedit ecclesie Gainge.*[204]
Item anno secundo regni sui dedit memoratus rex Eadwius Deo et beate Marie et huic domui Abbendonie et monachis ibidem Deo in perpetuum seruientibus Gainge, et carta sua confirmauit. Cuius carte tenor hic est:

B121. *Carta regis Edwi de Gaing.*
Charters of Abingdon Abbey, no. 58; above, c. 42.

[i. 189] fo. 47v fo. 48r **B122.** *De Henneritha, quomodo data erat.*
Eodem anno dedit rex Edwius Brihtrico | ministro suo in Hennæriþes decem mansas, et ille de consensu regis Deo et beate Marie et domui Abbendonie et monachis ibidem Deo seruientibus in puram et perpetuam elemosinam.[205] Et hec est carta regis donationem eius confirmans:

B114 [a] *an illustration of the king appears at the start of this charter*

B118 [a] *see above, c. 43*

B114. *Privilege of King Eadwig concerning the village of Abingdon and concerning the choosing of the abbot from the congregation itself.*
Charters of Abingdon Abbey, no. 83; above, c. 37.

B115. *Charter of King Eadwig concerning Abingdon.*
Charters of Abingdon Abbey, no. 52; above, c. 38.

B116. *How the king gave the church Hinksey.*[202]
Likewise, in the same year [956], King Eadwig gave and by his charter confirmed Hinksey, Seacourt, and Wytham to God and the blessed Mary and this house of Abingdon and the monks serving God there for ever. The terms of his charter are as follows:

B117. *Charter of King Eadwig concerning Hinksey.*
Charters of Abingdon Abbey, no. 59; above, c. 41.

B118. *Concerning the wood that King Eadwig gave to the church of Abingdon.*[203]
Likewise, in the first year of his reign [955–6], King Eadwig gave and by his charter confirmed a certain wood at Hawkridge to God and the blessed Mary and the house of Abingdon and the monks serving God there for ever, for constructing the church of St Mary of Abingdon, at the request of Æthelwold abbot of that monastery. The terms of his charter are as follows:

B119. *Charter of King Eadwig concerning Hawkridge.*
Charters of Abingdon Abbey, no. 57; above, c. 43.

B120. *How King Eadwig gave Ginge to the church.*[204]
Likewise, in the second year of his reign [956–7], the aforementioned King Eadwig gave and by his charter confirmed Ginge to God and the blessed Mary and this house of Abingdon and the monks serving God there for ever. The terms of his charter are as follows:

B121. *Charter of King Eadwig concerning Ginge.*
Charters of Abingdon Abbey, no. 58; above, c. 42.

B122. *Concerning Hendred, how it was given.*
In the same year King Eadwig gave ten hides in Hendred to Beorhtric his thegn, and that man by the king's consent gave them to God and the blessed Mary and the house of Abingdon and the monks serving God there, in pure and perpetual alms.[205] And this is the king's charter confirming this gift:

[202] Cf. above, c. 40. [203] Cf. above, p. 72. [204] Cf. above, p. 70.
[205] Beorhtric cannot be identified with any certainty.

B123. *Carta.*
Charters of Abingdon Abbey, no. 53.[206]

[i. 191] **B124**. *Quomodo rex Edwius dedit Brithnoþo Tadmertuna.*[207]
Concessit idem rex Eadwius eodem anno Birhtnoþo ministro suo in Tadmærtuna [a]nouem cassatos,[a] [208] et ipse de concessu regis Deo et beate Marie et domui Abbendonie et monachis ibidem Deo seruientibus in puram et perpetuam elemosinam. Et hec est carta regis hanc donationem confirmans:

B125. *Carta regis Edwi de Tademertuna.*
Charters of Abingdon Abbey, no. 67; above, c. 54.

[i. 194] fo. 49r **B126**. *De quinque cassatis in Taddemertune.*
Eodem anno dedit rex Eadwius Brihtrico ministro suo quinque cassatos in eadem Tademertuna, et ipse de concessu regis Deo et beate Marie et domui Abbendonie et monachis ibidem Deo seruientibus in puram et perpetuam elemosinam. Et hec est carta regis hanc donationem confirmans:

B127. *Carta regis Edwi de quinque cassatis in Tademertun.*
Charters of Abingdon Abbey, no. 66; above, c. 55.

[i. 197] fo. 49v **B128**. *Quomodo rex Edwius dedit Beornodo quinque cassatos in Tademertuna.*
Item eodem anno dedit memoratus rex Eadwius Beorthnodo principi quinque mansas in eadem Tadmertuna, et ipse de consensu regis Deo et beate Marie et domui Abbendonie et monachis ibidem Deo seruientibus in puram et perpetuam elemosinam. Et hec est carta regis hanc donationem confirmans:

B129. *Carta regis Edwii de quinque cassatis in Tademertuna.*
Charters of Abingdon Abbey, no. 73; above, c. 56.

[i. 200] fo. 50r **B130**. *Quomodo rex Edwius dedit Alfrico comiti Cuþesdune.*[209]
Eodem anno dedit rex Edwius Ælfero comiti Cuþenesdune decem mansarum, et ille de consensu regis Deo et beate Marie et domui Abbendonie et monachis ibidem Deo seruientibus in puram et

B124 [a–a] *the numeral and the word* cassatos *appear beyond the normal end of the written line*

[206] Sawyer, no. 581. This charter records Eadwig granting the above ten hides to Beorhtric. The incarnation date is given as 955, but 956 is more likely to be correct, which would match the indiction and the witness list. *Charters of Abingdon Abbey*, p. 223, states that it 'is probably authentic, although there are some minor difficulties'.

B123. *Charter.*
Charters of Abingdon Abbey, no. 53.[206]

B124. *How King Eadwig gave Tadmarton to Byrhtnoth.*[207]
The same King Eadwig in the same year granted nine hides[208] in Tadmarton to Byrhtnoth his thegn, and he himself, by the king's grant, gave it to God and the blessed Mary and the house of Abingdon and the monks serving God there, in pure and perpetual alms. And this is the king's charter confirming this gift:

B125. *Charter of King Eadwig concerning Tadmarton.*
Charters of Abingdon Abbey, no. 67; above, c. 54.

B126. *Concerning five hides in Tadmarton.*
In the same year King Eadwig gave five hides in that same Tadmarton to Beorhtric his thegn, and he himself, by the king's grant, gave it to God and the blessed Mary and the house of Abingdon and the monks serving God there, in pure and perpetual alms. And this is the king's charter confirming this gift:

B127. *Charter of King Eadwig concerning five hides in Tadmarton.*
Charters of Abingdon Abbey, no. 66; above, c. 55.

B128. *How King Eadwig gave five hides in Tadmarton to Byrhtnoth.*
Likewise, in the same year, the afore-mentioned King Eadwig gave five hides in that same Tadmarton to Byrhtnoth, a noble, and he himself, by the king's consent, gave it to God and the blessed Mary and the house of Abingdon and the monks serving God there, in pure and perpetual alms. And this is the king's charter confirming this gift:

B129. *Charter of King Eadwig concerning five hides in Tadmarton.*
Charters of Abingdon Abbey, no. 73; above, c. 56.

B130. *How King Eadwig gave Cuddesdon to Earl Ælfric.*[209]
In the same year King Eadwig gave Cuddesdon amounting to twenty hides to Ælfhere, an earl, and that man by the king's consent gave it to God and the blessed Mary and the house of Abingdon and the

[207] MS C does not provide introductions to these Tadmarton charters.

[208] The charter specifies ten hides, but the abbreviation in MS B for 'id est', which precedes the numeral, makes that numeral look like 'ix', hence the confusion.

[209] The rubricator seems to have entered the wrong name, as the charter which follows specifies Ælfhere as the grantee. MS C has a different section introducing the gift; above, c. 45.

perpetuam elemosinam. Et hec est carta regis hanc donationem confirmans:

B131. *Carta regis Edwii de Cuþenesdune, quomodo dedit comiti.*
Charters of Abingdon Abbey, no. 70; above, c. 46.

[i. 203] fo. 51^r^ **B132.** *Quomodo rex Edwius dedit Alfric Hannie uiginti cassatorum.*[210]
Item eodem anno dedit rex Ælfrico parenti suo Hannie uiginti mansarum, et ipse de consensu regis Deo et beate Marie et domui Abbendonie et monachis ibidem Deo seruientibus in puram et perpetuam elemosinam. Et hec est carta regis hanc donationem confirmans:

[i. 204] **B133.** *Carta regis Edwii de Hannie.*
Charters of Abingdon Abbey, no. 55 (i).[211]

[i. 207] fo. 52^r^ **B134.** *Quomodo rex Edwius dedit Eadrico Welliford duorum et uiginti cassatorum.*[212]
Item idem rex Edwius dedit Eadrico ministro suo Welliford duarum et uiginti mansarum,[a] et ipse de consensu regis Deo et beate Marie et domui Abbendonie et monachis ibidem Deo seruientibus in puram et perpetuam elemosinam. Et hec est carta regis hanc donationem confirmans:

B135. *Carta regis Eadwii duorum et uiginti cassatorum in Welliford.*
Charters of Abingdon Abbey, no. 64; above, c. 48.

[i. 210] fo. 52^v^ **B136.** *Quomodo Edwius rex dedit Alfsio Bennaham quinque et uiginti cassatorum.*[213]
Item idem rex Eadwius dedit Ælfsio ministro suo Bennaham quinque et uiginti cassatorum, et ipse de consensu regis Deo et beate Marie et domui Abbendonie et monachis ibidem Deo seruientibus in puram et perpetuam elemosinam. Et hec est carta regis hanc donationem confirmans:

B134 [a] *corr. from* mansas

---

[210] It is almost certain that the grantee was Ælfric Cild. He married the sister of Ælfhere, a royal kinsman; hence Ælfric was by marriage a royal kinsman, or, as the charter says, 'adoptiuus parens'. The witness list includes Ælfric's three brothers-in-law. On Ælfric, see also above, p. cxxiii.

[211] Sawyer, no. 597. This charter records Eadwig granting the above twenty hides to Ælfric, and receiving 60 *mancuses* in return. It is dated 956. It is repeated in a somewhat different version below, B161. Deficiencies in the latter version may have led to the production of the present one, but this cannot be certain; *Charters of Abingdon Abbey*, pp. 234–5. *Charters of Abingdon Abbey*, p. 235, states that 'in spite of these textual

monks serving God there, in pure and perpetual alms. And this is the king's charter confirming this gift:

B131. *Charter of King Eadwig concerning Cuddesdon, how he gave it to the earl.*

Charters of Abingdon Abbey, no. 70; above, c. 46.

B132. *How King Eadwig gave Hanney amounting to twenty hides to Ælfric.*[210]

Likewise, in the same year, the king gave Hanney amounting to twenty hides to Ælfric, his kinsman, and he by the king's consent gave it to God and the blessed Mary and the house of Abingdon and the monks serving God there, in pure and perpetual alms. And this is the king's charter confirming this gift:

B133. *Charter of King Eadwig concerning Hanney.*

Charters of Abingdon Abbey, no. 55 (i).[211]

B134. *How King Eadwig gave Welford amounting to twenty-two hides to Eadric.*[212]

Likewise, the same King Eadwig gave Welford amounting to twenty-two hides to Eadric his thegn, and he by the king's consent gave it to God and the blessed Mary and the house of Abingdon and the monks serving God there, in pure and perpetual alms. And this is the king's charter confirming this gift:

B135. *Charter of King Eadwig regarding twenty-two hides in Welford.*

Charters of Abingdon Abbey, no. 64; above, c. 48.

B136. *How King Eadwig gave Benham amounting to twenty-five hides to Ælfsige.*[213]

Likewise, the same King Eadwig gave Benham amounting to twenty-five hides to Ælfsige his thegn, and he by the king's consent gave it to God and the blessed Mary and the house of Abingdon and the monks serving God there, in pure and perpetual alms. And this is the king's charter confirming this gift:

difficulties, there can be little doubt that [the document] represents a genuine charter of 956'.

212 MS C has a different section introducing the gift; above, c. 47.

213 Ælfsige could also be the recipient of the grant of *Æscesburh*, above, B98–B99 (*Charters of Abingdon Abbey*, no. 48). The charter grants lands in the modern parish of Speen, Berkshire, including Marsh Benham, or perhaps the entirety of that modern parish; see *Charters of Abingdon Abbey*, pp. 304–5. For Abingdon holding two hides at Hoe Benham after 1066, see *DB* i, fo. 58^{v}; vol. ii. 156; for a 12th-c. administrative list mentioning Abingdon's possession of a ten-hide holding in Benham, see vol. ii. 389.

B137. *Carta regis Edwii de Bennaham.*
Charters of Abingdon Abbey, no. 72.[214]

[i. 212] fo. 53r **B138**. *Quomodo rex Edwius dedit Alfwino Middeltun quindecim cassatorum.*[215]

Item idem rex Eadwius dedit Ælfwino ministro suo Middeltun quindecim cassatorum, et ipse de consensu regis Deo et beate Marie et domui Abbendonie et monachis ibidem Deo seruientibus in puram et perpetuam elemosinam. Et hec est carta regis hanc donationem confirmans:

[i. 213] **B139**. *Carta regis Edwii de Middeltuna.*
Charters of Abingdon Abbey, no. 54; above, c. 50.

[i. 215] **B140**. *Quomodo Edwius rex dedit Brihtelmo Kenitun.*

fo. 53v Item idem rex dedit Byrhtelmo presbitero Chenitum, et ipse de consensu regis dedit[a] Deo et beate Marie et domui Abbendonie et monachis ibidem Deo seruientibus in puram et perpetuam elemosinam. Et hec est carta regis hanc donationem confirmans:

[i. 216] **B141**. *Carta regis Edwii de Kenitune.*
Charters of Abingdon Abbey, no. 56; above, c. 44.

[i. 218] **B142**.[a]
fo. 54r *Charters of Abingdon Abbey*, no. 76.[216]

fo. 54v **B143**. Item idem rex Eadwius dedit Ælfrico ministro suo Bægenweorðe quinque et uiginti cassatorum, et ipse de consensu regis Deo et beate Marie et domui Abbendonie et monachis ibidem Deo seruientibus in puram et perpetuam elemosinam.[217] Et hec est carta regis hanc donationem confirmans:

[i. 219] **B144**. *Carta regis Edwii de Baenwurþe.*
Charters of Abingdon Abbey, no. 60; above, c. 53.

B140 [a] *interlin.*

B142 [a] *the rubricator failed to supply a heading in the appropriate place*

---

[214] Sawyer, no. 591. This charter records Eadwig granting the above twenty-five hides to Ælfsige, his 'loyal man [*meo fideli*]'. It is dated 956. *Charters of Abingdon Abbey*, p. 303, states that it 'is almost certainly authentic'.

B137. *Charter of King Eadwig concerning Benham.*
Charters of Abingdon Abbey, no. 72.[214]

B138. *How King Eadwig gave Milton amounting to fifteen hides to Ælfwine.*[215]
Likewise, the same King Eadwig gave Milton amounting to fifteen hides to Ælfwine his thegn, and he by the king's consent gave it to God and the blessed Mary and the house of Abingdon and the monks serving God there, in pure and perpetual alms. And this is the king's charter confirming this gift:

B139. *Charter of King Eadwig concerning Milton.*
Charters of Abingdon Abbey, no. 54; above, c. 50.

B140. *How King Eadwig gave Kennington to Brihthelm.*
Likewise, the same king gave Kennington to Brihthelm the priest, and he by the king's consent gave it to God and the blessed Mary and the house of Abingdon and the monks serving God there, in pure and perpetual alms. And this is the king's charter confirming this gift:

B141. *Charter of King Eadwig concerning Kennington.*
Charters of Abingdon Abbey, no. 56; above, c. 44.

B142.
Charters of Abingdon Abbey, no. 76.[216]

B143. Likewise, the same King Eadwig gave Bayworth amounting to twenty-five hides to Ælfric his thegn, and he by the king's consent gave it to God and the blessed Mary and the house of Abingdon and the monks serving God there, in pure and perpetual alms.[217] And this is the king's charter confirming this gift:

B144. *Charter of King Eadwig concerning Bayworth.*
Charters of Abingdon Abbey, no. 60; above, c. 53.

[215] MS C has a different section introducing the gift; above, c. 49.

[216] Sawyer, no. 1292; *Anglo-Saxon Charters*, ed. Robertson, no. 31. MS C provides a Latin summary of this Old English text immediately after its version of the charter; above, p. 76, where this transaction is discussed. *Charters of Abingdon Abbey*, p. 315, suggests that the present Old English text may have been written on the same sheet as the preceding charter, perhaps as an endorsement or addition.

[217] MS C records Ælfric's gift of Bayworth to Abingdon with a different passage, above, p. 84.

[i. 222] fo. 55[r] **B145.** *Quomodo rex Edwius dedit Eadrico Pirianford sexdecim cassatorum.*[218]

Item idem rex Eadwius dedit Eadrico[a] ministro suo Pirianforda sexdecim mansatorum, et ipse de consensu regis Deo et beate Marie et domui Abbendonie et monachis ibidem Deo seruientibus in puram et perpetuam elemosinam. Et hec est carta regis hanc donationem confirmans:

B146. *Carta regis Edwii de Pirianford.*
Charters of Abingdon Abbey, no. 63.[219]

[i. 224] fo. 55[v] **B147.** *Quomodo rex Edwius dedit Alfero Wilmanlehttune.*

Item idem rex Eadwius dedit Alfero senatori Wilmanlehttune, et ipse de consensu regis dedit beate Marie et domui Abbendonie et monachis ibidem Deo seruientibus in puram et perpetuam helemosinam.[220] Et hec est carta regis hanc donationem confirmans:

B148. *Carta regis Edwi de Wilmaleahtun.*
Charters of Abingdon Abbey, no. 71.[221]

[i. 227] fo. 56[v] **B149.** *Quomodo rex Edwius dedit Edmundo Anningadune.*[222]

Item idem rex dedit Eadmundo senatori suo Annigadune, et ipse de consensu regis Deo et beate Marie et domui Abbendonie et monachis ibidem seruientibus in puram et perpetuam elemosinam. Et hec est carta regis hanc donationem confirmans:

B150. *Carta regis Edwii de Anningedune.*
Charters of Abingdon Abbey, no. 65.[223]

B145 [a] *interlin.*

[218] Pyrford, Surrey. This may be the same Eadric who received Welford, Berkshire, from Eadwig on the same occasion; above, cc. 47–8. *DB* i, fo. 32[r], records that Earl Harold had held Pyrford. Prior to his holding, it had been assessed at twenty-seven hides, but later for only sixteen 'ad libitum Heraldi'. The hidage mentioned here and in the charter which follows thus matches the reduced level following Harold's intervention. It may be that the charter was altered to reflect the reduction, or that Harold reduced it to a figure which had some earlier basis; see *Charters of Abingdon Abbey*, pp. 269–70.

[219] Sawyer, no. 621. This charter records Eadwig granting the above sixteen hides to Eadric. It is dated 956. *Charters of Abingdon Abbey*, p. 268, states that 'there is no good reason to object to' the charter concerning its authenticity. Apart from the presence of this charter in the archive, there is no other evidence of Abingdon interest in this land.

B145. *How King Eadwig gave Pyrford amounting to sixteen hides to Eadric.*[218]

Likewise, the same King Eadwig gave Pyrford amounting to sixteen hides to Eadric his thegn, and he by the king's consent gave it to God and the blessed Mary and the house of Abingdon and the monks serving God there, in pure and perpetual alms. And this is the king's charter confirming this gift:

B146. *Charter of King Eadwig concerning Pyrford.*
Charters of Abingdon Abbey, no. 63.[219]

B147. *How King Eadwig gave Wormleighton to Ælfhere.*

Likewise, the same King Eadwig gave Wormleighton to Ælfhere 'the senator', and he by the king's consent gave it to God and the blessed Mary and the house of Abingdon and the monks serving God there, in pure and perpetual alms.[220] And this is the king's charter confirming this gift:

B148. *Charter of King Eadwig concerning Wormleighton.*
Charters of Abingdon Abbey, no. 71.[221]

B149. *How King Eadwig gave Annington to Edmund.*[222]

Likewise, the same king gave Annington to Edmund, his 'senator', and he by the king's consent gave it to God and the blessed Mary and the house of Abingdon and the monks serving God there, in pure and perpetual alms. And this is the king's charter confirming this gift:

B150. *Charter of King Eadwig concerning Annington.*
Charters of Abingdon Abbey, no. 65.[223]

[220] In fact the land probably passed to Abingdon by grant of King Æthelred, above, c. 99 (p. 152).

[221] Sawyer, no. 588. This charter records Eadwig granting ten hides in Wormleighton to Ealdorman Ælfhere. It is dated 956. *Charters of Abingdon Abbey*, p. 300, states that it 'is probably authentic'. For further discussion of Wormleighton, see above, p. 152 n. 327.

[222] Annington, Sussex. A contemporary endorsement to the original charter concerning Annington refers to Edmund as an ealdorman. An ealdorman called Edmund was a regular witness of charters between 949 and 963. His ealdordom may have been in western Wessex; see *Charters of Abingdon Abbey*, p. 278.

[223] Sawyer, no. 624. The original charter also survives; London, British Library, Cotton Augustus ii. 45, reproduced in *BM Facs.*, iii. 20. It records Eadwig granting ten hides at Annington to Edmund, one of his great men ('cuidam meorum optimatum'). In the original the hidage has been altered to sixteen, and this is also the figure in the copy in the *History*. The charter is dated 956. Except for the alteration to the hidage, *Charters of Abingdon Abbey*, p. 277, seems to find the charter acceptable. Apart from the presence of this charter in the archive, there is no other evidence of Abingdon interest in this land.

[i. 229] **B151.** *Quomodo Edwius rex dedit Eadrico Peadenwurðe.*[224]
fo. 57r Item idem rex Eadwius dedit Eadrico Peadanwrðe, et ipse de
[i. 230] consensu regis Deo et beate Marie et domui Abbendonie et monachis ibidem Deo seruientibus in puram et perpetuam elemosinam. Et hec est carta regis hanc donationem confirmans:

B152. *Carta regis Eadwii de Pedanwrþe.*
Charters of Abingdon Abbey, no. 74.[225]

[i. 232] **B153.** *Quomodo rex Edwius dedit Aþelnoþo Fifhide.*[226]
fo. 57v Item idem rex Eadwius dedit Æþelnoðo Fifhidam, et ipse de consensu regis Deo et beate Marie et domui Abbendonie et monachis ibidem Deo seruientibus in puram et perpetuam elemosinam. Et hec est carta regis hanc donationem confirmans:

B154. *Carta regis Edwii de Fifhide.*
Charters of Abingdon Abbey, no. 61.[227]

[i. 234] **B155.** *Quomodo rex Edwius dedit Brihthelmo Stouwe quinque cassa-*
fo. 58r *torum.*
Eodem anno memoratus rex Eadwius dedit Brihtelmo cognato suo Stowe quinque mansarum, et ipse de consensu regis Deo et beate Marie et domui Abbendonie et monachis ibidem Deo seruientibus, eo tenore quo supra.[228]

B156. *Quomodo rex dedit Eadrico Pedanwyrþe.*
Item idem rex Eadwius dedit Eadrico ministro suo Peadanwyrðe, et ipse de consensu regis Deo et beate Marie et[a] domui Abbendonie et
[i. 235] monachis ibidem Deo seruientibus in puram et perpetuam elemosinam. Et hec est carta regis hanc donationem confirmans:

B157. *Carta regis Edwii de Pedanwurþe.*
Charters of Abingdon Abbey, no. 74.[229]

B156 [a] *interlin.*

---

[224] Padworth, Berkshire. Eadric's identity is hard to establish; see *Charters of Abingdon Abbey*, p. 310.

[225] Sawyer, no. 620. This charter records Eadwig granting five hides in Padworth to Eadric. It is dated 956. *Charters of Abingdon Abbey*, p. 310, comments that it 'is probably authentic'. It appears again, below, B157, probably through a straightforward error. Apart from the presence of this charter in the archive, there is no other evidence of Abingdon interest in this land.

[226] Æthelnoth's identity cannot be established with certainty.

[227] Sawyer, no. 603. This charter records Eadwig granting thirteen hides in Fyfield to his

B151. *How King Eadwig gave Padworth to Eadric.*[224]
Likewise, the same King Eadwig gave Padworth to Eadric, and he by the king's consent gave it to God and the blessed Mary and the house of Abingdon and the monks serving God there, in pure and perpetual alms. And this is the king's charter confirming this gift:

B152. *Charter of King Eadwig concerning Padworth.*
Charters of Abingdon Abbey, no. 74.[225]

B153. *How King Eadwig gave Fyfield to Æthelnoth.*[226]
Likewise, the same King Eadwig gave Fyfield to Æthelnoth, and he by the king's consent gave it to God and the blessed Mary and the house of Abingdon and the monks serving God there, in pure and perpetual alms. And this is the king's charter confirming this gift:

B154. *Charter of King Eadwig concerning Fyfield.*
Charters of Abingdon Abbey, no. 61.[227]

B155. *How King Eadwig gave Stowe amounting to five hides to Brihthelm.*
In the same year, the aforementioned King Eadwig gave Stowe amounting to five hides to Brihthelm, his kinsman, and he by the king's consent gave it to God and the blessed Mary and the house of Abingdon and the monks serving God there, on the same terms as above.[228]

B156. *How the king gave Padworth to Eadric.*
Likewise, the same King Eadwig gave Padworth to Eadric his thegn, and he by the king's consent gave it to God and the blessed Mary and the house of Abingdon and the monks serving God there, in pure and perpetual alms. And this is the king's charter confirming this gift:

B157. *Charter of King Eadwig concerning Padworth.*
Charters of Abingdon Abbey, no. 74.[229]

thegn Æthelnoth. It is dated 956. *Charters of Abingdon Abbey*, p. 262, states that it 'appears to be authentic'.

[228] A 16th-c. copy of the lost original charter of Eadwig concerning this grant is preserved as Cambridge, Corpus Christi College 111, pp. 159–60; *Charters of Abingdon Abbey*, no. 62. It records Eadwig granting the above hides at Church Stowe, Northamptonshire, to Brihthelm. Brihthelm was probably the bishop-elect of Wells; *Charters of Abingdon Abbey*, p. 266. It is unclear why the charter does not appear in the *History*; see above, p. lxviii. Apart from the presence of this document amongst the 16th-c. copies of Abingdon charters, there is no other evidence of Abingdon interest in this land.

[229] Sawyer, no. 620. It is dated 956. This charter has already appeared above, B152.

[i. 237] **B158.** *Quomodo rex Edwius dedit Wlfrico Cheorletun.*[230]
fo. 58v Item idem rex Eadwius dedit Wlfrico ministro suo Cheorletun, et ipse de consensu regis Deo et beate Marie et domui Abbendonie et monachis ibidem Deo seruientibus in puram et perpetuam elemosinam. Et hec est carta regis hanc donationem confirmans:

B159. *Carta regis Edwii.*
Charters of Abingdon Abbey, no. 69.[231]

[i. 238] **B160.** *Quomodo rex Edwius dedit Alfrio uiginti cassatos.*
fo. 59r Item idem rex Edwius dedit Alfrico parenti suo uiginti mansas, et ipse de consensu regis Deo et beate Marie et domui Abbendonie et monachis ibidem Deo seruientibus in puram et perpetuam elemosinam. Et hec est carta[a] regis hanc donationem confirmans:

[i. 239] **B161.** *Carta regis Edwii de uiginti cassatis.*
Charters of Abingdon Abbey, no. 55 (ii).[232]

[i. 242] **B162.** *Quomodo rex Edgarus dedit Alfeo Bochlande.*[233]
fo. 60r Tercio anno regni sui dedit rex Eadwius Ælfeho duci Bochlande, et ipse de consensu regis Deo et beate Marie et domui Abbendonie et monachis ibidem Deo seruientibus in puram et perpetuam elemosinam. Et hec est carta regis hanc donationem confirmans:

B163. *Carta regis Edgari de Bochelande.*
Charters of Abingdon Abbey, no. 75; above, c. 52.

[i. 245] **B164.** *Quo anno dedit rex Edwius Edrico Wurþe.*[234]
fo. 60v Quarto anno regni sui dedit rex Eadwius Edrico ministro suo Wurðe triginta mansarum, et ipse de consensu regis Deo et beate Marie et

B160 [a] cartha *MS*

---

[230] Probably Charlton in Grove, Berkshire. The grantee could be Wulfric Cufing; *Charters of Abingdon Abbey*, p. clxxx. Abingdon had no *Domesday* interest in lands at Charlton in Grove; *DB* i, fos. 57r, 60v, 61r, 62v.

[231] Sawyer, no. 634. This charter records Eadwig granting five hides in Charlton to Wulfric. It is dated 956. *Charters of Abingdon Abbey*, p. 292, states that it 'seems entirely acceptable'. Before the witness list, where one might have expected the vernacular boundary clause, appears the statement that 'the aforesaid land is separated by no fixed bounds, but the yokes [*iugera*] adjoin yokes'. Another charter granting five hides in Charlton to Abingdon, below, B223 (*Charters of Abingdon Abbey*, no. 118) contains a rather similar clause, and also states that the grant consists of 'common land [*communis terra*]'. All these statements suggest the existence of a strip-based common field system. See D. Hooke, *The Landscape of Anglo-Saxon England* (London, 1998), pp. 113–30.

[232] Sawyer, no. 597. A different version of this charter has already appeared above, B133, and is discussed there.

B158. *How King Eadwig gave Charlton to Wulfric.*[230]
Likewise, the same King Eadwig gave Charlton to Wulfric his thegn, and he by the king's consent gave it to God and the blessed Mary and the house of Abingdon and the monks serving God there, in pure and perpetual alms. And this is the king's charter confirming this gift:

B159. *King Eadwig's charter.*
Charters of Abingdon Abbey, no. 69.[231]

B160. *How King Eadwig gave twenty hides to Ælfric.*
Likewise, the same King Eadwig gave twenty hides to Ælfric, his kinsman, and he by the king's consent gave it to God and the blessed Mary and the house of Abingdon and the monks serving God there, in pure and perpetual alms. And this is the king's charter confirming this gift:

B161. *Charter of King Eadwig concerning the twenty hides.*
Charters of Abingdon Abbey, no. 55 (ii).[232]

B162. *How King Edgar gave Buckland to Ælfheah.*[233]
In the third year of his reign, King Eadwig gave Buckland to Ælfheah, an ealdorman, and he by the king's consent gave it to God and the blessed Mary and the house of Abingdon and the monks serving God there, in pure and perpetual alms. And this is the king's charter confirming this gift:

B163. *Charter of King Eadwig concerning Buckland.*
Charters of Abingdon Abbey, no. 75; above, c. 52.

B164. *In what year King Eadwig gave Longworth to Eadric.*[234]
In the fourth year of his reign, King Eadwig gave Longworth amounting to thirty hides to Eadric his thegn, and he by the king's

233 Edgar's name is most likely just a slip by the rubricator; see also above, B130. However, the witnesses are not entirely compatible with the charter's date of 957, and *Charters of Abingdon Abbey*, p. 313, suggests that the apparent simple error by the rubricator may reflect the instability of the text; see also above, cc. 51–2 and note. MS C has a different section introducing the gift; above, c. 51.

234 Eadric is probably the son of Ealdorman Ealhhelm, and brother of Ælfheah and Ælfhere; *Charters of Abingdon Abbey*, p. 329. See above, p. 50, for King Eadred's supposed restoration of Longworth to the abbey; p. 94 for a much more plausible charter recording restoration by Edgar. *Charters of Abingdon Abbey*, p. 329, suggests that Eadred's proposed grant was prevented by Eadwig, who granted the land to a thegn, before Edgar finally ensured that it was acquired by Abingdon. John, *Orbis Britanniae*, p. 197, suggests that we should believe the *History*'s statement in the present chapter that Eadric gave the land to Abingdon. He argues that at the time when Eadred booked Longworth to Abingdon, Eadric or a member of his family would have held it with some sort of precarious title. In 958

domui Abbendonie et monachis ibidem Deo seruientibus in puram et perpetuam elemosinam. Et hec est carta regis hanc donationem confirmans:

B165. *Carta regis Edwii de Wrþe.*
Charters of Abingdon Abbey, no. 80.[235]

[i. 247] fo. 61r **B166.** *Rex Edwius dedit Eadwoldo Draitun decem mansarum.*[236]
Eodem anno rex Eadwius dedit Eadwoldo ministro suo Drægtun decem mansarum, et ipse de consensu regis Deo et beate Marie et domui Abbendonie et monachis ibidem Deo seruientibus in puram et perpetuam elemosinam. Et hec est carta regis hanc donationem confirmans:

B167. *Carta regis Edwii de Draituna.*
Charters of Abingdon Abbey, no. 78.[237]

[i. 249] fo. 61v **B168.** *Rex Eadwius dedit Cinlaf uenator Escemere quatuor cassatorum.*[238]
Eodem die[a] dedit rex Eadwius Cynlaf uenatori suo Æscemere tredecim mansarum, et ipse de consensu regis domui Abbendonie, testibus supradictis testantibus.

B169. *Quomodo rex Edwius dedit Kinrico*[a] *duorum cassatorum.*
Item eodem anno dedit rex Eadwius Kynrico pincernario[239] Cern duorum cassatorum, et ipse de consensu regis Deo et beate Marie et
[i. 250] domui Abbendonie et monachis ibidem Deo seruientibus in puram et perpetuam elemosinam. Et hec est carta regis hanc donationem confirmans:

B168 [a] *over erasure, perhaps of* anno

B169 [a] *the place-name* Cern *may have been accidentally omitted here*

Eadwig persuaded Eadric to give Longworth to Abingdon. However, first he booked the land to Eadric. This temporary possession with full title meant that Eadric would receive the spiritual benefits due to a donor of bookland. Whilst John's suggestion cannot be disproved, it may seem a rather lengthy way to maintain trust in the *History*'s dubious and routine statement that the king gave the land to Eadric who gave it to Abingdon.

[235] Sawyer, no. 654. This charter records Eadwig (entitled 'rex Saxonum') granting the above hides to Eadric. It is dated 958. *Charters of Abingdon Abbey*, p. 328, states that it 'appears to be authentic'.

[236] Cf. above, c. 62, a charter of Edgar granting twenty hides at Drayton to Abingdon. This mentions that King Eadred, rather than Eadwig, had given ten hides (altered to twenty hides in MS B) to Eadwold, and Eadwold had restored it to Abingdon on his deathbed.

consent gave it to God and the blessed Mary and the house of Abingdon and the monks serving God there, in pure and perpetual alms. And this is the king's charter confirming this gift:

B165. *Charter of King Eadwig concerning Longworth.*
Charters of Abingdon Abbey, no. 80.[235]

B166. *King Eadwig gave Drayton amounting to ten hides to Eadwold.*[236]
In the same year, King Eadwig gave Drayton amounting to ten hides to Eadwold his thegn, and he by the king's consent gave it to God and the blessed Mary and the house of Abingdon and the monks serving God there, in pure and perpetual alms. And this is the king's charter confirming this gift:

B167. *Charter of King Eadwig concerning Drayton.*
Charters of Abingdon Abbey, no. 78.[237]

B168. *King Eadwig gave* Æscmere *amounting to four hides to Cynlaf the huntsman.*[238]
On the same day, King Eadwig gave *Æscmere* amounting to thirteen hides to Cynlaf his huntsman, and he by the king's consent gave it to the house of Abingdon, with the above witnesses witnessing.

B169. *How King Eadwig gave two hides to Cynric.*
Likewise, in the same year, King Eadwig gave *Cern* amounting to two hides to Cynric the cup-bearer,[239] and he by the king's consent gave it to God and the blessed Mary and the house of Abingdon and the monks serving God there, in pure and perpetual alms. And this is the king's charter confirming this gift:

Eadwold may be the thegn who witnessed certain charters of Eadwig; Keynes, *Atlas of Attestations*, table LI.

[237] Sawyer, no. 650. This charter records Eadwig granting the above hides to Eadwold. It is dated 958. *Charters of Abingdon Abbey*, p. 321, states that it 'is probably authentic'.

[238] The name *Æscmere* is preserved in Ashmansworth, Hampshire. This is next to Crux Easton, and it may be that record of the gift to Cynlaf is linked to Abingdon's interest in Crux Easton; see above, B13–B14, *Charters of Abingdon Abbey*, pp. 579–80 (iii). On the source for the *History*'s information, see above, p. xlii n. 169. For other mentions of *Æscmere*, see Sawyer, nos. 336, 1533.

[239] A Cynric *minister* also appears in MS B as a witness to B107, B114, B175, *Charters of Abingdon Abbey*, nos. 77, 83 (two Cynrics), 84. The compiler of MS B apparently derives the word 'pincernarius' from the use of 'propincernarius' in the charter that follows. *Cern* seems to have been the name of a stream, and thence of land by that stream. The land mentioned in this charter could be in the north of Pusey, Berkshire; EPNS, *Berkshire*, ii. 389–90, iii. 699. *DB* i, fo. 59^{v}, records Abingdon having two hides in Pusey.

B170. *Carta regis Edwii de Cern.*
Charters of Abingdon Abbey, no. 79.[240]

[i. 251] **B171.** *Quomodo rex Edwius ⟨dedit⟩ Wlfrico Dencheswrþe.*[241]
fo. 62r Item eodem anno dedit rex Eadwius Wlfrico ministro suo Dench-
[i. 252] eswrþe decem cassatorum, et ipse de consensu regis Deo et beate Marie et domui Abbendonie et monachis ibidem Deo seruientibus in puram et perpetuam elemosinam. Et hec est carta regis hanc donationem confirmans:

B172. *Carta regis Edwii de Dencheswrthe.*
Charters of Abingdon Abbey, no. 81.[242]

[i. 254] **B173.** *De morte Edwii regis.*[243]
fo. 62v Rege Eadwigo cedente in fatum sine liberis, diuina disponente clementia successit ei in regnum rex illustris Eadgarus frater eius uterinus. Iste uero rex Eadgarus, cum iam prouectus ad regni solium sceptrigera potiretur potestate, sic uet⟨e⟩rem hominem cum actibus suis[244] iugi meditatione[a] studuit exsuere, ut in ipso tam concupiscentia carnis quam concupiscentia oculorum pariter et superbia uite penitus adnullari uideretur. Licet enim etas uirens et forma decens, dignitas preminens et copia diuiciarum bonos mores sepius emollire et pudorem cordis soleant exstirpare, non est tamen aurum eius obscuratum[245] ob amorem rerum transeuntium, more fluentis aque, quin in omnibus et[b] per omnia diuinis obtemperatis preceptis et
fo. 63r quicquid ad hones|tatis et[c] dignitatis aumentum illi Deus misericorditer inperciit, totum ad ipsius honorem et[d] regni sui salubritatem, sagaciter accitare[e] satageret. Nec mora de nouo nouus miles effectus, rex Edgarus, donis nature insignitus et gratie, quasi pugil armatus contra diabolum monomachiam in hac conualle flebili[246] uiriliter sustinuit nec succubit, quia adiutor factus est ei et protector qui inbecilli Dauid de robusto Golia triumphum contulit.[247] Quid multa? Rex Edgarus, a beato Dunstano pariter et a sancto Adþelwoldo

B173 [a] *corr. from* meditationem *by erasure of final abbreviation mark* [b] *interlin.* [c] *mistakenly erased* [d] *interlin.* [e] *corr. from* accitaret *by erasure*

[240] Sawyer, no. 651. This charter records Eadwig granting the above hides to Cynric his cup-bearer ('propincernarius'). It is dated 958. *Charters of Abingdon Abbey*, p. 325, states that it 'can probably be accepted as authentic'. The witnesses include the king's steward (*discifer*) and butler (*pincerna*).

[241] See above, B91 (*Charters of Abingdon Abbey*, no. 41), for a charter of Eadred granting five hides in Denchworth to a man named Wulfric, most likely the beneficiary of this charter, Wulfric Cufing. The present charter may be a confirmation. See below, B186 (*Charters of Abingdon Abbey*, no. 86) for Wulfric's forfeiture of this and other estates, and their subsequent restoration by King Edgar in 960.

B170. *Charter of King Eadwig concerning* Cern.
Charters of Abingdon Abbey, no. 79.[240]

B171. *How King Eadwig gave Denchworth to Wulfric.*[241]
Likewise, in the same year, King Eadwig gave Denchworth amounting to ten hides to Wulfric his thegn, and he by the king's consent gave it to God and the blessed Mary and the house of Abingdon and the monks serving God there, in pure and perpetual alms. And this is the king's charter confirming this gift:

B172. *Charter of King Eadwig concerning Denchworth.*
Charters of Abingdon Abbey, no. 81.[242]

B173. *Concerning the death of King Eadwig.*[243]
When the childless King Eadwig yielded to death [959], by the disposition of divine clemency his uterine brother, the illustrious King Edgar, succeeded him in the kingdom. That King Edgar, indeed, when he had been conveyed to the throne of the kingdom and was enjoying the sceptre-bearing power, strove in constant meditation to shed 'the old man with his deeds',[244] thus that both lust of the body and lust of the eyes and likewise pride of life seemed to be entirely made nothing in him. For although vigorous age and seemly appearance, outstanding dignity and fullness of wealth are accustomed more often to weaken good behaviour and to eradicate modesty of heart, however his gold did not become dim[245] through love of transient things, like flowing water, but rather, obedient to divine commands in everything and every way, he strove keenly to do whatever God mercifully bestowed on him to increase honour and dignity, entirely for His honour and the good health of the kingdom. And without delay made anew a new knight, King Edgar, marked out with the gifts of nature and grace, like an armed champion manfully sustained single combat against the Devil in this tearful valley[246] and did not succumb, since He who conferred triumph on the weak David against the powerful Goliath was made his supporter and protector.[247] What's more, King Edgar was fittingly instructed by the blessed

[242] Sawyer, no. 657. This charter records Eadwig granting five hides in Denchworth to Wulfric. It is dated 958. *Charters of Abingdon Abbey*, p. 331, states that it 'appears to be authentic', whilst noting the difficulty of the existence of the earlier charter of Eadred.
[243] Cf. above, c. 59.
[244] Col. 3: 9 'expoliantes vos veterem hominem cum actibus suis'.
[245] Cf. Lam. 4: 1 'Quomodo obscuratum est aurum'.
[246] Cf. Ps. 83 (84): 7.
[247] For David and Goliath, see 1 Kgs (1 Sam.) 17.

ceterisque Anglie[f] sapientibus decenter instructus, improbos oppressit, rebelles redarguit, iustos et modestos medullitus dilexit, destructas Dei renouauit ecclesias ac honorifice ditauit, et monasteria circiter
[i. 255] quadraginta construi iussit, abiectis a[g] cenobiis clericis monachorum et sanctimonialium cateruas aggregauit. Proficiscens itaque rex de uirtute in uirtutem [h]inde ui⟨r⟩[h] [248] tantus ac talis est effectus, non minus predicabilis putaretur Anglis quam Romulus Romanis, Cirus Persis, Alexander Macedonibus, Artarxerses Parthis, Karolus magnus Francis.[249]

B174. *De priuilegio et cartis Edgari regis.*

Nunc uero de regis huius munificis liberalitatibus erga hanc sacratissimam domum Abbendonie, insimul et de libertatibus eius possessionumque ad eandem abbatiam pertinentium, sua auctoritate roboratis[a] mentionem facere duximus necessarium. Primo ergo ponendum est ipsius priuilegium,[250] deinde carte ponende quibus possessiones subsequentes huic domui confirmauit,[251] tercio carte hominum suorum qui de consensu suo cartas eisdem cartis confirmatas huic domui contulerunt,[252] et ab illo tempore usque ad presens tempus inconcusse permanent et gratia Dei perpetuum robur obtinebunt.[253] Quarto uero tam cartas eius quam suorum apponemus possessiones olim nostras confirmantes.[254] Que uero possessiones licet ad presens minime cedant in usus nostros, nichilominus tamen stetit per regem et suos quin carte eorum de eisdem possessionibus perpetuum robur obtinerent, si antiqui hostis uersutia, et hominum cupiditas ceca, insuper et potestas permisisset regia. Regis itaque Edgari priuilegii tenor hic est:

[i. 256] **B175.** *Priuilegium Edgari regis.*[a]

Charters of Abingdon Abbey, no. 84; above, c. 60.

[f] *corr. from* Anglice [g] *interlin.* [h–h] *the reading here is unclear and the text may be corrupt*

B174 [a] roborata *MS, perhaps misled by following c. 59 above*

B175 [a] *an illustration of the king appears at the start of this charter*

[248] The textual emendation, and therefore the translation, are necessarily speculative.

[249] The compiler here drew on John of Worcester, *Chronicle*, ii. 424: 'pacificus rex Eadgarus non minus memorabilis Anglis quam Romulus Romanis, Cirus Persis, Alexander Macedonibus, Arsaces Parthis, Karolus magnus Francis'.

[250] B175.

[251] B176–B183.

Dunstan and also by St Æthelwold and other wise men of England, and he crushed the ill-intentioned, rebuked rebels, from the depths of his heart loved the just and modest, renovated and honourably enriched God's ruined churches, ordered about forty monasteries to be constructed, and—once clerics had been expelled from the monasteries—gathered bands of monks and nuns. Proceeding from virtue to virtue he became thence a man[248] so great and of such quality that he was thought no less praiseworthy among the English than Romulus among the Romans, Cyrus among the Persians, Alexander among the Macedonians, Artaxerxes among the Parthians, and Charlemagne among the Franks.[249]

B174. *Concerning King Edgar's privilege and charters.*
Now, indeed, we have thought it necessary to mention this munificent king's generous gifts towards this most sacred house of Abingdon, and also its liberties and those of the possessions pertaining to that abbey, strengthened by his authority. To be placed first is his privilege,[250] next the charters whereby he confirmed subsequent possessions to this house,[251] third the charters of his men who by his consent conferred charters[252] on this house confirmed by Edgar's charters, which from that time until the present remain unshaken and by the grace of God will maintain their strength for ever.[253] Fourth, indeed, we place the charters both of him and of his men confirming our former possessions.[254] Although indeed these possessions at present yield nothing to our profit, nevertheless it was the responsibility of the king and his men that their charters concerning these possessions would have maintained their perpetual strength, if the cunning of the old enemy, the blind greed of men, and in addition royal power had permitted. And so the terms of King Edgar's privilege are as follows:

B175. *King Edgar's privilege.*
Charters of Abingdon Abbey, no. 84; above, c. 60.

[252] It seems likely that the scribe here meant to write 'terras' (lands) or some such word, rather than 'cartas' (charters).

[253] B184–B196.

[254] B197–B206. In fact all these are charters of the king, not of his men. The phraseology here may reflect 13th-c. assumptions about the likely existence of donors' charters recording their gifts to the Church. Of the places mentioned in those charters, only in Hendred did Abingdon have lands in the 12th or 13th c.; see vol. ii. 322, 388. However, the later lands may not be those which were granted to Abingdon by Edgar; see *Charters of Abingdon Abbey*, p. 224.

[i. 264] fo. 65v **B176.** *Carta regis Edgari de Mercham.*
Charters of Abingdon Abbey, no. 102; above, c. 60.

[i. 266] fo. 66r Frileford,[a] Appeltun, Leoie fuerunt tempore Edgari regis membra de Mercham, quarum mete partim hic distinguntur, partim alibi.[255]

Mete de Leia.[256] Ærest of þan hæcce to Dudemæres hele, of Dudemæres to merc lege, of merc lege to stan lege, of stan lege to þære dun lege, of þær dun lege swa eft innon þæne hæcce.

[i. 267] **B177.** *Carta regis Edgari de Cumenora.*
Charters of Abingdon Abbey, no. 111; above, c. 81.

[i. 270] fo. 66v **B178.** *Quomodo Wiham, Seuecurt, Henstesheie, Etun fuerunt membra de Cumenora.*
Fuerunt autem Wihtham, Seouecurt, Hensteseie, Eatun membra de Cumenora temporibus Eadgari regis Anglie, habentes cassatos quinque et uiginti.[257] Nunc uero Hensteseie membrum[a] est de Bertona, Wihteham et Seouecurt militibus date, Eatun omnino ablata.[258]
Mete de Eatun.
Charters of Abingdon Abbey, no. 151.[259]

B179. *Carta regis Eadgari de uiginti hidis in Draitun.*
Charters of Abingdon Abbey, no. 85; above, c. 62.

[i. 273] fo. 67v **B180.** *Carta regis Edgari de Hannie uiginti cassatarum.*
Charters of Abingdon Abbey, no. 112; above, c. 83.

B176 [a] *this sentence is preceded by a blank line, where the rubricator may have failed to enter a heading*

B178 [a] menbrum *MS*

---

[255] For comments on this passage, see above, p. 118 n. 261. The reference to bounds defined elsewhere could be to those of Appleton in Edmund's charter to Æthelstan Half-king, above, B70.

[256] This passage also forms the latter part of the boundary clauses of B239 and B258 (*Charters of Abingdon Abbey*, nos. 137, 146). These bounds also appear in MS C, fos. 201v–202r, in the quire of charter bounds at the end of that manuscript, in the main scribe's hand; see *Charters of Abingdon Abbey*, p. 589 (no. 46). The compiler of the later version of the *History* seems to have believed that it referred to a place called *Lege*, and hence associated it with the previous statement about the members of Marcham; Gelling, *Early Charters of the Thames Valley*, p. 65. The present bounds in fact describe an area of woodland linked to Chilton; see *Charters of Abingdon Abbey*, p. 538. In each of the following instances, 'lege', i.e. OE *leah*, could mean either clearing or wood; EPNS, *Berkshire*, iii. 768, 888, 935–6.

[257] How these twenty-five hides were distributed between the four named places is uncertain. A charter in Eadwig's name records his grant of twenty hides at Seacourt, Wytham, and Hinksey to Æthelwold; above, c. 41. Both *Domesday* and a charter of

B176. *Charter of King Edgar concerning Marcham.*
Charters of Abingdon Abbey, no. 102; above, c. 75.

Frilford, Appleton, Bessels Leigh were in King Edgar's time members of Marcham, the bounds of which are partly defined here, partly elsewhere.[255]

Bounds of Leigh.[256] First from the gate to Dudemær's nook, from Dudemær's to the boundary wood, from the boundary wood to the stone wood, from the stone wood to the hill wood, from the hill wood again as far as the gate.

B177. *Charter of King Edgar concerning Cumnor.*
Charters of Abingdon Abbey, no. 111; above, c. 81.

B178. *How Wytham, Seacourt, Hinksey, Eaton were then members of Cumnor.*
Moreover Wytham, Seacourt, Hinksey, and Eaton were members of Cumnor from the time of King Edgar of England, having twenty-five hides.[257] Now, indeed, Hinksey is a member of Barton, Wytham and Seacourt have been given to knights, Eaton completely taken away.[258]

The bounds of Eaton.
Charters of Abingdon Abbey, no. 151.[259]

B179. *Charter of King Edgar concerning twenty hides in Drayton.*
Charters of Abingdon Abbey, no. 85; above, c. 62.

B180. *Charter of King Edgar concerning Hanney amounting to twenty hides.*
Charters of Abingdon Abbey, no. 112; above, c. 83.

Coenwulf, above, c. 10, record ten hides at Eaton, but *DB* i, fo. 61v, makes clear that this was constituted of two five-hide parts. One of these five-hide units may have been included in the present total of twenty-five.

[258] No genuine charter associates Abingdon and Eaton. *DB* i, fo. 61v, shows that Eaton was not in Abingdon's hands *TRE*, and was held by Miles Crispin in 1086.

[259] Sawyer, no. 1569. As above, the compiler mistakenly associated two places with similar names. The Eaton mentioned in the previous section is Eaton in Appleton, whereas this boundary clause covers land on the Cherwell, probably to be associated with Wood Eaton, or Water Eaton, or nearby land in Oxfordshire; *Charters of Abingdon Abbey*, p. 577. The inclusion of a boundary clause in MS B not within a charter is unusual; it may have been written on a separate piece of parchment. Note that these bounds are also the final entry in the quire of MS C devoted to such bounds, fo. 202r; see also *Charters of Abingdon Abbey*, p. 590 (no. 57). The linguistic form of the bounds may suggest a date in the third quarter of the 11th c.; P. Kitson cited in *Charters of Abingdon Abbey*, p. 577.

[i. 276] fo. 68r **B181.** *Carta regis Edgari de Ora decem cassatarum.*
Charters of Abingdon Abbey, no. 113; above, c. 85.

[i. 279] fo. 68v **B182.** *Carta regis Edgari de Bedene.*
Charters of Abingdon Abbey, no. 103; above, c. 86.

[i. 281] fo. 69r **B183.** *Carta regis Edgari de Dencheswrþe.*
Charters of Abingdon Abbey, no. 104; above, c. 77.

[i. 283] fo. 69v **B184.** *Carta regis Edgari de Spersholt decem cassatorum.*
Charters of Abingdon Abbey, no. 97; cf. above, c. 139, and below, B279.[260]

[i. 286] fo. 70r **B185.** *Carta regis Edgari de Estune.*
Charters of Abingdon Abbey, no. 101.[261]

[i. 289] fo. 71r **B186.** *Carta regis Edgari de Æskeburi.*
Charters of Abingdon Abbey, no. 86.[262]

[i. 292] fo. 71v **B187.** *Carta regis Edgari de Wissele.*
Charters of Abingdon Abbey, no. 109; above, c. 88.

[i. 294] fo. 72r **B188.** *Carta regis Edgari de Licchelade.*
Charters of Abingdon Abbey, no. 105.[263]

[i. 297] fo. 73r **B189.** *Carta regis Edgari de Hamstede.*
Charters of Abingdon Abbey, no. 91.[264]

[260] On the repetition of this charter, see above, p. xlvi.

[261] Sawyer, no. 725. This charter records Edgar giving ten hides in Aston Upthorpe, Berkshire, to his queen Ælfthyrth. It is dated 964. *Charters of Abingdon Abbey*, p. 405, states that it 'is in some ways an unconventional text, but there is no good reason to question its authenticity'. Apart from the presence of this charter in the archive, there is no other evidence of Abingdon interest in this land.

[262] Sawyer, no. 687. The original charter also survives; London, British Library, Cotton Augustus ii 40, reproduced in *BM Facs.*, iii. 22. It records Edgar restoring to Wulfric Cufing estates that he had forfeited for a certain offence; *Æscesburh* (in this case identified by *Charters of Abingdon Abbey*, p. clxxvi, as primarily the area which became Woolstone), Denchworth, Garford, Chieveley, Stanmore, Chaddleworth, Boxford, Benham, all in Berkshire; Worting and Tichborne, Hampshire; Stedham, Tillington, Patching, Poynings, Newtimber, all in Sussex. It is dated 960. *Charters of Abingdon Abbey*, pp. 353–5, accepts the authenticity of the document. Wulfgar's disgrace presumably occurred between 958, when he was still receiving land-grants (see above, B172, and also Sawyer, no. 1491) and 960, the date of the present charter.

[263] Sawyer, no. 737. This charter records Edgar giving ten hides at Linslade, Buckinghamshire, to his kinswoman Ælfgifu. It is dated 966. *Charters of Abingdon Abbey*, p. 417, states that it 'appears to be authentic'. This Ælfgifu may have been King Eadwig's first

B181. *Charter of King Edgar concerning Oare amounting to ten hides.*
Charters of Abingdon Abbey, no. 113; above, c. 85.

B182. *Charter of King Edgar concerning Beedon.*
Charters of Abingdon Abbey, no. 103; above, c. 86.

B183. *Charter of King Edgar concerning Denchworth.*
Charters of Abingdon Abbey, no. 104; above, c. 77.

B184. *Charter of King Edgar concerning Sparsholt amounting to ten hides.*
Charters of Abingdon Abbey, no. 97; above, c. 139, and below, B279.[260]

B185. *Charter of King Edgar concerning Aston.*
Charters of Abingdon Abbey, no. 101.[261]

B186. *Charter of King Edgar concerning* Æscesburh.
Charters of Abingdon Abbey, no. 86.[262]

B187. *Charter of King Edgar concerning Whistley.*
Charters of Abingdon Abbey, no. 109; above, c. 88.

B188. *Charter of King Edgar concerning Linslade.*
Charters of Abingdon Abbey, no. 105.[263]

B189. *Charter of King Edgar concerning* Hamstede.
Charters of Abingdon Abbey, no. 91.[264]

wife, from whom he was divorced on grounds of consanguinity. The will of the beneficiary of this charter survives; Sawyer, no. 1484, *Anglo-Saxon Wills*, ed. Whitelock, no. 8. It records her bequeathing *Cæstæleshamme* (probably Chesham, Buckinghamshire) to Abingdon. There is no other evidence of Abingdon holding that land, assuming the bequest actually came into effect. Ælfgifu left Linslade to King Edgar. It is conceivable he gave it to Abingdon, but there is no other evidence for Abingdon having an interest in Linslade. However, it is notable that *DB* i, fo. 150^{v}, records Linslade being held *TRE* by Alwin, Queen Edith's man, suggesting the slight possibility that it had a continuing association with queens.

264 Sawyer, no. 698. This charter records Edgar granting three hides in *Hamstede* to his thegn Eadric. It is dated 961. *Charters of Abingdon Abbey*, p. 374, states that it 'can probably be treated as authentic'. Eadric may be the brother of Ealdormen Ælfhere and Ælfheah; see above, p. cxxiii. The land concerned cannot be identified with any certainty. *De abbatibus*, *CMA* ii. 282, records a certain 'Thovi' giving Abingdon land at Garsington and *Hamstede*. This appears amongst a set of entries concerning gifts in Abbot Ordric's time (1052–66). Such a gift by 'Thovi' seems plausible, but it need not concern the *Hamstede* of this charter; *Charters of Abingdon Abbey*, pp. 374–5.

[i. 299] fo. 73v **B190.** *Carta regis Edgari de septem cassatis de Kingestun.*
Charters of Abingdon Abbey, no. 114.[265]

[i. 300] fo. 74r **B191.** *Carta regis Edgari de Bragenfelda.*
Charters of Abingdon Abbey, no. 106.[266]

[i. 302] **B192.** *Carta regis Hedgari de Hocanedisce.*
Charters of Abingdon Abbey, no. 99.[267]

[i. 303] fo. 74v **B193.** *Carta regis Edgari de Æþedingetun.*
Charters of Abingdon Abbey, no. 90.[268]

[i. 305] fo. 75r **B194.** *Carta regis Edgari de Mordune.*
Charters of Abingdon Abbey, no. 94.[269]

[i. 308] fo. 75v **B195.** *Carta Edgari regis de Duclintun.*
Charters of Abingdon Abbey, no. 82.[270]

[i. 311] fo. 76r **B196.** *Carta Edgari regis de Boxora.*
Charters of Abingdon Abbey, no. 107; above c. 90.

[i. 314] fo. 77r **B197.** *Carta regis Edgari de Bedewinde.*[271]
Charters of Abingdon Abbey, no. 108; above, c. 61.

[i. 317] fo. 77v **B198.** *Carta regis Edgari de Hisseburna.*
Charters of Abingdon Abbey, no. 89; above, c. 64.

[265] Sawyer, no. 778. This charter records Edgar granting seven hides in Kingston, Berkshire, to his deacon Brihtheah. The absence of a boundary clause renders it impossible to be certain that this is Kingston Bagpuize. Gelling, *Early Charters of the Thames Valley*, p. 58, raises the possibility that it is Kingston Lisle. The charter is dated 970. *Charters of Abingdon Abbey*, p. 447, states that it 'is probably fundamentally authentic, although the lack of a boundary clause is surprising, and there is some possibility of reworking or revision in connection with the abbey's claim to Kingston Bagpuize'. See also above, notes to c. 92.

[266] Sawyer, no. 750. This charter records Edgar granting land in *Bragenfelda* to Byrhtnoth ealdorman of Essex. It is dated 967. *Charters of Abingdon Abbey*, p. 420, states that it 'is probably authentic'. For other charters in Byrhtnoth's favour preserved in the Abingdon archive, see above, cc. 54, 56. The land conveyed here is hard to identify as the charter includes neither hidage nor boundary clause. Apart from the presence of this charter in the archive, there is no other evidence of Abingdon interest in this land.

[267] Sawyer, no. 722. This charter records Edgar granting five hides in *Hocanedisce* to his thegn Wulfnoth. It is dated 963. *Charters of Abingdon Abbey*, p. 398, states that 'there is no reason to question [its] authenticity'. Wulfnoth cannot be identified with certainty. The place-name probably means 'Hoca's enclosure', but again, it cannot be identified with any certainty; *Charters of Abingdon Abbey*, p. 398. Apart from the presence of this charter in the archive, there is no other evidence of Abingdon interest in this land.

[268] Sawyer, no. 691. This charter records Edgar granting nine hides in *Ætheredingetune* to his thegn Ælfric. It is dated 961. *Charters of Abingdon Abbey*, p. 371, states that it 'would seem entirely authentic, were it not for the unfortunate detail of an attestation by Bishop Æthelwold'. This is inappropriate for a charter dated 961, since Æthelwold became a

B190. *Charter of King Edgar concerning seven hides at Kingston.* *Charters of Abingdon Abbey*, no. 114.[265]

B191. *Charter of King Edgar concerning* Bragenfelda. *Charters of Abingdon Abbey*, no. 106.[266]

B192. *Charter of King Edgar concerning* Hocanedisce. *Charters of Abingdon Abbey*, no. 99.[267]

B193. *Charter of King Edgar concerning* Ætheredingetune. *Charters of Abingdon Abbey*, no. 90.[268]

B194. *Charter of King Edgar concerning Moredon.* *Charters of Abingdon Abbey*, no. 94.[269]

B195. *Charter of King Edgar concerning Ducklington.* *Charters of Abingdon Abbey*, no. 82.[270]

B196. *Charter of King Edgar concerning Boxford.* *Charters of Abingdon Abbey*, no. 107. above c. 90.

B197. *Charter of King Edgar concerning Bedwyn.*[271] *Charters of Abingdon Abbey*, no. 108; above, c. 61.

B198. *Charter of King Edgar concerning Hurstbourne.* *Charters of Abingdon Abbey*, no. 89; above, c. 64.

bishop only in 963. It could be that his title was changed from *abbas* to *episcopus* in the process of copying, or that the name is an error for Ælfwold; *Charters of Abingdon Abbey*, pp. 371–2. The beneficiary may be Ælfric Cild, on whom see above, p. cxxiii. The place is probably Ardington, Berkshire, where in 1086 Robert d'Oilly held two manors, one assessed at nine hides *TRE*. The *TRE* holder of these nine hides was a free man named Sæwin; *DB* i, fo. 62r. In the 15th c. the abbot of Abingdon had some meadows there; Lyell, no. 13. Otherwise, apart from the presence of this charter in the archive, there is no evidence of Abingdon interest in this land

[269] Sawyer, no. 705. This charter records Edgar granting twenty hides at Moredon in Rodbourne Cheney, Wiltshire, to his thegn Eadwine. It is dated 962. *Charters of Abingdon Abbey*, p. 383, states that it 'is probably authentic'. For the previous and later history of the estate, see above, c. 102, *Charters of Abingdon Abbey*, pp. 383–4.

[270] Sawyer, no. 678. This charter records Edgar 'king of the Mercians' granting fourteen hides at Ducklington, Oxfordshire, to his thegn Eanulf, together with the old church at *Æstlea* and forty acres belonging to it and *Byrnanlea*. *Æstlea* or East Lea may be identified with Cokethorpe, *Byrnanlea* may underlie the name of Barleypark Farm and Wood; see EPNS, *Oxfordshire*, ii. 317; Blair, *Anglo-Saxon Oxfordshire*, pp. 130–1; *VCH*, *Oxfordshire*, xiii. 111, 140. The charter is dated 958. *Charters of Abingdon Abbey*, p. 334, states that 'there is every reason to think that [the document] is authentic'. Eanulf may have been a royal steward; see Sawyer, no. 768. Apart from the presence of this charter in the archive, there is no other evidence of Abingdon interest in this land.

[271] For the construction of the text of this charter in MS B, see *Charters of Abingdon Abbey*, pp. 427–8.

[i. 321] fo. 78v **B199.** *Carta regis Edgari de Suthhamtuna.*
Charters of Abingdon Abbey, no. 93; above, c. 65.

[i. 323] fo. 79r **B200.** *Carta regis Edgari de Fifhida.*
Charters of Abingdon Abbey, no 110; above, c. 79.

[i. 327] fo. 80r **B201.** *Carta regis Edgari de Esthalla.*
Charters of Abingdon Abbey, no. 96; above c. 70.

[i. 329] fo. 80v **B202.** *Carta Edgari regis de tribus hidis in Henneriþe.*
Charters of Abingdon Abbey, no. 92; above, c. 66.

[i. 331] fo. 81r **B203.** *Carta regis Edgari de decem hidis in Henneriþe.*
Charters of Abingdon Abbey, no. 100; above, c. 73.

[i. 334] fo. 81v **B204.** *Carta regis Edgari de Burgbeche.*
Charters of Abingdon Abbey, no. 88; above, c. 69.

[i. 337] fo. 82r **B205.** *Carta Edgari regis de Wasingetune.*
Charters of Abingdon Abbey, no. 98.[272]

[i. 340] fo. 83r **B206.** *Carta regis Edgari regis de Rimecunda.*
Charters of Abingdon Abbey, no. 87; above, c. 67.

[i. 343] **B207.** *De sancto Adþelwoldo.*

fo. 83v fo. 84r Nunc uero restat ut de uiro uenerabili | Aþelwoldo, tempore regis Eadgari istius loci abbate sanctissimo, mentionem faciamus, qualiter, post amplas possessiones Eadgari regis Anglorum illustrissimi, domum istam uenustissime ordinauerit, utputa prudens ac uigilans Domini nostri Ihesu Christi dispensator; uidelicet, quoad ordinis obseruantiam, et institutiones ordini admodum necessarias, similiter et con-[i. 344]suetudines omni memoria dignas. In primis itaque beatus Aþelwoldus, regnante rege Eadgaro, honorabile templum in honore sancte Dei genitricis semperque uirginis Marie in hoc loco construxit pariter et ad uotum consummauit.[273] Quo consummato, cum iam beatus Aþelwoldus nonnullos fratres ibi coadunasset, de communi consensu et pari uoluntate eorumdem misit quendam suum monac⟨h⟩um nomine Osgarum in transmarinas partes ad abbatiam Floriacensem propter

[272] Sawyer, no. 714. This charter records Edgar granting twenty-four hides in Washington to Bishop Æthelwold; see also above, p. cxxx. It is dated 963. *Charters of Abingdon Abbey*, p. 396, states that it 'appears to be authentic'. Before Edgar's death, Æthelwold exchanged an estate at Washington with Wulfstan Uccea, for lands in Huntingdonshire and Northamptonshire: Sawyer, no. 1377; *Anglo-Saxon Charters*, ed. Robertson, no. 37; *EHD*, i. no. 112. See above, B95 (*Charters of Abingdon Abbey*, no. 40), for

B199. *Charter of King Edgar concerning Southampton.*
Charters of Abingdon Abbey, no. 93; above, c. 65.

B200. *Charter of King Edgar concerning Fyfield.*
Charters of Abingdon Abbey, no. 110; above, c. 79.

B201. *Charter of King Edgar concerning Easthall.*
Charters of Abingdon Abbey, no. 96; above c. 70.

B202. *Charter of King Edgar concerning three hides in Hendred.*
Charters of Abingdon Abbey, no. 92; above, c. 66.

B203. *Charter of King Edgar concerning ten hides in Hendred.*
Charters of Abingdon Abbey, no. 100; above, c. 73.

B204. *Charter of King Edgar concerning Burbage.*
Charters of Abingdon Abbey, no. 88; above, c. 69.

B205. *Charter of King Edgar concerning Washington.*
Charters of Abingdon Abbey, no. 98.[272]

B206. *Charter of King Edgar concerning Ringwood.*
Charters of Abingdon Abbey, no. 87; above, c. 67.

B207. *Concerning St Æthelwold.*
Now, indeed, it remains for us to mention how the venerable man Æthelwold, most holy abbot of that monastery in King Edgar's time, after the extensive possessions of the most illustrious Edgar king of the English, arranged the affairs of that house very pleasingly, as a prudent and vigilant steward of our Lord Jesus Christ; that is, as to the observance of the ordered life, and the usages very necessary for the ordered life, and likewise the customs worthy of every memory. First, therefore, while King Edgar was reigning, the blessed Æthelwold built and also completed as he desired an impressive church in this place in honour of the holy mother of God and ever Virgin Mary.[273] Following the church's completion, and once he had brought together some brethren there, the blessed Æthelwold by common consent and joint will sent a certain one of his monks, named Osgar, overseas to the abbey of Fleury, in relation to the Rule of the

an earlier charter concerning Washington. The lands covered by the two charters are similar but not necessarily identical; *Charters of Abingdon Abbey*, p. 396.

[273] The passage 'honorabile . . . consummauit' is drawn directly from Wulfstan, *Life of Æthelwold*, c. 13, ed. Lapidge and Winterbottom, p. 24, with very minor changes. Again I deliberately follow Lapidge and Winterbottom's translation.

regulam beati Benedicti sub qua fratres istius loci Deo digne famulantes feliciter militarent. Attendens etiam diligenter beatus Aþelwoldus illud propheticum quo dicitur 'Domine, dilexi decorem domus tue'[274] (ut de domo exteriori ad presens intelligatur), quoad decentius potuit domum istam ornamentis ditauit preciosissimis.[275]

Dedit autem, ut ex antiquorum librorum accepimus attestatione,[276] calicem unum aureum immensi ponderis, ob honorem et reuerentiam corporis et sanguinis Domini nostri Ihesu Christi. Dedit etiam tres cruces admodum decoras ex argento et auro puro, que tempore werre regis Stephani sunt confracte, attestantibus monachis nostris uiam uniuerse carnis ingressis.[277] Ornauit etiam ecclesiam textis[278] tam ex argento puro quam ex auro obrizo, pariter et lapidibus preciosissimis, thurribulis et fialis,[279] peluibus fusilibus et candelabris ex argento[a] ductilibus, multisque bonis aliis tam usibus monachorum circa altare competentibus quam decentie ecclesiastice competentibus. Opitulante etiam piissimo rege Eadgaro, memorande memorie, abbas Aþelwoldus tabulam fecit argenteam precio adpreciatam trecentarum librarum, cuius etiam materiam forma exsuperabat artificialis, que etiam usque ad tempus Vincencii abbatis illesa permansit et incon-
[i. 345] fracta.[280] Interim uir Dei, mulieri forti consimilis,[281] sindonem fecit uendidit et tradidit Chananeo,[b][282] dum per sanctam conuersationem et deuotionem exemplum bone accionis prebuit discipulis suis, de bono in melius commutatis. Fecit etiam duas campanas propriis manibus, ut dicitur,[283] quas in hac domo posuit cum aliis duabus maioribus quas etiam beatus Dunstanus propriis manibus fecisse peribetur. Preterea fecit uir uenerabilis Aðelwoldus quandam rotam tintinnabulis plenam, quam auream nuncupant propter laminas ipsius deauratas, quam in festiuis diebus ad maioris excitationem deuocionis
fo. 84^{v} re|ducendo uolui constituit.[284] Fuerunt autem ista[c] super enumerata[d]

B207 [a] *corr. from* auro [b] *corr. from* Cananeo *by interlin.* [c] *interlin.* [d] *final two letters interlin.*

[274] Ps: 25 (26): 8. *De abbatibus* places these words in the mouth of Faritius at his death; *CMA* ii. 290.

[275] *De abbatibus* also describes the ornaments that Æthelwold gave to the church; *CMA* ii. 277–9. See also above, p. clxix, for this and what follows.

[276] These 'books' perhaps resembled the vernacular account of Æthelwold's gifts to Peterborough; *Anglo-Saxon Charters*, ed. Robertson, no. 39.

[277] According to *De abbatibus*, the crosses were four feet in length. The same text also mentions the breaking up and stripping of the crosses in Stephen's time; *CMA* ii. 278.

[278] Dodwell, *Anglo-Saxon Art*, p. 203, takes 'textis' to refer to texts, i.e. gospel texts. However, in that case the word should be 'textibus', not 'textis'. The *History* regularly and correctly treats 'textus', text, as fourth declension.

blessed Benedict, under which the brethren of that monastery worthily served and happily fought for God. So, diligently paying attention to that prophecy in which it is said 'Lord, I have loved the habitation of thy house',[274] (as is still understood from the outside of the house) Æthelwold enriched that house as fittingly as he could with most precious ornaments.[275]

Moreover he gave, as we have learnt from the witness of ancient books,[276] one gold chalice of immense weight, out of honour and reverence for the body and blood of our Lord Jesus Christ. He also gave three very beautiful crosses of pure silver and gold, which were broken in the time of war under King Stephen, when our monks who witnessed this had gone the way of all flesh.[277] He also decorated the church with cloths both of pure silver and of unadulterated gold,[278] and likewise with very precious stones, with censers and cruets,[279] with basins cast and candlesticks beaten from silver, and with many other goods, both fitting for the monks' uses around the altar and fitting for ecclesiastical propriety. Also, helped by the most pious King Edgar, whose memory should be commemorated, Abbot Æthelwold made a silver retable worth £300, the crafted form of which exceeded its matter; it remained unharmed and unbroken right up to the time of Abbot Vincent.[280] Meanwhile the man of God, like the virtuous woman,[281] 'maketh fine linen, selleth and delivereth it to the merchant',[282] while through holy religious life and devotion he presented an example of good action for his disciples, who were changed from good to better. He also made two bells with his own hands, so it is said, which he placed in this house with two other larger ones which the blessed Dunstan is also reputed to have made with his own hands.[283] Besides, the venerable man Æthelwold made a certain wheel full of little bells, which they call golden because of its gilded metal plates, and set down that on festival days to arouse greater devotion it be turned by moving back and forth.[284] Moreover,

[279] Small vessels to hold wine or water for use in the Eucharist, or holy water for other purposes.

[280] See also below, vol. ii. 230, 338; *De abbatibus*, *CMA* ii. 278.

[281] See Prov. 31: 10.

[282] Prov. 31: 24.

[283] Dodwell, *Anglo-Saxon Art*, p. 49, rejects the idea that Æthelwold possessed the skill to do such work in person, on the grounds that 'if Æthelwold had indeed possessed the skills and made these objects, they would certainly have been mentioned in the biography of him written by his contemporary, Wulfstan the Cantor, or in the related biography by Ælfric'.

[284] See also the description in *De abbatibus*, *CMA* ii. 278; this specifies that the gold and silver from it was worth £40 when it was destroyed after 1066. Dodwell, *Anglo-Saxon Art*, p. 32, suggests that this must be a revival of 'the old Israelite instrument of devotion—the timbrel'.

ornamenta, cum aumentatione bonorum aliorum, in ecclesia ista usque ad aduentum Normannorum in Angliam. Illo enim tempore erant in hac domo quidam monachi et sacriste de cenobio Gemmeticensi qui ornamenta quam plurima a beato Aþelwoldo laboriose adquisita et huic domui collata, tam aurea quam argentea, eruderato penitus argento a rota[e] memorata, secum in Normanniam fraudulenter asportauerunt.[285]

Attendens etiam diligentius uir uenerabilis Aþelwoldus illud autenticum quo dicitur 'de altari uiuant qui altari seruiunt',[286] similiter et illud euuangelicum 'dignus est operarius mercede sua'.[287] Singulis diebus horis statutis filiis suis in uinea Domini laborantibus annonam huiuscemodi sub certa astipulatione constituit.[288] Monachis Abbendonie ad mensam discumbentibus, unusquisque panem accipiat sibi deputatum de frumento puro quinque marcis parem in pondere, unde uersus ille 'Panis Abbendonie par marcis pondere quinque'. Ad istum panem frustum casei ad talem et tantam magnitudinem singulis diebus apponi constituit ut infra quinque dies pondus Abbendunense, quod tunc constabat ex uiginti duabus petris, ut ex antiquorum accepimus attestatione, penitus expenderetur.

Constituit etiam mon⟨a⟩chis istius loci Deo et beate Marie in
[i. 346] perpetuum seruientibus quaqua die duo genera leguminum ante generale, et pulmentum post generale; unum etiam generale et unam pitantiam eis constituit quibus ad refectionem sine crapula uesci possent.[289] In albis unam pitantiam plus quam in aliis diebus constituit, in cappis duas pitantias preter generale, in precipuis festiuitatibus tres pitantias preter generale, et in eisdem diebus artocreas, et ad cenam oblata constituit.[290] In quadragesimali uero

[e] *corr. from* aromata

[285] *De abbatibus* also mentions this incident, placing it soon after the Norman Conquest; *CMA* ii. 278. The Jumièges link probably was connected to Abbot Adelelm, or possibly Abbot Reginald, both of whom had been monks at that house; see vol. ii, pp. xl, xlii. The *History* elsewhere blames William I's queen for the removal of Abingdon ornaments; above, p. 224.

[286] Cf. 1 Cor. 9: 13.

[287] Luke 10: 7; see also 1 Tim. 5: 18.

[288] For comment on the remainder of this chapter, see above, p. clxxii.

[289] 'Generals' were the two dishes of cooked food specified in the Rule of St Benedict, c. 39, often with an additional third main dish. Pittances were additional dishes, of various foods, often of higher quality than generals. *Pulmentum*, here translated pottage, was a

the ornaments enumerated above, together with the increase of other goods, were in this church right up to the coming of the Normans to England. At that time there were in this house certain monks and sacrists from the monastery of Jumièges who deceitfully took away with them to Normandy very many ornaments laboriously acquired and conferred on this house by the blessed Æthelwold, both golden and silver, with the silver having been completely stripped from the aforementioned wheel.[285]

Also, the venerable man Æthelwold paid very diligent attention to that authority by which it is said that 'they live of the altar who wait at the altar'[286] and likewise to that Gospel by which it is said 'the labourer is worthy of his hire'.[287] Each day for his sons labouring in the vineyard of the Lord at the fixed hours he set down an allowance of the following sort, firmly corroborated.[288] When the monks of Abingdon were sitting at the table, each was to receive his allocation of pure wheaten bread equal in weight to five marks, whence the verse 'An Abingdon loaf is equal to five marks in weight'. To this bread he set down to be added a piece of cheese each day of such and so great a size that within five days should be entirely expended an Abingdon weight, which then consisted of twenty-two stone, as we have learnt from the testimony of aged men.

He also set down each day for the monks of that monastery serving God and the blessed Mary for ever two types of legumes before the generals, and a dish of pottage after the generals; he also set down one general and one pittance for those by whom they could be eaten without gluttony.[289] On festivals in albs, he set down one pittance more than on other days, on those in copes two pittances besides the generals, on the foremost festivals three pittances besides generals, and on those days he set down meat pies, and thin pastries for supper.[290] In place of cheese during Lent, indeed, he set down for

vegetable or cereal dish. For the various dishes, see B. Harvey, *Living and Dying in England 1100–1540: The Monastic Experience* (Oxford, 1993), pp. 10–11.

[290] Monks had either one or two meals a day, depending on the time of year and the liturgical status of the day. The first or only meal was called *prandium*, here translated as 'dinner'. The later was called *cena*, here translated as 'supper'. Of the four levels of feasts, those in albs were the second lowest; above them came those in copes, and at the top the half dozen greatest feasts of all; see *The Monastic Breviary of Hyde Abbey, Winchester*, ed. J. B. L. Tolhurst (6 vols., Henry Bradshaw Society, lix, lxx, lxxi, lxxvi, lxxviii, lxxx (1930–42)), vi. 146–7; *The Monastic Constitutions of Lanfranc*, rev. edn., ed. D. Knowles and C. N. L. Brooke (OMT, 2002), esp. pp. 70–104; Knowles, *Monastic Order*, p. 464. *Oblata* would normally refer to wafers used in the celebration of the Eucharist, but this is clearly not the meaning here; see also *Oxford English Dictionary*, *s.v.* Obley.

tempore, loco casei, constituit unicuique fratrum unam anguillam grossam cotidie, cum generale. In estate uero constituit ad cenam fratrum lac acidum in uasis pulcherrimis que 'Creches' uulgari onomate dicuntur,[292] a die que dicitur Hokedai usque ad festum sancti Michaelis,[291] qualibet die. A festo uero sancti Michaelis usque ad festum sancti Martini,[293] lac dulce secunda[f] die. Vas uero quod 'creche' nuncupatur septem polices continet quoad[g] profunditatem a summitate unius usque ad profundum lateris alterius. Constituit etiam placenta quinque diebus ebdomade Pasche, et in ebdomada Pentecostes quinque diebus, et in die sancti Marchii euuangeliste, tribus diebus rogationum, die ascensionis Dominice.

Ad mensuram potus monachorum, uir uenerabilis Aþelwoldus quandam assisam, non ultra rationabilem sufficientiam progredientem nec citra deficientem, constituendam perutile fore diiudicauit. fo. 85r Constituit | itaque cifum quendam magnum, flasconem et dimidium, scilicet duas caritates et eo amplius, in se plenarie continentem, quem cifum antiqui 'bollam Aþelwoldi' uocabant. Hac uero mensura[h] bis in die obbe monachorum implebantur, scilicet ad prandium et ad cenam. In festiuis etiam diebus constituit eis siue in albis siue in cappis idromellum, uidelicet ad prandium inter sex fratres sextarium et ad cenam inter duodecim fratres sextarium. In precipuis uero diebus quas apud nos principales obseruamus, scilicet natali Domini, in [i. 347] Pascha, [i]in Pentecoste, in assumptione[i] sancte Marie et in natiuitate eius, in natale apostolorum Petri et Pauli, in festiuitate omnium sanctorum, uinum illis constituit ad mensuram qua prius de idromello ad prandium, et ad cenam idromellum. Hec uero et his similia tam habundanter tamque circumspecte constituit ut non solum monachi quoad usum uictus sustentarentur, uerum etiam pauperes ex eorum reliquiis propensius recrearentur.

Preterea uidens uir uenerabilis quod in maxima parte diminute essent ueritates a filiis hominum et magis ac magis in posterum diminuende, timens sibi ac suis ne consuetudines inanteis assignate per processum temporis aut deteriorarentur, aut in peius mutarentur, uel etiam penitus adnullarentur, fecit quod potuit et firmiter prohibuit sub anatematis interminatione ne quis successorum suorum in peius mutare presumeret aut uariare, nisi forte zelo

[f] *over erasure* [g] qui ad *MS* [h] *corr. from* mensuram *by erasure of final abbreviation mark* [i–i] *over erasure*

[291] i.e. from the second Tuesday after Easter until 29 Sept.

each brother one large eel a day, with the generals. In summer, on each day from the day that is called Hock-day right up to the feast of St Michael,[291] he set down for the brethren's supper sour milk in most beautiful vessels which are called by the vernacular name of 'Creches';[292] from the feast of St Michael right up to the feast of St Martin,[293] sweet milk every second day. The vessel, indeed, which is called a 'Creche', contains seven inches in depth from the top of one side to the bottom of the other. He also set down loaves for five days in Easter week, five days in Whitsun week, and on the day of Mark the evangelist, the three days of Rogation, and the day of the Lord's Ascension.

As to the measure of the monks' drink, the venerable man Æthelwold judged that it would be very useful to set down a certain fixed allowance, neither passing nor falling short of a reasonable sufficiency. He therefore set down a certain great flagon, fully containing in itself a gallon and a half, that is two special measures and more, which flagon men of old used to call 'Æthelwold's bowl'. Twice a day, indeed, that is for dinner and for supper, the monks' drinking vessels were filled with this measure. Also, on festival days either in albs or in copes he set down for them mead, that is a sester between six brethren at dinner and a sester between twelve brethren at supper. On the foremost feast days, indeed, which we observe as principal amongst ourselves, that is Christmas, Easter, Whitsun, the Assumption of St Mary and her Nativity, the birth of the apostles Peter and Paul, the feast of All Saints, he set down wine for them at dinner in the amount which previously they had of mead, and mead for supper. These and things similar to them indeed, he set down so abundantly and so prudently that not only were the monks supported as to use of food, but also the poor were more readily revived from their leftovers.

Besides, the venerable man saw that truths were in the greatest part diminished by the sons of men and should be diminished more and more in future, and feared for himself and his men lest customs assigned earlier should either deteriorate through the passage of time, or be changed for the worse, or even be totally annulled; so he did what he could and firmly prohibited under threat of anathema that any of his successors should presume to change for the worse or

[292] This is most likely related to the OE 'cruce', referring to an earthenware pot; related words also appear in Old French, as 'cruie', 'cruise', 'cruche'.

[293] i.e. 29 Sept.–11 Nov.

caritatis succensus easdem consuetudines de bono in melius aumentare decreuisset.[294] Orauit etiam pro domo ista antequam ad episcopatum Wintoniensem uocatus esset orationem. Cuius orationis tenor hic est:

B208. *Oratio sancti Adelwoldi.*[295]

Deus eterne, ante cuius conspectum assistunt angeli, et cuius nutu reguntur uniuersa, protege Domine, quesumus, locum istum qui in nomine tuo et beate Marie constructum est, et per uirtutem nominis tui recedat ab eo uirtus inimicorum umbraque fantasmatum et incursio turbinum, percussio fulminum, lesio tonitruum, calamitas tempestatuum, omnisque spiritus procellarum. Preterea quesumus, [i. 348] Domine, ut non ignis domum istam consumat nec homo inicus[a] per superbiam eam destruat, sed tu, piissime Deus, conserua eam et guberna, multiplicique fructuum ubertate pinguescat, ut omnes habitantes in ea uoce et corde te imnizent et suaui modulatione nomen tuum magnificent, et super eos descendat benedictio tua et super locum istum, maneatque semper. Per Dominum nostrum.

B209. *Sanctus Adelwoldus factus est episcopus ab Adgaro rege.*[296]

Above, c. 71.

[i. 349] **B210.** *De morte Edgari regis.*[297]

fo. 85v Edgaro rege Anglorum illustrissimo uiam uniuerse carnis feliciter ingresso, cuius animo propitiatur Deus,[298] successit ei in hereditatem filius eius Edwardus, uir memorande memorie. Iste uero, per processum temporis, tam morum grauitate quam uite sanctitate pollebat, ut antequam humanitus ei contigisset in terra positus uitam angelicam actitare ab omnibus uideretur.[299] His enim dum regnaret, de Kingestuna Abbendunensi ecclesie septem hidas concessit et de concessu his litteris roborauit:

B208 [a] *for* iniquus

[294] See vol. ii. 332–6 on Abbot Faritius's changes to Æthelwold's arrangements.

[295] Wulfstan, *Life of Æthelwold*, ed. Lapidge and Winterbottom, p. lxxxv, states that 'this prayer does not occur in any earlier source, and the attribution to Æthelwold may well derive from genuine tradition. It bears no marks of Æthelwold's characteristic inclination towards ostentatious (especially Greek-based) vocabulary, yet it has a fine rhetorical sentence-structure, implying that its author was a Latinist of some competence. The question is best left open.' At *Life of Æthelwold*, p. lxxxv n. 158, the editors note that the prayer is also preserved in the so-called Abingdon Breviary of 1528. They do not discuss

modify these customs, unless, by chance, fired by the zeal of charity he decide to improve them from good to better.[294] He also prayed a prayer for this house before he was called to the bishopric of Winchester. The terms of his prayer are as follows:

B208. *Prayer of St Æthelwold.*[295]

Eternal God, before whose sight angels sit, and at whose will everything is ruled, Lord protect, we beseech, this monastery which has been built in Your name and the blessed Mary's, and through the might of Your name may there recede from it the might of enemies and the shadow of apparitions and the attack of whirlwinds, the striking of lightning bolts, the assault of thunder, the calamity of tempests, and every wind of storms. Besides, we beseech, Lord, that fire may not consume this house nor spiteful man destroy it through pride, but You, most pious God, guard and govern it, and let it grow rich with the manifold abundance of fruits, so that all living in it may sing Your praises with voice and heart and magnify Your name in sweet music, and may Your blessing descend on them and on this monastery, and remain for ever. Through our Lord.

B209. *St Æthelwold is made a bishop by King Edgar.*[296]

Above, c. 71.

B210. *Concerning the death of King Edgar.*[297]

When Edgar, most illustrious king of the English, happily went the way of all flesh, to whose soul may God be rendered favourable,[298] his son Edward succeeded him in his inheritance, a man whose memory should be commemorated [975]. Through the passage of time, indeed, that man exerted power by both the seriousness of his behaviour and the holiness of his life, so that before he had suffered the fate of mankind, placed on earth he was seen by all to lead the angelic life.[299] While he was reigning, he granted seven hides at Kingston to the church of Abingdon, and he strengthened the grant with these letters:

why it appears only in the later version of the *History*. Lapidge, 'Æthelwold as scholar and teacher', p. 100, describes the traditional link to Æthelwold as 'credible enough'.

[296] This is the first occasion in which MS B copies an entire section of narrative from MS C; see above, p. xxxviii.

[297] Cf. above, c. 91.

[298] Cf. Exod. 30: 16. Similar phrases were used in the liturgical commemoration of the dead.

[299] A phrase also used above, B83, concerning Æthelwold.

B211. *Carta sancti Edwardi martiris de septem hidis in Kingestune.*[a]
Charters of Abingdon Abbey, no. 116; above, c. 92.

[i. 352] fo. 86r **B212.** *Item carta Edwardi regis de tredecim hidis in Kingestun.*
Charters of Abingdon Abbey, no. 117.[300]

[i. 354] fo. 87r **B213** *Quomodo Osgarus abbas emit uiginti hidas in Kingestun.*
Above, c. 93.

[i. 356] **B214.**[a] Edwardo[301] rege Anglorum dolo Ælfthriþe nouerce sue ad celestia per martirium translato,[302] a sanctis archipresulibus Dunstano et Oswaldo et decem episcopis in Cingestune ad regni fastigium Aþelredus frater eius, filius Edgari et Ælfthriþe, consecratur.[303]
The remainder of this section is identical to c. 95 above, 'Qui, ubi imperitandi . . . fit obstaculo.'

[i. 357] **B215.** *De Edwino abbate.*[304]
The opening three sentences and the last sentence of this section are identical to c. 96 above, except that the name of Eadwine's brother is changed from Ælfric to Eadric, who is said to be son of Ælfhere, ealdorman of the Mercians. The passage 'Qua etiam tempestate . . . graue iniungit' is replaced by:
Nec tamen de his uindicta Dei abfuit diutius. Denique uir pro quo
fo. 87v monasterialis summa[305] ue|niit non multo post regiam offensam incurrens, a patria ista exul in Datiam depellitur, sed non multo post rediens Danos secum adduxit qui multo tempore patriam uastauerunt.

B216. *De morte Edwini abbatis.*
Above, c. 97.

B211 [a] *an illustration of the king appears at the start of this charter*

B214 [a] *the rubricator failed to provide a heading, although the appropriate space had been left*

[300] Sawyer, no. 828. This charter records Edward granting thirteen hides at Kingston Bagpuize to Bishop Ælfstan, probably of Ramsbury. The date given in the charter is 956, showing that the draftsman had been carelessly copying from an earlier diploma, probably B154 (*Charters of Abingdon Abbey*, no. 61). *Charters of Abingdon Abbey*, p. 456, states of this charter and the preceding one, that 'it is not easy to decide the status of these texts'. They could be classified as Abingdon forgeries made very soon after the purported grants, or they may be 'official and genuine (if incompetent) royal diplomas, drawn up at Abingdon between 975 and 978 with King Edward's permission'. See also the opinions on authenticity noted at the revised Sawyer, no. 828. The context of the charters may be a reorganization of the land; see above, p. 134 n. 285.

B211. *Charter of St Edward the martyr concerning seven hides in Kingston.*

Charters of Abingdon Abbey, no. 116; above, c. 92.

B212. *Likewise, the charter of King Edward concerning thirteen hides in Kingston.*

Charters of Abingdon Abbey, no. 117.[300]

B213. *How Abbot Osgar bought twenty hides in Kingston.*

Above, c. 93.

B214. When[301] Edward king of the English had been translated to Heaven[302] through martyrdom by the trickery of his step-mother Ælfthryth, his brother Æthelred, son of Edgar and Ælfthryth, was consecrated to the most exalted position in the kingdom by the saintly archbishops Dunstan and Oswald and by ten bishops at Kingston.[303]

The remainder of this section is identical to c. 95 above, 'When he acquired . . . defensive protection.'

B215. *Concerning Abbot Eadwine.*[304]

The opening three sentences and the last sentence of this section are identical to c. 96 above, except that the name of Eadwine's brother is changed from Ælfric to Eadric, who is said to be son of Ælfhere ealdorman of the Mercians. The passage 'Also at that time . . . for payment' is replaced by:

Nor, however, was God's vengeance absent for too long concerning these matters. Not long afterwards the man on behalf of whom the monastic command was sold[305] incurred royal displeasure and was expelled as an exile from this country to Denmark, but not long afterwards he returned and brought Danes with him who for a long time laid waste to this country.

B216. *Concerning the death of Abbot Eadwine.*

Above c. 97.

[301] Cf. above, c. 95.

[302] Cf. Edward the Confessor, below, p. 370.

[303] The passage 'a sanctis . . . ad regni fastigium' follows verbatim John of Worcester, *Chronicle*, ii. 430.

[304] This section is very similar to that in MS C, c. 96, above, except for the sentences 'Nor, however . . . to this country.' On Eadwine, and losses in his time, see above, pp. xcix, cxliv.

[305] The composers of the *History* do not use the unusual phrase 'monasterialis summa' elsewhere, and it could be a mistake. The only use of the word 'veniit' in the Bible is John 12: 5, when the speaker is Judas Iscariot.

[i. 358] **B217.** *De priuilegio Adelredi regis.*[a]
Charters of Abingdon Abbey, no. 124; above, c. 98.

[i. 367] fo. 89v **B218.** *Hucusque de ecclesie libertate; nunc uero de terrarum restitutionem subinferendum.*
Charters of Abingdon Abbey, no. 129; above, c. 99.

[i. 370] fo. 90v **B219.** *Carta Adelredi regis de Ernicote.*
Charters of Abingdon Abbey, no. 119.[306]

[i. 373] fo. 91r **B220.** *Carta regis Adelredi de Cerne.*
Charters of Abingdon Abbey, no. 128; above, c. 101.

[i. 377] fo. 92r **B221.** *Carta regis Adelred de Mordune.*
Charters of Abingdon Abbey, no. 135; above, c. 102.

[i. 382] fo. 93r **B222.** *Hec sunt terre que Adelredus rex dedit famulis suis, et ipsi de consensu regis ecclesie Abbendonensi.*[307]
Charters of Abingdon Abbey, no. 95.[308]

[i. 384] fo. 93v **B223.** *Carta regis Adelredi de Cheorletun.*
Charters of Abingdon Abbey, no. 118.[309]

[i. 386] fo. 94r **B224.** *Carta regis Adelredi de duabus hidis in Draitun et una in Suttun.*[310]
Charters of Abingdon Abbey, no. 120.[311]

B217 [a] *an illustration of the king appears at the start of this charter*

---

[306] Sawyer, no. 843. This charter records Æthelred granting two hides in Arncott, Oxfordshire, to Abingdon. It is dated 983. *Charters of Abingdon Abbey*, p. 463, states that 'as far as can be determined, [the document] is authentic'. *DB* i, fo. 156v, records Robert d'Oilly and Roger d'Ivry holding two hides in Arncott from Abingdon. For the post-Conquest history of the estate, see vol. ii. 34, 194, 266. This charter probably appeared on a missing folio of MS C.

[307] The heading applies not just to the charter which immediately follows, but to those in succeeding sections as well. The beneficiaries vary from major thegns such as Wulfric Spot to relatively minor thegns, to household officials; I have therefore chosen the relatively neutral 'followers' to translate 'famuli'; 'thegns' would be another possible translation.

[308] Sawyer, no. 833. This charter describes Æthelred granting woodland to his thegn, Leofric. It is dated 962 (a single numeral 'c' has slipped from the date in *Charters of Abingdon Abbey*, p. 385). *Charters of Abingdon Abbey*, pp. 385–6, describes it as 'a curious document. . . . the text as it stands must be regarded as spurious, even though the motivation for fabrication is unclear'. The witnesses are appropriate for the date 962, so the king's name ought to be Edgar. Given that the king's name appears three times in the text, this is presumably a deliberate change, not a slip. Leofric cannot be identified with any

B217. *Concerning King Æthelred's privilege.*
Charters of Abingdon Abbey, no. 124; above, c. 98.

B218. *Up to here concerning the church's liberty; now indeed is to be added concerning the restitution of lands.*
Charters of Abingdon Abbey, no. 129; above, c. 99.

B219. *Charter of King Æthelred concerning Arncott.*
Charters of Abingdon Abbey, no. 119.[306]

B220. *Charter of King Æthelred concerning Cerney.*
Charters of Abingdon Abbey, no. 128; above, c. 101.

B221. *Charter of King Æthelred concerning Moredon.*
Charters of Abingdon Abbey, no. 135; above, c. 102.

B222. *These are the lands that King Æthelred gave to his followers, and they by the king's consent gave to the church of Abingdon.*[307]
Charters of Abingdon Abbey, no. 95.[308]

B223. *Charter of King Æthelred concerning Charlton.*
Charters of Abingdon Abbey, no. 118.[309]

B224. *Charter of King Æthelred concerning two hides in Drayton and one in Sutton.*[310]
Charters of Abingdon Abbey, no. 120.[311]

certainty, nor can the location of the woods; for suggestions, see *Charters of Abingdon Abbey*, pp. 386–7.

[309] Sawyer, no. 839. This charter records Æthelred granting five hides at Charlton to his thegn Ælfgar. It is dated 982. *Charters of Abingdon Abbey*, p. 459, states that it 'is probably authentic'. Ælfgar cannot be identified with certainty, as he bears a common name. See above, B159 (*Charters of Abingdon Abbey*, no. 69) for King Eadwig granting five hides in Charlton to his thegn Wulfric. This may be the same estate. *Charters of Abingdon Abbey*, p. 293, notes that a man called Tovi held a total of five hides in Charlton in 1066 (*DB* i, fos. 60^{v}, 61^{r}), and suggests that these could be the five hides mentioned in this charter.

[310] It is unclear why the rubric differs from the charter as to the number of hides given.

[311] Sawyer, no. 851. This charter records Æthelred granting three hides in Drayton and one and a half hides in Sutton Courtenay to his man Wulfgar. It is dated 983. *Charters of Abingdon Abbey*, p. 466, states that it 'appears to be authentic'. The beneficiary is probably Wulfgar the king's butler; a problematic charter below, B231 (*Charters of Abingdon Abbey*, no. 130), states that Æthelred gave Abingdon three hides in Drayton and two at Sutton Courtenay, which had previously belonged to Wulfgar the butler. *DB* i, fo. 59^{r}, records Abingdon having one hide at Sutton Courtenay. It is possible that the small estate mentioned in this charter was related to the two-hide manor Drayton which Eadnoth the Staller held from Earl Harold *TRE*; *DB* i, fo. 60^{v}.

[i. 388] fo. 94v **B225.** *Carta regis Adelredi de duabus mansis in Dumbeltune.*[312]
Charters of Abingdon Abbey, no. 126.[313]

[i. 392] fo. 95v **B226.** *Carta regis Adelredi de Osanleia.*
Charters of Abingdon Abbey, no. 121.[314]

[i. 394] fo. 96r **B227.** *Carta regis Adelredi Eardulfeslea.*
Charters of Abingdon Abbey, no. 125.[315]

[i. 397] fo. 97r **B228.** *Carta Adelredi regis.*
Charters of Abingdon Abbey, no. 122.[316]

[i. 400] fo. 98r **B229.** *Carta regis Adelredi de Wttune.*
Charters of Abingdon Abbey, no. 123.[317]

[i. 404] fo. 98v **B230.** *Carta regis Adelredi de Bensingtun.*
Charters of Abingdon Abbey, no. 127.[318]

[i. 406] fo. 99v **B231.** *Carta Adelredi regis de tribus hidis in Draitun et duobus in Suttun.*
Charters of Abingdon Abbey, no. 130.[319]

312 Again there is an inconsistency between the rubric, which specifies a grant of two hides, and the charter, which specifies two and a half hides.

313 Sawyer, no. 886. The charter also survives as a single-sheet copy from the second half of the 13th c., London, British Library, Cotton Augustus ii. 48, and a 16th-c. copy of a lost single sheet, Cambridge, Corpus Christi College 111, pp. 175–8. This charter records Æthelred granting two and a half hides in Dumbleton to his thegn Wulfric. It also explains how a previous holder, Æthelsige, had forfeited the land to the king, who initially gave it to his man Hawase. It then passed to Wulfric son of Wulfrun, that is Wulfric Spot, a very wealthy thegn with extensive Mercian estates; *Anglo-Saxon Wills*, ed. Whitelock, pp. 152–3; *Charters of Burton Abbey*, ed. P. H. Sawyer (Anglo-Saxon Charters, 2; Oxford, 1979), pp. xxxviii–xliii. It is dated 995. *Charters of Abingdon Abbey*, p. 492, states that it 'seems entirely acceptable as an authentic charter of King Æthelred'. In his will, Wulfric probably left this land to Ælfric archbishop of Canterbury, who had also received twenty-four hides at Dumbleton from King Æthelred; below, B233, *Anglo-Saxon Wills*, ed. Whitelock, pp. 153–4. Ælfric in his own will left Dumbleton to Abingdon, with the exception of three hides to be retained for life by Ælfnoth the sitting tenant; above, c. 105, below, B235 (*Charters of Abingdon Abbey*, no. 133). *Charters of Abingdon Abbey*, p. 493, suggests that those hides may well 'essentially represent' the lands given to Wulfric in the present charter.

314 Sawyer, no. 852. This charter records Æthelred granting two hides in *Osanleia* to his thegn Ælfheah. It is dated 984. *Charters of Abingdon Abbey*, p. 468, states that it 'is probably authentic', although in the dating clause the indiction does not match the incarnation date, probably through scribal error. *Osanlea* cannot be identified with any certainty; *Charters of Abingdon Abbey*, p. 469. More than one thegn called Ælfheah appears in Æthelred's reign; note e.g. *Charters of Burton Abbey*, ed. Sawyer, no. 32. Apart from the presence of this charter in the archive, there is no other evidence of Abingdon interest in this land.

315 Oxfordshire. Sawyer, no. 883, trans. *EHD*, i. no. 118. This charter records Æthelred granting five hides to Æthelwig, the estate having previously been forfeited to the king. It is dated 995, the indiction probably being wrong through scribal error. *Charters of Abingdon Abbey*, p. 486, states that the document 'has a number of problems, and its authenticity is not beyond doubt'. Apart from the presence of this charter in the archive, there is no other

B225. *Charter of King Æthelred concerning two hides in Dumbleton.*[312]
Charters of Abingdon Abbey, no. 126.[313]

B226. *Charter of King Æthelred concerning* Osanleia.
Charters of Abingdon Abbey, no. 121.[314]

B227. *Charter of King Æthelred concerning Ardley.*
Charters of Abingdon Abbey, no. 125.[315]

B228. *King Æthelred's charter.*
Charters of Abingdon Abbey, no. 122.[316]

B229. *Charter of King Æthelred concerning Wootton.*
Charters of Abingdon Abbey, no. 123.[317]

B230. *Charter of King Æthelred concerning Benson.*
Charters of Abingdon Abbey, no. 127.[318]

B231. *Charter of King Æthelred concerning three hides in Drayton and two in Sutton.*
Charters of Abingdon Abbey, no. 130.[319]

evidence of Abingdon interest in this land. *DB* i, fo. 157^{r}, records that in 1086 Robert d'Oilly held Ardley from Earl Hugh of Chester, with an assessment of five hides. Note vol. ii. 24 for Earl Hugh acquiring land in Berkshire claimed by Abingdon; however, there is no evidence of such a claim to Ardley.

[316] Sawyer, no. 855. This charter records Æthelred granting eight hides on the river Kennet to his thegn Beorhtric. It is dated 984. *Charters of Abingdon Abbey*, p. 472, states that 'there seems no reason to suspect that [the document] is other than authentic'. The boundary clause, and the rubric to the charter in Edward the Confessor's name supposedly granting the land to Abingdon, above, c. 135, identify the land as Leverton.

[317] Sawyer, no. 858. This charter records Æthelred granting ten hides to his thegn Leofwine. It is dated 985. *Charters of Abingdon Abbey*, p. 475, states that it 'is clearly authentic'. Leofwine cannot be identified with certainty. Wootton may have been included in the twenty-five hides 'at Bayworth' which Eadwig gave Ælfric, above, c. 53. In *Domesday Book*, Wootton was probably included in the large manor of Cumnor, held by Abingdon; *DB* i, fo. 58^{v}.

[318] Sawyer, no. 887. This charter records Æthelred giving two hides at Benson, Oxfordshire, to three brothers who were his men, Eadric, Eadwig, and Ealdred. It is dated 996. *Charters of Abingdon Abbey*, p. 495, states that 'there is no good reason to question [the document's] authenticity'. Kelly points out, p. 496, that the two hides 'need not have been located within the present parish of Benson, but could have been carved from any property, close or distant, formerly dependent on the royal vill'. Apart from the presence of this charter in the archive, there is no other evidence of Abingdon interest in this land. In 1086 the king held eleven hides three virgates at Benson, a king's thegn [*minister*] called William one hide, Theodoric the goldsmith two hides; *DB* i, fos. 154^{v}, 160^{v}. For Abingdon receiving a mill at Benson in the mid- or late 1150s, see vol. ii. 316.

[319] Sawyer, no. 897. This charter records Æthelred granting three hides in Drayton and two in Sutton Courtenay to Abingdon. The previous holder is specified as Wulfgar the butler. The document is a very rare instance of a charter in favour of the abbey appearing

[i. 408] fo. 100r **B232.** *Carta regis Adelredi de Haseleie.*
Charters of Abingdon Abbey, no. 131.[320]

[i. 411] fo. 100v **B233.** *Quis abbatiam Burtune fundauit.*[321]
His diebus quidam minister Aþelredi regis Anglorum, dictus Wlfricus Spot, construxit abbatiam Burtun uocatam deditque ei omnem hereditatem paternam, appreciatam dcc. libras. Et ut hec donatio rata haberetur, dedit Aþelredo regi .ccc. mancas auri pro eius confirmatione, et unicuique episcopo quinque mancas, et duobus archiepiscopis decem mancas, insuper Alfrico archiepiscopo Chantuarie uillam Dumbeltonam, a predecessoribus suis ab ecclesia Abbendonensi iniuste ablatam, et unicuique abbati[a] libram auri, et unicuique et abbatisse quinque mancas.

B234. *Carta Adelredi regis de Dummeltun.*
Charters of Abingdon Abbey, no. 132; above, c. 104.

[i. 416] fo. 102r **B235.** *Testamentum Alfrici archiepiscopi.*
Charters of Abingdon Abbey, no. 133.[322]

[i. 417] **B236.** *Quod Latine sic interpretatur.*
Above, c. 105.

[i. 419] fo. 102v **B237.** *Carta regis Aþelredi de Waltham.*
Charters of Abingdon Abbey, no. 134.[323]

[i. 422] fo. 103v **B238.** *Carta regis Adelredi Hwittchureke.*[324]
Charters of Abingdon Abbey, no. 136.

B233 [a] abbatie *MS*

only in MS B. It is dated 1000. *Charters of Abingdon Abbey*, pp. 508–9, suggests of the charter's omission from MS C that 'it may simply have been overlooked, but there is some possibility that it did not come into existence until a later date. . . . There can be little doubt that [the document] was drawn up at Abingdon, and it seems most likely that it should be regarded as spurious, or at best dubious.' Kelly points out the lack of a proper royal style, conventional royal subscription, and also 'some surprising errors'. Another possibility is that this charter, like that concerning Arncott, above, B219, appeared on a missing folio of MS C; see above, above, p. xlvii.

[320] Sawyer, no. 902. This charter records Æthelred granting ten hides at Little Haseley, Oxfordshire, to his thegn Godwine, receiving in return payment of 30 *mancuses* of pure gold. It is dated 1002. *Charters of Abingdon Abbey*, p. 511, states that the document 'is probably authentic', although the indiction does not coincide with the incarnation date. The grantee cannot be identified with certainty, although he may be the son of Ealdorman Ælfheah, on whom see Williams, '*Princeps Merciorum gentis*', pp. 171–2. Apart from the

B232. *Charter of King Æthelred concerning Haseley.*
Charters of Abingdon Abbey, no. 131.[320]

B233. *Who founded the abbey of Burton.*[321]
In these days a certain thegn of Æthelred king of the English, called Wulfric Spot, built the abbey called Burton and gave it all his paternal inheritance, worth £700. So that this donation might be held strong, he gave 300 *mancuses* of gold to King Æthelred for his confirmation, and 5 *mancuses* to each bishop and 10 *mancuses* to the two archbishops, and also to Archbishop Ælfric of Canterbury the village of Dumbleton, unjustly taken from the church of Abingdon by his predecessors, and a pound of gold to each abbot and 5 *mancuses* to each abbess.

B234. *Charter of King Æthelred concerning Dumbleton.*
Charters of Abingdon Abbey, no. 132; above, c. 104.

B235. *Archbishop Ælfric's will.*
Charters of Abingdon Abbey, no. 133.[322]

B236. *Which is translated thus in Latin.*
Above, c. 105.

B237. *Charter of King Æthelred concerning Waltham.*
Charters of Abingdon Abbey, no. 134.[323]

B238. *Charter of King Æthelred concerning Whitchurch.*[324]
Charters of Abingdon Abbey, no. 136; cf. above, c. 140, and below, B280.

presence of this charter in the archive, there is no other evidence of Abingdon interest in this land.

[321] On possible sources for this section, see above, p. xlii.

[322] Sawyer, no. 1488; *Anglo-Saxon Wills*, ed. Whitelock, no. 18; also trans *EHD*, i. no. 126. The will is dateable to 1002 × 1005. For commentary, see above, c. 105, the Latin version of the will included in MS C.

[323] Sawyer, no. 915. This charter records Æthelred granting eight hides at Waltham St Lawrence to his reeve Ælfgar. Ælfgar had asked the king for the land in return for 300 *mancuses* of purest gold and silver. Gelling, *Early Charters of the Thames Valley*, p. 64, suggests that the price is too high, and should be 30 *mancuses*. However, we know too little about the background of the transaction for any certainty in this respect. The charter is dated 1007. *Charters of Abingdon Abbey*, p. 524, states that the document 'appears to be authentic'. See also above, B68 (*Charters of Abingdon Abbey*, no. 32), for a charter of Edmund recording his grant of thirty hides at Waltham to his thegn, Ælfsige; the present charter would concern a portion of that land. The eight hides may be those held by Queen Edith *TRE*; *DB* i, fo. 56^{v}.

[324] For the repetition of this charter, see above, p. xlvi.

[i. 425] fo. 104r **B239.** *Carta regis Adelredi de Chiltune.*
Charters of Abingdon Abbey, no. 137.[325]

[i. 428] fo. 105r **B240.** *De Alfifa que reddidit Chelgraue et Bulteswurþe.*
Above, c. 106.

[i. 429] **B241.** *De Alfled que reddidit Winkefeld.*
Above, c. 107.

B242. *De Edwio qui reddidit Bedene.*
Above, c. 108.

fo. 105v **B243.** *De prophetia sancti Dunstani.*[326]
Tempore uero istius Aþelredi, ut predixit beatus Dunstanus dum [i. 430] capiti eius regale imponeret diadema, subito facta est regni permutatio. Breui etenim tempore sex archiepiscopi, scilicet Dunstanus, Liuingus, Alfgarus, Siricius, Alfricus, Alfegus Cantuariensis ecclesie cathedram adepti archiepiscopalem cesserunt in fatum, ad hoc forte hac luce priuati, ne piorum patrum pia misericordia in posterum sibi insurgere filios uideret degeneres. Nec hoc solum, uerum etiam maiores natu et dignitate potentiores, immo cuiuscumque essent conditionis tam uiros quam mulieres tocius Anglie repentinus irruit pauor pariter et uastatio. Enimuero gens barbarica, scilicet Danorum, nauali uehiculo cum rege suo Swano in Angliam aduentasse perhibetur, que tantam ubique locorum ferocitatem exercuit pariter et impietatem ut nec dignitati uel etati, sexui parcerent aut conditioni. Quorum depopulationi simul et insultui cum gens Anglicana uideret se minime posse resistere, hii propter metum mortis, alii causa rei seruande, nonnulli etiam proditorie ad regem Danorum se contulerunt. Sicque factum est ut regnum ipsum in se diuisum flebiliter desolaretur.[327] Quid multa? Rex Aþelredus, uidens se alienatum tam a fidelitate quam a consortio suorum, Normanniam una cum uxore sua et liberis gressu petiit festinanti.[328] Regnauit itaque Swanus in Anglia

[325] Sawyer, no. 934. This charter records Æthelred granting five hides in Chilton to Byrhtwold bishop of Ramsbury, the estate having previously been forfeited to the king by a thegn called Wulfgeat. It is dated 1015. *Charters of Abingdon Abbey*, p. 538, states that the document 'is probably authentic'. See above, c. 133, for a very dubious charter of Edward the Confessor granting Chilton to Abingdon, and for further notes on the estate. Note also above, p. 330, for separate inclusion of the bounds of an area of woodland associated with Chilton.

[326] Cf. above, c. 109. On Dunstan's prophecies, see e.g. S. Keynes, 'The declining reputation of King Æthelred the Unready', in D. Hill, ed., *Æthelred the Unready: Papers*

B239. *Charter of King Æthelred concerning Chilton.*
Charters of Abingdon Abbey, no. 137.[325]

B240. *Concerning Ælfgifu who gave back Chalgrave and* Bulthesworthe.
Above, c. 106.

B241. *Concerning Eadflæd who gave back Winkfield.*
Above, c. 107.

B242. *Concerning Eadwine who gave back Beedon.*
Above, c. 108.

B243. *Concerning St Dunstan's prophecy.*[326]
In Æthelred's time, indeed, as the blessed Dunstan foretold while he was placing the royal diadem on his head, suddenly a transformation of the kingdom occurred. For in a short time six archbishops, that is Dunstan, Lyfing, Æthelgar, Sigeric, Ælfric, and Ælfheah, acquired the archiepiscopal throne of the church of Canterbury but then yielded to death, deprived of this light perhaps for this reason, so that the pious mercy of pious fathers might not see ignoble sons rise up against them in future. Nor this alone, but also sudden terror and ravaging too rushed down upon the greater by birth and the more powerful by rank, and also upon both the men and the women of the whole of England, of whatever standing. For a barbaric people, that is the Danes, are reported to have come by sea transport to England with their king, Swein, and everywhere exercised such ferocity and impiety too that they spared neither rank nor age, sex nor standing. When the English people saw they could not resist the Danes' devastation and assault at all, some went over to the king of the Danes for fear of death, others to preserve possessions, others still out of treachery. And so it happened that that kingdom divided against itself was lamentably brought to desolation.[327] What's more, when King Æthelred saw that he had lost the loyalty and company of his men, he swiftly sought Normandy, with his wife and children.[328] So

from the Millenary Conference (British Archaeological Reports, British Series, lix; 1978), pp. 227–53, at pp. 236–9.

[327] Matt. 12: 25 'Omne regnum divisum contra se desolabitur.'

[328] Emma in fact went to Normandy before Æthelred in 1013. The Æthelings too went to Normandy, perhaps separately from their mother. Æthelred travelled there after Christmas of that year; *ASC*, *s.a.* 1013. William of Malmesbury, *Gesta regum*, bk. ii, c. 178, ed. Mynors *et al.*, i. 304, says that the king travelled to Normandy in Jan. 1014. See also S. Keynes, 'The Æthelings in Normandy', *ANS*, xiii (1991), 173–205, at pp. 175–6.

paucis diebus, quia regno pariter et uita in[a] breui diuino arbitrio est priuatus. Verum post cuius decessum rex Anglorum Aþelredus, quam citius potuit a partibus remeans transmarinis, nullo contradicente, regno potitur prius habito.[329]

[i. 431] **B244.** *De morte Adelredi regis et de regno Edmundi regis filii sui.*
Above, c. 110.

[i. 433 n.] **B245.** *De morte Wlfgari abbatis.*[330]
fo. 106r Circa idem tempus domnus Wlfgarus abbas uiam uniuerse carnis ingressus est, cui successit Aþelwinus abbas, uir magne auctoritatis et equitatis assertor comprobatus, et iccirco Cnutoni regi familiaris est effectus.[331] Ad cuius etiam admonitiones memoratus rex multa bona huic ecclesie Abbendonie contulit. Dedit namque uillas que Mittune et Linford appellantur, cum omnibus ad se integre pertinentibus, sicut karte ipsius regis subsequentes attestantur. Quarum prima hec est:

[i. 436] **B246.** *Carta Cnutonis regis de Mittune.*[a]
Charters of Abingdon Abbey, no. 139.[332]

[i. 439] fo. 106v **B247.** *Carta regis Cnut de Linford.*
Charters of Abingdon Abbey, no. 138; above, c. 114.

[i. 442] fo. 107v **B248.** *Testamentum Adelredi regis.*[333]
As above, c. 115: 'Illibus diebus . . . largitus est'.

[i. 443] **B249.** *De donis Cnutonis regis.*[334]
Tecam etiam rex Cnuto de argento et auro ad honorem gloriosissimi martiris Vincentii Hispaniensis, cuius reliquie in hac continentur ecclesia fieri fecit. Dedit etiam memoratus rex huic domui duo signa grossa que usque in hodiernum tempus in ecclesia ista habentur. Abbas etiam Aþelwinus hoc tempore capsam unam, ad formam illius capse que per regem facta fuit, pari pene magnitudine condidit, in qua reliquias sanctorum a se diligenter adquisitas honorifice condidit. Fecit etiam crucem argenteam que adhuc in hac ecclesia habetur.

B243 [a] *interlin.*

B246 [a] *an illustration of the king appears at the start of this charter*

[329] Swein died 3 Feb. 1014. After some negotiation, Æthelred returned, having agreed that he would rule more justly than before; *ASC*, 'C', *s.a.* 1014.

[330] Cf. above, c. 111.

[331] On the problems of abbatial succession at this point, see above, p. c.

[332] Sawyer, no. 967. This charter records Cnut granting three hides in Myton,

Swein ruled for a few days in England, but was soon deprived of the kingdom and also life by divine judgement [3 Feb. 1014]. After his death, Æthelred king of the English returned from overseas regions as quickly as he could and, with no one contradicting, possessed the kingdom he had previously had.[329]

B244. *Concerning the death of King Æthelred and the reign of King Edmund his son.*

Above, c. 110.

B245. *Concerning the death of Abbot Wulfgar.*[330]

Around that time lord Abbot Wulfgar went the way of all flesh [1016], to whom succeeded Abbot Æthelwine, a man of great authority and a proven assertor of justice, and therefore made an intimate to King Cnut.[331] Also, urged by him, that king conferred many goods on this church of Abingdon. For he gave the villages called Myton and Lyford, with everything entirely pertaining to them, as the following charters of that king witness. Of these, this is the first:

B246. *Charter of King Cnut concerning Myton.*

Charters of Abingdon Abbey, no. 139.[332]

B247. *Charter of King Cnut concerning Lyford.*

Charters of Abingdon Abbey, no. 138; above, c. 114.

B248. *King Æthelred's testament.*[333]

As above, c. 115: 'In those days . . . large crystal.'

B249. *Concerning King Cnut's gifts.*[334]

King Cnut also had a reliquary of silver and gold made in honour of the most glorious martyr Vincent of Spain, whose relics are kept in this church. That king also gave to this house two large bells which are in this church to the present day. Also at this time Abbot Æthelwine constructed a reliquary of almost equal size, on the model of that made on the king's behalf, in which he honourably set the saints' relics which he had diligently acquired. He also made a silver cross which is still in this church.

Warwickshire, to Abingdon. It is dated 1033. *Charters of Abingdon Abbey*, pp. 547–9, examines the difficulties of accepting both this charter and c. 113, above, as genuine, although there is no certain reason for condemning either.

[333] The section that follows is in fact the grant of eight and a half hides and three reliquaries by a powerful man named Æthelweard.

[334] Cf. above, c. 111.

B250. *Quo tempore adlate sunt reliquie sancti Edwardi Abbendonie.*[335]
Tempore etiam Cnutonis regis reliquie sancti Eadwardi regis et martiris, que in[a] ista continentur ecclesia, ad hanc domum Abbendonensem mirifice sunt delate, prout in serie passionis et uite gloriosissimi martiris euidentissime continetur.[336]

B251. *De aduentu Siwardi abbatis.*[337]
Athelwino abbate diem clausit suppremum, successit ei Siwardus, ex [i. 444] Glestoniensi cenobio monachus, tam secularium quam ecclesiasticarum uigore admodum suffultus. Ob cuius etiam benignitatem, quam rex Cnuto ex ipsius pectore iugiter nouit exuberare, memoratus rex ecclesiam sancti Martini in Oxonefordia, cum uno prediolo, huic domui caritatiue contulit.[338]

B252. *Quomodo uoluit Siwardus abbas frangere ecclesiam sancti Adelwoldi.*[339]
Interea dum quadam die, more solito, abbas uenerabilis Siwardus deambularet in curia abbacie, attollens oculos suos ad ecclesiam et ad officinas quas beatus Aþelwoldus predecessor eius reedificauerat, proposuit in animo suo ecclesiam pariter cum officinis infringere et fo. 108r in | melius mutare necnon et ampliores reedificare. Quod cum in animo suo iam concepisset, uidens tamen nec se posse nec uelle huiusmodi opus aut sic infringere aut[a] aliud reparare sine regis gratia simul et licentia, ex consulto regem adiit petiturus[b] ab eo licentiam super huiusmodi negotio propensius exequendo. Nec mora quod a rege petiit, sine repulsu, maturius obtinuit. Itaque cum diucius deliberasset super huiusmodi negotio incoando, attendens diligenter uite sanctitatem uenerabilis uiri Aþelwoldi predecessoris sui, qui ipsum opus incoauerat pariter et consummauerat, timuit idem opus infringere, admodum pauidus ne super huiuscemodi facto gloriosissimi confessoris incurreret offensam. Quid multa? De consilio fratrum suorum, indictis sibi aliquot dierum ieiuniis, diuinam implorabant clementiam insuper et beati Aþelwoldi patrocinium, quatinus diuinitus eis esset manifestatum, aut de ueteri remanendo,

B250 [a] *interlin.*

B252 [a] *followed by* sic, *del. by expunction* [b] *corr. from* potiturus

[335] Cf. above, p. 182.
[336] Oxford, Bodleian Library, Digby 146, contains a version of the *Passio* of Edward the martyr in a 12th-c. hand probably from Abingdon; C. E. Fell, *Edward King and Martyr* (Leeds, 1971), p. vi. This does not mention the transfer of Edward's body to Wareham and its later translation to Shaftesbury, but nor does it specify that the relics were brought to

B250. *At what time St Edward's relics were brought to Abingdon.*[335]
Also in King Cnut's time the relics of St Edward king and martyr, which are kept in this church, were marvellously brought to this house of Abingdon, as is contained most clearly in the account of the passion and life of the most glorious martyr.[336]

B251. *Concerning the coming of Abbot Siward.*[337]
When Abbot Æthelwine had passed away [1030], Siward, a monk from the monastery of Glastonbury, succeeded him, strongly supported with vigour concerning both worldly and ecclesiastical matters. Also, because of his kindness, which King Cnut knew to flow copiously and constantly from his heart, that king charitably conferred on this house the church of St Martin in Oxford, with one small estate.[338]

B252. *How Abbot Siward wished to demolish St Æthelwold's church.*[339]
Meanwhile, one day the venerable Abbot Siward was walking in the abbey court as was his habit and raised his eyes to the church and the domestic buildings which the blessed Æthelwold his predecessor had rebuilt, and he mentally proposed to demolish the church and also the domestic buildings, to change them for the better and to rebuild them larger. After conceiving this in his mind, but seeing that without the king's grace and also permission he was neither capable of demolishing nor would wish to demolish such work or to build again another, he deliberately went to the king to seek from him permission concerning pursuing such business the more readily. He immediately obtained what he sought from the king, without rejection. When he had longer considered beginning this business, and paying diligent attention to the holiness of life of the venerable man Æthelwold his predecessor, who had begun and also completed this work, he feared to demolish it, very frightened lest he incur the anger of the most glorious confessor over such a deed. What's more, by his brethren's counsel, they imposed several days of fasting on themselves and implored divine clemency and also the patronage of the blessed Æthelwold, that it be divinely made manifest to them what was

Abingdon. Perhaps the compiler of the *History* had access to another version of the passion and life of Edward, or perhaps he was himself concocting an rival version to the Shaftesbury claim to Edward's relics.

337 Cf. above, c. 112.

338 The small estate is presumably Lyford; see above, c. 114, B247.

339 On this chapter, see above, pp. l–li.

aut nouo monasterio construendo, quid eis pocius expediret. Et factum est. Post aliquot dies, uiro uenerabili Siwardo abbate in [i. 445] lectulo suo quiescenti, apparuit ei beatus Aþelwoldus in sompnis, dicens 'Quid mente uolutes, quid in posterum de ecclesia mea pariter et edificiis[c] meis diruendis ac iterum reedificandis cogitando tecum deliberes bene noui, et iccirco ueni tibi consulere quid commodius sit agendum super huiuscemodi negotio exequendo. Non est itaque tui temporis hoc meum opus infringere aut aliud edificare. Quod ut certius fidem meis dictis adhibeas, attende diligentius, quod quidam de transmarinis partibus ueniet pater et pastor istius loci futurus, qui ipsum opus infringet et nouum incoabit; sed hoc ipsum non perficiet.[340] Post hunc uero, uenient et alii duo similiter loci pastores futuri, qui multa bona tam edificiis quam in aliis huic loco competentibus admodum necessarii actitare satagent.[341] Quibus cedentibus in fatum, non erit quispiam per diuturnam temporis protelationem in[d] hoc loco pastor et abbas futurus qui consimili modo hunc locum bonis studeat ampliare. Nouissimis uero diebus, erit quidam similiter istius loci abbas futurus qui in Christi uisceribus[342] hunc locum tanto amplexabitur affectu ut, bona bonis accumulans, edificia diruens et in melius reedificans, ecclesiam condecorans, ordinem seruans, de consuetudinibus nichil minuens sed pocius aumentans,[343] Deum timens, moribus pollens, uite sanctitate precluus, pius pater et pastor uocari dignus, in pace pectoris pacem prestolabitur eternitatis.'[344] His auditis Siwardus, a sompno expergefactus,[345] gratias Deo agere et a proposito suo desistere incepit, et pecuniam quam ad ipsum fo. 108v opus inchoandum coadunauerat diligenter | studuit erogare pauperibus.

[i. 446] **B253**. *De morte Cnutonis regis.*[346]

Mortuo Cnutone rege[a] necnon et Haraldo filio eius, ex concubina genito, regnauit Hardecnutus filius eius ex Emma (quondam Aþelredi regis regina). Iste ad monitionem Siwardi abbatis dedit huic domui Ferbergam et carta sua confirmauit. Cuius carte tenor hic est:

[c] edeficiis *MS* [d] *corr. from* etiam

B253 [a] *corr. from* regis

[340] i.e. Reginald; see vol. ii, p. cii.

[341] i.e. Faritius and Vincent; see vol. ii, pp. cii–ciii.

[342] Phil. 1: 8.

[343] Cf. the argument put into Abbot Faritius's mouth justifying his changes to Æthelwold's food provisions; vol. ii. 334.

[344] i.e. Hugh. The final phrase is also used of King Ceadwalla, above, p. 238.

better for them, about either letting the old remain or building a new monastery. And so it happened. After a few days, when the venerable man Abbot Siward was resting on his bed, the blessed Æthelwold appeared to him in his sleep, saying 'What you turn over in your mind, what you are contemplating by thinking about in future destroying my church and also my buildings and rebuilding again, I know well and therefore I have come to counsel you as to what it is more suitable to do concerning pursuing such business. So, it is not for your time to demolish my work or build another. So that you may display greater faith in my sayings, wait very diligently, that a certain future father and shepherd of this monastery will come from overseas, who will demolish this work and begin a new one; but he will not complete this.[340] After this man, indeed, there will also come two other men likewise shepherds of the monastery, who—greatly needed—will busy themselves doing many good deeds both about buildings and about other matters relating to this monastery.[341] When they yield to death, for a very long period of time there will be no future pastor and abbot in this monastery who will in similar fashion strive to increase this monastery with good deeds. In most recent times, indeed, there will likewise be a future abbot of this monastery who will embrace this monastery in 'the bowels of Christ'[342] with such emotion that piling good things on good, destroying buildings and rebuilding them for the better, adorning the church, preserving the ordered life, diminishing nothing of the customs but rather augmenting them,[343] God-fearing, strong in behaviour, outstanding in holiness of life, a pious father and worthy of being called shepherd, in peace of heart will await the peace of eternity.'[344] When he had heard these things, Siward awoke from sleep[345] and began to give thanks to God and to desist from his proposal, and strove diligently to bestow on the poor the money which he had gathered for beginning that work.

B253. *Concerning the death of King Cnut.*[346]

When King Cnut and also his son Harold, born from a concubine, had died [1035, 1040], Harthacnut, his son from Emma (formerly King Æthelred's queen) reigned. Urged by Abbot Siward, he gave and confirmed by his charter Farnborough to this house. The terms of his charter are as follows:

[345] A phrase also used of Robert d'Oilly after his illuminating dream; vol. ii. 330.

[346] Cf. above, c. 116.

B254. *Carta Hardecnuti de Fernberga.*[a]
Charters of Abingdon Abbey, no. 141; above, c. 117.

[i. 450] **B255.** *De morte Ardecnuti regis.*[347]
fo. 109v [i. 451] Successit Hardecnuto Anglorum regi beatissimus Eadwardus frater eius, Aþelredi quondam Anglorum regis et Emme filius.[348] Annitentibus Edsio Dorobernensi archiepiscopo et Liuingo Wigornensi episcopo et Godwino comite, cuius filiam accepturus erat in reginam,[349] Lundonie leuatur in regem[350] et ab archiepiscopis Edsio Dorobernensi[a] et Alfrico Eboracensi archiepiscopo aliisque ferme totius Anglie primatibus prima die Pasche unguitur in regem Wintonie.[351] Cuius beneficia que domui Abbendonie contulit inferius annotabimus.

B256. *De sancto Eadwardo rege.*[352]
Anno secundo regni Eadwardi regis, Edsius archiepiscopus Dorobernie, Godwino comite mediante, ab Eadwardo rege impetrauit ut sese causa imbecillitatis proprie labori cedere antisticii, Siwardum [i. 452] uero ex Abbendonia abbatem, utpote discretum[a] religiosumque uirum, in episcopum Rouecestrie sacratum, suo loco substitui et uice illius uniuersa dispensari concederet. Quo facto Aþelstanus, cenobii predicti tunc edituus, eidem preponitur.

B257. *Carta Edwardi regis de octo hidis iuxta Chinete.*[a]
Charters of Abingdon Abbey, no. 145; cf. above, c. 135, and below, B275.[353]

[i. 455] **B258.**[a]
fo. 110v *Charters of Abingdon Abbey*, no. 146; cf. above, c. 133, and below, B288.[354]

B254 [a] *an illustration of the king appears at the start of this charter*

B255 [a] *corr. from* Dorobernensis

B256 [a] *corr. from* diseretum

B257 [a] *an illustration of the king appears at the start of this charter*

B258 [a] *the rubricator failed to provide a heading for this charter which starts at the top of fo. 110v, even though a space had been left at the bottom of fo. 110r*

---

[347] Cf. above, c. 118.
[348] Edward was Harthacnut's half-brother, Emma being mother to both of them.
[349] Edward married Edith, daughter of Godwine, on 23 Jan. 1045; *Handbook of British Chronology*, p. 29.
[350] The phrase 'Lundonie leuatur in regem' follows verbatim John of Worcester, *Chronicle*, ii. 534.

B254. *Charter of Harthacnut concerning Farnborough.*
Charters of Abingdon Abbey, no. 141; above, c. 117.

B255. *Concerning the death of King Harthacnut.*[347]
There succeeded to Harthacnut king of the English the most blessed Edward his brother, son of Æthelred (formerly king of the English) and Emma.[348] Supported by Eadsige archbishop of Canterbury and Lyfing bishop of Worcester and Earl Godwine, whose daughter he was to receive as queen,[349] he was raised to being king at London,[350] and on the first day of Easter [3 Apr. 1043] was anointed as king at Winchester by archbishops Eadsige of Canterbury and Ælfric archbishop of York, and the other leading men of almost the whole of England.[351] We will record below the endowments that Edward conferred on the house of Abingdon.

B256. *Concerning St Edward the king.*[352]
In the second year of King Edward's reign, Eadsige archbishop of Canterbury, through the mediation of Earl Godwine, sought from King Edward that he grant that Eadsige yield from the toil of his bishopric because of his own weakness, and indeed that Abbot Siward, from Abingdon, as a discrete and devout man, consecrated as bishop of Rochester, be substituted in his place and everything be administered on his behalf. When this was done, Æthelstan, then sacrist of the aforesaid monastery, was put in charge of it.

B257. *Charter of King Edward concerning eight hides next to the Kennet.*
Charters of Abingdon Abbey, no. 145; above, c. 135, and below, B275.[353]

B258.
Charters of Abingdon Abbey, no. 146; cf. above, c. 133, and below, B288.[354]

[351] The passage 'ab archiepiscopis . . . in regem Wintonie' draws heavily on John of Worcester, *Chronicle*, ii. 534. Ælfric Puttoc was archbishop of York 1023–51; *Handbook of British Chronology*, p. 224. For the coronation, see Barlow, *Edward the Confessor*, pp. 60–70.
[352] Cf. c. 119 above.
[353] The present copy is a fuller version than that which appears below, B275, and in MS C, above, c. 135. It is possible that the absence of proem and exposition in the copy of MS C led the compiler of MS B to fail to recognize its identity with his other, full version.
[354] The present copy is a fuller version than that which appears below, B288, and in MS C, above, c. 133. It is possible that the absence of proem and exposition in the copy of MS C led the compiler of MS B to fail to recognize its identity with his other, full version. See also above, B176, for a portion of a boundary clause which may be drawn from this charter.

[i. 457] fo. 111^r **B259**. *De contentione Lechamstede.*
Above, c. 120.

[i. 458] **B260**. *Responsio Siwardi episcopi de Lechamstede.*
Above, c. 120.

[i. 459] fo. 111^v **B261**. *De uilla Leuekenore.*
Above, c. 121.

[i. 461] fo. 112^r **B262**. *De morte Siwardi episcopi.*
Above, c. 122.

[i. 462] **B263**. *De morte Adelstani abbatis.*
Above, c. 123.

fo. 112^v **B264**. *De Sperauoc abbate.*
Above, c. 124.

[i. 463] **B265**. *De Rodulfo episcopo.*
Above, c. 125.

[i. 464] **B266**. *De Ordrico abbate.*
Above, c. 126.

fo. 113^r **B267**. *Carta regis Eadwardi Anglice.*
Charters of Abingdon Abbey, no. 148; above, c. 127.

[i. 465] **B268**. *Interpretatio in Latinum*
Above, c. 128.

B269. *Carta regis Edwardi de hundredo de Hornimere.*
Charters of Abingdon Abbey, no. 149; above, c. 129.

[i. 466] **B270**. *Interpretatio in Latinum.*
Above, c. 130.

B271. *De quatuor cassatis de Sanford.*
Charters of Abingdon Abbey, no. 144.[355]

[i. 469] **B272**. *De morte Godwini comitis.*[356]
fo. 114^r Mortuo Godwino comite, successit ei Haroldus filius eius. Cuius suggestione, abbate Ordrico optinente, rex Anglorum Eadwardus

[355] Sawyer, no. 1022. This charter records King Edward the Confessor granting four hides 'in communi terra' at Sandford(-on-Thames) to Earl Godwine. It is dated 1050. *Charters of Abingdon Abbey*, p. 561, states that it 'would appear to be authentic'. *Charters of Abingdon Abbey*, p. 562, notes that it is possible that these four hides were properly

B259. *Concerning the dispute over Leckhampstead.*
Above, c. 120.

B260. *Bishop Siward's response concerning Leckhampstead.*
Charters of Abingdon Abbey, no. 143; above, c. 120.

B261. *Concerning the village of Lewknor.*
Above, c. 121.

B262. *Concerning the death of Bishop Siward.*
Above, c. 122.

B263. *Concerning the death of Abbot Æthelstan.*
Above, c. 123.

B264. *Concerning Abbot Spearhafoc.*
Above, c. 124.

B265. *Concerning Bishop Rodulf.*
Above, c. 125.

B266. *Concerning Abbot Ordric.*
Above, c. 126.

B267. *King Edward's charter in English.*
Charters of Abingdon Abbey, no. 148; above, c. 127.

B268. *Translation into Latin.*
Above, c. 128.

B269. *Charter of King Edward concerning the hundred of Hormer.*
Charters of Abingdon Abbey, no. 149; above, c. 129.

B270. *Translation into Latin.*
Above, c. 130.

B271. *Concerning four hides at Sandford.*
Charters of Abingdon Abbey, no. 144.[355]

B272. *Concerning the death of Earl Godwine.*[356]
When Earl Godwine died, his son Harold succeeded him. At his suggestion, Edward king of the English granted and by his charter confirmed Sandford across the river Thames amounting to four hides

Abingdon lands, seized by Godwine, but more likely that Abingdon acquired them after Godwine's tenure, and possibly only after 1066; see also above, c. 132 (*Charters of Abingdon Abbey*, no. 147) for a spurious charter of the Confessor granting these four hides to Abingdon.

356 Cf. c. 131 above.

ecclesie Abbendonensi Samford transflumen Tamisie quatuor hidarum concessit et carta sua confirmauit. Que ita inscripta est:

B273. *Carta quatuor hidarum de Samford.*
Charters of Abingdon Abbey, no. 147; above, c. 132.

[i. 473] fo. 114v **B274**. *Rex Edwardus dedit Leofwartun.*
Above, c. 134.

B275. *Carta regis Edwardi.*
Charters of Abingdon Abbey, no. 145; above, c. 135, and cf. B257.[357]

[i. 474] fo. 115r **B276**.[a]
Above, c. 136.

[i. 476] fo. 115v **B277**. *Carta decem cassatorum de Lecamstede.*[358]
Above, c. 137, and cf. above, B72.

[i. 477] fo. 116r **B278**.[a]
Above, c. 138.

[i. 478] **B279**. *Carta de Speresholt decem cassatorum.*
Charters of Abingdon Abbey, n. 97; above, c. 139, and cf. above, B184.

[i. 479] **B280**. *Carta de Hwitcyrce.*
Charters of Abingdon Abbey, no. 136; above, c. 140.

[i. 480] fo. 116v **B281**.[a]
Above, c. 141.

[i. 481] fo. 117r **B282**.[a]
Above, c. 141.

B283.[a]
Above, c. 141.

[i. 482] **B284**. *De morte Edwardi regis.*[359]
Above, c. 142.

B276 [a] *rubricated heading of minims*

B278 [a] *short rubricated heading of minims*

B281 [a] *rubricated heading of minims*

B282 [a] *rubricated heading of minims*

B283 [a] *rubricated heading of minims*

to the church of Abingdon, under the charge of Abbot Ordric. This was written thus:

B273. *Charter regarding four hides at Sandford.*
Charters of Abingdon Abbey, no. 147; above, c. 132.

B274. *King Edward gave Leverton.*
Above, c. 134.

B275. *King Edward's charter.*
Charters of Abingdon Abbey, no. 145; above, c. 135, B257.[357]

B276.
Above, c. 136.

B277. *Charter regarding ten hides at Leckhampstead.*[358]
Cf. *Charters of Abingdon Abbey*, no. 37; above, c. 137, and cf. B72.

B278.
Above, c. 138.

B279. *Charter concerning Sparsholt amounting to ten hides.*
Charters of Abingdon Abbey, no. 97; above, c. 139, and cf. above, B184.

B280. *Charter concerning Whitchurch.*
Charters of Abingdon Abbey, no. 136; above, c. 140, and cf. above, B238.

B281.
Above, c. 141.

B282.
Above, c. 141.

B283.
Above, c. 141.

B284. *Concerning the death of King Edward.*[359]
Above, c. 142.

[357] See above, pp. xlv–xlvi, for charters repeated in MS B.
[358] For the appearance in MS B of two versions of this charter of King Edmund, see above, p. xlvi n. 193.
[359] This is also the heading for B290 below.

B285. *De Ordrico abbate.*

Abbas[360] etiam Ordricus, postquam domum sibi commissam honorifice gubernasset, et a memoria principum apostolorum (quo deuotionis gratia perrexerat) ad sua remeasset, diutina egritudine decoctus diem sortitur ultimum, circa sollempnitatem sancti Vincentii martiris.[a]

Tunc duo subrogati sunt, Haroldus comes scilicet in regem Anglorum, et Ealdredus, hactenus exteriorum preposituram Abbendonie agens, inibi in abbatem monachorum.

In proximo autem Paschali festo, sidus insolitum, quod cometem
[i. 483] uocant, unius continuatione septimane apparuit, quo auspicatum est futurum quiddam maximum et inopinatum. Nec fefellit opinio, nam mense Septembrio instante rex Norweie, eodem denominatus uocabulo quo rex Anglie, scilicet Haroldus, Angliam appulit, regnum illic sibi uendicare pro lucro reputans, suffragium ferente fratre nostri regis Haroldi Tosti comite. Quibus Eboracem ultra urbem rex Anglorum occurrens, utrumque una cum auxiliariis eorum bello extinxit.

Huius uix soluto fine uictorie, ecce, comitem Normannie Willelmum sibi imminere apud Hastingas[b] bellumque paratum inferre, ni maturius regno cedat, ex nuntio discit. Rectiorem se causam[c] illo
fo. 117v regnandi in Anglia habere al|legans, dum pro consanguinitatis linea rex Eadwardus, iam defunctus, sibi regnum reliquerit sub ipsius etiam attestatione et concessu. Ille nuntium paruipendens, ac suis nimium uiribus fidens, minus prouide quam decuerat aggressus comitem, sensit superiorem, quem insulso ausu rebatur inferiorem. Itaque in bello corruens, tam ipse quam cuncti eius socii secum interire.

[i. 487] **B286.**[a] Hucusque de terris et possessionibus quas antiqui reges et regine insimul et homines eorum, tam tempore Anglorum quam Danorum, in puram et perpetuam elemosinam Deo et beate Marie et huic domui Abbendonie monachisque ibidem in perpetuum Deo seruientibus dederant et cartis suis firmiter confirmauerant, Deo iuuante, quoad melius potuimus in his duobus libris precedentibus

B284 [a] *space suitable for a heading left here* [b] *over erasure* [c] eam *MS*

B286 [a] *the rubricator failed to provide a heading, although the appropriate space had been left*

B285. *Concerning Abbot Ordric.*
Also[360] Abbot Ordric, after he had honourably governed the house entrusted to him, and had returned home from the shrine of the princes of the apostles (to which he had gone for the sake of devotion), was worn out by a long-lasting illness and was allotted his final day, around the solemn feast of St Vincent the martyr.

Then two men were chosen in place of their predecessors, that is Earl Harold as king of the English, and Ealdred, who had hitherto acted as provost of the external affairs of Abingdon, as abbot of the monks herein.

However, at the next festival of Easter, an unusual star, which they call a comet, appeared for the duration of one week, and by this it was divined that something most important and unexpected would happen. And that belief was not mistaken, for, with the month of September upon them, the king of Norway, called by the same name as the king of England, that is Harold, landed in England, considering claiming the realm there for his benefit, aided by Earl Tostig, brother of our King Harold. The king of England hurried to meet them beyond the town of York, and in battle killed them both with their supporters.

With this victory scarcely complete, behold, he learnt from a messenger that William count of Normandy was threatening him and prepared to join battle at Hastings, unless he immediately ceded the kingdom. He argued that he had a greater right than William to reign in England, since King Edward, now deceased, had by his own statement and grant left the kingdom to him because of the line of kinship. He belittled the messenger, put too much trust in his strength, and attacked the count less prudently than was fitting, but discovered William was the superior, whom with stupid rashness he had thought inferior. And so falling in battle, both Harold and his allies with him died.

B286. Up to here, in these two preceding books, as best we could, by God's help, we have made a record concerning the lands and possessions which old kings and queens and also their men, both in the time of the English and of the Danes, gave and firmly confirmed by their charters in pure and perpetual alms to God and the blessed Mary and this house of Abingdon and the monks serving God there

[360] This chapter is closely based on c. 143, the common material being here indicated by underlining.

annotauimus. Ceterum uero singulas cartas singulorum regum successiue regnantium necnon et omnium aliorum beneficia sua huic domui conferentium locis competentibus studiose posuimus. Verum quod si quis mortalium de supradictis terris et possessionibus miretur, nunc datis, nunc ablatis, at nunc possessis iterum recuperatis, legat libros in ordine, nec quicquam ibi inueniet contrarium quod animum suum iuste debeat ducere in ambiguum.

Explicit liber secundus.

[i. 488] **B287.** *Incipit liber tercius.*[361]
Item,

Then as above, c. 132, following charter: 'Idem rex . . . Wiltoniensi donauerat.'

B288. *Carta regis Edwardi de Cildatun.*
Charters of Abingdon Abbey, no. 146; above, c. 133, B258.[362]

[i. 489] fo. 118r **B289.**[a] Pertactatis itaque in duobus supradictis uoluminibus sufficienter, pro uiribus nostris pariter et modulo scientie nostre,[363] beneficiis ab antiquis regibus Anglorum insimul et eorum hominibus huic sacratissime domui illatis et eorumdem cartis firmiter confirmatis, nunc superest ut post[b] aduentum Normannorum in Angliam singulorum regum in ordine succedentium libertates insimul et beneficia huic sacratissime domui Abbendonie gratis data et gratanter accepta, presentibus et futuris hec eadem scire desiderantibus, quoad succincius poterimus, Deo iuuante, innotescere procuramus.

B290. *De morte Edwardi regis.*[364]
Igitur Edwardo rege Anglorum anno .mlxv. Dominice incarnationis ad celestia translato,[365] successoreque eius Haroldo pridie idus Octobris a Willelmo Normannorum duce bello prostrato, Willelmus dux Normannie ab Aldredo Eboracensi archiepiscopo die natalis Domini in Westmonasterio honorifice coronatus est,[366] prius tamen, ut ipse archiepiscopus ab eo exigebat, ante altare sancti Petri, coram
[i. 490] clero et populo, iureiurando promittens se uelle sanctas Dei ecclesias

B289 [a] *the rubricator failed to provide a heading, although the appropriate space had been left* [b] *interlin.*

[361] On MS B's confused division into books, see above, p. lxix.
[362] On the repetition of this charter in MS B, see above, p. xlvi n. 194.

for ever. Moreover, we have carefully placed in the proper places each charter of each king reigning in succession and also of all others conferring their endowments on this house. But if indeed any mortal man wonders about the above lands and possessions, now given, now taken away, but now recovered and possessed, let him read the books in order, and he will find nothing contrary there which ought justly to lead his mind to doubt.

End of Book II.

B287. *Book III begins.*[361]
Likewise,
then as above, c. 132, following charter: 'The same king . . . bishop of Wilton.'

B288. *Charter of King Edward concerning Chilton.*
Charters of Abingdon Abbey, no. 146; above, c. 133, B258.[362]

B289. Therefore, having in the two volumes above covered sufficiently, according to our strength and also the extent of our knowledge,[363] the endowments bestowed by the old kings of the English and also their men on this most sacred house and firmly confirmed by their charters, it now remains for us, with God's help, to attend to noting down, as far as we can very succinctly, the liberties and also the endowments given freely to this most sacred house of Abingdon and graciously received, of each king in order of succession after the coming of the Normans to England, for men present and future who wish to know these matters.

B290. *Concerning the death of King Edward.*[364]
Therefore, when Edward king of the English had been translated[365] to the heavens in the year of our Lord 1065, and his successor Harold had been brought down in battle on 14 October [1066] by William duke of the Normans, William duke of Normandy was crowned[366] with due ceremony by Ealdred archbishop of York on Christmas day at Westminster, first, however, promising on oath before the altar of St Peter in the presence of clergy and people, as the archbishop himself required of him, that he wished to defend the holy churches

[363] A phrase also used above, B8.
[364] This is also the heading for B284 above.
[365] Cf. Edward the martyr, above, p. 346.
[366] The remainder of this sentence follows John of Worcester, *Chronicle*, ii. 606, closely from 'in Westmonasterio' and verbatim from 'coram clero'.

ac rectores illarum defendere, necnon cunctum populum sibi subiectum iuste ac regali prouidentia regere, rectam legem statuere et tenere, rapinas iniustaque iuditia penitus interdicere. Hec omnia Deo uouit, sed nichil horum tenuit. Nam episcopos omnes Anglie, preter Aldredum archiepiscopum Eboracensem et Wlstanum episcopum Wigornensem, deposuit, abbates etiam omnes, quos nulla euidenti causa nec concilia nec leges seculi dampnabant, suis honoribus priuauit.[367] Anglorum pene omnes nobiles, pecuniarum contractum sibi assumentes, extera[a] ad regna conuolarunt. Quorum mox terre in regium proscripte sunt fiscum.

Eorum unus, Blachemannus presbiter de quo in Ordrici abbatis cronicis retulimus, cognito imperii permutatu, impatiens more Anglia[b] digreditur.[368] At abbas Ealdredus, dominum nouiter regno potitum hinc recogniturus, de prefato presbitero quid euenerit quidue de ecclesia tenuerit illinc insinuaturus, curiam regis adiit, a quo et benigne suscipitur. Ceterum de presbiteri negotio in tantum explicuit ut, preter insule Andresie portionem, reliqua iuri ecclesie permitterentur; is[c] enim locus regio proprie receptui ad tempora abbatis Faritii perdurauit.[369] His ita peractis, suarum securus rerum, abbas domi resedit.

Above, c. 143: 'Vt de his . . . opere redimitis.'

[i. 491] **B291.** *De molendino de Cudesdun.*

fo. 118v Apud uillam Cuthesdunam, terris episcopio Lincolniensi pertinentibus conterminam,[370] orta pro exclusa cuiusdam molendini ipsi
[i. 492] Cuthesdunæ adiacenti contentione, uolentibus hominibus episcopii exclusam destrui, abbatie uero nolentibus. Petrus, tunc ad contuendum episcopium constitutus iam eo antistite defuncto, capellanus quidem regis sed post Cestrensis episcopus,[371] multitudine stipatus armatorum, abbas quoque Ealdredus cuneo laicorum et monachorum comitatus deuotorum, secum reliquias sancti Vincentii martiris habens, ad ipsum locum ultra citraque molendinum, sue quisque in portione telluris, statum contionatorium capiendo,[372] conuenerunt;

B290 [a] *corr. from* extra *by interlin.* [b] *corr. from* Anglica [c] his *MS*

[367] Ealdred was archbishop of York 1061–9, Wulfstan (II) bishop of Worcester 1062–95; *Handbook of British Chronology*, p. 224.

[368] Cf. MS C's treatment of Blæcmann, above, c. 143. For the mention 'in the chronicles of Abbot Ordric', see above, c. 136, B276.

[369] See vol. ii. 72–6.

of God and their rulers, and to rule the whole people subject to him justly and by royal foresight, to establish and maintain right law, and to forbid totally rapine and unjust judgements. All these things he swore to God, but he held none of them. For he deposed all the bishops of England, besides Ealdred archbishop of York and Wulfstan bishop of Worcester, and he also deprived of their high office all abbots, whom neither councils nor the laws of the world condemned for any evident cause.[367] Almost all the nobles of the English fled to foreign kingdoms, taking for themselves a restricted amount of money. Soon their lands were forfeited to the royal treasury.

When one of them, the priest Blæcmann to whom we referred in the chronicles of Abbot Ordric, learnt of the change of regime, he left England, impatient of delay.[368] But Abbot Ealdred, partly to recognize the lord who had newly possessed the realm, and partly to indicate what had happened concerning that priest and what he held of the church, went to the court of the king, by whom he was kindly received. Moreover, he untangled the matter of that priest to such a degree that, besides part of the island of Andersey, the rest were allowed to the church's property. For that place lasted until Abbot Faritius's time as a royal haven.[369] With matters completed thus the abbot resided again in the house, secure in his possessions.

Above, c. 143: 'When this abbot . . . in magnificent work.'

B291. *Concerning the mill of Cuddesdon.*

At the village of Cuddesdon, next to lands pertaining to the bishopric of Lincoln,[370] a dispute arose over the sluice belonging to Cuddesdon mill; the men of the bishopric wished to destroy the sluice, but those of the abbey did not wish this. So Peter, a chaplain of the king, indeed, and afterwards bishop of Chester,[371] who was then appointed to watch over the bishopric after the bishop's death, closely surrounded by a mass of armed men, and also Abbot Ealdred accompanied by a band of devoted laymen and monks, and having with him the relics of St Vincent the martyr, met at that place on either side of the mill (for the site was of this sort), each on part of their own estate, taking up the position of suitors.[372] Some of the

[370] Probably Great Milton, Oxfordshire; see vol. ii. 172–4 for continuing trouble in this area after the Norman Conquest.

[371] Peter was consecrated bishop of Lichfield in 1072, the see was transferred to Chester in 1075, and he died in 1085; *Handbook of British Chronology*, p. 253.

[372] For another use of *contionator* in this sense, see *Liber Eliensis*, bk. ii, c. 34, ed. Blake, p. 109.

huiusmodi enim loci situs. Illorum uero quidam equis insidentes et garrientes, istorum uniuersi solotenus pedibus consistentes et in
fo. 119r sancto cuius aderant pia pignera multam | confidentiam habentes. O Dei sanctorumque eius confidentiam, quam in se confidentibus subuenialem! Siquidem cum arbitrorum presentium examine res eo procederet uti abbas super reliquias quas attulerat ipse iurando faceret quod pars sua rectius iret, ille genuflectit[a] sursum dextramque tetendit. Cum ecce, in parte oblocutorum cepit terra firma concuti, dura emolliri, adeo ut equorum pedes infra ipsam mollitiem implicarentur. Turbo etiam perualidus de manibus hastas tenentium excutiens in aera proicere, et inter se ui turbinis illidentes, mirabile uisu, confringere. Quare illi, iam stupidi sueque uite diffisi, clamant, uouent numquam de causa pro qua conflictum inierant ultra inserendum sermonem, incolumes tantum miseratione presentis sancti permitterentur reuerti inde ad propria, insani capitis fore cuius ausus impelleret eadem repetere. Ita rectitudo ecclesie sancti Vincentii martiris, publice propalata, dedit apud Abbendunense monasterium celebriorem extunc haberi sue uenerationis cultum.

[i. 493] **B292.** *De captione Aldredi abbatis.*[a]

Above, c. 144.

B291 [a] *corr. from* genuflectet

B292 [a] *the rubricator included a heading, although no appropriate space had been left* former, indeed, were mounted on horses and chattering, all of the latter just stood on their own feet and had great trust in the saint whose holy relics were present. O trust of God and His saints, how supportive of those trusting in Him! When, indeed, by judgement of the judges present it came about that the abbot was to make an oath on the relics which he had brought that his side was the more just, he knelt and stretched upwards his right hand. When, lo, on the opponents' side the firm ground began to shake, the hard ground to soften, so much so that the feet of the horses became stuck in the softness. Also a very strong wind plucked the spears from the hands of those holding them, and threw them into the air, dashed them against one another and broke them by the force of the wind, in a marvellous sight. Therefore those men, now shocked and despairing of their lives, shouted out and vowed that never again would discussion be started about the case for which they had entered the conflict, nor would any crazed daring impel repetition of these matters. They asked only that they be permitted, by the mercy of the saint who was present, to return thence safe to their homes. So the justness of the church of St Vincent the martyr, publicly made widely known, made the cult of his veneration be held thenceforth more famous at the monastery of Abingdon.

B292. *Concerning the capture of Abbot Ealdred.*
Above, c. 144.

CONCORDANCES

These concordances provide easy cross-reference to the two versions of the *History*, to Sawyer's *Anglo-Saxon Charters*, and to Kelly's *Charters of Abingdon Abbey*. Cross-reference to Stevenson's Rolls Series edition, and to the folios of the manuscripts of the *History*, are given in the margins of the Latin text of my edition. Sawyer and Kelly provide references to other editions of the charters.

CONCORDANCE I: MS C

MS C	MS B	Sawyer	Kelly	Charter Beneficiary
1				
2			51B	
3	B9	241	4	Abbot Hæha
4	B9	241	4	Abbot Hæha, etc.
5		239	2	Abbot Hæha
6		252	1	Abbot Hæha and Cilla
7	B10	1179	3	Cilla
8	B30	93	5	Abingdon
9				
10		166	8	Abingdon
11	B18	183	9	Abingdon
12	B26	278	11	Abingdon
13	B28	302	14	(decimation charter)
14				
15	B34	1201	17	Cuthwulf
16	B32	335	15	Æthelwulf
17				
18	B41	355	18	Deormod
19	B47	404	22	Abbot Cynath
20	B48	409	25	Abingdon
21	B50	408	27	Abingdon
22	B49	410	26	Abingdon
23	B52	1208	28	Abingdon
24				
25		460	31	Ælfhild
26				
27				
28	B85	567	51	Abingdon
29				
30				
31				
32				
33				
34				
35	B101	558	45	Wulfric
36				

MS C	MS B	Sawyer	Kelly	Charter Beneficiary
37	B114	658	83	Abingdon
38	B115	605	52	Abingdon
39				
40				
41	B117	663	59	Abingdon
42	B121	583	58	Abingdon
43	B119	607	57	Abingdon
44	B141	614	56	Brihthelm, priest
45				
46	B131	587	70	Ælfhere
47				
48	B135	622	64	Eadric
49				
50	B139	594	54	Ælfwine
51				
52	B163	639	75	Ælfheah
53	B144	590	60	Ælfric
54	B125	617	67	Byrhtnoth
55	B127	618	66	Beorhtric
56	B129	611	73	Byrhtnoth
57				
58	B78	482	35	Sæthryth
59				
60	B175	673	84	Abingdon
61	B197	756	108	Abingdon
62	B179	682	85	Abingdon
63				
64	B198	689	89	Abingdon
65	B199	701	93	Abingdon
66	B202	700	92	Abingdon
67	B206	690	87	Abingdon
68				
69	B204	688	88	Abingdon
70	B201	708	96	Abingdon
71	B209			
72				
73	B203	724	100	Abingdon
74				
75	B176	734	102	Abingdon
76				
77	B183	733	104	Abingdon
78				
79	B200	758	110	Abingdon
80				
81	B177	757	111	Abingdon
82				
83	B180	759	112	Abingdon
84				
85	B181	760	113	Abingdon
86	B182	732	103	Abingdon
87				

MS C	MS B	Sawyer	Kelly	Charter Beneficiary
88	B187	769	109	Wulfstan
89				
90	B196	761	107	Ælfwine
91				
92	B211	829	116	Abingdon
93	B213	1216	115	Abingdon
94				
95	(cf. B214)			
96	(cf. B215)			
97	B216			
98	B217	876	124	Abingdon
99	B218	937	129	Abingdon
100				
101	B220	896	128	Abingdon
102	B221	918	135	Abingdon
103				
104	B234	901	132	Archbishop Ælfric
105	B236	(1488)	(133)	various incl. Abingdon
106	B240			
107	B241			
108	B242			
109				
110	B244			
111				
112				
113		973	140	Abingdon
114	B247	964	138	Abingdon
115	(cf. B248)			
116				
117	B254	993	141	Abingdon
118				
119				
120	B259–60	incl. 1404	incl. 143	writ in Abingdon's favour
121	B261			
122	B262			
123	B263			
124	B264			
125	B265			
126	B266			
127	B267	1065	148	Abingdon
128	B268			
129	B269	1066	149	Abingdon
130	B270			
131				
132	B273, B287	1025	147	Abingdon
133	B288	1023	146	Abingdon
134	B274			
135	B275	1020	145	Abingdon
136	B276			
137	B277	665	37	Eadric
138	B278			

MS C	MS B	Sawyer	Kelly	Charter Beneficiary
139	B279	713	97	Æthelsige
140	B280	927	136	Leofric
141	B281–3			
142	B284			
143	B285, B290			
144	B292			

CONCORDANCE 2: MS B

MS B	MS C	Sawyer	Kelly	Charter Beneficiary
B1				
B2				
B3				
B4				
B5				
B6				
B7				
B8				
B9	3, 4	241	4	Abbot Hæha
B10	7	1179	3	Cilla
B11				
B12				
B13				
B14		268	7	Lulla
B15				
B16				
B17				
B18	11	183	9	Abingdon
B19				
B20		269	6	Beorhtric/Hemele
B21				
B22		202	13	Ælfheah
B23				
B24		1271	12	King Berhtwulf, Æthelwulf
B25				
B26	12	278	11	Abingdon
B27				
B28	13	302	14	decimation charter
B29				
B30	8	93	5	Abingdon
B31				
B32	16	335	15	Æthelwulf (duplicate of B89)
B33				
B34	15	1201	17	Cuthwulf
B35				
B36		225	20	Eadric
B37				
B38				
B39				
B40				

MS B	MS C	Sawyer	Kelly	Charter Beneficiary
B41	18	355	18	Deormod
B42				
B43		999	142	Ælfstan
B44				
B45		369	19	Tata
B46				
B47	19	404	22	Abbot Cynath
B48	20	409	25	Abingdon
B49	22	410	26	Abingdon
B50	21	408	27	Abingdon
B51				
B52	23	1208	28	Abingdon
B53				
B54		413	23	Ælfric
B55		1604	24	Wulfnoth
B56				
B57		411	29	Ælfheah
B58				
B59		396	21	Ealdred
B60				
B61		448	30	Eadwulfu
B62				
B63				
B64			31A	(Ælfhild)
B65				
B66		471	33	Wulfric
B67				
B68		461	32	Ælfsige
B69				
B70		480	34	Æthelstan
B71				
B72		491	37	Eadric (different version of c. 137, B277)
B73				
B74		494	38	Ælfheah
B75				
B76		496	36	Bishop Ælfric
B77				
B78	58	482	35	Sæthryth
B79				
B80		500	39	Ordulf
B81				
B82				
B83				
B84				
B85	28	567	51	Abingdon
B86				
B87		542	42	Wulfric
B88				
B89	16	335	15	Æthelwulf (duplicate of B32)
B90				

MS B	MS C	Sawyer	Kelly	Charter Beneficiary
B91		529	41	Wulfric
B92				
B93		539/338a	16	Cuthred
B94				
B95		525	40	Eadric
B96				
B97		552	44	Wulfric
B98				
B99		561	48	Ælfsige and Eadgifu
B100				
B101	35	558	45	Wulfric
B102				
B103		560	49	Ælfric
B104				
B105		564	50	Ælfheah
B106				
B107		577	77	Wulfric
B108				
B109		559	47	Ælfwine
B110				
B111		578	46	Ælfgar
B112				
B113				
B114	37	658	83	Abingdon
B115	38	605	52	Abingdon
B116				
B117	41	663	59	Abingdon
B118				
B119	43	607	57	Abingdon
B120				
B121	42	583	58	Abingdon
B122				
B123		581	53	Beorhtric
B124				
B125	54	617	67	Byrhtnoth
B126				
B127	55	618	66	Beorhtric
B128				
B129	56	611	73	Byrhtnoth
B130				
B131	46	587	70	Ælfhere
B132				
B133		597	55 (i)	Ælfric (different version of B161)
B134				
B135	48	622	64	Eadric
B136				
B137		591	72	Ælfsige
B138				
B139	50	594	54	Ælfwine
B140				
B141	44	614	56	Brihthelm

MS B	MS C	Sawyer	Kelly	Charter Beneficiary
B142	(cf. 44 for Latin summary)	1292	76	exchange between Brihthelm and Æthelwold
B143				
B144	53	590	60	Ælfric
B145				
B146		621	63	Eadric
B147				
B148		588	71	Ælfhere
B149				
B150		624	65	Edmund
B151				
B152		620	74	Eadric (duplicate of B157)
B153				
B154		603	61	Æthelnoth
B155				
B156				
B157		620	74	Eadric (duplicate of B152)
B158				
B159		634	69	Wulfric
B160				
B161		597	55 (ii)	Ælfric (different version of B133)
B162				
B163	52	639	75	Ælfheah
B164				
B165		654	80	Eadric
B166				
B167		650	78	Eadwold
B168				
B169				
B170		651	79	Cynric
B171				
B172		657	81	Wulfric
B173				
B174				
B175	60	673	84	Abingdon
B176	75	734	102	Abingdon
B177	81	757	111	Abingdon
B178		1569	151	(bounds only)
B179	62	682	85	Abingdon
B180	83	759	112	Abingdon
B181	85	760	113	Abingdon
B182	86	732	103	Abingdon
B183	77	733	104	Abingdon
B184		713	97	Æthelsige (different version of c. 139, B279)
B185		725	101	Queen Ælfthryth
B186		687	86	Wulfric
B187	88	769	109	Wulfstan
B188		737	105	Ælfgifu
B189		698	91	Eadric
B190		778	114	Brihtheah, deacon

MS B	MS C	Sawyer	Kelly	Charter Beneficiary
B191		750	106	Byrhtnoth
B192		722	99	Wulfnoth
B193		691	90	Ælfric
B194		705	94	Eadwine
B195		678	82	Eanulf
B196	90	761	107	Ælfwine
B197	61	756	108	Abingdon
B198	64	689	89	Abingdon
B199	65	701	93	Abingdon
B200	79	758	110	Abingdon
B201	70	708	96	Abingdon
B202	66	700	92	Abingdon
B203	73	724	100	Abingdon
B204	69	688	88	Abingdon
B205		714	98	Bishop Æthelwold
B206	67	690	87	Abingdon
B207				
B208				
B209	71			
B210				
B211	92	829	116	Abingdon
B212		828	117	Bishop Ælfstan
B213	93			
B214	(cf. 95)			
B215	(cf. 96)			
B216	97			
B217	98	876	124	Abingdon
B218	99	937	129	Abingdon
B219		843	119	Abingdon
B220	101	896	128	Abingdon
B221	102	918	135	Abingdon
B222		833	95	Leofric
B223		839	118	Ælfgar
B224		851	120	Wulfgar
B225		886	126	Wulfric
B226		852	121	Ælfheah
B227		883	125	Æthelwig
B228		855	122	Beorhtric
B229		858	123	Leofwine
B230		887	127	Eadric, Eadwig, Ealdred
B231		897	130	Abingdon
B232		902	131	Godwine
B233				
B234	104	901	132	Archbishop Ælfric
B235	(cf. c. 105)	1488	133	various incl. Abingdon
B236	105	(1488)	(133)	various incl. Abingdon
B237		915	134	Ælfgar
B238		927	136	Leofric (different version of c. 140, B280)
B239		934	137	Bishop Byrhtwold
B240	106			

MS B	MS C	Sawyer	Kelly	Charter Beneficiary
B241	107			
B242	108			
B243				
B244	110			
B245				
B246		967	139	Abingdon
B247	114	964	138	Abingdon
B248	(cf. 115)			
B249				
B250				
B251				
B252				
B253				
B254	117	993	141	Abingdon
B255				
B256				
B257		1020	145	Abingdon (different version of c. 135, B275)
B258		1023	146	Abingdon (different version of c. 133, B288)
B259	120			
B260	120	1404	143	writ in Abingdon's favour
B261	121			
B262	122			
B263	123			
B264	124			
B265	125			
B266	126			
B267	127	1065	148	Abingdon
B268	128			
B269	129	1066	149	Abingdon
B270	130			
B271		1022	144	Godwine
B272				
B273	132	1025	147	Abingdon
B274	134			
B275	135	1020	145	Abingdon (different version of B257)
B276	136			
B277	137	665	37	Eadric (different version of B72)
B278	138			
B279	139	713	97	Æthelsige (different version of B184)
B280	140	927	136	Leofric (different version of B238)
B281	141			
B282	141			
B283	141			
B284	142			
B285	143			
B286				
B287	132			

MS B	MS C	Sawyer	Kelly	Charter Beneficiary
B288	133	1023	146	Abingdon (different version of B258)
B289				
B290	143			
B291				
B292	144			

INDEX OF BIBLICAL AND CLASSICAL QUOTATIONS AND ALLUSIONS

(I) IN NARRATIVE SECTIONS

(II) IN CHARTERS EDITED IN THIS VOLUME[1]

[1] Note that this index does not include charters only calendared in the present volume.

INDEX

To avoid providing many entries for undifferentiated personal names, I have included a brief, generally formulaic, indication of each individual's place in the *History*. The word 'witness' following a personal name indicates that the individual appears in the *History* only as a witness to a document or transaction. Separate entries are given for thegns of different kings; these may separate references to thegns who spanned reigns.

The index covers both volumes of this edition, the individual volumes being distinguished by small capital I and II.